Wissenschaftliche Untersuchungen
zum Neuen Testament

Herausgeber / Editor
Jörg Frey

Mitherausgeber / Associate Editors
Friedrich Avemarie · Judith Gundry-Volf
Martin Hengel · Otfried Hofius · Hans-Josef Klauck

184

Richard H. Bell

The Irrevocable Call of God

An Inquiry into Paul's Theology of Israel

Mohr Siebeck

RICHARD H. BELL, born 1954; 1979 PhD Theoretical Atomic Physics; 1991 Promotion in Theologie (Tübingen); Senior Lecturer at the University of Nottingham, UK.

ISBN 3-16-148009-0
ISSN 0512-1604 (Wissenschaftliche Untersuchungen zum Neuen Testament)

Die Deutsche Bibliothek lists this publication in the Deutsche Nationalbibliographie; detailed bibliographic data is available in the Internet at *http://dnb.ddb.de*.

The book was printed by Gulde-Druck in Tübingen on non-aging paper and bound by Buchbinderei Spinner in Ottersweier.

Printed in Germany.

To my good friend Jennie

In gratitude

Preface

My thoughts on Paul's view of Israel have changed dramatically over the
years in two respects. When I studied theology at Wycliffe Hall in Oxford,
the "new perspective" on Paul was starting to dominate British scholarship
and like many others I adopted this new approach. There was a certain
excitement in arguing that the traditional Lutheran approach to Paul was
mistaken. We could now set the record straight: Judaism was not a religion
of works-righteousness and neither was Paul criticizing Judaism for being
such. I was particularly attracted to the work of N.T. Wright (now Bishop of
Durham) who argued that Paul's criticism of Judaism was not for works-
righteousness but for "national righteousness", i.e. trying to confine God's
grace to herself and not sharing it with the Gentiles. As I started my curacy
in the Diocese of London I studied Romans in detail and decided that one of
the best ways to understand this great epistle was to preach through it. I am
very grateful to the people of St Margaret's Edgware for listening attentively
and giving helpful responses (a salutary reminder that there are many dedicated and enthusiastic theologians in our Church congregations). I applied
the new perspective to Romans and when I reached Romans 9.29 took a
holiday. It was to be a theological holiday. I spent some time in Bonn reading German protestant work on Paul, then travelled further through Germany
eventually reaching the charming town of Tübingen where I had arranged to
meet Professors Hofius and Stuhlmacher. Meeting them and reading their
work (and that of Professor Martin Hengel) was to change the direction of
my theological thinking. When I returned to England and to Romans (at
Romans 9.30!) I found myself taking a more traditional "Lutheran" approach
and I (and the congregation) discovered that my sermons were beginning to
make much more sense of the text. (My consolation about those earlier
"new perspective" sermons is that I happen to have a "high" view of preaching, i.e. even if the exegesis of the text is not right, God can nevertheless
speak to his people.)

The second way in which I have changed my mind regards the issue of
Israel as the people of God. In my days as a Physics undergraduate when I
started reading the bible in earnest for the first time, I slowly built up the

picture in my mind that the Church was the "new Israel" and since the Jews had rejected the gospel they were no longer the people of God. When it came to middle eastern politics I remember arguing with Jewish friends that the theological status of Jews was irrelevant to the situation in the middle east. The promises had all been revoked. It was with some irritation that I heard some Christians affirm that the Jews were still the "people of God". Again, if I may refer back to my sermons on Romans, I remember vigorously preaching a "subsitution model" when I came to Romans 2.25-29. However, when I later did detailed study on Romans I changed my mind. I consider it a great mercy that in God's providence I have put my ideas into print *after* changing my mind!

When my curacy came to an end I spent four years in Tübingen on my doctorate on Romans 9-11. During that time I had the privilege of having Professor Stuhlmacher as my "Doktorvater" and the joy of attending the lectures of Professor Hofius on Romans, and various seminars and Oberseminars of Professor Hengel. I would like once more to record my gratitude to these New Testament scholars who demonstrated that study of the New Testament can be both wissenschaftlich and of service to the Church.

In this present work on Paul and Israel many aspects of Pauline theology enter the discussion. At certain points in the work I felt that a whole monograph should be devoted to the issue at hand. But I have attempted to bring together various aspects of Pauline theology as they relate to the Israel question and hope that my synthesis will be of value to both New Testament and systematic theologians. I have been working on this book on and off for the last six years. The final form of the work has emerged as I taught "Paul and Israel" to third year theology students at the University of Nottingham. I have taught it to five different groups of students and I wish to thank them for their interest in the subject and for their searching questions. Dr Matthew Howey, one of my former PhD students, attended these lectures and I thank him for correcting an earlier form of the manuscript. Peter Watts, who gained both BA and MA degrees in theology at the University of Nottingham, corrected the final versions and made helpful comments on the content. He then undertook the mammoth task of creating the indices using Nota Bene 7.0. I thank him for his dedication to this task especially since in the final stages he was also working as a school academic tutor and had to work on the indices at evenings and weekends. It has been a great privilege to work with Peter. He is a man of many talents: theologian, IT expert, trumpeter and a virtuoso on the computer keyboard.

Dr James Crossley and Dr Stephen Travis read the section on Jesus and Israel and made helpful comments. I am especially grateful to Professor Friedrich Avemarie for reading through most of chapter 3 and offering his valuable critical comments. I also thank Mr Ed Ball and Professor Maurice Casey, colleagues in Old Testament and New Testament respectively in the department of theology. It has been a great pleasure to work with them and I thank them for many informal chats. Some of the material from chapter 5 was presented to the New Testament seminar group at the University of Durham shortly before I submitted the manuscript to the publisher. I am grateful for the perceptive comments made by members of that esteemed group. In the light of some of these comments, I have, at one or two points, made some last minute changes.

The approach of this work is primarily theological. Historical questions are addressed in as much as they throw light on the theological issues. The work involves a fair amount of exegesis, but where issues have been treated in detail in my works *Provoked to Jealousy* or *No one seeks for God,* a summary of the exegesis found there is given. But in some cases I offer a fairly detailed treatment. Although at one or two points I have made slightly different exegetical judgements to those found in my earlier works, there is no significant change in my position. But at certain points I have sharpened my arguments and related the exegesis to new theological problems and literature.

Chapters 9 and 10 are an attempt to relate Pauline theology to some current theological problems. To do this is of course a risk. But when I have spoken to non-theologians about this project on Paul and Israel, I have often been asked about controversial issues such as the holocaust, the promise of the land of Israel and mission to Jews (in the sense of evangelism). One of the great privileges of working in a University is the opportunity to seek for truth. It is surely part of the social responsibility of someone working in a University to engage in this quest. To address questions such as the holocaust and the land is a risk; but I hope readers will agree with me that it is a risk worth taking.

I would like to thank Professors Hengel, Hofius and Frey for accepting this work in the WUNT series. I am also grateful to the staff of Mohr Siebeck for their customary efficiency. They have patiently dealt with all sorts of delays for which the author alone is responsible.

I thank the University of Nottingham for the semester of study leave in 2001 in which I was able to do intensive work on the book. In particular I thank colleagues who kindly took over my administrative responsibilities at that time. I also thank those who have acted as head of department during the writing of this book, Professors Alan Ford, Hugh Goddard and Maurice Casey. They have all encouraged a happy atmosphere in which to work.

I thank my sons, Jack and Cameron. They have helped me in more ways than they realise. In addition to simply being there, they have demonstrated extraordinary patience. They have allowed me to work on this book at evenings and weekends and spent many hours with me at the University. I thank them in particular for help in photocopying and sorting out piles of paper. They, like me, can now give a sigh of relief: "Vollendet das ewige Werk"! This book is dedicated to Jennie, my friend, who has helped me in so many ways. She has spent many hours with Jack and Cameron and without her help I could not have set up the study at home where, over the last two and a half years, the book was completed. I also thank her parents, Pat and Keith Tinsdeall, for their kindness and help in so many practical ways. This will never be forgotten.

Finally I want to say a big thank you to my mother, now in her mid-eighties. She is a remarkable person and is an inspiration to so many. Just before the book was completed she managed to get through a painful operation and demonstrated yet again her determination to live life to the full.

Shavuoth, 2005   Richard H. Bell
Nottingham

Table of Contents

Abbreviations

1. Biblical books

The abbreviations used for books of the OT, NT and Apocrypha will be readily understood.

2. Pseudepigrapha and Early Christian Writings

2 Bar.	Syriac Apocalypse of Baruch
1 En.	1 Enoch
4 Ezr.	4 Ezra
Jub.	Jubilees
Apoc. Moses	Apocalypse of Moses
LAB	Liber Antiquitatum Biblicarum
Ps. Sol.	Psalms of Solomon
Test. Sim.	Testament of Simeon
Test. Jud.	Testament of Judah
Test. Reub.	Testament of Reuben
Test. Zeb.	Testament of Zebulun
Test. Ben.	Testament of Benjamin
Test. Job	Testament of Job
Barn.	Epistle of Barnabas
1 Clem.	1 Clement

3. Dead Sea Scrolls

CD	Damascus Document
1QH	Hymns of Thanksgiving
1QpHab	Pesher Habakkuk
1QS	Community Rule
4QFlor	Florilegium
4QMMT	Some of the Precepts of the Law
4QpNah	Pesher Nahum
4QTest	Testimonia

4. Tractates of the Mishnah, Tosephta, Babylonian and Palestinian Talmudim

For the Mishnah, Tosephta, Babylonian and Palestinian Talmudim the letters m., t., b. and y. are placed before the tractate respectively.

Abod. Zar.	Abodah Zarah
ARN	Aboth Rabbi Nathan
Bab. Bat.	Baba Bathra
Bab. Met.	Baba Metzia
Ber.	Berakoth
Ket.	Ketuboth
Kid.	Kiddushin
Mak.	Makkoth
Men.	Menahoth
Pes.	Pesahim
Sanh.	Sanhedrin
Shab.	Shabbath
Sot.	Sotah
Yad.	Yadaim
Yeb.	Yebamoth

5. Midrashim

Gen. R.	Midrash Genesis Rabbah
Ex. R.	Midrash Exodus Rabbah
Lev. R.	Midrash Leviticus Rabbah
Num. R.	Midrash Numbers Rabbah
Mek. Ex.	Mekhilta Exodus
Mek. R. Sim.	Mekhilta R. Simeon ben Yoḥai
Sifre Dt.	Sifre Deuteronomy
Sifre Num.	Sifre Numbers
Midr. Ps.	Midrash on the Psalms
Leq. t.	Leqach tob
Pes. R.	Pesikta Rabbati

6. Reference Works

ABD	D.N. Freedman (ed.), *The Anchor Bible Dictionary*, 6 vols, New York: Doubleday 1992
ANEP	J.B. Pritchard (ed.), *The Ancient Near East in Pictures*, Princeton: Princeton University Press ²1969, (¹1954)
ANRW	H. Temporini and W. Haase (ed.), *Aufstieg und Niedergang der römischen Welt*, Berlin/New York: Walter de Gruyter 1972ff.

BA   W. Bauer, *Wörterbuch zum Neuen Testament*, Berlin/New York: Walter de Gruyter [6]1988 (bearbeitet von K. und B. Aland)

BAG   W. Bauer, W.F. Arndt, and F.W. Gingrich, *Greek-English Lexicon of the New Testament*, Chicago/London: University of Chicago Press 1961

BCFT   G.C.D. Howley, F.F. Bruce, and H.L. Ellison (ed.), *A Bible Commentary for Today*, London/Glasgow: Pickering & Inglis 1979

BDB   F. Brown, S.R. Driver, and C.A. Briggs, *A Hebrew and English Lexicon of the Old Testament based on the Lexicon of W. Gesenius*, Oxford: Clarendon Press 1978 (repr.)

BDF   F. Blass and A. Debrunner, *A Greek Grammar of the New Testament*, translated and revised by R.W. Funk, Chicago/London: University of Chicago Press 1961

CCHS   B. Orchard et al. (ed.), *A Catholic Commentary on Holy Scripture*, London: Thomas Nelson 1953

DOTTE   W.A. Van Gemeren (ed.), *New International Dictionary of Old Testament Theology & Exegesis*, 5 vols, Grand Rapids: Zondervan 1997

Denzinger   H. Denzinger, *Enchiridion symbolorum definitionum et declarationum de rebus fidei et morum* (ed. P. Hünermann), Freiburg: Herder 1991

EB(C)   T.K. Cheyne - J. Sutherland Black (ed.), *Encyclopaedia Biblica*, 4 vols, London: A. & C. Black 1899-1903

EM   T. Gaisford (ed.), *Etymologicum Magnum*, Oxford: OUP 1848.

EDNT   H. Balz - G. Schneider (ed), *Exegetical Dictionary of the New Testament*, 3 vols, Grand Rapids: Wm. B. Eerdmans 1990-93

EJud   *Encyclopaedia Judaica*, 16 vols, Jerusalem: Keter Publishing House 1978 (repr.), ([1]1971-72)

GK   E. Kautzsch (ed.), *Gesenius' Hebrew Grammar* ET, Oxford: Clarendon Press [2]1910 (revised by A.E. Cowley)

HAW   W. Otto (ed.), *Handbuch der Altertumswissenschaft* (begründet von I. v. Müller, fortgesetzt von R. v. Pöhlmann), München: C.H. Beck [6]1924

HDB   J. Hastings (ed.), *A Dictionary of the Bible*, 5 vols, Edinburgh: T. & T. Clark 1898-1904

HGR   J. Hastings (ed.), *Dictionary of the Bible* revised by F.C. Grant and H.H. Rowley, Edinburgh: T. & T. Clark [2]1963

HWP   J. Ritter and K. Gründer (ed.), *Historisches Wörterbuch der Philosophie*, Basel: Schwabe & Co. 1971ff

IB   G.A. Buttrick (ed.), *The Interpreter's Bible*, 12 vols, New York/Nashville: Abingdon-Cokesbury Press 1952-57

IDB   G.A. Buttrick (ed.), *The Interpreter's Dictionary of the Bible*, 4 vols, New York/Nashville: Abingdon-Cokesbury Press 1962

IDBSup	Supplementary volume to IDB, 1976
ISBE	G.W. Bromiley (ed.), *The International Standard Bible Encyclopedia*, 4 vols, Grand Rapids: Wm B. Eerdmans 1979-88.
Jastrow	M. Jastrow, *A Dictionary of the Targumim, the Talmud Babli and Yerushalmi, and the Midrashic Literature*, 2 vols, New York: Pardes Publishing House 1950
JE	I. Singer (ed.), *Jewish Encyclopedia*, 12 vols, London/New York: Funk and Wagnalls 1901-6.
KBS	L. Koehler, W. Baumgartner, and J.J. Stamm, *Hebräisches und Aramäisches Lexikon zum Alten Testament*, 3 vols, Leiden: E.J. Brill 1967-83
KP	K. Ziegler and W. Sontheimer (ed.), *Der Kleine Pauly: Lexikon der Antike*, 5 vols, München: Deutscher Taschenbuch Verlag 1979
LPGL	G.W.H. Lampe (ed.), *Patristic Greek Lexicon*, Oxford: Clarendon Press 1961-68
LSJ	H.G. Liddell and R. Scott, *Greek-English Lexicon*, Oxford: Clarendon Press 1985 (revised by H.S. Jones and R. McKenzie with a Supplement 1968)
LEHC	J. Lust, E. Eynikel, K. Hauspie and G. Chamberlain, *A Greek-English Lexicon of the Septuagint: Part I, A-I*, Stuttgart: Deutsche Bibelgesellschaft 1992
LThK[1]	M. Buchberger (ed.), *Lexikon für Theologie und Kirche*, 10 vols, Freiburg: Herder 1930-38.
LThK[2]	J. Höfer and K. Rahner (ed.), *Lexikon für Theologie und Kirche*, 11 vols, Freiburg: Herder 1957-67
MTH	J.H. Moulton, N. Turner and W.F. Howard, *A Grammar of New Testament Greek*, 4 vols, Edinburgh: T. & T. Clark 1978-80 (repr.), ([1]1908-76)
NIB	L.E. Keck et al. (ed.), *The New Interpreter's Bible*, 12 vols, Nashville: Abingdon Press 1994ff.
NIDNTT	C. Brown (ed.), *The New International Dictionary of New Testament Theology*, 3 vols, Exeter: Paternoster Press 1975-78
PW	*Paulys Realencyclopädie der classischen Altertumswissenschaft*, Neue Bearbeitung von G. Wissowa, W. Kroll, K. Mittelhaus et al., Stuttgart: Alfred Druckenmüller Verlag 1894ff., 2. Reihe 1914ff.
PWSup	Supplement to PW, 1903ff.
RE[3]	A. Hauck (ed.), *Realencyklopädie für protestantische Theologie und Kirche*, 22 vols, Leipzig: J.C. Hinrichs'sche Buchhandlung [3]1896-1909.
RGG[1]	F.M. Schiele and L. Zscharnack (ed.), *Die Religion in Geschichte und Gegenwart: Handwörterbuch in gemeinverständlicher Darstellung*, 5 vols, Tübingen: J.C.B. Mohr (Paul Siebeck) [1]1909-13.

RGG²	H. Gunkel and L. Zscharnack (ed.), *Die Religion in Geschichte und Gegenwart: Handwörterbuch für Theologie und Religionswissenschaft*, 7 vols, Tübingen: J.C.B. Mohr (Paul Siebeck) ²1927-32.
RGG³	K. Galling (ed.), *Die Religion in Geschichte und Gegenwart: Handwörterbuch für Theologie und Religionswissenschaft* (UTB), 7 vols, Tübingen: J.C.B. Mohr (Paul Siebeck) 1986 (repr.), (³1959)
SVF	Ioannes ab Arnim (ed.), *Stoicorum veterum fragmenta*, 4 vols, Stuttgart: In aedibus B.G. Teubner ²1964 (¹1903-24).
TDNT	G. Kittel and G. Friedrich (ed.), *Theological Dictionary of the New Testament* ET, 10 vols, Grand Rapids, Michigan: Wm. B. Eerdmans 1964-76
THAT	E. Jenni and C. Westermann (ed.), *Theologisches Handwörterbuch zum Alten Testament*, 2 vols, München: Chr. Kaiser Verlag/Zürich: Theologischer Verlag 1 1971; 2 1976.
ThWNT	G. Kittel and G. Friedrich (ed.), *Theologisches Wörterbuch zum Neuen Testament*, 10 vols, Stuttgart: W. Kohlhammer 1933-78
TRE	G. Krause and G. Müller (ed.), *Theologische Realenzyklopädie*, 27 vols, Berlin/New York: Walter de Gruyter 1977-97

7. Sources

ANF	A. Roberts, J. Donaldson and A.C. Coxe (ed.). *Ante-Nicene Fathers*, 10 vols, Peabody: Hendrickson 1994 (repr.), (¹1885-1896)
AV	Authorised Version
APOT	R.H. Charles (ed.), *The Apocrypha and Pseudepigrapha of the Old Testament in English*, 2 vols, Oxford: OUP 1977 (repr.), (¹1913).
BHS	Biblia Hebraica Stuttgartensia
BSELK	*Die Bekenntnisschriften der evangelisch-lutherischen Kirche*, Göttingen: Vandenhoeck & Ruprecht ¹⁰1986
CCSL	Corpus Christianorum, Series Latina
CIJ	J.B. Frey (ed.), *Corpus Inscriptionum Iudaicarum*, 2 vols, Rom: Pontificio Istituto di Archeologia cristiana 1 1936; 2 1952
CIL	Corpus Inscriptionum Latinarum, Berlin 1893-1934
CSEL	Corpus Scriptorum Ecclesiasticorum Latinorum
FaCh	Fathers of the Church
GCS	Die griechischen christlichen Schriftsteller der ersten drei Jahrhunderte
GNT³	K. Aland, et al. (ed.), *The Greek New Testament*, New York: United Bible Societies ³1975
GNT⁴	K. Aland et al. (ed.), *The Greek New Testament*, Stuttgart: Deutsche Bibelgesellschaft ⁴1993.
JB	Jerusalem Bible
LCC	Library of Christian Classics
LCL	Loeb Classical Library

LW	J. Pelikan and H.T. Lehmann (ed.), *Luther's Works*, Philadelphia: Fortress Press
MPG	J.-P. Migne, *Patrologia Graeca*
MPL	J.-P. Migne, *Patrologia Latina*
NA[26]	K. Aland et al., (ed.), *Novum Testamentum Graece*, Stuttgart: Deutsche Bibelstiftung [26]1979
NA[27]	K. Aland et al., (ed.), *Novum Testamentum Graece*, Stuttgart: Deutsche Bibelstiftung [27]1993
NEB	New English Bible
NIV	New International Version
NK[2]	N. Nestle and G.D. Kilpatrick (ed.), *H KAINH ΔIAΘHKH*, London: British and Foreign Bible Society [2]1958, ([1]1954)
NPNF1	P. Schaff (ed.), *Nicene and Post-Nicene Fathers: First Series*, 14 vols, Peabody: Hendrickson 1994 (repr.), ([1]1886-1889).
NPNF2	P. Schaff and H. Wace (ed.), *Nicene and Post-Nicene Fathers: Second Series*, 14 vols, Peabody: Hendrickson 1994 (repr.), ([1]1890-1900).
NRSV	New Revised Standard Version
OCT	Oxford Classical Texts
OECT	Oxford Early Christian Texts
OTP	James H. Charlesworth (ed.), *The Old Testament Pseudepigrapha*, 2 vols, London: Darton, Longman & Todd 1 1983; 2 1985
RSV	Revised Standard Version
RT	Rabbinische Texte
RV	Revised Version
SC	Sources chrétiennes
WA	*D. Martin Luthers Werke, kritische Gesamtausgabe*, Weimar: Hermann Böhlaus Nachfolger
WH	B.F. Westcott and F.J.A. Hort (ed.), *The New Testament in the Original Greek*, London: Macmillan 1881.
ZB	Die Zürcher Bibel, i.e. *Die heilige Schrift des Alten und des Neuen Testaments*, Zürich: Verlag der Zürcher Bibel 1987.

8. Periodicals

AELKZ	Allgemeine evangelisch-lutherische Kirchenzeitung
AJP	American Journal of Philology
AJS	American Journal of Sociology
AusBR	Australian Biblical Review
BBR	Bulletin for Biblical Research
Bib	Biblica
BJRL	Bulletin of the John Rylands Library, University of Manchester
BTB	Biblical Theology Bulletin
BThZ	Berliner Theologische Zeitschrift
BZ	Biblische Zeitschrift

CBQ	Catholic Biblical Quarterly
CTJ	Calvin Theological Journal
EvTh	Evangelische Theologie
ExpT	Expository Times
ETL	Ephemerides theologicae Lovanienses
GGA	Göttingische gelehrte Anzeigen
GPM	Göttinger Predigtmeditationen
HBT	Horizons in Biblical Theology
HTR	Harvard Theological Review
HUCA	Hebrew Union College Annual
IMJ	The Israel Museum Journal
JAC	Jahrbuch für Antike und Christentum
JBL	Journal of Biblical Literature
JCH	Journal of Contemporary History
JJS	Journal of Jewish Studies
JPJ	Journal of Progressive Judaism
JSNT	Journal for the Study of the New Testament
JSS	Journal of Semitic Studies
JTS	Journal of Theological Studies
Jud	Judaica
KantSt	Kant Studien
KuD	Kerygma und Dogma
NovT	Novum Testamentum
NTS	New Testament Studies
RQ	Revue de Qumran
RSO	Rivista degli studi orientali
RTR	Reformed Theological Review
SEÅ	Svensk Exegetisk Årsbok
SJT	Scottish Journal of Theology
SPAW.PH	Sitzungsberichte der preußischen Akademie der Wissenschaften, Philosophisch-historische Klasse
SR	Studies in Religion
TE	Theological Educator
ThBei	Theologische Beiträge
ThBl	Theologische Blätter
ThLZ	Theologische Literaturzeitung
ThR	Theologische Rundschau
ThStKr	Theologische Studien und Kritiken
ThZ	Theologische Zeitschrift
VC	Vigilae Christianae
VF	Verkündigung und Forschung
VT	Vetus Testamentum
WTJ	Westminster Theological Journal
WuD	Wort und Dienst
ZAW	Zeitschrift für die alttestamentliche Wissenschaft

ZNW	Zeitschrift für die neutestamentliche Wissenschaft
ZThK	Zeitschrift für Theologie und Kirche

9. Series

AB	Anchor Bible
ABRL	Anchor Bible Reference Library
ABPB	Aachener Beiträge zu Pastoral- und Bildungsfragen
ACJD	Abhandlungen zum christlich-jüdischen Dialog
AGAJU	Arbeiten zur Geschichte des antiken Judentums und des Urchristentums
ALGHJ	Arbeiten zur Literatur und Geschichte des hellenistischen Judentums
AnBib	Analecta Biblica
AMNSU	Arbeiten und Mitteilungen aus dem Neutestamentlichen Seminar zu Upsala
ArB	Aramaic Bible
ATD	Das Alte Testament Deutsch
AThANT	Abhandlungen zur Theologie des Alten und Neuen Testaments
AzTh	Arbeiten zur Theologie
BEThL	Bibliotheca ephemeridum theologicarum Lovaniensium
BEvTh	Beiträge zur evangelischen Theologie
BFCTh	Beiträge zur Förderung christlicher Theologie
BHTh	Beiträge zur historischen Theologie
BIS	Biblical Interpretation Series
BJS	Brown Judaic Studies
BKAT	Biblischer Kommentar: Altes Testament
BKT	Bibliothek klassischer Texte
BMANT	Beiträge zur Wissenschaft vom Alten Testament
BNTC	Black's New Testament Commentaries
BS	Biblical Seminar
BüSH	Bücherei der Salzburger Hochschulwochen
BZAW	Beihefte zur Zeitschrift für die alttestamentliche Wissenschaft
CB	Century Bible
CBC	Cambridge Bible Commentary
CCWJCW	Cambridge Commentaries on Writings of the Jewish and Christian World 200BC to AD200
CGTC	Cambridge Greek Testament Commentary
CB.NT	Coniectanea Biblica: New Testament Series
CNT	Commentaire du Noveau Testament
CNTC	Calvin's New Testament Commentaries
ConNeo	Coniectanea Neotestamentica
CRINT	Compendia rerum Iudaicarum ad Novum Testamentum
CSCT	Columbia Studies in the Classical Tradition
CSHJ	Chicago Studies in the History of Judaism
CThM	Calwer Theologische Monographien

EHS.Th	Europäische Hochschulschriften, Reihe 23: Theologie
EKGB	Einzelarbeiten aus der Kirchengeschichte Bayerns
EKK	Evangelisch-katholischer Kommentar zum Neuen Testament
ET	Erlanger Taschenbücher
Étbib	Études bibliques
FFNT	Foundations and Facets: New Testament
FRLANT	Forschungen zur Religion und Literatur des Alten und Neuen Testaments
FzB	Forschung zur Bibel
GL	German Library
GNT	Grundrisse zum Neuen Testament: NTD Ergänzungsreihe
HzAT	Handbuch zum Alten Testament
HzNT	Handbuch zum Neuen Testament
HThKNT	Herders theologischer Kommentar zum Neuen Testament
HThKNTSup	Herders theologischer Kommentar zum Neuen Testament, Supplementbände
HTS	Harvard Theological Studies
HUTh	Hermeneutische Untersuchungen zur Theologie
ICC	International Critical Commentary
JAL	Jewish Apocryphal Literature
JSNTSup	Journal for the Study of the New Testament Supplement Series
JSPSup	Journal for the Study of the Pseudepigrapha Supplement Series
KzAT	Kommentar zum Alten Testament
KEK	Meyers kritisch-exegetischer Kommentar über das Neue Testament
KzNT	Kommentar zum Neuen Testament
LD	Lectio Divina
LEC	Library of Early Christianity
LDSS	Literature of the Dead Sea Scrolls
LJC	Library of Jewish Classics
LL	Lutterworth Library
LLJC	Littman Library of Jewish Civilization
MMTM	Makers of the Modern Theological Mind
MNTC	Moffatt New Testament Commentary
MRvB.BÖA	Monographische Reihe von 'Benedictina': Biblisch-ökumenische Abteilung
MThS	Marburger theologische Studien
MTL	Marshall's Theological Library
NBST	Neukirchener Beiträge zur Systematischen Theologie
NCB	New Century Bible
NClB	New Clarendon Bible
NICNT	New International Commentary on the New Testament
NICOT	New International Commentary on the Old Testament
NIGTC	New International Greek Testament Commentary
NLC	New London Commentary
NovTSup	Novum Testamentum Supplements
NSBT	New Studies in Biblical Theology

NTD	Das Neue Testament Deutsch
NTL	New Testament Library
NTR	New Testament Readings
OBS	Oxford Bible Series
OCT	Outstanding Christian Thinkers
OTL	Old Testament Library
OTM	Oxford Theological Monographs
PAB	Potsdamer altertumswissenschaftliche Beiträge
P.SBG	Prophezei: Schweizerisches Bibelwerk für die Gemeinde
PVTG	Pseudepigrapha Veteris Testamenti Graece
QD	Quaestiones Disputatae
RNT	Regensburger Neues Testament
SAS	Studien des apologetischen Seminars
SBB	Stuttgarter biblische Beiträge
SBLDS	Society of Biblical Literature Dissertation Series
SBS	Stuttgarter Bibelstudien
SBT	Studies in Biblical Theology
SCJ	Studies in Christianity and Judaism
SD	Studies and Documents
SIJD	Schriften des Institutum Judaicum Delitzschianum
SJ	Studia Judaica
SJC	Studies in Judaism and Christianity
SJLA	Studies in Judaism and Late Antiquity
SLJC	The Schiff Library of Jewish Classics
SNTSMS	Society for New Testament Studies Monograph Series
SNTU	Studien zum Neuen Testament und seiner Umwelt
SPIB	Scripta Pontificii Instituti Biblici
SPS	Sacra Pagina Series
SSS	Semitic Study Series
StDel	Studia Delitzschiana
STDJ	Studies on the Texts of the Desert of Judah
StNT	Studien zum Neuen Testament
SNTW	Studies of the New Testament and Its World
StPB	Studia post-biblica
SVTP	Studia in Veteris Testamenti Pseudepigrapha
ThBü	Theologische Bücherei
ThExH	Theologische Existenz heute
ThHK	Theologischer Handkommentar zum Neuen Testament
ThSt	Theologische Studien
TNTC	Tyndale New Testament Commentaries
TPINTC	Trinity Press International New Testament Commentaries
TeolSt	Teologiske Studier
TSAJ	Texte und Studien zum Antiken Judentum
TTL	Theological Translation Library
TU	Texte und Untersuchungen zur Geschichte der altchristlichen Literatur
TWB	Third Way Books

UTB	Uni-Taschenbücher
WBC	Word Biblical Commentary
WC	Westminster Commentaries
WdF	Wege der Forschung
WMANT	Wissenschaftliche Monographien zum Alten und Neuen Testament
WUNT	Wissenschaftliche Untersuchungen zum Neuen Testament
YJS	Yale Judaic Series
ZBK	Zürcher Bibelkommentare

Chapter 1

Paul: A Hebrew of Hebrews

1. Paul's Birth, Upbringing and Education

Paul was born around the beginning of the Christian era[1] in Tarsus. Although we only know the place of his birth from Acts (9.11; 21.39; 22.3; cf. 9.30; 11.25), it is corroborated by Gal. 1.21. Here Paul says that after his visit to Jerusalem (three years after his conversion) he went into "the regions of Syria and Cilicia". One could interpret this as Paul's returning to the city of his birth since Tarsus was at this time administered by the governor of Syria, Syria-Cilicia forming a double province. For although Cilicia was made a province (with Tarsus as capital) after Pompey's victory over the pirates in 67 BC, it was later divided with the rich plainland of eastern Cilicia (Cilicia Pedias, Cilicia Campestris, "Plain Cilicia") united with Syria; on the other hand western Cilicia (Cilicia Tracheia, "Rough Cilicia"), a wild and mountainous region, was allotted to client kings. The double province existed from around 25 BC (when eastern Cilicia was joined to Syria) until 72 AD. In that year the last of the client kings of western Cilicia abdicated

---

[1] His birth date is estimated from Acts 7.58, where Paul is described as a "young man" (νεανίας) and Phlm 9, where Paul describes himself as an "old man" (πρεσβύτης) (the context I believe favours a reference to his age rather than his being an ambassador). According to *BA* νεανίας can refer to someone between the ages of 24 and 40. Philemon was most probably written from Ephesus in the period 53-55 AD (cf. P. Stuhlmacher, *Der Brief an Philemon* (EKK 18), Zürich/Braunschweig: Benziger Verlag/Neukirchen-Vluyn: Neukirchener Verlag ³1989, (¹1975), p. 21; E. Lohse, *Colossians and Philemon* (Hermeneia) ET, Philadelphia: Fortress Press 1971, p. 188). According to J. Murphy-O'Connor, *Paul: A Critical Life*, Oxford/New York: OUP 1997, p. 4, "for Paul's contemporaries, any male in his late fifties or early sixties would have been considered 'elderly'". R. Riesner, *Paul's Early Period: Chronology, Mission Strategy, Theology* ET, Grand Rapids/Cambridge: Wm B. Eerdmans 1998, p. 214, points out that if Paul were born around the turn of the century, it would fit well with his father's acquisition of the *civitas Romana*.

and the region was joined to eastern Cilicia to form a province under Vespasian.[2] Therefore for the whole of Paul's lifetime, the area of Cilicia in which Tarsus stood was part of this double province of Syria-Cilicia. Tarsus, standing in this plainland, was just ten miles from the coast and situated on the river Cydnus. Lying to the north were the Taurus mountain range and the Cilician Gates (just 30 miles away). The major trade route from Syria to central Asia minor ran across Cilicia Pedias and through these gates. In addition to being near this major trade route, Tarsus was an intellectual centre, being the home of great men such as the Stoic philosopher Athenodorus, the teacher of Augustus. In every respect Tarsus was indeed "no mean city" (Acts 21.39).

At some point Paul moved to Jerusalem. The key text is Acts 22.3, which appears at the beginning of Paul's speech given to the Jerusalem crowds shortly after he had been arrested. The translation as given in the RSV is:

---

[2] See, e.g., F.F. Bruce, *Paul: Apostle of the Free Spirit*, Exeter: Paternoster 1977, p. 33. Such a view whereby the union of Cilicia with Syria is placed under Augustus (advanced by Baronius, *Annales Ecclesiastici* (1588) and T. Mommsen, *Res Gestae Divi Augusti*, [2]1883, p. 173) is criticised by E.J. Bickerman, "Syria and Cilicia", *AJP* 68 (1947) 356 (353-62). Bickermann argues that "Cilicia Campestris was added to Syria sometime between A.D. 18 and 35 and separated from the latter before the spring of 55, probably at the end of 54" (359). See also "The Date of Fourth Maccabees" in *Studies in Jewish and Christian History I* (AGJU 9.1), Leiden: E.J. Brill 1986, 279-80 (275-81). Bickermann appeals to Tacitus, Annales 2.58 (referring to events of 18 AD) and Annales 13.8 (events of early 55 AD) to suggest that at these times there was an independent Cilicia. Hence he limits the double province to the period 20-54 AD. He has been rightly criticized by M. Hengel and A.M. Schwemer, *Paulus zwischen Damaskus und Antiochien: Die unbekannten Jahre des Apostels* (WUNT 108), Tübingen: J.C.B. Mohr (Paul Siebeck) 1998, p. 42. They suggest that the Tacitus texts do not point to an independent Cilicia. See also E.M.B. Green, "Syria and Cilicia–A Note", *ExpT* 71 (1959-60) 52-53, who suggests that τὰ κλίματα τῆς Συρίας καὶ τῆς Κιλικίας refers to one district and believes it is significant that א* 33 and a few other MSS omit the second article. C.J. Hemer, *The Book of Acts in the Setting of Hellenistic History* (ed. by C.H. Gempf) (WUNT 49), Tübingen: J.C.B. Mohr (Paul Siebeck) 1989, p. 172, considers whether the chronology of the double province has relevance for Acts 23.34 (dated sometime in the period 57-59 AD).

I am a Jew, born at Tarsus in Cilicia, but brought up in this city at the feet of Gamaliel, educated according to the strict manner of the law of our fathers, being zealous for God as you all are [to] this day.[3]

This translation is based on taking the structure of the verse as follows:

1 Ἐγώ εἰμι	ἀνὴρ Ἰουδαῖος
2 γεγεννημένος	ἐν Ταρσῷ τῆς Κιλικίας
3 ἀνατεθραμμένος δὲ	ἐν τῇ πόλει ταύτῃ παρὰ τοὺς πόδας Γαμαλιὴλ
4 πεπαιδευμένος	κατὰ ἀκρίβειαν τοῦ πατρῴου νόμου
5 ζηλωτὴς ὑπάρχων τοῦ θεοῦ	καθὼς πάντες ὑμεῖς ἐστε σήμερον

Such a structure is supported by du Toit,[4] who gives a number of stylistic reasons for accepting this.[5] However, as du Toit points out, most modern text editions[6] and commentators put the *caesura* before παρὰ τοὺς πόδας Γαμαλιήλ.[7] One such structure could then be the following:[8]

1	Ἐγώ εἰμι ἀνὴρ Ἰουδαῖος
2	γεγεννημένος ἐν Ταρσῷ τῆς Κιλικίας
3	ἀνατεθραμμένος δὲ ἐν τῇ πόλει ταύτῃ
4	παρὰ τοὺς πόδας Γαμαλιὴλ πεπαιδευμένος κατὰ ἀκρίβειαν τοῦ πατρῴου νόμου
5	ζηλωτὴς ὑπάρχων τοῦ θεοῦ
6	καθὼς πάντες ὑμεῖς ἐστε σήμερον

---

[3] C. Burchard, "Fußnoten zum neutestamentlichen Griechisch", *ZNW* 61 (1970) 169 n. 65 (157-71), points out that "σήμερον betont nicht den Zeitpunkt im Gegensatz gegen ein Gestern oder Morgen, denn das gibt keinen Sinn". He suggests rather "bis auf den heutigen Tag" and compares Joseph and Asenath 4.7: ἔστι δὲ οὗτος ὁ Ἰωσὴφ ἀνὴρ θεοσεβὴς καὶ σώφρων καὶ παρθένος ὡς σὺ σήμερον.

[4] See A.B. du Toit, "A Tale of Two Cities: 'Tarsus or Jerusalem' Revisited", *NTS* 46 (2000) 384 (375-402).

[5] Du Toit, "Two Cities", 384, points out that in such a structure lines 2-4 begin with a perfect participle and that it is characteristic of Luke's style to have an accumulation of circumstantial participles where the participle "almost invariably appears in the first part of each phrase".

[6] *GNT³, GNT⁴, NA²⁶, NA²⁷, NK².*

[7] Contrast *WH* who take ἀνατεθραμμένος δὲ ἐν τῇ πόλει ταύτῃ παρὰ τοὺς πόδας Γαμαλιήλ as a unit.

[8] This could be a chiastic structure. Du Toit, "Two Cities", 383, points to the problems in viewing this as a consciously intended chiasmus.

1   I am a Jew,
2   born at Tarsus in Cilicia,
3   but brought up in this city,
4   educated at the feet of Gamaliel according to the strict manner of the law of our fathers,
5   being zealous for God
6   as you all are to this day.

Such a structure is reflected in the translations and commentaries of Stählin,[9] Wikenhauser,[10] Haenchen,[11] Bruce,[12] Schneider,[13] Pesch,[14] Roloff,[15] Lüdemann[16] and Barrett.[17] Du Toit finds such a structure unsatisfactory mainly because placing παρὰ τοὺς πόδας Γαμαλιήλ at the beginning of line 4 "disturbs the rhythmic flow of the Greek" and makes the line "very long and cumbersome".[18] But I wonder whether such a structure is so problematic. Although line 4 may be long, it may be that κατὰ ἀκρίβειαν τοῦ πατρῴου νόμου should be taken with ζηλωτὴς ὑπάρχων τοῦ θεοῦ as suggested by Burchard[19] and Marshall.[20] This would then give:

---

[9] G. Stählin, *Die Apostelgeschichte* (NTD 5), Göttingen: Vandenhoeck & Ruprecht ³1968, (¹1936), p. 281.

[10] A. Wikenhauser, *Die Apostelgeschichte* (RNT 5), Regensburg: Friedrich Pustet ⁴1961, (¹1956), p. 244.

[11] E. Haenchen, *Die Apostelgeschichte* (KEK 3), Göttingen: Vandenhoeck & Ruprecht ⁷1977, (¹1956), p. 595.

[12] F.F. Bruce, *The Book of the Acts* (NICNT), Grand Rapids: Wm B. Eerdmans ²1988, (¹1954), p. 414.

[13] G. Schneider, *Die Apostelgeschichte* (HThKNT 5), 2 vols, Freiburg/Basel/Wien: Herder 1 1980; 2 1982, 2:316, 320.

[14] R. Pesch, *Die Apostelgeschichte* (EKK 5), 2 vols, Zürich/Einsiedeln/Köln: Benziger Verlag/Neukirchen-Vluyn: Neukirchener Verlag 1986, 2:228, 233.

[15] J. Roloff, *Die Apostelgeschichte* (NTD 5), Göttingen: Vandenhoeck & Ruprecht 1981, pp. 318, 322.

[16] G. Lüdemann, *Early Christianity according to the Traditions in Acts* ET, London: SCM 1989, p. 238. However, in *Paul, Apostle to the Gentiles: Studies in Chronology* ET, London: SCM 1984, p. 39 n. 72, he doubts whether the author is giving reliable historical information.

[17] C.K. Barrett, *The Acts of the Apostles* (ICC), 2 vols, Edinburgh: T. &. T. Clark 1994-98, 2:1029.

[18] Du Toit, "Two Cities", 383.

[19] C. Burchard, *Der dreizehnte Zeuge: Traditions- und kompositionsgeschichtliche Untersuchungen zu Lukas' Darstellung der Frühzeit des Paulus* (FRLANT 103), Göttingen: Vandenhoeck & Ruprecht 1970, p. 32; "Fußnoten", 168-69.

[20] I.H. Marshall, *The Acts of the Apostles* (TNTC), Leicester: IVP 1980, p. 354, who,

1   Ἐγώ εἰμι ἀνὴρ Ἰουδαῖος
2   γεγεννημένος ἐν Ταρσῷ τῆς Κιλικίας
3   ἀνατεθραμμένος δὲ ἐν τῇ πόλει ταύτῃ
4   παρὰ τοὺς πόδας Γαμαλιὴλ πεπαιδευμένος
5   κατὰ ἀκρίβειαν τοῦ πατρῴου νόμου ζηλωτὴς ὑπάρχων τοῦ θεοῦ
6   καθὼς πάντες ὑμεῖς ἐστε σήμερον

Such a structure also brings out a clearer internal chiasmus in lines 3-4:

3   ἀνατεθραμμένος
          δὲ ἐν τῇ πόλει ταύτῃ
4   παρὰ τοὺς πόδας Γαμαλιὴλ
    πεπαιδευμένος

Further, by placing παρὰ τοὺς πόδας Γαμαλιήλ before the participle πεπαιδευμένος, emphasis is placed on the fact that Paul was educated by one of the most prestigious Pharisees of the time.[21] This education was most probably his education as a Pharisee.[22] It has been suggested that the reference is more to his "Erziehung zum Gentleman"[23] which could include

referring to Acts 21.20; Rom. 10.2; Gal. 1.14; Phil. 3.6 writes that "religious zeal was expressed in meticulous observance of the law". See also K. Lake and H.J. Cadbury, in F.J. Foakes Jackson and K. Lake (ed.), *The Beginnings of Christianity, Part I: The Acts of the Apostles, Vol. IV*, London: Macmillan 1933, p. 279.

[21] R.C.H. Lenski, *The Interpretation of the Acts of the Apostles*, Minneapolis: Augsburg Publishing House 1961 (repr.), (¹1934), p. 902, writes: "by no less a person than Gamaliel was Paul educated".

[22] See W.C. van Unnik, "Tarsus or Jerusalem: The City of Paul's Youth", in *Sparsa Collecta: The Collected Essays of W.C. van Unnik (Part One)* (NovTSup 29), Leiden: E.J. Brill 1973, 259-320. Cf. also G. Schneider, παιδεύω, *EWNT* 3:4 (3-4), who understands the verb in Acts 22.3 as "trained". Although the idea of ordination to be a Rabbi comes in the period after 70 AD (see M. Hengel, *The Charismatic Leader and his Followers* (SNTW) ET, Edinburgh: T. & T. Clark 1981, p. 44 n. 22), the scribal beth-hammidrash (see οἶκος παιδείας in Sir. 51.23) had existed for some time (see Hengel, *Pre-Christian Paul*, p. 28). On the use of the term "Rabbi", see R. Riesner, *Jesus als Lehrer: Eine Untersuchung zum Ursprung der Evangelien-Überlieferung* (WUNT 2.7), Tübingen: J.C.B. Mohr (Paul Siebeck) ³1988, (¹1981), pp. 266-74.

[23] Burchard, *Der dreizehnte Zeuge*, p. 32.

early education.[24] If this were to be the case, problems concerning chronology could arise.[25]

I therefore believe that the triadic structure points to Paul being "born" (γεγεννημένος) in Tarsus, but "brought up" (ἀνατεθραμμένος) in Jerusalem and "educated" (πεπαιδευμένος) at the feet of Gamaliel. But how old was Paul when he moved to Jerusalem? W.C. van Unnik argued that the move from Tarsus to Jerusalem "took place quite early in Paul's life, apparently before he could peep round the corner of the door and certainly before he went roaming on the streets".[26] Crucial to his argument is that ἀνατρέφειν ("to bring up") is quite different to παιδεύειν ("to educate"). ἀνατρέφειν "takes place in the parental home, and in it mother and father play the leading part".[27] He concludes that in Acts 22.3, "ἀνατεθραμμένος can refer only to Paul's upbringing in the home of his parents from the earliest years of his childhood until he was of school age; πεπαιδευμένος refers to the instruction which he received in accordance with Eastern custom 'at the feet of'

---

[24] See K. Haacker, "Werdegang des Apostels Paulus", *ANRW* 2.26.2 (1995) 857 (815-938), who argues that παιδεύειν/παιδεία refers to "eine höhere Allgemeinbildung und keine spezielle Berufsausbildung". He suggests that Gamaliel could have run a sort of boarding-school for children of pious families (as his grandson Gamaliel II had done) (859 n. 203). Such an idea is obviously rather speculative. I see no problem in using παιδεύειν/παιδεία for his education as a Pharisee. As van Unnik, "Tarsus or Jerusalem", demonstrated, the root can be used for specialist training (see, for example, the use of ἐκπαιδεύειν for instruction in Roman law in Gregory Thaumaturgus, *Panegyric on Origen* 62).

[25] If Paul were born in say 5 AD (a relatively late estimate) and if Gamaliel began teaching in Jerusalem in 25 AD (the estimate of P. Billerbeck (with H.L. Strack), *Kommentar zum Neuen Testament aus Talmud und Midrasch*, 4 vols, München: C.H. Beck-'sche Verlagsbuchhandlung 1-3 ³1961; 4 ²1956, 2:636, followed, e.g., by J. Gnilka, *Paulus von Tarsus. Zeuge und Apostel* (HThKNTSup 6), Freiburg/Basel/Wien: Herder 1996, p. 28), then the earliest age at which Paul could study under Gamaliel would be 20. The only way the chronology could work is if one took Oepke's scheme that Paul was born 10 AD at the earliest (A. Oepke, "Probleme der vorchristlichen Zeit des Paulus", in K.H. Rengstorf (ed.), *Das Paulusbild in der neueren deutschen Forschung* (WdF 24), Darmstadt: Wissenschaftliche Buchgesellschaft 1982, 445 (410-46)) and Gamaliel was active 20-50 AD (441).

[26] Van Unnik, "Tarsus or Jerusalem", 301.

[27] Van Unnik, "Tarsus or Jerusalem", 286.

Gamaliel".[28] Since schooling started at the age of six to seven,[29] his ἀνατροφή must have taken place before he was seven and therefore necessitated a move to Jerusalem at a very young age.

Such an argument has been challenged by du Toit. He questions van Unnik's understanding of the participles ἀνατεθραμμένος and πεπαιδευμένος. He concludes his survey of the use of τροφή and cognates by saying that although conventionally it focused on the initial stage of upbringing at home, it could also overlap with παιδεία or the whole upbringing process.[30] Preferring the first structure referred to above, he argues that ἀνατεθραμμένος δὲ ἐν τῇ πόλει ταύτῃ παρὰ τοὺς πόδας Γαμαλιήλ forms a unit. Since Gamaliel was involved in his "upbringing" (ἀνατεθραμμένος), Paul did not have to move to Jerusalem at such an early age.

Du Toit then goes further. He argues that in terms of accumulative probabilities, "the bulk of information tilts the scale decidedly in favour of Tarsus as the place where he learned to speak Greek, grew up into the Greek Bible, appropriated the basics of Greek style and rhetoric and acquired a rudimentary knowledge of popular Greek philosophy".[31] This argument *could* be correct but I believe it is *unlikely* to be so. First of all, there are, as I have suggested, good arguments for taking πεπαιδευμένος with παρὰ τοὺς πόδας Γαμαλιήλ. Secondly, the participles ἀνατεθραμμένος and πεπαιδευμένος could well be distinguishing the processes of "bringing up" and "teaching". However, I accept that some sort of elementary schooling could be included in the use of ἀνατεθραμμένος in Acts 22.3.[32] Thirdly,

---

[28] Van Unnik, "Tarsus or Jerusalem", 295.

[29] See H.I. Marrou, *A History of Education in Antiquity* ET, London: Sheed and Ward 1956, pp. 102, 142-43 regarding Greek education. Regarding Jewish education, M. Hengel, *Judentum und Hellenismus*, Tübingen: J.C.B. Mohr (Paul Siebeck) [2]1973, ([1]1969), p. 151, points out that according to the tradition of Rab, the school age was also set at six to seven years.

[30] Du Toit, "Two Cities", 379, points out that τρέφω and related terms were "originally and conventionally used for the pre-school stage" (see, e.g., Philo, *Spec. leg.* 2.229). But he gives a number of examples where τρέφω κτλ can overlap with παιδεία or even replace or include it.

[31] Du Toit, "Two Cities", 401.

[32] On Lk. 4.16, Riesner, *Jesus als Lehrer*, pp. 242, writes: "Der Ausdruck (ἀνα)τρέφειν schließt keineswegs aus, daß Jesus in seinem Heimatort eine gründliche Elementarschulausbildung erhielt". Riesner, like du Toit, "Two Cities", gives cases where the verb can be used for education which does not take place in the home. See, however, the comments of F. Bovon, *Das Evangelium nach Lukas: 1. Teilband Lk 1,1-*

all the signs are that Paul had Aramaic/Hebrew as a mother tongue (Phil. 3.5; 2 Cor. 11.22) and that Greek philosophy had little *direct* influence on Paul,[33] suggesting that he may well have moved to Jerusalem at a young age. Du Toit *is* correct to write that "Acts 22.3 does not require a conclusion that the historical Paul grew up from his earliest years as a thoroughbred, exclusively Aramaic speaking Jerusalem Jew."[34] However, not even van Unnik seems to go this far for he does not claim Paul was "exclusively Aramaic speaking".[35] Rather he writes that "Aramaic was his earliest and principal tongue".[36] And although I believe Paul did move to Jerusalem relatively early in his life, I would certainly not wish to say that Paul was an "exclusively Aramaic speaking Jerusalem Jew". It is true that Paul has a good command of Greek. But Greek could have been used by Paul in Jerusalem.[37] Although Hengel's views on the hellenization of Palestine[38] have been ques-

---

9.50 (EKK 3.1), Zürich: Benziger Verlag/Neukirchen-Vluyn: Neukirchener Verlag 1989, p. 210 n. 13: "In einem biographischen Kontext bedeutet τρέφω, wie auch ἀνατρέφω, nicht einfach 'ein Kind ernähren' und auch nicht nur 'ein Kind aufziehen', diese Verben bezeichnen vielmehr den Zeitabschnitt der Kindheit, den das Kind zu Hause verbringt, wo es von seiner Mutter und seinem Vater ernährt und zunächst einmal aufgezogen wird". In Acts 7.21, the verb ἀνατρέφω would most naturally refer to the upbringing of Moses, here in the home of his adoptive mother, Pharaoh's daughter.

[33] This is not to deny, of course, that later in Paul's missionary work among Gentiles he engaged directly with educated non-Jews.

[34] Du Toit, "Two Cities", 401.

[35] An exception here is R.A. Martin, *Studies in the Life and Ministry of the Early Paul and Related Issues*, Lewiston/Queenston/Lampeter: Mellen Biblical Press 1993, who claims that it was only after his conversion that the strict Pharisee Paul learnt Greek (see for example *Studies*, pp. 15-16; 30-31; 86-102).

[36] Van Unnik, "Tarsus or Jerusalem", 304.

[37] Acts 6.9 mentions that Jerusalem had a synagogue of freedmen which included Cilicians. Riesner, *Early Period*, pp. 153-54, following the lead of H.J. Cadbury, *The Book of Acts in History*, London: A. & C. Black 1955, p. 73, suggests Luke assumed Paul was a member of this synagogue.

[38] Hengel, *Judentum und Hellenismus*, passim (*Judaism and Hellenism: Studies in their Encounter in Palestine during the Early Hellenistic Period* ET, 2 vols, London: SCM 1974).

tioned by some[39] his major views have been overwhelmingly accepted and there can be no doubt that Jerusalem was considerably hellenized, even though the majority of its inhabitants spoke Aramaic.[40] Hengel estimated that there were at the minimum 10-20% of the Jerusalem population who had Greek as a mother tongue and working with a population of 80-100,000 gives the minimum number as between 8,000 and 16,000.[41] This is a considerable number. Paul could therefore have a good command of Greek if he did grow up in Jerusalem.

To sum up so far, although I cannot be quite so precise as van Unnik, I believe he is right in putting the move early in Paul's childhood.[42] But what about his education in Jerusalem? Some have doubted whether Paul had a Jerusalem education; this education is only mentioned in Acts and, it is argued, the author is often unreliable.[43] Further G. Strecker believes on the basis of Gal. 1.22 ("And I was still not known by sight by the Churches of Judea") that Paul had never been in Jerusalem before the apostolic council

---

[39] See A. Momigliano, "Review of *Judentum und Hellenismus*, by M. Hengel", *JTS* 21 (1970) 149-53; L.H. Feldman, "Hengel's *Judaism and Hellenism* in Retrospect", *JBL* 96 (1977) 371-82; F. Millar, "The Background to the Maccabean Revolution: Reflections on Martin Hengel's *Judaism and Hellenism*", *JJS* 29 (1978) 1-21. For an overview and critique of these responses to Hengel's work, see L.L. Grabbe, *Judaism from Cyrus to Hadrian*, 2 vols, Minneapolis: Fortress Press 1992, 1:150-53.

[40] Du Toit refers to a study by D. Fiensy, "The Composition of the Jerusalem Church", in R. Bauckham (ed.), *The Book of Acts in Its Palestinian Setting* (The Book of Acts in its First Century Setting vol. 4), Grand Rapids: Wm B. Eerdmans/Carlisle: Paternoster, 213-36, to draw out the point that Aramaic was the "main language of Palestinian Jewry" ("Two Cities", 377). Yet the chapter of Fiensy emphasizes the importance of Greek culture in Jerusalem.

[41] M. Hengel, *The 'Hellenization' of Judaea in the First Century after Christ* (in collaboration with C. Markschies) ET, London: SCM/Philadelphia: TPI 1989, p. 10.

[42] M. Hengel, *The Pre-Christian Paul*, London: SCM 1991, p. 39, although not agreeing with van Unnik, nevertheless grants that he "has Luke on his side". Hengel wishes to place the move to Jerusalem later. He points to Paul's command of Greek (p. 35), although this could be consistent with being brought up in Jerusalem, since, as Hengel himself points out, Greek schooling was also available in Jerusalem (p. 39).

[43] I will refer to the author of Luke-Acts as "Luke". This does not commit us to Luke, the companion of Paul, being the author, although I believe it is very probable that he was. For a fine discussion of Luke as historian of Paul's journeys (and defence of the view that Luke was the author) see C.-J. Thornton, *Der Zeuge des Zeugen: Lukas als Historiker der Paulusreisen* (WUNT 56), Tübingen: J.C.B. Mohr (Paul Siebeck) 1991.

(Gal. 2.1ff.), the exception being the very short visit to Peter in Gal. 1.18.[44] Jerusalem had only a population of 25,000[45] and if he was "not known by sight" Strecker argues that Paul cannot have been in Jerusalem and suggests that Paul's education took place in the diaspora.[46]

There are three problems with Strecker's approach. First, he misuses Gal. 1.22, a matter I will deal with below. Secondly, he assumes that Jerusalem was the sort of place where everyone knew everyone else. This is manifestly not the case even if one were to work with Strecker's low estimate of a population of 25,000.[47] In fact recent studies suggest a much bigger population. A minimum of around 60,000 has been suggested at the time of the early Church.[48] Thirdly, although it is possible that Paul received some of his elementary education in Tarsus in a Jewish Greek school, it is virtually impossible that he received his Pharisaic education in the diaspora. There is no evidence of Pharisaic schools in the diaspora before 70 AD.[49] It is instructive to consider Alexandria, the second city of the empire and the biggest centre of Jewish learning in the diaspora. Could there have been Pharisaic schools here? There is the following polemic of the Pharisee Abtalion (teacher of Hillel) against Alexandria in the Mishnah, Aboth 1.11:

---

[44] G. Strecker, "Befreiung und Rechtfertigung: Zur Stellung der Rechtfertigungslehre in der Theologie des Paulus", in J. Friedrich, W. Pöhlmann and P. Stuhlmacher (ed.), *Rechtfertigung: Festschrift für Ernst Käsemann zum 70. Geburtstag*, Tübingen: J.C.B. Mohr (Paul Siebeck)/Göttingen: Vandenhoeck & Ruprecht 1976, 482 n. 10 (479-508).

[45] Strecker takes this number from J. Jeremias (see *Jerusalem in the Time of Jesus* ET, Philadelphia: Fortress Press 1969, p. 84).

[46] Strecker, "Befreiung und Rechtfertigung", 482 n. 10.

[47] Hengel, *Pre-Christian Paul*, p. 24.

[48] Hengel, *Pre-Christian Paul*, p. 24, refers to J. Wilkinson, "Ancient Jerusalem: Its Water Supply and Population", *PEQ* 106 (1974) 33-51 and M. Broshi, "La Population de l'ancienne Jérusalem", *RB* 82 (1975) 5-14. They suggest a population growing from 32,000 in the Hasmonaean period to 80,000 in 66 AD. W. Reinhardt, "The Population Size of Jerusalem and the Numerical Growth of the Jerusalem Church", in R. Bauckham (ed.), *The Book of Acts in Its Palestinian Setting* (The Book of Acts in its First Century Setting vol. 4), Grand Rapids: Wm B. Eerdmans/Carlisle: Paternoster 1995, 263 (237-65), believes that around 30 AD the conceivable lower limit is 60,000 and that the figure may have reached 100-120,000 in the forties.

[49] See Hengel, *Pre-Christian Paul*, pp. 33-34. Contrast Strecker, "Befreiung", 482 n. 10, who has argued that there were Pharisaic schools in the Diaspora (see also K. Berger, "Jesus als Pharisäer und frühe Christen als Pharisäer", *NovT* 30 (1988) 231-62).

Abtalion said: Ye sages, give heed to your words lest ye incur the penalty of exile and ye be exiled to a place of evil waters, and the disciples that come after you drink (of them) and die, and the name of Heaven be profaned.[50]

The "place of evil waters" is most probably Alexandria situated on the coast at the west end of the Nile delta. It is unlikely that there was a Pharisaic school in Alexandria or indeed elsewhere in the dispersion before 70 AD. Strangely Mt. 23.15 has been used to argue for Pharisaic schools in the diaspora.[51]

Woe to you, scribes and Pharisees, hypocrites! for you traverse sea and land to make a single proselyte, and when he becomes a proselyte you make him twice as much a child of hell as yourselves.

But Mt. 23.15 does *not* point to Pharisees being permanently settled in the diaspora. On the contrary, the perspective is from the land of Israel and if the Pharisees were already in the diaspora, there would be no need to "traverse sea and land".

So far I have almost exclusively relied upon the testimony of Acts. But what is Paul's own perception of his upbringing and education? In Phil. 3.5-6 he writes that he was

---

[50] H. Danby (ed.), *The Mishnah*, Oxford: OUP 1985 (repr.), (¹1933), p. 447. This text, incidentally, shows that Abtalion did not consider himself to be in "exile" in Jerusalem (see M.A. Seifrid, "The 'New Perspective on Paul' and Its Problems", *Themelios* 25.2 (2000) 10 (4-18)). This puts in question the idea of N.T. Wright that Israel regarded the Babylonian exile as continuing into the present day (see N.T. Wright, *The New Testament and the People of God*, London: SPCK 1992, pp. 268-79).

[51] Strecker, "Befreiung und Rechtfertigung", 482 n. 10. The text does raise important questions about Jewish missionary activity. M. Goodman, "Jewish Proselytizing in the First Century", in J. Lieu, J. North and T. Rajak (ed.), *The Jews among Pagans and Christians in the Roman Empire*, London/New York: Routledge 1992, 53-78, is extremely sceptical about such activity and solves the "problem" of Mt. 23.15 by suggesting that προσήλυτος here means a Jew converted to the Pharisaic sect (60-63). The problem with this solution, however, is that προσήλυτος was, since the LXX, a fixed religious term for a Gentile who had become a full member of the people of God through circumcision (see K.G. Kuhn, προσήλυτος, *TDNT* 6:727-44) and there is no clear indication in the text that the term is to be understood in a different sense (see U. Luz, *Das Evangelium nach Matthäus (Mt 18-25)* (EKK 1.3), Zürich/Düsseldorf: Benziger Verlag/Neukirchen-Vluyn: Neukirchener Verlag 1997, p. 324). J. Jeremias, *Jesu Verheißung für die Völker* (Franz Delitzsch-Vorlesungen 1953), Stuttgart: W. Kohlhammer Verlag 1956, p. 15, believes "Das Logion entstammt alter aramäischer Überlieferung" and points to the various semitisms (n. 61).

. . . circumcised on the eighth day, of the people of Israel, of the tribe of Benjamin, a
Hebrew born of Hebrews; as to the law a Pharisee, 6 as to zeal a persecutor of the
church, as to righteousness under the law blameless.

Here Paul presents seven things he was proud of, and he begins by listing
four privileges which he inherited.[52] First, "circumcised on the eighth day"
indicates that neither Paul nor his parents were Gentiles and that they
observed the law strictly in that Paul was circumcised on the eighth day precisely (Gen. 17.12, Lev. 12.3). Secondly, "of the people of Israel" indicates
that neither he nor his parents were proselytes. They belonged to the Jewish
people from birth.[53]

Thirdly, he writes that he is "of the tribe of Benjamin" (cf. Rom. 11.1).[54]
Although there are texts which suggest that Benjamin split off from Judah (1
Kgs 12.20), generally it is portrayed as being faithful to Judah (1 Kgs 12.21,
23; 2 Chron. 11.10, 12, 23; 14.8; 15.2, 8-9).[55] Indeed according to Jos.
15.8; 18.16, 23 (but contradicted by 15.63), Jerusalem belonged to Benjamin.[56] Saul/Paul could be proud of belonging to such a tribe. Not only was
the first king of Israel from this tribe but Benjaminites "were renowned for

---

[52] In Phil. 3.2-6 Paul is making the point that if anyone had reason to have "confidence in the flesh" (3.4) it was Paul himself. He is attacking Jewish Christians (whom
he calls "dogs", "evil workers", "those who mutilate the flesh" (3.2)) who were compelling Christians to keep the Jewish law and be circumcised (see chapter 4, section 4.1
below). Paul had an even better pedigree (3.5-6) yet for the sake of Christ counts it as
loss (3.7).

[53] G.B. Caird, *Paul's Letters from Prison* (NClB), Oxford: OUP 1976, p. 135, prefers
the translation "an Israelite by race" since γένος, the word used here, refers to racial
descent whereas λαός refers to "people" which would include proselytes.

[54] On Benjamin as a tribe see K.-D. Schunck, *Benjamin. Untersuchungen zur Entstehung und Geschichte eines israelitischen Stammes* (BZAW 86), Berlin: Walter de
Gruyter 1963.

[55] The discrepancy between 1 Kgs 12.20 and 12.21, 23 is variously explained. One
possibility is that vv. 21-24 are a later addition reflecting the post-exilic situation that
tribes of Judah and Benjamin lived in the area around Jerusalem (see G.H. Jones, *1 and 2
Kings, Volume I* (NCB), Grand Rapids: Wm B. Eerdmans/London: Marshall, Morgan &
Scott 1994 (repr.), (¹1984), p. 255). Chronicles would also reflect the post-exilic situation.

[56] This may again be reflecting post-exilic circumstances. We read in 1 Chronicles that
after the exile Benjaminites "dwelt in Jerusalem" (9.3; see also the genealogies in vv. 7-9
and cf. Neh. 11.7-9).

their prowess in battle".[57] Had Luke said that Paul was a Benjaminite, many scholars would no doubt dismiss such a connection. But since Paul himself claims this ancestry, many are ready to consider it. Interestingly Rabbi Judah ha Nasi, the editor of the Mishnah, claimed to be a Benjaminite. Therefore his great-great grandfather, Gamaliel I, Paul's teacher (according to Acts 22.3) would also be a Benjaminite.[58] It is striking that extensive genealogies are given in 1 Chronicles for the tribe of Benjamin (1 Chron. 7.6-12; 8; 9.3, 7-9) (in contrast, genealogies for Dan and Zebulon are omitted). Braun writes that "[a]lthough most, if not all, of these genealogies stem from the remote past, we may assume that the interest in such geneaologies was keenest among those who wished to establish their own relationship to Israel through the tribe of Benjamin".[59] The most famous descendant of Benjamin in Israel's history was undoubtedly king Saul. Despite the suggestion in 1 Chron. 10.6 that all of Saul's house died ("Thus Saul died; he and his three sons and all his house died together"), his genealogy is given in 8.33-40 through 13 generation. Japhet estimates that Ulam (the first born of the last generation mentioned) would be living around the end of the seventh century, shortly before the exile (cf. 9.1).[60] 1 Chron. 8.40: "The sons of Ulam were men who were mighty warriors, bowmen, having many sons and grandsons, one hundred and fifty. All these were Benjaminites". Perhaps Paul's family had a family tree which traced their origin through Ulam and Saul.[61] Paul/Saul was therefore named after his most illustrious ancestor.

---

[57] S.J. De Vries, *1 Kings* (WBC 12), Waco: Word Books 1985, p. 158. See 1 Chron. 8.40.

[58] See Hengel, *Pre-Christian Paul*, pp. 26-27.

[59] R. Braun, *1 Chronicles* (WBC 14), Waco: Word Books 1986, p. 128.

[60] S. Japhet, *I & II Chronicles* (OTL), London: SCM 1993, p. 199.

[61] On the question of genealogies see Jeremias, *Jerusalem*, pp. 275-302. He believes that there were many instances where lay families had written records of genealogical descent and that these were often accurate. M.D. Johnson, *The Purpose of the Biblical Genealogies* (SNTSMS 8), Cambridge: CUP 1969, pp. 99-108, is much more sceptical. He believes that "feelings of attachment to individual tribes, . . . with the exception of the priests and Levites, were not strong in post-biblical Judaism, although, as in the case of Paul, there are exceptions to this generalization" (p. 105). He believes that in post-biblical Judaism the laity usually had oral rather than written genealogies (p. 106). The case of priests was different: he believes Josephus is to be trusted that careful and formal genealogical records were kept in Jerusalem (p. 99).

The fourth privilege Paul lists is that he is "a Hebrew born of Hebrews". There has been some debate concerning the precise meaning of the word "Hebrew" (Εβραῖος). The term only occurs in the New Testament in three places: Acts 6.1; Phil. 3.5; 2 Cor. 11.22. Gutbrod believes the stress is on descent and not language (although the descent may also include language).[62] In a discussion of Phil. 3.5 and 2 Cor. 11.22, Harvey argues that "'Hebrews' is a designation used by those who claim to be conservative and non-innovative".[63] However, in his discussion of Acts 6-7 he seems to think that "Hebrews" and "Hellenists" *are* terms referring to the use of language (although he is unsure whether there is an "ideological" difference between the two groups).[64] I suggest that in Phil. 3.5 and 2 Cor. 11.22 the stress is also most probably on the linguistic significance of the term.[65] Also the term can be used for Jews of Palestinian origin or who have a close relationship with Palestine.[66] So in Phil. 3.5 and 2 Cor. 11.22 Paul is stressing that he is not a diaspora Jew speaking a foreign language — he is a Hebrew/Aramaic speaking Jew.[67] This gives support to the position of van Unnik described above. Further, according to Phil. 3.5, his parents were Hebrew/Aramaic speaking Jews. This raises a number of important issues. There is a tradition in Jerome[68] that Paul's parents came from the neighbourhood of Gischala in Galilee and were carried off to Tarsus in the upheavals of war.[69] Although

---

[62] See W. Gutbrod in G. von Rad, K.G. Kuhn and W. Gutbrod, Ἰσραήλ κτλ, *TDNT* 3:389-90 (356-91).

[63] G. Harvey, *The True Israel: Uses of the Names Jew, Hebrew and Israel in Ancient Jewish and Early Christian Literature* (AGAJU 35), Leiden/New York/Köln: E.J. Brill 1996, p. 132.

[64] Harvey, *True Israel*, pp. 132-36.

[65] See C.F.D. Moule, "Once More, Who Were the Hellenists", *ExpT* 70 (1958-59) 100-2; Hengel, *Pre-Christian Paul*, pp. 117-18 n. 146.

[66] M. Hengel, "Between Jesus and Paul", in *Between Jesus and Paul: Studies in the Earliest History of Christianity*, London: SCM 1983, 10 (1-29). Cf. D. Georgi, *Die Gegner des Paulus im 2. Korintherbrief: Studien zur religiösen Propaganda in der Spätantike* (WMANT 11), Neukirchen-Vluyn: Neukirchener Verlag 1964, pp. 51-63, especially pp. 52-54, who notes that originally the term "Hebrew" was used for the language and writing of Palestinian Jews and then the geographical and cultural characteristics, i.e. people of a Palestinian origin, culture and tradition.

[67] Hengel, *Pre-Christian Paul*, p. 26.

[68] Jerome, *Ad Philemonem* 5.23.

[69] Cf. Jerome, *De viris illustribus* 5.

there are some problems with this tradition from Jerome (it includes the idea that Paul himself was born in Galilee) it could throw some interesting light on Paul's statement here that he is a Hebrew speaking Jew of Hebrew speaking parents[70] and could account for how Paul's father gained Roman citizenship (i.e. by being emancipated by a Roman citizen). It does however pose a problem in that Paul, according to Acts 22.28, was born a Roman citizen. But if Paul's parents were Hebrew speaking it could throw some light on the rather neglected statement of the Lucan Paul in Acts 23.6: "I am a Pharisee, a son of Pharisees" (ἐγὼ Φαρισαῖός εἰμι, υἱὸς Φαρισαίων).[71] This assertion that he was a son of Pharisees could of course be a Lucan invention. However, is there any reason for doubting the veracity of this[72] especially in view of the fact that the term "Pharisee" was not sharply defined?[73]

So far Paul has mentioned all the things associated with his birth and upbringing, things over which he had no control. Then he goes on to mention the personal decisions he took in his life as a Jew. He was a Pharisee, a persecutor of the Church, and he considered himself blameless under the law. In the pages that follow I will be investigating in more detail these three special aspects of Paul. But already I think there can be hardly any doubt about Paul's Jewish credentials.

In view of this one has to place Paul in the mainstream of Palestinian Judaism. Palestinian Judaism was of course hellenized. Paul like many Jews could speak and write fluent Greek. But Paul was certainly not in the category of a thoroughly hellenized Jew like Philo of Alexandria. He was a "Hebrew of Hebrews" (cf. 2 Cor. 11.22) and a member of the Pharisaic

---

[70] Cf. Riesner, *Early Period*, p. 153.

[71] The term "son" (υἱός) is to be taken literally (see Burchard, *Der dreizehnte Zeuge*, p. 39).

[72] Hengel and Schwemer, *Paulus*, p. 260, write: "Es besteht kein Grund, an diesen Angaben zu zweifeln". See also Burchard, *Der dreizehnte Zeuge*, p. 39. He points out that this is the first time in Acts that Paul's connection with Pharisaism is mentioned and thinks the tradition is to be trusted.

[73] R. Deines, *Die Pharisäer* (WUNT 101), Tübingen: J.C.B. Mohr (Paul Siebeck) 1997, p. 540, writes: "Pharisäer ist, wer sich selbst als Pharisäer bezeichnet, oder von anderen als solcher bezeichnet wird".

movement, which had a major influence on Palestinian Judaism in this period.[74]

2. Paul the Pharisee

We possess writings associated with Pharisaic groups[75] and material which contains the traditions of the Pharisees;[76] but when it comes to individual identifiable Pharisaic writings we have the works of just two: Josephus and Paul. And *if* Mason is correct to believe that Josephus was not a Pharisee,[77] we have just Paul. Although he wrote his letters as a Christian, it is nevertheless possible to glean something of his Pharisaic views. Rom. 2.1-16 is particularly interesting, for Paul seems to be writing from Jewish presuppositions. These verses form part of the argument of Rom. 1.18-3.20, where Paul is demonstrating that no one will be justified on the basis of their works[78] so preparing the ground for the "righteousness of God" which has been "manifested apart from law" (Rom. 3.21). In Rom. 2.1-16 Paul seems to argue that if justification is by works, a perfect obedience is necessary. We see this in Rom. 2.12-13:

---

[74] M. Smith, "Palestinian Judaism in the First Century" in M. David (ed.), *Israel: Its Role in Civilisation*, New York: Harper 1956, 67-81, and J. Neusner, "Josephus's Pharisees", in *Ex Orbe Religionum. Studia Geo Widengren*, Leiden: E.J. Brill 1972, 224-44 (= *From Politics to Piety*, Englewood Cliffs, N.J.: Prentice-Hall 1973, 45-66), dispute the influence the Pharisees had on the Jewish people before 70 AD. Contrast Hengel, *Pre-Christian Paul*, pp. 44-45, who argues that the Pharisees were the leading spiritual group since the end of the second century BC. See also M. Hengel and R. Deines, "E.P.Sanders' 'Common Judaism', Jesus, and the Pharisees", *JTS* 46 (1995) 4 (1-70), who criticize Sanders, among other things, for underestimating the influence of the Pharisees, and Deines, *Pharisäer*, p. 554, who understands the Pharisees as "*die grundlegende und prägende religiöse Strömung innerhalb des palästinischen Judentums zwischen 150 v. und 70 n. Chr. . . .*" (Deines' emphasis). See also S. Mason, *Flavius Josephus on the Pharisees: A Composition-Critical Study* (StPB 39), Leiden/New York: E.J. Brill 1991, who concludes that "Josephus consistently represents the Pharisees as the dominant religious group among the Jews, who had the support of the masses" (p. 372) and that he is unlikely to have made this up (p. 373).

[75] E.g. the Psalms of Solomon (see the discussion in chapter 3 below).

[76] E.g. the Mishnah and the Babylonian and Palestinian Talmuds.

[77] See my discussion of Josephus in chapter 3 below.

[78] See the conclusion in Rom. 3.20: "For no human being will be justified in his sight by works of the law, since through the law comes knowledge of sin".

All who have sinned without the law will also perish without the law, and all who have sinned under the law will be judged by the law. 13 For it is not the hearers of the law who are righteous before God, but the doers of the law who will be justified.

This demand for a perfect obedience in v. 13 corresponds exactly to what we find in Gal. 3.10[79] and Gal. 5.3.[80] This suggests that Paul was certainly one of the stricter Pharisees. But could this demand for a "perfect obedience" include "repentance"? Paul does speak of repentance in Rom. 2.4-5:

Or do you presume upon the riches of his kindness and forbearance and patience? Do you not know that God's kindness is meant to lead you to repentance? 5 But by your hard and impenitent heart you are storing up wrath for yourself on the day of wrath when God's righteous judgment will be revealed.

However, such repentance seemed to play at most a minor part in Paul's consideration of the final judgement and Paul seems very pessimistic that Israel (and the Gentiles)[81] will in fact repent.[82] In this respect he shares the views of some of the Apocalypses (cf. 1 Enoch 91-105).[83] There is no problem in Paul the Pharisee sharing apocalyptic views[84] and there are, as I hope

---

[79] Gal. 3.10: "Indeed those who rely on works of law (ἐξ ἔργων νόμου) are under a curse; for it is written, 'Cursed be everyone who does not persevere in doing everything written in the book of the law'". The quotation is from Dt. 27.26 (modified by 28.58). See chapter 4 below for a discussion of Gal. 3.10.

[80] Gal. 5.3: "I testify again to every man who receives circumcision that he is bound to keep the whole law".

[81] I argued in *No one seeks for God: An Exegetical and Theological Study of Romans 1.18-3.20* (WUNT 106), Tübingen: J.C.B. Mohr (Paul Siebeck) 1998, pp. 137-38, that Rom. 2.1-16 is addressed to Jew *and* Gentile.

[82] See R.H. Bell, "Teshubah: The Idea of Repentance in Ancient Judaism", *JPJ* 5 (1995) 47-48 (22-52).

[83] See Bell, "Teshubah", 30-31.

[84] W.D. Davies, *Paul and Rabbinic Judaism: Some Rabbinic Elements in Pauline Theology*, London: SPCK [2]1955, ([1]1948), pp. 9-10, argues that the Pharisaic interest in resurrection, the age to come, and the king messiah suggests that apocalyptic was not alien to Pharisaic Judaism. See also W.D. Davies, "Apocalyptic and Pharisaism", in *Christian Origins and Judaism*, London: Darton, Longman & Todd 1972, 19-30, and D.S. Russell, *The Method and Message of Jewish Apocalyptic* (OTL), London: SCM 1964, pp. 25-27.

will become clear in the present study, good reasons for seeing Paul the Christian as an apocalyptic theologian.[85]

This concern of Paul for a perfect obedience to the law is related to what he writes in Phil. 3.6: "as to righteousness under the law blameless". This does however bring us on to some important distinctions which have to be made concerning the issue of "perfect obedience". For it would be a mistake to believe Paul is claiming here that he was sinless. Fifty years ago Mitton wrote this:

> In Ph 3[6] he is defending himself, his apostleship, and his interpretation of the gospel, against men who claim that their Jewish status and their strict Pharisaic obedience to the Law give them the right to pass judgment on him, who, in their eyes is either an upstart or a renegade, and so has no authority or proper standing. For the sake of his converts and his further missionary activities, Paul must answer their charges plainly. So he speaks, not of the inner failures which only he and God know of, but of his earlier acknowledged success as a Pharisee, when he was required to offer outward obedience to certain specific moral and ritual regulations.[86]

Despite all the work that has subsequently been done on Paul and his "robust conscience",[87] Mitton is surely correct to maintain that Paul did know of "inner failures". In a similar way, Espy understands "blameless" in Phil. 3.6 to be something other than "without sin". Paul's "'blamelessness' was a state of being *without fault* - which in regard to the Law would appear to suggest an extreme scrupulosity, a life without the omission of even the least observance".[88] A hint of this extreme scrupulosity can be found in the aorist participle γενόμενος which is probably best understood as ingressive

---

[85] See U. Wilckens, "Die Bekehrung des Paulus als religionsgeschichtliches Problem", *ZThK* 56 (1959) 286 (273-93); W.G. Kümmel, "Jesus und Paulus", in *Heilsgeschehen und Geschichte: Gesammelte Aufsätze 1933-1964* (MThS 3), Marburg: N.G. Elwert Verlag 1965, 450 (439-56); E. Käsemann, "On the Subject of Primitive Christian Apocalyptic", in *New Testament Questions of Today* (NTL) ET, London: SCM 1969, 131 (108-37).

[86] C.L. Mitton, "Romans vii. Reconsidered - II", *ExpT* 65 (1953/54) 100 (99-103).

[87] I am of course thinking of K. Stendahl's essay "The Apostle Paul and the Introspective Conscience of the West", in *Paul among Jews and Gentiles and Other Essays*, London: SCM 1976, pp. 78-96 (= *HTR* 56 (1963) 199-215). Interestingly this paper was given at the Annual Meeting of the American Psychological Association. The earliest form of the essay appeared as "Paulus och Samvetet" (Paul and Conscience) in *SEÅ* 25 (1960) 62-77.

[88] J.M. Espy, "Paul's 'Robust Conscience' Re-examined", *NTS* 31 (1985) 165 (161-88).

(Phil. 3.6b: κατὰ δικαιοσύνην τὴν ἐν νόμῳ γενόμενος ἄμεμπτος). Therefore at a certain point in time Paul reached what he thought was the state of being "blameless". We noted above the ἀκρίβεια of Paul as a Pharisee (Acts 22.3: κατὰ ἀκρίβειαν τοῦ πατρῴου νόμου)[89] and Espy rightly points to Jesus' teaching that although one can "tithe mint and dill and cummin", sin can involve neglecting the more important matters (Mt. 23.23). "Jesus does not condemn scrupulosity which carries tithing into the smallest matters, but he points to the large areas within the Law which no exactness can analyse into precise commandments, and which no scrupulosity can comprehend or grasp (cf. Matt 22.34-40)".[90] Although Paul was later to argue that "the law is holy, and the commandment is holy and just and good" (Rom. 7.12), in a sense the law is clearly inadequate for defining a holy life.[91]

Therefore the pre-Christian Paul, although being "blameless" regarding righteousness under the law, was far from being "sinless". Such a view is confirmed when one considers that Paul must have known (probably by heart) the prayers of penitence in Dan. 9.3-27 and 4 Ezra, and the penitential Psalms[92] which demonstrated the frailty of the human person. This brings me to the point made by some scholars that Paul's "blamelessness" was achieved not just by keeping the law but also by repentance and sacrifice in cases where he broke the law.[93] This is certainly possible. But, as I will argue in chapter 3, there were limits to the atoning value of repentance and sacrifice. Perhaps a more effective form of atonement would be by performing "good works" (cf. Sir. 3.3-4, 14-15). But whatever means of atonement Paul used, if he did break the law frequently he would hardly describe himself as "blameless" even if he had atoned for these sins.

---

[89] Note also Acts 26.5, where Paul is reported to say that "according to the strictest party of our religion (κατὰ τὴν ἀκριβεστάτην αἵρεσιν τῆς ἡμετέρας θρησκείας) I have lived as a Pharisee".

[90] Espy, "Robust Conscience", 165.

[91] On the difficult issue of Paul's understanding of the law, in particular how his view on the law changed as a result of theological reflection on the death of Christ under the law, see chapter 2 below.

[92] The most famous penitential Psalm is Ps. 51 and Paul quotes Ps. 51.4 (Ps. 50.6 LXX) in Rom. 3.4.

[93] So T.R. Schreiner, "Paul and Perfect Obedience of the Law: An Evaluation of the View of E.P. Sanders", *WTJ* 47 (1985) 260-61 (245-78), points to the possibility of offering sacrifices.

One could perhaps compare Paul to the sectaries of Qumran. As Gundry points out, "The people at Qumran out-Phariseed the Pharisees; yet among them a deep sense of personal sin co-existed with the conviction that they were the righteous".[94] Paul clearly felt he belonged to the righteous. He writes in Gal. 1.14: "I advanced in Judaism beyond many of my own age among my people, so extremely zealous was I for the traditions of my fathers". His zeal was both in the study of the law and in the doing of the law (clearly you have to study the law in order to know how to do the law). The "traditions of my fathers" (αἱ πατρικαί μου παραδόσεις) are probably both the written and oral torah of the Pharisees.[95] He was an outstanding Jew and he was blameless "from the standpoint of outside observers".[96] And for Paul the Pharisee, that is precisely what mattered. According to the synoptic gospels,[97] this outer righteousness was of the utmost importance for

---

[94] R.H. Gundry, "The Moral Frustration of Paul before his Conversion: Sexual Lust in Romans 7:7-25", in Donald A. Hagner and Murray J. Harris (ed.), *Pauline Studies: Essays presented to Professor F.F. Bruce on his 70th Birthday*, Exeter: Paternoster 1980, 234 (228-45). Although the sectaries could speak of תְּמִימִם (see 1QS 8.1: the smallest congregation should be made up of 3 priests and 12 laymen who are perfect), texts such as 1QH 1.21-27; 3.23-25; 4.29-30; 1QS 9.9-11 refer to their deep consciousness of sin.

[95] Many commentators wish to confine the meaning to the oral traditions. See J.B. Lightfoot, *St. Paul's Epistle to the Galatians*, Peabody: Hendrickson 1993 (repr.), (¹1865), p. 82, who points to the expressions of Josephus τὰ ἐκ παραδόσεως τῶν πατέρων (*Ant.* 13.297) and ἡ πατρῴα παράδοσις (*Ant.* 13.408), whereby the pharisaic traditions are distinguished from the written torah. See also E.D.W. Burton, *The Epistle to the Galatians* (ICC), Edinburgh: T. & T. Clark 1988 (repr.), p. 48 and R.Y.K. Fung, *The Epistle to the Galatians* (NICNT), Grand Rapids: Eerdmans 1988, p. 57. Jesus also is recorded as making a distinction between the "traditions of the elders" (παράδοσις τῶν πρεσβυτέρων) in Mt. 15.2; Mk 7.3, 5 and the law of Moses. Paul, however, is not making such a distinction and is most likely referring to both written and oral torah. See F. Mußner, *Der Galaterbrief* (HThKNT 9), Freiburg/Basel/Wien: Herder 1974, p. 80: "gegenüber den heidenchristlichen Lesern seines Briefes braucht er ja nicht scharf zu differenzieren".

[96] Gundry, "Moral Frustration", 234.

[97] The gospels contain much anti-Pharisaic polemic. Nevertheless, they give useful information about the ritual purity in eating and dietary laws (Mk 7.1-23) and on exact tithing, etc. (Mt. 23.1-36) (see J. Neusner, *From Politics to Piety: The Emergence of Pharisaic Judaism*, Englewood Cliffs, N.J.: Prentice-Hall 1973 (repr.: New York: Ktav 1979), p. 78).

the Pharisees (Mt. 23.1-36; Lk. 11.37-54).[98] The inner Paul, like the Pharisees of Mt. 23.27, may have been "full of dead men's bones and all uncleanness" but Paul nevertheless considered himself a fine Pharisee. If there was frustration and failure in Paul's pre-Christian life, it did not lead him to despair but caused him to arm himself "more firmly for further warfare under the banner of the Torah".[99] Paul therefore was a successful Jew and had a relatively "robust conscience".[100]

One possible problem with this view is Romans 7. See, for example, Rom. 7.14, 24: "I am carnal, sold under sin. . . . Wretched man that I am!

---

[98] It seems that the Pharisees wished to imitate the priests and apply the priests' standards of ritual purity to the whole nation, thus fulfilling Ex. 19.6a ("you shall be to me a kingdom of priests and a holy nation"). See M. Hengel, "Der vorchristliche Paulus", *ThBei* 21 (1990) 182-83 (174-95).

[99] So E. Käsemann, *Romans* ET, London: SCM 1980, p. 203, portrays the life of the pious man in Qumran.

[100] Despite my earlier criticisms of Stendahl, he has drawn attention to problems in comparing Paul with the monk Luther. See his essay "Paul Among Jews and Gentiles", in *Paul among Jews and Gentiles and Other Essays*, pp. 12-23, which is based on lectures given in 1963 (Austin Presbyterian Seminary) and 1964 (Colgate Rochester Divinity School). Stendahl criticizes those who understand Paul as a first century Luther. Luther before his conversion was a man of despair, full of guilt, who lived under the burdensome demands of the "law" (p. 12). He was plagued by an introspective conscience (pp. 78-96). Paul by contrast was a happy successful Jew before his conversion (or, as Stendahl puts it, before his call (pp. 7-23)). According to Stendahl, the introspective conscience really first began with Augustine, "the first truly Western man" (p. 16), who was introspective enough to write a spiritual biography. The introspective conscience reached its climax in the religious world with the Reformation and in the secular world with Freud. In contrast to the west, the eastern Churches know little of this introspection (p. 17). Stendahl, as is the case in many polemical works, has overstated his case. For a critique, see Espy, "Robust Conscience", 161-88. Espy is right to criticize Stendahl's arguments that the *Christian* Paul had a robust conscience (163-64), but I do not find his arguments against the *pre-Christian* Paul having a robust conscience entirely convincing. A number of important issues are raised by C.K. Barrett, "Paul and the Introspective Conscience", in W.P. Stevens (ed.), *The Bible, the Reformation and the Church: Essays in Honour of James Atkinson* (JSNTSup 105), Sheffield: Sheffield Academic Press 1995, 36-48. He rightly points out that "[a] conscience is nothing if not introspective; there is nowhere else it can look but within, that is, into an awareness of previous actions (which of course must include words and thoughts) and of their relation to some accepted standard of right and wrong" (39). The question though is: "Did the inward investigating gaze of his conscience cause Paul acute unhappiness, a sense of hopelessness, of perdition?" (40-41). I will return to the issue of uncertainty of salvation in Judaism (including the ideas of Schürer and others) in chapter 3 below.

Who will deliver me from this body of death". However, this text is only a problem if it is taken as a straightforward autobiographical account of Paul's pre-Christian life.[101] Such a view is rightly rejected by Kümmel who argued that the first person singular in Rom. 7.7-25 is not to be understood autobiographically but stylistically.[102] To be more precise Rom. 7.7-13 refers to Adam[103] and is written in the past (apart from 7.7a, 12). That the story is told in the supra-individual "I" means that "we are implicated in the story of Adam".[104] Rom. 7.14-25 then concerns man in the shadow of Adam,[105] and is written mainly in the present.[106] The "I" of Rom. 7.7-25a is

---

[101] E.g., A. Deißmann, *Paulus: Eine kultur- und religionsgeschichtliche Skizze*, Tübingen: J.C.B. Mohr (Paul Siebeck) ²1925, pp. 75-76, 139; A.D. Nock, *St. Paul*, London: Thornton Butterworth 1938, pp. 67-68; Gundry, "Moral Frustration"; D.J.W. Milne, "Romans 7:7-12, Paul's Pre-conversion Experience", *RTR* 43 (1984) 9-17.

[102] There is a long tradition of understanding Romans 7.14-25 as *Christian* experience (either Paul's own Christian experience or Christian experience generally) spanning from the Patristic period (Methodius, Ambrose, Ambrosiaster, Augustine) through the Middle Ages (Aquinas) and Reformation (Luther, Calvin) and down to the present day. For 20th century advocates, see K. Barth, *A Shorter Commentary on Romans* ET, London: SCM 1959, pp. 84-87; A. Nygren, *Commentary on Romans* ET, Philadelphia: Fortress Press 1949, pp. 284-303; C.K. Barrett, *A Commentary on the Epistle to the Romans* (BNTC), London: A. & C. Black ²1991, (¹1957), pp. 131-44; J.I. Packer, "The 'Wretched Man' in Romans 7", in F.L. Cross (ed.), *Studia Evangelica II*, Berlin 1964, 621-27; Cranfield, *Romans*, 1:340-47; J.D.G. Dunn, "Rom. 7,14-25 in the theology of Paul", *ThZ* 31 (1975) 257-73, and Dunn, *Romans* (WBC 38), 2 vols, Dallas, Texas: Word Books 1988, pp. 375-412. Among those who have supported such a view are some theological giants. But there have been dissenters (e.g. Greek exegetes, Pietists) and since Kümmel's ground breaking work many have given powerful arguments against this view. I do not have space to discuss this view in detail. But it is important to stress that the change from past to present does not necessarily support this view for there is a much more convincing explanation for this change in tense (see below).

[103] See Käsemann, *Romans*, p. 196: "In the full sense only Adam lived before the commandment was given. Only for him was the coming of the divine will in the commandment an occasion for sin as he yielded covetously to sin and therefore 'died'". See also R. Schnackenburg, "Römer 7 im Zusammenhang des Römerbriefs", in E.E. Ellis and E. Gräßer (ed.), *Jesus und Paulus: Festschrift für Werner Georg Kümmel zum 70. Geburtstag*, Göttingen: Vandenhoeck & Ruprecht 1975, 293-94 (283-300).

[104] Käsemann, *Romans*, p. 196.

[105] Käsemann, *Romans*, pp. 200-1; Schnackenburg, "Römer 7", 295.

[106] O. Hofius, "Der Mensch im Schatten Adams. Römer 7,7-25a", in *Paulusstudien II* (WUNT 143), Tübingen: J.C.B. Mohr (Paul Siebeck) 2002, 120 (104-154), writes: "Hier wird mithin nicht ein Ereignis erzählt, sondern ein Tatbestand geschildert. Die Gegenwartsaussagen V. 14-23 beschreiben Vers für Vers, was für Adam selbst seit

to be related to the "we" of Rom. 7.5:[107] "While we were living in the flesh, our sinful passions, aroused by the law, were at work in our members to bear fruit for death". Hofius writes that it "ist a priori ausgeschlossen, daß es sich in Röm 7,7-25a um individuelle Rede handelt und hier etwa das 'Ich' des Paulus in einer persönlichen und autobiographisch orientierten Confessio zu Wort kommt".[108] Paul may have experienced some tensions before becoming a Christian (in view of his use of penitential Psalms etc.) but these tensions are not to be read off from Romans 7. Further, the texts point in one overall direction: Paul considered himself to be a successful Pharisee.

3. Paul the Persecutor of the Church

The suggestion that Paul was a strict Pharisee receives some confirmation from his violent persecution of the Church. No one can doubt that Paul was a violent persecutor of the Church. This is referred to in his letters. So in Phil. 3.6 he writes: "as to zeal a persecutor of the Church" (κατὰ ζῆλος διώκων τὴν ἐκκλησίαν). Paul was zealous for God, like Phinehas[109] and Elijah[110] before him, and in persecuting the Church he clearly thought he was doing a service to God (cf. Jn 16.2).[111] Then in Gal. 1.13 he writes: "For you have heard of my former life in Judaism, how I persecuted the church of God violently and tried to destroy it". It is no coincidence that in the following verse Paul speaks about his advance in Judaism.[112] This pic-

---

seinem Fall und in gleicher Weise von Adam her für einen *jeden* adamitischen Menschen gilt" (Hofius' emphasis).

[107] Hofius, "Mensch im Schatten Adams", 110.

[108] Hofius, "Mensch im Schatten Adams", 110.

[109] See Num. 25.7-13; Sir. 45.23; 1 Mac. 2.54; 4 Mac. 18.12. See also Ps. 106.30.

[110] See 1 Kgs 18.20-40; 19.10, 14; Sir. 48.1-2.

[111] On Paul's zeal for God, see R.H. Bell, *Provoked to Jealousy: The Origin and Purpose of the Jealousy Motif in Romans 9-11* (WUNT 2.63), Tübingen: J.C.B. Mohr (Paul Siebeck) 1994, pp. 301-11.

[112] W. Grundmann, "Paulus, aus dem Volke Israel, Apostel der Völker", *NovT* 4 (1960) 267 (267-91), writes that "die Aussagen über die Verfolgung der Gemeinde und über die Fortschritte im Judentum koordiniert sind".

ture of Paul violently persecuting the Church is supported by Acts (e.g. Acts 8.3) which also picks up the link between persecution and zeal.[113]

Although no one seems to doubt that Paul persecuted the Church, there have been two areas of controversy regarding which Christians he persecuted. First, did Paul persecute Judaean Churches? Secondly, did he engage in a general persecution, i.e. a persecution of both Hebrew and Greek speaking Jewish Christians?

That Paul persecuted the Judaean Churches has been questioned by Conzelmann,[114] Bornkamm[115] and Becker[116] on the basis of Gal. 1.22. I quote Gal. 1.22-23:

And I was still not known by sight by the Churches of Judea; 23 they only heard it said, 'He who once persecuted us is now preaching the faith he once tried to destroy'.

So it is inferred that Paul cannot have persecuted the Judaean Churches. But Paul in Gal. 1.22 is speaking of himself as an apostle and wishes to say that *as an apostle* he was unknown to the Churches of Judaea.[117] Gal. 1.23 is crucial in deciding whether Paul persecuted the Judaean Churches: "only they heard it said, 'He who once persecuted us is now preaching the faith he once tried to destroy'" (μόνον δὲ ἀκούοντες ἦσαν ὅτι ὁ διώκων ἡμᾶς ποτε νῦν εὐαγγελίζεται τὴν πίστιν ἥν ποτε ἐπόρθει). F.F. Bruce points out that the ὅτι is recitativum and that

. . . the words which it introduces do not convey the direct speech of those from whom the reports ultimately emanated, but the direct speech of those in Judaea who received and disseminated the reports. It was not the new converts in Syria and Cilicia (see v. 21) that referred to Paul as '*our* former persecutor'; it was the Judaean churches.[118]

---

[113] Some have tried to argue that the pictures of Paul as persecutor are quite different in the letters and in Acts. For a critique of such views see Bell, *Provoked to Jealousy*, pp. 295-96, n. 28.

[114] H. Conzelmann, *Geschichte des Urchristentums* (GNT 5), Göttingen: Vandenhoeck & Ruprecht [6]1989, p. 65.

[115] G. Bornkamm, *Paul* ET, London: Hodder and Stoughton 1985 (repr.), ([1]1971), p. 15.

[116] J. Becker, *Paulus: Der Apostel der Völker*, Tübingen: J.C.B. Mohr (Paul Siebeck) 1989, p. 40.

[117] See A.J. Hultgren, "Paul's Pre-Christian Persecutions of the Church: Their Purpose, Locale, and Nature", *JBL* 95 (1976) 105-7 (97-111).

[118] F.F. Bruce, *The Epistle of Paul to the Galatians: A Commentary on the Greek Text* (NIGTC), Exeter: Paternoster 1982, p. 105. See also Burchard, *Der dreizehnte Zeuge*, p. 50 and Fung, *Galatians*, p. 83. A. Oepke, *Der Brief des Paulus an die Galater*

In fact Hengel and Schwemer argue that the report comes from the Hellenists who had been driven out of Judaea.[119]

As regards the second point, I do not believe Paul engaged in a general persecution. Rather he persecuted the Hellenistic Jewish Christians. They were Jewish Christians who spoke Greek and their theological perspective was somewhat different to those who spoke Hebrew/Aramaic.[120] Although these Hellenists probably honoured the decalogue, they were critical of the temple and had a liberal attitude towards the ceremonial law.[121] Such an attitude would have infuriated Paul. For it was not that long ago that Jews had defended their laws and their temple with their blood against the Greek (!) Antiochus Epiphanes. Although Judaism itself was becoming hellenized as early as the third century BC,[122] it must have struck Paul that these very

---

(ThHK 9), Berlin: Evangelische Verlagsanstalt 1937, p. 29, and Mußner, *Galaterbrief*, p. 99, argue that the Judaean Churches are included in the "us" (ἡμᾶς) in Gal. 1.23.

[119] M. Hengel and A.M. Schwemer, *Paul Between Damascus and Antioch*, London: SCM 1997, p. 37. They also argue that "Judaea" refers to the whole Roman province which included not only biblical Judaea but also Samaria, Peraea, Galilee and the coastal cities (p. 36).

[120] One key reason why this divergence of theology came about was because they held separate services. Although Luke's picture in Acts 6-8 has come in for some criticism, Gnilka, *Paulus*, p. 36, believes we have here "eine denkwürdige Entwicklung".

[121] See M. Hengel, "The Origins of the Christian Mission", in *Between Jesus and Paul*, London: SCM 1983, 56 (48-64). See also P. Stuhlmacher, *Das paulinische Evangelium: I. Vorgeschichte*, Göttingen: Vandenhoeck & Ruprecht 1968, p. 251 n. 2. F. Hahn, *Der urchristliche Gottesdienst* (SBS 41), Stuttgart: Verlag katholisches Bibelwerk 1970, pp. 50-51, questions whether such a distinction between ceremonial and ethical law can be made. However, although someone such as Paul himself may not have made such a distinction, some groups in early Christianity probably did make it. It is also worth adding that just as Palestinian Judaism was a "complex Judaism" (see the discussion below, chapter 3), so the Hellenist Christians were not a monolithic entity. Among their number were probably also those who had a conservative view of the law. However, this fact does not destroy the theory of the general distinction between Hebrews and Hellenists (as C.C. Hill, *Hellenists and Hebrews: Reappraising Division within the Earliest Church*, Minneapolis: Fortress Press 1992, p. 193, suggests). See H. Räisänen, "Die 'Hellenisten' der Urgemeinde", *ANRW* 2.26.2:1476, 1490 (1468-1516).

[122] Hengel, *Judaism and Hellenism*, 1:310, concludes that "as early as the third century BC an encounter between Hellenistic civilization and the Jewish upper classes took place which was probably more intensive than our scanty sources indicate to us".

Jews who were not keeping the law had *Greek* as a mother tongue. Was there a possible association with Antiochus Epiphanes?[123]

So although the Hebrew Jewish Christians faced some persecution, it was the Hellenists who seem to have borne the brunt.[124] This is suggested further by Acts 8.1:[125]

And Saul was consenting to his (Stephen's) death. And on that day a great persecution arose against the church in Jerusalem; and they were all scattered throughout the region of Judea and Samaria, except the apostles.

There are in fact three reasons why a general persecution does not seem to have taken place.[126] First, if Paul persecuted the Hebrew speaking Jewish Christians, why would he spare their leaders, the apostles?[127] Secondly, in

---

[123] This suggestion was made by my student Andrew Grundy. Cf. D.E.H. Whiteley, *The Theology of St. Paul,* Oxford: Blackwell [2]1974, ([1]1964), p. 78, who notes that when Paul himself changed his views on the law when he became a Christian, "it must have seemed to some of his former associates that he was wantonly throwing away the religious and national heritage which his ancestors in the time of Antiochus Epiphanes had defended with their life's blood".

[124] Cf. Bruce, *Acts,* p. 162. Note that the persecution faced in Acts 12.1-4 was occasioned by the particular political situation facing Agrippa I (see Hengel and Schwemer, *Between Damascus and Antioch,* pp. 244-57). Concerning this issue of the persecution of Jewish Christians who were faithful to the law, see chapter 2 below.

[125] Hill, *Hellenists and Hebrews,* pp. 38-39, questions the historicity of Acts 8.1: "the entire sequence of events it initiates is bereft of historical realism". But is it really so implausible that Hellenists were scattered "throughout the region of Judea and Samaria"?

[126] Cf. Roloff, *Apostelgeschichte,* p. 129.

[127] R. Bauckham, "James and the Jerusalem Church", in R. Bauckham (ed.), *The Book of Acts in Its Palestinian Setting* (The Book of Acts in its First Century Setting vol. 4), Grand Rapids: Wm B. Eerdmans/Carlisle: Paternoster, 429 (415-80), argues that "Luke's text is not concerned to claim that the apostles escaped persecution. This is not the most natural reading of the text for a reader who observes that, at other points in Acts, it is precisely the apostles who are targets of persecution (4:1-3; 5:17-18; 12:1-19). Given that 'all' is hyperbolic (as 8:3 makes clear it must be), the real point is that, whereas many prominent members of the Jerusalem church were *permanently* dispersed to other parts of the country (cf. 8:40; 11:19-20), the apostles remained the leaders of the Jerusalem church". Ingenious though this interpretation is, I wonder whether it is plausible. It is true that the apostles faced persecution in Acts 4.1-3 and 5.17-18 but it does not appear as severe as that of 8.1-3 (on 12.1-19, see the discussion in chapter 2 below). In fact the response of Gamaliel in Acts 5.35-39 seems positively irenic. Further, it is significant that the prominent members who were dispersed were precisely the Hellenists.

the following text only Hellenists are mentioned among the dispersed Christians (Acts 8.4-5; 11.19ff.). Thirdly, the text of Acts assumes the existence of a Jerusalem Church (Acts 8.14; 9.26ff.) after this persecution.[128]

If Paul persecuted only the Hellenists, a possible problem is solved. It has been said that if Paul was educated at the feet of Gamaliel (Acts 22.3) how can it be that Paul was a violent persecutor of the Church yet Gamaliel his teacher is so tolerant according to Acts 5.35-39?[129] According to this text, after Peter and the Apostles refused to keep silent about the good news of Jesus, Gamaliel advised the council:

Men of Israel, take care what you do with these men. 36 Before these days Theudas arose, giving himself out to be somebody, and a number of men, about four hundred, joined him; but he was slain and all who followed him were dispersed and came to nothing. 37 After him Judas the Galilean arose in the days of the census and drew away some of the people after him; he also perished, and all who followed him were scattered. 38 So in the present case I tell you, keep away from these men and let them alone; for if this plan or this undertaking is of men, it will fail; 39 but if it is of God, you will not be able to overthrow them. You might even be found opposing God!

However, the difference in the approach of Gamaliel and Paul should not surprise us for two reasons. First, a pupil can be very different to his teacher.[130] Secondly, and the one relevant to the issue of persecution, is that Gamaliel was faced with Hebrew Christians who kept the Jewish law

---

[128] E. Larsson, "Die Hellenisten und die Urgemeinde", *NTS* 33 (1987) 222 (205-25), believes that there was a general persecution, but does not seem to have considered the second and third points made above. M.A. Seifrid, *Justification by Faith: The Origin and Development of a Central Pauline Theme* (NovTSup 68), Leiden: E.J. Brill 1992, pp. 159-61, also argues for a general persecution. Fundamental to his position is the rejection of M. Hengel's view of the Hellenists (see Hengel, "Between Jesus and Paul"). For a defence of Hengel, see C. Marvin Pate, *The Reverse of the Curse: Paul, Wisdom, and the Law* (WUNT 2.114), Tübingen: J.C.B. Mohr (Paul Siebeck) 2000, pp. 156-64 (against Seifrid) and pp. 164-66 (against Larsson).

[129] See H. Conzelmann *Die Apostelgeschichte* (HzNT 7), Tübingen: J.C.B. Mohr (Paul Siebeck) ²1972, (¹1963), pp. 48 and 135.

[130] This is a universal phenomenon. Hengel, *Pre-Christian Paul*, p. 28, points out that those who studied in Marburg between 1920 and 1950, even the theological conservatives, went above all to Rudolf Bultmann's lectures. As regards Gamaliel, b. Shab. 30b speaks of a "certain disciple" who "scoffed at him". Rabbis, like most teachers, had rebellious pupils. It is just possible that this disciple in b. Shab. 30b was Paul (see J. Klausner, *From Jesus to Paul* ET, New York: Macmillan 1944, (¹1939), pp. 310-11; F.F. Bruce, *New Testament History*, New York: Doubleday & Co. 1980 (repr.), (¹1969), p. 237).

whereas Paul, as I have argued above, was faced with Hellenistic Jewish Christians who did not keep the ceremonial law and were critical of the temple. Gamaliel and Paul therefore faced quite different situations.

I therefore see no reason why Paul should not have studied under Gamaliel.[131] Indeed he is an obvious teacher for Paul since he was the leading Pharisaic teacher at that time.[132]

4. The Major Influences upon Paul

Having viewed Paul's upbringing and education and life as a Pharisee, we are in a position to assess the major influences upon Paul. I suggest that up to the time of his conversion, the major single literary influence upon him was the "Hebrew Bible". I use quotation marks here because I do not believe the canon of the Hebrew Bible had been closed during Paul's lifetime.[133] The "Torah" was closed under Ezra.[134] When the "Prophets" came to an end in the Persian period, the ideas of a prophetic canon and an expanding canon emerged.[135] The third part of the canon, the "Writings", was not closed until around 100 AD.[136] The closing of the canon could be

---

[131] I do not think that Paul's silence about an education under Gamaliel is a problem as J. Knox, *Chapters in a Life of Paul*, London: SCM [2]1989, ([1]1950), p. 21, suggests. Knox also thinks that an education under Gamaliel would suit an important redactional interest of Luke-Acts: "the interest in Christianity as the continuation and fulfillment of authentic Judaism and in the city of Jerusalem as the place where the transition took place".

[132] His great reputation is reflected in these words of m. Sot. 9.15: "When Rabban Gamaliel the Elder died, the glory of the Law ceased and purity and abstinence died".

[133] Against R.T. Beckwith, *The Old Testament Canon of the New Testament Church*, London: SPCK 1985, who argues that the Jewish canon reached its final form in the time of Judas Maccabaeus (p. 406). See also E.E. Ellis, *The Old Testament in Early Christianity*, Tübingen: J.C.B. Mohr (Paul Siebeck) 1991, pp. 40-41.

[134] H. Gese, "Das biblische Schriftverständnis", in *Zur biblischen Theologie: Alttestamentliche Vorträge*, Tübingen: J.C.B. Mohr (Paul Siebeck) [3]1989, ([1]1977), 25 (9-30).

[135] H. Gese, "Die dreifache Gestaltwerdung des Alten Testaments", in *Alttestamentliche Studien*, Tübingen: J.C.B. Mohr (Paul Siebeck) 1991, 21 (1-28). Gese dates the closure of this prophetic canon in the third century BC ("Gestaltwerdung", 18).

[136] H. Gese, "Erwägungen zur Einheit der biblischen Theologie", in *Vom Sinai zum Zion: Alttestamentliche Beiträge zur biblischen Theologie* (BEvTh 64), München: Chr. Kaiser Verlag [3]1990, ([1]1974), 16 (11-30).

related to the discussion which took place in Jabneh[137] regarding the books which "render the hands unclean".[138] Although the debate went on into the second century,[139] it seems that the closing of the canon was taking place around 100 AD and the closing of the Jewish canon could have been, at least in part, a response to the Christians and their use of the "Septuagint".[140] If this view is correct, then at the time of Paul, there was no closed Old Testament canon. This is the case not only for the Hebrew but also for the Greek.[141]

---

[137] On Jabneh, E. Schürer, *The History of the Jewish People in the Age of Jesus Christ* (revised and edited by G. and P. Vermes, F. Millar, M. Goodman and M. Black), 3 vols, Edinburgh: T. & T. Clark 1973-86, 1:524-26.

[138] See m. Yad. 3.5: "R. Simeon b. Azzai said: I have heard a tradition from the seventy-two elders on the day when they made R. Eleazar b. Azariah head of the college [of Sages], that the Song of Songs and Ecclesiastes both render the hands unclean" (Danby, *Mishnah*, p. 782). Interestingly, the problems with Song of Songs and Ecclesiastes could account (at least in part) for what appears to be a smaller canon in Josephus, *Contra Apionem* 1.37-43. He speaks of 22 books whereas Palestinian Judaism speaks of 24. See M. Hengel, "Die Septuaginta als 'christliche Schriftensammlung', ihre Vorgeschichte und das Problem ihres Kanons" (unter Mitarbeit von R. Deines), in M. Hengel und A.M. Schwemer (ed.), *Die Septuaginta zwischen Judentum und Christentum* (WUNT 72), Tübingen: J.C.B. Mohr (Paul Siebeck) 1994, 261 (182-284).

[139] P. Schäfer, *The History of the Jews in Antiquity: The Jews of Palestine from Alexander the Great to the Arab Conquest*, Luxembourg: Harwood Academic Publishers 1995, p. 139-40, points out that discussion concerning Song of Songs, Ecclesiastes, Esther, Daniel and Ecclesiasticus continued into the so-called Usha period (i.e. after the Bar Kochba revolt).

[140] Cf. H. Gese, "Hermeneutische Grundsätze der Exegese biblischer Texte", in *Alttestamentliche Studien*, Tübingen: J.C.B. Mohr (Paul Siebeck) 1991, 259 (249-65). Schäfer, *History of the Jews*, pp. 139-40, believes that Christian theology may have exaggerated the influence of Christianity on the Rabbis at Jabneh. If Christianity did have such an influence why did the discussion concerning certain biblical books continue into the Usha period. "From the rabbinic point of view, Christianity doubtless had no significance whatsoever during the Jabneh period and certainly did not constitute a reason for fixing the canon" (p. 139). Whether Schäfer is right or not, it obviously does not change the fact that there was no closed Old Testament canon in Paul's day.

[141] Hengel, "Die Septuaginta als 'christliche Schriftensammlung'", 183, writes: "Eine genuin *jüdische, vorchristliche* Schriftensammlung in *griechischer* Sprache von *kanonischer* Geltung, die – auch im Bereich der Geschichtsbücher und Weisheitsschriften – eindeutig und klar abgrenzbar ist und sich durch ihren größeren Umfang von dem hebräischen Bibelkanon unterscheidet, läßt sich nicht nachweisen, und erst recht nicht, daß ein derartiger 'Kanon' bereits im vorchristlichen Alexandrien ausgebildet worden sei" (Hengel's emphasis). Towards the end of his article, Hengel makes this important theological point: "Muß das Alte Testament nicht auf das Neue hin in gewisser Hinsicht

Paul therefore grew up a "Hebrew of Hebrews" with Aramaic/Hebrew as his major tongue. Together with the Hebrew Bible he also learned the various Pharisaic understandings of scripture which shine through even in the letters he wrote as a Christian.[142] The fact that his first Bible was the "Hebrew Bible" *may* account for the fact that with one possible exception,[143] when he quotes from scripture, he only quotes from those works now in the "Hebrew Bible". If his primary "Bible" were some form of Septuagintal text, one may perhaps expect quotations from so-called apocryphal works (even though there was no clear pre-Christian Septuagintal canon). However, one cannot make too much of this for the argument would apply to almost every single New Testament author.

But if this "Hebrew Bible" was so important for Paul, why is it that when he quotes from the scriptures the form he usually follows is that of the Septuagint? The various monographs on Paul's use of scripture give different statistics concerning Paul's quotations from the Hebrew Bible or Septuagint, but whichever author is followed, Paul seems to have a clear preference for

---

offenbleiben und ist nicht im Neuen Testament selbst eine Gestalt wie die des eschatologischen Propheten Johannes Baptista das wichtigste Beispiel für diese Offenheit des Alten zum Neuen, Endgültigen, hin? 'Das Gesetz und die Propheten gehen bis Johannes', sagt der Jesus der Logionquelle (Lk 16,16 vgl. Mt 11,13)" ("Septuaginta", 283).

[142] The Rabbinic parallels to Paul have been extensively studied and a number will be discussed in the pages that follow. The work which towers above all others is that of the Brandenburg pastor P. Billerbeck (with H.L. Strack), *Kommentar zum Neuen Testament aus Talmud und Midrasch*, 4 vols, München: C.H. Beck'sche Verlagsbuchhandlung 1-3 ³1961; 4 ²1956. He deals with parallels between rabbinic literature and the Pauline corpus in pp. 1-670 of volume 3, first published in 1926. I shall say more about this great scholar in chapter 3 below. Mention should also be made of the pioneering work of the Anglican Priest John Lightfoot, whose work *Horae Hebraicae et Talmudicae* was published between 1658 and 1674. Of the Pauline corpus he dealt only with Romans (published posthumously) and 1 Corinthians. As S.C. Neill comments, "he was the first systematically and methodically to apply his Talmudic knowledge to the elucidation of the New Testament text" (S.C. Neill, *The Interpretation of the New Testament, 1861-1961*, Oxford: OUP ²1966, (¹1964), p. 294). An English translation is *Commentary on the New Testament from the Talmud and Hebraica*, 4 vols, Peabody: Hendrickson 1995 (repr. from the OUP edition of 1859). Lightfoot's "philosophy" behind this work can be found in vol. 2 pp. 3-6.

[143] Gese, "Gestaltwerdung", 25, suggests that 1 Cor. 2.9 includes a quotation from Sir. 1.10.

the Septuagint. Let me start by giving the quotation statistics of Stanley.[144] According to his analysis, if one were to work just with *quotations* from the Old Testament, 34 of the 83 quotations correspond to Septuagintal texts where the Masoretic text is followed. Of the remaining 49, 44 follow the Septuagint where it diverges from the Hebrew. This leaves just five texts where there is a measure of agreement with the Masoretic text against the Septuagint (Rom. 10.15; 11.4; 12.19; 1 Cor. 3.19; 15.54). To this list once can add Rom. 11.35 (Job 41.11a; MT 41.3a).[145] Stanley believes that in such cases direct resort to the Hebrew is "unlikely".[146] I am not so sceptical at least in the case of Rom. 10.15 since I argued elsewhere that Paul could well have worked from the Hebrew text of Is. 52.7.[147] But it is striking that Paul is loyal to the Greek text even when it manifests errors in contrast to the Masoretic text (e.g. Gal. 3.17) and when the Hebrew would be more congenial to Paul's argument.[148]

I suggest that Paul, the "Hebrew of Hebrews", made a deliberate decision to move over to using the Septuagint when he became apostle to the Gentiles.[149] Paul had surely used Septuagintal texts before his conversion.

---

[144] C.D. Stanley, *Paul and the Language of Scripture: Citation technique in the Pauline Epistles and contemporary literature* (SNTSMS 74), Cambridge: CUP 1992, p. 67.

[145] Stanley does not include it since it lacks "the special markers that would identify it as a quotation to Paul's readers" (Stanley, *Scripture*, p. 191). It is listed as a quotation by E.E. Ellis, *Paul's Use of the Old Testament*, London/Edinburgh: Oliver and Boyd 1957, p. 151. C.E.B. Cranfield, *A Critical and Exegetical Commentary on the Epistle to the Romans* (ICC), 2 vols, Edinburgh: T. & T. Clark 1 ²1977, (¹1975); 2 1979, 2:591, believes Paul is either quoting from the Hebrew or from a Greek version other than the LXX. It is also possible that he quotes from a special recension of the LXX. D.-A. Koch, *Die Schrift als Zeuge des Evangeliums: Untersuchungen zur Verwendung und zum Verständnis der Schrift bei Paulus* (BHTh 69), Tübingen: J.C.B. Mohr (Paul Siebeck) 1986, pp. 57ff, believes Paul had a special recension of Isaiah, Job and 1 Kings. On Rom. 11.35 see *Schrift*, pp. 72-73.

[146] Stanley, *Scripture*, p. 67,

[147] Bell, *Provoked to Jealousy*, pp. 88-89.

[148] O. Michel, *Paulus und seine Bibel* (BFCTh 2.18), Darmstadt: Wissenschaftliche Buchgesellschaft ²1972, (Gütersloh: Bertelsmann ¹1929), p. 68. See, e.g., 1 Cor. 2.16, Is. 40.13 where, it is argued, the Masoretic "spirit of the Lord" (Greek equivalent πνεῦμα κυρίου) would suite Paul's purposes better than the LXX νοῦς κυρίου.

[149] If I may offer a brief anecdote, at the age of 32 when I moved to Germany I made use of the German rather than the English Bible. I also discovered that I became more fluent in German than in my mother tongue English.

Indeed as a Pharisee, he may well have taught Greek speaking Jews in Jerusalem including those diaspora Jews who came to Jerusalem for instruction on the law.[150] But after his call to be apostle to the Gentiles, I think he made a policy decision to work mainly from Septuagintal texts. If Paul moved over to using the Septuagint, there are two important questions to address. The first question is that *if* Paul considered scripture to be inspired, would he have considered the Septuagintal texts to be the inspired version.[151] My response to this is that it is unlikely that Paul worked with ideas of the inspiration of scripture. The idea of scripture being God-breathed occurs only in the deutero-Pauline letter 2 Tim. 3.16. The emphasis on the work of the Spirit is decidedly different in Paul.[152]

The second question is whether Paul the Christian worked with a larger bible than that of the later Jewish Tanak (which corresponds in size to the protestant Old Testament). The Septuagintal texts of the fourth and fifth centuries roughly consists of the books corresponding to the Old Testament and the Apocrypha.[153] As has already been stressed, it is unlikely that some

---

[150] See Hengel, *Pre-Christian Paul*, p. 58: "Nowhere did so many Greek-speaking Jews and Gentile sympathizers from all over the empire gather together so constantly as in Jerusalem. . . The signficance of Jerusalem as the metropolis of world Judaism between Herod and 70 CE can hardly be overestimated".

[151] This view was to become the predominant view in the early Church. So Augustine, *De civitate Dei*, 18.43, argued that the same Spirit which was at work in the Prophets was at work in the 70 translators of the Septuagint.

[152] See, for example, 1 Cor. 2.6-16. 2 Cor. 4.13 could be relevant for the question of inspiration. G. Fee, *God's Empowering Presence: The Holy Spirit in the Letters of Paul*, Peabody: Hendrickson 1994, p. 323 translates it as follows: "But having the same Spirit of faith that is in keeping with what is written, 'I believed, therefore I spoke,' we also believed, and therefore we speak". He therefore understands πνεῦμα as Holy Spirit (cf. V.P. Furnish, *II Corinthians* (AB 32A), New York: Doubleday 1984, p. 258). He rightly understands 2 Cor. 4.13 as saying that "[Paul] and the Psalmist share the same faith, because they share the same Spirit who engendered such faith". However, he goes beyond this in claiming that the Old Testament is "inspired" (p. 324).

[153] B.M. Metzger, *An Introduction to the Apocrypha*, New York: OUP 1957, pp. 3-4, lists the following 14-15 documents which make up the Apocrypha: First and Second Esdras, Tobit, Judith, Additions to Esther, Wisdom, Ecclesiasticus, Baruch, Letter of Jeremiah, Prayer of Azariah and the Song of the Three Young Men, Susanna, Bel and the Dragon, Prayer of Manasseh, First and Second Maccabees. The number varies according to whether the Letter of Jeremiah is included in the book of Baruch. Copies of the Septuagint contain 12 or so books in addition to those of the Hebrew canon. These extra 12 are roughly the same as those in the Apocrypha. The differences are as follows. 1. Some Septuagint manuscripts include 3 and 4 Maccabees and Psalm 151 which are

form of pre-Christian Septuagintal closed canon existed. But Christian usage of Greek Old Testament texts including works which were to be later classified as "apocryphal" probably did lead to some sort of concept of "Greek Bible". Different Christian communities would obviously have different "scriptural libraries".[154] But nevertheless some picture can be built up of a "Greek Bible" of the early Christian writers against which the Rabbis in the late first century reacted in reducing this to the "Hebrew" canon.[155] Paul, during his long period of study after his conversion, probably developed his own "Septuagintal canon" which most likely included "apocryphal" works (e.g. Wisdom, Sirach). Within this Septuagint Paul clearly had preferences for certain books which are to be found in the later Hebrew canon (e.g. Deuteronomy, Isaiah, Psalms). It has been pointed out above that with one possible exception, Paul quotes only from books which were to form the Hebrew canon.[156] But his pattern of quotation does not mean his canon as apostle to the Gentiles was so restricted for he alludes extensively to books from the apocrypha, one of the most striking examples being the allusions to Wisdom in Rom. 1.18ff.[157]

So although Paul usually used the Septuagint as apostle to the Gentiles, I suggest that the bible he grew up with, the one with which he felt most comfortable, was the Hebrew Bible. This would cohere with Paul's own witness that he was Ἑβραῖος ἐξ Ἑβραίων. But it is also important to emphasize that Paul was bi-lingual, fluent in both Greek and Hebrew. Although there were a number of prominent early Christians who were bi-lingual,[158] it was by no

---

not in the Apocrypha. 2. The apocalypse 2 Esdras (4 Ezra) is not in any Septuagint manuscript. 3. The Prayer of Manasseh is not in all copies of the Septuagint and when present is found among the Odes.

[154] See M. Hengel, *The Septuagint as Christian Scripture: Its Prehistory and the Problem of Its Canon* (with the assistance of R. Deines; introduction by R. Hanhart) ET, Edinburgh/New York: T. & T. Clark 2002, p. 111.

[155] See, for example, the "loci citati vel allegati" in the appendix IV of NA^{27}.

[156] For a useful table of quotations see Koch, *Schrift*, p. 33.

[157] See the references to Wisdom in the index of Bell, *No one seeks for God.* p. 331.

[158] Hengel, *Pre-Christian Paul*, pp. 55-56, gives the following examples of "Hebrews" with a very good command of Greek: John Mark, Silas/Silvanus, Simon Peter and James, the brother of Jesus. However, he considers Paul to have Greek as a mother tongue.

means common in the post-apostolic or patristic period.[159] But whether he used the Hebrew or not, it is clear that in studying passages of Paul's letter in the following chapters much attention will be paid to the Old Testament context.

The Old Testament is therefore the key literary influence on Paul. Greek philosophy on the other hand seems to have had little direct influence on him. In the seven letters of Paul (Romans, 1 and 2 Corinthians, Galatians, Philippians, 1 Thessalonians and Philemon) there is just one quotation from a Greek philosopher: "Do not be deceived: 'Bad company ruins good morals'" (1 Cor. 15.33). It is unlikely that Paul found this quotation of Menander, Thais, by reading his works. It is more likely that he learnt it in the Hellenistic synagogue.[160] It is significant that although Hengel tends to see Paul's move to Jerusalem later than van Unnik suggests[161] he doubts very much whether Paul had ever seen a Greek tragedy or mime and finds no sign of knowledge of classical Greek literature in his letters.[162] Similarly I am very sceptical that Paul was versed in ancient rhetoric. There is no shortage of books written on Paul and rhetoric. Norden was to some extent correct in seeing Paul as someone whose rhetoric was "of the heart".[163] Du Toit feels that Norden's view is too simplistic and points to Paul's use of antitheses, mentioning Rom. 2.7-10, "a textbook example of the so-called double antithesis (bound together by an overall *chiasmus* in vv. 6 and 11!)"[164] Paul

---

[159] The common assumption that Origen was bi-lingual in Greek and Hebrew is almost certainly wrong. See R.H. Bell, "Origen, Eusebius and an -οω Verb", *JTS* 44 (1993) 157-62.

[160] Cf. Hengel, *Pre-Christian Paul*, pp. 2-3. He points out that in Paul's time this saying from Menander had become a detached saying (p. 94 n. 28). It is instructive to consider W. von Christ, *Geschichte der griechischen Litteratur 2.2: Die nachklassische Periode der griechischen Litteratur von 100 bis 530 nach Christus (umgearbeitet von W. Schmid u. O. Stählin)* (HAW 7.2.2), München: C.H. Beck ⁶1924, pp. 1134-35. In this section (revised by Stählin), a considerable hellenistic influence upon Paul in Tarsus is assumed yet we read: "Seine Sprache zeigt keinen Einfluß litterarischer Bildung; auch die Zitate aus der poetischen Litteratur des Griechen (1 Kor. 15,33; Act. 17,28; Tit. 1.12) verdankt er nicht eigener Lektüre . . ."

[161] See, for example, Hengel, *Pre-Christian Paul*, p. 34.

[162] See, for example, Hengel, *Pre-Christian Paul*, p. 2.

[163] E. Norden, *Die antike Kunstprosa vom VI. Jahrhundert v. Chr. bis in die Zeit der Renaissance*, Stuttgart/Leipzig: B.G. Teubner 1995 (repr. of ³1915), pp. 502, 509.

[164] Du Toit, "Two Cities", 395.

does show some sophistication but why could he not gain the basis for this style simply from the Old Testament?[165] Du Toit further points to Paul's use of the "diatribe" to establish Greek pagan rhetorical influence. Norden I believe was quite right in his judgement that Paul's letters have a greater elegance than the gospels but not such that he gained by reading Greek authors. On the specific issue of the diatribe I am somewhat sceptical as to whether Paul employed this.[166] In fact the lack of classical rhetoric is striking not only in Paul but in the vast majority of early Christian writings.[167]

What about the larger context of paganism? Again although there have been theories about Paul deriving aspects of his theology from mystery cults etc. they have been shown to be seriously lacking. When viewing "Paul and paganism" Wright correctly stresses that Paul did not so much *derive* his ideas from this world of thought but rather *confronted* paganism with the gospel which he derived from Judaism in the light of the Christ event.[168]

Thus the picture we have of Paul coheres I believe with the view that there was an early move to Jerusalem. It is striking that Paul in his letters never refers to Tarsus apart from the reference to the "regions of Syria and Cilicia" (Gal. 1.21) and that a recent book by Wallace and Williams, attempting to put Paul in the context of the culture of his day, believes that "Paul's obvious connections are all with Jerusalem".[169] They argue that

---

[165] Du Toit admits earlier that the features of chiasmus and "hyperbolic contrasts" demonstrates semitic influence (393).

[166] See Bell, *No one seeks for God*, pp. 185-86.

[167] As Hengel and Schwemer, *Paul Between Damascus and Antioch*, p. 171, conclude: "the striking thing about Paul and the whole of earliest Christianity is that we do not find a deeper philosophical-oratorical education and a style corresponding to what we meet in Philo, Justus of Tiberias or Josephus. Luke and the author of Hebrews are exceptions here. The wave of philosophical education first broke with the earliest Christian Gnostics, Basilides, Carcoprates and Valentinus and then with the Apologists after Justin. This also applies to higher oratorical training. The significance of the rhetoric of the schools on Paul is much exaggerated today, following a fashionable trend".

[168] See N.T. Wright, *What Saint Paul Really Said*, Oxford: Lion 1997, p. 79: "The direction of Paul's message was confrontation with paganism; he had good news for them, but it was good news which undermined their worldview and replaced it with an essentially Jewish one, reworked around Jesus". Wright gives as an example Phil. 2.10-11. The idea of "Jesus Christ is Lord" is *derived* from a Jewish context but *confronts* the pagan view of Caesar being "Lord" (p. 88).

[169] R. Wallace and W. Williams, *The Three Worlds of Paul of Tarsus*, London/New York: Routledge 1998, p. 180.

"Since citizenship in the ancient world went by descent rather than domicile, there is no intrinsic reason why Paul, the citizen of Tarsus (Acts 21.39), need ever have visited the city, much less lived there".[170] Paul's stay in Tarsus mentioned in Acts 9.30 and 11.25 could simply be explained by the fact that he had relatives there.[171] I would not wish to deny that Paul was born in Tarsus; far from it. But it is interesting that his ties are with Jerusalem.[172] I suggest therefore that Paul moved to Jerusalem fairly early in his childhood. This was the conclusion I arrived at on the basis of the discussion of Acts 22.3 above.[173] And in Jerusalem itself Paul moved in the two worlds of Judaism and Hellenism, the Hellenistic influence coming through Judaism.

Other literary influences apart from the Septuagint and the Hebrew scriptures include works like Psalms of Solomon[174] and apocalypses like 1 Enoch and 4 Ezra.[175] However, as I will argue in chapter three below, such works influence Paul in that he reacts *against* much of the theology found in them.

What about non-literary influences? Clearly his upbringing in a law keeping family and his Pharisaic education stamped his intellect and character. But for the Christian Paul, there is one experience which towered above everything else: his meeting with the risen Christ on the Damascus Road. And when we speak of the derivation of Paul's theology it should never be

---

[170] Wallace and Williams, *Three Worlds*, p. 180.

[171] There may be a problem with 9.30 since it is at the end of the problematic first post-conversion visit to Jerusalem of Acts. As is well known it does not fit at all well with the first post-conversion visit mentioned in Galatians (Gal. 1.18-19). But it does cohere with Gal. 1.21.

[172] See, for example, Acts 23.16 which speaks of the son of Paul's sister who appears to live in Jerusalem (see Pesch, *Apostelgeschichte*, 2:248).

[173] Acts 26.4 would support this conclusion if τε has an explicative sense: "All the Jews know my manner of life from my youth, which was from the beginning (ἀπ' ἀρχῆς) within my own nation, namely (τε) in Jerusalem". See Bruce, *Acts*, p. 462; Pesch, *Apostelgeschichte*, 2:272. However, Lake and Cadbury, *Acts*, p. 315, translate τε as "and": "All Jews know the life which from the beginning I led from my youth in my nation and in Jerusalem". They comment that ἔθνος refers to the nation in Cilicia and is contrasted with Jerusalem. See also Du Toit, "Two Cities", 388-89.

[174] These Psalms, sometimes incorrectly considered part of the Septuagint, probably arose in Pharisaic circles.

[175] As noted above, there are good reasons for viewing Paul as an apocalyptic theologian.

forgotten that he developed it from the Old Testament and Judaism but in the light of the Christ event and in the light of his conversion. And it is to his conversion and his subsequent new attitude to Israel that we now turn.

Chapter 2

Paul: The Christian Missionary, persecuted by the Jews

1. The Conversion of Paul

We saw in the last chapter that Paul was a violent persecutor of the Church. It was to extend his persecuting activity that Paul travelled to Damascus to persecute Hellenistic Jewish Christians there. However, his journey to Damascus was interrupted by a life changing experience.[1] The glorified Christ appeared to him. In Acts there are three accounts of his conversion (Acts 9.1-19; 22.1-21; 26.2-23) and, as is well known, there are various contradictions in the three accounts.[2] There are also references to his conversion in the letters (e.g. Gal. 1.16; 1 Cor. 15.8; 2 Cor. 4.4-6).

In 1 Cor. 15.8, after describing the resurrection appearances to "Cephas", to "the twelve", to "more than five hundred brethren", to James, and to "the apostles", he writes: "last of all, as to one untimely born, he appeared also to me" (ἔσχατον δὲ πάντων ὡσπερεὶ τῷ ἐκτρώματι ὤφθη κἀμοί). The use of the verb ὤφθη gives the clue to the nature of these resurrection appearances. The verb ὀφθῆναι, "appear", is used in the LXX for the appearance of God himself or of his angels before human beings. In these instances the concern

---

[1] According to the chronology I am following, Paul would be about 30 years old. He was converted around 31-32 AD, most probably within 18 months of the resurrection. See Bell, *Provoked to Jealousy*, p. 287 n. 5. We may consider Schlatter and Oepke for examples of two alternative (and extreme) chronologies. A. Schlatter, *Die Geschichte der ersten Christenheit*, Stuttgart: Calwer Verlag [6]1983, ([1]1926), p. 114, thinks that Paul as persecutor was probably over 40. His conversion was therefore not to be understood as "das Erlebnis eines jugendlichen Schwärmers"! Oepke, "Probleme der vorchristlichen Zeit", 446, believes Paul was around 20 at his conversion (he dates Paul's birth at 10 AD at the earliest (445)).

[2] So in Acts 9.7 Paul's companions hear the voice but do not see the light; in 22.9 they see the light but do not hear the voice. According to Hengel and Schwemer, *Between Damascus and Antioch*, p. 342 n. 166, "Luke wants to indicate that different versions were in circulation".

is not simply with seeing but is bound up with a verbal revelation. For example, the ἄγγελος κυρίου appears to Moses in Ex. 3.2, 4ff. Ex. 3.2: "And the angel of the LORD appeared to him in a flame of fire out of the midst of the bush". The Greek aorist passive here (ὤφθη) is equivalent to the niphal form of ראה (וַיֵּרָא) and means to let oneself be seen. וַיֵּרָא מַלְאַךְ יְהוָֹה אֵלָיו ; ὤφθη δὲ αὐτῷ ἄγγελος κυρίου. The expression ὀφθῆναί τινι in 1 Cor. 15.5-8 points to the appearance of the risen Jesus to chosen individuals and groups, and one so chosen was Paul himself. Therefore the revelation given to Paul would not be seen by a bystander. It is interesting that Luke, although giving a different emphasis to the conversion of Paul, seems to recognize that Paul received a revelation which the onlookers did not receive.[3] If the appearance to Paul was an appearance of the ascended and exalted Jesus, so were the appearances to the disciples. Paul makes no distinction in 1 Cor. 15.5-8 between the appearance to him and the earlier appearances to the disciples. So the resurrection appearances were appearances of the risen Jesus to certain chosen individuals or groups. However, the appearances are not to be simply explained away as subjective visions. Paul, for example, makes a clear distinction between the resurrection appearance he received on the Damascus Road and the visions (ὀπτασίαι) and revelations (ἀποκαλύψεις) he speaks of in 2 Cor 12.1ff.[4] The resurrection appearances therefore stand between objective appearances which any bystander would also see and Paul's spiritual experiences as in 2 Cor. 12.1-10.[5]

---

[3] According to Acts Paul was accompanied on his journey to Damascus. But only Paul received the vision of the risen Christ and as far as we know he was the only one to be converted. As noted above (n. 2), the text of Acts is a little confused for in Acts 9.7 the men travelling with Paul heard the voice but saw no one whereas in Acts 22.9 Paul says they saw the light but did not hear the voice. Whichever is correct, one is left with the impression that only Paul met with the risen Christ.

[4] Such a distinction was made by P. Althaus. See P. Althaus, *Die Wahrheit des kirchlichen Osterglaubens: Einspruch gegen E. Hirsch*, Gütersloh: C. Bertelsmann 1940 (second edition 1941); see also W. Pannenberg, *Jesus – God and Man* ET, Philadephia: The Westminster Press 1968, p. 94. Hirsch objected to Althaus' argument, pointing out that the word ὀπτασία is used in Acts 26.19 for Paul's vision (but note this is is Luke's usage, not Paul's). For further discussion of the Hirsch-Althaus debate, see M. Meiser, *Paul Althaus als Neutestamentler: Eine Untersuchung der Werke, Briefe, unveröffentlichten Manuskripte und Randbemerkungen* (CThM A15), Stuttgart: Calwer Verlag 1993, pp. 343-54, especially p. 348.

[5] See P. Stuhlmacher, *Biblische Theologie des Neuen Testaments, Band 1: Grundlegung. Von Jesus zu Paulus*, Göttingen: Vandenhoeck & Ruprecht 1992, p. 174.

In another text, 2 Cor. 4.4-6, Paul alludes to the first day of creation, likening this to the blinding light he experienced on the Damascus Road (cf. Acts 9.3; 22.6, 9; 26.13). Then on another occasion he says simply "have I not seen our Lord Jesus?" (1 Cor. 9.1: οὐχὶ ᾽Ιησοῦν τὸν κύριον ἡμῶν ἑόρακα;).

Paul and the author of Acts clearly have a different emphasis regarding the Damascus Road experience.[6] However, I believe the differences have been often exaggerated.[7] But whatever the differences, one thing does seem clear from the texts: it was believed that the risen Christ appeared to Paul. Further, what may be legitimately called a conversion[8] seems to have occurred out of the blue. I find the various psychological explanations for Paul's conversion unconvincing[9] as I do the naturalistic explanations.[10] I am

---

[6] See Deißmann, *Paulus*, pp. 103-5; A.F. Segal, *Paul the Convert: The Apostolate and Apostasy of Saul the Pharisee*, New Haven/London: Yale University Press 1990, pp. 14-16.

[7] Hengel and Schwemer, *Between Damascus and Antioch*, pp. 38-43, point to key ways in which Luke and Paul cohere on the matter of his conversion. Both have the brilliant light; also Luke has the audition and Paul obviously saw the revelation of Jesus Christ (Gal. 1.12) as a "word event".

[8] For a defence of the term "conversion" see Bell, *Provoked to Jealousy*, p. 286 n. 1. See further Segal, *Paul the Convert*, p. 72: "Conversion is an appropriate term for discussing Paul's religious experience, although Paul did not himself use it". However, Segal makes the mistake of seeing Paul's vision in the light of Jewish visionary experience as found from Ezekiel through to Merkabah. Although there are similarities between Ezek. 1.28; 2.1-3 and Luke's account (Segal, *Paul the Convert*, p. 9), Hengel and Schwemer, *Between Damascus and Antioch*, p. 341 n. 165, rightly comment that the parallels Segal finds are more akin to 2 Cor. 12.1ff than Paul's vision before Damascus.

[9] See, for example, the application of T. Kuhn, *The Structure of Scientific Revolutions*, Chicago/London: The University of Chicago Press 1962 by M. Heirich, "Change of Heart: A Test of Some Widely Held Theories of Religious Conversion", *AJS* 83 (1977) 653-680. See also G. Lüdemann, *The Resurrection of Jesus*, London: SCM 1995, pp. 16-19, 102-7, 119-21, 172-73. For general criticism of such psychological explanations see E.J. Bickerman, "A propos de la phénoménologie religieuse" in *Studies in Jewish and Christian History III* (AGJU), Leiden: E.J. Brill 1986, 224 (212-24), and more specifically concerning his conversion, J.G. Gager, "Some Notes on Paul's Conversion", *NTS* 27 (1981) 697-703.

[10] The first attempt I have found to give a naturalistic interpretation of Paul's conversion is the work of the nineteenth century liberal C. Holsten, *Zum Evangelium des Petrus und des Paulus*, Rostock: Rittersche Hofbuchhandlung 1868 (for some of the history behind this work, see P. Mehlhorn, "Holsten", *RE*³ 8:282 (281-86). Apparently he saw himself together with Hilgenfeld as the last of the Tübingen school (see K. Bauer, "Holsten", *RGG*² 2:1998). Some of the older works on Paul discuss Holsten's theory (e.g. A.

even sceptical about attempts to portray the pre-Christian Paul as someone experiencing conflicts which somehow prepared him for his conversion.[11]

It is easy to underestimate the trauma of this life-changing experience on the Road to Damascus.[12] Paul was overwhelmed by Jesus Christ in his glory.[13] He realized that this was the same Jesus who had suffered the ignoble death of crucifixion. For the pre-Christian Paul, a crucified messiah was unthinkable (partly in view of Dt. 21.23).[14] Since such an accursed Jesus had been vindicated by God in the heavenly court, Paul had to rethink his view of the law. The precise nature of this reappraisal of the law has been a matter of dispute and I mention two interpretations which I believe are plausible. The first is that Christ was condemned under the law but this verdict was reversed through the exaltation of Christ so leading to the view that somehow the law was at fault. So Luz writes: *"Wenn der gekreuzigte Jesus von der Tora verflucht wird, so wird deutlich, daß Gott zur Tora selbst Nein gesagt hat, wenn er diesen Gekreuzigten auferweckte".*[15] Kim puts forward a similar argument: "Paul realized that the crucified Jesus of Nazareth was not accursed by God as the law had pronounced (Dtn 21.23), but, on the contrary, exalted by him as his own Son (cf. Rom 1.3f.). This means that God reversed or annulled the verdict of the law upon Jesus. Paul was thus compelled to recognize that it is no longer the Torah but Christ

---

Sabatier, *The Apostle Paul: A Sketch of the Development of His Doctrine* ET, London: Hodder and Stoughton [4]1899, pp. 64-67).

[11] See Bell, *Provoked to Jealousy*, p. 296, nn. 29, 30.

[12] Cf. C. Dietzfelbinger, *Die Berufung des Paulus als Ursprung seiner Theologie* (WMANT 58), Neukirchen-Vluyn: Neukirchener Verlag 1985, p. 115, who is critical of Wrede, Schweitzer and Strecker, for not taking full account of the Damascus Road experience in their consideration of Paul's theology.

[13] See, for example, Phil. 3.12. Most commentators rightly see a reference to Paul's conversion here. See also J. Dupont, "The Conversion of Paul, and its Influence on His Understanding of Salvation by Faith", in W. Ward Gasque and R.P. Martin (ed.), *Apostolic History and the Gospel: Biblical and Historical Essays presented to F.F. Bruce on his 60th Birthday*, Exeter: Paternoster 1970, 180-81 (176-94).

[14] The importance of this text will be discussed below.

[15] U. Luz, "Das Neue Testament", in R. Smend and U. Luz, *Gesetz. Biblische Konfrontationen* (KT 1015), Stuttgart/Berlin/Köln/Mainz: W. Kohlhammer Verlag 1981, 91 (58-139) (emphasis of Luz).

who truly represents the will of God, that Christ has superseded the Torah as the revelation of God".[16]

The problem with this view is that although there is a certain historical plausibility to it (i.e. Christ was condemned by a human court according to the law but after his conversion Paul came to see that the verdict of this human court was overturned through the resurrection), the Pauline texts themselves suggest another understanding. This brings me to a second and more satisfactory view: the law comes to an end not because of its failure but rather because the law has a time-limited function to condemn until the revelation of Christ (Gal. 3.15-4.7).[17] And if we bring in Rom. 10.4, it means that the law in fact continues to condemn those who do not believe in Christ even after the Christ event.[18] For Paul it is not the law which is at fault but rather the seeking of salvation through the law which is wrong.[19] He came to see that the law functions simply as a condemning word.

How are these *texts* then to be related to the change in Paul's actual *thinking*. I suggest that after Paul's conversion he realized that his terrible mistake in persecuting Christians had been based on a fundamental misconception: he had not realized that the law had a time-limited function. Therefore it was not that the law was at fault as Bruce suggests in writing that the law "led him to sin". Bruce continues: "It was his devotion to the law that made him such a zealous persecutor of the church: his persecuting zeal was but one aspect of his zeal for the law".[20] Rather it was Paul's misunderstanding of the function of the law which was at fault. One may also add that Jesus died under the law. But he died not because of his own guilt but for *our sake* he was accursed (Gal. 3.13). He identified so much with a fallen humanity, being sent in the form of sinful flesh (Rom. 8.3), that he died under the law.

---

[16] S. Kim, *The Origin of Paul's Gospel* (WUNT 2.4), Tübingen: J.C.B. Mohr (Paul Siebeck) 1981, p. 274.

[17] See H.-J. Eckstein, *Verheißung und Gesetz. Eine exegetische Untersuchung zu Galater 2,15-4,7* (WUNT 86), Tübingen: J.C.B. Mohr (Paul Siebeck) 1996, p. 163.

[18] The sense of this much disputed verse is that Christ brings the condemning function of the law to an end but only for those who have faith. It is highly unlikely that Paul means to say that Christ brings the *saving* function of the law to an end since for Paul the law can have no saving function since all are in Adam.

[19] Eckstein, *Verheißung*, p. 65.

[20] F.F. Bruce, "What the Law could not do", in *Paul: Apostle of the Free Spirit*, Exeter: Paternoster 1977, 189 (188-202).

The gospels portray his death as a miscarriage of justice, something reflected by Paul in 1 Cor. 2.8. But in another sense he died "justly" under the law but not so much because of what he *did*[21] but because of his identification with sinful human nature, i.e. who he *was*.[22] The theological consequences of this are not always appreciated.[23]

So I suggest that soon after Paul's conversion, he realized that the law no longer has a claim on the Christian. "For I through the law died to the law" (Gal. 2.19a: ἐγὼ γὰρ διὰ νόμου νόμῳ ἀπέθανον). This has been variously understood but the most likely meaning is that Paul, by dying with Christ (see 2.19b), has died to the law through the law in the sense that Christ stood under the curse of the law. Paul participated in this death under the judgement of the law. The death on the cross is, as Eckstein writes, "zugleich und in einem die *Bestätigung* des Gesetzes und die *Befreiung* von ihm – *durch das Gesetz* stirbt der Mensch *dem Gesetz*".[24] The link between διὰ νόμου and Christ's death on the cross is not only suggested by the expression Χριστῷ συνεσταύρωμαι but also by the parallel in Rom. 7.4: καὶ ὑμεῖς ἐθανατώθητε τῷ νόμῳ διὰ τοῦ σώματος Χριστοῦ.[25]

One issue which has to be considered is whether Dt. 21.23 played any part in Paul's reappraisal of the law. The above discussion has assumed that

---

[21] I do not intend to enter the discussion as to whether Jesus was a law observant Jew. For a recent discussion of the matter see J.G. Crossley, *How Understanding the Importance of the Law in the Teaching of Jesus and in Earliest Christianity Can Help Date the Second Gospel*, Nottingham Ph.D. Dissertation 2002.

[22] H. Gese, "Sühne", righly stresses the ontological view of sin of the Priestly writer which is reflected in Paul's own understanding. Jesus our sacrifice has to go through a "Todesgericht"; atonement is "ein Zu-Gott-kommen durch das Todesgericht hindurch" (Gese, "Sühne", 104).

[23] I have explored some of the implications of Rom. 8.3, 2 Cor 5.19, 21 and Rom. 3.25 in "Sacrifice and Christology in Paul", *JTS* 53 (2002) 1-27. One of my conclusions is that in becoming a human person Christ was made to be a sinner in a "cosmic" sense (but not necessarily in an ethical sense).

[24] Eckstein, *Verheißung und Gesetz*, p. 66 (Eckstein's emphasis).

[25] Eckstein, *Verheißung und Gesetz*, p. 66. Eckstein, *Verheißung und Gesetz*, p. 65, is rightly critical of some of Bruce's work on Gal. 2.19. So Bruce writes that "the law had led him into sin. In the revelation of Jesus Christ on the Damascus road the moral bankruptcy of the law was disclosed" (*Galatians*, p. 143). Eckstein points out that it is not the law which led Paul astray but the blindness of Paul (see especially 2 Cor. 4.4). There are nevertheless points of agreement between Bruce and Eckstein regarding the relationship of Gal. 3.13 to 2.19.

it did. But this point has been disputed by Tuckett. One of his objections is that according to the logic of the scheme "corollaries about the Law inevitably follow from the conviction that Jesus was Messiah/Lord/accepted by God or whatever" but in fact "a sizeable part of the early Christian church failed to draw such corollaries".[26] It is true that many in the early Church failed to draw these conclusions. However, Seifrid correctly points out: "It is not necessarily the case that the conclusions which Paul might have drawn about the Law from this text would have been transparent to every Jewish Christian".[27] Further there are a number of texts in Galatians which suggest that Dt. 21.23 did in fact have a crucial rôle to play in Paul's new understanding of the law. Gal. 2.19a, for example, has to be understood in the light of Christ becoming a curse for us (Gal. 3.13) and the believer being crucified with Christ in Gal. 2.20.[28]

Right from the start Christ's person and work were therefore of fundamental importance[29] and they became inextricably intertwined with his theology not only of law but also of justification.[30] Therefore the justification of the ungodly, which was to become so central in Paul's theology, developed out of the Damascus Road experience.[31]

Paul's conversion can be viewed as an act of the grace of God. Paul contributed absolutely nothing to his conversion. It should therefore come as no surprise that Paul was to stress the grace of God more than any other New

---

[26] C.M. Tuckett, "Deuteronomy 21,23 and Paul's Conversion", in A. Vanhoye (ed.), *L'apôtre Paul: Personnalité, style et conception du ministère* (BEThL 73), Leuven: Leuven University Press 1986, 348-49 (345-50).

[27] Seifrid, *Justification by Faith*, p. 166.

[28] See Bruce, *Galatians*, p. 143; R.C. Tannehill, *Dying and Rising with Christ: A Study in Pauline Theology* (BZNW 32), Berlin: Alfred Töpelmann 1967, p. 59.

[29] Cf. M. Hengel and A.M. Schwemer, *Paul between Damascus and Antioch*, London 1997, p. 98: "The starting point could only be the person of the exalted Christ who had encountered Paul before Damascus and his saving work. At the beginning stands a personal encounter, a being overwhelmed by the crucified and exalted Christ".

[30] See Bornkamm, *Paul*, p. 117, argues that "to show that Christological statements cannot be separated from soteriological ones or, better expressed, to set out the gospel concerning Christ *as* a gospel of justification, and vice versa, is a decisive concern of his whole theology". See also Bornkamm, *Paul*, pp. 248-49; "Paulus", *RGG*[3] 5:177 (166-90).

[31] See Kim, *Origin of Paul's Gospel*, pp. 269-311. See also Dietzfelbinger, *Berufung*, pp. 114-16.

Testament theologian. We shall also see that this experience was one of the clues for him in Romans as to how Israel will be finally saved.

2. Paul's Missionary Work among the Jews

Paul was called to be the "apostle to the Gentiles". Nevertheless it is certain that he evangelized Jews also. Acts describes a number of occasions when Paul preached in the synagogue; then, on being rejected by the Jews, he would turn to the Gentiles. So in Acts 13.16b-41 Paul preached in the synagogue in Pisidian Antioch. However, because the Jews rejected Paul's message, Paul and Barnabas turned to preach to the Gentiles. See Acts 13.46:

> And Paul and Barnabas spoke out boldy, saying, 'It was necessary that the word of God should be spoken first to you. Since you thrust it from you, and judge yourselves unworthy of eternal life, behold, we turn to the Gentiles'.

Then according to Acts 14.1-7 Paul and Barnabas preached in the synagogue in Iconium. The city was divided, some siding with the Jews and others with "the Apostles" (14.4). Paul and Barnabas fled when they heard of a plan by both Jews and Gentiles to molest and stone them. In Acts 17.1-5 we read how Paul preached in the synagogue of Thessalonica for three Sabbaths. Again in Bereoa, Paul and Silas preached in the synagogue (Acts 17.10). Although these Jews of Bereoa "received the word with all eagerness" (17.11), Jews came from Thessalonica to stir up and incite the crowds (17.13). Likewise in Acts 18.4 Paul preached in the synagogue in Corinth. He "argued in the synagogue every sabbath, and persuaded both Jews and Greeks".

But are such reports historically reliable? Does it not seem hard to imagine that Paul, especially after the agreement of the apostolic council (Gal. 2.9), should preach first in the synagogues and then, only after he has been cast out, should turn to the Gentiles?

The accounts in Acts, however, ring true, for it would be understandable for Paul to use the network of synagogues in the diaspora. First, he could there find temporary accommodation and employment.[32] Second, it provided

---

[32] M. Hengel, "Die Synagogeninschrift von Stobi", *ZNW* 57 (1966) 171-72 (145-83), discusses the way synagogues could be used for accommodation and as an agency for obtaining employment.

him with an opportunity to preach. I can see no reason to doubt the custom of the ruler of the synagogue inviting someone to give a "word of exhortation" after the reading of the lessons.[33] Further, we know that synagogue preaching was seen as an extremely important means of religious propaganda, sermons being addressed to both Jews and Gentiles.[34] Third, Paul found in the synagogues the God-fearers (φοβούμενοι τὸν θεόν or σεβόμενοι τὸν θεόν) who were open to the gospel.[35] Therefore I think the picture in Acts that Paul first preached in the synagogues and then later turned to the Gentiles is to be considered reliable.[36]

Further, there is implicit support in the letters for the view that Paul evangelized Jews. First, 1 Cor. 9.20 suggests that Paul, even in his later mis-

---

[33] In Acts 13.15 the ἀρχισυνάγωγοι (on this term see Schürer/Vermes et al., *Jewish People*, 2:434-36 and compare Acts 18.8, 17) invite Paul and Barnabas to give a word of exhortation after the reading of the law and prophets. G.F. Moore, *Judaism in the First Centuries of the Christian Era: The Age of the Tannaim*, 3 vols, Cambridge, Mass.: Harvard University Press 1 1927; 2 1927; 3 1930, 1:305, does not doubt the veracity of Paul preaching in the syagogues: "Preaching in the synagogue was not the prerogative of any class, nor was any individual regularly appointed to conduct this part of the service". See also M. Hengel, *The Charismatic Leader and his Followers* (SNTW) ET, Edinburgh: T. & T. Clark 1981, p. 45: "Intrinsically every Jew familiar with the Law was entitled to speak in it. Only after 70 A.D. – in connection with the exclusion of the mînîm – do limitations to this right become discernible". Also Schürer/Vermes et al., *Jewish People*, 2:434, point out that at this time parts of the service including the preaching "were still performed by members of the congregations themselves, which accounts for Jesus (and Paul) being able to speak in various synagogues". I. Elbogen, *Der jüdische Gottesdienst in seiner geschichtlichen Entwicklung*, Hildesheim: Georg Olms Verlagsbuchhandlung [4]1962, p. 197, believes the idea of asking visitors to preach rings true since in the diaspora there may be a lack of suitable people to preach.

[34] See Hengel and Schwemer, *Between Damascus and Antioch*, pp. 73-75. As an example they give the pseudo-Philonic sermon *De Jona*, discussed by F. Siegert in *Drei hellenisch-jüdische Predigten. Ps.-Philon, 'Über Jona', 'Über Jona' (Fragment) und 'Über Simson' II. Kommentar* (WUNT 61), Tübingen: J.C.B. Mohr (Paul Siebeck) 1992.

[35] Acts 13.16, 26; 14.1; 16.14; 17.4, 12, 17; 18.4, 7. On the controversy as to the identification of the God-fearers, see Bell, *Provoked to Jealousy*, pp. 327-28. Literature not cited there includes J.A. Overman, "The God-Fearers: Some Neglected Features", *JSNT* 32 (1988) 17-26; M.C. de Boer, "God-Fearers in Luke-Acts", in C.M. Tuckett (ed.), *Luke's Literary Achievement: Collected Essays* (JSNTSup 116), Sheffield; Sheffield Academic Press 1995, 50-71; Levinskaya, *Diaspora Setting*, pp. 51-82.

[36] For further detailed defence of the basic historicity of these passages, see Bell, *Provoked to Jealousy*, pp. 311-25.

sionary work, did preach to Jews as well as to Gentiles:[37] "To the Jews I became as a Jew, in order to win Jews; to those under the law I became as one under the law—though not being myself under the law—that I might win those under the law". Secondly, 2 Cor. 11.24 points to the synagogue flogging Paul endured: "Five times I have received at the hands of the Jews the forty lashes less one". This synagogue flogging was inflicted for a variety of offences.[38] It is not clear why Paul received these floggings, but we know that in the third century, flogging was inflicted upon a scholar who had deserved the synagogue ban,[39] and it could be that this may have happened earlier in isolated cases.[40] The context suggests that Paul had received these beatings because he was a Christian. One therefore wonders whether Paul received these beatings because of his preaching. In view of the silence about such beatings in Acts, it may be that they belong to the early period of Paul's missionary activity.[41]

3. Paul persecuted by Jews

Paul, therefore, experienced persecution at the hands of the Jews. This involved not only the life threatening punishment of the 39 lashes[42] but also other forms of physical and psychological punishment. According to Acts 14.19 Paul was stoned and dragged out of the city of Lystra, the people supposing he was dead. This stoning may be that mentioned in 2 Cor. 11.25. Note also that Paul refers in 2 Cor. 11.26 to the danger he faced from his own people.

---

[37] See G. Bornkamm, "The Missionary Stance of Paul in I Corinthians 9 and in Acts", in L.E. Keck and J.L. Martyn (ed.), *Studies in Luke-Acts: Essays presented in honor of Paul Schubert*, London: SPCK 1968, 200 (194-207).

[38] See m. Mak. 3.1-9.

[39] Billerbeck, *Kommentar*, 4:319, 320.

[40] C.K. Barrett, *A Commentary on The Second Epistle to the Corinthians* (BNTC), London: A. & C. Black ²1979, (¹1973), p. 296.

[41] Cf. Riesner, *Early Period*, p. 267, who suggests that "some of the persecutions and tribulations" of 2 Cor. 11.24ff. derive from the period when Paul used Tarsus as a base for his missionary work. See also Hengel and Schwemer, *Between Damascus and Antioch*, p. 158.

[42] According to m. Sanh. 3.14, the scourger is not culpable should the person being scourged die, provided that he did not give him one stripe too many.

It therefore seems beyond doubt that Paul received the most savage persecution at the hands of the Jews. Further, he was persecuted by Jews not only for evangelizing Jews but also for evangelizing Gentiles.

Why was Paul so persecuted? There were three reasons. The first is his liberal attitude to the law. This liberal attitude manifested itself in three ways. First, he himself did not always keep the Mosaic law.[43] Secondly, he taught that it was not necessary for other Jews to keep the law.[44] Thirdly, he taught that Gentiles could become members of God's people without keeping the law.[45] We have already seen that the pre-Christian Paul persecuted the Hellenists because of their liberal attitude to the law.[46] Paul's new view on the law was even more radical and it is therefore scarcely surprising that he was persecuted for this reason.

Just as the persecution of the Hellenists could be contrasted with the way the Hebrew speaking Jewish Christians were largely exempt from persecution, so we can contrast Paul and James. Paul was persecuted for his attitude to the law. With James it was somewhat different. James had a conservative view of the law. Assuming that the letter of James was written by him, he believed that Jewish Christians should keep the whole law[47] although his view on which laws the Gentiles should keep is less clear.[48] Generally speaking James, the brother of Jesus, seems to have striven to build up a peaceful relationship with the Jewish people. The hostility to Christians in

---

[43] See, e.g., 1 Cor. 9.21; 10.27. Paul belonged to the "strong" (i.e. those who felt they did not have to keep the Jewish law) of Rom. 14.1-15.6 (see Bell, *Provoked to Jealousy*, pp. 72-73).

[44] Again Rom. 14.1-15.6 refers to the "weak" who kept the Jewish law and the "strong" who felt they did not have to keep it. There were clearly Jewish Christians (such as Prisca and Aquila) who belonged to this "strong" group. See Bell, *Provoked to Jealousy*, pp. 72-73.

[45] In particular he did not insist on the pre-requisite of circumcision. This, from a human perspective, would make the gospel attractive to "God-fearers".

[46] See chapter one above.

[47] On this see R. Bauckham, *James: Wisdom of James, disciple of Jesus the sage* (NTR), London/New York: Routledge 1999, pp. 142-47.

[48] Bauckham, *James*, p. 148, believes that James essentially agreed with Paul that Gentiles did not have to accept circumcision and be obligated to keep the whole law (Gal. 2.1-10; Acts 15.1-29).

Jerusalem seems to be due to the high priestly families who felt insecure.[49] But as regards the Pharisees, those who were strict in keeping the law, he seems to have had a good relationship. In fact when James was martyred, the Pharisees objected.[50]

The second reason is that Paul preached a crucified messiah. This idea of a crucified messiah was scandalous. We know from 4QpNah 1.7-8; Temple Scroll 64.6-13, that Jews at this time were applying Dt. 21.23 to crucifixion.

Dt. 21.22-23: And if a man has committed a crime punishable by death and he is put to death, and you hang him on a tree, (23) his body shall not remain all night upon the tree, but you shall bury him the same day, for a hanged man is accursed by God; you shall not defile your land which the LORD your God gives you for an inheritance.

According to this text a man was first put to death and *then* hanged on a tree.[51] Likewise m. Sanh. 6.4, which quotes Dt. 21.23, explains that stoning is followed by hanging.[52] However, in the two Qumran texts the order is

---

[49] Hengel and Schwemer, *Between Damascus and Antioch*, p. 255, note that the "persecution of the Christians by Agrippa I in Jerusalem was a 'momentous interlude' for the earliest community there. After the persecution, for around twenty years it was able to recover and consolidate itself under the leadership of James the brother of the Lord, but from now on it had to take special heed of the changed situation in the Holy City under the new unhappy rule of the procurators, a situation which was becoming more radical. Now the charge of belonging to the 'lawbreakers' (Josephus, *Antt.* 20,200) could quickly be made when different views clashed, especially as the high-priestly families, still powerful but feeling very insecure, continued to be hostile to the Christians. The cautious attitude of James, who wanted to avoid causing any offence in Jerusalem on the question of the law, and the zeal of his supporters, who wanted to extend this attitude outside Judaea as well, along with the intensified view of some–perhaps in Jerusalem most– Jewish Christians that all Gentile Christians should be circumcised, is probably connected with this persecution. It would also be understandable if James had attempted to make closer links with that opposition in Jerusalem to which Peter perhaps owed his life, i.e. the Pharisaic circles faithful to the law, by his own strict personal obedience to the law".

[50] Josephus, *Ant.* 20.201, writes that "Those of the inhabitants of the city who were considered the most fair-minded and who were strict (ἀκριβεῖς) in observance of the law were offended at this" (Josephus (LCL), 10:109).

[51] See, for example, S.R. Driver, *A Critical and Exegetical Commentary on Deuteronomy* (ICC), Edinburgh: T. & T. Clark 1973 (repr. of [3]1901, [1]1895), p. 248.

[52] See Danby, *Mishnah*, p. 390. Note however that the precise details of the methods of stoning as given in m. Sanhedrin does not correspond to methods which may have been used in incidents referred to in Jewish and Christian texts of the New Testament period. See J. Blinzler, "The Jewish Punishment of Stoning in the New Testament Period", in E. Bammel (ed.), *The Trial of Jesus: Cambridge Studies in honour of C.F.D. Moule* (SBT 2.13), London: SCM 1970, 147-61.

reversed. So in the Temple Scroll the order is: "you shall hang him on the tree and he will die". I quote 64.9b-13a:

> If there were a man with a sin punishable by death and he escapes (10) amongst the nations and curses his people / and / the children of Israel, he also you shall hang on the tree (11) and he will die. Their corpses shall not spend the night on the tree; instead you shall bury them that day because (12) they are accursed by God and man, those hanged on a tree; thus you shall not defile the land which I (13) give you for inheritance.[53]

This text picks up both the idea that the hanged man is cursed (Dt. 21.23a) and that Israel is not to defile the land (Dt. 21.23b). But in view of the order hanging–dying it is probable that it is referring to the punishment of crucifixion. That the man is put to death by hanging is confirmed by the reference to the witnesses in 64.7-9a:[54]

> If there were to be a spy against his people who betrays his people to a foreign nation or causes evil against his people, 8 you shall hang him from a tree and he will die. On the evidence of two witnesses and on the evidence of three witnesses 9 shall he be executed and they shall hang him on the tree.[55]

That Temple Scroll 64.6-13 refers to crucifixion receives some confirmation from another Qumran text, 4QpNah 1.7-8:

> '[And chokes prey for its lionesses; and it fills] its caves [with prey] and its dens with victims' (Nah. ii.12a-b). Interpreted, this concerns the furious young lion [who executes revenge] on those who seek smooth things and hangs men alive, 8 . . . formerly in Israel. Because of a man hanged alive on [the] tree, He proclaims, 'Behold I am against [you, says the Lord of Hosts'].[56]

The reference here is to Alexander Jannaeus (the "furious young lion") who crucified 800 Pharisees.[57] This punishment is then related to Dt. 21.23. Finally, Paul himself clearly alludes to Dt. 21.23 in Gal. 3.13:

---

[53] F.G. Martínez, *The Dead Sea Scrolls Translated* ET, Leiden: E.J. Brill, 1994, p. 178.

[54] O. Betz, "Jesus and the Temple Scroll", in J.H. Charlesworth (ed.), *Jesus and the Dead Sea Scrolls*, New York: Doubleday 1992, 84 (75-103), points out that the idea of witnesses, absent in Dt. 21.23, is brought in from Dt. 17.6-7.

[55] Martínez, *Dead Sea Scrolls*, p. 178.

[56] G. Vermes, *The Dead Sea Scrolls in English*, Sheffield: JSOT Press ³1987, (¹1962), p. 280. There is some debate as to how to reconstruct the missing text. See Y. Yadin, "Pesher Nahum 4QpNahum Reconsidered", in *IEJ* 21 (1971) 4 (1-12) and J.A. Fitzmyer, "Crucifixion in Ancient Palestine, Qumran Literature and the New Testament", *CBQ* 40 (1978) 502 (493-513).

[57] See Josephus, *Bellum* 1.97-98; *Antiquitates* 13.380-83.

Christ redeemed us from the curse of the law, having become a curse for us—for it is written, 'Cursed be every one who hangs on a tree'.

In view of the horror of crucifixion and the tradition of Dt. 21.23, the cross never became a symbol of Jewish suffering.[58] A crucified messiah was unthinkable. Far from expecting a suffering messiah, Psalm of Solomon 17 expects a triumphant messiah who would liberate Israel from the Romans.[59]

However, this understanding of applying Dt. 21.23 to Christ has not been universally accepted. Tuckett argues that not all victims of crucifixion would be regarded as cursed in the light of Dt. 21.23. He argues that 4QpNah 1.7-8 may be "expressing abhorrence at the act of hanging men alive, but the abhorrence need only be at the inhuman cruelty of the punishment itself".[60] However, there seems little doubt, despite the lacuna in the text, that crucifixion is interpreted in terms of Dt. 21.23. Further, the crucial point regarding Jesus is that he was proclaimed as a crucified messiah. As Seifrid comments, "Deut 21:23 need not have been universally applicable to have been relevant to the case of Messianic claimants. It is the particular notion of a crucified Messiah which appears to have been objectionable to Jews according to Paul's statements".[61]

The third reason Paul was persecuted by Jews is because he claimed that salvation was to be found in Jesus alone. Salvation was not even to be found through Jesus *and* the law.[62] In a Jewish culture only God could save. So in Is. 43.11 we read: "I, I am the LORD, and besides me there is no saviour". So Paul was attributing something in particular to Jesus, i.e. that he was the saviour, which can only be attributed to God. That Paul preached a divine Jesus is confirmed by his letters. Most New Testament scholars have been willing to believe that according to Paul Jesus was to some extent divine. Many, however, have drawn back from asserting that Paul believed in the full divinity of Jesus. There are, however, strong arguments to support the view that Paul believed in Jesus' full divinity. First, Paul seems to have

---

[58] M. Hengel, *The Cross of the Son of God*, London: SCM 1986, p. 176.

[59] See especially Ps. Sol. 17.21-25.

[60] Tuckett, "Deuteronomy 21,23", 347.

[61] Seifrid, *Justification by Faith*, p. 166.

[62] This was probably the view of Paul's opponents in Galatia.

believed that Jesus was pre-existent, a view found clearly in Phil. 2.6-7.[63] Secondly, Paul applies a number of Yahweh texts to Jesus.[64] Thirdly, it seems to be likely that Paul actually refers to Christ as God in Rom. 9.5.[65]

---

[63] There has been some controversy as to whether this text supports Christ's pre-existence. J.D.G. Dunn, *Christology in the Making: An Inquiry into the Origins of the Doctrine of the Incarnation*, London: SCM [2]1989, ([1]1980), pp. 114-21, has questioned whether Paul has in view a pre-existent Christ here. For critical responses see L.D. Hurst, "Re-enter the Pre-existent Christ in Philippians 2.5-11?", *NTS* 32 (1986) 449-57; C.A. Wanamaker, "Philippians 2.6-11: Son of God or Adamic Christology?", *NTS* 33 (1987) 179-93; N.T. Wright, "ἁρπαγμός and the Meaning of Philippians 2:5-11", *JTS* 37 (1986) 321-52; O. Hofius, *Der Christushymnus Philipper 2,6-11* (WUNT 17), Tübingen: J.C.B. Mohr [2]1991, [1](1976), pp. 113-22. See also M. Hengel, "Präexistenz bei Paulus?", in C. Landmesser, H.-J. Eckstein and H. Lichtenberger (ed.), *Jesus Christus als die Mitte der Schrift* (BZNW 86), Berlin/New York: Walter de Gruyter 1997, 479-518. An extremely useful collection of essays can be found in R.P. Martin and B.J. Dodd (ed.), *Where Christology Began: Essays on Philippians 2*, Louisville: Westminster John Knox Press 1998.

[64] See, e.g., Rom. 10.12-13; Phil. 2.11. Note that in Rom. 10.9-13, the lord (κύριος) Paul speaks of is Jesus and in Rom. 10.13 he applies a Yahweh text to Jesus. Note also that in Phil. 2.10-11 there is an allusion to Is. 45.23. Phil. 2.10-11 reads: ". . . so that at the name of Jesus every knee shall bow in heaven, and on earth and under the earth 11 and every tongue confess 'Jesus Christ is Lord' to the glory of God the Father" (my translation). Cf. Is. 45.23:

"By myself I have sworn,
from my mouth has gone forth in righteousness
a word that shall not return:
'To me every knee shall bow,
every tongue confess.'"

Paul has applied the words which originally referred to Yahweh to Jesus. For a discussion of these and other "Yahweh texts" where Jesus is the referent, see D.B. Capes, *Old Testament Yahweh Texts in Paul's Christology* (WUNT 2.47), Tübingen: J.C.B. Mohr (Paul Siebeck) 1992, pp. 115-160.

[65] There has been some dispute about the punctuation. One way of reading it is as in the RSV: "to them (i.e. the Israelites) belong the patriarchs, and of their race is the Christ. God who is over all be blessed for ever. Amen". The footnote gives the alternative: "Christ, who is God over all, blessed for ever". For a defence of this alternative see, for example, O. Cullmann, *The Christology of the New Testament* ET, London: SCM [2]1963, ([1]1959), pp. 312-13. For a more detailed treatment see B.M. Metzger, "The Punctuation of Rom. 9.5", in B. Lindars and S. Smalley (ed.), *Christ and Spirit in the New Testament: In Honour of Charles Francis Digby Moule*, Cambridge: CUP 1973, 95-112, and M.J. Harris, *Jesus as God: The New Testament Use of Theos in Reference to Jesus*, Grand Rapids: Baker Book House 1992, pp. 143-72. See also the discussion of Rom. 9.1-5 in chapter 4 below.

Fourthly, Paul worships Jesus and uses language of Jesus which one would usually apply only to God.[66]

That Paul considered Christ to be fully divine has not been universally accepted. The two main reasons why Christ's full divinity has been questioned is that Rom. 1.3-4 could suggest adoptionism and that there are certain texts which seem to imply that Jesus is subordinate to God. Regarding the first point, the text of Rom. 1.3-4 is: "the gospel concerning his Son, who was descended from David according to the flesh and designated Son of God in power according to the Spirit of holiness by his resurrection from the dead, Jesus Christ our Lord". Does it not appear that it was only at the resurrection that Jesus was appointed Son of God? But we have to be ask whether "in power" (ἐν δυνάμει) qualifies "Son of God" or "designated". If it qualifies "designated" the sense is: "designated in power Son of God". This would imply adoptionism. Only at the resurrection would he be designated Son of God, and so designated in power. But if "in power" qualifies "Son of God" the sense is: "designated Son-of-God-in-power".[67]

---

[66] On this see R.T. France, "The Worship of Jesus: A Neglected Factor in Christological Debate", in H.H. Rowdon (ed.), *Christ the Lord: Studies in Christology presented to Donald Guthrie*, Leicester: IVP 1982, 30-32 (17-36). He points out that Christians in 1 Cor. 1.2 are defined as "those who call on the name of our Lord Jesus Christ" (compare the phrase "to call upon the name of the Lord" used for worship of God in Gen. 4.26; 13.4; Ps. 105.1; Jer. 10.25; Jl 2.32). He also points to Jesus' divine functions. Two notes of caution are necessary. First, worship of Jesus does not necessarily mean the worshipper of Jesus considered him to be fully divine. So James, the brother of Jesus, worshipped Jesus, but did not have a Christology which would be as high as Paul's. Even if the low Christology of the Ebionites does not go back to James (as R. Bauckham, "James and Jesus", in B. Chilton and J. Neusner (ed.), *The Brother of Jesus: James the Just and His Mission*, Louisville: Westminster John Knox Press 2001, 135 (100-135), argues), his Christology seems to entail a belief that Jesus is messiah who will return to judge humankind according to their works. This brings me to the second cautionary note which concerns Christ's "divine functions". Jesus carrying out certain "divine functions" does not necessarily point to his divinity. So although Christ is judge (Rom. 2.16), a rôle usually taken by God, it must be recognized that judgement can be delegated to a figure who is not fully divine (e.g. the Son of Man of 1 Enoch). Nevertheless, it is striking that Paul can speak of praying to Christ as κύριος (Rom. 10.13-14; 2 Cor. 12.8-9), sinning against Christ (1 Cor. 8.12), tempting Christ (1 Cor. 10.9) and refers to the day of Christ (1 Cor. 1.8), the Church of God (1 Cor. 10.32) and of Christ (Rom. 16.16), the Spirit of God (1 Cor. 2.11) and of Christ (Rom. 8.9).

[67] See Cranfield, *Romans*, 2:62.

This means that we do not have adoptionism.[68] At the resurrection he was designated Son of God in power as opposed to his being Son of God in weakness in his earthly existence.[69] This would seem to be the natural reading in view of the beginning of Rom. 1.3: "(the gospel) concerning his Son" (περὶ τοῦ υἱοῦ αὐτοῦ).[70] A second reason for questioning Christ's full divinity is the existence of certain Pauline texts which point to Christ's subordination to the Father. But a frequent problem in the discussion is that it is assumed that the subordination is ontological and not functional. So statements about Jesus' subordination are seen as implying that he was not fully God. Such texts however are concerned with his function, not with his ontological status.[71]

However, the claim that Paul was persecuted because of his high Christology has been questioned. James Dunn has in fact argued that Christology was hardly an issue of contention between Paul and non-

---

[68] See D.P. Bailey, *Jesus as the Mercy Seat: The Semantics and Theology of Paul's Use of Hilasterion in Romans 3:25*, Cambridge Ph.D. Dissertation 1999, p. 206, for an instructive comparison of Rom. 1.4 and 3.25. So in Rom. 1.4 we have ὁ θεὸς ὥρισεν (subject and verb), αὐτόν (object), υἱὸν θεοῦ ἐν δυνάμει (complement) and then two prepositional phrases; in Rom. 3.25 we have again ὁ θεὸς προέθετο (subject and verb), αὐτόν (object), ἱλαστήριον διὰ πίστεως (complement) and then again two prepositional phrases.

[69] On this see Cranfield, *Romans*, 1:62.

[70] Note also that there is a Greek word for adoption (or adoption as sons), υἱοθεσία. This term however is only used for Christians. Christ is God's own son (see τοῦ ἰδίου υἱοῦ in Rom. 8.32).

[71] One of the key texts here is 1 Cor. 15.24, 28: "Then comes the end, when he (Jesus) delivers the kingdom to God the Father after destroying every rule and every authority and power. . . . 28 When all things are subjected to him, then the Son himself will also be subjected to him who put all things under him, that God may be everything to every one". J. Ziesler, *Pauline Christianity* (OBS), Oxford/New York: OUP 1990, pp. 39-40, comments: "Things traditionally said about God may now be properly said about Christ, but not that he is God, for the element of subordination remains". However, 1 Cor. 15.24, 28 is addressing questions about Jesus' function (that he is subject to his father, not whether he is fully God or not). One may compare Paul's view of women. Although he believed that women were subject to their husbands (1 Cor. 11.3; cf. Eph. 5.22-24), he nevertheless believed that a woman was just as much a human being as a man. Cf. G.D. Fee, *The First Epistle to the Corinthians* (NICNT), Grand Rapids: Wm B. Eerdmans 1987, p. 760: "As in [1 Cor.] 3:22-23 and 11:3, the language of the subordination of the Son to the Father is functional, referring to his 'work' of redemption, not ontological, referring to his being as such".

Christian Jews[72] although he admits that Christology was the decisive factor which gave rise to the final "parting of the ways" at the beginning of the second century.[73] My response to Dunn is twofold. First, Paul's view of Christ was far more exalted than Dunn allows.[74] And if, according to Dunn, John's Christology could give rise to a parting of the ways,[75] why could Paul's Christology not do precisely the same? Secondly, Dunn seems to assume Paul worked with a Jewish view of God which did not appear to change as a result of his conversion.[76] So Dunn writes:

. . . we could readily speak of the substructure of Paul's theology as the story of God and creation, with the story of Israel superimposed upon it. On top of that again we have the story of Jesus, and then Paul's own story, with the initial intertwining of these last two stories as the decisive turning point in Paul's life and theology.[77]

I find such an analysis misleading. One cannot simply speak of superimposition for as a result of his Damascus Road experience Paul's view of God clearly changed.[78] And on the specific issue of Christology, there are, con-

---

[72] See J.D.G. Dunn, "How Controversial Was Paul's Christology?", in M.C. De Boer (ed.), *From Jesus to John: Essays on Jesus and New Testament Christology in Honour of Marinus de Jonge* (JSNTSup 84), Sheffield: JSOT Press 1993, 167 (148-67).

[73] See, for example, J.D.G. Dunn, *The Partings of the Ways Between Christianity and Judaism and their Significance for the Character of Christianity*, London: SCM 1991, pp. 228-29.

[74] See the discussion above.

[75] Dunn, *Partings*, pp. 228-29.

[76] We see the same view in E.P. Sanders, *Paul and Palestinian Judaism: A Comparison of Patterns of Religion*, London: SCM 1977, p. 509: "From him [Paul] we learn nothing new or remarkable about God. . . . it is clear that Paul did not spend his time reflecting on the nature of the deity".

[77] See J.D.G. Dunn, *The Theology of Paul the Apostle*, London/New York: T. & T. Clark 2003 (repr.), ([1]1998), p. 18.

[78] F. Watson, "The Triune Divine Identity: Reflections on Pauline God-Language, in Disagreement with J.D.G. Dunn", *JSNT* 80 (2000) 99-124. Although I consider this to be a fine rebuttal of Dunn's position, I would wish to qualify Watson's statement: "Fundamental to his Jewish heritage is a non-Platonic ontology in which being and act are identical" (106). Whilst being is very much related to act, I suggest that act is dependent on ontology. Compare the idea that soteriology depends on Christology (see Bell, "Sacrifice and Christology", 11-12).

trary to Dunn, texts in Paul which point to his Christology being a bone of contention.[79]

Paul therefore was persecuted fiercely by Jews because of his liberal attitude to the law, his preaching of "Christ crucified" and his high Christology. From a human perspective it is therefore understandable that in one passage of his letter to the Thessalonians, Paul lashes out at the Jews. It is to this text, 1 Thes. 2.13-16, that we now turn.

4. A Study of 1 Thessalonians 2.13-16

4.1. Introduction

This text has been considered to be one of the most "anti-Jewish" passages in the New Testament.[80] It runs as follows:

13 Because of this, we also thank God constantly for this, that when you received the word of God which you heard from us, you accepted it not as a human word but as what it really is, the word of God, which is at work in you believers. 14 For you, brethren, became imitators of the churches of God in Christ Jesus which are in Judea; for you suffered the same things from your own countrymen as they did from the Jews, 15 who killed both the Lord Jesus and the prophets, and drove us out, and displease God and oppose all men 16 by hindering us from speaking to the Gentiles that they may be saved — so as always to fill up the measure of their sins. But God's wrath has come upon them at last![81]

---

[79] Dunn denies that 1 Cor. 1.23 points to a "crucified messiah" being in itself a stumbling block in itself to Jews. Rather, he claims "[i]t was the prospect of accepting that claim for themselves which was the stumbling block" ("How Controversial", 155). But is this a distinction non-Christian opponents of Paul would make? When it comes to the issue of Paul's high Christology, Dunn finds it "striking" that there "is the total absence of any indication that Paul's Christology of exaltation was a sticking point with his Jewish (Christian) opponents" ("How Controversial", 162). Paul's high Christology clearly involved more than a belief in Christ's exaltation. And Paul's high Christology essentially accounts for many of the controversies he had with both Christian and non-Christian Jews. So, e.g., his opponents in Galatians appear to claim that salvation was through Christ *and* the law; salvation through Christ alone was insufficient. Paul's response that salvation is through faith in Christ alone is based on his high Christology.

[80] See, e.g., H. Schreckenberg, *Die christlichen Adversos-Judaeos-Texte und ihr literarisches und historisches Umfeld (1.-11. Jh.)* (EHS.Th 172), Frankfurt am M./Bern/New York: Peter Lang 1982, p. 133: "Das ist vielleicht die schärfste antijüdische Polemik des ganzen Neuen Testaments".

[81] My own translation.

One of the most striking ideas in this passage is that the Jews killed the Lord Jesus; this idea was to become an important justification in later Church history for the Christian persecution of Jews.[82] But we should not jump to conclusions in "condemning" such a text. Although some questions will be raised later on, it should be made clear from the start that Paul does not advocate any form of Jewish persecution.

Nevertheless, these words have been an acute embarrassment for a number of scholars. Even the conservative scholar F.F. Bruce can write this on 1 Thes. 2.15: "Such sentiments are incongruous on the lips of Paul . . . nor can he be readily envisaged as subscribing to them even if they were expressed in this form by someone else".[83] Some scholars such as Pearson have tried to avoid the problem which these words cause by arguing that 1 Thes. 2.13-16 is an interpolation.[84] Among Pearson's arguments is support for Baur's thesis[85] that 2.16c ("But God's wrath has come upon them forever"; ἔφθασεν δὲ ἐπ᾽ αὐτοὺς ἡ ὀργὴ εἰς τέλος) refers to the destruction of Jerusalem in 70 AD,[86] although Pearson rejects Baur's proposal that the whole letter is un-Pauline.[87]

Pearson's arguments have been rightly criticized by Hurd,[88] who, commenting on 2.16c, rightly cautions that we must

---

[82] See the excursus below on the Jewish responsibility and guilt for the death of Jesus.

[83] F.F. Bruce, *1 & 2 Thessalonians* (WBC 45), Waco: Word Books 1982, p. 47.

[84] See B.A. Pearson, "1 Thessalonians 2:13-16: A Deutero-Pauline Interpolation", *HTR* 64 (1971) 79-94; H. Boers, "The Form Critical Study of Paul's Letters: 1 Thessalonians as a Case Study", *NTS* 22 (1976) 151-52 (140-58). For an overview of research see W. Trilling, "Die beiden Briefe des Apostels Paulus an die Thessalonicher: Eine Forschungsübersicht", *ANRW* 2.25.4 (1987) 3390-92 (3365-3403).

[85] F.C. Baur, *Paulus, der Apostel Jesu Christi*, 2 vols, Leipzig: Fues's Verlag (L.W. Reisland) 1 ²1866, 2 ²1867, 2:97.

[86] Pearson, "1 Thessalonians 2:13-16", 82-83. Note also Knox, *Chapters*, p. 73: ". . . 2:16b, if taken most naturally, would suggest a date outside Paul's lifetime entirely!" S.G.F. Brandon, *The Fall of Jerusalem and the Christian Church*, London: SPCK ²1957, (¹1951), pp. 92-93, considered that 1 Thes. 2.14-16 was an interpolation made by a Gentile Christian, and followed Baur in assuming a reference to the events of 70 AD in 2.16.

[87] Pearson, "1 Thessalonians 2:13-16", 79-83.

[88] J.C. Hurd, "Paul Ahead of His Time: 1 Thess. 2:13-16", in P. Richardson (ed.), *Anti-Judaism in Early Christianity: Volume 1: Paul and the Gospels* (SCJ 2), Ontario: Wilfrid Laurier University Press 1986, 21-36.

. . . warn ourselves against the fallacy of supposing that the text ought to be referring to the event which seems to us the most obvious candidate: the sack of Jerusalem and the destruction of the Temple. . . . If we connect the text with the events of 70 C.E., we must first make it probable on other grounds that it was written after 70 C.E. and not vice versa.[89]

To this may be added a number of points in favour of its authenticity. First, there is no textual evidence that 1 Thes. 2.13-16 is an interpolation.[90] Secondly, although some have felt that the passage interrupts the argument from 2.12 to 2.17, the passage can sit conveniently in its present context.[91] Thirdly, the passage is largely consistent with Paul's style[92] and vocabulary,[93] although there is some non-Pauline vocabulary and some minor divergences from Paul's usual style. Fourthly, a number of theological motifs in this passage cohere well with other parts of 1 Thessalonians and other letters of Paul.[94]

But we are still left with the problem that there is some non-Pauline vocabulary and style in this passage and ideas which seem foreign to Paul's theological outlook. The best way of dealing with this is to suggest that Paul

---

[89] Hurd, "Paul Ahead of His Time", 35. See also W.D. Davies, "Paul and the People of Israel", in *Jewish and Pauline Studies*, London: SPCK 1984, 125 (123-152 = *NTS* 24 (1978) 4-39).

[90] See the first of K. Aland and B. Aland's "Twelve basic rules for textual criticism", in *The Text of the New Testament: An Introduction to the Critical Editions and to the Theory and Practice of Modern Textual Criticism* ET, Grand Rapids: Eerdmans/Leiden: E.J. Brill 1987, p. 275: "Textual difficulties cannot be solved by conjecture, or by pointing to glosses or interpolations, etc., where the textual tradition itself shows no break; such attempts amount to capitulation before the difficulties and are themselves violations of the text".

[91] C.A. Wanamaker, *The Epistles to the Thessalonians: A Commentary on the Greek Text* (NIGTC), Grand Rapids: Wm B. Eerdmans/Exeter: Paternoster 1990, pp. 108-9, believes the verses form a digression. On the other hand T. Holtz, *Der erste Brief an die Thessalonicher* (EKK 13), Zürich/Einsiedeln/Köln: Benziger Verlag/Neukirchen-Vluyn: Neukirchener Verlag 1986, p. 94, finds a causal connection betwen 2.1-12 and 2.13-16.

[92] See J.A. Weatherly, "The Authenticity of 1 Thessalonians 2.13-16: Additional Evidence", *JSNT* 42 (1991) 91-98 (79-98). Weatherly is critical of the work of D. Schmidt, "1 Thess 2:13-16: Linguistic Evidence for an Interpolation", *JBL* 102 (1983) 269-79.

[93] See G. Lüdemann, *Paulus und das Judentum* (ThExH 215), München: Chr. Kaiser Verlag 1983, who points to the use of κωλύειν (cf. Rom. 1.13; 1 Cor. 14.39); ἔθνη (used 45 times by Paul); λαλεῖν (used 52 times by Paul); σῴζειν (used 19 times by Paul).

[94] See, for example, the comment below on 1 Thes. 2.13.

took over earlier tradition. This would account for the non-Pauline vocabulary and some stylistic peculiarities. The non-Pauline vocabulary is:

1. Although Paul uses the verb "kill" (ἀποκτείνειν) elsewhere on three occasions, this is the only place where he uses it for the death of Jesus.

2. Elsewhere Paul uses the verb διώκειν for "persecute" but only here does he use ἐκδιώκειν.

3. The word "contrary" (ἐναντίος) is used by Paul only here.

4. The expressions ἀναπληρῶσαι αὐτῶν τὰς ἁμαρτίας ("to fill up their sins") and φθάνειν ἐπί τινα . . . εἰς τέλος ("to come upon someone . . . forever") are non-Pauline.

This non-Pauline vocabulary is restricted to vv. 15-16. Paul has therefore probably taken over traditional material and supplemented it by vv. 13-14 and by 2.16a: "by hindering us from speaking to the Gentiles that they may be saved" (κωλυόντων ἡμᾶς τοῖς ἔθνεσιν λαλῆσαι ἵνα σωθῶσιν).[95]

I want to consider two possible parallels to 1 Thes. 2.13-16 from the synoptic tradition: Mk 12.1-9 and Mt. 23.29-38. Steck[96] and Lüdemann[97] have drawn attention to the following parallels between 1 Thes. 2.13-16 and Mk 12.1-9: both have the killing of the prophets (1 Thes. 2.15; Mk 12.1b-5); both refer to the killing of Jesus (1 Thes. 2.15; Mk 12.8); both speak of retribution coming upon the Jews (1 Thes. 2.16; Mk 12.8).

Another possible parallel to 1 Thes. 2.13-16 is the tradition now found in Matthew 23. This has been argued by scholars such as Dibelius,[98] Orchard,[99] Dodd,[100] Schippers[101] and D. Wenham.[102] So in Mt. 23.29-38

---

[95] See W.G. Kümmel, "Das literarische und geschichtliche Problem des ersten Thessalonicherbriefes", in *Heilsgeschehen und Geschichte, Band I: Gesammelte Aufsätze 1933-1964* (MThS 3), Marburg: N.G. Elwert Verlag 1965, 412 (406-16).

[96] O.H. Steck, *Israel und das gewaltsame Geschick der Propheten* (WMANT 23), Neukirchen-Vluyn: Neukirchener Verlag 1967, p. 276.

[97] Lüdemann, *Paulus und das Judentum*, p. 23.

[98] M. Dibelius, *An die Thessalonicher I-II. An die Philipper* (HzNT 11), Tübingen: J.C.B. Mohr (Paul Siebeck) ³1937, p. 11.

[99] J.B. Orchard, "Thessalonians and the Synoptic Gospels", *Bib* 19 (1938) 23 (19-42).

[100] C.H. Dodd, "Matthew and Paul", in *New Testament Studies*, Manchester: Manchester University Press 1953, 64-65 (53-66).

[101] R. Schippers, "The Pre-Synoptic Tradition in 1 Thessalonians II.13-16", *NovT* 8 (1966) 232-34 (223-34).

[102] D. Wenham, "Paul and the Synoptic Apocalypse", in R.T. France and D. Wenham (ed.), *Gospel Perspectives: Studies in History and Tradition in the Four Gospels, Volume II*, Sheffield: JSOT Press 1981, 361 (345-75).

and in 1 Thes. 2.15-16 there are four key words in common which are used in a parallel fashion: "to kill" (ἀποκτείνειν); "prophet" (προφήτης); "persecute" ((ἐκ)διώκειν); "fill up" ((ἀνα)πληροῦν). Further, there are four parallel ideas in these texts.

1. Both have the idea of killing the prophets (to which Paul adds killing Jesus).[103] See 1 Thes. 2.15 and Mt. 23.37.

2. Paul says Jews "persecute us" (ἡμᾶς ἐκδιωξάντων, 1 Thes. 2.15) and in Mt. 23.34 Jesus says "you persecute from city to city" (διώξετε ἀπὸ πόλεως εἰς πόλιν).

3. The phrase in 1 Thes. 2.16 "so as always to fill the measure of their sin" (εἰς τὸ ἀναπληρῶσαι αὐτῶν τὰς ἁμαρτίας πάντοτε) is similar to Mt. 23.32 "Fill up the measure of your fathers" (ὑμεῖς πληρώσατε τὸ μέτρον τῶν πατέρων).

4. The judgement of 1 Thes. 2.16c "But God's wrath has come upon them at last" (ἔφθασεν δὲ ἐπ᾽ αὐτοὺς ἡ ὀργὴ εἰς τέλος) parallels Mt. 23.36 "Truly, I say to you, all this will come upon this generation" (ἥξει ταῦτα πάντα ἐπὶ τὴν γενεὰν ταύτην) and 23.38 "Behold your house is forsaken and desolate" (ἰδοὺ ἀφίεται ὑμῖν ὁ οἶκος ὑμῶν).

If Paul is dependent on this material (traditionally assigned to "Q") then, it is claimed, a number of oddities in the text of 1 Thes. 2.13-16 can be explained.[104] So why should Paul pick on Judaean Jews when writing to Thessalonica? A possible explanation is that Paul is using tradition originally directed to Judaean Jews. Another peculiarity is that Paul uses ἀποκτείνειν for the death of Jesus. But if Paul had used the Q tradition of killing the prophets (see Mt. 23.37 // Lk. 13.34: "O Jerusalem, Jerusalem, killing the prophets . . . " (ἡ ἀποκτείνουσα τοὺς προφήτας)) then he may simply have added Jesus to the prophets.[105] It is further claimed that the use of earlier tradition can account for the extremely strong language Paul uses against the Jews.[106]

The taking over of earlier tradition would also to some extent explain the ideas in 1 Thes. 2.13-16 which seem so foreign to Paul. But even if Paul took over earlier tradition, he has decided to use this tradition and the

---

[103] On this addition see below.

[104] Interestingly both 1 Thessalonians and Q are dated to around 50 AD.

[105] See Wenham, "Paul and the Synoptic Apocalypse", 362.

[106] See Wenham, "Paul and the Synoptic Apocalypse", 362.

exegete and theologian can still be left with a sense of embarrassment. There is also the additional factor (rarely discussed) that Paul accuses the Jews of the very things he did. He stood in the tradition of those who killed Jesus and the prophets in his savage persecution of the Christians. It is striking that many elements in 1 Thes. 2.14-16 are there also at the end of Stephen's speech in Acts 7.51-53:

You stiff-necked people, uncircumcised in heart and ears, you always resist the Holy Spirit. As your fathers did, so do you. 52 Which of the prophets did not your fathers persecute? (τίνα τῶν προφητῶν οὐκ ἐδίωξαν οἱ πατέρες ὑμῶν;) And they killed those who announced beforehand the coming of the Righteous One (καὶ ἀπέκτειναν τοὺς προκαταγγείλαντας περὶ τῆς ἐλεύσεως τοῦ δικαίου), whom you have now betrayed and murdered, 53 you who received the law as delivered by angels and did not keep it (οἵτινες ἐλάβετε τὸν νόμον εἰς διαταγὰς ἀγγέλων καὶ οὐκ ἐφυλάξατε).

Luke then narrates the killing of Stephen (7.54-8.1):

Now when they heard these things they were enraged, and they ground their teeth against him. 57 . . . they cried out with a loud voice and stopped their ears and rushed together upon him. 58 Then they cast him out of the city and stoned him; and the witnesses laid down their garments at the feet of a young man named Saul.

Paul may not have thrown stones but according to Acts 8.1 "Saul was consenting to his death".[107]

I will argue in chapter 6 that the views expressed in 1 Thes. 2.13-16 on the Jews cannot be reconciled with Romans 9-11. But positing an interpolation is no way to deal with this problem. Rather, it is better to work with the idea of a development in Paul's thinking, a development which will be

---

[107] There is no space here to discuss the involved historical questions of this passage. Stephen's speech is unusual in several respects. It is long (it makes up 5% of Acts) and appears to be an independent unit (Roloff, *Apostelgeschichte*, p. 117, refers to "dieses sperrige Traditionsstück"). I do not think the authenticity of this speech can be questioned on the grounds that it is not in fact a *defence* made by Stephen before his accusers (cf. Roloff, *Apostelgeschichte*, p. 118) since Stephen may in fact have had the intention to go on the offensive! Steck, *Geschick*, p. 266, does not believe that this final section I have quoted (7.51-53) is Luke's own composition since it is not part of Luke's redactional interest. Steck, *Geschick*, p. 279: "Schon *Lk* ist der traditionelle Vorstellungskontext der Aussage vom gewaltsamen Geschick der Propheten nicht mehr vertraut". Further, Steck, *Geschick*, p. 266, believes that the ending is an integral part of the tradition of "Stephen's speech" which Luke took over (Steck accepts the three stage composition process put forward by F. Hahn, *Christologische Hoheitstitel: Ihre Geschichte im frühen Christentum* (FRLANT 83), Göttingen: Vandenhoeck & Ruprecht ²1964, (¹1963), pp. 382-85).

traced in chapter 8. 1 Thessalonians is most likely Paul's first extant letter and Romans most likely his last. Although there is only five to seven years between the writing of these letters, a development in Paul's thinking during this period is certainly possible.

To many, it would perhaps be a relief if 1 Thes. 2.13-16 were an interpolation. But I do not find the arguments in its favour convincing. I will later consider some of the theological issues (or problems) involved in 1 Thes. 2.13-16. But it is perhaps worth stressing now that this passage is strictly speaking "inner-Jewish polemic".[108] The text would carry a quite different sense had it been written after the clear separation of Judaism and Christianity.[109] Further, compared to other contemporary "anti-Jewish" polemic Paul criticism of "the Jews" is mild.[110]

I now consider this passage verse by verse.

4.2. 1 Thessalonians 2.13

Paul begins by thanking God that the Thessalonians received the gospel not as the word of man but as the word of God. Some of the wording is striking (and rather complex). He speaks of the word of God which is delivered and

---

[108] Contrast David Flusser in the forward to C. Thoma, *A Christian Theology of Judaism* (SJC), New York: Paulist Press 1980, p. 17, who writes this about "anti-semitism" in the New Testament: "Do not tell me that such statements and ideas are merely inner-Jewish disputes or prophetic scoldings. All of them sound Greek and not Hebrew, that is, they emerged among Gentile Christians, even though one or the other redactor may have been a Christian of Jewish descent". Such comments may be relevant to say Jn 8.41-47; they are not relevant though to 1 Thes. 2.13-16.

[109] Cf. R. Kampling, "Eine auslegungsgeschichtliche Skizze zu 1 Thess 2,14-16", in D.-A. Koch and H. Lichtenberger (ed.), *Begegnungen zwischen Christentum und Judentum in Antike und Mittelalter. Festschrift für Heinz Schreckenberger* (SIJD 1), Göttingen: Vandenhoeck & Ruprecht 1993, 185-87 (183-213).

[110] See L.T. Johnson, "The New Testament's Anti-Jewish Slander and the Conventions of Ancient Polemic", *JBL* 108 (1989) 441 (419-41), who writes that "by the measure of Hellenistic Conventions, and certainly by the measure of contemporary Jewish polemic, the NT's slander against fellow Jews is remarkably mild".

perceived through the preaching (λόγος ἀκοῆς παρ' ἡμῶν τοῦ θεοῦ).[111] He refers then to the gospel mentioned earlier in the letter (1 Thes. 1.5; 2.2, 4, 8, 9). The apostolic preaching, not to be identified with the word of God, is then the chosen instrument of God through which his word is manifest in the world.[112]

4.3. 1 Thessalonians 2.14

The Thessalonians became imitators of the churches of God in Judaea[113] not through a conscious choice but simply through the circumstances they found themselves in.[114] Paul compares the persecution the Thessalonians suffered from their countrymen to that which the Judaean Christians suffered from the Jews.

Some have claimed that the contrast between the "Jews" and "your own countymen" means that the Thessalonians were persecuted only by Gentiles.[115] However, I believe Marshall is correct in understanding "your own countrymen" in a local and not racial sense.[116] So Paul is probably referring to opposition from both Jews[117] and Gentiles.[118] In this sense then it is not unnatural for Paul to introduce a discussion about the Jews. If Paul

---

[111] O. Hofius, "Wort Gottes und Glaube bei Paulus", in *Paulusstudien* (WUNT 51), Tübingen: J.C.B. Mohr (Paul Siebeck) 1989, 153 n. 41 (148-74), analyses the Greek as follows: τοῦ θεοῦ is a genitivus auctoris of λόγος; παρ' ἡμῶν belongs to ἀκοῆς and represents a genitivus auctoris; the genitive ἀκοῆς signifies where the λόγος τοῦ θεοῦ is to be perceived. Wanamaker, *1 & 2 Thessalonians*, p. 111, wrongly suggests that the first genitive "of God" is redundant in the sentence. Concerning ἀκοή, he suggests that it refers to what is heard ("preaching") rather than the act of hearing.

[112] See Hofius, "Wort Gottes", 153.

[113] The term Judea may refer also to the areas of Galilee and Samaria: i.e. Paul is referring to Palestine. See *BAG* p. 379 ('Ιουδαία 2.).

[114] L. Morris, *The First and Second Epistles to the Thessalonians* (NICNT), Grand Rapids: Wm B. Eerdmans ²1991, (¹1959), p. 82; Wanamaker, *1 & 2 Thessalonians*, p. 112.

[115] See E. Haenchen, *The Acts of the Apostles* ET, Oxford: Basil Blackwell 1971, p. 513 (*Apostelgeschichte*, pp. 452-53).

[116] I.H. Marshall, *1 and 2 Thessalonians* (NCB), Grand Rapids: Wm B. Eerdmans 1983, pp. 78-79.

[117] Cf. Acts 17.5-10.

[118] For some of the political background concerning the Gentile opposition described in Acts 17.6-9 see R. Jewett, *The Thessalonian Correspondence: Pauline Rhetoric and Millenarian Piety* (FFNT), Philadelphia: Fortress Press 1986, pp. 123-25.

had no thought of Jewish opposition in Thessalonica in mind his polemic against the Jews would be rather irrational.

Paul's reference to persecution of Judaean Christians by Jews suggests a recent persecution. It has been argued that there was no significant persecution of Christians in Judaea before the Jewish war, thus adding fuel to the debate about the authenticity of this passage.[119] However, Reicke comes to the conclusion that in the period 33 to 54 "Christians were repeatedly the victims of Jewish patriotism and zealotism".[120] Further, Jewett points out that during the procuratorship of Ventidius Cumanus (48-52) the Zealot movement grew in strength and their target would be anyone who had connections with Gentiles and who were polluting Israel.[121] Did not Phinehas after all kill the Israelite and the foreign woman (a Midianite) with whom he was in union? Was not Paul, who had close contact with Gentiles, an ideal target? It may be that the attempt made on his life described in Acts 23.12-22 was by Zealots.[122] Therefore, although the Jerusalem Christians developed good relations with the Pharisees (see above), they were subject to persecution by other Jewish groups.

Note that Paul in this passage Paul uses the term "Jews" (Ἰουδαῖοι). This is a general term. The other terms he uses elsewhere are "Israelites" (Ἰσραηλεῖται) and "Hebrews" (Ἑβραῖοι).[123] "Israelities" refers to the elect people of God, a term used significantly in Romans 9-11.[124] The term "Hebrew", as I argued in chapter 1 above, denotes the people of Palestinian

---

[119] See Pearson, "1 Thessalonians 2:13-16", 87.

[120] B. Reicke, "Judaeo-Christianity and the Jewish establishment, A.D. 33-66" in E. Bammel and C.F.D. Moule (ed.), *Jesus and the Politics of His Day*, Cambridge: CUP 1984, 149 (145-52).

[121] R. Jewett, "The Agitators and the Galatian Congregation", *NTS* 17 (1970-71) 204-5 (198-212).

[122] See Schlatter, *Geschichte der ersten Christenheit*, pp. 254-55; R. Pesch, *Die Apostelgeschichte* (EKK 5), 2 vols, Zürich/Einsiedeln/Köln: Benziger Verlag/Neukirchen-Vluyn: Neukirchener Verlag 1986, 2:248 (on Acts 23.12-13). Cf. M. Hengel, *The Zealots: Investigations into the Jewish Freedom Movement in the Period from Herod I until 70 A.D.* ET, Edinburgh: T. & T. Clark 1989, p. 47 n. 189, p. 215 n. 362, p. 351.

[123] On the terms Israelites and Hebrews see Georgi, *Gegner*, pp. 51-63. Another term is "Seed of Abraham" (Σπέρμα Ἀβραάμ) which Georgi also discusses (*Gegner*, pp. 63-82).

[124] See Bell, *Provoked to Jealousy*, pp. 173-74.

origin, culture, tradition and especially language. One question is how wide Paul's reference was in referring to the "Jews". The reference can certainly be limited to non-Christian Jews but whether the term can be further narrowed is a moot point. Marshall considers Marxsen's point that Paul was referring to particular Jews, those who had been hostile to God's messengers and not Jews in general.[125] However, Marshall concedes that the thesis of Marxsen that Paul is thinking of individual Jews who persecute missionaries is weak. Marshall writes: "More probably Paul is thinking collectively of the Jews as a people who by and large were opposed to the gospel and had turned against God during their history".[126]

A further attempt to restrict the reference is to be found in the work on the "antisemitic comma" between v. 14 and v. 15.[127] A comma at the end of v. 14 sets off in English a non-restrictive relative clause (although the same does not happen in Greek).[128] The question is whether the Greek articular participle at the beginning of v. 15 is restrictive (ὑπὸ τῶν Ἰουδαίων, 15 τῶν ἀποκτεινάντων . . .). Gilliard, appealing to Dana and Mantey, believes that the articular participle is restrictive. In discussing the restrictive participle they explain that it:

> . . . may denote an affirmation that distinguishes the noun which it qualifies as in some way specifically defined, or marked out in its particular identity. *This use approximates the function of a restrictive relative clause, and may usually be so translated in English.* It is to be differentiated from the ascriptive use in that, while the ascriptive participle only assigns a quality or characteristic, the restrictive denotes distinctiveness.[129]

My question though is whether a restrictive understanding makes much sense of the flow of Paul's argument in vv 14-15. If it were restrictive it would mean that the Jews who persecuted Christians in Judaea were the same as those who killed Jesus and the prophets and who drive out Paul and

---

[125] See Marshall, *1 and 2 Thessalonians*, pp. 82-83, and W. Marxsen, *Der erste Brief an die Thessalonicher* (ZBK), Zürich: Theologischer Verlag 1979, pp. 48-51.

[126] Marshall, *1 and 2 Thessalonians*, p. 83

[127] See F.D. Gilliard, "The Problem of the Antisemitic Comma Between 1 Thessalonians 2.14 and 15", *NTS* 35 (1989) 481-502.

[128] Gilliard, "Comma", 487. Obviously any comma placed at the end of v. 14 would be a later addition. Gilliard estimates this to be no earlier than the ninth century.

[129] H.E. Dana and J.R. Mantey, *A Manual Grammar of the Greek New Testament*, New York: Macmillan 1927, pp. 224-25, quoted in Gilliard, "Antisemitic Comma", 489 (Gilliard's emphasis).

his fellow workers, oppose all men and hinders Paul from speaking to the Gentiles. This is unlikely.

4.4. 1 Thessalonians 2.15

Here Paul writes that the Jews killed the Lord Jesus. 1 Thessalonians is probably the earliest extant letter of Paul, although some have dated Galatians earlier.[130] It also may be the earliest book of the New Testament.[131] It is therefore probably the first extant text to claim that the Jews killed Jesus. Even if Galatians were written earlier, it contains no reference to Jews being responsible for Jesus' death. The question therefore arises as to where Paul got this idea from. It would be foolish to claim that Paul made it up and I know of no one who has ever suggested this. As a persecutor of the Church he must have known that Jesus was executed as a deceiver of the people and that since this was a Jewish charge the Jews had some rôle in his trial. Further, in 1 Thes. 2.15 Paul was most probably taking over early Christian tradition that the Jews had a crucial rôle in the death of Jesus, even though it was the Roman authorities who actually carried out the sentence of crucifixion. The crucial opportunity for Paul to learn something of the trial of Jesus would be in his meeting with Cephas and James in Jerusalem, three years after his conversion (Gal. 1.18-19).[132]

So in claiming that the Jews killed the "Lord Jesus", Paul is stating a historical fact. Although he has omitted to say in 1 Thessalonians 2 that the Gentile rulers were also responsible, he does clearly imply this in 1 Cor. 2.7-8:

---

[130] According to Bruce, *Galatians*, p. 55, the letter was written in 48 AD on the eve of the Apostolic conference of Acts 15.6-29. See also Fung, *Galatians*, p. 28 and his discussion of the dating (pp. 9-28).

[131] Note however that some have argued for an early dating of the gospels. See, for example, J. Wenham, *Redating Matthew, Mark and Luke: A Fresh Assault on the Synoptic Problem*, London: Hodder & Stoughton 1991, who dates Matthew around 40 AD and Mark around 45 AD. Such early dating is not restricted to conservative scholars. See P.M. Casey, *Aramaic Sources of Mark's Gospel* (SNTSMS 102), Cambridge: CUP 1998, who regards a dating of Mark around 40 AD as "highly probable" (p. 260), and Crossley, *Law*.

[132] Although it may be the case that no canonical gospel had been written by 50 AD, there was oral tradition about the Jews' rôle in the trial of Jesus and there may have been earlier written sources or proto-gospels. For further discussion of the Jews' rôle in the death of Jesus, see the excursus below (section 4.6).

But we impart a secret and hidden wisdom of God, which God decreed before the ages for our glorification. None of the rulers of this age (οὐδεὶς τῶν ἀρχόντων τοῦ αἰῶνος τούτου) understood this; for if they had, they would not have crucified the Lord of glory".[133]

The claim therefore that there is no mention in the authentic letters of Paul of a Roman rôle in the death of Jesus is not strictly correct.[134]

Although Paul makes the serious charge that the Jews killed the Lord Jesus he does not say that Jews should be persecuted. This to many readers may seem an obvious and unnecessary point to make. However, in view of the way people have made the New Testament writers responsible for the many evil things that have happened to Jewish people, it is necessary to make this point explicit.[135]

---

[133] Some have taken the "rulers of this age" (ἄρχοντες τοῦ αἰῶνος τούτου) to be the demonic powers. See J. Weiß, *Der erste Korintherbrief* (KEK 5), Göttingen: Vandenhoeck & Ruprecht 1977 (repr.), (⁹1910), pp. 53-54; O. Cullmann, *Christ and Time: The Primitive Christian Conception of Time and History* ET, Philadelphia: Westminster Press 1964, pp. 191-206; G.B. Caird, *Principalities and Powers*, Oxford: Clarendon Press 1956, pp. 82-83; F.F. Bruce, *1 and 2 Corinthians*, Grand Rapids: Wm B. Eerdmans 1996 (repr.), (¹1971), p. 38. Such views have come in for some criticism. See F. Lang, *Die Briefe an die Korinther* (NTD 7), Göttingen: Vandenhoeck & Ruprecht 1986, pp. 42-43, who points out that Paul uses ἄρχοντες for political rulers (Rom. 13.3ff.) whereas he uses ἀρχαί for demonic powers (Rom. 8.38). See also Fee, *First Epistle to the Corinthians*, pp. 103-4. The "rulers of this age" referred to, who crucified Christ, are both Jewish and Gentile political leaders (e.g. Pilate and Caiaphas). However, I would not wish to exclude the idea of demonic overtones. As A.C. Thiselton, *First Epistle to the Corinthians* (NIGTC), Grand Rapids/Cambridge: Wm B. Eerdmans/Carlisle: Paternoster 2000, p. 238, comments: "Even if Paul's language *denotes* human leaders, *connotations* remain of a structural power either by cumulative inbuilt fallenness or by association with still stronger cosmic forces". He also points to Reinhold Niebuhr's view that "corporate evil takes a qualitative leap beyond the sum of all individual acts of evil" (Thiselton's summary; cf. R. Niebuhr, *Moral Man and Immoral Society*, London: SCM 1963).

[134] For an example of such a claim see J.T. Carroll and J.B. Green, *The Death of Jesus in Early Christianity*, Peabody: Hendrickson 1995, p. 190.

[135] On the relation between the Jews' alleged deicide and their persecution, see the discussion in section 4.7 and in chapter 9 below.

Paul goes on to say the Jews killed the prophets.[136] This is a theme found in the Old Testament itself and elsewhere in Paul (see Rom. 11.3).[137] As we have seen it also occurs in Mt. 23.29-38 and Mk 12.1-9. One should also remember the neglected *Vitae prophetarum* which mentions a number of violent deaths of prophets at the hands of their own people.[138]

Paul goes on to say the Jews "drove us out". Since the verb, unlike the following verbs, is an aorist Paul may have some particular event in mind, probably his being driven out by Jews in Thessalonica.[139]

Then Paul says the Jews "displease God and oppose all men". Bruce calls this "a piece of indiscriminate anti-Jewish polemic",[140] comparing Tacitus, *Hist.* 5.5.2:

. . . the Jews are extremely loyal toward one another, and always ready to show compassion, but toward every other people they feel only hate and enmity.[141]

But, as pointed out earlier, Paul's polemic is inner-Jewish polemic and therefore does not properly parallel Tacitus here.[142] Another conservative New Testament scholar, I.H. Marshall, however, denies any "anti-Semit-

---

[136] Strictly speaking the prophets could go with "drove out" rather than with "kill". So E.J. Bicknell, *The First and Second Epistles to the Thessalonians* (WC), London: Methuen & Co. 1932, p. 27, understands the sentence "who both killed the Lord Jesus and drove out the prophets and us". He considers the addition of "prophets" after "Jesus" an anticlimax. However, this understanding is unlikely to be correct in the light of the strong tradition of the killing of the prophets.

[137] It is unlikely that Paul is thinking of Christian prophets (James son of Zebedee or Stephen) as K. Lake, *The Earlier Epistles of St. Paul: Their Motive and Origin*, London: Rivingtons 1911, p. 87 n. 2, suggests.

[138] See A.M. Schwemer, *Studien zu den frühjüdischen Prophetenlegenden Vitae Prophetarum Band I: Die Viten der großen Propheten Jesaja, Jeremia, Ezekiel und Daniel* (TSAJ 49), Tübingen: J.C.B. Mohr (Paul Siebeck) 1995, pp. 79-82. She suggests that the tradition in the *Vitae prophetarum* cannot be later than the first half of the first century AD and that the formation of the work itself cannot have taken place long after that (p. 69). Those prophets in *Vitae prophetarum* who met a violent end at the hands of their own countrymen are Zechariah ben Jehoiada (cf. 2 Chr. 24.20-22), Isaiah (sawn in two by Manasseh, cf. Heb. 11.37), Jeremiah, Ezekiel, Amos and Micah.

[139] Marshall, *1 and 2 Thessalonians*, p. 79.

[140] Bruce, *1 & 2 Thessalonians*, p. 47.

[141] Tacitus (LCL), 3:181-83.

[142] Cf. Kampling, "Auslegungsgeschichtliche Skizze", 186.

ism" in Paul's language.[143] But the essence of Paul's accusation that Jews "displease God and oppose all men" can only be discerned by considering 1 Thes. 2.16a.

4.5. 1 Thessalonians 2.16

How then do Jews "displease God and oppose all people". The answer is "by hindering us from speaking to the Gentiles that they may be saved". This is an important point and finds support in the Patristic exegesis. Kampling considers the exegesis of this passage in the early Church and concludes: "Keiner der hier genannten Autoren, wenn er überhaupt darauf zu sprechen kommt, deutete die Menschenfeindschaft anders denn als Hinderung der Mission".[144] Acts recounts many such occasions when the Jews were hindering the mission of Paul.[145] Paul takes this so seriously because in his view it is exclusively through preaching that Gentiles come to salvation. For Paul the gospel comes through the preached word, and faith can only come into being by hearing the gospel (Rom. 10.17). It is, after all, the preached word which creates faith in the hearer.[146] Therefore Paul sees the Jews as jeopardizing the salvation of the Gentiles. By such serious action Paul believes the Jews have filled up the measure of their sins. The wording here is striking in that other eschatological passages speak of a measure as being filled until a certain point; when this point is reached then

---

[143] Marshall, *1 and 2 Thessalonians*, p. 83: "The man who wrote Rom. 9:1-5; 10:1 is hardly likely to have been guilty of anti-Semitism at any time". But this does not allow for the possibility that Paul changed his mind.

[144] Kampling, "Auslegungsgeschichtliche Skizze", 212. He considers Ignatius, Barnabas, Justin, Melito, Clement of Alexandria, Tertullian, Origen, Eusebius, Ambrosiaster, John Chrysostom, Jerome, Pelagius and Theodoret.

[145] See Acts 13.45-50; 14.2, 19; 17.5-9, 13; 18.12 (some of these texts are briefly discussed at the beginning of this chapter).

[146] See, for example, the genitive τὸ ῥῆμα τῆς πίστεως (Rom. 10.8), which is best understood as the word which creates faith (as opposed to the word which "demands faith" as R. Bultmann, πιστεύω κτλ, *TDNT* 6:213 (174-228) suggested). See Hofius, "Wort Gottes", 159-60.

God's judgement falls.[147] This is found, for example, in Gen. 15.16 which many commentators believe Paul is alluding to. However, here in 1 Thes. 2.16 "the quantity of sins which calls forth judgement *has already been completed*".[148] Further, passages which speak of a measure being filled allow the idea of the possibility of repentance. Paul, however, seems to have excluded this. "1 Thess 2:16 . . . collapses entirely the period of time remaining before the eschaton and leaves the sinners mentioned in the passage no time to reform".[149] And so Paul writes: "But God's wrath has come upon them at last (εἰς τέλος)!". This is the translation of the RSV. *BAG* give the following meanings for εἰς τέλος: 1. in the end, finally; 2. to the end, until the end; 3. forever; 4. decisively, fully. Of these possibilities, I would opt for either the first ("finally") or the third ("forever"). Solution 1 ("finally") is supported by Dodd[150] and Best[151] and suits the context well. Solution 3 is also possible in view of the Septuagintal use.[152] I therefore prefer the translation: "But God's wrath has come upon them finally/forever". In chapter 6 below I shall discuss Rom. 11.25-32 which speaks of Israel's salvation. If one opts for solutions 1 or 3 it seems impossible to reconcile 1 Thes. 2.16 to Rom. 11.25-32. But there are two ways in which a harmonization could be attempted. First, one could adopt solution 2 and argue that the Jews are under God's wrath "until the end".[153] However, as Best points out, this

---

[147] The idea here is that of the "eschatological measure" which will be discussed in more detail in chapter 6 below (see discussion of Rom. 11.25). See also R. Stuhlmann, *Das eschatologische Maß im Neuen Testament* (FRLANT 132), Göttingen: Vandenhoeck & Ruprecht 1983, and J. Jeremias, "Einige vorwiegend sprachliche Beobachtungen zu Röm 11,25-36", in L. de Lorenzi (ed.), *Die Israelfrage nach Röm 9-11* (MRvB.BÖA 3), Rom: Abtei von St Paul vor den Mauern 1977, 196-97 (193-216).

[148] J.W. Simpson, "The Problems Posed By 1 Thessalonians 2:15-16 And A Solution", *HBT* 12 (1990) 45 (42-72).

[149] Simpson, "Problems", 46.

[150] C.H. Dodd, "The Mind of Paul: II", in *New Testament Studies*, Manchester: Manchester University Press 1953, 120 (83-128), writes that according to 1 Thes. 2.16, "'the Wrath' has fallen *finally* on the Jews,—εἰς τέλος implying that this sentence of reprobation cannot ever be reversed".

[151] E. Best, *A Commentary on the First and Second Epistles to the Thessalonians* (BNTC), London: A. & C. Black 1979 (repr.), ([1]1972), p. 121.

[152] Pss. 76.9; 78.5; 102.9 LXX (see Wanamaker, *1 & 2 Thessalonians*, p. 117).

[153] F. Hahn, *Mission in the New Testament* (SBT 47) ET, London: SCM 1965, p. 106 n. 3, believes this to be the most probable understanding.

can hardly be the correct interpretation since the context implies a certain finality about what takes place.[154] The second is to adopt a particular interpretation of solution 4 ("fully").[155] Again, Best sees a problem in that the expression εἰς τέλος should really have a temporal element since 16c parallels 16b ("so as *always* to fill up the measure of their sins"). Both these attempts to harmonize 1 Thes. 2.16 and Rom. 9-11, I believe, fail. I therefore conclude that Paul's view concerning Israel in 1 Thes. 2.16 is bleak in the extreme.

In the introduction above I rejected Pearson's view that 1 Thes. 2.16c refers to the destruction of Jerusalem in 70 AD.[156] But if the reference is not to 70 AD, what else can it refer to? E. Bammel believes it refers to the expulsion by Claudius of Jews from Rome,[157] an event which probably occurred in 49 AD.[158] R. Jewett believes it refers to the death in the temple courts of 20,000 to 30,000 Jews at the passover of 49 AD.[159] Perhaps this is somewhat more plausible since Paul's focus is on Judaea. But although these two events happened just a year before Paul was writing 1 Thes-

---

[154] Best, *Thessalonians*, p. 122.

[155] See T. Holtz, *Der erste Brief an die Thessalonicher* (EKK 13), Zürich/Einsiedeln/ Köln: Benziger Verlag/Neukirchen-Vluyn: Neukirchener Verlag 1986, p. 110, who writes in relation to Rom. 11.25-32: "Dem widerstreitet 1Thess 2,16 nicht, εἰς τέλος ('gänzlich') schreibt das Gericht über die Juden nicht für das Eschaton fest!"

[156] Pearson, "1 Thessalonians 2:13-16",

[157] E. Bammel, "Judenverfolgung und Naherwartung: Zur Eschatologie des Ersten Thessalonicherbriefs", *ZThK* 56 (1959) 295, 306 (294-315).

[158] If is plausible that a reference could be made to this in 1 Thessalonians. The letter was most likely written from Corinth (Best, *Thessalonians*, pp. 7-11) and it is there that Paul met Priscilla and Aquila who had come from Italy "because Claudius had commanded all the Jews to leave Rome" (Acts 18.2). Cf. Bammel, "Judenverfolgung", 305-6.

[159] Jewett, "Agitators and the Galatian Congregation", 205 n. 5. This was first suggested by J.A. Bengel, *Gnomon Novi Testamenti*, Berlin: Gust. Schlawitz 1855 (³1773), pp. 519-20, although he gives the date as 48 AD. See Josephus, *Antiquitates* 20.105-112 (112 gives the number of 20,000) and *Bellum* 2.224-27 (227 gives a number of at least 30,000). According to Josephus the crowds were provoked by the lewdness of a Roman soldier who was standing guard on the porticoes of the temple (according to *Antiquitates* 20.108 he uncovered his genitals but according to *Bellum* 2.224 he turned "his backside to the Jews, and made a noise in keeping with his posture"). A riot ensued and panic set in as Cumanus, the procurator, sent in reinforcements. In attempting to escape from the temple into the town, the Jews trampled each other to death.

salonians and could be seen as especially relevant and fresh in the mind of the Thessalonians (if they knew of such events) they were local phenomena.[160] This therefore leads me to consider whether the verse refers to any historical event at all. I agree with Best that Paul is not speaking of a past historical event; rather Paul is asserting that "judgement is about to overtake the Jews".[161] Best writes:

Paul is led to this conclusion not by some historical event but by the inner logic of what he has written about the sins of the Jews combined with his belief, apparent elsewhere in the epistle, that the End is only a short time away.[162]

Likewise, Marshall thinks that Paul "is writing about an imminent judgement rather than a past one".[163] So Paul expresses the future as though it had already happened.[164] Paul also may well have been influenced by the synoptic apocalypse tradition.[165] Note also that 1 Thes. 2.16 has almost exactly the same wording as the parallel in T. Levi 6.11 ('Εφθασε δὲ ἡ ὀργὴ κυρίου ἐπ' αὐτοὺς εἰς τέλος "But the wrath of God ultimately came upon them"). Like 1 Thes. 2.16, this text may not be referring to a specific event.

4.6. The Jews' Rôle in the Death of Jesus

Paul claims that the Jews "killed the Lord Jesus". I think it unlikely that Paul invented this. He is probably referring to earlier tradition as suggested above.

There are two ways Paul may have viewed the Jews' killing of Jesus: first, the trial before Caiaphas and the Sanhedrin; secondly, the crowds crying before Pilate to have Jesus crucified. I turn to the first of these.

There has been a sharp debate concerning the rôle of the Jews in the trial and condemnation of Jesus. One Jewish view is that the gospel accounts of the trial and death of Jesus have been grossly distorted, whereby blame is

---

[160] Although the destruction of the temple in 70 AD was local, it obviously carried much more significance.

[161] This is a perfectly natural way to take the aorist ἔφθασεν.

[162] Best, *Thessalonians*, p. 120.

[163] Marshall, *Thessalonians*, p. 82.

[164] Cf. A. Oepke, "Die Briefe an die Thessalonicher", in H.W. Beyer, P. Althaus, H. Conzelmann, G. Friedrich and A. Oepke, *Die kleineren Briefe des Apostels Paulus* (NTD 8), Göttingen: Vandenhoeck & Ruprecht [13]1972, 165 (157-87).

[165] See the discussion above in the introduction to 1 Thes. 2.13-16.

placed squarely on the shoulders of the Jews whereas Pilate is essentially whitewashed.[166] Some Christian scholars have come to share this view. So according to J.D. Crossan, the passion narratives are so theologically biased that the historicity of much of it has to be seriously questioned.[167]

The passion narratives certainly are theologically coloured and I would not argue for the historicity of all the details. Nevertheless, I believe the basic elements have a historical core, in particular that the Sanhedrin did have a rôle in the trial and condemnation of Jesus.[168] This last issue has been somewhat fraught with difficulties for on the one hand according to Jn 18.31 the Jews say "It is not lawful for us to put any man to death" yet on the other hand it seems the Jews were permitted to carry out executions for certain religious offences. So some have questioned the truth of Jn 18.31[169] and argued that the Sanhedrin had the power to put someone to death; since Jesus was executed by the Romans it is inferred that the Sanhedrin had no rôle in condemning him.[170] So Winter believes that "Jn 18_{31b} provides no

---

[166] G. Lindeskog, *Die Jesusfrage im neuzeitlichen Judentum. Ein Beitrag zur Geschichte der Leben-Jesu-Forschung* (AMNSU 8), Uppsala: Almquist & Wiksell 1938, p. 280, points to the influential work of L. Philippson, *Haben die Juden Jesum wirklich gekreuzigt?* Berlin 1866. His influence can be seen, for example, in J. Klausner, *Jesus von Nazareth: Seine Zeit, sein Leben und seine Lehre* GT, Berlin: Jüdischer Verlag 1930 (second edition 1934; Hebrew 1922; English 1925), pp. 469-83.

[167] J.D. Crossan, *Who Killed Jesus? Exposing the Roots of Anti-Semitism in the Gospel Story of the Death of Jesus*, New York: Harper Collins 1995.

[168] In the trial of Jesus most things are up for debate including the question whether one can even talk of "a Sanhedrin" at the time of the Roman Prefecture. See the judicious discussion of this in R.E. Brown, *The Death of the Messiah: A Commentary on the Passion Narratives in the Four Gospels* (ABRL), 2 vols, New York: Doubleday 1994, 1:340-48. Brown believes that there was just one assembly (not two) at the time of Jesus' trial (1:345-47) and that the "council" in Josephus corresponds to the "Sanhedrin" in the New Testament (1:343). Such an assembly consisted of chief priests, scribes and rulers or influential citizens and "played a major administrative and judicial role in Jewish self-governance in Judea" (1:343).

[169] See the discussion on penal jurisdiction in Palestine before 70 AD in J. Juster, *Les Juifs dans l'Empire romain*, 2 vols, Paris: Librairie Paul Geuthner 1914, 2:127-49. See also H. Lietzmann, "Der Prozeß Jesu", in K. Aland (ed.), *Kleine Schriften II: Studien zum Neuen Testament* (TU 68), Berlin: Akademie Verlag 1958, 251-63 (= *SPAW.PH* 14 (1934) 313-322); "Bemerkungen zum Prozeß Jesu II", in *Schriften II*, 269-76 (= *ZNW* 31 (1932) 78-84); T.A. Burkill, "The Competence of the Sanhedrin", *VC* 10 (1956) 80-96; "The Trial of Jesus", *VC* 12 (1958) 1-18; P. Winter, *On the Trial of Jesus* (SJ 1), Berlin: de Gruyter 1961, 73-90.

[170] This is the contention of Juster, *Juifs*, 2:134-36.

evidence at all of the facts of history – the assertion denying the competence of Jewish law courts to administer capital punishment has its basis in the theological scheme devised by the Fourth Evangelist".[171] And the theological interest is to place responsibility on the Jews. Winter writes: "To hold the Jews responsible and yet explain why Jesus did not die by stoning or any other Jewish form of administering the death penalty, the Fourth Evangelist without the slightest hesitation deprives the Jews of all authority to carry out a judicial sentence of death".[172]

Although New Testament scholars frequently question the historicity of something which seems to be in the redactional interest of an Evangelist,[173] caution is necessary. For the very redactional concern may have its roots in history. And this may be the case in the trial of Jesus, even though the responsibility of the Jewish people has been exaggerated. But let me return to the specific issue of Jn 18.31.

A good case can be made that the Jews generally could not enact the death penalty at the time of Jesus' trial even though they could carry out trials.[174] The known instances of enacting the death penalty at this time are few and far between.[175] They are the killing of James the brother of John by the sword,[176] the stoning of Stephen,[177] the stoning of James in 62 AD,[178] and the burning of a priest's daughter who had committed adultery.[179] These cases, however, may be the "exceptions which prove the rule" that during the period 6-66 AD the Sanhedrin did not have the right to exact capital

---

[171] Winter, *Trial*, p. 88 (emphasized in Winter).

[172] Winter, *Trial*, p. 89.

[173] E.P. Sanders and M. Davies, *Studying the Synoptic Gospels*, London: SCM/Philadelphia: TPI 1989, pp. 304-15.

[174] R. Schnackenburg, *Das Johannesevangelium, III Teil: Kommentar zu Kap. 13-21* (HThKNT 4.3), Freiburg/Basel/Wien: Herder [6]1992, ([1]1975), p. 280 (on Jn 18.31). See also D.R. Catchpole, "The Problem of the Historicity of the Sanhedrin Trial", in E. Bammel (ed.), *Trial of Jesus: Cambridge Studies in honour of C.F.D. Moule* (SBT 2.13), London: SCM 1970, 63 (47-65).

[175] Note, however, that Josephus, our main source, is by no means exhaustive for this period and is indeed sometimes patchy.

[176] See Acts 12.2. The reference "with the sword" probably means he was beheaded (see F.V. Filson, *A New Testament History* (NTL), London: SCM Press 1965, p. 194).

[177] Acts 7.54-8.2.

[178] Josephus, *Antiquitates* 20.200.

[179] See m. Sanh. 7.2.

punishment. The stoning of Stephen seems to have been an example of mob justice.[180] The stoning of James was done between the death of the procurator Festus and the arrival of his successor Albinus. In fact the high priest Ananus who convened the Sanhedrin was deposed.[181] The priest's daughter, according to Jeremias, was probably executed during the reign of Agrippa I (41-44 AD) when the Jews had their own independent state.[182] Also James the brother of John was executed in this period.[183] That the Jews did not have the right to execute in this period receives confirmation from Jewish tradition. First, there are texts which point to the fact that 40 years before the destruction of Jerusalem, the power of life and death was taken away from the Jews.[184] The number 40 is probably given as a round number, the reference presumably being to beginning of the Roman procuratorship in 6 AD.[185] Secondly, according to the Scroll of Fasting (Megillath Taanith),[186]

---

[180] See Klausner, *From Jesus to Paul*, p. 292; Hengel, *Pre-Christian Paul*, p. 70.

[181] The question though still remains whether he was deposed simply for convening the Sanhedrin without the consent of Albinus (which Josephus, *Antiquitates* 20.201-203 suggests) or whether it was also because he passed the sentence of death without having the authority to do so.

[182] See J. Jeremias, "Zur Geschichtlichkeit des Verhörs Jesu vor dem Hohen Rat", in *Abba: Studien zur neutestamentlichen Theologie und Zeitgeschichte*, Göttingen: Vandenhoeck & Ruprecht 1966, 140 (139-44). Jeremias argues for this dating for according to t. Sanh. 9.11, R. Eliezer ben Zadok, who witnessed it, was lifted on his father's shoulders to see this spectacle (see also b. Sanh. 52b). According to Jeremias' reckoning, he would have been a child during the reign of Agrippa I (Jeremias, "Geschichtlichkeit", 141). H. Lietzmann, "Bemerkungen zum Prozeß Jesu. II", in K. Aland (ed.), *Kleine Schriften II: Studien zum Neuen Testament* (TU 68), Berlin: Akademie Verlag 1958, 273-74 (269-76), is probably correct in believing that Jeremias' argument is possible but far from conclusive.

[183] For a useful overview of Herod Agrippa and the New Testament, see Bruce, *New Testament History*, pp. 258-64.

[184] See y. Sanh. 1.1 (18a) (J. Neusner, *Talmud of the Land of Israel, vol. 31: Sanhedrin and Makkot* (CSHJ), London/Chicago: University of Chicago Press 1984, p. 12); y. Sanh. 7.2 (24b) (Neusner, *Talmud: Sanhedrin and Makkot*, p. 201); b. Sanh. 41a.

[185] E. Lohse, συνέδριον, *TDNT* 7:866 (860-71).

[186] See Meg. Taan. 6. A convenient text may be found in G.H. Dalman, *Grammatik des jüdisch-palästinischen Aramäisch und aramäische Dialektproben*, Darmstadt: Wissenschaftliche Buchgesellschaft 1981 (repr.), (²1905) (see *aramäische Dialektproben*, p. 2 (section VI) and the comment on p. 43).

after the Romans had been driven out of Jerusalem in 66 AD, the Jews returned to executing their criminals.[187]

Despite this, however, there still remain possible problems for a text like Jn 18.31 for there do seem to be cases where Jews were able to carry out certain executions. It can be reasonably argued that Stephen's death was a result of lynch justice. But it seems that further persecution of Hellenists continued also outside of Judaea.[188] Schlatter therefore may be right in suggesting that the Jews' right to put Hellenists to death was only possible because the Roman authorites allowed it.[189] Also the execution of those (even Romans) who entered the "court of Israel" (i.e. going beyond the "court of the Gentiles") was applicable also to this period of 6 AD to 66 AD.[190] But again this was only done on the express permission of the Roman authorities.[191]

Therefore I can give a qualified assent to Jn 18.31. Brown believes that it has to be understood in a nuanced way.[192] As far as Jesus' execution is concerned, Brown considers a number of significant points.[193] In view of the large crowds present at the passover feast the Jewish authorities may well have decided that it was risky for them to execute Jesus. It would provoke

---

[187] Jeremias, "Geschichtlichkeit", 144. Note, however, that P. Winter, "The Trial of Jesus and the Competence of the Sanhedrin", *NTS* 10 (1963-64) 495 (494-99), puts a different interpretation on Meg. Taan. 6. He argues that the passage "contains information to the effect that the revolutionary Jewish party ursurped judicial powers to deal with its opponents". Meg. Taan. 6 "is far too incomplete in its information to base on this passage any deductions concerning the distribution of judicial competence between Roman and Jewish courts, as it was in existence before the 22nd Ellul".

[188] So Damascus, where Paul was sent, belonged to Syria, not Judaea.

[189] See Schlatter, *Die Geschichte der ersten Christenheit*, pp. 98-100 (see also A. Schlatter, *Der Evangelist Johannes. Wie er spricht, denkt und glaubt: Ein Kommentar zum vierten Evangelium*, Stuttgart: Calwer Verlag ⁴1975, (¹1930), pp. 338-39).

[190] See Josephus, *Bellum*, 6.124-26; *Antiquitates* 15.417.

[191] See Josephus, *Bellum* 6.126, where Titus says to the Jews: "And did we not permit you to put to death any who passed it (i.e. the balustrade), even were he a Roman". Grabbe, *Judaism*, 2:393, suggests that the wording of the inscription "more likely suggests a warning not of legal liabilities but of practical consequences, for instance, lynching by a mob of loyal Jews outraged at such a desecration" (he refers to E.J. Bickerman, "The Warning Inscription of Herod's Temple", *JQR* 37 (1946-47) 394-98 (387-405)).

[192] Brown, *Death of the Messiah*, 1:371.

[193] Brown, *Death of the Messiah*, 1:371-72.

an angry reaction in the crowds. Further they knew that the Romans would execute him by crucifixion therefore making Jesus accursed by God.[194] A further reason for handing Jesus over to the Romans is that at Passover Pilate was in Jerusalem and it would be highly undiplomatic to by-pass him. Both the Gospels and Josephus suggest Caiaphas had a close relationship with the Roman administration, a suggestion made highly plausible by the fact that Caiaphas had an unusually long term as high priest.[195]

Therefore I believe it plausible that the Sanhedrin tried Jesus, sentenced him to death and handed him over to Pilate for crucifixion. Perhaps what is not so clear is the rôle the Jewish crowds had in crying before Pilate for Jesus to be crucified. In the gospels this crying out for Jesus to be crucified is tied up with the Barabbas episode,[196] and many have been reluctant to give credence to this. For we have no evidence outside the New Testament for this custom of releasing a prisoner at the time of passover (which has become known as the *privilegium paschale*). However, the idea seems reasonable especially since passover was celebrating the release of Israel from

---

[194] I work with the assumption that the Jews found Jesus guilty of being a messianic pretender who was leading the people astray. Cf. A. Strobel, *Die Stunde der Wahrheit* (WUNT 21), Tübingen: J.C.B. Mohr (Paul Siebeck) 1980, who argues that the Jewish and Roman judicial proceeding against Jesus are probably historically authentic and based on the accusation that Jesus was a false prophet and religious seducer (מַדִּיחַ; πλάνος) or an inciter (מֵסִית; ἀποστάς). Such a person must, according to Dt. 13.1-11, be sentenced to death. Note that πλάνος is used in Mt. 27.63 and πλανάω in Jn 7.12. See also Justin Martyr (*Dialogue* 69.7; 108.2, describing Jesus as a λαοπλάνος and πλάνος respectively). As far as Jesus' messianic claims were concerned, these were a problem for both the Jewish authorities and the Romans. The Romans earlier had political problems (and would continue to have problems) with such "messianic" figures (see Hengel, *Zealots*, pp. 290-98) and crucifixion would be an entirely appropriate punishment for such a "king of the Jews". Note that crucifixion was a political (and military) punishment (Hengel, *Cross of the Son of God*, p. 178) and in Roman times it was practised above all on dangerous criminals and members of the lowest classes (p. 180).

[195] He was high priest for 18 years. Compare this with the fact that according to Josephus, *Antiquitates* 20.250, there were 28 priests between the time of Herod and the destruction of the temple (he calculates this as as period of 107 years, i.e. 37 BC to 70 AD). See also B. Chilton, "Caiaphas", *ABD* 1:805 (803-6).

[196] Mk 15.6-11, 12-15; Mt. 27.15-21, 22-26; Lk. 23.13-19, 20-25; Jn 18.38b-40; 19.1, 4-16; see also Acts 3.14.

bondage[197] and m. Pesahim 8.6[198] may be an enigmatic hint of this custom. Further there is no compelling reason for rejecting the story of Barabbas as told in the gospels.[199]

I return now to Paul. Apart from 1 Thes. 2.15, the only other possible reference to a Jewish part in Jesus' death is 1 Cor. 11.23b which could be translated "on the night he was betrayed". It is striking that apart from various texts where Lord and Jesus stand in a predicative position (1 Cor. 12.3; Rom. 10.9; Phil. 2.11), 1 Thes. 2.15 and 1 Cor. 11.23 are the only texts where "Lord Jesus" is used. Although 1 Cor. 11.23 could refer to betrayal, there is no reference to Judas Iscariot, a point which H. Maccoby thinks is highly significant.[200] Maccoby thinks the figure of Judas who betrayed Jesus was made up between Paul's letters and the writing of the gospels.[201] He finds confirmation in that Paul speaks of "the twelve" witnessing the resurrection (1 Cor. 15.5) and not eleven.[202] But reference is probably made to the "twelve" because this was the eschatological number corresponding to the twelve tribes of Israel.[203] In fact Paul never elsewhere refers to "the twelve" and is probably here using earlier tradition.[204] Although Paul makes

---

[197] See R.H. Gundry, *Mark: A Commentary on His Apology for the Cross*, Grand Rapids: Wm B. Eerdmans 1993, p. 935.

[198] "They may slaughter . . . for one whom they have promised to bring out of prison".

[199] Cf. Hengel, *Zealots*, pp. 340-41; O. Betz, *Was wissen wir von Jesus?*, Wuppertal/Zürich: R. Brockhaus Verlag ²1991, (¹1965), p. 105. Brown, *Death of the Messiah*, 1:819-20, is slightly more sceptical. He suggests that the idea of the *privilegium paschale* is a secondary development, but that there may well have been a Barabbas whom Pilate released at the time of Jesus' crucifixion. Brown suggests that Christians then developed this story into the form we now have in the gospels. It is to be noted (as does Winter, *Trial*, p. 98), that there was nothing to stop Pilate releasing both Jesus and Barabbas.

[200] H. Maccoby, *Judas Iscariot and the Myth of Jewish Evil*, New York: Free Press 1992, p. 24.

[201] Maccoby, *Judas*, pp. 141-42.

[202] Some texts do give eleven (D F G latt), but this is clearly a "correction". There is little weight in the argument of Weiß, *Der erste Korintherbrief*, p. 350, that the reference to the twelve is a gloss.

[203] See Mt. 19.28 and Lang, *Korinther*, p. 212.

[204] The twelve were only significant in the years of the early Church (C.K. Barrett, *A Commentary on the First Epistle to the Corinthians* (BNTC), London: A. & C. Black ²1971, (¹1968), p. 342).

no reference to the fact that a *Jew* or *Jews* "betrayed him" it seems likely that Paul did know of the betrayal of Jesus by a Jewish disciple.[205] But there is another possible interpretation of 1 Cor. 11.23. The verb παραδίδωμι can also mean "hand over" or "deliver up". If the passive is here avoided by circumlocution, then Paul may be saying Jesus was delivered up by God,[206] a point I will return to in the next section. We therefore have a parallel to Rom. 4.25 (cf. Rom. 8.32), in which case 1 Cor. 11.23 could allude to Isaiah 53.[207] The two key verses alluded to are 53.6b (καὶ κύριος παρέδωκεν αὐτὸν ταῖς ἁμαρτίαις ἡμῶν) and 53.12 (ἀνθ᾽ ὧν παρεδόθη εἰς θάνατον ἡ ψυχὴ αὐτοῦ). Many commentators allow a dual reference,[208] some believing that the primary reference is to Judas' betrayal of Jesus and a secondary reference to Jesus being handed over by God (Paul alluding to Isaiah 53),[209] others believing the primary reference is to Jesus being handed over by God.[210]

4.7. Jewish Responsibility and Guilt for the Death of Jesus

As has already been mentioned Christian persecution of Jews has often been based on the assumption that they were responsible for Jesus' death. Historically it seems that the Jews were responsible in two respects. First, although the Jewish authorities did not have the authority to execute Jesus, they did have the authority to pass a sentence of death.[211] Secondly, I think there is a

---

[205] On Judas, see G.W. Buchanan, "Judas Iscariot", *ISBE* 2:1151-53.

[206] Such a solution though is rejected by T.C. Edwards, *A Commentary on the First Epistle to the Corinthians*, London: Hodder and Stoughton 1897, p. 292, who thinks the reference is exclusively to Judas.

[207] See J. Jeremias, *The Eucharistic Words of Jesus* ET, London: SCM 1966, pp. 112-13.

[208] For example H. Conzelmann, *Der erste Brief an die Korinther* (KEK 5), Göttingen: Vandenhoeck & Ruprecht ²1981, (¹1969), p. 240 n. 44, wishes to understand παραδίδωμι in both senses. Also, although as noted above Jeremias sees an allusion to Isaiah 53 he uses the term "betrayed" in the translation of 1 Cor. 11.23 (*Eucharistic Words*, p. 74 n. 4) implying a reference to Judas Iscariot. Also, he believes that 1 Cor. 11.23 may indicate an early tradition about Judas (*Eucharistic Words*, pp. 94-95).

[209] See Bruce, *1 and 2 Corinthians*, p. 111.

[210] See A. Robertson and A. Plummer, *A Critical and Exegetical Commentary on the First Epistle of St. Paul to the Corinthians* (ICC), Edinburgh: T. & T. Clark ²1914, (¹1911), p. 243. See also Thiselton, *First Epistle to the Corinthians*, pp. 869-70.

[211] See J. Blinzler, *The Trial of Jesus* ET, Cork: Mercier Press 1959, p. 159.

historical core to the gospel accounts that crowds of Jews in Jerusalem were crying out for the death of Jesus, even though some of the details may be historically untrue.[212] *Historically*, therefore, it seems that some Jews in Jerusalem in 30 AD, together with Pilate, were responsible for Jesus' death. And if they were responsible, they were also certainly guilty. But there are two crucial points to add here.

The first is that although *historically* the Jews were responsible, *theologically* Jesus was delivered over by God.[213] He did not spare his own son (Rom. 8.32). Jesus' death was a sacrifice for sin and to blame human beings for Jesus' death can miss the whole point of his sacrificial death.[214] Is Paul in danger of doing this in 1 Thes. 2.15?

The second additional point is that it is one thing to say that *some* Jews in Jerusalem in 30 AD were responsible for Jesus' death. It is quite another

---

[212] See, for example, the words of Mt. 27.25 where the Jews answer to Pilate "His blood be on us and on our children". They are secondary and certainly seem to tie in with Matthew's redactional interest concerning the Jews. Cf. D. Hill, *The Gospel of Matthew* (NCB), London: Oliphants 1972, p. 351. This is one of the most difficult texts in the New Testament regarding the Jews. However, the author is not asserting a simple collective guilt of all Jews for Jesus' death. See J. Gnilka, *Das Matthäusevangelium* (HThKNT 1), 2 vols, Freiburg/Basel/ Wien: Herder 1 1986, 2 1988, 2:459: "Mit diesem Ruf erklärt sich das ganze Volk bereit, das Unheil des vergossenen Blutes des Christus Jesus auf sich und seine Nachkommenschaft zu übernehmen. Mt hat das über Israel hereinbrechende Unheil in zwei Dingen verwirklicht gesehen: 1. An die Stelle des Gottesvolkes Israel ist die universale Kirche getreten, an die Stelle des λαός das ἔθνος aus den Völkern (vgl. 21,43). 2. Über Israel ist im Jüdisch-Römischen Krieg die Katastrophe hereingebrochen. Land, Stadt und Tempel wurden dem Volk genommen. Mt sieht diese Ereignisse in einer unheilsgeschichtlichen Dimension (vgl. 23,37-39)". A stronger apology for Matthew is found in the statement that Mt. 23.35-36 and 27.25 "converge to delimit the retribution to the period of Jesus' contemporaries and the ensuing generation" (Carroll and Green, *Death of Jesus*, p. 47 n. 27). One wonders whether this is wishful thinking by authors who have a high regard for the theological outlook of the first gospel.

[213] This is the case even if 1 Cor. 11.23 refers to Judas.

[214] Cf. G. Lindeskog, "Der Prozess Jesu im jüdisch-christlichen Religionsgespräch", in O. Betz, M. Hengel and P. Schmidt (ed.), *Abraham unser Vater: Juden und Christen im Gespräch über die Bibel. Festschrift für Otto Michel zum 60. Geburtstag*, Leiden: E.J. Brill 1963, 335-36 (325-36): "Und es muß überall und zu jeder Zeit von den Verkündern des Evangeliums klar und deutlich und überzeugend gepredigt werden, daß die Juden als Nation keine Schuld am Kreuz Christi haben. . . . Gott übernimmt – um paulinisch zu sprechen – die Verantwortung für das Kreuz Christi. Er allein und kein Mensch ist dessen mächtig. Denn wäre es nicht so, dann hätte das Kerygma von der Versöhnung keinen Sinn".

thing to claim that *all* Jews are somehow responsible. In 1 Thes. 2.15 Paul is not blaming all Jews for Jesus' death. But he is clearly drawing the principle from the Jews' involvement in Jesus' death that Jews are rejecting God and his agents. This is a view which Paul continued to hold for it is found in Romans, probably his last letter. In Rom. 11.2 Paul writes how Elijah pleads with God against Israel: "Lord, they have demolished thy altars, and I alone am left, and they seek my life" (Rom. 11.3, quoting 1 Kgs 19.10).

It is the case that in the history of the Church, Jews have been persecuted because they were considered responsible for Jesus' death.[215] However, as I have already stressed, Paul does not draw the conclusion that Jews should be persecuted. It is also worth reflecting on the fact that Christian antisemitism, in particular the charge of deicide, is found in a much stronger form outside the New Testament. So in the Gospel of Peter Herod commands that Jesus be crucified (1.2) and Joseph must seek Herod's permission for the body of Jesus (2). In the Gospel of Nicodemus (Acts of Pilate) responsibility for Jesus' death is firmly place on the Jews and it is stressed on a number of occasions that Pilate is not guilty of his blood.[216] Then there is the Homily on Pascha (72, 79, 81) of Melito of Sardis:

It is he that has been murdered.
And where has he been murdered? In the middle of Jerusalem.
By whom? By Israel.
Why? Because he healed their lame
and cleansed their lepers
and brought light to their blind
and raised their dead. . . .
You prepared for him sharp nails and false witnesses
and ropes and scourges
and vinegar and gall
and sword and forceful restraint as against a murderous robber. . . .
And you killed your Lord at the great feast. . . .
O lawless Israel, what is this unprecedented crime you committed.[217]

We will also see that his rhetoric against the Jews is matched by that of John Chrysostom.[218]

---

[215] This will be discussed in more detail in chapter 9 below.

[216] On the legends of Pilate, see C.H. Moehlman, *The Christian-Jewish Tragedy: A Study in Religious Prejudice*, Rochester, New York: Leo Hart 1933, pp. 45-88.

[217] S.G. Hall (ed.), *Melito of Sardis: On Pascha and Fragments* (OECT), Oxford: Clarendon Press 1979, pp. 39, 45.

[218] See chapter 9 below.

To gain a perspective one must realise that 1 Thes. 2.14-16 played "nur eine relativ untergeordnete Bedeutung im altkirchlichen Antijudaismus".[219] Further, the persecution of Jews and the attitude of antisemitism[220] have had reasons other than the charge of deicide. As Brown points out, there was a strong anti-Judaism among pagans in the ancient world and this was carried over when pagans became Christians in large numbers.[221] One early example of this is the Church in Rome.[222] Further, the overriding reason for modern antisemitism is not the rôle Jews played in the death of Jesus. Rather it is based on economic, ethnic and nationalistic components.[223] Further the basis for antisemitism in the Third Reich was a pseudo-scientific racial theory

---

[219] Kampling, "Auslegungsgeschichtliche Skizze", 212.

[220] The use of the word "antisemitism" is not entirely fortunate and its use for the first century is anachronistic. The term was first used by Wilhelm Marr in his pamphlet *Der Judenspiegel* (1862) and in 1879 he brought the term into political use by founding the "League of Anti-Semites" ("Antisemiten Liga"). The term was therefore originally used in connection with a racial theory. As S.J.D. Cohen, *From Maccabees to the Mishnah* (LEC 7), Philadelphia: Westminster Press 1987, p. 48, points out, such antisemitism was unknown in the ancient world. Characteristics of different nations were explained by their climate, soil and water. But since it is so well established it will be used together with the word "anti-Judaism". Throughout this work I shall write this word "antisemitism" rather than anti-Semitism, partly because it is not the opposite of "Semitism" and partly because the term "antisemite" is used for a hater of Jews and not a hater of "Semites" as such (which of course include not only Jews but also Arabs, Phoenicians, Akkadians, Babylonians, etc). On this issue see H. Maccoby, *A Pariah People: The Anthropology of Antisemitism*, London: Constable 1988, p. 45. On problems with the concept of antisemitism, see N.R.M. de Lange and C. Thoma, "Antisemitismus I", *TRE* 3:114-15 (113-19).

[221] Brown, *Death of the Messiah*, 1:384 n. 132.

[222] Concerning the history of anti-Judaism in Rome, see W. Wiefel, "The Jewish Community in Ancient Rome and the Origins of Roman Christianity", in K.P. Donfried (ed.), *The Romans Debate*, Peabody: Hendrickson ²1991, (¹1977), 85-101. For examples of this antisemitism, see Tacitus, *Historiae* 5.1-13. He accuses the Jews of laziness because they not only rest on the sabbath (cf. Juvenal, *Satires* 14.105-6) but also every seventh year (*Historiae* 5.4), and also accuses them of various "base and abominable" customs (for example their sitting apart at meals, their hatred of other nations, and their propensity to lust (5.5)).

[223] See H. Arendt, *The Origins of Totalitarianism*, Cleveland: World Publishing Company ²1958, (¹1951), pp. 11-53.

about Jews.[224] It is true that there are cases where a "Christian" anti-semitism has been mixed with a racial antisemitism (e.g. at the end of the 19th century and during the Third Reich).[225] But nevertheless it is essential to distinguish between these two types of antisemitism.[226]

I do not want to whitewash the New Testament authors or the Church. But it is a gross injustice if one imagines that the central reason for persecution of Jews has been their rôle in the death of Jesus. Matthew's gospel and John's gospel may have unwittingly contributed something towards antisemitism in Germany. But the central argument for antisemitism in the Third Reich was a pseudo-scientific racial theory.[227] Further, it has been claimed that some Church leaders have justified the mass murder of Jews in

---

[224] Cf. M. Saperstein, *Moments of Crisis in Jewish-Christian Relations*, London: SCM/Philadelphia: TPI 1989, pp. 40-41: "The intellectual origins of Nazi antisemitism are to be found in pseudo-scientific racist and mystical-romantic-nationalist ideologies of the nineteenth century, not in the teachings of Augustine, Innocent III, or even Martin Luther". This is not to deny though that figures like Luther were exploited by the nazis. Also in the late nineteenth century Christian anti-semitism was mixed with the new racial form of antisemitism. For further discussion of nazi antisemitism see chapter 9 below.

[225] K. Scholder, writing in 1988, wrote: "As far as I can see, complete clarity has yet to be arrived at as to the development of the relationship between religious and racial antisemitism in the nineteenth century" (*A Requiem for Hitler and Other New Perspectives on the German Church Struggle* ET, London: SCM 1989 (German 1988), pp. 175-76). He suggests that the linking factor may be the social and economic problems of the nineteenth century and gives Adolf Stöcker, the Berlin Court and Cathedral preacher, as an example of someone who combined these two types of antisemitism.

[226] The case of Gerhard Kittel is instructive. In his serious academic work one can believe him when he writes: "My position in the Jewish question is based on Holy Scripture and the tradition of the primitive Christian Church" (quoted in J.R. Porter, "The Case of Gerhard Kittel", *Theology* 50 (1947) 401 (401-6)). It is true that he also lapsed into a racial antisemitism (see the very unsympathetic treatment of W.F. Albright, "Gerhard Kittel and the Jewish question in antiquity", in *History, Archaeology and Christian Humanism*, London: A. & C. Black 1965, 233-40 (229-40), where he criticizes Kittel's book *Das antike Weltjudentum* (Forschungen zur Judenfrage 7), Hamburg: Hanseatische Verlagsanstalt 1943, written in collaboration with Eugen Fischer). Nevertheless, his two sorts of antisemitism are essentially distinct.

[227] Maccoby, *Pariah People*, wishes to see more continuity between Christian antisemitism and that of the nazis. He argues that modern antisemitism "shows a strong tendency to identify the Jews with whatever diabolic force is required by a dualistic ideology. . . . It cannot be a coincidence that this dualistic schema echos that of traditional Christianity" (p. 48). He therefore describes the "Jew-phobia of modern political ideologies" as "post-Christian antisemitism" (p. 48).

the Holocaust on the grounds of alleged deicide.[228] There is, however, no clear evidence for such a claim.[229]

I will return to the Holocaust in chapters 9 and 10 below. But perhaps it is worth repeating the point of Steven Katz:

> . . . that Paul and the authors of the various Gospels – with the exception of Luke – as well as almost all the persons mentioned in their narratives, including Jesus, would have been maligned as racial criminals by the biocentric norms of the Third Reich, and therefore marked for inevitable murder. . . . The extermination of thousands of Jewish Christians . . . in the death camps poignantly indicates that something fundamental was operative in the Nazi *Weltanschauung* that had no place in its Christian predecessor.[230]

---

[228] See I. Greenberg, "Cloud of Smoke, Pillar of Fire: Judaism, Christianity, and Modernity after the Holocaust", in E. Fleischner (ed.), *Auschwitz: Beginning of a New Era? Reflections on the Holocaust*, New York: Ktav 1977, 11-12, 441-42 n. 7 (7-53, 441-46). See also R.L. Rubenstein, *After Auschwitz*, Indianapolis: Bobbs-Merrill 1966, pp. 55-56. Rubenstein essentially accuses Heinrich Grüber, Dean of the Evangelical Church in Berlin, of seeing the Holocaust as a punishment for deicide.

[229] See Saperstein, *Moments of Crisis*, p. 41; p. 75 n. 11.

[230] S.T. Katz, *Kontinuität und Diskontinuität zwischen christlichem und national-sozialistischem Antisemitismus*, Tübingen: J.C.B. Mohr (Paul Siebeck) 2001, p. 14.

Chapter 3

Paul's Critique of Israel's Religion

1. The Present Debate

In the previous chapter the issue of "antisemitism" was raised in relation to 1 Thes. 2.15-16 and the charge of deicide. But is not Paul's theology antisemitic through and through? For did not Paul find something fundamentally wrong in Israel's religion? Most would generally agree that Paul was critical of Judaism and that he "broke away" from his earlier religion. And even those who play down a "break" with Judaism acknowledge that Paul did find something wrong with Judaism.[1] But what was his critique of Judaism?

The traditional protestant answer that Judaism was a religion of works-righteousness goes back to Martin Luther. The Jew had to earn salvation by doing works of the law and Paul responded to such a works-righteousness by declaring: "For we hold that a person is justified by faith apart from works of law" (Rom. 3.28). So commenting on Rom. 3.27-28, Luther writes:

The law of works necessarily puffs up and induces glorying, for a man who is righteous and who has kept the law without a doubt has something about which he can boast and be proud. Now Jews believe that they have attained this status because they do outwardly what the law orders or prohibits.[2]

Luther goes on in his lectures on Romans to argue "works of the law are works in which the persons who do them trust as if they are justified by doing them, and thus are righteous on account of their works".[3] After dis-

---

[1] So Dunn, for example, plays down Paul's "break" with Judaism ("The New Perspective on Paul", *BJRL* 65 (1983) 102 (95-122); *Theology of Paul the Apostle*, pp. 335-89) but nevertheless believes he was critical of Judaism as it was manifest at that time. For further discussion, see below section 8.

[2] W. Pauck (ed.), *Martin Luther: Lectures on Romans* (LCC 15), Philadelphia: The Westminster Press 1961, p. 118.

[3] Pauck (ed.), *Luther: Lectures on Romans*, p. 119.

cussing some Old Testament texts Luther argues that "the righteousness of God is offered to us apart from our merits and works".[4] Luther believed he had made a great discovery and his view of justification by faith is arguably the most important theological truth to emerge from the time of the Reformation.[5] But the premise of his theology of justification by faith through grace is that Judaism understood salvation to be by works.

Luther's understanding of Judaism and of justification in Paul has influenced theologians to this day (including some Roman Catholics). One of the key Lutheran scholars who argued that Judaism was a religion of works-righteousness was Ferdinand Weber.[6] Weber's view of Judaism as a religion of "legalism"[7] was continued by Emil Schürer,[8] Wilhelm Bousset,[9]

---

[4] Pauck (ed.), *Luther: Lectures on Romans*, p. 120.

[5] This is a theological judgement. Historically, justification was the chief concern of the early period of the Reformation but for reformed theologians other important concerns arose. For an overview, see A.E. McGrath, *Reformation Thought*, Oxford: Blackwell ³1999, (¹1988).

[6] F. Weber, *System der altsynagogalen palästinischen Theologie aus Targum, Midrasch und Talmud* (ed. by F. Delitzsch and G. Schnedermann), Leipzig: Dörffling & Franke 1880, revised as *Jüdische Theologie auf Grund des Talmud und verwandter Schriften*, Leipzig: Dörffling & Franke 1897.

[7] I will discuss this term in section 6 below. In using the term here I mean a negative sort of legalism

[8] E. Schürer, *Geschichte des jüdischen Volkes im Zeitalter Jesu Christi*, 4 vols, Leipzig: J.C. Hinrichs'sche Buchhandlung ⁴1901-11, (¹1886-90). For a translation of the second edition, see E. Schürer, *A History of the Jewish People in the Time of Jesus Christ*, 3 vols, Peabody: Hendrickson 1994 (repr.), (Edinburgh: T. & T. Clark ¹1890). Schürer's work has also been extensively revised. See E. Schürer, *The History of the Jewish People in the Age of Jesus Christ* (revised and edited by G. and P. Vermes, F. Millar, M. Goodman and M. Black), 3 vols, Edinburgh: T. & T. Clark 1973-86. Much of his negative view of Judaism does not survive in this reworked version. In the preface to volume 2 of the revised Schürer, one reads: ". . . in the domain of value judgments, the editors have endeavoured to clear the notorious chapter 28, *Das Leben unter dem Gesetz*—here re-styled as 'Life and the Law'— and the section on the Pharisees (§26 I) of the dogmatic prejudices of nineteenth-century theology" (*The History of the Jewish People in the Age of Jesus Christ*, 2:v; see also 2:464 n. 1). I will later consider whether this criticism of Schürer is entirely justified.

[9] W. Bousset, *Die Religion des Judentums im neutestamentlichen Zeitalter*, Berlin: Reuther & Reichard 1903. This was edited by H. Greßmann: *Die Religion des Judentums im späthellenistischen Zeitalter* (HzNT 21), Tübingen: J.C.B. Mohr (Paul Siebeck) ³1926.

Paul Billerbeck[10] and Rudolf Bultmann[11]. Taking this view of Judaism, it is then argued that Paul contrasts Christianity, a religion of grace, with Judaism, a religion of works-righteousness. Bultmann, for example, understood the faith-works antithesis as a contrast between faith as "the radical renunciation of accomplishment"[12] ("der radikale Verzicht auf die Leistung")[13] and the earning of salvation by works of the law.[14] In fact, the Jew comes to represent the religious person whose sin is to attempt to justify himself by works of the law. So Bultmann's pupil, Käsemann, writes:

> . . . in and with Israel he [Paul] strikes at the hidden Jew in all of us, at the man who validates rights and demands over against God on the basis of God's past dealings with him and to this extent is serving not God but an illusion.[15]

Likewise another pupil, Bornkamm, believes that Paul's opponent in Rome is the Jew and his understanding of salvation.[16] He writes:

---

[10] P. Billerbeck, (H.L. Strack), *Kommentar zum Neuen Testament aus Talmud und Midrasch*, 4 vols, München: C.H. Beck'sche Verlagsbuchhandlung 1-3 [3]1961; 4 [2]1956. This work is often referred to as "Strack-Billerbeck" and was earlier even referred to as "Strack's final work". However it was Billerbeck who actually wrote it. Strack himself was a great inspiration for the work, had helped in the printing and distribution of the work (see *Kommentar*, 4:V-VI) and had checked the first volume (see *Kommentar*, 1:V), but was not involved in the writing of the work. See J. Jeremias, "Billerbeck, Paul", *TRE* 6:641-42 (640-42). I will therefore refer to the work as "Billerbeck".

[11] R. Bultmann, *Das Urchristentum im Rahmen der antiken Religionen*, Zürich: Artemis Verlag [5]1986, ([1]1949). For an English translation see R. Bultmann, *Primitive Christianity in its Contemporary Setting* ET, London: Collins 1960.

[12] R. Bultmann, *Theology of the New Testament* ET, 2 vols, London: SCM 1 1952; 2 1955, 1:316.

[13] R. Bultmann, *Theologie des Neuen Testaments* (UTB 630), Tübingen: J.C.B. Mohr (Paul Siebeck) [9]1984 (durchgesehen und ergänzt von O. Merk), ([1]1948), p. 316.

[14] See Bultmann's article on καυχάομαι κτλ, *TDNT* 3:645-54.

[15] E. Käsemann, "Paul and Israel", in *New Testament Questions of Today* (NTL) ET, London: SCM 1969, 186 (183-87). For a critical discussion of Käsemann's view of Judaism, see P.F.M. Zahl, *Die Rechtfertigungslehre Ernst Käsemanns* (CThM B13), Stuttgart: Calwer Verlag 1996 (especially the "Exkurs I: Die Typologie des Judentums bei Käsemann", pp. 45-58). For a partial defence of Käsemann, see below. See also D.V. Way, *The Lordship of Christ: Ernst Käsemann's Interpretation of Paul's Theology* (OTM), Oxford: Clarendon Press 1991, pp. 180-82.

[16] G. Bornkamm, "The Letter to the Romans as Paul's Last Will and Testament", in K.P. Donfried (ed.), *The Romans Debate*, Peabody: Hendrickson [2]1991 ([1]1977), 26 (16-28).

For Paul, the Jew represents man in general, and indeed man exactly in his highest poten-
tial: the pious man who knows God's demand in the law but who has yet failed to meet
God's claim and is lost in sin and death.[17]

Paul therefore addresses the Jew "hidden within each Christian".[18] So
according to this line of thinking, the Jew for Paul represents the religious
human being who tries to make a claim upon God. By means of the law, the
Jew believes he can accumulate merit.[19] H. Ridderbos writes:

The law is the unique means to acquire for oneself merit, reward, righteousness before
God, and the instrument given by God to subjugate the evil impulse and to lead the good
to victory. It can rightly be said, therefore, that for the Jews the law was the pre-eminent
means of salvation, indeed the real 'substance of life'.[20]

Critics of this line of thinking have maintained one of two things: either
Paul, although a Jew, did not understand Judaism; or those standing in the
tradition of Luther have neither understood Judaism nor Paul. The first position is represented by Schoeps.

Schoeps writes of "Paul's fundamental misapprehension":[21] "Paul succumbed to a characteristic distortion of vision which had its antecedents in
the spiritual outlook of Judaic Hellenism".[22] So when Paul speaks of "law"
he reduces what for Jews was "both law and teaching" to "the ethical (and
ritual) law" and "wrested and isolated the law from the controlling context
of God's covenant with Israel".[23] He concludes:

Because Paul had lost all understanding of the character of the Hebraic *berith* as a part-
nership involving mutual obligations, he failed to grasp the inner meaning of the Mosaic
law, namely, that it is an instrument by which the covenant is realized.[24]

---

[17] Bornkamm, "Testament", 26.

[18] Bornkamm, "Testament", 26.

[19] I will discuss the meaning of "merit" below (e.g. in the discussion about Sirach).

[20] H.N. Ridderbos, *Paul: An Outline of His Theology* ET, London: SPCK 1977, p.
132, pointing to Bousset and Greßmann, *Religion des Judentums*, 1926, p. 119 and Billerbeck, *Kommentar*, 3:126ff.

[21] H.-J. Schoeps, *Paul: The Theology of the Apostle in the Light of Jewish Religious
History* ET, London: Lutterworth Press 1961, p. 213.

[22] Schoeps, *Paul*, p. 213.

[23] Schoeps, *Paul*, p. 213.

[24] Schoeps, *Paul*, p. 218.

It is certainly the case that in the Old Testament itself law and ברית are intimately related.[25] So the law itself is called the סֵפֶר הַבְּרִית (Ex. 24.7) just as the decalogue is called דִּבְרֵי הַבְּרִית (Ex. 34.28). But has Paul misunderstood the link between law and ברית? One of Paul's fundamental points in his teaching of the law is that it has a condemning function (2 Cor. 3.6b-9). It is true that the law is a means by which the ברית is established. But if the law is not kept, then Israel is condemned (Dt. 27.15-26). Perhaps it is Schoeps' own understanding of covenant and law which needs questioning. He speaks of a *foedus aequum*:

As a theopolitical event the Sinaitic *berith* is a sacral legal act of reciprocity, in the contraction of which both partners stand on one platform and speak on equal terms, recognizing each other (Deut. 26:17-18). This expresses fairly pregnantly what is to be understood by the election of Israel.[26]

Is this really the case? Kutsch in fact argues that such reciprocity is to be found nowhere in the Old Testament. The relationship of God and people is one of lord and servant. He writes:

In diesem Gott-Volk-Verhältnis setzt Verpflichtungen allein Gott. Dabei kann Gott die Durchführung seiner *bᵉrît* = 'Zusage' von der Erfüllung bestimmter Bedingungen (Dtn 7,9; 1Kön 8,23), das Gott-Volk-Verhältnis von der Bewahrung seiner *bᵉrît* 'Verpflichtung' (Ex 19,5; vgl. Ps 132,12) abhängig machen. Aber der Mensch kann nicht durch die Erfüllung dieser Bedingungen Gott zur Einhaltung seiner Zusage verpflichten; die Einhaltung hat allein darin ihre Garantie, daß Gott zu seinem Wort steht.[27]

We will see a fundamental switch in this idea as we move to later Jewish literature. There are certainly later Jewish texts which precisely suggest that keeping the commandments obligates God to save Israel.

Before leaving this issue of "reciprocity", let us consider the case of Ex. 24.7-8 which is often taken to imply a "reciprocity". Kutsch argues that ברית has nothing to do with such "reciprocity":

Das übliche Verständnis des Textes geht . . . hier von der Bedeutung 'Bund' für *bᵉrît* aus. Ein 'Bund' zwischen Jahwe und dem Volk wird 'geschlossen', Mose hat ihn vermittelt: der 'Sinai-Bund'. Als Bestätigung dient das zweimalige Blutsprengen: einerseits an

---

[25] Schoeps, *Paul*, p. 214. I refrain from using Schoeps' translation "covenant"; I will shortly consider the best way to translate ברית.

[26] Schoeps, *Paul*, p. 214.

[27] E. Kutsch, בְּרִית, *THAT* 1:350 (339-52). See also E. Kutsch, "Gesetz und Gnade. Probleme des alttestamentlichen Bundesbegriffs", *ZAW* 69 (1967) 32 (18-35).

den Altar, andererseits auf das Volk. Durch das 'Bundesblut' werden die 'Bundes-
partner' – Jahwe, vertreten durch den Altar, und das Volk – miteinander verbunden.[28]

Kutsch argues that one reason this line of thinking has received such support
is because ברית has been mistranslated as "Bund", implying a reciprocity.
Indeed, the sense of Ex. 24.8 is that if the Israelites do not keep the "words"
which Yahweh demands, then their blood shall be shed, i.e. they will suffer
the penalty of death.[29] Such a view finds support in the Rabbinic writings.[30]
Again we see how this corresponds to Paul's view that the law has a condemning function. So in Ex. 24.3-8 ברית is not a "Bund" but a "Bestimmung" (determination), "Verpflichtung" (obligation).[31] And what is often
translated as "book of the covenant" (סֵפֶר הַבְּרִית) contains the commandments which Israel is to keep and corresponds to סֵפֶר הַתּוֹרָה (as can be seen
by comparing 2 Kgs 23.2b, 21b with 22.8a, 11a).[32] Here ברית signifies the
"obligation" and to be more precise not the act of obligation but rather the
content, i.e. that which the people are to do.[33] It is therefore hardly surprising that in later Rabbinic "covenant" (ברית) instead of pointing to God's
electing grace had become synonymous with "law" (תורה) in the sense of
commandments.[34] Paul refers to this "covenant" as ἡ παλαιὰ διαθήκη, and

---

[28] E. Kutsch, *Neues Testament-Neuer Bund? Eine Fehlübersetzung wird korrigiert*,
Neukirchen-Vluyn: Neukirchener Verlag 1978, p. 28. Kutsch cites several commentators
who propose this view (e.g. H. Holzinger, B. Baentsch, G. Beer, M. Noth) to which one
can add B.S. Childs, *Exodus* (OTL), London: SCM 1974, p. 506, J.P. Hyatt, *Exodus*
(NCB), London: Marshall, Morgan & Scott/Grand Rapids: Wm B. Eerdmans ²1980,
(¹1971), p. 257, and J.I. Durham, *Exodus* (WBC 3), Waco: Word Books 1987, p. 343.

[29] Kutsch, *Neues Testament*, p. 32.

[30] Kutsch, *Neues Testament*, pp. 32-37.

[31] Kutsch, *Neues Testament*, p. 30.

[32] Kutsch, *Neues Testament*, p. 30.

[33] Kutsch, *Neues Testament*, p. 30. He points out that correspondingly in Deuteronomy ברית refers to the decalogue (Dt. 4.13; 5.2).

[34] See below the example of Lev. R. 28.6. See also Mek. Ex. on Ex. 12.6 (Pisha 5):
"For one who worships idols breaks off the yoke, annuls the covenant and mispres-
resents the Torah. And whence do we know that he who transgresses all the commandments breaks off the yoke, annuls the covenant, and misrepresents the Torah? From the
scriptural passage: 'That thou shouldest enter into the covenant of the Lord thy God'
(Deut. 29.11), for 'the covenant' here simply means the Torah, as it is said: 'These are
the words of the covenant which the Lord commanded Moses' (Deut. 28.69)" (J.Z.
Lauterbach (ed.), *Mekilta de-Rabbi Ishmael* (SLJC), 3 vols, Philadelphia: JPS 1 ²1949,
(¹1933); 2 ²1949, (¹1933); 3 ²1949, (¹1935), 1:37-38). One may also consider Sir. 17.11-
14, where law and covenant are essentially synonyms. However, it needs stressing also

his "old covenant" is precisely the law.[35] One therefore needs to ask whether Paul really misunderstands the Old Testament and Rabbinic Judaism as Schoeps suggests?

But there are passages in Paul's letters regarding the law which would understandably dismay a non-Christian Jewish reader. For we find him not only attacking the Judaism of his time but also questioning some key theological principles found in the Old Testament itself. So we find him rejecting the whole principle of righteousness based on law as found in Lev. 18.5[36] and we find him advocating a pessimistic anthropology which goes far beyond that found in Rabbinic Judaism and even beyond that found in the Old Testament.[37] But this does not so much expose Paul as someone who misunderstood Palestinian Judaism. Rather we see someone grappling with the "Old Testament" in the light of the Christ event. He most likely came to his pessimistic anthropology through the following sequence of events: I have participated in Christ's death and resurrection; I have become a new creation and my old self has been destroyed; therefore I must have participated in Adam's sin. Paul was one of the greatest original theologians of all time. One does not have to resort to a hypothesis that "Paul succumbed to a characteristic distortion of vision which had its antecedents in the spiritual outlook of Judaic Hellenism" as Schoeps does.[38] In any case the view that Paul knew only the Judaism of the diaspora, a Judaism which was colder and more pessimistic than "Rabbinic Judaism", has been shown to be wanting.[39]

Another position which is related to that of Schoeps is that of Räisänen who argues that Paul misrepresents Judaism although in this case Paul has not so much misunderstood Judaism but has misrepresented it in order to promote the Gentile mission. So according to Paul Judaism was legalistic

---

that in the Rabbinic literature, ברית could take on a variety of nuances. See the discussion below.

[35] See the discussion of 2 Corinthians 3 in chapter 6, section one, below.

[36] See Rom. 10.5 and the discussion in Bell, *Provoked to Jealousy*, pp. 189-91.

[37] See Bell, *No one seeks for God*, pp. 118-131.

[38] Schoeps, *Paul*, p. 213.

[39] Such a view is put forward by C.G. Montefiore, *Judaism and St. Paul: Two Essays*, New York: Arno Press 1973 (repr.), ([1]1914), pp. 93-129. For criticism of such a view see Bell, *Provoked to Jealousy*, pp. 288-89.

but this was an unfair caricature.[40] Whether this central point was a mis-representation remains to be seen in the following discussion. But in view of the various charges made against Paul that he misunderstood Judaism, one ought to bear in mind the words of Barrett: "He is a bold man who supposes that he understands first-century Judaism better than Paul did . . ."[41]

Whereas Schoeps accused Paul of not understanding Judaism, a number of other scholars have accused Christians, especially those in the Lutheran tradition, of neither understanding Judaism nor Paul. What then has been the criticism of this traditional "Lutheran"[42] understanding of Paul? E.P. Sanders writes:

> One must note in particular the projection on to Judaism of the view which Protestants find most objectionable in Roman Catholicism: the existence of a treasury of merits established by works of supererogation. We have here the retrojection of the Protestant-Catholic debate into ancient history, with Judaism taking the role of Catholicism and Christianity the role of Lutheranism.[43]

According to Sanders, Paul's criticism of Judaism is that Judaism is not Christianity.[44] Salvation is only through Christ and therefore cannot be through the law. Further, he argues that in both Judaism and Paul "getting-in" is by grace, whereas "staying-in" is by works, an issue which will be pursued below. Sanders describes Judaism as "covenantal nomism",[45] and *to some extent* Sanders is happy to use this description for Paul's theology.[46]

---

[40] See H. Räisänen, *Paul and the Law* (WUNT 29), Tübingen: J.C.B. Mohr (Paul Siebeck) 1983, pp. xxvi-xxix.

[41] C.K. Barrett, *Paul: An Introduction to His Thought* (OCT), London: Cassell 1994, p. 78.

[42] I use quotation marks to indicate those Lutherans who have kept more or less to Luther's understanding of Judaism and justification. There are of course Lutherans who have turned their back on Luther's teaching at this point. One such person was K. Stendahl (see *Paul among Jews and Gentiles*) who for some years was Lutheran bishop in Stockholm.

[43] Sanders, *Paul and Palestinian Judaism*, p. 57.

[44] Sanders, *Paul and Palestinian Judaism*, p. 552.

[45] Sanders, *Paul and Palestinian Judaism*, p. 75, defines "covenantal nomism" as "the view that one's place in God's plan is established on the basis of the covenant and that the covenant requires as the proper response of man his obedience to its commandments, while providing means of atonement for transgression".

[46] Sanders, *Paul and Palestinian Judaism*, p. 513. I write "to some extent" because in the end Sanders prefers to understand Paul's soteriology as "participation theology". Note that M.D. Hooker, "Paul and 'Covenantal Nomism'", in M.D. Hooker and S.G.

Sanders' work has had great influence on Anglo-Saxon New Testament scholarship.[47] As far as the British context is concerned he has influenced scholars such as J.D.G. Dunn,[48] J. Ziesler,[49] N.T. Wright,[50] F. Watson,[51] J.M.G. Barclay[52], and B.W. Longenecker.[53] They have been critical of Sanders at certain points but I believe it is true to say that Sanders has been a decisive influence upon their work. So J.D.G. Dunn speaks of "The New Perspective on Paul".[54] N.T. Wright considers that since the publication of *Paul and Palestinian Judaism*, "the entire flavour of Pauline studies has

---

Wilson (ed.), *Paul and Paulinism: Essays in honour of C.K. Barrett*, London: SPCK 1982, 47-56, has been quoted by some to support the idea that "covenantal nomism" is entirely appropriate for Paul. However, as D.A. Hagner, "Paul & Judaism: Testing the New Perspective", in P. Stuhlmacher, *Revisiting Paul's Doctrine of Justification: A Challenge to the New Perspective*, Downers Grove: IVP 2001, 98 (75-105), points out, Hooker actually writes: "Clearly we cannot speak of 'covenantal nomism' in Paul's case, since that would run counter to Paul's basic quarrel with the Law".

[47] He has also influenced some theologians as well as New Testament scholars.

[48] See e.g. J.D.G. Dunn, *Romans* (WBC 38), 2 vols, Dallas, Texas: Word Books 1988.

[49] See J. Ziesler, *Paul's Letter to the Romans* (TPINTC), London: SCM/Philadelphia: Trinity Press International 1989; *Pauline Christianity* (OBS), Oxford/New York: OUP 1990, pp. 103-4.

[50] See N.T. Wright, *The Messiah and the People of God: A Study in Pauline Theology with Particular Reference to the Argument of the Epistle to the Romans*, Oxford D. Phil. Thesis 1980; *The Climax of the Covenant: Christ and the Law in Pauline Theology*, Edinburgh: T. & T. Clark 1991.

[51] See F. Watson, *Paul, Judaism and the Gentiles: A Sociological Approach* (SNTSMS 56), Cambridge: CUP 1986. Note, however, that Watson has now moved away from his sociological approach and from Sanders' position. In fact he gave an address at the British New Testament conference held in Manchester in 2001 entitled "Not the New Perspective". He comments that "in relation to the new perspective, I seem not to be one of the elect, the saints who are immune from apostasy and who infallibly persevere to the end".

[52] J.M.G. Barclay, *Obeying the Truth: A Study of Paul's Ethics in Galatians*, Edinburgh: T. & T. Clark 1988.

[53] B.W. Longenecker, *Eschatology and the Covenant: A Comparison of 4 Ezra and Romans 1-11* (JSNTSup 57), Sheffield: JSOT Press 1991. Longenecker, however, seems to take a more nuanced approached in his book *The Triumph of Abraham's God: The Transformation of Identity in Galatians*, Edinburgh: T. & T. Clark 1998.

[54] The title of Dunn's article in *BJRL* 65 (1983) 95-122, the published form of his Manson Memorial Lecture given at the University of Manchester in 1982.

been changed, quite probably permanently".[55] That Sanders has exercised enormous influence cannot be denied. Whether this new period can be described as "this bright post-Sanders epoch" is another matter.[56]

Sanders' approach has not gone unchallenged. Interestingly he has not only been criticized by Christian scholars[57] but also by Jewish scholars.[58] I now turn to the question of whether Sanders' view of Palestinian Judaism is viable. There are in fact a number of issues to untangle. First I will look at the specific issue of salvation by works. This will be followed by consider-

---

[55] S. Neill and T. Wright, *The Interpretation of the New Testament, 1861-1986*, Oxford/New York: OUP 1988, p. 424.

[56] Wright, *Interpretation*, p. 373. Wright's allusion is to S. Neill's comments on "Strack-Billerbeck" in the original edition. "In the dark days before Strack-Billerbeck we referred to Rabbinic matters cautiously, if at all; in this bright post-Strack-Billerbeck epoch, we are all Rabbinic experts, though at second hand" (p. 292).

[57] See, for example, H. Hübner, "Pauli theologiae proprium", *NTS* 26 (1980) 445-73; R.H. Gundry, "Grace, Works and Staying Saved in Paul", *Bib* 66 (1985) 1-38; J. Gundry Volf, *Paul and Perseverance: Staying in and Falling Away* (WUNT 2.37), Tübingen: J.C.B. Mohr (Paul Siebeck) 1989; M.A. Seifrid, *Justification by Faith: The Origin and Development of a Central Pauline Theme* (NovTSup 68), Leiden: E.J. Brill 1992; M.A. Seifrid, *Christ, our Righteousness: Paul's Theology of Justification* (NSBT 9), Downers Grove: IVP 2000; S. Kim, *Paul and the New Perspective: Second Thoughts on the Origin of Paul's Gospel*, Grand Rapids/Cambridge: Wm B. Eerdmans 2002.

[58] Most notably J. Neusner. See his reviews of *Paul and Palestinian Judaism* and *Paul, the Law and the Jewish People* in J. Neusner, *Ancient Judaism: Debates and Disputes* (BJS), Chico: Scholars Press 1984, pp. 127-41; 195-203. See also J. Neusner, *Sifre to Deuteronomy: An Introduction to the Rhetorical, Logical and Topical Program* (BJS 124), Atlanta, Georgia 1987, pp. 174-78 (on p. 177 n. 7 he accuses Sanders of ignoring his review of *Paul and Palestinian Judaism*). Neusner's criticisms include bringing to the Rabbinic sources "the issues of Pauline scholarship and Paul" (p. 129) and carrying out what he calls "Billerbeck-scholarship", i.e. culling sayings from various Rabbinic sourses and ignoring the context (p. 131). Ironically P. Billerbeck is a bête noire for Sanders (see below). Neusner concludes that "in regard to Rabbinic Judaism, Sanders' book is so profoundly flawed as to be hopeless and, I regret to say it, useless in accomplishing its stated goals of systematic description and comparison" (p. 137). Sanders has, however, also received support from Jewish scholars. So L. Dean, "Paul's 'Erroneous' Description of Judaism", in L. Swidler, L.J. Eron, G. Sloyan, L. Dean (ed.), *Bursting the Bonds? A Jewish-Christian Dialogue on Jesus and Paul*, Maryknoll, New York: Orbis Books 1990, 142 n. 2 (136-42), points approvingly to Sanders' *Paul and Palestinian Judaism* as a "most thorough treatment of the error of claiming that Judaism was legalistic". Further, Segal, *Paul the Convert*, pp. 125, 169, 262-64, and "Covenant in rabbinic writings", *SR* 14 (1985) 53-55 (53-62), gives qualified support to some of Sanders' work.

ing Paul's response to Judaism and the particular issue of "legalism" and the "pious Jew".

2. Did Jews Believe in Salvation by Works?

Sanders claims that Judaism did not teach salvation by works. Rather, there is an agreement between Paul and Palestinian Judaism: "salvation is by grace but judgement is according to works; works are the condition of remaining 'in', but they do not earn salvation".[59] Whether this is an accurate description of Paul's "pattern of religion" remains to be seen. But first let us examine Jewish texts to see if the description fits. In the space available I cannot deal with all the relevant texts, but I will deal with a representative sample and with texts which may appear to be a "problem" for my position.

2.1. Apocrypha and Pseudepigrapha
In this section I consider the Apocrypha and Pseudepigrapha but not the texts which one calls apocalypses. These will be discussed in the next section.

In Sirach there is reference to the election of Israel.[60] However here, as in many other Jewish texts, one asks what the basis of this election is. Ironically, a key to the idea of election is free choice. One of the innovative theological aspects of Sirach is that human free will is propositionally formulated.[61] Human freedom means that human beings determine their own destiny. So in Sir. 15.15-17 we read:

15 If you will, you can keep the commandments,
and to act faithfully is a matter of your own choice.
16 He has placed before you fire and water:
stretch out your hand for whichever you wish.
17 Before a man are life and death,
and whichever he chooses will be given to him.

Here the will of the human being stands in the foreground. This is seen in the use of the noun יֵצֶר, introduced in 15.14 as a fundamental anthropologi-

---

[59] Sanders, *Paul and Palestinian Judaism*, p. 543.

[60] E.g. Sir. 17.17: "He appointed a ruler for every nation, but Israel is the Lord's own portion" (cf. Dt. 32.8-9).

[61] See Sir. 15.11-20 and Hengel, *Judaism and Hellenism*, 1:140.

cal term,[62] and also in the verb חפץ. Although the ideas of Sir. 15.16-17 find a similarity in Dt. 30.15,19, Sirach emphasises the rôle of the human will.[63] It is in the light of this that one is to understand a text such as Sir. 33.11-12:

11 In the fulness of his knowledge the Lord distinguished them (i.e. all human beings)
and appointed their different ways;
12 some of them he blessed and exalted,
and some of them he made holy and brought near to himself;
but some of them he cursed and brought low,
and he turned them out of their place.

This text probably refers to the call of Abraham and his descendants (and the call of priests, those he "made holy") and the rejection of the Gentiles, the Canaanites being particularly in view (those he "turned out").[64] But why are the Gentiles cursed? Skehan and Di Lella write: "God curses some people because they have chosen the path of wickedness; it is not that they are wicked because God has cursed them".[65] Conversely, God chose Abraham and his descendants because of their works. In fact Abraham was understood as one who kept "the law of the Most High" (Sir. 44.20). Any idea of election is therefore based on human works.

Sirach seems to give a key rôle to what one can legitimately call human merit.[66] The term "merit" is of course associated with certain medieval theological discussions (e.g. regarding *meritum de condigno* and *meritum de congruo*). I am using the term in the sense of "salvific human action" in the sense that God has to reward such human action. This merit theology is found not only in connection with the idea of election just discussed but also

---

[62] U. Wicke-Reuter, *Göttliche Providenz und menschliche Verantwortung bei Ben Sira und in der Frühen Stoa* (BZAW 298), Berlin/New York: de Gruyter 2000, pp. 117-19, defends the view that here יצר means "will" in a neutral sense and is not to be understood in the later rabbinic sense of יצר הרע.

[63] Wicke-Reuter, *Göttliche Providenz*, p. 121, points to three aspects here: first, the three-fold use of the verb חפץ; secondly, the element of decision is emphasized by the two sets of opposites, fire and water (v. 16), life and death (v. 17). Thirdly, the address to the people of Israel in Dt. 30 becomes a general anthropological principle of free choice.

[64] P.W. Skehan and A.A. Di Lella, *The Wisdom of Ben Sira* (AB 39), New York: Doubleday 1986, p. 400.

[65] Skehan and Di Lella, *Ben Sira*, p. 83.

[66] Cf. D.A. Carson, *Divine Sovereignty and Human Responsibility: Biblical Perspectives in Tension* (MTL), London: Marshall, Morgan & Scott 1981, pp. 49-50.

in other respects. So human works can atone for sins.[67] See, for example, Sir. 3.3-4, 14-15:[68]

3 Whoever honours his father atones for sins,
4 and whoever glorifies his mother is like one who lays up treasure.
14 For kindness to a father will not be forgotten,
and against your sins it will be credited to you;
15 in the day of your affliction it will be remembered in your favour
as frost in fair weather, your sins will melt away.

Boccaccini notes here "a radical shift in the conception of the retributory principle from that expressed by Ezekiel, for whom merits could not be accumulated".[69] Sirach is the first extant text to affirm that merits can compensate for transgressions.[70] And it is in Sirach that we see the beginning of the view that almsgiving in particular can atone for sins. See Sir. 3.30:

Water extinguishes a blazing fire: so almsgiving atones for sin.

Likewise, fasting (Sir. 34.26), forgiving others (Sir. 28.1-7), and possibly death (Sir. 18.22) can atone for one's sins.[71]

Within Sirach one can find a form of universalism. So although Wisdom makes her dwelling in Jacob, she calls to all (Sir. 24.19). The extravagant

---

[67] See W.O.E. Oesterley, *An Introduction to the Books of the Apocrypha*, London: SPCK 1946 (repr.), ([1]1935), p. 91.

[68] G.H. Box and W.O.E. Oesterley, *APOT* 1:324, comment: "We are met here with the beginnings of the development (especially in one direction) of the Jewish doctrines of atonement and mediation which assumed great importance in later times. The honouring of father and mother was the fulfilling of a *mitzvah*, or 'commandment', of the Law, which being a meritorious act, effected atonement".

[69] G. Boccaccini, *Middle Judaism: Jewish Thought 300 B.C.E. to 200 C.E.*, Minneapolis: Fortress Press 1991, p. 117.

[70] Boccaccini, *Middle Judaism*, p. 117.

[71] The meaning of Sir. 18.22b is unclear. G.H. Box and W.O.E. Oesterley in *APOT* 1:380 translate the verse as: "Delay not to pay thy vow in due time, And wait not till death to be justified (καὶ μὴ μείνῃς ἕως θανάτου δικαιωθῆναι)". They comment: "As in later Rabbinical literature, Death is regarded as a means of atonement". A similar translation is given by G. Sauer (ed.), *Jesus Sirach (Ben Sira)* (JSHRZ 3.5), Gütersloh: Gütersloher Verlagshaus Gerd Mohn 1981, p. 550: "Laß dich nicht daran hindern, ein Gelübde zur rechten Zeit zu erfüllen, und warte nicht bis zum Tode, um darin als gerechtfertigt zu gelten". A different translation however is given by Skehan and Di Lella, *Sirach*, p. 287: "Let nothing prevent the prompt payment of your vows, wait not to fulfill them when you are dying". The RSV has: "and do not wait until death to be released from it" (cf. ZB). Note that we possess no Hebrew for this verse. See H.-P. Rüger, "Apokryphen I", *TRE* 3:305 (289-316).

language of 24.13-34[72] suggests that Wisdom reaches out into the whole world.[73] Providence takes on a universal perspective.[74] Also it is possible for any (presumably even a Gentile) not to sin (Sir. 15.20).[75] Further Sir. 10.19 shows it is possible to find good people among all nations. Sir. 10.19:

> What race is worthy of honour? The human race.
> What race is worthy of honour? Those who fear the Lord.
> What race is unworthy of honour? The human race.
> What race is unworthy of honour? Those who transgress the commandments.

T.A. Burkill can even write that on the basis of 10.19: "the conception of race can be construed entirely in terms of piety and morals".[76] Note also that although the emphasis in retribution is on this world, the Greek version does bring in a reference to the hereafter.[77]

The book of Tobit also endorses merit theology.[78] First, Tobit is clearly a pious Jew who knows he is pious (even though Tob. 3.3-5 includes a confession of Tobit's sin).[79] See Tob. 1.3, 16-17:

> I, Tobit, walked in the ways of truth and righteousness all the days of my life, and I performed many acts of charity to my brethren and countrymen who went with me into the land of the Assyrians, to Nineveh. . . . 16 In the days of Shalmaneser I performed many

---

[72] See for example the images of growing trees (v. 14: "I grew tall like a cedar in Lebanon, and like a cypress on the heights of Hermon"), of rivers which gush forth (v. 30: "I went forth like a canal from a river and like a water channel into a garden. I said 'I will water my orchard and drench my garden plot'; and lo, my canal became a river, and my river became a sea") and light shining out (v. 32: "I will again make instruction shine forth like the dawn, and I will make it shine afar").

[73] Cf. Sauer, *Jesus Sirach*, p. 491, who writes that although Wisdom is only to be found in Israel, Jerusalem and the temple, it flows out from here "in die Völkerwelt, auch in die hellenistische!"

[74] See the discussion of Sir. 39.12-35 in Wicke-Reuter, *Göttliche Providenz*, pp. 75-79.

[75] Cf. Bousset and Greßmann, *Religion des Judentums*, p. 82.

[76] T.A. Burkill, "Ecclesiasticus", *IDB* 2:21 (13-21). This view is disputed by Sanders, *Palestinian Judaism*, p. 330 n. 3.

[77] See Skehan and Di Lella, *Ben Sira*, pp. 86, 201-2 (on 7.17b) and pp. 531-32 (on 48.11b).

[78] It is perhaps surprising that Luther had praise for Tobit and Judith. See H. Bornkamm (ed.), *Luthers Vorreden zur Bibel*, Göttingen: Vandenhoeck & Ruprecht [3]1989, pp. 154-56; pp. 147-49.

[79] G.W.E. Nickelsburg, *Jewish Literature between the Bible and the Mishnah*, Philadelphia: Fortress Press 1981, p. 33, who adds that his harsh judgement of his wife (2.11-14) further indicates "that our author's righteous man is not a perfect man".

acts of charity to my brethren. 17 I would give my bread to the hungry and my clothing to the naked; and if I saw any one of my people dead and thrown out behind the wall of Nineveh, I would bury him.

As in Sirach, almsgiving can atone for sin.[80] See Tob. 12.9:

For almsgiving delivers from death, and it will purge away every sin.

ἐλεημοσύνη γὰρ ἐκ θανάτου ῥύεται, καὶ ἀποκαθαριεῖ πᾶσαν ἁμαρτίαν.

The term ἐλεημοσύνη may not just be confined to almsgiving and the translation "acts of mercy" in both 12.8 and 12.9 is possible.[81] Therefore "almsgiving" or "acts of kindness" leads to salvation from death (ἐκ θανάτου ῥύεται).[82] In 12.8 the angel stresses that δικαιοσύνη and ἐλεημοσύνη are concerned with human deeds (12.8) and promises that δικαιοσύνη and ἐλεημοσύνη lead to positive ends (cf. 4.10).[83] These verses from Tobit 12 are part of the speech of the angel (12.6-15). The soteriological message of Tobit is present throughout the work but is fully developed here in the speech of the angel. The conclusion is clear: "So ist es möglich, durch das Tun von Barmherzigkeit die eigene Rettung auszulösen".[84]

Turning to Judith we see that God rewards those who do not sin. So in the speech of Achior, the leader of the Ammonites, we read (Jud. 5.17):

As long as they did not sin against their God they prospered, for the God who hates iniquity is with them.

---

[80] M. Rabenau, *Studien zum Buch Tobit* (BZAW 220), Berlin/New York: Walter de Gruyter 1994, p. 127, correctly sees almsgiving (ἐλεημοσύνη) as a "decisive leading idea" ("entscheidende[r] Leitgedanke") in the book of Tobit.

[81] See S. von Stemm, *Der betende Sünder vor Gott. Studien zu Vergebungsvorstellungen in urchristlichen und frühjüdischen Texten* (AGAJU 45), Leiden/Boston/Köln: E.J. Brill 1999, pp. 165-66, may well be right in believing that ἐλεημοσύνη is not confined to "almsgiving".

[82] This expression could mean either being saved from a premature death (C.A. Moore, *Tobit* (AB 40A), New York/London/Toronto/Sydney/Auckland: Doubleday 1996, p. 270) or being saved from a difficult life situation (von Stemm, *Sünder*, p. 168, points to Tobit's blindness or the demonic oppression of Sarah). The Vulgate, however, understands deliverance from eternal damnation: *quoniam elemosyna a morte liberat et ipsa est quae purgat peccata et faciet invenire vitam aeternam*. This, according to Moore, *Tobit*, p. 270, is a misunderstanding since "neither here nor elsewhere in the Greek versions of Tobit is belief in an afterlife affirmed".

[83] Again in Tob. 4.9-10 reference is made to this life.

[84] Von Stemm, *Sünder*, p. 180.

It may be objected that this text, like many others in the Apocrypha, is simply reflecting deuteronomic theology.[85] So Deuteronomy 27-28 speaks of blessing for obedience and cursing for disobedience. However, Carson I believe is right to question whether the theology of Judith is so deuteronom-istic.[86] Deuteronomy emphasizes God's grace. See Dt. 7.7-8:

> It was not because you were more in number than any other people that the LORD set his love upon you and chose you, for you were the fewest of all peoples; 8 but it is because the LORD loves you, and is keeping the oath which he swore to your fathers, that the LORD has brought you out with a mighty hand, and redeemed you from the house of bondage, from the hand of Pharaoh king of Egypt.

It is such elements which are played down in Judith and other later Jewish literature. Although it is the case that obedience to God does not necessarily bring Israel victory (Jud. 8.15-17)[87] yet at the same time there does seem to be a quasi-mechanical view that obedience will lead to victory. So Judith boasts (Jud. 8.18, 20) that "never in our generation, nor in these present days, has there been any tribe or family or people or city of ours which wor-shipped gods made with hands . . . But we know no other god but him, and therefore we hope that he will not disdain us or any of our nation". In con-trast, in Dt. 8.1-9.6 it is stressed that Israel dispossessed the nations because of God's promise to the fathers, not because of her righteousness.[88] Like Tobit, Judith is a figure of immense piety. As Moore writes: "What makes her unique among biblical heroines is her piety and the particular outward forms that piety took, i.e., strenuous fasting, constant prayer, celibacy, and great concern for observing the laws of *kašrût*. In this respect, none of the

---

[85] See M.S. Enslin and S. Zeitlin, *The Book of Judith* (JAL 7), Leiden: E.J. Brill/ Philadelphia: Dropsie University 1972, p. 90. See also pp. 83-84 (on Jud. 4.13).

[86] Carson, *Divine Sovereignty*, p. 50, who is critical of M.S. Enslin, *The Book of Judith* (JAL 8), Leiden: E.J. Brill 1972, pp. 33, 83-84, 90.

[87] See Nickelsburg, *Jewish Literature*, p. 107: "The God of Judith is the deliverer of his people, yet he remains sovereign and *not obligated* to act in their behalf".

[88] Carson, *Divine Sovereignty*, p. 50. See, in particular, Dt. 9.4-5: "Do not say in your heart, after the LORD your God has thrust them out before you, 'It is because of my righteousness that the LORD has brought me in to possess this land'; . . . 5 Not because of your righteousness or uprightness of your heart are you going in to possess their land; but because of the wickedness of these nations the LORD your God is driving them out from before you, and that he may confirm the word which the LORD swore to your fathers, to Abraham, to Isaac, and to Jacob".

other biblical heroines are like her, not Miriam, Deborah, Jael or Esther".[89]
In short, the figure of Judith and the whole book reflects a Pharisaic piety.[90]
I turn now to the Psalms of Solomon. These are especially important for
they were probably written in Pharisaic circles.[91] Sanders quotes Ps. Sol.
9.9-10 to show that God chose the descendants of Abraham and that a
covenant was made with them.[92] See Ps. Sol. 9.9-10:

---

[89] Moore, *Judith*, p. 62.

[90] A.E. Cowley, *APOT* 1:247, describes the book as "strongly Pharisaic". See also
Moore, *Judith*, pp. 31, 62.

[91] The Psalms contain ideas which are certainly those of the Pharisees. So there is the
resurrection of the dead in Ps. Sol. 3.12; 13.11; 14.9-10. Further the historical picture
fits the Pharisees very well. These Psalms were probably written by devout Jews hor-
rified at the invasion of their country by Pompey (63 BC) and corruption in political and
religious leadership. So certain Jews (and presumably Gentiles) had profaned the
sanctuary (1.8); the "sons of Jerusalem" (possibly the priests) had defiled the sanctuary
and profaned the offerings (2.3) and defiled themselves with improper intercourse (2.13);
Jews were committing incest and adultery (8.9-10); Priests were stealing from the
sanctuary and walking on the place of sacrifice (8.11-12), their sin surpassing that of the
Gentiles (8.13). The rulers opened the gates to Pompey (8.16-18) (cf. *Antiquitates*
14.59) and welcomed him. The sinners, the Jewish opponents of the devout, are probably
the Hasmonean Sadducees. They usurped the monarchy (17.5-8, 22) and were not
scrupulous in ritual purity (1.8; 2.3, 5; 7.2; 8.12; 17.45) and were too willing to adopt
foreign customs (8.22). The highly influential work of J. Wellhausen, *Die Pharisäer und
die Sadducäer: Eine Untersuchung zur inneren jüdischen Geschichte*, Göttingen:
Vandenhoeck & Ruprecht ³1967, (¹1874), established the links between the Ps. Sol. and
Pharisees, a view which many have supported down to this day (e.g. Nickelsburg, *Jewish
Literature*, pp. 203-12). His views though have not gone unchallenged. O. Eißfeldt, *The
Old Testament: An Introduction* ET, Oxford: Basil Blackwell 1966, pp. 610-13, saw
many links with the Qumran texts as did A. Dupont-Sommer, *The Essene Writings from
Qumran* ET, Oxford: Basil Blackwell 1961, p. 296. On Wellhausen's work see Deines,
Pharisäer, pp. 40-67. Recent studies which have supported the Pharisaic link are J.
Schüpphaus, *Die Psalmen Salomos: Ein Zeugnis Jerusalemer Theologie und
Frömmigkeit in der Mitte des vorchristlichen Jahrhunderts* (ALGHJ 7), Leiden: E.J.
Brill 1977 and M. Winninge, *Sinners and the Righteous: A Comparative Study of the
Psalms of Solomon and Paul's Letters* (CB.NT 26), Stockholm: Almqvist & Wiksell
1995.

[92] E.P. Sanders, *Judaism: Practice and Belief 63BCE-66CE*, London: SCM/Philadel-
phia: TPI 1992, p. 263.

For you chose the descendants of Abraham above all the nations,
and you put your name upon us, Lord,
and it will not cease forever.
10 You made a covenant with our ancestors concerning us,
and we hope in you when we turn our souls toward you.[93]

Again one needs to ask what the basis of this election was. A clue is found just a few verses earlier in Ps. Sol. 9.4-5:

Our works (are) in the choosing and power of our souls,
to do right and wrong in the works of our hands,
and in your righteousness you oversee human beings.
5 The one who does what is right saves up life for himself with the Lord,
and the one who does what is wrong causes his own life to be destroyed;
for the Lord's righteous judgments are according to the individual and the household.[94]

Such verses seriously relativize what Ps. Sol. 9.9-10 says about the covenant. Maier writes that "die Darlegung der Willensfreiheit im Rahmen des neunten Salomopsalmes einen auffallend starken Ton trägt".[95] In fact Ps. Sol. 9.4-5 parallels Sir. 15.14-17.[96] The salvation of the individual is therefore not so much dependent on membership of the nation Israel; the crucial issue is behaviour and, as Ps. Sol. 9.4-5 makes clear, this is dependent on the individual's free will. The Psalms make it clear that the salvation of God is only for the pious, and not for sinners (Ps. Sol. 12.6; 17.23); and among the sinners are Jews.[97] It is those who do "righteous deeds" who are "pious". See Ps. Sol. 9.3: "the righteous deeds of your holy ones are before you, O Lord".[98] Therefore it is not the covenant which is the fundamental category for the Psalms of Solomon, but rather the question of whether one is pious or not. Further, as Seifrid writes, "the Israel of the Messianic king-

---

[93] R.B. Wright, *OTP*, 2:661. Kutsch, *Neues Testament*, p. 73 argues that διαθήκη here is to be understood as "Gottes (Setzung =) Zusage" (see p. 73 n. 148).

[94] R.B. Wright, *OTP*, 2:660.

[95] G. Maier, *Mensch und freier Wille nach den jüdischen Religionsparteien zwischen Ben Sira und Paulus* (WUNT 12), Tübingen: J.C.B. Mohr (Paul Siebeck) 1971, p. 340.

[96] Maier, *Mensch und freier Wille*, pp. 335-40.

[97] See n. 91 above.

[98] Translation of S.J. Gathercole, *Where is Boasting? Early Jewish Soteriology and Paul's Response in Romans 1-5*, Grand Rapids/Cambridge U.K.: Wm B. Eerdmanns 2002, pp. 64-65, who rightly renders δικαιοσύναι as "righteous deeds" rather than "righteousness" (as in R.B. Wright, *OTP*, 2:660).

dom is conceived as a sanctified body, from which 'sinners' have been removed".[99]

There are some texts in these Psalms which speak of God being merciful to the righteous, although it is not entirely clear whether the idea is that God is merciful in judgement itself or whether he is merciful in that he delivers the righteous from the oppression of the unrighteous.[100] But whatever the case, the author of the Psalms of Solomon clearly believed that the "righteous" had merited this position. I believe Seifrid is correct to argue for the absense of saving righteousness in the Psalms of Solomon.[101] The gift of life in 9.4-5 is based not on the righteousness of God[102] but goes back to the person's own righteousness, i.e. his righteous deeds.

There can therefore be little support for "covenantal nomism" in the Psalms of Solomon. "The Psalmist is a moral rigorist. It is by scrupulous purity of life that one makes oneself pleasing to God."[103]

---

[99] Seifrid, *Justification by Faith*, p. 128. He points to Ps. Sol. 17.26-27, 43-44; 18.1-5.

[100] See Ps. Sol. 2.33-35: "Praise God, you who fear the Lord with understanding, for the Lord's mercy is upon those who fear him with judgment. 34 To separate between the righteous and the sinner to repay sinners forever according to their actions 35 And to have mercy on the righteous (keeping him) from the humiliation of the sinner, and to repay the sinner for what he has done to the righteous" (translation of R.B. Wright, *OTP*, 2:654). See also 13.9-12, where "the Lord's mercy is upon the devout" (v. 12) but this mercy involves discipline.

[101] Seifrid, *Justification by Faith*, pp. 119-120, argues for there being a *iustitia distributiva* but a complete absence of *iustitia salutifera* in the Psalms of Solomon.

[102] As von Stemm, *Sünder*, p. 192, n. 36, contends. He argues that ἐν (τῇ) δικαιοσύνῃ (σου) (9.4) is used to describe God himself and serves on the other hand to describe the "Gerichtshandelns Gottes". "Damit referiert die Vokabel δικαιοσύνη primär auf ein Attribut der Taten Gottes als auf eine Tat selbst" (p. 192). "Sowohl ζωή als auch ἀπώλεια gelten als Wirkung der göttlichen δικαιοσύνη, denn die 'Gerechtigkeit' ist Ursprung und Merkmal des göttlichen Gerichtes zugleich" (p. 192). Likewise he argues that "das Attribut δίκαιος überwiegend als Verhältnisbegriff eingesetzt wurde, um das angemessene Verhalten gegenüber einer zwischenmenschlichen oder auch einer religiösen Norm zu charakterisieren, so wird auch in den Psalmen Salomos das Gerechtsein eines Menschen aus dem Gegenüber zu Gott verstanden, was zusätzlich auch an der Verwendung des Substantives δικαιοσύνη gezeigt werden kann" (pp. 186-87).

[103] R.B. Wright and V. Schwartz, *OTP*, 2:645.

Turning to the Wisdom of Solomon, one can again find a theology of salvation by works. However, some verses may suggest that the book supports
a salvation by grace. See especially 15.1-2:

But thou, our God, art kind and true,
patient, and ruling all things in mercy.
2 For even if we sin we are thine, knowing thy power;
but we will not sin, because we know that we are accounted thine.

One problem of much of the discussion of such a text is that it is assumed
that the righteous are to be equated with "Israel" and the unrighteous with
"Gentiles" in the book of Wisdom.[104] However, in Wisdom 1-5 apostate
Jews also belong to the ungodly[105] and the idea of a righteous Gentile is not
to be excluded.[106] The picture in Wisdom is therefore that the "elect" are
those Jews who have been faithful to the law.

Pseudo-Philo's Biblical Antiquities (*Liber Antiquitatum Biblicarum*) has
been viewed as putting forward most clearly "grace which is bestowed upon
those in covenant relationship with God".[107] There certainly is talk of mercy
and grace. However, we have to ask what the basis of this mercy is. One
reason God made a covenant with Israel is because of Abraham's prior
faithfulness. Pseudo-Philo, unlike Genesis, relates Abraham to the story of
the tower of Babel (LAB 6-7). Abraham and eleven others refused to take
part in the building of the tower, such a building implying idolatry. Eleven
take refuge in the mountains and only Abraham trusts God enough to remain
and face the wrath of the builders. Abraham is cast into a furnace but God

---

[104] See for example A. Nygren's discussion of the parallels between Rom. 2.1-6 and
Wisdom 11-15 (*Commentary on Romans* ET, Philadelphia: Fortress Press [6]1983,
([1]1949), pp. 113-17). See also Dunn, *Romans*, 1:90-91.

[105] See Wis. 1.16-2.20 and G. Siegfried, "Wisdom, Book of", *HDB*, 4:929 (928-31).
In fact the conclusion of J.P. Weisengoff, "The Impious of Wisdom 2", *CBQ* 11 (1949)
64-65 (40-65), is that the "view according to which the 'impious' are identified primarily
with apostate Jews but with their pagan associates not excluded, rests on solid foundations".

[106] Cf. L.L. Grabbe, *Wisdom of Solomon*, Sheffield: Sheffield Academic Press 1997,
p. 51.

[107] See Longenecker, *Eschatology*, p. 24. See also H. Jacobson, *A Commentary on
Pseudo-Philo's Liber Antiquitatum Biblicarum with Latin Text and English Translation*
(AGAJU 31), 2 vols, Leiden/New York/Köln: E.J. Brill 1996, 1:241-42: "If there is a
single predominant theme in LAB, it is the following: No matter how much the Jewish
people suffer, no matter how bleak the outlook appears, God will never completely abandon His people and in the end salvation and triumph will be the lot of the Jews".

delivers him. As a reward God chooses Abraham and brings him to Canaan, and establishes a "covenant" with him.[108] So God says "I will bless his seed and be lord for him as God forever" (7.4).[109] Another reason for choosing Israel is the fact that Abraham and Isaac were obedient when God "demanded [Abraham's] son as a holocaust". So "because he [Abraham or Isaac] did not refuse, his offering was acceptable before me, and on account of his blood I chose them" (18.5).[110] Feldman points to certain similarities between the acount in Pseudo-Philo and in Josephus[111] and writes that:

. . . both Josephus and Pseudo-Philo look upon the sacrifice as payment due to God. Moreover, both Josephus and LAB stress Isaac's joy in being sacrificed, his free and voluntary acceptance of his role, and the significance of the sacrifice for the destiny of Israel, namely that because Isaac did not resist, his offering (LAB 18.5) was acceptable to God and that God chose Israel because of his blood.[112]

It may be noted in passing that Paul's view of Jesus' sacrificial death has no notion of "merit".[113]

LAB 31.2 may appear to stress God's grace: "Even if my people have sinned, nevertheless I will have mercy on them".[114] This is a striking verse but actually refers to mercy in battle.[115] There are also some signs of

---

[108] Again Kutsch, *Neues Testament*, p. 73 nn. 145, 150, argues that "covenant" in LAB 4.11; 7.4 and 8.3, is to be understood as "Gottes (Setzung =) Zusage".

[109] On this passage see F.J. Murphy, "The Eternal Covenant in Pseudo-Philo", *JSP* 3 (1988) 44-45 (43-57).

[110] Translation of D.J. Harrington, *OTP*, 2:325. The phrase *non contradixit* could refer to Abraham or Isaac. I believe it refers to Isaac's willingness to be sacrificed since the passage appears to emphasize the obedience of both Abraham and Isaac (see Jacobson, *Pseudo-Philo*, 1:582-83).

[111] See below for a brief discussion of Josephus.

[112] L.H. Feldman, "*Josephus'* Jewish Antiquities *and Pseudo-Philo's* Biblical Antiquities", in L.H. Feldman and G. Hata (ed.), *Josephus, the Bible and History*, Detroit: Wayne State University Press 1989, 63 (59-80).

[113] See Bell, "Sacrifice and Christology"; "Rom 5.18-19 and Universal Salvation", *NTS* 48 (2002) 422-23 (417-32). See also the comments of O. Hofius on the ὑπακοή of Christ in Rom. 5.19: ". . . Christi ὑπακοή ist die heilschaffende Tat seiner freiwilligen Selbsthingabe in den Tod und eben damit das Ereignis der Gnade Gottes (V. 15bβ.17b) und der Erweis seiner Liebe (Röm 5,8) selbst" ("Die Adam-Christus-Antithese und das Gesetz", in *Paulusstudien II* (WUNT 143), Tübingen: J.C.B. Mohr (Paul Siebeck) 2002, 85 (62-103), Hofius' emphasis).

[114] Quoted by Longenecker, *Eschatology*, p. 24.

[115] The context is the defeat and death of Sisera.

synergism and limits to grace. So mercy is shown to Gideon "on account of those who have fallen asleep" (35.3).[116] Also the emphasis is on *unintentional sins* being set right (22.6).[117]

Law is a central concept in Pseudo-Philo. It is true that according to Pseudo-Philo, "the Law is not a collection of unbearable injunctions but that which 'teaches' God's ways", something "one must 'enter' and 'walk in', not unlike the covenant".[118] Indeed in a number of texts where it is claimed that reference is to the "covenant" or "covenant relationship", the word translated "testamentum" actually means "law".[119] So LAB 11.1, translated by Harrington as "I will give a light to the world and illumine their dwelling places and establish my covenant with the sons of men and glorify my people above all nations",[120] is actually referring to the law.[121] A similar parallelism between light and law is seen in 2 Bar. 17.4[122] and LAB 11.1 goes on to stress that the eternal statutes "will be a light for the righteous, but will be punishment for the impious".[123] Likewise behind the word testamentum we should understand "law" in texts such as LAB 11.3, 32.8.[124] The law therefore will act as as punishment for the impious and

---

[116] Harrington, *OTP*, 2:349n. compares 2 Mac. 8.15. See also Jacobson, *Pseudo-Philo*, 2:914, who writes that there "appears to be an allusion to the concept of 'merits of the patriarchs'".

[117] On the forgiveness of unintentional sins see R.H. Bell, "Sin Offerings and Sinning with a High Hand", *JPJ* 4 (1995) 25-59.

[118] J.R. Levison, "Torah and Covenant in Pseudo Philo's *Liber Antiquitatum Biblicarum*", in F. Avemarie and H. Lichtenberger (ed.), *Bund und Tora: Zur theologischen Begriffsgeschichte in alttestamentlicher, frühjüdischer und urchristlicher Tradition* (WUNT 92), Tübingen: J.C.B. Mohr (Paul Siebeck) 1996, 123 (111-27). Levison here discusses Pseudo-Philo 16 which concerns Korah's rebellion (Num 16.1-3). According to LAB, Korah and his company object to the law about tassels (cf. the immediately preceding section Num. 15.37-41). "Why is an unbearable law imposed upon us?" (LAB 16.1). The seven sons of Korah respond, saying that "if we walk in [God's] ways, we will be his sons. But if you are unbelieving, do your own way" (LAB 16.5). Rejection of the law is essentially unbelief.

[119] I am assuming that Pseudo-Philo was originally written in Hebrew, translated into Greek and then into the extant Latin. See Harrington, *OTP* 2:298-99.

[120] Referred to by Longenecker, *Eschatology*, p. 24, and partially quoted by Sanders, *Practice*, p. 264 (Harrington's translation, *OTP* 2:318).

[121] Kutsch, *Neues Testament*, p. 74 n. 165.

[122] Kutsch, *Neues Testament*, p. 74 n. 165.

[123] Jacobson, *Pseudo-Philo*, 1:108.

[124] Kutsch, *Neues Testament*, p. 74 n. 166.

Jews are numbered among the impious as well as among the pious.[125] All will be judged according to their works.[126] The law is the fundamental factor in salvation and the "covenant" is only preserved if Israel obeys the law.[127] The importance of keeping the law for salvation is often played down in the secondary literature on Pseudo-Philo. So Murphy writes that "Israel's sin cannot nullify God's plans".[128] But the grim story of the burning of 6110 sinners of Israel who were considered to be unworthy to fight against the Philistines (which has no equivalent in the Old Testament) demonstrates that there are cases where those who sin are to be judged and will find no mercy (LAB 25-26).[129] The same can be said for the story of Korah's rebellion

---

[125] Jacobson, *Pseudo-Philo*, 1:447, rightly stresses that one cannot equate the pious with all Jews.

[126] Gathercole, *Boasting*, p. 79, points to LAB 64.7 (Samuel, on being raised by the witch of Endor, says "I thought that the time to receive the reward of my works had arrived") and 3.10 (which refers to the judgement of the dead according their deserts). Gathercole rightly argues (against K. Yinger, *Paul, Judaism, and Judgement according to Deeds* (SNTMS 105), Cambridge: CUP 1999, p. 80) that this latter text is not simply concerned with the punishment of the wicked.

[127] So C. Dietzfelbinger, *Pseudo-Philo: Antiquitates Biblicae* (JSHRZ 2.2), Gütersloh: Gütersloher Verlagshaus Gerd Mohn ²1979, (¹1975), p. 97, writes: "[Das Gesetz] ist *der* Heilsfaktor für Israel und seine Geschichte; durch das Gesetz wird der Bund konstituiert, und im Halten des Gesetzes wird der Bund bewahrt" (Dietzfelbinger's emphasis). But Israel has fallen into sin, the most serious being idolatry and marrying foreign women. "Heil liegt für Israel darum ausschließlich in der Hinwendung zum Gesetz, und Geschichte ist der Raum ständiger Begegnung Israels mit dem Gesetz. Daß diese Begegnung negativ ausfiel, ist Grund des vergangenen und gegenwärtigen Unheils. Daß solche Begegnung aber auch in Gegenwart und Zukunft dem Volk ermöglicht wird, ist Grund für die Hoffnung künftigen und endgültigen Heils" (Dietzfelbinger, *Pseudo-Philo*, p. 97).

[128] Murphy, "Eternal Covenant", 45.

[129] Each tribe had sinners who had committed a particular sin. Such sins include the *desire* to do various things (e.g. make the golden calf (Judah), sacrifice to gods of the Canaanites (Reuben), test the tent of meeting (whether or not it is holy) (Levi) and eat their own children (Zebulun)) or the making of forbidden things (Dan, Naphtali), committing adultery (Gad), and taking the idols of the Amorites (Asher).

(LAB 16)[130] even though their rejection of a particular law may be considered tantamount to "unbelief".[131]

Yet despite this nomistic emphasis, there is more emphasis on grace in Pseudo-Philo than in many other intertestamental Jewish writings.[132] Note that although Cohn reintroduced Pseudo-Philo to the world of scholarship in 1898,[133] the work was not included in editions of the Apocrypha and Pseudepigrapha made by Charles[134] or by Kautzsch.[135] It was neither made use of in Billerbeck[136] nor by Bousset-Greßmann.[137] Relatively recent works such as Carson's on *Divine Sovereignty*[138] have also not explicitly referred to it. But even if scholars such as Carson had referred to it, I do not think their conclusions would have been different. Pseudo-Philo is just one work among many and is to be viewed as somewhat exceptional.[139] Also one can-

---

[130] Although this story in LAB has a parallel in Num. 16.1-35, the rebellion in Num. 16.3 consists in Korah objecting to Moses exalting himself, whereas in LAB 16.1 Korah and his companions object, as we have seen, about the law of tassels being "an unbearable law imposed upon us".

[131] Levison, "Torah", 123. E. Reinmuth, "Beobachtungen zum Verständnis des Gesetzes im Liber Antiquitatum Biblicarum (Pseudo-Philo)", *JSJ* 20 (1989) 168 (151-70), points to "Befleckung" (defilement) as a central opposition to law in LAB. So in the context of Korah's rebellion we have in 16.3: *Et nunc fortiter contaminatum sunt cogitationes hominum.* See also 25.1 in the context of who should go up to fight against the Philistines.

[132] LAB 30.7 is particularly striking (words ascribed to Deborah): "And behold now the LORD will take pity on you today, not because of you but because of his covenant that he established with your fathers and the oath that he has sworn not to abandon you forever".

[133] L. Cohn, "An Apocryphal Work Ascribed to Philo of Alexandria", *JQR* 19 (1898) 277-332.

[134] R.H. Charles (ed.), *The Apocrypha and Pseudepigrapha of the Old Testament in English*, 2 vols, Oxford: OUP 1977 (repr.), ([1]1913).

[135] E. Kautzsch (ed.), *Die Apokryphen und Pseudepigraphen des Alten Testaments*, 2 vols, Tübingen/Freiburg/Leipzig: J.C.B. Mohr (Paul Siebeck) 1900.

[136] Billerbeck, *Kommentar*.

[137] Bousset and Greßmann, *Religion des Judentums*.

[138] Carson, *Divine Sovereignty*.

[139] As regards the relationship of Pseudo-Philo to apocryphal and pseudepigraphical works, Harrington (*OTP*, 2:302) points out that in *form* Pseudo-Philo is closest to Jubilees, the Qumran Genesis Apocryphon, and Josephus' Antiquities. As regards apocalyptic language it stands closest to 4 Ezra and 2 Baruch. M.R. James, *The Biblical Antiquities of Philo*, London: SPCK 1917, pp. 46-58, sets out parallels between Pseudo-Philo and 2 Baruch and between Pseudo-Philo and 4 Ezra and concludes that all three works

not exclude the possibility that this work contains Christian influences and even interpolations.[140]

Turning to the books of Maccabees, we find in 1 Maccabees the view, as Oesterley puts it, that "God helps those who help themselves".[141] There is at the same time a transcendent view of God and a large scope for human free will. This may appear to be a contradiction since if God is more sovereign one would expect there to be less scope for human free will. However, I think that Oesterley's explanation is highly plausible. He writes:

> Just as there was a disinclination, on account of its transcendent holiness, to utter the name of God, and instead to substitute paraphrases for it, so there arose also a disinclination to ascribe action among men directly to God, because of His inexpressible majesty. One result of this was the further tendency to emphasize and extend the scope of human free-will. These tendencies were only beginning to exert their influence, but they largely explain the religious characteristics of the book.[142]

This can also be applied to other works from this period as we shall see.

As is well known, the book deals with reward from the perspective of "this world". So in Mattathias' speech before his death in 1 Mac. 2.49b-68, he relates righteousness to "worldy" rewards.[143] So he asks: "Was not

---

emanate from the same circle. But Harrington (*OTP*, 2:302) notes that there are ideas common to 4 Ezra and 2 Baruch which are absent in Pseudo-Philo. Harrington argues that the most one can say is that the authors of 4 Ezra and 2 Baruch may have known Pseudo-Philo. A similar judgement is made by M.E. Stone, *Fourth Ezra* (Hermeneia), Minneapolis: Fortress Press 1990, p. 40.

[140] There are some important verbal parallels with the New Testament. See Harrington, *OTP* 2:301-2; James, *Biblical Antiquities*, pp. 59-60; L.H. Feldman, Prolegomenon, lvi-lviii (in Ktav repr. of James, 1971). See, however, Jacobson, *Pseudo-Philo*, 1:449, who says that more important parallels to, for example, *tribus diebus* (11.2) can be found in the Old Testament. One could also make a case that the sacrifice of Christ influenced the sacrifice of Isaac in Pseudo-Philo (18.5; 32.1-4; 40.2-3). Usually the converse has been suggested. See Schoeps, *Paul*, pp. 141-49. For a critique of Schoeps' tradition history see P.R. Davies and B.D. Chilton, "The Aqedah: A Revised Tradition History", *CBQ* 40 (1978) 514-46, a work which by implication would be critical of my suggestion, since it downplays any hint of expiation.

[141] W.O.E. Oesterley, *APOT* 1:61.

[142] Oesterley, *APOT* 1:61.

[143] An exception is Elijah: "because of great zeal for the law he was taken up into heaven" (2.58) (cf. Gathercole, *Boasting*, p. 52). But it is still the case that 1 Maccabees has no eschatology and makes no comment about existence after death (K.-D. Schunck, "Makkabäer/Makkabäerbücher", *TRE* 21 738 (736-45)). J.A. Goldstein, *1 Maccabees* (AB 41), Garden City, New York: Doubleday & Co. 1976, p. 12, may be going too far

Abraham found faithful when tested, and it was reckoned to him as righteousness?" By relating Gen. 15.6 to Gen. 22.1-19 it is shown that Abraham's righteous status depends on his "works".[144] Although the stress is on "this world" this relationship between works and a righteous status is not irrelevant to our enquiry. For Phinehas receives an *"everlasting* priest-hood" because "he was deeply zealous" (2.54) and David "because he was merciful, inherited the throne of the kingdom *for ever*" (2.57). Those who perform good deeds "receive great honour and an *everlasting name*" (2.51).[145]

2 Maccabees reflects a Pharisaic standpoint.[146] The writer stresses the personal piety of Israel. So laws were kept in Jerusalem because of the piety of the high priest (3.1) and the Jews were "invulnerable, because they fol-lowed the laws ordained by him [God]" (8.36). But disaster comes to Israel because the leaders or people of Israel forsook the law/covenant (4.7, 11-15, 25, 34, 39, 50; 5.6).[147] The author does stress that "these punishments were designed not to destroy but to discipline our people" (6.12).[148] It is true also that Israel is God's "portion" (1.26). Nevertheless, good works are essential for Israel and the scheme of sin and retribution is the context of the author's "frequent moralizing comments".[149]

---

when he infers that the "author completely rejected the belief in immortality or resurrec-tion since he does not allude to either even where a believer could hardly have avoided doing so (2:62-64)". Goldstein, *1 Maccabees*, p. 238, translates 2.58 as: "Elijah for his acts of zeal on behalf of the Torah was taken up *as if* into heaven" (my emphasis). He comments (*1 Maccabees*, p. 241): "At least from the time of the Greek translation of Kings, there were Jewish authorities who were reluctant to believe that Elijah, a mortal, had been taken up all the way into heaven (cf. Ps 115:16)".

[144] This is a view contradicted by Paul. See the discussion in chapter 4 below on Gal. 3.6.

[145] See Gathercole, *Boasting*, p. 52.

[146] Metzger, *Apocrypha*, p. 146.

[147] Nickelsburg, *Jewish Literature*, p. 119.

[148] Nickelsburg, *Jewish Literature*, p. 119, p. 154 n. 58, compares similar ideas in Tobit and Psalms of Solomon.

[149] Nickelsburg, *Jewish Literature*, p. 118. He refers to 2 Mac. 3.1; 4.16-17, 26, 38, 42; 5.10, 19-20; 6.12-16; 15.32-33.

Jubilees[150] is interesting in that the author seems to have a deterministic view when discussing God's control of history.[151] Yet at the same time he believes that human beings are responsible for their sins. The author manages to live with both views. So "when [the author] makes God the speaker of the prophetic words in chapter 1, they are no longer prophetic words. They become facts present in the foreknowledge of God. Prophetic words are not necesarily inevitable; but there is no avoiding what God knows to be the future. The fact that certain predictions are inscribed on heavenly tablets (5:13) implies the same fixed order of events".[152] Also although human beings commit evil, the actual causes of evil are superhuman beings. In this way the author develops a theodicy in that God is not directly responsible for evil.[153] So certain biblical traditions are recast: it was Mastema (the prince of evil spirits, 10.8), not God, who initiated the idea of tempting Abraham to kill Isaac (17.15-18.13); Mastema, not God, provoked the Egyptians to pursue Israel (48.12; cf. Ex. 14.8-9), and tried to kill Moses on his way to Egypt (48.2-3; cf. Ex. 4.24).[154]

---

[150] Although Jubilees does share ideas with apocalyptic, there are significant differences. So in neither Charles nor Charlesworth is Jubilees classified under apocalyptic. O.S. Wintermute, *OTP*, 2:36-37, points to M. Testuz, *Les Idées religieuses du livre des Jubilés*, Geneva 1960, pp. 11-12, who concluded that Jubilees was a work of composite genre. But see also A. Nissen, "Tora und Geschichte im Spätjudentum", *NovT* 9 (1967) 241-77, who gives five points in favour of Jubilees being apocalyptic. Russell, *Method and Message of Jewish Apocalyptic*, p. 54, writes: "Jubilees is not, strictly speaking, an apocalyptic book; but it belongs to the same milieu and must be taken into serious account in dealing with that literature". See below for further discussion of apocalyptic. C. Rowland, *The Open Heaven: A Study in Apocalyptic in Judaism and Early Christianity*, London: SCPK 1982, pp. 51-52, believes Jubilees definitely is an apocalypse in view of the "way in which this whole story is placed in the context of God's revelation to Moses on Sinai" (p. 51). Note that according to Rowland "[a]pocalyptic seems essentially to be about the revelation of the divine mysteries through visions or some other form of immediate disclosure of heavenly truths" (p. 70). For the purpose of this inquiry, it is not necessary to decide on this issue.

[151] See Russell, *Method and Message of Jewish Apocalyptic*, p. 230. He points to Jub. 4.19, where Enoch "saw what was and what will be in a vision of his sleep as it will happen among the children of men in their generations until the day of judgment" (I have used Wintermute's translation, *OTP*, 2:62).

[152] Wintermute, *OTP*, 2:47.

[153] See Wintermute, *OTP*, 2:47.

[154] Wintermute, *OTP*, 2:47-48. One should however note that generally the demons or impure spirits affect Gentiles rather than Israel (see J.C. VanderKam, "Anthropological Gleanings from the Book of Jubilees", in U. Mittmann-Richert, F. Avemarie and G.S.

In view of this theological scheme, how are we to view the question of "salvation"? The first point to make is that although Jubilees seems so different to 1 Maccabees, there is an element in common. God is becoming increasingly transcendent such that the action of human beings is something they do because of their free will. Jubilees brings in another dimension though. The transcendence of God has given rise to intermediary figures.[155] And there is a development of reward and merit theology. In Jubilees a righteous status is bestowed on those who do good deeds. So Simeon and Levi are praised for killing the Shechemites (contrast Gen. 49.5-7!): "And it was a righteousness for them and it was written down for them for righteousness" (30.17).[156] Levi was rewarded. "And Levi and his sons will be blessed forever because he was zealous to do righteousness and judgment and vengeance against all who rose up against Israel. And thus a blessing and righteousness will be written (on high) as a testimony for him in the heavenly tablets before the God of all" (30.18-19).[157]

There is therefore a merit and reward theology. But how is it that Sanders again claims that there is stress on the covenant and election in Jubilees? He first quotes Jub. 1.17-18 ("And I will build My sanctuary in their midst . . . And I will not forsake them nor fail them; for I am their God"). However, this is in response to their repentance (Jub. 1.15). The initiative is with human beings. The second text quoted is Jub. 1.25: "And they shall be called children of the living God, and every angel and every spirit shall know, yea, they shall know that these are My children and I am their Father in uprightness and righteousness . . . ". But again this is in response to the repentance of Israel. See Jub. 1.23: ". . . they will return to me in all uprightness and with all of (their) heart and soul . . . ".

Although Jubilees may not strictly belong to "apocalyptic literature", it now provides a useful bridge to this literature.

Oegema (ed.), *Der Mensch vor Gott. Forschungen zum Menschenbild in Bibel, antikem Judentum und Koran. Festschrift für Hermann Lichtenberger zum 60. Geburtstag*, Neukirchen-Vlyun: Neukirchener Verlag 2003, 127 (117-32)).

[155] Cf., Wintermute, *OTP*, 2:47: "Between God and man, Jubilees introduces us to a host of angels and demons".

[156] Wintermute, *OTP*, 2:113.

[157] Wintermute, *OTP*, 2:113. VanderKam, "Anthropological Gleanings", 124-26, points to the extensive rewriting of Genesis 34 in Jubilees 30.

2.2. Apocalyptic literature

In apocalyptic[158] there is the view that salvation is by works. This is made explicit in 2 Bar. 51.7: "Miracles, however, will appear at their own time to those who are saved because of their works and for whom the Law is now a hope . . ."[159]

There are ideas of election in apocalyptic but it seems election is based on human righteousness.[160] Election is seen "in terms of merit, namely, that the people is chosen because none is more worthy".[161] So in 2 Baruch, election is based on human worth. 2 Bar. 48.20: "For these are the people whom you have elected, and this is the nation of which you found no equal." In what sense did God find no equal? In theory it could be her beauty, her faith or her forefathers. But in view of the overall argument of 2 Baruch I suspect that she was most worthy because of her "works". And even if the reference is not to works, we are now a long way from Gen. 12.1-4 where "the election of Abraham, the progenitor of the covenanted people of Israel, comes suddenly and without warning" and catches us "unprepared"[162] or Dt. 7.6-8

---

[158] Here and in a number of places below I refer to "apocalyptic". I use this term to refers to the kind of material found in apocalypses (cf. J.J. Collins, "Genre, Ideology and Social Movements in Jewish Apocalypticism", in J.J. Collins and J.H. Charlesworth (ed.), *Mysteries and Revelations: Apocalyptic Studies since the Uppsala Colloquium* (JSPSup 9), Sheffield: JSOT Press 1991, 13 (11-32)). For a helpful summary of the genre of apocalypses, see K. Koch, "Einleitung", in K. Koch and J.M. Schmidt (ed.), *Apokalyptik* (WdF 365), Darmstadt: Wissenschaftliche Buchgesellschaft 1982, 12-13 (1-29). But in using "apocalyptic" in this narrow sense, I do not intend to suggest that groups such as the Qumran sectaries did not have "apocalyptic" ideas even though the number of apocalypses found there are few (cf. J.J. Collins, *Apocalypticism in the Dead Sea Scrolls* (LDSS), London/New York: Routledge 1997, p. 9). It has become customary to use the term "apocalypticism" for the world view which may be extrapolated from apocalypses (P.D. Hanson, "Apocalypticism", *IDBSup* 30-31 (28-34); J.J. Collins, "Early Jewish Apocalypticism", *ABD* 1:283 (282-88)).

[159] Translation of A.F.J. Klijn, *OTP*, 1:638.

[160] See, e.g., 1 En. 51.2: "And he shall choose the righteous and the holy ones from among (the risen dead), for the day when they shall be selected and saved has arrived". Such a view of election seem perfectly logical for writings which stress salvation by works.

[161] G. Schrenk, ἐκλέγομαι, *TDNT* 4:170 (168-76).

[162] D. Novak, *The Election of Israel: The Idea of the Chosen People*, Cambridge: CUP 1995, p. 115.

where "the people of Israel themselves cannot claim any inherent qualities that could be seen as reasons for their election by God".[163]

But even if 2 Bar. 48.20 does not refer to "works", one can make the general point that the "elect" now means the "righteous".[164] Carson writes: "God may be 'gracious' to his people, but it is no longer grace in defiance of demerit and rooted in the sovereign goodness of God. Rather, it is a kind response to merit".[165] So God does then appear to be gracious to the "righteous" and disciplines them. But the righteous are elected precisely because of their "works".

It has been claimed that in apocalyptic the righteous are judged by mercy whereas the sinners are punished according to strict rules of justice. This view is misleading in the extreme. So Sanders has claimed to find the idea of judgement according to grace in 2 Bar. 84.11[166]: "For if he judges us not according to the multitude of his grace, woe to all us who are born".[167] However, it is crucial to consider the context which concerns keeping the law.[168] Further, other texts tell that the righteous have a store of good works for the final judgement:

For the righteous justly have good hope for the end and go away from this habitation without fear because they possess with you a store of good works which is preserved in treasuries (14.12; cf. 24.1).[169]

---

[163] Novak, *Election*, p. 116.

[164] Carson, *Divine Sovereignty*, p. 68. Note also that in a range of apocalyptic literature, the "righteous" are those who keep the law. See J. Stock-Hesketh, "Law in Jewish Intertestamental Apocalyptic", Nottingham Ph.D. Thesis 1993. See, for example, pp. 103-7 (on 1 En. 72-82) and pp. 317-21 (on 2 Baruch).

[165] Carson, *Divine Sovereignty*, p. 69. Note also that although in 2 Bar. 84.10 the readers are encouraged to pray that the Mighty One may accept them in mercy, he (the Mightly One) is also asked to remember the integrity of the fathers.

[166] See E.P. Sanders, "The Covenant as a Soteriological Category and the Nature of Salvation in Palestinian and Hellenistic Judaism", in R. Hamerton-Kelly and R. Scroggs (ed.), *Jews, Greeks and Christians: Religious Cultures in Late Antiquity*, Leiden 1976, 17-20 (11-44).

[167] Translation of Klijn, *OTP*, 1:651.

[168] See, for example, 2 Bar. 84.6b-8: "if you obey the things which I have said to you, you shall receive from the Mighty One everything which has been prepared and has been preserved for you. 7 Therefore let this letter be a witness between me and you that you may remember the commandments of the Mighty One, and that it also may serve as my defense in the presence of him who has sent me. 8 And remember Zion and the Law . . . and do not forget the festivals and the sabbaths".

[169] Klijn, *OTP*, 1:626.

Works such as 2 Baruch and 4 Ezra are important for understanding the Judaism which Paul attacked even though they were written late in the first century.[170] However, there has been a debate about the precise theology of 4 Ezra and how it relates to Jewish tradition.[171] So E.P. Sanders attempted to marginalize the work, claiming that its view of works was exceptional.[172] This was continued by B.W. Longenecker in his work on 4 Ezra and Romans 1-11.[173] So Longenecker was critical of those such as G.R.S. Mead, A.L. Thompson and M.A. Knibb, who argued that the author of 4 Ezra stayed with tradition.[174] Note, however, that Longenecker has changed his mind, now claiming that 4 Ezra after all was not a peripheral work;

---

[170] The two works have an intimate relationship. In fact some believe that 4 Ezra was a source for 2 Baruch (B. Violet, *Die Apokalypsen des Esra und des Baruch in deutscher Gestalt* (GCS 18), Leipzig: J.C. Hinrichs'sche Buchhandlung 1924, p. lv) whereas others argue for the opposite (P. Bogaert, *L'Apocalypse syriaque de Baruch* (SC 144-45), 2 vols, Paris: Cerf 1969, 1:26-27).

[171] One of the problem with 4 Ezra is where to locate the theological views of the author and indeed whether the work is intended to portray a particular theological view. Although he has been criticized by M.E. Stone, I think there is much to the suggestion of E. Brandenburger, *Die Verborgenheit Gottes im Weltgeschehen* (AThANT 68), Zürich: Theologischer Verlag 1981, that the purpose of the apocalypse is to promote the views of Uriel in visions 1-3, views which are accepted by Ezra and expressed by him in his final speech (14.28-36). M.E. Stone, "On Reading an Apocalypse", in J.J. Collins and J.H. Charlesworth (ed.), *Mysteries and Revelations: Apocalyptic Studies since the Uppsala Colloquium* (JSPSup 9), Sheffield: JSOT Press 1991, 68-72 (65-78), finds Brandenburger's view unconvincing. Although he keeps stressing that Ezra is the "hero" in visions 1-3, it is surely beyond doubt that the views of the angel do represent the views of the author.

[172] Sanders, *Palestinian Judaism*, p. 409: "In IV Ezra . . . we see an instance in which covenantal nomism has collapsed. All that is left is legalistic perfectionism".

[173] See Longenecker, *Eschatology*, p. 152: "The author of 4 Ezra has advanced a new understanding of the character of Jewish existence without the temple: salvation is not a national privilege but an individual responsibility worked out with great effort by works of merit".

[174] See, for example, A.L. Thompson, *Responsibility for Evil in the Theodicy of IV Ezra* (SBLDS 29), Missoula: Scholars Press 1977, p. 318, who argues that the closing episodes "represent his acceptance of the traditional basis of salvation, namely, the merit and obedience of the individual". See also Knibb in M.A. Knibb and R.J. Coggins, *The First and Second Books of Esdras* (CBC), Cambridge: CUP 1979, p. 182: "the author of 2 Esdras 3-14, in common with other Jews of his day, believed that by the strict observance of the law it was possible for an individual to acquire, as it were, a credit balance of good works and to earn thereby the reward in the world to come of life" (comment on 7.77).

rather it is "to be located more centrally within the spectrum of Jewish life in the first century".[175]

There are indeed strong arguments for 4 Ezra (and 2 Baruch) belonging to the mainstream of Jewish tradition. 4 Ezra and 2 Baruch are related to Jewish tradition in two respects. First, much of their content is the same as that of other Jewish apocalyptic and, it has to be stressed, such apocalyptic was not on the margins of Judaism.[176] Secondly, as Stone points out in his commentary, 4 Ezra "conforms to the exegetical or theological ideas preserved in the rabbinic tradition".[177] I maintain that 4 Ezra and 2 Baruch belong to mainstream Judaism precisely in that they teach salvation by works.[178] Such a view can be clearly seen in, for example, the third vision (4 Ezr. 6.35-9.25). It is hard to find here any mercy on sinners.[179]

To summarize this section I would say that although apocalyptic has distinctive ideas, it cannot be isolated as peculiar in regard to issues of works-righteousness.[180] The idea of a merit theology is found in other streams of

---

[175] B.W. Longenecker, *2 Esdras*, Sheffield: Sheffield Academic Press 1995, p. 102. See also L.L. Grabbe, "Chronography in 4 Ezra and 2 Baruch", in K.H. Richards (ed.), *Society of Biblical Literature 1981 Seminar Papers*, Chico: Scholars Press 1981, 49-63; L.L. Grabbe, "The Social Setting of Early Jewish Apocalypticism", *JSP* 4 (1989) 27-47; P.R. Davies, "The social world of apocalyptic writings", in R.E. Clements (ed.), *The World of Ancient Israel*, Cambridge: CUP 1989, 251-71. Longenecker points out that such views (i.e. that apocalyptic did not arise among groups on the fringes) cohere well with the work of M.A. Knibb, "Apocalyptic and Wisdom in 4 Ezra", *JSJ* 13 (1982) 56-74.

[176] Hengel and Deines, "E.P. Sanders' 'Common Judaism', Jesus, and the Pharisees", 54, criticize Sanders for neglecting the eschatological expectation, including his neglect of 4 Ezra and 2 Baruch. In fact earlier in the article Hengel and Deines put forward their fundamental criticism of Sanders: he has marginalized the Pharisees thereby giving rise to a "Sadducean tendency" in his "presentation of 'common Judaism' as a religion of the temple and the priesthood" ("E.P. Sanders' 'Common Judaism', Jesus, and the Pharisees", 4).

[177] Stone, *Fourth Ezra*, p. 38.

[178] Note incidentally that although "faith" does occur in 4 Ezra, the term is used interchangeably with "works" (see Stone, *Fourth Ezra*, pp. 296, 397). So 7.77 speaks of storing up a "treasure of works" whereas 6.5 speaks of storing up "treasures of faith". Stone rightly argues that this contrasts starkly with Paul's faith/works dichotomy as in Rom. 3.27 (p. 296). For 4 Ezra faith is itself a work (cf. Jas 2.21-23).

[179] See, for example, 4 Ezr. 7.58-115.

[180] So Sanders has to say that 4 Ezra is an exception to the rule of "covenantal nomism". Ziesler, *Pauline Christianity*, pp. 104-5, sees both 2 Baruch and 4 Ezra as being atypical of Judaism. They were written after 70 AD and Ziesler concludes that they

Judaism. We have seen it already in the non-apocalyptic works of the Apocrypha and Pseudepigrapha. We will also find it in Qumran and in the Rabbinic literature.

2.3. Essene texts from Qumran

The Essene texts of Qumran[181] seem unusual in that there is in fact a strong teaching on election.[182] The sectaries see themselves as the elect of God.[183] Yet even here we occasionally find traces of merit theology.[184] So those who wish to join the community may do so by a free decision: "This is the rule for the men of the Community who freely volunteer to convert from all evil and to keep themselves steadfast in all he (i.e. God) prescribes in compliance with his will".[185] Then if they do "the right" they will gain righteousness (salvation). This is seen clearly in 4QMMT, מִקְצָת מַעֲשֵׂי הַתּוֹרָה "Some of the precepts of the law". In this fragment the teacher of righteousness writes to his opponent in Jerusalem: he says that he has

C 26 . . . written 27 a part of the commandments of the law (מקצת מעשי התורה), which we believe to be especially important, for your good (salvation?) and the good (salvation?) of your people (i.e. Israel) (לטוב לך ולעמך).

The teacher of righteousness then wishes that the wicked priest

C 30 . . . finds joy at the end of time in that you find our words correct 31 and that this may be reckoned to you as righteousness (ונחשבה לך לצדקה) when you do the right and

---

"may therefore reflect an increased pessimism and failure of nerve, not to mention an oppressive sense of the sin which must have brought about such a shocking disaster" (*Pauline Christianity*, p. 105). Incidentally, Ziesler believes that Paul anyway was not attacking the sort of Judaism found in these works.

[181] In the following I will be assuming that those of the Qumran community were Essenes. For a defence of this view see G. Vermes, *The Dead Sea Scrolls: Qumran in Perspective*, London: SCM [3]1994, ([1]1977), pp. 111-18.

[182] In my study of repentance in ancient Judaism, Qumran was one of the exceptions to the general rule that repentance was seen as a meritorious work (see Bell, "Teshubah", 34).

[183] See 1QS 11.7-8: "To those whom God has selected he has given them as everlasting possession; until they inherit them in the lot of the holy ones. 8 He unites their assembly to the sons of the heavens in order (to form) the counsel of the Community and a foundation of the building of holiness to be an everlasting plantation throughout all future ages" (Martínez, *Dead Sea Scrolls*, p. 18).

[184] 1QS 3.6ff; 1QpHab 8.1-3.

[185] 1QS 5.1 (Martínez, *Dead Sea Scrolls*, p. 8).

the good before God (בעשותך הישר והטוב) for your good (salvation?) (טוב) and 32 the good (salvation?) of your people.

Parts of this translation, which is based on that of H. Stegemann, may be disputed. Compare the translation given by Qimron and Strugnell:

C 26 We have (indeed) sent you 27 some of the precepts of the Torah according to our decision, for your welfare and the welfare of your people. For we have seen (that) 28 you have wisdom and knowledge of the Torah. Consider all these things and ask Him that He strengthen 29 your will and remove from you the plans of evil and the device of Belial 30 so that you may rejoice at the end of time, finding that some of our practices are correct. 31 And this will be counted as a virtuous deed of yours, since you will be doing what is righteous and good in His eyes, for your own welfare and 32 for the welfare of Israel.[186]

The key difference in the translations is whether טוב is to be understood as "salvation" or as "welfare". In favour of "salvation" is the fact that the text is clearly concerned with the last things, i.e. finding "joy at the end of time". Also this טוב is related to צדקה, which can mean very much the same as salvation in various texts in the Psalms and Deutero-Isaiah.[187] But in favour of Qimron and Strugnell is that the noun טוב can mean "welfare" in the Hebrew Bible. I have found no other texts where טוב unequivocely means salvation. But in Sifre Zutta on Num. 10.32 טוב can mean the reward of the righteous.[188] Perhaps the wisest translation for טוב is simply "good",[189] but in view of the eschatological emphasis in the passage, I would favour the interpretation "salvation" rather than "welfare". Note that although the idea

---

[186] E. Qimron and J. Strugnell (ed.), *Discoveries in the Judaean Desert X: Qumran Cave 4, V: Miqṣat Ma'aśe Ha-Torah* (DJD 10), Oxford: OUP 1994, p. 63.

[187] See Bell, *No one seeks for God*, p. 1 n. 2. Note also the translation I have given for 4QMMT above: "reckoned to you as righteousness". Cf. Rom. 4.3: "For what does the scripture say? 'Abraham believed God, and it was reckoned to him as righteousness'" (τί γὰρ ἡ γραφὴ λέγει; Ἐπίστευσεν δὲ Ἀβραὰμ τῷ θεῷ καὶ ἐλογίσθη αὐτῷ εἰς δικαιοσύνην). Paul quotes Gen. 15.6. The Hebrew is :וְהֶאֱמִן בַּיהוָה וַיַּחְשְׁבֶהָ לּוֹ צְדָקָה. Cf. ונחשבה לך לצדקה of 4QMMT.

[188] See the translation of F. Avemarie, *Tora und Leben: Untersuchungen zur Heilsbedeutung der Tora in der frühen rabbinischen Literatur* (TSAJ 55), Tübingen: J.C.B. Mohr (Paul Siebeck) 1996, p. 531: "'Und wenn du mit uns gehst, dann (werden wir) dies Gute, (das uns der Herr erweisen wird, auch dir erweisen.)' . . . Eine andere Auslegung: Das 'Gute' ist die Belohnung der Gerechten, denn es heißt: 'Wie groß ist dein Gutes, das du denen aufbewahrt hast, die dich fürchten!' (Ps 31,20). – Er verhieß ihm, daß seine Kinder an alledem Anteil hätten".

[189] Qimron and Strugnell, *Miqṣat Ma'aśe Ha-Torah*, p. 84, compare טוב in C27, 31-32, to Dt. 6.24.

of resurrection itself is not common in the Essene texts from Qumran, nevertheless the idea does exist that there is salvation after death.[190]

If I am right in interpreting טוב as salvation, there is a strong parallel to what I believe is the emphasis in Paul's use of ἔργα νόμου: the relation of such works to salvation at the final judgement (a Jewish view which Paul rejects, e.g. Rom. 3.20). But whether the idea in 4QMMT C27, 32, is "salvation" or "welfare", it seems clear that the "precepts of the law" here involve the whole torah. Note, however, that here the idea is not so much the works as actually done (as in Paul), but the demands of the law.[191]

---

[190] See H. Lichtenberger, "Auferstehung in den Qumranfunden", in F. Avemarie and H. Lichtenberger (ed.), *Auferstehung – Resurrection* (WUNT 135), Tübingen: J.C.B. Mohr (Paul Siebeck) 2001, 91 (79-91): "Der Tenor der Texte . . . läßt keinen Zweifel daran, daß die qumran-essenische Gemeinschaft auch über den Tod des einzelnen hinaus an eine Teilhabe am Heil glaubte, auch wenn sie dies nicht mit dem Gedanken der leiblichen Auferstehung von den Toten in Verbindung brachte". The expression which may point to a future salvation in MMT is "at the end of time". Note, however, that the Hebrew term is באחרית העת (C30). A. Steudel, *Der Midrasch zur Eschatologie aus der Qumrangemeinde (4QMidrEschat*[a.b]*)* (STDJ 13), Leiden/New York/Köln: E.J. Brill 1994, p. 163, argues that the term אחרית הימים, often taken as a synomyn for אחרית העת (Qimron and Strugnell, *Miqṣat Ma'aśe Ha-Torah*, p. 63 n. 30), refers not to a time of salvation but the time immediately before. "אחרית הימים meint in 4QMidrEschat – wie in Qumran überhaupt – *nicht* Heilszeit, *auch nicht* ein *punkuelles* Ende der Geschichte; auch ist *nicht* 'Zukunft' damit gemeint, wie es von neueren Übersetzungen vorgeschlagen wird. Sondern אחרית הימים meint eine begrenzte Zeitspanne, nämlich die letzte Zeitepoche der von Gott vorhergeplanten in Perioden ablaufenden Geschichte" (Steudel's emphasis). Therefore she translates the phrase אחרית הימים "die letzte Zeitepoche". Even if אחרית העת carries the same sense, it is still nevertheless clear that righteousness/salvation is dependent on the performance in doing works of law.

[191] This point was made in one of the first works which compared Galatians with 4QMMT, H.-W. Kuhn, "Die Bedeutung der Qumrantexte für das Verständnis des Galaterbriefs", in G.J. Brooke (ed.), *New Qumran Texts and Studies: Proceedings of the First Meeting of the International Orgnization for Qumran Studies, Paris 1992* (STDJ 15), Leiden/New York/Köln: E.J. Brill 1994, 174-75 (169-221). But contrast M. Bachmann, "4QMMT und Galaterbrief, מעשי התורה und ΕΡΓΑ ΝΟΜΟΥ", *ZNW* 89 (1998) 99-113 (91-113), who argues that ἔργα νόμου in Paul is best understood, as in 4QMMT, as "Regelungen des Gesetzes" or "Halakhot" (100). On the other hand, J.D.G. Dunn, "4QMMT and Galatians", *NTS* 43 (1997) 150 (147-53) believes Galatians and 4QMMT have similar understandings but מעשי התורה should not be understood as "precepts of the Torah" but as "works of the Torah". Qimron and Strugnell, *Miqṣat Ma'aśe Ha-Torah*, p. 139, note that in MMT laws are not referred to as מצוות but rather מעשים (B2) and מעשי התורה (C27). They also note that the singular מעשה is used in Ex. 18.20 to refer to law in general; it is only from the second temple period and onwards that the plural מעשים is commonly used for commands of the bible.

2.4. Josephus

Traditionally, Josephus has been taken to be a Pharisee.[192] It has been largely assumed that *Vita* 12b refers to Josephus' "conversion" to the Pharisees: ἐννεακαιδέκατον δ᾽ ἔτος ἔχων ἠρξάμην [τε] πολιτεύεσθαι τῇ Φαρισαίων αἱρέσει κατακολουθῶν, ἣ παραπλήσιός ἐστι τῇ παρ᾽ Ἕλλησι Στωικῇ λεγομένῃ. So Thackeray translates this passage as: "Being now in my nineteenth year I began to govern my life by the rules of the Pharisees, a sect having points of resemblance to that which the Greeks call the Stoic school".[193] Some have doubted whether Josephus actually became a Pharisee at that age.[194] Mason is much more radical in claiming that "Josephus was not, and never claimed to be, a Pharisee. He was an aristocratic priest . . ."[195] Mason argues that πολιτεύεσθαι does not mean "to conduct oneself"; rather it has to be understood as "take part in public life".[196] How did he take part in public life? By "following the Pharisaic school" (τῇ Φαρισαίων αἱρέσει κατακολουθῶν). According to Mason, the point Josephus makes is not that he joined the Pharisaic party but rather that he used the Pharisaic party as a stepping stone for his public career. If Josephus were not a member of the Pharisaic sect, the problem that he is negative towards the Pharisees may be solved.

Mason has received some support for his position[197] but it is by no means compelling. Mason's translation of πολιτεύεσθαι may well be right.[198] But this does not exclude Josephus actually *becoming* a Pharisee. Perhaps he became one because he saw that his ambitions would be better served with this group since they were popular with the people.[199] Further Mason argues

---

[192] For a recent defence of Josephus' Pharisaic allegiance, see T. Rajak, *Josephus: The Historian and His Society*, London: Duckworth 1983, pp. 30-34.

[193] Josephus (LCL) 1:7.

[194] See S.J.D. Cohen, *Josephus in Galilee and Rome: His Vita and Development as a Historian* (CSCT 8), Leiden: E.J. Brill 1979, p. 107. Hengel, *Zealots*, p. 371 n. 286, also doubts the veracity of *Vita* 12b, although he believes it natural that after the war Josephus would join the Pharisees as the only surviving party and therefore would be writing his works as a Pharisee.

[195] Mason, *Josephus*, p. 374.

[196] Mason, *Josephus*, pp. 347-49.

[197] See, e.g., the review by N.L. Collins in *NovT* 34 (1992) 303-7.

[198] Mason points to the various German translations which understand ἠρξάμην πολιτεύεσθαι as Josephus' entry into public life.

[199] Cf. L.H. Feldman, "Josephus", *ABD* 3:982 (981-998).

that just because Josephus "followed" the Pharisees does not mean he *became* one. He gives the parallel of the Sadducees that "whenever they come in a position of leadership, they defer, albeit unwillingly and by necessity (ἀκουσίως . . . καὶ κατ' ἀνάγκας), to what the Pharisee says, because otherwise they would become intolerable to the masses" (*Antiquitates* 18.17). And, he argues, if they "defer" to the Pharisees yet remain "relentless opponents", then Josephus, in "following" the Pharisaic school, does not necessarily become a Pharisee either.[200] But a little earlier Josephus makes it clear that he has something very specific in mind with Sadducees deferring to Pharisees. For the Pharisees are "extremely influential among the townsfolk; and all prayers and sacred rites of divine worship are performed according to their exposition" (*Antiquitates* 18.15).[201] And, of course, they defer "unwillingly". There is nothing in the text of *Vita* 12b to suggest that Josephus was doing anything analogous.

I shall therefore work with the assumption that Josephus was a Pharisee; and if this assumption is correct, he is the only other Pharisee known to us by name apart from Paul to leave written material.[202] And we find in his writings a theology which can legitimately be called a "merit theology". At the beginning of *Antiquitates* he writes:

. . . the main lesson to be learnt from this history by any who care to peruse it is that men who conform to the will of God, and do not venture to transgress laws that have been excellently laid down, prosper in all things beyond belief, and for their reward are offered by God felicity; whereas in proportion as they depart from the strict observance of these laws, things (else) practicable become impracticable, and whatever imaginary good thing they strive to do ends in irretrievable disasters.[203]

It may be objected that if this is called merit theology, it is precisely what one finds in parts of the Old Testament. Does not Dt. 28 speak of blessings and cursings? Does not Proverbs teach that those who do God's will prosper? To some extent that may be true but one has to bear in mind that the Old Testament presents a spectrum of views, and passages like Dt. 28

---

[200] Mason, *Josephus*, p. 354.

[201] Cf. Deines, *Pharisäer*, p. 53 n. 34.

[202] A.J. Saldarini, *Pharisees, Scribes & Sadducees in Palestinian Society*, Edinburgh: T.& T. Clark, p. 134: "Paul is the only person besides Josephus whose claim to be a Pharisee is preserved".

[203] *Antiquitates* 1.14 (Josephus (LCL), 4:9).

and the book of Proverbs are at one end of it.[204] Josephus, however, writes a fairly consistent history of the Jews based on this merit theology. He even develops the idea of a treasury of merits. So Josephus considerably expands the speech of Abijah in 2 Chr. 13.4b-12 in *Antiquitates* 8.276-81. Abijah says that Rehoboam should have been forgiven:

... for the sake of his father Solomon and the benefits you have received from him. For the merits of the fathers should be a palliation of the sins of their children.[205]

This is not in the original speech of 2 Chr. 13.4b-12. Linked with such a theology which stresses merit is boasting in one's achievement. So Moses says regarding God's choice of Aaron to be high priest:

For my part, had the weighing of this matter been entrusted to me, I should have adjudged myself worthy of the dignity, alike from that self-love that is innate in all, as also because I am conscious of having laboured abundantly for your salvation. But now God himself has judged Aaron worthy of this honour and has chosen him to be priest, knowing him to be the most deserving among us.

Again this is not to be found in the Old Testament. Carson writes that in view of this, "it is not surprising that there is nothing of gracious election in Josephus, and little enough of any kind of election".[206] God does show favour to Israel but this seems to depend on the merits of the Patriarchs.[207] One could make the point that Josephus may play down election for diplomatic reasons: his Roman audience may see election as an expression of Jewish nationalism. However, this is an unlikely explanation. Josephus was proud of his nation.

2.5. Philo

Sanders quotes from Philo's *De specialibus legibus* 1.303 to prove his point that Philo can be seen in terms of covenantal nomism:[208]

---

[204] But, as we have seen, Deuteronomy also speaks of God's grace as in Dt. 7.7-8.

[205] *Antiquities* 8.278 (Josephus (LCL), 5:721).

[206] Carson, *Divine Sovereignty*, p. 113.

[207] Josephus' "Patriarchal narratives" stress the meritorious religious achievement of the Fathers (see, for example, *Antiquitates* 1:222-36, on the binding of Isaac where the piety (θρησκεία) of both Abraham and Isaac is emphasized). See R.J. Daly, "The Soteriological Significance of the Sacrifice of Isaac", *CBQ* 39 (1977) 45-75, who describes the Aqedah in Josephus as "highly moralizing" (57) and serving to emphasize the "meritorious religious achievement of Abraham and Isaac" (59).

[208] See Sanders, *Practice*, p. 263.

Yet out of the whole human race He chose as of special merit and judged worthy of preeminence over all, those who are in a true sense men, and called them to the service of Himself, the perennial fountain of things excellent . . .[209]

But again one has to ask what concept of "election" is used here. The text is clear that God chose those who merited it. Again, we have synergism, not grace.[210] One reason for this was clearly a theological position which, as we have seen, was prevalant. Further, for a Graeco-Roman audience, praising virtue and merit was normal whereas election and grace were irrational.

There is much more one can say about Philo but since Philo's Judaism is quite different to that of the pre-Christian Paul[211] I will move on to the Rabbinic literature which presents special problems.

2.6. Rabbinic literature

Of all the Jewish strands, Rabbinic literature and the Judaism it represents is the most difficult to assess. It is difficult for a number of reasons. First, it is often difficult to date the material. Much of the material is considerably later than Paul and there is the question of whether a particular view can be extrapolated back into the first century particularly, before 70 AD.[212] Secondly, the material often seems contradictory. Not only does one find the approach "Rabbi A said this; Rabbi B said this", but within a particular

---

[209] Philo (LCL), 7:275.

[210] I. Abrahams, *Studies in Pharisaism and the Gospels, First Series*, Cambridge: CUP 1917, p. 146, argues that Philo, like other Jewish writers, has "something like the *synergism* of Erasmus, which as his opponent saw was radically opposed to the Pauline theory of grace". Regarding Philo he points to *De exsecrationibus* 164 (435), which concerns how "[r]epentance and confession lead to grace" (Abrahams, *Studies*, p. 146; see Philo (LCL), 8:417). This text is perhaps not so striking as 152 (433) which moralizes Dt. 28.43: "The proselyte exalted aloft by his happy lot will be gazed at from all sides, marvelled at and held blessed by all for two things of highest excellence, that he came over to the camp of God and that he has won a prize best suited to his merits, a place in heaven firmly fixed, greater than words dare describe . . ." (Philo (LCL), 8:409). Note that *De exsecrationibus* (Περὶ ἀρῶν) is often viewed as attached to the "Exposition" of *De praemiis et poenis* as a sort of epilogue (see Schürer/Vermes et al., *Jewish people*, 3.2:853-54). E.R. Goodenough, "Philo's Exposition of the Law and his De Vita Mosis", *HTR* 27 (1933) 118-25 (109-25), regarded it as separate work.

[211] As pointed out in chapter 1 above, Philo was a thoroughly hellenized Jew.

[212] On the problem of determining "Pharisaic teaching" before 70 AD, see Hengel, *Pre-Christian Paul*, pp. 42-45.

work and in neighbouring statements there are contradictions.[213] Thirdly, there is such a vast amount of material to consider.

At this point I ought to pause for a moment for in speaking of salvation in Rabbinic Judaism I am perhaps guilty of imposing a Christian concept on Jewish literature. It must first be stressed that the importance (or lack of importance) of salvation cannot be established by a simple word study. For example, it is true that the verb "save" (ישׁע) and its cognates occur seldom in the Rabbinic writings.[214] But this in itself proves little and one must also consider the possiblity that the Christian use of the name "Jesus" (ישׁוע) discouraged Rabbinic use.[215] Compared to "save", the terms "redeem" and "redeemer" occur more often and usually refer to the exodus from Egypt and the final salvation of Israel.[216] But if there is any single term in Rabbinic literature which corresponds to Christian "salvation", it is "life" (חיים).[217] But again searching for the *word* is not always the right way to proceed. A more appropriate way is to look for the *idea*. So Moore, for example, points out that "a lot in the World to Come" is the "nearest approximation in rabbinical Judaism to the Pauline and Christian idea of salvation, or eternal life".[218] As we shall see the idea is certainly there and it is appropriate to speak of "salvation" in Rabbinic Judaism; indeed Avemarie argues that it is especially appropriate because it does not limit the discussion to any particular linguistic terms.[219]

I have already indicated earlier in this chapter that Sanders is highly critical of the traditional Lutheran understanding of Judaism as a religion of works-righteousness. His work has for some scholars produced something like a revolution. Although Sanders presents a special synthesis regarding "covenant" and "nomism", 50 years before Sanders' book on *Paul and Palestinian Judaism* G.F. Moore had stressed the electing grace of God found in the tannaitic literature. So Moore writes that Israel's salvation

---

[213] See Aboth 1.3 and Aboth 2.1 (see Avemarie, *Tora und Leben*, p. 578).

[214] Avemarie, *Tora und Leben*, pp. 1-2. Avemarie gives an overview of the occurrences on p. 1 n. 5.

[215] Avemarie, *Tora und Leben*, p. 2 n. 6, who acknowledges M. Hengel for this insight.

[216] Avemarie, *Tora und Leben*, p. 2.

[217] Avemarie, *Tora und Leben*, p. 2.

[218] Moore, *Judaism*, 2:94.

[219] Avemarie, *Tora und Leben*, p. 3.

depends simply on the fact that they are chosen by God. Moore writes that a part in the "World to Come"

> . . . is ultimately assured to every Israelite on the ground of the original election of the people by the free grace of God, prompted not by its merits, collective or individual, but solely by God's love, a love that began with the Fathers.[220]

One of the problems with such an approach is that there are many texts which contradict it and which affirm the key rôle of good works in gaining salvation. One can approach the issue of "works" in two ways: firstly by examining more closely the Rabbinic idea of "election"; secondly by examining the rôle works themselves play in salvation.

Turning to the issue of election, it needs first to be stressed that there are cases where someone can enter the "World to Come" without being "elected" by God. Here we have the case of the proselyte and the righteous Gentile. In the case of a proselyte, there is no election at all. He simply enters the covenant voluntarily.[221] In the case of righteous Gentiles, there was the view that they also can enter the "World to Come". I have discussed this issue elsewhere together with some Rabbinic texts[222] but I add another example, that of "Antoninus".[223] He is reported to ask R. Judah ha-Nasi:

> 'Shall I enter the world to come?' 'Yes!' said Rabbi. 'But,' said Antoninus, 'is it not written, *There will be no remnant to the house of Esau?*' 'That,' he replied, 'applies only to those whose evil deeds are like to those of Esau.' We have learnt likewise: *There will be no remnant to the House of Esau*, might have been taken to apply to all, therefore Scripture says distinctly – *To the house of Esau*, so as to make it apply only to those who act as Esau did.[224]

Such cases are important since they point to the fact that the Rabbis can work with an idea of salvation by works without bringing in ideas of election.[225]

---

[220] Moore, *Judaism*, 2:94-95. Cf. *Judaism*, 2:319.

[221] As Sanders, *Paul and Palestinian Judaism*, pp. 206-8, recognizes.

[222] See Bell, *No one seeks for God*, pp. 181-82.

[223] The identity of this Antonine emperor is unclear. Many identify him with Marcus Aurelius (I. Epstein, *Judaism: A Historical Presentation*, Harmondsworth: Penguin 1977 (repr.), (¹1959), p. 121).

[224] b. Abod. Zar. 10b, discussed by F. Avemarie, "Erwählung und Vergeltung. Zur optionalen Struktur rabbinischer Soteriologie", *NTS* 45 (1999) 116-17 (108-26).

[225] See Avemarie, "Erwählung und Vergeltung", 115.

But even in the election of Israel, the Rabbis demonstrate a considerable degree of synergism.[226] According to Sanders,[227] the Rabbis gave three reasons why God chose Israel: (i) God offered the covenant and law to all nations but only Israel accepted it; (ii) God chose Israel because he found some merit either in the Patriarchs or in the exodus generation or in a future generation; (iii) God chose Israel for his own name's sake. Even if these are the reasons for choosing Israel (I will argue that the election of Israel is *not* in fact important in the Rabbinic literature), there is considerable synergism, and only the third could possibly be compared to the election of Christians as understood by Paul.

But on close attention, it is seen that the texts which Sanders discusses *do not concern the election of Israel*. Concerning the first of the above explanations, the Rabbis do not ask why God chose Israel; rather, they ask why Israel has the Torah and the other nations do not. In the text that Sanders quotes, Mek. Ex. 19.2 (Baḥodesh 1),[228] the word or concept of election does not appear. The same can be said of the other texts quoted to support explanation (i). In fact a number of texts that Sanders quotes to support a teaching on election, mostly from Mekhilta Exodus,[229] deal with the question of why God delivered Israel out of Egypt or more specifically why he divided the Red Sea although Sanders in his commentary constantly speaks of "election".[230] Sanders' key word "covenant" does occur in one text where Sanders discusses explanation (ii) (Lev. R. 28.6). But here covenant (בְּרִית), as is often the case in Rabbinic literature, means "commandment" and has no connection with election.[231] Should Sanders' basic concept of "covenan-

---

[226] See, for example, the discussion on Sifre Deuteronomy in chapter 7 of Bell, *Provoked to Jealousy*.

[227] Sanders, *Paul and Palestinian Judaism*, pp. 87-101.

[228] Lauterbach, *Mekilta de-Rabbi Ishmael*, 2:198-200.

[229] See Mek. Ex. Pisḥa 5 (to 12.6), 16 (to 13.4); Mek. Ex. Beshallaḥ 3 (to 14.15), 6 (to 14.31); Mek. Ex. Simeon b. Yoḥai to Ex. 6.2; Ex. R. 15.4.

[230] On this point see Avemarie, *Tora und Leben*, p. 42: "Diese Texte erörtern, wie gesagt, Gründe für das Exoduswunder; von 'God's choosing of Israel', wie Sanders wiederholt insinuiert (89, 91; vgl. 90, 92), handeln sie nicht". The covenant with Israel, of course, precedes the exodus.

[231] "And which covenant is it? The commandment of the sheaf", as quoted in Sanders, *Paul and Palestinian Judaism*, p. 93. Note, however, that F. Avemarie, "Bund als Gabe und Recht", in F. Avemarie and H. Lichtenberger (ed.), *Bund und Tora: Zur theologischen Begriffsgeschichte in alttestamentlicher, frühjüdischer und urchristlicher Tradi-*

tal nomism"[232] be expressed as "nomistic nomism"?[233] Another possible meaning of בְּרִית is circumcision. The text of Sifra Nedabah parasha 2.3 (commenting on Lev. 1.2), quoted by Sanders,[234] makes perfect sense if בְּרִית is translated as circumcision.[235] In fact there is only one text quoted by Sanders where "covenant" in Sanders' sense is actually found, namely Sifre Zutta: "He will keep with you the covenant of your fathers".[236]

Although the words election and covenant are not common in Rabbinic Judaism the *idea* of the covenant with Israel is there[237] but, as I have already stressed, there is considerable synergism. Also, if the discussion is taken back to Abraham (and this would be entirely appropriate since any stress in the Rabbinic literature on "covenant" is found with Abraham)[238], one has to

---

tion (WUNT 92), Tübingen: J.C.B. Mohr (Paul Siebeck) 1996, 211 (163-216), finds a variety of nuances for the term ברית: "Der Vielzahl von Bünden, von denen schon in der Schrift die Rede ist, entspricht es, daß der Bundesbegriff der rabbinischen Überlieferung eine Fülle möglicher Bedeutungsgehalte auf sich vereinigt, die je nach Zusammenhang in ganz verschiedenen Betonungen und Kombinationen zur Geltung gebracht werden können".

[232] E.g. Sanders, *Paul and Palestinian Judaism*, p. 427.

[233] Cf. Stuhlmacher, *Biblische Theologie*, 1:255, who regards "covenantal nomism" as a tautology. For a different view see Avemarie, "Bund als Gabe und Recht", 215 n. 275.

[234] Sanders, *Paul and Palestinian Judaism*, p. 84: "Just as [native-born] Israelites accept the covenant, also the proselytes accept the covenant. Apostates are excluded since they do not accept the covenant".

[235] Cf. Avemarie, "Bund als Gabe und Recht", 199-200. Avemarie's translation brings out the Hebrew participle: "'Wie die Kinder Israels Annehmende des Bundes (מקבלי ברית) sind, so sind auch die Proselyten Annehmende des Bundes. Ausgeschlossen sind die Apostaten, die nicht Annehmende des Bundes sind" (199). He suggests that "Bund" refers not to the "Sinaibund" but rather "Beschneidung". Note that although Sanders, *Palestinian Judaism*, p. 84, translates ברית as "covenant", he does recognize that the expression later on which he has translated as "broken the covenant" may refer to effacing circumcision.

[236] Quoted in Sanders, *Paul and Palestinian Judaism*, p. 105. Avemarie, *Tora und Leben*, p. 41, comments: "Es ist möglich, daß hierin eine Bundestheologie in nuce liegt; ein 'Bundesnomismus' aber wohl kaum, denn von der Tora, vom Gehorsam, von der Intention, von Sühne und von Reue ist hier nicht die Rede".

[237] A similar phenomenon occurs regarding the Old Testament itself. So ברית may not mean "covenant" but the idea is certainly there that Yahweh has done something for Israel (e.g. Ex. 20.2).

[238] See Avemarie, "Bund als Gabe und Recht", 191-96.

ask why God chose Abraham.[239] A concept which frequently occurs in the Rabbinic literature is the idea of the merits of the Fathers.[240] So, for example, Lev. R. 29.7, referring explicitly to the day of solemn rest on the first day of the seventh month (i.e. the New Year, Lev. 23.24), tells Israel to recall the merit of the Patriarchs.[241] Lev. R. 36.2 says that "As the vine is propped up by dry stakes and is itself fresh, so Israel rely upon the merit of their forefathers, although these are asleep. Hence it is written, 'Then will I remember my covenant with Jacob'".[242] Gen. R. 56.2 is striking in that Abraham, Israel (in Egypt) and Hannah and others are rewarded for worshipping![243] So "the Torah was given only as a reward for worshipping" and "the dead will come to life again only as a reward for worshipping".[244] Merit is found not only in Abraham but also in Isaac[245] and Jacob.[246] It is worth considering the fact that in contrast to this Rabbinic view, the Patriarchs in Genesis are generally not portrayed as righteous.[247] In fact Jacob is portrayed as a scoundrel. The power of these Patriarchal narratives

---

[239] See Avemarie, "Bund als Gabe und Recht", 191-96.

[240] See E.E. Urbach, *The Sages - Their Concepts and Beliefs* ET, 2 vols, Jerusalem: Magnes Press, Hebrew University 1975, pp. 497-99, on the importance of the merits of the Fathers.

[241] Lev. R. 29.7: "And when are you to recall the merit of the Patriarchs and be acquitted in judgment? 'In the seventh month'" (J. Israelstam and J.J. Slotki (ed.), *Midrash Rabbah: Leviticus*, London/New York: Soncino ³1983, p. 375). See Urbach, *Sages*, pp. 504-5.

[242] Israelstam and Slotki, *Leviticus*, p. 459.

[243] H. Freedman (ed.), *Midrash Rabbah: Genesis*, 2 vols, London/New York: Soncino ³1983, 1:492-93.

[244] Freedman, *Genesis*, 1:492-93.

[245] So in the binding of Isaac, not only did Abraham earn merit but also Isaac in allowing himself to be sacrificed. See Urbach, *Sages*, p. 502, who points out that Isaac becomes the centre of the story.

[246] Note also that the merits of later generations can help earlier generations. See Midr. Ps. 114.5 (W.G. Braude, *The Midrash on the Psalms* (YJS 13), 2 vols, New Haven: Yale University Press 1959, 2:217-18): "Another comment on 'When Israel came forth out of Egypt': Through what merit did the children of Israel come forth out of Egypt? . . . Through the merit of Hananiah, Mishael, and Azariah . . . Through the merit of the generation of Isaiah . . ."

[247] The stories concerned with Abraham's obedience to God are exceptions (see Gen. 12.4a; 22.1-14).

lies in the fact that despite their shortcomings, God chose Abraham, Isaac and Jacob.[248] Later Judaism, however, was to whitewash them.[249]

Having looked at election I turn to the second issue, the rôle of works themselves in salvation. Here the question of "falling away" is of central importance. In many of the texts it seems easy to fall away from salvation.[250] So even working on Sanders' premises that works keep you "in" it seems that if you do not produce the works you will be excluded from salvation.[251] If that is the case the value of the "election" seems to be seriously relativized.

Is it then the case that the view put forward by Weber and Billerbeck is correct after all? There is little doubt in my mind that the view of these scholars is supported by a number of texts. But it is not the whole truth. So Avemarie concludes:

Unhaltbar ist . . . die Grundthese des Systems von Weber und Billerbeck, daß Israel die Gebote *nur* dazu empfangen habe, um sich durch ihre Erfüllung Verdienste zu verschaffen und damit die Teilhabe am ewigen Leben zu sichern.[252]

Avemarie points to texts which have little interest in obeying the Torah as a means to salvation:

Gelegentlich aber bleiben Gebot, Forderung und Gehorsam beiseite, die Tora erscheint nicht als Weg und Mittel, sondern als das begehrte Gut selbst – ein Gut, das Israel längst zuteil geworden ist, mit dem Gott es vor allen Völkern ausgezeichnet hat, dessen es sich in unmittelbarer Gewißheit freuen und rühmen darf und das ihm als sein Erbe ewig unveräußerlich bleiben wird.[253]

But such texts do not occur frequently in Rabbinic literature (just as texts that express the view that God chose Israel simply because he loves Israel do not occur frequently). Nevertheless, one can say that the view of Weber and Billerbeck is onesided. But equally onesided is the approach of Moore:

---

[248] Conversely, those who seem to be righteous (e.g. Hagar) are rejected. One of the remarkable things about the Patriarchal narratives is that there is no theological comment on the fact that God has chosen the unrighteous.

[249] For example a number of texts stress that if the Patriarchs did sin they did so in ignorance. So T. Jud. 19.3-4 stresses that Judah "acted in ignorance". T. Zeb. has Zebulon say: "Nor do I recall having committed a transgression, except what I did to Joseph in ignorance".

[250] See the question of deliberate sins and the scope of repentance discussed below.

[251] On the rôle of sacrifice, repentance and day of atonement, see below section 5.

[252] Avemarie, *Tora und Leben*, p. 581 (my emphasis).

[253] Avemarie, *Tora und Leben*, p. 530 (my emphasis).

Ebenso unhaltbar ist auf der anderen Seite die These G.F.Moores, daß sich die Teilhabe der Israeliten an der kommenden Welt allein darauf gründe, daß sie als Israeliten das erwählte Volk Gottes sind.[254]

But how are these two sides to be synthesized? Avemarie rejects the approach of Sanders. The essence of his argument is that rather than having some overarching scheme of "covenantal nomism" there are Rabbinic texts which speak of "covenant" and others which speak of "nomism". These two views stand side by side and no attempt appears to be made to bring them together.[255] Further, "covenantal nomism" is a misleading term[256] and does not open up the Jewish texts.[257]

I believe that it is difficult to escape the conclusion that Rabbinic Judaism was a religion of salvation by works (even if there are elements of God's election of Israel). And in the discussion below (sections 4, 5 and 6) I will argue that Rabbinic Judaism can be described as a religion of "works-righteousness". The question though is whether we can extrapolate back from Rabbinic writings (the earliest being the Mishnah, 200 AD) to the time of Paul. Some of the tradition in these texts clearly goes back to Paul's time, although deciding what is early tradition is not always easy. One simply cannot assume that something ascribed to a certain Rabbi (say a near contemporary of Paul such as Gamaliel I or his son Simon) is accurately ascribed. One also has to reckon with the possibility that the anonymous traditions of the Mishnah (i.e. that which was accepted without question) is actually early, as Hengel and Deines have suggested.[258] But despite these problems of methodology, I think one can say with some confidence that the Pharisaism to which Paul belonged did believe in salvation by works and his

---

[254] Avemarie, *Tora und Leben*, p. 582.

[255] See Avemarie, *Tora und Leben* and Seifrid, *Christ our Righteousness*, who has built upon Avemarie's work. For a useful overview of Seifrid's view, see "The 'New Perspective on Paul' and Its Problems".

[256] See the definition given above, section 1.

[257] Cf. the comments of O. Hofius in M. Hengel and U. Heckel (ed.), *Paulus und das antike Judentum: Tübingen-Durham-Symposium im Gedenken an den 50. Todestag Adolf Schlatters* (WUNT 58), Tübingen: J.C.B. Mohr (Paul Siebeck) 1991, 314: "O. HOFIUS bezweifelt, daß der Begriff 'Bundesnomismus' ein für die Erschließung frühjüdischer Texte sinnvoller und für die Paulus-Exegese brauchbarer Begriff sei".

[258] Hengel and Deines, "E.P. Sanders' 'Common Judaism', Jesus, and the Pharisees", 14.

religion, like that of the Rabbis after 70 AD, can be legitimately described as one of "works-righteousness".

3. Conclusions concerning Salvation in Early Judaism

To conclude the discussion so far on Judaism, I believe that all strands of Judaism at about the time of Paul supported salvation by works and to this extent the religion of the Jews can be called a religion of works-righteousness.[259] This is not to deny that there were different forms of Judaism in the first century AD. Indeed rather than speaking of a harmonious 'Common Judaism' (essentially a common denominator) as Sanders does (or to go to the other extreme and speak of diverse Judaisms), it is more appropriate to speak of "complex Judaism".[260] But all the strands of Judaism I have studied show that salvation was to a large extent by works.

In the above discussion I have considered texts which are roughly contemporary with Paul (written in the period 200 BC to 100 AD) and I have considered the Rabbinic literature (dated 200 AD onwards), considering how the "soteriology" can be traced back to Paul. Another possible approach is to view salvation from the "Old Testament"[261] onwards, thereby giving a different perspective on the issues. The pervasive view among Old Testament scholars is that once a written law was in existence (i.e. the law of the Pentateuch) Israel's religion became less spontaneous and more "fossilized" and "legalistic". Such a view goes back to Wellhausen. Once a documentary hypothesis of the Pentateuch had developed with the "prophets" *preceding* the "law" (which took its final form in the post-exilic period), then a development could legitimately be found.[262] So Wellhausen wrote of

---

[259] The other aspect to works-righteousness is legalism and a performance religion. I approach this question in section 6 below ("Legalism, the 'Pious Jew' and Uncertainty of Salvation").

[260] See Hengel and Deines, "E.P. Sanders' 'Common Judaism', Jesus, and the Pharisees", 53.

[261] I here use the "Old Testament" in the sense of the Tanak (the Law, Prophets and Writings) which corresponds in scope to the Protestant Old Testament. On the issue of the canon see chapter 1 section 4.

[262] Note that prior to Wellhausen adherents of the documentary hypothesis believed that J, E and P were early and roughly contemporary. Wellhausen set out to establish that P was not to be dated around 1000 or 900 BC like J or E but was post-exilic, reflecting the age of Ezra and Nehemiah.

Israel's history as beginning as a spontaneous joyful religion but which "degenerated" into a fossilized legalistic religion.[263] Although many Old Testament scholars have not been as extreme as Wellhausen, there is no doubt that nearly all have accepted that once a written law was in existence, Israel's religion was destined to become more legalistic. Consider, for example, Bright's view of the history of Israel. He writes: "The exaltation of the law did not betoken any loss of interest in the cult, but rather resulted in a heightened diligence in its prosecution—after all, the law required it".[264] Concerning the day of atonement he writes:

> Its ritual (Lev., ch. 16), which developed various ancient rites, gave expression to that keen sense of the burden of sin which postexilic Jews felt in a way perhaps impossible for old Israel. The great judgment of the exile, and Israel's present estate, served as a constant reminder of the enormity of transgressing the divine commands and, as heightened concern for the law heightened also the fear of breaking it, produced a deeply felt need for continual expiation".[265]

Likewise, he writes: "The law did not, as once was the case, describe existing practice; it prescribed practice. Though the cult was engaged in joyfully, it was less a spontaneous expression of the national life, more a fulfilling of the law's requirements".[266] Further, with the exaltation of the law in the post-exilic period, there is a tendency "to loosen law from the context of the covenant form in which it originally belonged, and to view it as something eternally existing and immutable".[267] Then Bright goes on to discuss the legalism which entered Judaism in the post-exilic period.[268] A roughly similar approach can be found in the earlier work of Eichrodt[269] and von

---

[263] See J. Wellhausen, *Prolegomena to the History of Ancient Israel* ET, Cleveland/New York: World Publishing Company 1957. Note that J.H. Hayes and F. Prussner, *Old Testament Theology*, London: SCM 1985, p. 140, have misquoted Wellhausen. They write that Wellhausen described Judaism "as 'a mere empty chasm over which one springs from the Old Testament to the New'". But Wellhausen (p. 1) in fact wrote this was the view of "dogmatic theology" and does not share this view himself.

[264] J. Bright, *A History of Israel* (OTL), London: SCM ²1972, (¹1960), p. 437.

[265] Bright, *History of Israel*, p. 437.

[266] Bright, *History of Israel*, p. 438.

[267] Bright, *History of Israel*, p. 442.

[268] Bright, *History of Israel*, p. 444.

[269] See W. Eichrodt, *Theology of the Old Testament* (OTL) ET, 2 vols, London: SCM 1961-67 (*Theologie des Alten Testaments*, 2 vols, Stuttgart: Ehrenfried Klotz Verlag/Göttingen: Vandenhoeck & Ruprecht 1 ⁷1962; 2 ⁴1961, (originally appeared as 3

Rad.[270] An interesting exception to this trend is Gese who, taking a tradition-historical approach, stresses the continuity of the traditions right through into the New Testament period.[271] But although I have the greatest admiration for Gese's biblical theology programme, it is perhaps at its weakest when it does not sufficiently emphasize some of the *discontinuities* between Old and New Testaments.[272]

---

vols, 1 [1]1933; 2 [1]1935; 3 [1]1939)), 2:313: "In later Judaism *fear* forms the basis of the individual's relationship with God. Nevertheless this is a matter not so much of numinous awe as of a rationally justified anxiety in face of the omnipresent and omniscient divine judge, who watches strictly over the fulfilment of his law, and promises his rewards only to impeccable obedience" (Eichrodt's emphasis). Later (2:315) he writes that "a right coexistence of fear and love in the heart of Man is regarded as the normal attitude toward God, fear seeming necessary to guard one from contempt for the Law, while love helps one to overcome the weariness, indeed hatred, inspired by its oppresive burden and compulsion". Such views have their roots in the post-exilic theology. See the whole section "The Personal Relationship with God in the Post-Exilic Period" (2:301-15).

[270] See G. von Rad, *Old Testament Theology* (OTL) ET, 2 vols, London: SCM 1975, 1:91: "What gives Deuteronomy its characteristic stamp is just the very fact that in the directions it gives and the comforts it offers, it refers to the problems raised by a definite moment in Israel's history. But now this flexibility of Jahweh's revelation, allowing it to gear itself to the place and time and condition of the Israel at the time addressed, ceases. The law becomes an absolute entity, unconditionally valid irrespective of time or historical situation. But this made the revelation of the divine commandments something different from what it had been hitherto. This was no longer the helpful directing will of the God who conducted his people through history; rather it is now beginning to become the 'law' in the theological sense of the word. . . . Israel had to serve the commandments. . . . We do not as yet see any legal casuistry proper. But when the law was made absolute, the path to such casuistry, with its intrinsic consequences, had to be followed out".

[271] So on the issue of law, Gese finds continuity between the Old Testament and New Testament ("Das Gesetz", in *Zur biblischen Theologie: Alttestamentliche Vorträge*, Tübingen: J.C.B. Mohr (Paul Siebeck) [3]1989, ([1]1977), 55-84), an approach also adopted by P. Stuhlmacher ("Das Gesetz als Thema biblischer Theologie", in *Versöhnung, Gesetz und Gerechtigkeit: Aufsätze zur biblischen Theologie*, Göttingen: Vandenhoeck & Ruprecht 1981, 136-65).

[272] I will discuss Gese's approach in chapter 8 below. But for now, consider these words: "The gulf supposedly between the Old and New Testaments does not exist traditio-historically at all, and no dubious bridges are needed to span it. There is a difference between the Old and New Testaments insofar as the New Testament represents the goal and end, the *telos* of the path of biblical tradition. . . . There is no opposition in content or in tradition history between the Old Testament and the New Testament. The Old Testament prepares for the New in every respect: the doctrine of the new covenant, the structure of Christology, etc." ("Tradition and Biblical Theology", in D.A. Knight (ed.), *Tradition and Theology in the Old Testament*, London: SPCK 1977, 322 (301-

4. Paul's Response to Salvation by Works in Judaism

So far I have considered Jewish texts. Let us now consider what Paul says about Jewish religion. In my mind there is no doubt that he believed that Judaism was a religion of salvation by works. I argued in chapter 1 that Rom. 2.1-16 is based on Jewish presuppositions. He assumes that the final judgement depends on works (2.6-11, 12-16). But Paul also took an extreme view in that he believed that a perfect obedience to the law was necessary for acquittal at the final judgement. This suggests that Paul was at an extreme position of the Pharisaic spectrum, probably taking a view similar to the "Shammaite" position rather than the "Hillelite". For in Rabbinic Judaism the general view is not that a perfect obedience is necessary; rather, the general view was most probably that there should be a majority of good deeds.[273] Such a view regarding the majority of good deeds is clearly indicated in R. Akiba's saying in Aboth 3.16 (3.15). The text as translated by Danby is: "All is foreseen, but freedom of choice is given; and the world is judged by grace, yet all is according to the excess of works".[274] According to this translation there are two paradoxes. Elsewhere I have suggested that a better translation is: "All is known, and freedom of choice is given; the world is judged by good nature (fairness), and all is according to excess of works".[275] So the text is not saying that God foresees but rather watches, examines, to see what human beings do. Therefore the world is judged by fairness. Aboth 3.16 (3.15) therefore points clearly to the principle of judge-

---

26)). Sometimes there is a continuity of tradition and this is one of the things I established in Paul's use of Dt. 32.1-43 (Bell, *Provoked to Jealousy*, pp. 200-85). But this is not always the case even in the "doctrine of the new covenant" or "the structure of Christology". See, e.g, the discussion of Christology in chapter 10 section 2 below.

[273] Note, however, that even if Paul had taken a more lenient view (say the principle of the majority of works) he would still come to the conclusion that no one will be acquitted since he has such a pessimistic anthropology.

[274] Danby, *Mishnah*, p. 452. הַכֹּל צָפוּי וְהָרְשׁוּת נְתוּנָה: וּבְטוֹב הָעוֹלָם נִדּוֹן: וְהַכֹּל לְפִי רֹב הַמַּעֲשֶׂה.

[275] See Bell, *No one seeks for God*, pp. 241-42.

ment according to the majority of works,[276] and certainly a similar idea is being put forward by R. Eleazar in Aboth 4.22: "And know that everything is according to the reckoning".[277] However, this idea that judgement is according to the majority of works is found in only a few texts. But although this view is not frequently explicitly stated, it may well have been widespread and is reflected in the idea that it is essential to accumulate as many good works as possible. See also Gen. R. 9.9 (on 1.31) which speaks of heaping up fulfilments of the law: "Thus for him who heaps up fulfilments of the law and good works (מסגל במצות ומעשים טובים), Gan Eden is there; but for him who does not heap up fulfilments of the law and good works (מסגל במצות ומעשים טובים) Gehinnom is there".[278]

So it appears that in Rabbinic Judaism, perfect obedience was not generally required. But there was obviously a spectrum of opinion. There may well have been a few Rabbis/Pharisees[279] who regarded virtually perfect obedience as necessary for salvation and one such person was Paul of Tarsus who belonged to the "right wing" of the Rabbinic spectrum.[280]

---

[276] See Avemarie, *Tora und Leben*, p. 39, for a critique of Sanders' treatment of this passage (see Sanders, *Paul and Palestinian Judaism*, p. 139, who can only conclude that "Aboth 3.15 remains enigmatic"). Avemarie suggests that Sanders' problem here is trying to harmonize Aboth 3.15 with y. Kid. 61d and b. Sanh. 81a. In a personal comunication he tells me that S. Safrai, "And All is According to the Majority of Deeds" (Hebrew), *Tarbiz* 53 (1983-84) 33-40, takes the original (though it is weakly attested in the MS tradition) to be "and not according to the majority of deeds".

[277] Danby, *Mishnah*, p. 455.

[278] Translation of G. Bertram, ἔργον, *TDNT* 2:648 (635-55). Cf. Gen. R. 9.10. See also Billerbeck, *Kommentar*, 4:11.

[279] I assume some degree of continuity between the Pharisees before 70 AD and the "Rabbis". But S.J.D. Cohen, "The Significance of Yavneh: Pharisees, Rabbis, and the End of Jewish Sectarianism", *HUCA* 54 (1984) 27-53, argues for discontinuity. P. Schäfer, "Der vorrabbinische Pharisäismus", in M. Hengel and U. Heckel (ed.), *Paulus und das antike Judentum: Tübingen-Durham-Symposium im Gedenken an den 50. Todestag Adolf Schlatters* (WUNT 58), Tübingen: J.C.B. Mohr (Paul Siebeck) 1991, 125-72, has some sympathy for the views of Cohen, especially his criticism of Neusner. However, in the debate, 172-75, M. Hengel argues for continuity. For example he makes the point that according to Josephus, the New Testament and Essene sources the Pharisees were highly influential; in fact their movement was the most influential between the Maccabean revolt and the destruction of Jerusalem. "Where should the Sages of Jabneh find the point of contact to unite the people, if not here?" (173).

[280] Cf. Phil. 3.6.

Compare Gamaliel II[281] who wept when he came to the end of the 13 requirements of Ezek. 18.5-9. He said: "Only he who does all these things shall live, but not merely one of them" (b. Sanh. 81a).[282]

Paul the Christian responded to this Jewish view by affirming that justification is not (and cannot be) through works of law but by grace and through faith. There are a number of texts where Paul discusses this (see, for example, Phil. 3.9; Rom. 3.21-31; Gal. 2.16) and I have elsewhere discussed in some detail Paul's critique of justification by works of law.[283] Paul's view is diametrically opposed to that of Judaism. He had a *sola fide, sola gratia* theology, and this can even be seen in the way he applied this to the salvation of the Jewish people. In this connection it must be stressed that a text such as Rom. 11.29 cannot be used to demonstrate the non-Christian Jewish view of God's grace.[284] This is the view of Paul the Christian Jew. Further, Rom. 11.26 shows that Paul's soteriology differed radically from that of Rabbinic Judaism. According to m. Sanh. 10.1, the Jew is saved by works; according to Paul, the Jew is saved by grace.[285]

---

[281] But note that Paul's teacher was Gamaliel I.

[282] See the similar story in b. Mak. 24a regarding Ps. 15.5b: "he that doeth these things shall never be moved". "Whenever R. Gamaliel came to this passage he used to weep, saying: [Only] one who practised all these shall not be moved; but anyone falling short in any of these [virtues] would be moved!" b. Mak. 24a says that David reduced the 613 commandments to eleven in Ps. 15. Galamiel's words do not exclude occasional disobedience followed by repentance. Rather, they point to the expectation that the main principles of the Torah (as given by Ezekiel and David) would be kept. Note that in both b. Sanh. 81a and b. Mak. 24a the words of Gamaliel are reported in Aramaic whereas the context is Hebrew. Also whereas in b. Sanh. 81a the text commented upon is Ezek. 18.5-9 and Gamaliel's words are followed by a quotation from R. Akiba, in b. Mak. 24a the text is Ps. 15.5b and the response to Gamaliel comes from "his colleagues".

[283] See, e.g., Bell, *No one seeks for God*, pp. 262-73. See also section 6 below.

[284] See Sanders, *Practice*, p. 264, who quotes Rom. 11.28-29 to support the view that "Paul provides excellent evidence of the assumption of a covenantal relationship between God and Israel". He also quotes Rom. 9.4-5. This text *may* parallel a Jewish view, although it would be wrong to jump to any conclusion about "covenantal nomism" (Sanders, *Practice*, p. 264). But in fact no clear parallel has been found in the Jewish literature (see the discussion of this passage in chapter 4 below). Avemarie, *Tora und Leben*, p. 536 n. 29, compares Mekhilta Ex. Amalek/Jethro 2 to Ex. 18.27.

[285] See the discussion in chapters 6 and 7 below.

5. Sacrifice, Repentance and Day of Atonement

It may be objected that all I have said above may seem reasonable based on the texts I have chosen but I have ignored three fundamental aspects of Jewish theology which show God to be gracious: sacrifice, repentance and the day of atonement. Were these not three fundamental ways in which the Israelite could gain forgiveness of sins? So sacrifice would include the sin offering and the burnt offering (including the continual burnt offering, offered every day, morning and evening, in the temple, Ex. 29.38-42; Num. 28.3-8). Although in the Old Testament texts not all sacrifices were explicitly atoning sacrifices, one could make a case that the sacrificial system as a whole was concerned with atonement.[286] Further, there is evidence that certain sacrifices such as the passover lamb later came to be understood as an atoning sacrifice.[287] Then in addition to sacrifice there was repentance,

---

[286] See the discussion of the term λατρεία (Rom. 9.4) in chapter 4 below.

[287] In the biblical texts the passover lamb does not appear to have had an atoning significance and some, like B.H. McLean, "The Absence of an Atoning Sacrifice in Paul's Soteriology", *NTS* 38 (1992) 531-53, have argued that it never became one. However it can be argued that in later tradition the passover was considered an atoning sacrifice. L. Morris, *The Apostolic Preaching of the Cross*, Leicester: IVP ³1965, pp. 130-33, points to various rabbinic texts. "So God said to Israel: 'I am now occupied in judging souls, and I will tell you how I will have pity on you, through the blood of the Passover and the blood of the circumcision, and I will forgive you. . . .'" (Ex. R. 15.12, S.M. Lehrman (ed.), *Midrash Rabbah: Exodus*, London/New York: Soncino ³1983, p. 176). In Num. R. 13.20, Num. 7.46 is quoted. "'One male of the goats for a sin-offering' (Num. 7.46). This was in allusion to the Paschal sacrifice which the Holy One, blessed be He, commanded them to offer from the goats as a token of withdrawal from idolatry." (Num. R. 13.20, J.J. Slotki (ed.), *Midrash Rabbah: Numbers*, 2 vols, London/New York: Soncino ³1983, 2:554). Further in Josephus, *Antiquitates* 2.312 we read that the Israelites in Egypt "in readiness to start, sacrificed, purified the houses with the blood . . .". This, according to Morris, refers to the passover as a purification ritual. See also Pesahim 10.6: "R. Akiba adds: Therefore, O Lord our God and the God of our fathers, bring us in peace to the other set feasts and festivals which are coming to meet us, while we rejoice in the building up of thy city and are joyful in thy worship; and may we eat there of the sacrifices and of the Passover offerings whose blood has reached with acceptance the wall of thy Altar, and let us praise thee for our redemption and for the ransoming of our soul . . . ". These texts suggest that there was some development in the understanding of the passover such that by Jesus' time the passover was seen to have an atoning function. We see this precisely in Jn 1.29, 36.

an important part of Jewish life, whereby God would forgive sins. Then there was the day of atonement which combined sacrifice and repentance.[288]

However, sacrifice, repentance and the day of atonement may not rescue Judaism from being a religion of salvation by works. Why? Because *in Paul's time* it is most likely that these means of atonement were only valid for unwitting sins. I stress *in Paul's time* because it seems that in later texts such as the Mishnah, Tosephta and Palestinian and Babylonian talmuds, a more lenient view had developed alongside the stricter one.[289] So in texts which are roughly contemporary with Paul, i.e. in texts from the Apocrypha, Pseudepigrapha, Dead Sea Scrolls and Josephus, we find a strict view that the sin offering was only valid for unwitting sins. Likewise repentance only seems to be valid for unwitting sins. Why should there be such a difference of view? One reason seems to be that those texts which are especially hard on the "sinner" come from times when there was considerable opposition between the parties.[290] So we find this in Psalms of Solomon,[291] 1 Enoch (especially 91-105),[292] Jubilees,[293] 4 Ezra and 2 Baruch[294] and Qumran

---

[288] Note that although the Ark of the Covenant was lost with the destruction of Solomon's temple, the High Priest entered the Holy of Holies as if the Ark was still there. See Gese, "Sühne", 105.

[289] Elsewhere ("Sin Offerings", 49-52) I pointed out that although we can find a moral rigour associated with the Pharisees in Psalms of Solomon, Gospels, Acts and Josephus, the Rabbinic literature gives a greater variety of views including a more lenient one.

[290] Cf. E. Sjöberg, *Gott und die Sünder im palästinischen Judentum*, Stuttgart/Berlin: W. Kohlhammer 1938, p. 263.

[291] For details of the historical context of these Psalms, see above.

[292] These chapters have been dated to the late Hasmonean period. V. Tcherikover, *Hellenistic Civilisation and the Jews* ET, Philadelphia: JPS 1959, pp. 258-59, sees references in 94-105 to the time of Alexander Jannaeus (104-78) (see 95.7; 96.8; 97.8-10; 98.2; 98.12 (note that the chapter references below 100 on pp. 258-59 are out by 10 – I assume this is a translation error). G.W.E. Nickelsburg, *Resurrection, Immortality, and Eternal Life in Intertestamental Judaism* (HTS 26), Cambridge, Mass.: Harvard University Press 1972, p. 113, also believes a likely historical setting of the chapters is the reign of Alexander Jannaeus (or possibly the later part of the reign of John Hyrcanus (110-105)). R.H. Charles, *The Book of Enoch*, Oxford: Clarendon Press 1893, p. 263, believes the author of 91-104 belongs to the Pharisaic party and dates the section to either 95-79 or 70-64 during which the Pharisees were oppressed by both rulers and Sadducees (p. 264).

[293] Wintermute, *OTP*, 2:46, suggests a dating of Jubilees around 161-40 BC. Jubilees is highly critical of the programme of Hellenisation. Following F.M. Cross, *The Ancient*

texts.[295] This rigorist view is also found in the depiction of the Pharisees in Josephus and in the Gospels and Acts; they tell of a time when they were in conflict with the Sadducees. So in the gospels we see Jesus' conflict with the Pharisees over issues of repentance.[296] Acts stresses the strict nature of the sect of the Pharisees (e.g. 22.3; 26.5) as does Josephus.[297] On the other hand Rabbinic literature seems much more lenient towards "sinners". This was because there was little party strife in the period during which the tradition was committed to writing.

But there is another important point to make as regards repentance. There is a view in Philo, Josephus, and in Apocryphal, Pseudepigraphal and Rabbinic literature that repentance was to a greater or lesser extent seen as a meritorious work. This can be seen in five ways. First, repentance can be linked to outer penitential acts (see T. Reub. 1.9-10, T. Sim. 3.4, T. Jud. 15.4 and LAE 4-10, 17). Secondly, repentance and good works are often

---

Library of Qumran and Modern Biblial Studies, Garden City, New York: Doubleday ²1961, pp. 199-200, he suggests that Jubilees is a product of one of the "proto-Essene (presumably Hasidic) communities".

[294] Although written after 70 AD these two apocalypses reflect the situation in Israel before the fall of Jerusalem. Note that M. Hengel thinks 2 Baruch and 4 Ezra come from Pharisaic scribes ("The Scriptures in Second Temple Judaism", in D.R.G. Beattie and M.J. McNamara (ed.), *The Aramaic Bible: Targums in their Historical Context* (JSOT-Sup 166), Sheffield: JSOT Press 1994, 174 (158-75)). Some, of course, would wish to divorce "rabbinic Judaism" from "apocalyptic". See also the discussion above, section 2.2.

[295] The sectaries of Qumran believed that they alone ("the penitents of the desert") were the true Israel. They also had links to the apocalyptic tradition. See the words of Cross, *Qumran*, p. 199: "The concrete contacts in theology, terminology, calendrical peculiarities, and priestly interests, between the editions of Enoch, Jubilees, and the Testaments of Levi and Naphtali found at Qumran on the one hand, and the demonstrably sectarian works of Qumran on the other, are so systematic and detailed that we must place the composition of these works within a single line of tradition". He also writes: "The Essenes prove to be the bearers, and in no small part the producers, of the apocalyptic tradition of Judaism" (p. 98).

[296] The Pharisees appear to exclude certain types of people (e.g. tax collectors) from repentance. See also Lk. 15.7, which J. Jeremias, *The Parables of Jesus* ET, London: SCM ³1972, (¹1954), p. 135, understands as: "Thus God, at the Last Judgement, will rejoice more over one sinner who has repented, than over ninety-nine respectable persons (δίκαιοι), who have not committed any gross sin".

[297] See A.I. Baumgarten, "The Name of the Pharisees", *JBL* 102 (1983) 413-17 (411-28).

bracketed together as meritorious acts.[298] Thirdly, the idea that repentance can function as a sacrifice may lead to the idea of repentance as a meritorious act. So rather than a sacrifice atoning for sins it is one's repentance and penitance that atones.[299] Fourthly, the view that repentance operates *ex opere operato* or *ex opere operantis* is found in Rabbinic literature. Such is the power of repentance that it "overrides a prohibition of the Torah" (R. Joḥanan b. Nappaḥa, b. Yom. 86b) and transforms deliberate sins into merits (Resh Lakish, b. Yom. 86b). Linked with this is the quantification of sin and forgiveness. So in y. Yom. 8.7 (45c), we read that for desecrating God's name neither repentance for Yom Kippur atones but repentance and Yom Kippur will atone for one third, chastisement a third and death the final third. Fifthly, repentance texts which emphasize the rôle of free will. A good example here is Ps. Sol. 9. There has been some controversy as to whether repentance is seen here as a human work.[300] However, in view of the stress on the freedom of the will in Ps. Sol. 9.4-5 perhaps the approach of Braun (admittedly one which is not fashionable) is more to the point that repentance is seen as a work.[301] That the Psalms of Solomon deal with repentance as a "work" which can earn God's mercy is also suggested by the external penitential acts (e.g. Ps. Sol. 3.8). However, there are cases in the intertestamental literature where there is little or no idea of a meritorious repentance.[302] There is little indication of meritorious

---

[298] So repentance and good works are the intercessor of human beings (b. Shab. 32a); repentance and good works are the only things which accompany one into death (Midr. Tan. Dt. 3.23); repentance and good works are a shield against retribution (Ab. 4.11).

[299] Cf. b. Ber. 17a: "When R. Shesheth kept a fast, on concluding his prayer he added the following: Sovereign of the Universe, Thou knowest full well that in the time when the Temple was standing, if a man sinned he used to bring a sacrifice, and though all that was offered of it was its fat and blood, atonement was made for him therewith. Now I have kept a fast and my fat and blood have diminished. May it be to Thy will to account my fat and blood which have been diminished as if I had offered them before thee on the altar, and do Thou favour me".

[300] Those who deny the "performance" nature of repentance include Winninge, *Sinners*, pp. 42, and von Stemm, *Sünder*.

[301] H. Braun, "Vom Erbarmen Gottes über die Gerechten", in *Gesammelte Studien zum Neuen Testament und seiner Umwelt*, Tübingen: J.C.B. Mohr (Paul Siebeck) [2]1967, 33-34 (8-69). One does not have to be a Bultmannian to arrive at such a conclusion. See also the earlier work of Sjöberg, *Gott und die Sünder*, 261.

[302] Cf. Sjöberg, *Gott und die Sünder*, p. 256.

repentance in Qumran and perhaps the clearest expression of the grace of God is seen in the prayer of Manasseh.[303]

6. Legalism, the "Pious Jew" and Uncertainty of Salvation

Not only has the Lutheran tradition portrayed Judaism as a religion of salvation by works; it has also portrayed Judaism as a religion of legalism and of the Jew boasting in his good works and making a claim upon God. Further there is the claim that Judaism was a religion which because of its stress on salvation by works could offer no assurance of salvation. What are we to say to this?

I turn first to the issue of legalism. I have used this word sparingly above since it is only now that I am attempting to clarify the use of the word. The Shorter Oxford English Dictionary gives the following theological definition: "Adherence to the Law as opposed to the Gospel; the doctrine of justification by works, or teaching which savours of it". In fact the term "legalism" can refer not only to keeping the law (or trying to keep it) but also to a constellation of aspects which, at least from a Christian perspective, are negative. One of these is externalism and casuistry; another is the attitude that one is earning salvation by doing good works and which can give rise to an attitude of boasting and self-righteousness. Attempts have been made to distinguish between a "negative" and "positive" legalism. So Räisänen dis-

---

[303] Some believe that Prayer of Manasseh was a Christian composition (J.A. Fabricius, J.-P. Migne, F. Nau). However, J.H. Charlesworth in *OTP*, 2:628, believes such a view "is no longer persuasive". A definite argument against would be the sentiment in v. 8 (mentioned above) that the Patriarchs require no repentance since they did not sin. A better case could be made for Joseph and Aseneth being in part a Christian composition (e.g. a Christian revision or having Christian interpolations). For example, Joseph's prayer for Aseneth in 8.10-11 (". . . and renew her by your spirit, and form her anew by your hidden hand, and make her alive again by your life, and let her eat your bread of life, and drink your cup of blessing . . .", C. Burchard, *OTP*, 2:213) sounds remarkably Christian (see also 15.4). For example the verb "to make alive again" (ἀναζωοποιεῖν) is only found in Christian texts hitherto (except possibly Testament of Abraham A18.11). Note, however, that the anthropology is optimistic and the concept of sin corresponds to that of many "intertestamental" writings (cf. C. Burchard, *Joseph und Aseneth* (JSHRZ 2.4), Gütersloh: Gütersloher Verlagshaus Gerd Mohn 1983, p. 603). For example Aseneth sins unwittingly (6.7; 12.5; 13.13). On the question of interpolations see T. Holtz, "Christliche Interpolationen in 'Joseph and Aseneth'", *NTS* 14 (1967-68) 482-97.

tinguishes a "hard" or "anthropocentric" legalism (as in Bultmann's view of Judaism) from a "soft" or "torah-centric" legalism. Hard legalism is the view found, for example, in Moule: legalism is "the intention to claim God's favour by establishing one's own rightness" and the law is "a system of human achievement".[304] Soft legalism, on the other hand, "consists of the observance of precepts" but "is free of any boasting or a self-righteous attitude".[305] Richard Longenecker speaks of "acting legalism" and "reacting nomism". The former is "an ordering of one's life in external and formal arrangments according to the Law in order to gain righteousness and/or appear righteous"; the latter is "the moulding of one's life in all its varying relations acording to the Law in response to the love and grace of God".[306] But these distinctions are even a simplification for "legalism" can take on a whole spectrum of meanings between the two extremes from the most "negative" to the most "positive". In the following pages I will, unless otherwise indicated, be using the term legalism towards the "negative" end of the spectrum, i.e., to mean "hard" or "anthropocentric" legalism.

Regarding this anthropocentric legalism, one can make the empirical point that all religions, however much they stress "grace", have the tendency to move towards legalism including many forms of Christianity. So in Christianity there is a constant temptation to move from a *sola gratia* and *sola fide* theology to a theology in which one earns one's salvation.[307] Legalism seems to go hand in hand with ideas of merit.[308] This move towards a merit

---

[304] C.F.D. Moule, "Obligation in the Ethic of Paul", in W.R. Farmer, C.F.D. Moule and R.R. Niebuhr (ed.), *Christian History and Interpretation: Studies presented to John Knox*, Cambridge: CUP 1967, 393, 397 (389-406).

[305] H. Räisänen, "Legalism and Salvation by the Law", in S. Pedersen (ed.), *Die paulinische Literatur und Theologie. The Pauline Literature and Theology* (TeolSt 7), Aarhus: Aros/Göttingen: Vandenhoeck & Ruprecht 1980, 64 (63-83).

[306] R.N. Longenecker, *Paul, Apostle of Liberty*, Grand Rapids: Baker Book House 1980 (repr.), (¹1964), p. 78.

[307] J.R.W. Stott, *Romans*, Leicester: IVP 1994, p. 28, makes the point that although the *Book of Common Prayer* and the Thirty-nine Articles stress justification by faith, many Anglicans believe in some sort of works-righteousness. In my judgement this commentary written for the series "The Bible Speaks Today" by an Anglican clergyman who has preached on Romans throughout his productive ministry and has introduced so many to Paul's liberating message of justification by faith has more insight into Paul's gospel than many publications produced by full-time academic New Testament scholars (even though I disagree with Stott on a number of points).

[308] In a slightly different context T.F. Torrance writes that legalism leads "to the

theology may reflect a general anthropological tendency that one feels one ought to earn something rather than simply receiving a free gift.[309] There are also versions of Christianity which embody casuistry and externalism. However, such forms of Christianity do not correspond to Paul's witness to Christ.

As far as Jewish legalism is concerned, we can first of all say, as I have argued above, that all forms of Judaism at the time of Paul believed in salvation by works to a greater or lesser extent. Works played a fundamental rôle in salvation. Further, it is striking to contrast Paul's neglect of legal definition in his Christian theology with the preoccupation of the Pharisees and Rabbis with this.[310] Although there were many types of Judaism in Paul's time I think it is fair to say that all types were to a greater or lesser extent "legalistic" in the sense that they not only held to salvation by works but

---

growth of Pelagian notions of merit and fulfilled duty" (see his chapter on "The Roman Doctrine of Grace and the Point of View of Reformed Theology", in *Theology in Reconstruction*, London: SCM 1965, 179 (169-91)).

[309] Cf. D.J. Davies, *Studies in Pastoral Theology and Social Anthropology*, Birmingham: University of Birmingham ²1990, (¹1986), p. 11: "There is something in the very notion of merit that attracts human interest and appeals both to sense and reason". One of the greatest ironies is that in Anselm's view of the atonement, ideas of merit enter to explain this event which should form the basis of a sola gratia theology. Cf. Davies, *Studies*, p. 14.

[310] See, for example, the making of a "fence around the law" (Aboth 1.1 (see C. Taylor, *Sayings of the Jewish Fathers* (LJC), New York: Ktav ²1969, (¹1897), p. 11 n. 1)) and the "tradition of the elders" (Mk 7.3; Mt. 15.2 (see Billerbeck, *Kommentar*, 1:691-95)). The preoccupation of Pharisees with the details of the law is clearly seen in the key words ἀκρίβεια (Acts 22.3) and ἀκριβής (Acts 26.5). Although ἀκριβῶς is used in connection with Christian conduct in Eph. 5.15, it has no legal connotation. Note also the use of θρησκεία in Acts 26.5. This word, very popular with an author like Josephus (see above), occurs just four times in the New Testament. The scarcity of this word (and synonyms) may have some connection with the lack of a "cultic approach" to God (cf. W. Radl, θρησκεία, *EDNT* 2:154-55) but it may also be related to the rejection of synergism (cf. K.L. Schmidt, θρησκεία, *TDNT* 3:158 (155-59)). It is striking that the only positive uses of θρησκεία (religion) are in Jas 1.26-27 which is precisely a book in the New Testament with synergistic tendencies. Also the one occurrence of θρησκός (religious) is in Jas 1.26.

also that they were concerned with legal definitions (e.g. rules for keeping the sabbath).[311]

Jewish legalism can be found in both New Testament and Rabbinic texts. As far as Paul is concerned, there are texts such as Rom. 3.27-4.5[312] and Rom. 9.30-10.4[313] which point to Judaism being a legalistic religion, the former, as we shall see, pointing to a negative form of legalism. Further there are New Testament texts which refer specifically to the related issue of the "pious Jew"[314] who felt he had a claim upon God.[315] There has been some debate though as to whether this view can be found in Paul. I maintain that it can. First, in Phil. 3.5-6 Paul points to his personal accomplishments as a Jew and it is difficult to escape the implication of self-righteousness in the pre-Christian Paul.[316] Secondly, there is the important discussion of Rom. 2.1-16 and 2.17-24. In Rom. 2.1-4 Paul is attacking the self-righteous human being (who could be a Jew or a Gentile), arguing that although this person may think he is righteous, he is in fact no better than those who sin blatantly.[317] Then in Rom. 2.17-24, the focus is on the self-righteous Jew.[318] Thirdly one can point to Paul's discussion of "boasting". Bultmann's article on καυχάομαι is one of the most famous in Kittel's dictionary of the New Testament.[319] Although I cannot agree with Bultmann on every point his

---

[311] For a cross section of views, see Jub. 50.6-13; CD 10.1-12.5; m. Shab. 7; m. Erubin (on m. Shabbath and Erubim, a good overview is given by J. Neusner, *The Four Stages of Rabbinic Judaism*, London/New York: Routledge 1999, pp. 120-56). See also E. Lohse, σάββατον κτλ, *TDNT* 7:11-14 (1-35); G.F. Hasel, "Sabbath", *ABD* 5:853-54 (849-56).

[312] Discussed in Bell, *No one seeks for God*, chapter 7, especially pp. 264-68.

[313] Discussed in Bell, *Provoked to Jealousy*, pp. 186-91.

[314] I use quotation marks because much German discussion (especially of the Bultmann school) uses the term "der fromme Jude".

[315] Lk. 1.5-6 obviously raises some important and interesting questions regarding such "pious Jews".

[316] On this text see Gundry, "Grace, Works and Staying Saved in Paul", 13-14, and P.T. O'Brien, *The Epistle to the Philippians: A Commentary on the Greek Text* (NIGTC), Grand Rapids: Wm B. Eerdmans 1991, pp. 395-96.

[317] See Bell, *No one seeks for God*, pp. 138-40.

[318] See Bell, *No one seeks for God*, pp. 184-93.

[319] R. Bultmann, καυχάομαι κτλ, *TDNT*, 3:645-54. Note that Kittel's dictionary has come in for criticism not only on grounds of semantics (see J. Barr, *The Semantics of Biblical Language*, Oxford: OUP 1961) but also for its antisemitism. See, for example, P.M. Casey, "Some Anti-Semitic Assumptions in the *Theological Dictionary of the New*

overall conclusion is, I believe, correct: boasting in Paul does involve boasting in the performance of works. The key text is Rom. 3.27ff. and the debate centres on the question whether Paul is speaking of the Jew boasting in his performance of the law (Bultmann's view) or boasting in his having the law and boasting in his election (Sanders).[320] Unfortunately many make the mistake of stopping at the end of Romans 3.[321] But if we continue the argument into Romans 4 I believe the inescapable conclusion is that Paul understood boasting here to mean boasting in the performance of doing the law. So in Rom. 4.2 he writes: "For if Abraham was justified by works, he has something to boast about, but not before God".[322] Then in Rom. 4.4: "Now to one who works, his wages are not reckoned as a gift but as a due". Bultmann's view seems to be vindicated at this point.[323]

In connection with this question of the pious Jew there is an important distinction to be made when we talk of works-righteousness from a Christian perspective. Luther's view is that the Jews tried to fulfil the law and did not succeed. We find this in Paul of course: there is no justification by works of the law because all men and women are in Adam and all "fall short of the glory of God" (Rom. 3.23). This can be called a quantitative criticism of works-righteousness.[324] It is simply impossible to fulfil the law. But Bultmann believed Paul went a stage further. Certainly, according to Paul, men and women are incapable of fulfilling the law. "But Paul goes much further still; he says not only that man *can* not achieve salvation by works of the Law, but also that he is not even *intended* to do so."[325] This is often referred

---

Testament", *NovT* 41 (1999) 280-91. Note, however, the judgement of S.C. Neill, *The Interpretation of the New Testament, 1861-1961*, Oxford: OUP [2]1966, ([1]1964), p. 224: "[Bultmanns's] articles in Kittel's great *Wörterbuch* are among the best". I will return to the question of Kittel's antisemitism in chapter 9 below.

[320] Sanders, *Paul, the Law, and the Jewish People*, p. 33.

[321] This, of course, is one of the hazards of working with chapter divisions.

[322] On the exegetical details see Bell, *No one seeks for God*, pp. 267-68.

[323] On Rom. 3.27ff. see Bell, *No one seeks for God*, pp. 264, 266-68. In my discussion of Rom. 2.17, 23, I argued that Paul believes the Jew boasts both in his possession of the law and in his performance of the law (see pp. 186-88). A number of my points have been supported by the most recent discussion of boasting by Gathercole, *Boasting*.

[324] Cf. D. Moo, "Paul and the Law in the Last Ten Years", *SJT* 40 (1987) 297-98 (287-307).

[325] Bultmann, *Theology of the New Testament*, 1:263 (Bultmann's emphasis).

to as the qualitative criticism.[326] So if the Jew fulfils the law from A to Z, that is one of the gravest sins he could commit. For the pious Jew then boasts in his performance and feels he has a claim upon God. This idea of the self-righteous Jew is found not only in Bultmann but also in his pupils, Käsemann and Bornkamm.[327]

In view of this discussion I believe that Bultmann's and Käsemann's view of the pious Jew who boasted in his righteousness is not entirely mistaken. Their view of the Jew is, however, only half the truth. According to Paul the Jew did represent the religious man, but he also represented man receiving the promises of God. For a balanced view of Israel this latter point needs stressing and will be discussed in chapters 4, 6 and 7 below.

I turn now to other texts which concern the pious Jew. The gospels refer to pious Pharisees. First, they are attacked for their legalism and hypocrisy. It is of interest that although the "new Schürer" refers to Schürer's "questionable value judgements"[328] in section 28 ("Das Leben unter dem Gesetz"), it is admitted that:

> . . . the great accumulation of commandments and obligations could lead to pettiness, formalism, and an emphasis on outward observance rather than true integrity. Even though rhetorically exaggerated and representing the standpoint of a Galilean charismatic, a number of the sayings attributed to Jesus by Matthew and Luke undoubedly expose the excesses and abuses to which a legally motivated religion tended to lead.[329]

Reference is then made to a number of texts including Jesus' attack on the Pharisees in Mt. 23.1-36. But more relevant for our inquiry is the parable of the Pharisee and the Publican, Lk. 18.9-14:

---

[326] Such a qualitative criticism (together with the quantitative criticism) is found also in Luther (see P. Althaus, *Die Theologie Martin Luthers*, Gütersloh: Güterloher Verlagshaus Gerd Mohn [6]1983 ([1]1962), pp. 111-12). So on Gal. 2.16, Luther argues that "if though couldest do the work of the law according to this commandment: 'Thou shalt love the Lord thy God with all thy heart,' &c. (not to say here that no man yet ever did or could do so), yet thou shouldest not be justified before God; for a man is not justified by works of the law" (P.S. Watson (ed.), *A Commentary on St. Paul's Epistle to the Galatians by Martin Luther*, London: James Clarke 1961 (repr.), ([1]1953), p. 128; *WA* 40.1:218). However, this qualitative critique became predominant in Bultmann's analysis.

[327] See the discussion of their views at the beginning of this chapter.

[328] See Schürer/Vermes et al., *History of the Jewish People*, 2:464 n. 1. See also n. 8 above.

[329] Schürer/Vermes et al., *History of the Jewish People*, 2:486.

He (Jesus) also told this parable to some who trusted in themselves that they were righteous and despised others: 10 "Two men went up into the temple to pray, one a Pharisee and the other a tax collector. 11 The Pharisee stood and prayed thus with himself, 'God, I thank thee that I am not like other men, extortioners, unjust, adulterers, or even like this tax collector. 12 I fast twice a week, I give tithes of all that I get.' 13 But the tax collector, standing far off, would not even lift up his eyes to heaven, but beat his breast, saying, 'God, be merciful to me a sinner!' 14 I tell you, this man went down to his house justified rather than the other; for every one who exalts himself will be humbled, but he who humbles himself will be exalted".

One can add other texts, both Jewish and Christian, to support the existence of the "pious Jew". Whatever special pleading Sanders may offer,[330] b. Ket. 104a and y. Ber. 4.4 (8b) clearly indicate an attitude of boasting. In the former, Rabbi Judah ha Nasi boasts before God in his study of the Torah; in the latter, Rabbi Samuel b. Naḥum boasts that not one of his 248 limbs has offended against God. And, of course, one can compare Paul's pre-Christian attitude reflected in Phil. 3.5-6.

One text which is particularly striking, bringing together a boastful attitude and an anxiety about salvation, is b. Ber. 28b. First I draw attention to a prayer of R. Neḥunia b. ha-Ḳaneh which has similarities to Lk. 18.11.[331]

I give thanks to Thee, O Lord my God, that Thou hast set my portion with those who sit in the Beth ha-Midrash and Thou has not set my portion with those who sit in [street] corners, for I rise early and they rise early, but I rise early for words of Torah and they rise early for frivolous talk; I labour and they labour, but I labour and receive a reward and they labour and do not receive a reward; I run and they run, but I run to the life of the future world and they run to the pit of destruction.[332]

Although this does refer to God who "set his portion", the passage emphasizes the works of R. Neḥunia b. ha-Ḳaneh, his reward, and his pride. This prayer is followed by the story of R. Eliezer who fell ill and his disciples came to him to seek advice as to how to "win the life of the future world". This is then immediately followed by the story of R. Joḥanan ben Zakkai. He had fallen ill and his disciples came to visit him. They asked: "Lamp of

---

[330] Sanders, *Paul and Palestinian Judaism*, pp. 229-30.

[331] See Billerbeck, *Kommentar*, 2:240 on Lk. 18.11.

[332] See the parallel in y. Ber. 4.2 (7d.29-41), where R. Neḥunia b. ha-Kaneh, is specifically mentioned as saying this prayer (in b. Ber. 28b, it is not clear that R. Neḥunia b. ha-Ḳaneh used this prayer). R. Neḥunia b. ha-Ḳaneh belonged to the first generation of the tannaim (see H.L. Strack and G. Stemberger, *Einleitung in Talmud und Midrasch*, München: Verlag C.H. Beck [7]1982, p. 75). Avemarie, *Tora und Leben*, pp. 346-47, believes it unlikely that these prayers actually go back to R. Neḥunia.

Israel, pillar of the right hand, mighty hammer! Wherefore weepest thou?"
He replied:

> If I were being taken today before a human king who is here today and tomorrow in the
> grave, whose anger if he is angry with me does not last for ever, who if he imprisons me
> does not imprison me for ever and who if he puts me to death does not put me to ever-
> lasting death, and whom I can persuade with words and bribe with money, even so I
> would weep. Now that I am being taken before the supreme King of Kings, the Holy
> One, blessed be He, who lives and endures for ever and ever, whose anger, if He is angry
> with me, is an everlasting anger, who if He imprisons me imprisons me for ever, who if
> He puts me to death puts me to death for ever, and whom I cannot persuade with words
> or bribe with money — nay more, when there are two ways before me, one leading to
> Paradise and the other to Gehinnom, and I do not know by which I shall be taken, shall I
> not weep?

His final blessing is that the fear of heaven may come upon his disciples.
The dating of these texts does not directly concern me.[333] But what is important is what they tell of Rabbinic soteriology. The death-bed story of
Johanan ben Zakkai was commented upon by Bultmann and by Rengstorf,
and both have received criticism from Sanders for the conclusions they
come to. So Bultmann writes that one of the consequences of a "legalistic
conception of obedience was that the prospect of salvation became highly
uncertain".[334] Rengstorf comments: "It belongs to a religion of works that its
adherents cannot have assurance".[335] Sanders questions these conclusions,
believing rather that the death-bed scene shows rather that "the Rabbi felt
close to God, had a real perception of living in his sight, and was conscious
of his own unworthiness".[336] Even if this is correct, one cannot escape the
conclusion that according to this scene there was a lack of assurance. Note
that a sense of unworthiness does not inevitably lead to a lack of assurance.

---

[333] J. Neusner, *Development of a Legend: Studies on the Traditions concerning
Yohanan ben Zakkai* (StPB 16), Leiden: E.J. Brill 1970, pp. 221-223, sets out a synopsis
(y. Abod. Zar. 3.1 (42c); y. Sot. 9.16 (24c); ARN 25; b. Ber. 28b). The material on the
uncertainty of R. Johann's salvation (quoted above) which is only in ARN 25 and b. Ber.
28b is, according to Neusner, *Legend*, p. 224, a late invention.

[334] Bultmann, *Primitive Christianity*, pp. 82-83.

[335] K.H. Rengstorf, in R. Bultmann and K.H. Rengstorf, ἐλπίς κτλ, *TDNT* 2:527 (517-
35). However, contrast G. Bornkamm, "Der Lohngedanke im Neuen Testament", in
Studien zu Antike und Urchristentum. Gesammelte Aufsätze Band II (BevTh 28),
München: Chr. Kaiser Verlag ³1970, (¹1959), 77 (69-92), who argues that the giving of
the law gives the "pious" person too much security. Friedrich Avemarie brought this to
my attention (see also *Tora und Leben*, p. 14 n. 10).

[336] Sanders, *Paul and Palestinian Judaism*, p. 229.

One only has to think of Luther's death-bed words: "We are beggars. That is true".[337]

In view of this lack of assurance, it is understandable that for some Jews (or perhaps many) who were concerned about the World to Come, life could be a torment and the law was seen as a burden. So in Mt. 23.4, Jesus is reported to say of the Pharisees: "They bind heavy burdens, hard to bear, and lay them on men's shoulders; but they themselves will not move them with their finger". According to Hagner, this "points clearly to the Pharisees' distinctive oral Torah with its difficult and complicated casuistry".[338] Examples could be the Pharisees' teaching on clean and unclean, tithing, fasting, prayer and hallowing of the sabbath and holy days.[339]

In view of this material on boasting and lack of assurance, one wonders whether Schürer's now largely maligned words[340] do not have *some* truth in them. He writes:

> Life was a continual torment to the earnest man, who felt at every moment that he was in danger of transgressing the law . . . On the other hand, pride and conceit were almost inevitable for one who had attained to mastership in the knowledge and treatment of the law.[341]

I argued in chapter 1 that Paul considered himself to be a successful Jew with a relatively robust conscience. He was therefore probably more guilty of "pride and conceit" than being subjected to "continual torment". Yet even Paul was aware of his failings and there were probably many who found life a "continual torment". Schürer's description of "life under the law" has been

---

[337] The German is: "Wir sind Bettler. Das ist wahr". As H. Lilje, *Martin Luther in Selbstzeugnissen und Bilddokumenten*, Hamburg: Rowohlt 1965, p. 124, points out, behind these words is faith in God, "der die Hoffnung der Geringen, der Trost der Sünder, das Leben der Sterbenden ist, und der den Bettlern die leeren Hände füllt".

[338] D. Hagner, *Matthew 14-28* (WBC 33B), Dallas: Word Books 1995, p. 660.

[339] Cf. Billerbeck, *Kommentar*, 1:911 and the Rabbinic material given in 1:912-13.

[340] I am not here thinking of the remarks by the editors of the new Schürer. See above.

[341] Schürer, *History of the Jewish People*, 2.2:125 (§28).

criticized as onesided.[342] And one reason it may be considered onesided is that he decided to end his History with the Bar Kochba revolt and used mainly the Greek sources. The later Rabbinic literature was used as supplementary literature.[343] Since the Rabbinic sources demonstrate a broader view, and included more lenient views regarding the forgiveness of sins (see above), to some extent this onesidedness for describing the Judaism of Paul's time was acceptable. I therefore think that Schürer's view on "life under the law" has some truth in it.[344] If this view of Judaism is accepted (even as a partial picture), the message of Paul makes perfect sense. In Christ he could preach a message of salvation by grace, a salvation ultimately independent of works, a salvation which excludes all boasting, and a salvation which brings assurance of salvation.

7. "Getting-in" and "Staying-in" in Paul

According to Paul salvation is by grace. Further it is grace from beginning to end. I stress this because some have seen the Christian life as beginning with grace but continuing with works. For example, some forms of Pietism have the idea that at the beginning of the Christian life, at conversion, God is gra-

---

[342] G.F. Moore, "Christian Writers on Judaism", *HTR* 14 (1921) 239 (197-254) objects to Schürer's emphasis on the "incredible externalizing of the religious and moral life". See also Avemarie, *Tora und Leben*, p. 20 n. 34, who thinks that "Schürers knappe Bemerkungen zum jüdischen Gesetzesgehorsam (II 545-551) verraten mehr über Theologie im wilhelminischen Deutschland als über antikes Judentum".

[343] M. Hengel, "Der alte und der neue 'Schürer'", *JSS* 35 (1990) 27 (19-72). Hengel points out that he only thoroughly knew the Mishnah. For the later sources he tended to rely on secondary literature. However, note that "[s]eine zahlreichen Rezensionen aus dem Bereich des rabbinischen Judentums zeigen . . . sein sicheres und in der Regel sachliches Urteil" (27).

[344] As noted above, even the editors or the "new Schürer" accept the dangers of a "legally motivated religion" (2:486).

cious but after that it is essentially up to the Christian to do good works.[345] This sounds remarkably like the gospel of Paul according to E.P. Sanders. He makes a distinction between "getting in" the covenant and "staying in" the covenant. According to Sanders' understanding of Paul, the Christian gets in by grace and stays in by works. Although I do not like the distinction between "getting-in" and "staying-in"[346] I will nevertheless consider Paul in connection with these two concepts since they are now so prevalent in the secondary literature.

"Getting-in" had to be by grace for Paul because he believed human beings were so twisted and so totally corrupt that the only way to save them was through God's grace.[347] Judaism had no such doctrine of the total corruption of humankind[348] and therefore could envisage a religion where getting in was partly on the basis of works. Hence we find the synergism in Rabbinic Judaism as discussed above.

What about "staying-in"? Sanders' claims that for Paul as well as for Palestinian Judaism, "salvation is by grace but . . . works are the condition of remaining 'in'".[349] As far as Paul is concerned, Sanders is certainly wrong.[350] As far as Palestinian Judaism is concerned, can one really say salvation is by grace? Even working from Sanders' premises, one must argue that if works of the law are the means of staying in the covenant and if

---

[345] I have met some Christians in the Pietist movement in Germany who were clearly troubled by the fear of losing their salvation. In fact some go to the rather extreme view that Pietism has broken people psychologically. In the late 1980s I discovered a piece of graffiti in the Gentleman's toilet in the Tübingen Protestant Faculty. Roughly translated it ran as follows: "those burdened with guilt in the Tübingen psychiatric hospital would like to thank the Württemberg Pietism". But one should not forget the positive rôle that "Württemberg Pietism" has played (both the "Altpietismus" and the frequently denigrated "Neupietismus").

[346] Gundry, "Grace, Works, and Staying Saved in Paul", 12, questions this distinction. He writes: "Sanders' bisection of getting in and staying in cuts a line through Paul's religion where the pattern shows a whole piece of cloth".

[347] On Paul's view of the "fall" see Bell, *No one seeks for God*, pp. 125-131.

[348] On Jewish views of the "fall" see Bell, *No one seeks for God*, pp. 118-125.

[349] Sanders, *Paul and Palestinian Judaism*, p. 543.

[350] See Gundry Volf, *Paul and Perseverance*, who argues that according to Paul, "staying in" for the Christian is *not* by works.

exclusion from the covenant means loss of salvation, then salvation is by works and not, as Sanders claims, by grace.[351]

8. Concluding Reflections

This is perhaps the appropriate point to reflect on wider issues the new perspective raises. One of the first points to raise is the naïvity of the approach. We can see this in the fact that an "objectivity" is claimed.[352] Sanders writes: "I have been engaged for some years in the effort to free history and exegesis from the control of theology".[353] Yet has not the modern interest in community and Jewish Christian dialogue and the disinterest in issues of sin and guilt influenced the exegesis of those in the new perspective? John Barclay points to three aspects of our present "social and ideological environment which undergird the new perspective and encourage its reception". These are "Theological Respect for Judaism", "Community as the Goal of Christian Faith" and "Multicultural Concerns".[354] Barclay, in pointing to these influences, is not "attempting to disqualify the historical study" which he believes has been the "hallmark" of the new perspective.[355] However, for me these influences do raise important question since the Paul of the new perspective is made to sound "surprisingly liberal, Western and pluralist".[356] This is indeed strange in view of the supposed distance between Paul and ourselves which Stendahl emphasizes.[357] As Matlock suggests, Luther's

---

[351] For further comments on Sanders' work on Palestinian Judaism, see the discussion of Sifre Dt. in Bell, *Provoked to Jealousy*, chapter 7.

[352] R.B. Matlock, "Almost Cultural Studies? Reflections on the 'New Perspective' on Paul", in J.C. Exum and S.D. Moore (ed.), *Biblical Studies/Cultural Studies: The Third Sheffield Colloquium* (JSOTSup 266), Sheffield: Sheffield Academic Press 1998, 439-42 (433-59).

[353] E.P. Sanders, *Jesus and Judaism*, London: SCM 1985, pp. 333-34.

[354] See J.M.G. Barclay, "'Neither Jew nor Greek': Multiculturalism and the New Perspective on Paul", in M.G. Brett (ed.), *Ethnicity and the Bible* (BIS 19), Leiden/New York/ Köln: E.J. Brill 1996, 203-5 (197-214).

[355] Barclay, "Multiculturalism and the New Perspective on Paul", 203 n. 19.

[356] Matlock, "Almost Cultural Studies", 442.

[357] See K. Stendahl, "Biblical Theology, Contemporary", in *IDB* 1:420 (418-32).

Paul comes to grief more for his failure to fit the twentieth century than the first.[358]

The new perspective is therefore partly driven by "political correctness". In fact much modern scholarship on Judaism seems to be partly driven by a desire to say positive things about Judaism. So Matlock points to the irony that Charlesworth, whilst wishing to argue for scientific objectivity, "to describe and not to prescribe",[359] clearly wants to say positive things about Judaism. So the term "late Judaism" is to be replaced by "early Judaism". Many would no doubt agree that this is appropriate. But his rationale is that "['Early Judaism'] has the connotation of being alive with refreshing new insights . . . Early Jews were brilliantly alive with penetrating speculations into almost every facet of our world and universe".[360] As Matlock asks: "Descriptive, not prescriptive?"[361] Similar political correctness is also found among Christian scholars who seem to go out of their way to say positive things about Islam and avoid negative aspects.

But this political correctness regarding Judaism sometimes backfires in that complements are paid to Judaism when in fact such complements turn out to be rather condescending. So Jews are portrayed as liberal protestants.[362] This is seen, for example, when Dunn argues that "Judaism is first and foremost a religion of grace. . . . Somewhat surprisingly, the picture which Sanders painted of what he called 'covenantal nomism' is remarkably like the classic Reformation theology of works–that good works are the consequence and outworking of divine grace, not the means by which that grace is first attained".[363] Note also the section of Sanders' work *Judaism: Practice and Belief, 63BCE–66CE*, which is entitled "A Religion of Grace".[364] Alexander, in his review of Sanders' *Jesus and Judaism*, points out that Sanders assumes that grace is superior to "legalism". But what is wrong with "legalism" (at the "soft" end of the spectrum) from a Jewish perspec-

---

[358] Matlock, "Almost Cultural Studies", 442.

[359] J.H. Charlesworth, *Old Testament Pseudepigrapha and the New Testament* (SNTSMS 54), Cambridge: CUP 1985, p. 58.

[360] Charlesworth, *Pseudepigrapha and the New Testament*, p. 59.

[361] Matlock, "Almost Cultural Studies", 441.

[362] See Matlock, "Almost Cultural Studies", 438-39.

[363] J.D.G. Dunn, "The Justice of God: A Renewed Perspective on Justification by Faith", *JTS* 43 (1992) 7-8 (1-22).

[364] See pp. 275-78 and bottom of 277!

tive? Many Jews do not have any problem with the view that Judaism is legalistic in this sense. I vividly recall the day when I told my local orthodox Rabbi about the work of Sanders and others in the new perspective. He dismissed it immediately, commenting that "we Jews believe in salvation by works". As Alexander comments "what is wrong with 'legalism', once we have got rid of abusive language about 'hypocrisy' and 'mere externalism'?"[365] See also his concluding remarks in an article on "Torah and Salvation in Tannaitic Literature": "Tannaitic Judaism can be seen as fundamentally a religion of works-righteousness, and it is none the worse for that. The superiority of grace over law is not self-evident and should not simply be assumed".[366] From a Jewish perspective, then, there is really nothing wrong with salvation by works.[367] However, from Paul's Christian perspective, there is a problem. For Paul had both a quantitative and a qualitative critique of works.[368]

Another questionable aspect of the new perspective, particularly as found in the work of Dunn, is that Paul was opposing an exclusivism. This, incidentally, tends almost to the point of making justification a social gospel.[369] So Dunn writes that "this discovery of the horizontal and social dimension of justification by faith indicates that such social concerns lie at the heart of this so characteristic and fundamentally Christian and Protestant doctrine. Which is also to say that the obligation to such social and political concern lies at the heart of our faith".[370] In the following chapter I shall question whether this relativizing of the election of Israel can actually be found in Romans and whether Paul actually criticized Israel for "national righteousness" (i.e. attempting to restrict God's grace to herself). But there is a very simple reason why it would make little sense for Paul to oppose

---

[365] P.S. Alexander, Review of E.P. Sanders, *Judaism: Practice and Belief, 63BCE-66CE, JJS* 37 (1986) 105 (103-6).

[366] P.S. Alexander, "Torah and Salvation in Tannaitic Literature", in D.A. Carson, P.T. O'Brien and M.A. Seifrid (ed.), *Justification and Variegated Nomism, Volume I: The Complexities of Second Temple Judaism* (WUNT 2.140), Tübingen: J.C.B. Mohr (Paul Siebeck)/Grand Rapids: Baker 2001, 300 (261-301).

[367] I will return to this point in chapter 11 below.

[368] See also E. Lohse, "Theologie der Rechtfertigung im kritischen Disput - zu einigen neuen Perspektiven in der Interpretation der Theologie des Apostels Paulus", *GGA* 249 (1997) 77 (66-81) on Phil. 3.7-9.

[369] Lohse, "Theologie der Rechtfertigung im kritischen Disput", 79.

[370] Dunn, "Justice of God", 21.

"exclusivism". If he did this he could be legitimately accused of replacing one form of exclusivism with another. For his predestinarian theology implies that there *is* a form of exclusivism. This therefore seriously puts in question Dunn's whole approach.[371]

I believe therefore that Luther was not so mistaken in his understanding of Paul's remarkable theology. He was one of the great exponents of Paul and those of us in the Protestant tradition should never forget what we owe to him.[372] Sadly, it has become fashionable in certain circles to vilify this great reformer and theologian. His industry both in his service to the Church and to the University were awe-inspiring, an industry which was matched by his theological brilliance.[373]

In view of the above discussions I believe that the traditional protestant view of Judaism and Paul is roughly correct. Judaism was a religion of works-righteousness. In case all those who held such views are tarnished with the brush of antisemitism, it is worthwhile stressing here that many who had a negative view of Judaism were nevertheless opponents of antisemitism. One example is Bultmann. He participated in the formation and continuation of the Confessing Church and signed the Barmen Declaration. It is highly significant that his Faculty in Marburg unanimously rejected the Aryan Paragraph in a statement largely written by Bultmann himself. Further, in lectures to students he denounced the defamation of German

---

[371] Note, however, that Dunn finds support in M. Bockmuehl, "1QS and Salvation at Qumran", in D.A. Carson, P.T. O'Brien and M.A. Seifrid (ed.), *Justification and Variegated Nomism, Volume I: The Complexities of Second Temple Judaism* (WUNT 2.140), Tübingen: J.C.B. Mohr (Paul Siebeck)/Grand Rapids: Baker 2001, 414 n. 116 (381-414).

[372] Luther has, of course, had a large influence on certain modern Catholic exegetes as well.

[373] Luther's stature as one of the Church's greatest theologians has often not been appreciated in my own Church, the Church of England. I consider it one of the scandals of the *The Alternative Service Book*, 1980, that under lesser festivals and commemorations, Luther is simply not mentioned except that 31 October is devoted to "Saints and Martyrs of the Reformation Era". On the other hand, "Charles I, King, Martyr, 1649" and "Thomas More, Martyr, 1535", have their special days! See *The Alternative Service Book*, Cambridge: CUP/London: Clowes, SPCK 1980, pp. 18-21. The situation is somewhat improved in *Common Worship: Services and Prayers for the Church of England*, London: Church House Publishing 2000. Under "Holy Days", Martin Luther is commemorated on 31 October (p. 14) (and John Calvin on 26 May, p. 10).

Jews.[374] Another scholar who had a negative view of Judaism who is worth considering here is Paul Billerbeck. He, like his teacher H.L. Strack,[375] was an emphatic opponent of antisemitism. It is unfortunate that in some quarters it has become fashionable to denigrate the work of this great scholar. Billerbeck has been a target of Sanders' polemic. It is sobering to read the comments of M. Hengel and R. Deines that Billerbeck "did more to spread the knowledge of rabbinic texts in academic theology than any other Christian theologian, including Sanders".[376]

However, where much Protestant understanding of Paul and Judaism has gone wrong is in the understanding of the *status* of the Jewish people. Indeed, for the major part of the history of the Church, it has been affirmed that the Jews have been disinherited. They are no longer the people of God.[377] It is to an investigation of this issue that I now turn.

---

[374] See W. Schmithals, *Die Theologie Rudolf Bultmanns. Eine Einführung*, Tübingen: J.C.B. Mohr (Paul Siebeck) 1966, pp. 300-305; M. Ashcraft, *Rudolf Bultmann* (MMTM), Peabody: Hendrickson 1972, pp. 17-18; E. Dinkler, "Die christliche Wahrheitsfrage und die Unabgeschlossenheit der Theologie als Wissenschaft. Bemerkungen zum wissenschaftlichen Werk Rudolf Bultmanns", in O. Kaiser (ed.), *Gedenken an Rudolf Bultmann*, Tübingen: J.B.C. Mohr (Paul Siebeck) 1977, 25-30 (15-40; E. Jüngel, "Glauben und Verstehen. Zum Theologiebegriff Rudolf Bultmanns", in *Wertlose Wahrheit. Zur Identität und Relevanz des christlichen Glaubens. Theologische Erörterungen III* (BevTh 107), München: Chr. Kaiser Verlag 1990, 20-21 (16-77). M. Hengel, "A Gentile in the Wilderness: My Encounter with Jews and Judaism", in J.H. Charlesworth (ed.), *Overcoming Fear between Jews and Christians*, New York: Crossroad 1992, 77 (67-83), points out that "Bultmann's closest friend of his youth, with whom he exchanged many letters, was a Jew who fell in World War I". See also E. Gräßer, "Antijudaismus bei Bultmann? Eine Erwiderung", *Der Alte Bund im Neuen: Exegetische Studien zur Israelfrage im Neuen Testament* (WUNT 35), Tübingen: J.C.B. Mohr (Paul Siebeck) 1985, 201-11, who closes his article with substantial quotations from the speech given by the Jewish philosopher Hans Jonas at a memorial service for Rudolf Bultmann on 16 November 1976.

[375] On Strack's opposition to antisemitism, see R. Gutteridge, *Open thy Mouth for the Dumb! The German Evangelical Church and the Jews*, Oxford: Basil Blackwell 1976, pp. 328-29.

[376] Hengel and Deines, "E.P. Sanders' 'Common Judaism', Jesus, and the Pharisees", 69.

[377] Luther's own view will be studied in the pages which follow.

Chapter 4

Is Israel Still the People of God?

1. The Term "People of God"

In asking whether Israel remains the "people of God" I need to consider first whether this is a reasonable and natural question. Paul does not in fact have a particular preference for the word λαός.[1] Out of the 142 occurrences in the New Testament, it occurs 11 times in the Pauline letters generally considered authentic and once in Titus. It is striking that in the genuine letters it appears six times in Romans 9-11 (Rom. 9.25 (twice), 26; 10.21; 11.1, 2). Otherwise it appears twice in Romans 15 (15.10, 11), twice in 1 Corinthians (10.7; 14.21), once in 2 Corinthians (6.16) and finally in the deutero-Pauline Titus (2.14). In the genuine letters the word is always introduced into the discussion because of an Old Testament quotation.[2] In most instances the term λαός is used of Israel. But in 2 Cor. 6.16 and 1 Cor. 14.21 the term is by implication used for the Church of Jews and Gentiles and in Rom. 9.25-26 it refers to the inclusion of Gentiles in the people of God.[3] It is striking that the term does not appear in Galatians since, as we shall see, the use of the term would be fitting for Paul's argument.

Although the term λαός is not frequently used by Paul I think it is fair to say that the idea is often present. So although the term is not used in Galatians, Paul implies that the Church of Jews and Gentiles is the one new

---

[1] On the use of λαός in the New Testament, see H. Strathmann in R. Meyer and H. Strathmann, λαός, TDNT 4:50-57 (29-57).

[2] See G. Delling, "Merkmale der Kirche nach dem Neuen Testament", 13 (1966-67) 302 (297-316). In the case of Tit. 2.14, the word is probably introduced because of an allusion to Ezek. 37.23 (see G.W. Knight, *Commentary on the Pastoral Epistles* (NIGTC), Grand Rapids: Eerdmans/Carlisle: Paternoster 1992, p. 328).

[3] See Bell, *Provoked to Jealousy*, pp. 185-86, for a discussion of Rom. 9.24-29. Cf. W. Klaiber, *Rechtfertigung und Gemeinde: Eine Untersuchung zum paulinischen Kirchenverständnis* (FRLANT 127), Göttingen: Vandenhoeck & Ruprecht 1982, pp. 27-28.

λαός θεοῦ.[4] We therefore now turn to the question whether the Church is not only the new people of God but whether she replaces Israel as the people of God.

2. The Church replaces Israel?

When Jesus marvelled at the faith of the centurion who was asking Jesus to heal his servant, he said (Mt. 8.10b-12):

> Truly, I say to you, not even in Israel have I found such faith. 11 I tell you, many will come from east and west and sit at table with Abraham, Isaac, and Jacob in the kingdom of heaven, 12 while the sons of the kingdom will be thrown into the outer darkness; there men will weep and gnash their teeth.

Most commentators assume (rightly, I believe), that Matthew refers to Gentiles coming from east and west[5] either to Zion or to the kingdom of God[6] whilst the "sons of the kingdom", i.e. the Jews who have refused to

---

[4] See Strathmann, λαός, 56.

[5] So, e.g., U. Luz, *Das Evangelium nach Matthäus (Mt 8-17)* (EKK 1.2), Solothurn/Düsseldorf: Benziger Verlag/Neukirchen-Vluyn: Neukirchener Verlag [2]1996, ([1]1990), p. 15, writes: "Die Heiden von Ost und West werden sich dem Gott Israels zuwenden". An exception to this widespread interpretation is W.D. Davies and D.C. Allison, *A Critical and Exegetical Commentary on the Epistle to the Gospel According to Saint Matthew* (ICC), vol. II, Edinburgh: T. & T. Clark 1991, pp. 27-28. They believe that "as spoken by Jesus, Mt 8.11f. par. was intended to draw a stark contrast not between unbelieving Jews and believing Gentiles but between privileged and unprivileged Jews" (p. 28). Matthew's view is not that different for he did not think the point lay "in the salvation of the Gentiles as opposed to the damnation of all Jews but in the salvation of the seemingly unfortunate as opposed to the 'sons of the kingdom', the wise and privileged who have lived in the Eretz Israel and beheld the Messiah, and yet do not believe" (p. 28).

[6] For a discussion of these options see M. Theobald, "Mit verbundenen Augen? Kirche und Synagoge nach dem Neuen Testament", in *Studien zum Römerbrief* (WUNT 136), Tübingen: J.C.B. Mohr (Paul Siebeck) 2001, 371 n. 10 (367-95). He refers to G. Lohfink and M. Reiser (who see the idea of the pilgrimage to Zion here) and to J. Schlosser and J. Becker (who dispute this). So J. Becker, *Jesus of Nazareth* ET, New York/Berlin: Walter de Gruyter 1998, p. 68, writes that the text "implies that one experiences the Kingdom of God in a final sense not by making a pilgrimage to Zion but, rather, by entering the Kingdom of God". J. Schlosser, "Die Vollendung des Heils in der Sicht Jesu", in H.-J. Klauck (ed.), *Weltgericht und Weltvollendung. Zukunftsbilder im Neuen Testament* (QD 150), Freiburg/Basel/Wien: Herder 1994, 65 (54-84), argues against Reiser that there is no allusion to Is. 66.23-24 in Mt. 8.11.

accept the Messiah,[7] are cast out. A similar view of the rejection of Israel and substitution by Gentiles can be seen in the parable of the labourers in the vineyard. Jesus says this (Mt. 21.43):

Therefore I tell you, the kingdom of God will be taken away from you and given to a nation producing the fruits of it.

According to the context this is addressed to the leaders, but the idea of the kingdom being taken away from the whole Jewish people is not far away.[8] The impression given is that Israel is disinherited (Jewish Christians being an exception) and those Gentiles who accept Jesus are now the people of God. These texts give rise to the view that the Christian Church (of Jews and Gentiles) replaces Israel, often referred to as the substitution model.[9] Such a view is widely held. But is it to be found in Paul?

Some scholars have maintained that Paul did have such a view. So Conzelmann writes that:

. . . in Paul's thought the conception of the church as the new people of God and the true people of God stand side by side. It is the new people of God where the conception of the dismissal of Israel from salvation history is the dominant factor.[10]

N.T. Wright appears to understand Paul to have a substitution model. He argues that the basis of Israel's jealousy (see Rom. 10.19; 11.11, 14) is that

---

[7] See D.A. Hagner, *Matthew 1-13* (WBC 33A), Dallas: Word Books 1993, p. 206. I do not think "sons of the kingdom" can be restricted to the Jewish leaders (as Davies and Allison, *Matthew II*, p. 28, suggest).

[8] Luz, *Matthäus III*, p. 225, writes: "Schon von der deuteronomistischen Prophetenmordtradition her ist es ja ganz Israel, das die zu ihm gesandten Propheten abgelehnt und getötet hat. Die Leser/innen haben vielleicht 8,12 noch im Gedächtnis: Dort war Israel 'Söhne der βασιλεία', nicht etwa nur seine Führer".

[9] See B. Klappert, *Israel und die Kirche: Erwägungen zur Israellehre Karl Barths* (ThExH 207), München: Chr. Kaiser Verlag 1980, pp. 14-17, who sums up such as view as follows: "Die Kirche als das neue Gottesvolk ersetzt das Israel der Erwählung Gottes".

[10] H. Conzelmann, *An Outline of the Theology of the New Testament* (NTL) ET, London: SCM 1969, p. 251 (original in *Grundriß der Theologie des Neuen Testaments* (UTB 1446), Tübingen: J.C.B. Mohr (Paul Siebeck) [4]1987 (revised by A. Lindemann), ([1]1967), p. 278). See also L. Cerfaux, "Le privilège d'Israël selon saint Paul", in *Recueil Lucien Cerfaux: Études d'Exégèse et d'Histoire Religieuse de Monseigneur Cerfaux réunies à l'occasion de son soixante-dixième anniversaire* (BEThL 6-7), 2 vols, Gembloux: Éditions J. Duculot 1954, 2:363 (339-64), who writes: "Le Christ venu, Israël s'efface" and "les privilèges du judaïsme trouvent leur épanouissement dans l'Église chrétienne" (Cerfaux, "Privilège", 341).

her covenant privileges have been *transferred* to the Church.[11] Such a view could account for the jealousy of Israel for the Gentile Christians, but the question is whether Paul thought in terms of a transfer of covenant privileges.[12]

In most letters of Paul we get no clear idea of how he related Israel to the Church. So, for example, in 1 Thessalonians, probably Paul's earliest extant letter, Paul shows that he has a negative view of Israel's future in 2.16.[13] But the letter does not give any clear indication as to whether Paul considered the Jews to be no longer the people of God. However, there are two letters, Galatians and Romans, in which we can gain a fairly good picture of Paul's view, and it is to these letters that I now turn.

3. Substitution Models in Galatians?

3.1. Galatians 3-4

Of all books in the New Testament, Galatians is the one which has the most "negative view" of the Jewish law.[14] Even the reading of the letter today can offend; how much more then would it offend in the early history of the Christian Church.[15] Further, because the letter has a negative view of the

---

[11] Wright, *Messiah and the People of God*, p. 193.

[12] P. von der Osten-Sacken, "Antijudaismus um Christi willen?", *BThZ* 4 (1987) 107-120 (review of E. Gräßer, *Der Alte Bund im Neuen*), 111, objects to the use of the word "Privilegien" (for the list in Rom. 9.4-5, for example) and suggests instead "Gnadengaben" (Rom. 11.29). There may be some weight to his suggestion although it should be noted that Rom. 11.29 most likely refers to the election of and promise to *Abraham* (see the discussion of 11.29 in chapter 7 below). Because the term "privileges" is so well established in the secondary literature I will continue to use the term.

[13] See the discussion above in chapter 2.

[14] The precise nature of this "negative view" will be investigated below.

[15] James, the brother of Jesus, although giving Paul the "right hand of fellowship" at the conference in Jerusalem (Gal. 2.9), fell out with Paul probably after hearing of (or reading) Galatians. Cf. M. Hengel, "Der Jakobusbrief als antipaulinische Polemik", in *Paulus und Jakobus. Kleine Schriften III* (WUNT 141), Tübingen: J.C.B. Mohr (Paul Siebeck) 2002, 536 (511-48), who suggests that James wrote his anti-Pauline letter between 58 and 62 AD, and refers to J.J. Wettstein, *Novum Testamentum Graecum*, 2 vols, Amsterdam 1752, 2:659, who believes that James wrote his letter after Paul wrote his letters to the Galatians and to the Romans (but before 1 Peter, which he took to be genuine).

law, including its rôle being superceded by the gospel, by implication it may be suggesting that Israel's rôle as the people of God has also been superceded (or that Israel is indeed no longer the people of God). The demotion of the law may imply the demotion of the people of the law. Also if Paul argues for the inferiority of the law to the gospel, this may again have some implication for the people of the law vis-à-vis the people of the gospel.

The central section of Galatians, 2.15-5.12, concerns the superiority of the gospel over the law.[16] The texts and points which are particularly relevant to our inquiry will now be investigated.

3.1.1. Galatians 3.6-7

Abraham was justified by faith, a faith which excluded merit (Gal. 3.6). Paul quotes Gen. 15.6 and Paul understands this verse to mean "Abraham believed *in God* and it was reckoned to him as righteousness". Paul's use of Gen. 15.6 is quite different to the ancient Jewish view, where Abraham believed what God said (i.e. that his descendants will be as numerous as the stars) and he was rewarded.[17] There was also the Jewish tradition that Gen. 15.6 is fulfilled in the offering of Isaac in Gen. 22.1-19.[18] Hofius rightly

---

[16] The central section is taken by Fung to be 2.15-5.12, which he entitles "Exposition of the Doctrine of Justification by Faith" (*Galatians*, p. 112). H. Schlier takes 3.1-5.12 as the unit, the theme being "Das Gesetz und der Glaube" (*Der Brief an die Galater* (KEK 7), Göttingen: Vandenhoeck & Ruprecht [14]1971, ([10]1949), p. 118).

[17] See Billerbeck, *Kommentar*, 3:199-201; Lightfoot, *Galatians*, pp. 158-64. See especially, Mek. Ex. to 14.31 (Lauterbach, *Mekilta*, 1:252-53): "For as a reward for the faith with which Israel believed in God, the Holy Spirit rested upon them and they uttered the song; as it is said: 'And they believed in the Lord . . . Then sang Moses and the children of Israel' (Ex. 14.3[1]; 15.1). R. Nehemiah says: Whence can you prove that whosoever accepts even one single commandment with true faith is deserving of having the Holy Spirit rest upon him? We find this to have been the case with our fathers. For as a reward for the faith with which they believed, they were considered worthy of having the Holy Spirit rest upon them, so that they could utter the song, as it is said: 'And they believed in the Lord . . . Then sang Moses and the children of Israel'. And so also you find that our father Abraham inherited both this world and the world beyond only as a reward for the faith with which he believed, as it is said: 'And he believed in the Lord', etc. (Gen. 15.6)". Note also the tradition that God divided the Red Sea as a reward for Abraham's faith. See Mek. Ex. to 14.15 (Lauterbach, *Mekilta*, 1:220): "Shema'yah says: 'The faith with which their father Abraham believed in Me is deserving that I should divide the sea for them'. For it is said: 'And he believed in the Lord' (Gen. 15.6)".

[18] See 1 Mac. 2.52: "Was not Abraham found faithful when tested, and it was reckoned to him as righteousness". See also Jas 2.21-23.

stresses that according to Paul there are not two stages here: believing God (or in God) and then receiving a reward of righteousness. Paul has telescoped these two stages into one.[19] It soon becomes clear that this faith in God is also faith in Christ.

From this is in then argued that the "sons of Abraham" are actually those who believe in Christ (Gal. 3.7). So in Gal. 3.7 Paul writes: "You must recognize (γινώσκετε),[20] then, that it is the people of faith (οἱ ἐκ πίστεως) who are sons of Abraham". It is in fact *exclusively* Christians (οἱ ἐκ πίστεως) who are children of Abraham.

3.1.2. Galatians 3.8

The gospel was preached beforehand to Abraham. So in Gal. 3.8 Paul writes: "And the scripture foreseeing (προϊδοῦσα δὲ ἡ γραφή) that God would justify the Gentiles by faith (ὅτι ἐκ πίστεως δικαιοῖ τὰ ἔθνη ὁ θεός), declared the gospel beforehand to Abraham, saying, 'All the nations shall be blessed in you' (προευηγγελίσατο τῷ Ἀβραὰμ ὅτι Ἐνευλογηθήσονται ἐν σοὶ πάντα τὰ ἔθνη)".[21] Although the subject of the verbs προορᾶν and προευαγγελίζεσθαι is ἡ γραφή, God is actually the subject.[22] And the gospel

---

[19] See O. Hofius, "'Rechtfertigung des Gottlosen' als Thema biblischer Theologie", in *Paulusstudien* (WUNT 51), Tübingen: J.C.B. Mohr (Paul Siebeck) 1989, 129 (121-47): "[Paulus] hört in Gen 15,6 nicht *zwei* Sätze – einen über Abrahams Tat und einen anderen über Gottes diese Tat anerkennende Reaktion –, sondern er hört hier *einen einzigen* Satz, der als ganzer Gottes heilvolles Handeln an Abraham beschreibt. Abrahams Glaube ist für Paulus der durch das Wort Gottes (Gen 15,1b.4b.5) gewirkte Glaube, so daß Gott 'zur Gerechtigkeit anrechnet', was er selbst geschenkt hat und was in keinem auch noch so sublimen Sinn ein menschliches ἔργον ist" (Hofius' emphasis).

[20] I take this as an imperative rather than an indicative (cf. Bruce, *Galatians*, p. 153; Fung, *Galatians*, p. 138).

[21] The quotation is a conflation of Gen. 12.3c and 18.18b (cf. 22.18a). Gen. 12.3c has the expression πᾶσαι αἱ φυλαὶ τῆς γῆς whereas 18.18b has πάντα τὰ ἔθνη τῆς γῆς which suits Paul's argument in Gal. 3.8. It may be that Paul understood πάντα τὰ ἔθνη "nicht als Beschreibung der Vielzahl der einzelnen Völkerschaften der Erde . . . , sondern als Bezeichnung für die Gesamtheit der Nichtjuden ('Heiden')" (Koch, *Schrift*, p. 124). This may then account for Paul's omission of τῆς γῆς from 18.18b.

[22] One may compare Gal. 3.22a: ἀλλὰ συνέκλεισεν ἡ γραφὴ τὰ πάντα ὑπὸ ἁμαρτίαν. The sense here is that God has (in the scripture and according to the witness of scripture) "imprisoned all under sin". Cf. the parallel, Rom. 11.32, where God is explicitly the subject: συνέκλεισεν γὰρ ὁ θεὸς τοὺς πάντας εἰς ἀπείθειαν. See also Rom. 9.17a: λέγει γὰρ ἡ γραφὴ τῷ Φαραὼ, which means "God speaks (as the Scripture witnesses) to Pharaoh".

which was preached to Abraham was the same gospel Paul was preaching.[23] So rather than the gospel coming after the law, the gospel indeed preceded the law (see point 7 below). Abraham was therefore a justified sinner and believed in Christ.[24] This raises the question as to how Abraham believed in Christ. One possible option is to argue with Hanson that "Abraham believed in God-in-Christ; he was justified by God-in-Christ, the pre-existent, pre-incarnate Christ, of course".[25] But how can one believe in a pre-incarnate Christ, a Christ who has not been crucified and a Christ who has not even participated in the human condition? In the discussion below on 1 Cor. 10.1-13 I will again probe the question of how Christ is related to the history of Israel. But as far as Abraham's faith is concerned, I think the reality of Abraham's "faith" can only be realized through Christ. Conversely we will see that the reality of Israel's disobedience in the wilderness can only be seen in terms of "tempting Christ" (1 Cor. 10.9).

3.1.3. Galatians 3.10-12

In the next section, Gal. 3.10-13, Paul argues that those who rely on works of law are under a curse. Gal. 3.10-12 are formulated antithetically to 3.6-9.[26] For in vv. 7 and 9 Paul speaks of those who are saved ἐκ πίστεως but in v. 10 he speaks of those who seek justification ἐξ ἔργων νόμου. Also in vv. 8-9 he speaks of blessing whereas in v. 10 he speaks of the curse (κατάρα). So he writes: "Indeed those who rely on works of law (ἐξ ἔργων νόμου) are under a curse (ὑπὸ κατάραν εἰσίν); for it is written 'Cursed (ἐπικατάρατος) be everyone who does not persevere in doing everything written in the book of the law'".[27] These words are addressed not only to Jews who do not believe in Christ but also to those Jewish Christians who are insisting that Christians must keep the law. They are now under a curse. They also threaten any Gentile Christians who are considering justification by law (cf.

---

[23] A.T. Hanson, "Abraham the Justified Sinner", in *Studies in Paul's Technique and Theology*, London: SPCK 1974, 64 (52-66), rightly argues that the verb προευ-ηγγελίσατο means "preaching the gospel by anticipation" not "preaching a preliminary gospel".

[24] Hanson, "Justified Sinner", 66.

[25] Hanson, "Justified Sinner", 66.

[26] Eckstein, *Verheißung und Gesetz*, p. 121.

[27] The quotation is from Dt. 27.26 but has been modified in the light of Dt. 28.58. See Eckstein, *Verheißung und Gesetz*, p. 125.

Gal. 5.2-4).[28] The implication of the quotation from Dt. 27.26 is that if justification is to be by law, then a perfect obedience is necessary. So a curse is
on everyone "who does not persevere in doing *everything* written in the
book of the law". The word πᾶσιν is significant. Paul, as in other texts,
believes a perfect obedience of the law is necessary (cf. Rom. 2.12-13; Gal.
5.3). But to argue that a perfect obedience is required does not mean that
one has to take the view that Paul is putting forward an empirical
argument.[29] For Paul believes that *in principle* no one can keep the law. Further, the law was never meant to have a saving function. For human beings
were under the power of sin *before* the law of Moses was given.[30] Although
in Galatians Paul does not explicitly discuss the origin of sin as he does in
Romans (see 5.13a: ἄχρι γὰρ νόμου ἁμαρτία ἦν ἐν κόσμῳ . . . 14a ἀλλὰ
ἐβασίλευσεν ὁ θάνατος ἀπὸ Ἀδὰμ μέχρι Μωϋσέως) he does nevertheless
make clear that *in principle* righteousness through the law is excluded (Gal.
3.21b; 2.16; 3.11, 18).

Before proceeding I should add that although a principal part of Paul's
argument concerning the law is developed from his Christology and soteriology, and in fact he could only come to his conclusions regarding the law on
the basis of these, part of his argument also regards the impossibility of
keeping the law.[31]

Paul in 3.11 writes that it is evident that absolutely no one (οὐδείς) is justified before God by law. He establishes this by a quotation from Hab. 2.4b:

---

[28] Gundry Volf, *Paul and Perseverance*, p. 214, rightly stresses though that Paul is
convinced that the Gentile Christians will not in fact take this step of being justified by
law (see Gal. 5.10).

[29] This is what is suggested by Räisänen, *Paul and the Law*, pp. 94-95, 109.

[30] See Eckstein, *Verheißung und Gesetz*, p. 130.

[31] So Eckstein, *Verheißung und Gesetz*, p. 133, writes concerning Gal. 3.10-14, "daß
Paulus *von der Christologie und der Soteriologie her* die Aussagen über die Bedeutung
der Tora und die Situation des Menschen vor Gott entfaltet – oder wie er es dann in Phil
3,8 formuliert: Um der überragenden Erkenntnis Christi Jesu willen und durch Christus
erachtet der Apostel das, was ihm vorher als Gewinn erschien, als Verlust" (Eckstein's
emphasis). However, I think Paul's argument is more complex. For part of the argument
in Galatians certainly involves the impossibility of keeping the whole law. Even in Phil.
3.2-11, there is an element of showing that there is something fundamentally wrong in
establishing a righteousness based on law, even though the emphasis is on "the surpassing worth of knowing Christ Jesus". For I argued in chapter 3 above that in Phil. 3.5-6
Paul boasts in his personal accomplishments as a Jew and it is difficult to escape the
implication of Paul's self-righteousness as a Pharisee.

"He who is righteous by faith shall live" (Ο δίκαιος ἐκ πίστεως ζήσεται).[32] But a problem arises here. Is Paul's argument as follows: "because Scripture says that it is he who is righteous (that is, justified) by *faith* that will live, it follows that no one is justified by works of the law (irrespective of one's success or failure in keeping it)"?[33] In answer to this one must say first of all that it is clear throughout the letters of Paul that no one can succeed in keeping the law. But secondly, in view of the so called qualitative critique of the law, it is clear that no one is even intended to be justified by works.

In Gal. 3.12 Paul makes it clear that faith and law are entirely different principles. "But the law is not based on faith; rather 'he who does them will live in them'" (ὁ δὲ νόμος οὐκ ἔστιν ἐκ πίστεως, ἀλλ᾽ Ὁ ποιήσας αὐτὰ ζήσεται ἐν αὐτοῖς). So according to Hab. 2.4b, he who is righteous by faith shall live, but according to Lev. 18.5 the one who does the commandments shall live.[34] The former is the correct way.

3.1.4. Galatians 3.13-14

In Gal. 3.13-14 Paul picks up the positive statement of 3.6-9 and the antithetic negative statements of 3.10-12. I have already discussed 3.13 in chapter 2 above and here I simply want to focus on the link between 3.13 and 3.14. Christ redeemed us (Χριστὸς ἡμᾶς ἐξηγόρασεν)[35] from the curse of the law (i.e. the condemning function of the law) by becoming a curse on our behalf (i.e. he fully identified with the human condition). Then in v. 14

---

[32] There are numerous questions regarding Paul's use of Hab. 2.4b. I take Paul's septuagintal text to be (ὁ δὲ δίκαιος ἐκ πίστεως μου ζήσεται). The most striking change to the LXX is the omission of μου. The sense is therefore changed from God's faithfulness to faith in Christ. Note that earlier he uses the objective genitives πίστις Ἰησοῦ Χριστοῦ and πίστις Χριστοῦ (Gal. 2.16) and πίστις τοῦ υἱοῦ τοῦ θεοῦ (Gal. 2.20). Then after this he simply uses the absolute πίστις to refer to faith *in Christ* (Gal. 3.2, 5, 7, 8, 9, 12, 14, 23, 24, 25, 26). See Eckstein, *Verheißung und Gesetz*, p. 138.

[33] Fung, *Galatians*, p. 145.

[34] Compare Rom. 10.5-10 where Paul sets Lev. 18.5 against Dt. 30.12-14. See Bell, *Provoked to Jealousy*, pp. 190-91.

[35] The ἡμᾶς refers to both Jews and Gentiles. See Eckstein, *Verheißung und Gesetz*, pp. 152-53, who is rightly critical of those such as T.L. Donaldson, "The 'Curse of the Law' and the Inclusion of the Gentiles", *NTS* 32 (1986) 94-112, who argue that ἡμᾶς refers solely to Jews. Donaldson's view is adopted by Longenecker, *Triumph*, p. 93, who thereby argues that there is "a salvation-historical perspective on Israel's past". See the discussion below on Rom. 15.8-9.

he writes "in order that the blessing of Abraham might come to the Gentiles in Christ Jesus, in order that we might receive the promise of the Spirit through faith". So the overcoming of the curse of the law results in the blessing of Abraham coming to the Gentiles. Paul again is thinking back to Gen. 12.1-3 and it is significant that this text follows the primordial history of Gen. 2-11 with its "Unheilsgeschichte".[36] Paul's emphasis is therefore on the reversal of the curse on the Gentiles and the blessing they receive. This has come about not through the law but through the cross of Christ.

3.1.5. Galatians 3.15-16

The section Gal. 3.15-18 makes some fundamental points regarding our enquiry and I begin with 3.15-16. Paul argues *a minori ad maius*.[37] Gal. 3.15: "Brothers, I give a human analogy; even in the case of the decree of a human being, once it is ratified no one annuls it (οὐδεὶς ἀθετεῖ) or adds to it (ἢ ἐπιδιατάσσεται)". I have translated διαθήκη as "decree"[38] and the background of the term on the human level may be the Mattanah (מַתָּנָה).[39] But whatever the background of διαθήκη may be, Paul's point is clear. So he writes in Gal. 3.16: "Now the promises were made to Abraham and to his seed. It does not say, 'And to seeds', referring to many; but to one, 'And to your seed', which is Christ" (τῷ δὲ Ἀβραὰμ ἐρρέθησαν αἱ ἐπαγγελίαι καὶ τῷ σπέρματι αὐτοῦ. οὐ λέγει, Καὶ τοῖς σπέρμασιν, ὡς ἐπὶ πολλῶν, ἀλλ᾽ ὡς ἐφ᾽ ἑνός, Καὶ τῷ σπέρματί σου, ὅς ἐστιν Χριστός). Paul's point in v. 16 is that the promises (αἱ ἐπαγγελίαι)[40] were made (by God) to Abraham and his "seed", and the "seed" far from being the people of Israel, i.e. the physical

---

[36] Cf. G. von Rad, *The Problem of the Hexateuch and other essays* ET, Edinburgh/London: Oliver & Boyd 1966, p. 65.

[37] See J. Calvin, *The Epistles of Paul The Apostle to the Galatians, Ephesians, Philippians and Colossians* (CNTC 11), Grand Rapids: Wm B. Eermans 1993 (repr.), (¹1965), p. 56: "This is an argument from the less to the greater. Human contracts (hominum contractus) are regarded as binding; how much more what God has established?"

[38] Cf. Eckstein, V*erheißung und Gesetz*, p. 175.

[39] See E. Bammel, "Gottes ΔΙΑΘΗΚΗ (Gal. III.15-17) und das jüdische Rechtsdenken", *NTS* 6 (1959-60) 313-19. Bammel is supported by Kutsch, *Neues Testament*, pp. 137-38. For an evaluation, see Eckstein, *Verheißung und Gesetz*, pp. 174-88.

[40] The plural is used because although there was one fundamental promise to Abraham (Gen. 12.1-3) it is repeated in various forms (Gen. 18.18; 22.18; 26.4; 28.14).

descendants, actually refers to Christ and by implication those who are in Christ. So Schneider writes that Paul disrupts the concept of Israel "by enunciating the principle that the promise which Abraham received on the basis of faith applies to 'the seed' (Gl. 3:16), i.e. Christ. Hence believers who belong to Christ and are one in Him (Gl. 3:28) are heirs of Abraham's promise".[41] Likewise, Oepke writes: "Er preßt den Singular σπέρματι im Gegensatz zum Plural, deutet ihn auf das *Individuum* Christus und springt von dem letzteren über auf die an ihm hängende, in ihm befaßte *Gemeinschaft*".[42] Such an argument is, however, challenged by Eckstein. He objects that Jesus is not the receiver of the blessing but the mediator of it.[43] However, I do not think there is a problem so long as Christ is seen as a representative of the Church of Jews and Gentiles. Further, if Eckstein's approach is adopted, a distinction has to be made between the way promises were made to "Abraham" and the way they were made "to his seed", Christ.[44] So the verb ἐρρέθησαν of Gal. 3.16 which occurs only once must really take on two meanings, one in reference to Abraham (to whom the promise was "spoken", "made") and another in reference to Christ (to whom the promise "refers"). It is the case that in v. 19 the promise is not *made* to Christ but *refers* to Christ.[45] But Paul in v. 16 seems to be saying that the promise was *made* to Christ but as a representative figure.

---

[41] J. Schneider, κλάδος, *TDNT* 3:721 (720-22).

[42] Oepke, *Galater*, p. 61 (Oepke's emphasis). Cf. Burton, *Galatians*, pp. 181-82.

[43] Eckstein, *Verheißung und Gesetz*, p. 183: "Während nun Abraham und die υἱοὶ Ἀβραάμ (3,7) – d.h. das σπέρμα Ἀβραάμ im kollektiven Sinne (3,29) – dieser εὐλογία als der Überwindung des Fluches bedürfen, kann das von Jesus Christus als dem einzigartigen σπέρμα Ἀβραάμ keineswegs ausgesagt werden. Er hat nicht wie Abraham selbst den Segen *zugesprochen bekommen* (3[,]6.9.16.18), sondern ihn durch sein stellvertretendes Sterben am Kreuz *verwirklicht* (3,13f.). Er ist nicht Segens*empfänger*, sondern der *eine* Segens*mittler* . . ." (Eckstein's emphasis).

[44] Eckstein, *Verheißung und Gesetz*, p. 184, writes: "Die Worte τῷ Ἀβραάμ ἐρρέθησαν αἱ ἐπαγγελίαι besagen, wie V. 18b erklärt, daß Abraham das Erbe auf Grund der Verheißung von Gott geschenkt worden ist. Die Worte ἐρρέθησαν αἱ ἐπαγγελίαι καὶ τῷ σπέρματι αὐτοῦ hingegen werden in V. 19 durch die Wendung τὸ σπέρμα ᾧ ἐπήγγελται aufgenommen; und das bedeutet: Christus ist der *eine* Nachkomme Abrahams, durch den und in dem der Segen Gottes gemäß der Verheißung zu den Heiden kommt – derjenige, auf den sich die Segensverheißung von Gen 12,3/22,18 usw. bezieht".

[45] Cf. *BA*, 568.

3.1.6. Galatians 3.17-18

Paul's next point (in 3.17) is that the law was added 430 years after the covenant made with Abraham (3.17) and cannot invalidate that covenant. The figure of 430 years comes from Ex. 12.40 (LXX).[46] Paul then concludes the section 3.15-18 by stressing in v. 18 that the inheritance (ἡ κληρονομία) comes through the promise, not through the law. The term κληρονομία comes from the promise to Abraham of the land (Gen. 15.7: εἶπεν δὲ πρὸς αὐτόν Ἐγὼ ὁ θεὸς ὁ ἐξαγαγών σε ἐκ χώρας Χαλδαίων ὥστε δοῦναί σοι τὴν γῆν ταύτην κληρονομῆσαι).[47]

3.1.7. Galatians 3.19a, b

The law was "added (προσετέθη) because of transgressions (τῶν παρα-βάσεων χάριν)" (3.19b). This is Paul's first response to his question τί οὖν ὁ νόμος; which can be translated as "Then what is the nature of the law" (3.19a).[48] It is difficult to avoid the conclusion that the giving of the law has a shadow side to it, even perhaps a sinister side. This sinister aspect is not necessarily implied by the use of the verb "was added" (προσετέθη). The verb may well have a fairly neutral sense.[49] But the context does suggest a rather sinister intent. For it was added (by God!) "because of transgressions" (τῶν παραβάσεων χάριν) (3.19). Now the law's function in both Gal. 3.19 and Rom. 5.20 is to show sin to be sin and to condemn the sinner.[50] It was added to imprison sinners.[51] But I wonder whether that is all there is to it.

---

[46] The MT gives 430 years for the time the Israelites lived in *Egypt*. But Ex. 12.40 LXX has: ἡ δὲ κατοίκησις τῶν υἱῶν Ισραηλ, ἣν κατῴκησαν ἐν γῇ Αἰγύπτῳ καὶ ἐν γῇ Χανααν, ἔτη τετρακόσια τριάκοντα.

[47] See the parallel text in Rom. 4.13. See chapter 10 for a discussion of Israel's claim to the land.

[48] The interrogative pronoun τί is therefore understood as predicative rather than adverbial and ἐστίν is assumed (Eckstein, *Verheißung und Gesetz*, pp. 190-91). Contrast Mußner, *Galaterbrief*, p. 245 who understands τί adverbially and includes (προσετέθη) in the question: "Warum wurde also das Gesetz *hinzugefügt*?" (Mußner's emphasis).

[49] So Eckstein, *Verheißung und Gesetz*, p. 191, is critical of Oepke, *Galater*, p. 63, who, appealing to the use of νόμος δὲ παρεισῆλθεν in Rom. 5.20a and the use of παρεισῆλθον with the subject "false brothers", understands Gal. 3.19 as "das Gesetz hat sich hintenherum *eingeschlichen*" (Oepke's emphasis).

[50] Cf. O. Hofius, "Das Gesetz des Mose und das Gesetz Christi", in *Paulusstudien* (WUNT 51), Tübingen: J.C.B. Mohr (Paul Siebeck) 1989, 62 (50-74).

[51] Cf. Eckstein, *Verheißung und Gesetz*, pp. 192-93.

For once the law was added, a new possibility for sinning was opened: the desire to fulfil the law, make a claim upon God and to boast. So "because of transgressions" (τῶν παραβάσεων χάριν) in Gal. 3.19 includes the idea of provoking and increasing transgression as one finds in Rom. 7.7-8, 13.[52] A parallel idea is found in Rom. 5.20.[53] Then in Gal. 3.19b Paul writes that the law was added until the seed came (i.e. Christ) to whom the promise "had been made" (ἄχρις οὗ ἔλθῃ τὸ σπέρμα ᾧ ἐπήγγελται). However, does it make much sense *here* to speak of a promise made to Christ?[54] Perhaps a better translation is "to whom the promise referred"[55] or "to whom the promise had been referred" (bringing out the perfect sense of ἐπήγγελται).[56] Paul therefore stresses that the law is not everlasting.[57]

3.1.8. Galatians 3.19c

Paul continues in 3.19c that the law "was ordained by/through angels through an intermediary" (διαταγεὶς δι' ἀγγέλων ἐν χειρὶ μεσίτου). The intermediary is clearly Moses (see Dt. 5.5). But in what sense are God and the angels involved in "ordaining" of the law? Some have argued that according to Gal. 3.19 God was not involved at all in the giving of the law. It is certainly the case that the verb διατάσσω has the sense "ordain" rather than simply "mediated" or "promulgated".[58] But what is the sense of δι'

---

[52] Cf. Fung, *Galatians*, pp. 159-60.

[53] So R. Bultmann, "Adam und Christus nach Römer 5", in *Exegetica. Aufsätze zur Erforschung des Neuen Testaments*, Tübingen: J.C.B. Mohr (Paul Siebeck) 1967, 439 (424-44), writes: "Das Gesetz . . . bringt die Sünde zutage: τῶν παραβάσεων χάριν προσετέθη (Gal 3,19). Denn es weckt die schlummernde Sünde ([Röm] 7,7-11), die durch das Gesetz den Tod wirken soll, ἵνα γένηται καθ᾽ ὑπερβολὴν ἁμαρτωλός ([Röm] 7,13). Die Grundsünde des Menschen ist ja das καυχᾶσθαι, und eben dieses, das sich beim Juden auf das Gesetz gründet, soll zerschlagen werden".

[54] Contrast Gal. 3.16 where I argued above that there are good grounds for understanding the promise to be made to Christ but to Christ as a representative figure.

[55] Cf. Fung, *Galatians*, p. 160, who refers to the NIV.

[56] The perfect also serves to stress the abiding validity of the promise. See Bruce, *Galatians*, p. 176; Schlier, *Galater*, p. 154.

[57] So he contradicts the ancient Jewish view as found, for example, in Bar. 4.1; 2 Bar. 77.15; 4 Ezr. 9.37; 1 En. 99.2. Also compare Sir. 24.9 and 24.23 (identification of pre-existent wisdom with the law).

[58] This is a point H. Maccoby, *The Mythmaker: Paul and the Invention of Christianity*, London: Weidenfeld & Nicholson 1986, pp. 188-89, makes to argue that according to Gal. 3.19 God was not involved in giving the law.

ἀγγέλων. The preposition διά can be understood in a causative sense.[59] And Oepke may be right to understand διά as serving "zur Bezeichnung eines Urhebers zweiten Grades",[60] so distinguishing δι' ἀγγέλων from ὑπ' ἀγγέλων. Others understand διά as instrumental.[61] I think it is difficult to exclude a causal element in δι' ἀγγέλων but this must not be seen as excluding the activity of God. Delling is right to argue that "God allowed angels to formulate its [i.e. the Law's] statutes; the Law is only decreed by angels. But the fact that it is not ordained directly by God in its details does not mean for Paul that it was not instituted by God in intention".[62] Despite the rather sinister aspects of the adding of the law (in that it brings condemnation), it must be stressed that the law was added by God.[63] But Gal. 3.19 does speak of an inferiority of the law in that it comes *indirectly* through angels whereas God speaks his promise to Abraham directly.[64] This is clarified in v. 20 (although it is a verse which has caused numerous difficulties with commentators): ὁ δὲ μεσίτης ἑνὸς οὐκ ἔστιν, ὁ δὲ θεὸς εἷς ἐστιν. This is best translated: "But the mediator is not mediator of a single person. But God is one". So Moses was a mediator of many (i.e. the angels).

---

[59] See A. Oepke, διά, *TDNT* 2:67-69 (65-70).

[60] Oepke, *Galater*, p. 64.

[61] So Schlier, *Galater*, p. 155; Mußner, *Galaterbrief*, p. 247; Bruce, *Galatians*, p. 176-77. See also Burton, *Galatians*, p. 189, who translates: "being enacted through the agency of angels in the hand of a mediator", and Lightfoot, *Galatians*, p. 145: "ordered, or administered by the medium of angels". Eckstein, *Verheißung und Gesetz*, p. 201, thinks the instrumental sense is more likely but does not rule out the causal.

[62] G. Delling, τάσσω κτλ, *TDNT*, 8:35 (27-48).

[63] Contrast, H. Hübner, *Law in Paul's Thought* (SNTW) ET, Edinburgh: T. & T. Clark 1984, p. 27, who believes that "the angels are authors of the Law" and that they are "demonic beings who in contrast to God do not desire the salvation of mankind". Note that such a view is unlikely in view of the fact that Paul is adopting a Jewish tradition of angels mediating the law. See Dt. 33.2 LXX; Ps. 67.18 LXX. Note also that this tradition is found elsewhere in the New Testament. Heb. 2.2 speaks of the "message declared by angels" (ὁ δι' ἀγγέλων λαληθεὶς λόγος). Acts 7.38 refers to the angel which spoke to Moses at Mount Sinai. See also Acts 7.53, which closes this speech of Stephen: ". . . you who received the law as delivered by angels and did not keep it" (οἵτινες ἐλάβετε τὸν νόμον εἰς διαταγὰς ἀγγέλων καὶ οὐκ ἐφυλάξατε). The relevance of this text for 1 Thes 2.14-16 was discussed in chapter 2 above.

[64] See Gal. 3.16-18 and the discussion above on Gal. 3.8 (i.e. that God is actually the subject of προορᾶν and προευαγγελίζεσθαι).

By contrast God, who is one, required no mediator when he made his promise to Abraham (cf. v.18) but spoke to him directly.[65]

3.1.9. Galatians 3.21-25

The law is not against the promises of God (3.21), but it did act as a custodian (παιδαγωγός) (3.24) until the point in time when Christ came.[66] The law was not a "pedagogue" in the sense that it had an educative function. Rather Paul is emphasizing the confining and restrictive roles of the παιδαγωγός.[67] We may compare the image of v. 23: "Before faith came we were guarded and confined under law, until the revelation of the faith that was to come" (Πρὸ τοῦ δὲ ἐλθεῖν τὴν πίστιν ὑπὸ νόμον ἐφρουρούμεθα συγκλειόμενοι εἰς τὴν μέλλουσαν πίστιν ἀποκαλυφθῆναι). But now that "faith has come" (3.25) we are no longer under such a παιδαγωγός. The law has been surpassed in the history of salvation.[68]

3.1.10. Galatians 3.29

In Gal. 3.29 Paul states that "if you are Christ's, then you are Abraham's offspring, heirs according to promise" (εἰ δὲ ὑμεῖς Χριστοῦ, ἄρα τοῦ Ἀβραὰμ σπέρμα ἐστέ, κατ᾽ ἐπαγγελίαν κληρονόμοι). This underlines what Paul said earlier in 3.7 and functions as a resumé. But a new element has entered the argument because in v. 27 he brings in the idea of being baptized into Christ. Christians (whether Jew or Gentile) are the seed of Abraham because they are in Christ who is himself the seed of Abraham (3.16).

3.1.11. Galatians 4.1-7

The Christian is no longer a "slave" but a "son". This is stressed in two ways. First in Gal. 4.1-7 Paul uses the image of the "heir" as a slave who subsequently gains adoption as a son.[69] The Galatians were "slaves to the

---

[65] See the diagram in Mußner, *Galaterbrief*, p. 249.

[66] Cf. Hofius, "Das Gesetz des Mose und das Gesetz Christi", 64 n. 51.

[67] The παιδαγωγός (literally "boy-leader") was usually a slave who conducted the freeborn youth to and from school and had some oversight over his behaviour.

[68] But it needs to be stressed that the law was never a means of salvation. Cf. Hofius, "Das Gesetz des Mose und das Gesetz Christi", 64 n. 51.

[69] The precise background to this section is disputed. See e.g. J.M. Scott, *Adoption as Sons of God: An Exegetical Investigation into the Background of ΥΙΟΘΕΣΙΑ in the Pauline Corpus* (WUNT 2.48), Tübingen: J.C.B. Mohr (Paul Siebeck) 1992, pp. 121-86.

elemental spirits of the universe" (ὑπὸ τὰ στοιχεῖα τοῦ κόσμου ἤμεθα δεδουλωμένοι) (Gal. 4.3). For the Jews, the term "elemental spirits" refers to the law of Moses; for the Gentiles, the term refers to their gods who, according to 4.8, are no real gods.[70] Paul then speaks of redemption in vv. 4-5: "But when the time had fully come, God sent forth his Son, born of woman, born under the law, 5 to redeem those who were under the law, so that we might receive adoption as sons" (ὅτε δὲ ἦλθεν τὸ πλήρωμα τοῦ χρόνου, ἐξαπέστειλεν ὁ θεὸς τὸν υἱὸν αὐτοῦ, γενόμενον ἐκ γυναικός, γενόμενον ὑπὸ νόμον, 5 ἵνα τοὺς ὑπὸ νόμον ἐξαγοράσῃ, ἵνα τὴν υἱοθεσίαν ἀπολάβωμεν). The expression γενόμενον ὑπὸ νόμον points to the fact that Jesus Christ took upon himself the curse of the law[71] and by doing so was identifying himself with humanity;[72] and the redemption he refers to in v. 5 is for Jews *and Gentiles*. And those who have been redeemed can cry "Abba! Father!" (4.6b) and are no longer a slave but a son "and if a son then an heir" (4.7b). So the heirs are not the Jews but those Jews and Gentiles who have been redeemed by Christ.

3.1.12. Galatians 4.21-31

The second analogy Paul uses to show that Christians are not slaves but free sons is that of Sarah and Hagar (4.21-31).[73] Abraham had two sons by these two women: Ishmael was the son of the slave Hagar; Isaac was the son of the free woman Sarah. Hagar bore her son κατὰ σάρκα but Sarah bore her

---

[70] Cf. E. Plümacher, στοιχεῖον, *EDNT* 3:278 (277-78).

[71] Cf. Gal. 3.13. However, the curse of the law upon Christ cannot simply be restricted to his death on calvary. See my argument in "Sacrifice and Christology", 14-16.

[72] Contrast the view of Mußner, *Galaterbrief*, p. 270, who argues Paul is stressing "daß er nicht nur Mensch unter den Menschen wurde, sondern darüber hinaus Jude und als solcher dem Gesetz unterstellt".

[73] This has variously been called an "allegory" (Burton, *Galatians*, p. 251; Schoeps, *Paul*, p. 234) or "typology" (Bruce, *Galatians*, p. 217). Fung, *Galatians*, p. 218, following H.L. Ellison, *The Message of the Old Testament*, Grand Rapids: Wm B. Eerdmans 1969, p. 70, rightly calls this an analogy. The Greek has ἅτινά ἐστιν ἀλληγορούμενα (3.24) but A.T. Hanson, "Birth with Promise", in *Studies in Paul's Technique and Theology*, London: SPCK 1974, 91 (87-103), rightly points out "just as τύπος in Paul does not necessarily mean 'type', so we are not justified in assuming that ἀλληγορούμενα means 'are an allegory'". After engaging in a study of the verb, he takes it to mean "these things are intended to convey a deeper meaning" ("Birth with Promise", 94).

son δι᾽ ἐπαγγαλίας (v. 23). The analogy is that these women refer to two covenants (δύο διαθῆκαι) (v. 24). The word διαθήκη, often translated as "covenant", is "a world order decreed by divine institution".[74] It is often assumed that these "covenants" are the old and new covenants. But the διαθήκη . . . ἀπὸ ὄρους Σινᾶ probably refers to the "law" in the sense of the legal material found in Ex. 20.1-17 and following.[75] Further, the other διαθήκη, rather than referring to the "new covenant", may well refer to the covenant God made with Abraham. These two διαθῆκαι, therefore, can be considered to be simultaneous "covenants", for the covenant which Christians enjoy was originally that made with Abraham (and Sarah and Isaac). In Gal. 4.25 Paul writes that Hagar is Mount Sinai in Arabia.[76] But why would Paul wish to bring in Arabia? Various suggestions have been made, but the best interpretation is that v. 25a has a sort of concessive force and δέ of v. 25b has an adversative force: "It is true that this Hagar represents mount Sinai in Arabia, but she is to be identified with the Jerusalem so strongly propagated by the heretical teachers".[77] Thereby Paul relates "Sinai" to "Jerusalem". So Hagar represents the "covenant" of the law (cf. Ex. 24.7-8) and the law itself, and she corresponds to the present Jerusalem (συστοιχεῖ δὲ τῇ νῦν Ἰερουσαλήμ). The verb συστοιχέω, a hapax legomenon in early Christian literature, means "to stand in the same rank or line, of soldiers" or "correspond" (LSJ). Here the sense is the former, and many commentators therefore rightly place the concepts in columns:[78]

---

[74] H.D. Betz, *Galatians* (Hermeneia), Philadelphia: Fortress Press 1979, p. 244. Cf. Kutsch, *Neues Testament*, p. 159, who understands the διαθήκη related to Hagar as "Setzung".

[75] O. Hofius, "Gesetz und Evangelium nach 2. Korinther 3", in *Paulusstudien* (WUNT 51), Tübingen: J.C.B. Mohr (Paul Siebeck) 1989, 76-77 (75-120).

[76] There is some dispute over the original reading. However, the harder reading given in *NA*[27] is the more probable reading: τὸ δὲ Ἀγὰρ Σινᾶ ὄρος ἐστὶν ἐν τῇ Ἀραβίᾳ. Cf. Betz, *Galatians*, p. 244.

[77] See H.N. Ridderbos, *The Epistle to the Galatians* (NLC) ET, London: Marshall, Morgan & Scott 1976 (repr.), ([3]1961), pp. 177-78, who also discusses the textual variants.

[78] See, e.g., Betz, *Galatians*, p. 245. The columns I present bear some resemblance to those of Betz.

Hagar	Sarah
son of the slave woman	son of the free woman
born according to the flesh	born through the promise
"covenant" of Sinai	covenant with Abraham (?)
present Jerusalem	heavenly Jerusalem
slavery	freedom
born according to the flesh	born according to the Spirit
persecute	persecuted
cast out	inherit

But it has been suggested that since the cognate συστοιχία can mean coordinate pairs such as odd and even, right and left,[79] it may be that "present Jerusalem" should be in the *opposite* column to "Hagar".[80] This is rather unlikely; Paul means to say that Hagar "belongs to the same column as the present Jerusalem".[81] And ἡ νῦν Ἰερουσαλήμ refers to the city Jerusalem as "das geistliche Zentrum der Judenschaft".[82] And this Jerusalem is not the ideal city of David or Solomon;[83] rather it is associated with slavery! And it is a present slavery (δουλεύει). So she (Hagar) is in slavery with her children (δουλεύει γὰρ μετὰ τῶν τέκνων αὐτῆς). On the other hand Sarah is the Jerusalem "above" (ἡ ἄνω Ἰερουσαλήμ) and is free (ἐλευθέρα ἐστίν) (v. 26a). Further, she is "our mother" (ἥτις ἐστὶν μήτηρ ἡμῶν) (v. 26b). Paul here is clearly replacing the synagogue with the Church. For the Jewish self-

---

[79] See LSJ. Aristotle, *Metaphysics* 986a, when discussing the Pythagorean tables of opposites, writes: "Others of this same school hold that there are ten principles, which they enunciate in a series of corresponding pairs (κατὰ συστοιχίαν): (i.) Limit and the Unlimited; (ii.) Odd and Even; (iii.) Unity and Plurality; (iv.) Right and Left; . . . (H. Tredennick (ed.), *Aristotle: Metaphysics, Books I-IX* (LCL), London/Cambridge Mass.: Harvard University Press 1996 (repr.), ([1]1933), pp. 34-35).

[80] See L. Gaston, "Israel's Enemies in Pauline Theology", *NTS* 28 (1982) 404 (400-23). One of Gaston's purposes is to question the anti-Judaic character of Galatians. But even if his attempt to place "present Jerusalem" in the opposite column to "Hagar", Paul still has many negative things to say about the Sinai covenant.

[81] See J.D.G. Dunn, *The Epistle to the Galatians* (BNTC), London: A. & C. Black 1993, p. 252.

[82] Mußner, *Galaterbrief*, p. 325. I am not so sure of Mußner's suggestion that Paul may have in mind Jerusalem as a centre of "Judenchristenheit".

[83] Mußner, *Galaterbrief*, p. 325.

understanding was that they were the free ones.[84] Further, the Jews claimed Jerusalem as their mother.[85] Now she is the mother of Christians. Paul then quotes Is. 54.1, which is apposite for his purposes:

Rejoice, O barren one who does not bear;
break forth and shout, you who are not in travail;
for the children of the desolate one are many more
than the children of the one who has a husband.

Paul applies this to Sarah (who originally was barren, Gen. 16.1); further, Hagar, when she conceived, looked with contempt at Sarah (Gen. 16.4). Paul has therefore completed his συσοιχία.[86] It is quite clear that Paul wishes to create an opposition between the Church of Jews and Gentiles on the one hand and non-Christian Jews on the other. But within this non-Christian Jewish group he includes his Jewish Christian enemies. Paul therefore "wants to create a dualistic polarity between 'Judaism' and 'Christianity,' in order to discredit his Jewish-Christian opposition".[87]

Paul in vv. 28-31 draws out the devastating consequences of this analogy. Addressing the Galatians in the second person, he tells them that they are children of promise, like Isaac. Children of promise are those Jewish Pauline Christians and the Gentile Christians (hence Paul addresses them as ἀδελφοί). And just as then, when the one born "according to the flesh" persecuted the one born "according to the Spirit", so it is now (v. 29). Although there is no story in the Old Testament about Ishmael "persecuting" Isaac, some have understood the pi'el participle מְצַחֵק of Gen. 21.9 to mean "mocking".[88] If it is translated "playing", Isaac is supplied as an object (following

---

[84] See m. Aboth 6.2: "'And the tables were the work of God, and the writing was the writing of God, graven (haruth) upon the tables'. Read not 'haruth' but 'heruth' (freedom), for thou findest no freeman excepting him that occupies himself in the study of the Law; and he that occupies himself in the study of the Law shall be exalted . . ." (Danby, *Mishnah*, p. 459).

[85] See Is. 50.1; 51.17-18; 54.1 (quoted in Gal. 4.27); 60.4; Jer. 50.12; Ps. 87.5. See also 4 Ezr. 10.7 and the material in Billerbeck, *Kommentar*, 3:574.

[86] Betz, *Galatians*, p. 249.

[87] Betz, *Galatians*, p. 246.

[88] See G. Wenham, *Genesis 16-50* (WBC 2), Dallas, Texas: Word Books 1994, p. 82. But J. Skinner, *A Critical and Exegetical Commentary on Genesis* (ICC), Edinburgh: T. & T. Clark ²1930, (¹1910), p. 322, argues that "mock" would require a following בְּ.

LXX, Vulgate).[89] But however the text is translated, traditions developed to account for Sarah's anger in her demand for Hagar and Ishmael to be expelled (Gen. 21.10, quoted in Gal. 4.30).[90] Note also that in the Genesis text itself Hagar held Sarah in contempt (Gen. 16.4). Perhaps this was then projected onto the relationship between their respective sons. But Gen. 21.9 is clearly the most important text, since the following verse is quoted in Gal. 4.30: "Cast out the slave and her son; for the son of the slave shall not inherit with the son of the free woman". The words "of the free woman" (τῆς ἐλευθέρας) are not in the LXX and are clearly Paul's own addition. Betz rightly argues that "cast out" (ἔκβαλε) must be taken seriously.[91] But who is to be cast out? Clearly Paul believes that all Jews who do not believe in Christ are to be cast out.[92] Some, however, believe that such a conclusion can only be reached if the situation which Paul is addressing is ignored,[93] i.e. that Paul is attacking the Judaizers who are insisting that Gentile Christians be circumcised.[94] In response one must say that Paul's line of argument in Galatians 4 is precisely that because Jews are to be cast out, the Jewish Christians who oppose Paul must also be cast out.[95] The final part of Paul's argument in 4.22-31 can therefore be put like this:

Hagar the slave bears a son who persecutes the son of Sarah, the free woman. She and her son are cast out by divine command. The unbelieving Jews, enslaved to the Torah,

---

[89] E.A. Speiser, *Genesis* (AB), Garden City, New York: Doubleday & Co. 1964, translates Gen. 21.9 as: "When Sarah noticed that the son whom Hagar the Egyptian had borne to Abraham was playing with her son Isaac" (p. 153) and writes "his 'playing' with Isaac need mean no more than that the older boy was trying to amuse his little brother". He suggests that "with her son Isaac" may have been lost in MT by haplography (מצחק is a play on the name יצחק).

[90] See Billerbeck, *Kommentar*, 3:575-76. So according to R. Yishmael, "מצחק means nothing other than bloodshed" (t. Sot. 6.6 (304)).

[91] Betz, *Galatians*, pp. 250-51.

[92] See Oepke, *Galater*, p. 87: "Hagar, dh das ungläubige Israel, wird ausgestoßen und vom (messianischen) Erbe ausgeschlossen"; U. Luz, *Das Geschichtsverständnis des Paulus* (BEvTh 49), München: Chr. Kaiser Verlag 1968, p. 285: "Hier ist die Verwerfung der Juden explizit ausgesprochen".

[93] See Mußner, *Galaterbrief*, p. 332.

[94] See again Mußner, *Galater*, p. 332, and R.N. Longenecker, *Galatians* (WBC 41), Dallas, Texas: Word Books 1990, p. 217.

[95] Note that Mußner, *Galater*, p. 332, and Longenecker, *Galatians*, p. 217, both say Paul cannot be casting out all Jews because of what he writes in Rom. 9-11. But this does not take account of a possible change in Paul's view (see Betz, *Galatians*, p. 251).

persecute believing Christians, who are free in Christ. The unbelieving Jews are rejected by God.[96]

But Paul may also be implying that if the Galatians Gentiles succumb to the demands of the Judaizers and opt for Judaism rather than Paul's view, they will effectively exclude themselves.[97] The passage is concluded in v. 31 by Paul's assertion that the Galatian Christians are not children of the slave woman, but of the free woman.

Gal. 4.21-31 has been rightly seen as attacking Judaism, and it can even be inferred that Paul is bringing Judaism to an end.[98] Perhaps Paul is even attacking the Jewish people.[99] This is also the case even if Paul used the story of Abraham and his two sons Isaac and Ishamel because his opponents had used it.[100] Paul's argument in Gal. 4.21-31 has been a source of embarrassment for Christians.[101]

---

[96] Hanson, "Birth with Promise", 95.

[97] Betz, *Galatians*, p. 251.

[98] Lightfoot, *Galatians*, p. 184: "The Law and the Gospel cannot coexist; the Law must disappear before the Gospel. . . The Apostle thus confidently sounds the death-knell of Judaism".

[99] See the references in Gaston, "Israel's Enemies", 419 n. 15. It is, however, worth noting that Gaston has misrepresented the views of W.M. Ramsay, *A Historical Commentary on St. Paul's Epistle to the Galatians*, London: Hodder and Stoughton ²1900, p. 431. Ramsay does not find the passage "unnecessarily insulting and offensive to Jews, weak as an argument, and not likely to advance his purpose" as Gaston suggests. Rather, according to Ramsay, the passage *would* be so *if* "this passage were to be taken simply in its relation to the preceding and following parts of the Epistle, as rising spontaneously in Paul's mind in the sequence of his own philosophical argument".

[100] C.K. Barrett, "The Allegory of Abraham, Sarah, and Hagar in the Argument of Galatians", in J. Friedrich, W. Pöhlmann, and P. Stuhlmacher (ed.), *Rechtfertigung: Festschrift für Ernst Käsemann zum 70. Geburtstag*, Tübingen: J.C.B. Mohr (Paul Siebeck)/Göttingen: Vandenhoeck & Ruprecht 1976, 10 (1-16), suggests that Paul used this passage from Genesis because his opponents were using it to argue that "the Jews, who live by the law of Moses, are the heirs of Abraham and it is to Jews that the promise applies".

[101] So J.L. Martyn, "The Covenants of Hagar and Sarah: Two Covenants and Two Gentile Missions", *Theological Issues in the Letters of Paul* (SNTW), Edinburgh: T. & T. Clark 1997, 192-93 (191-208), points to the exclusion of this text (together with 1 Thes. 2.14-15; Gal. 3.19-20; 2 Cor. 3.6, 14) from the declaration of the Rheinland Synod, 1980. I take his point that the declaration does work with its own canon but one also has to bear in mind that the declaration is not long, being just over two pages in Klappert and Starck, *Umkehr und Erneuerung*, pp. 264-66. Perhaps one may add that Barth's silence concerning Gal. 4.21-31 is not so "remarkable" in *CD* 4.1:637-42 (just

3.1.13. Galatians 3-4: Conclusions

The whole argument of Galatians 3-4 is devastating and Christian familiarity with the text has perhaps made us forget the original impact of this text. So the law, far from keeping one from sin (the traditional Jewish view), acts as the condemning word of God. And the gospel has replaced the law in salvation history (Gal. 3.19-25). Indeed the gospel was prior to the law. And the fundamental point for our enquiry is that just as the gospel has replaced the law, so also Christians (both Jew and Gentile) have replaced Israel.[102] Jews who do not believe in Christ are the sons of slavery. The children of Abraham are now *exclusively* those who believe in Christ.

3.2. Galatians 6.16

Another text in Galatians relevant to the question whether Paul has a substitution model is Gal. 6.16.[103] The text in the RSV is: "Peace and mercy be upon all who walk by this rule, upon the Israel of God" (καὶ ὅσοι τῷ κανόνι τούτῳ στοιχήσουσιν, εἰρήνη ἐπ᾽ αὐτοὺς καὶ ἔλεος καὶ ἐπὶ τὸν Ἰσραὴλ τοῦ θεοῦ). According to this translation καί before ἐπὶ τὸν Ἰσραὴλ θεοῦ is taken as epexegetic. The "Israel of God" is therefore taken to mean the Church of Jews and Gentiles.[104] However, three other proposals have been supported

---

less than six pages are devoted to the argument of Galatians) as Martyn suggests. Martyn, "Covenants", 193 n. 6, points to H. Jansen, "Allegorie van slavernij en vrijheid", in T. Baarda, H. Jansen, S.J. Noorda and J.S. Vos (ed), *Paulus en de andere joden*, Delft: Meinema 1984, 107 n. 20 (75-113).

[102] Luz, *Geschichtsverständnis*, p. 285: "Paulus steht hier vor der Notwendigkeit, die Radikalität und Einzigkeit der göttlichen Gnade in einer Situation klar zu machen, wo sich das Gesetz als zweiter, besserer oder zusätzlicher Weg zum Heil anzubieten schien. Hier muß Paulus klarstellen: Das Gesetz führt, wird es als Heilsweg verstanden, nicht zum Heil, sondern schließt Heil aus. In der Konsequenz dieser Ausführungen läge: Das Judentum *ist* verworfen. Der Grund dieser – allerdings nicht gezogenen – Konsequenz ist: Die Gnade ist der einzige Zugang zu Gott. Und zugleich hält Paulus energisch die Kontinuität von Gottes Handeln fest: Indem die Verheißung im Christusgeschehen wirksam wird, löst Gott sein altes, in der Schrift vorherverkündetes Handeln ein. *Daß in Gl. 3 und 4 der Heilsweg Israels so radikal preisgegeben und zugleich der Gottesvolkgedanke so radikal festgehalten wird, ist nicht zufällig, sondern entspricht sich gegenseitig*" (Luz's emphasis).

[103] For a survey of opinions, see G. Schrenk, "Was bedeutet 'Israel Gottes'?", *Jud* 5 (1949) 81-94, and P. Richardson, *Israel in the Apostolic Church* (SNTSMS 10), Cambridge: CUP 1969, pp. 74-84.

[104] N.A. Dahl, "Der Name Israel: Zur Auslegung von Gal. 6,16", *Jud* 6 (1950) 161-70.

which all go against the substitution theory. One is that the "Israel of God" refers to Jewish Christians.[105] The second is that "Israel of God" refers to "the remnant according to the election of grace" who "even though as yet unenlightened are the true Israel of God".[106] The third is that the "Israel of God" ('Ισραὴλ τοῦ θεοῦ) means "all Israel" (πᾶς 'Ισραήλ) as in Rom. 11.26.[107]

I believe that in the light of the whole argument in Galatians, the reference is most likely to the Church of Jews and Gentiles, thereby implying a substitution model. We have already seen that Paul in Galatians 3-4 has argued that the Church of Jews and Gentiles replaces Israel. Further Paul has been at pains in these chapters to stress that national distinctions no longer count. So it is the people of faith who are sons of Abraham (3.7). There is neither Jew nor Greek for all are one in Christ Jesus (3.28). If such distinctions do not count it would be odd for Paul to wish peace and mercy upon those in the Church according to their ethnic distinctions. This is especially so since Paul in the previous verse argues that neither circumcision nor uncircumcision counts for anything, and what does count is the new creation (καινὴ κτίσις). Some have argued that Paul's whole argument leads up to 6.15.[108] Whether or not this is the case it is clear that what Paul writes in Gal. 6.11-18 is integrally related to the earlier part of his letter.[109] Some confirmation

---

[105] See G. Schrenk's response to Dahl in "Der Name Israel: Der Segenswunsch nach der Kampfepistel", *Jud* 6 (1950) 170-90. Cf. Richardson, *Israel*, p. 83: "The 'Israel of God' is, when Galatians is written, a part of the Israelite nation".

[106] See Burton, *Galatians*, p. 358. Burton translates Gal. 6.16 as: "And as many as walk by this rule, peace be upon them, and mercy upon the Israel of God" (p. 357). A distinction is therefore made between those who walk by the principle of Gal. 6.15 and the elect of Israel. For criticism of Burton, see Fung, *Galatians*, p. 310.

[107] See Mußner, *Galaterbrief*, p. 417 n. 61. For Mußner's understanding of πᾶς 'Ισραήλ see F. Mußner, *Traktat über die Juden*, München: Kösel-Verlag 1979, pp. 52-57 and "'Ganz Israel wird gerettet werden' (Röm 11,26)", *Kairos* NF 18 (1976) 241-55.

[108] See Betz, *Galatians*, p. 321. See also J.A.D. Weima, "Gal. 6,11-18: a Hermeneutical Key to the Galatian Letter", *CTJ* 28 (1993) 90-107; "The Pauline Letter Closings: Analysis and Hermeneutical Significance", *BBR* 5 (1995) 177-98; C.A. Ray, "The Identity of the 'Israel of God'", *TE* 50 (1994) 105-14.

[109] Fung, *Galatians*, p. viii, considers Gal. 6.11-18 to be the "Summary and Conclusion" of the letter. Others like F.J. Matera, "The Culmination of Paul's Argument to the Galatians: Gal. 5.1-6.17", *JSNT* 32 (1988) 79-91, consider chapters 5 and 6 to be the culmination.

of this understanding of "Israel of God" can be found in Beale's argument that Is. 54.10 and its context forms an appropriate background to the ideas of "new creation" and "Israel of God" in Gal. 6.15-16.[110] For Paul has already used Is. 54.1 in Gal. 4.27 for the redefined "Israel" which consists of Jews and Gentiles.

3.3. *Galatians: Conclusion*

In conclusion, Galatians seems to put forward a view that the Church of Jews and Gentiles replaces Israel as the people of God. Before turning to Romans to see if a similar view of substitution is to be found, I consider briefly some texts from the Corinthian correspondence and Philippians.

4. 1 and 2 Corinthians and Philippians

4.1. *Controversy with Judaizers in Philippians and 2 Corinthians*

Philippians and 2 Corinthians do not put forward the sort of substitution theory found in Galatians but neither do they make clear that Israel's election remains firm. The fact that there is no clear substitution theory is perhaps significant for in these letters Paul is, as in Galatians, having to contend with Judaizers. He could therefore be tempted, as in Galatians, to make negative comments about Israel. However, his negative comments seem to be reserved for the Judaizers themselves.

In Phil. 3.2 Paul warns[111] the Philippian Christians of the "dogs" who are also termed "evil workers" and "mutilation".[112] Paul is referring to one

---

[110] G.K. Beale, "Peace and Mercy Upon the Israel of God: The Old Testament Background of Galatians 6,16b", *Bib* 80 (1999) 204-23.

[111] The threefold βλέπετε is to be translated "beware of", not "consider" or "take due not of" (as suggested by G.D. Kilpatrick, "ΒΛΕΠΕΤΕ, Philippians 3:2", in M. Black and G. Fohrer, *In Memoriam Paul Kahle* (BZAW 103), Berlin: A. Töpelmann 1968, 146-48; Caird, *Paul's Letters from Prison*, p. 133; G.F. Hawthorne, *Philippians* (WBC 43), Waco: Word Books 1983, p. 125).

[112] I take Phil. 3.2-4.1 to be an original part of the letter (contra F.W. Beare, *The Epistle to the Philippians* (BNTC), London: A. & C. Black 1959, pp. 100-41, who understands it as "an interpolated fragment").

group whom I take to be Judaizers,[113] not Jews in general.[114] It is difficult to conceive of a situation whereby Jews were trying to persuade Gentile Christians to become Jewish proselytes.[115] However, we know from Galatians (and 2 Corinthians) that Judaizers were a serious threat and it seems that we are dealing with such opponents here also. They do not appear to be a local group; rather they are a distant threat.[116] In Phil. 3.2-3 Paul contrasts these "dogs", "evil workers" and "mutilation" with what is often translated as the "true circumcision". Robinson argues that when Paul speaks of ἡ περιτομή in Phil. 3.2, he is referring to Jewish Christians who, like Paul, "have the spiritual reality of which their outward circumcision is the sign"[117] and believes Phil. 3.15-16 and 17-21 refer to such Jewish Christians. However, this is a rather unnatural reading and the Gentile readers are unlikely to have understood the term in this way.[118] Paul most likely refers to all Christians,

---

[113] J.J. Müller, *The Epistle of Paul to the Philippians* (NICNT), Grand Rapids: Eerdmans 1991 (repr.), (¹1955), p. 106; G.D. Fee, *Paul's Letter to the Philippians* (NICNT), Grand Rapids: Eerdmans 1995, p. 294; O'Brien, *Philippians*, pp. 353-57, seems to take the reference to be to Judaizers (p. 357), but he does not exclude the idea that "mutilation" could refer to "Jews, Judaizing Christians, or Gentile proselytes circumcised later in life" (p. 354). R.P. Martin, *Philippians* (NCB), London: Oliphants 1976, p. 125, thinks the opponents are Jewish-Christian gnostic emissaries. J. Gnilka, *Der Philipperbrief* (HThKNT 10.3), Freiburg/Basel/Wien: Herder ⁴1987, (¹1968), p. 188, believes they are not simply Jews, but people "die mit ihrer Predigt eine gefährliche Synthese von Jüdischem und Christlichem und noch anderen Elementen anbieten".

[114] Those who believe the reference is to Jews include E. Lohmeyer, *Der Brief an die Philipper* (KEK 9), Göttingen: Vandenhoeck & Ruprecht ¹⁴1974, (⁸1930), pp. 124-26; Caird, *Paul's Letters from Prison*, pp. 130-34; G.F. Hawthorne, *Philippians* (WBC 43), Waco: Word Books 1983, pp. xliv-xlvii, 125; D.E. Garland, "The Composition and Unity of Philippians: Some Neglected Factors", *NovT* 27 (1985) 167-69.

[115] Further, as Fee, *Philippians*, p. 294 n. 38 points out, it is unlikely that Gentile Christians would be attracted to becoming Jewish proselytes "since that is what most of them avoided as God fearers".

[116] Cf. P. Bonnard, *L'épîtres de saint Paul aux Philippiens et l'épître aux Colossiens* (CNT), Neuchâtel: Delachaux et Nestle 1950, p. 9.

[117] D.W.B. Robinson, "'We are the circumcision'", *AusBR* 15 (1967) 30-32 (28-35).

[118] Note that one of Robinson's arguments is that "the circumcision" always refers to "'Jews' in an actual sense" and that "[o]n no occasion is it used figuratively" ("Circumcision", 30). It is the case that if ἡ περιτομή is taken in Phil. 3.2 to refer to Christians generally, then this is an exception. However, note that in Rom. 2.26 the term περιτομή is used in a figurative sense. See the exegesis below on Rom. 2.25-29.

believing Jews and Gentiles. They, but not the Judaizers, are the "circumcision" (περιτομή); Judaizers are the "mutilation" (κατατομή).

Many commentators assume that Paul in Philippians is virtually asserting
that Israel has been disinherited. So O'Brien writes: "The nation's claim to
be ἡ περιτομή is false; in truth it is ἡ κατατομή".[119] But this does not sufficiently take into account the polemical context and the fact that Paul is
attacking Judaizers, not Jews in general. Undoubtedly, Paul is saying that a
Christian is a "spiritual Jew". But it is by no means clear that the Jew is disinherited. It is instructive to consider John Chrysostom's use of Phil. 3.2-3a
to argue that the Jews have been disinherited. He says in his First Discourse
against the Jews:

> Although those Jews had been called to the adoption of sons, they fell to kinship with
> dogs; we who were dogs received the strength, through God's grace, to put aside the
> irrational nature which was ours and to rise to the honor of sons. How do I prove this?
> Christ said: 'It is not fair to take the children's bread and to cast it to the dogs.' Christ
> was speaking to the Canaanite woman when He called the Jews children and the Gentiles
> dogs. (2) But see how thereafter the order was changed about: they became dogs, and
> we became the children. Paul said of the Jews: 'Beware of the dogs, beware of the evil
> workers, beware of the mutilation. For we are the circumcision.' Do you see how those
> who at first were children became dogs?[120]

It is understandable that Chrysostom should apply Phil. 3.2-3 in this way
since he was faced with the situation of Christians being attracted to
Judaism and synagogue worship. In Antioch Christians were therefore being

---

[119] O'Brien, *Philippians*, p. 359.

[120] Chrysostom, *Adversus Iudaeos* 1.2.1-2 in P.W. Harkins (ed.), *Saint John
Chrysostom: Discourses against Judaizing Christians* (FaCh 68), Washington: Catholic
University of America Press 1977, pp. 5-6 (*PG* 48:845). The title *Adversus Iudaeos* is
that given in *PG*. Note, however, that these sermons were not addressed against Jews as
such but against Christians who were being attracted to Judaism. Hence Harkins feels
justified in giving the title "Discourses against Judaizing Christians" (see Harkins, *Discourses*, p. xxxi n. 47). See also F. Millar, "Jews of the Graeco-Roman Diaspora", in J.
Lieu, J. North and T. Rajak (ed.), *The Jews among Pagans and Christians in the Roman
Empire*, London/New York: Routledge 1992, 115 (97-123): "His sermons, though
inevitably hostile in tone, are not directed against the Jews of Antioch as such, but
against Christians from his congregation who allowed themselves to be drawn into participating in the Jewish festivals . . ."

led astray not by Jewish Christians but by non-Christian Jews.[121] Chrysostom clearly read his own situation into the text of Phil. 3.2-3.

Likewise it has been argued that since Paul speaks of Christians as "those worshipping by the Spirit of God" (οἱ πνεύματι θεοῦ λατρεύοντες)[122] that ἡ λατρεία, the service of God, is now performed by the Church and not by Israel.[123] Philippians may not have the positive view of Israel's λατρεία as in Rom. 9.4, but to make these assertions about the simple transfer of the λατρεία from Israel to the Church is going beyond the evidence of the text.[124] Philippians does not seem to put forward an explicit substitution model. The same seems to be the case in 2 Corinthians.

There has been considerable debate about Paul's opponents in 2 Corinthians. The three main views are that they were Judaizers,[125] Gnostics,[126] or Christian propagandists from a Hellenistic-Jewish background.[127] There have also been attempts to refine or even combine some of these views. So Murphy-O'Connor suggests that although the intruders were Judaizers they allied themselves with the "Spirit-people" of Corinth and in order to make themselves attractive to this group they "preached themselves" (2 Cor. 4.5; 10.12) by demonstrating their visions (12.1) and miracles

---

[121] Millar, "Jews", 115, writes that "the annual cycle of festivals was indeed observed by the synagogue community of Antioch, and in such a way as to attract the attention, favourable or hostile, of their Christian neighbours". One reason Judaism was attractive was because the synagogues were revered as being the place where the Law and the Prophets were kept (Chrysostom, *Discourse* 1.5.2).

[122] Note that πνεύματι is instrumental (so πνεύματι θεοῦ means "by the Spirit of God"). Some early scribes unnecessarily changed θεοῦ to θεῷ to avoid the implication that the Spirit is worshipped.

[123] Cf. O'Brien, *Philippians*, pp. 360-61.

[124] It is perhaps significant that although O'Brien, *Philippians*, p. 360 n. 84, mentions Rom. 9.4 and Acts 26.7 in passing in connection with the Septuagintal use of λατρεύω, he fails to draw on the significance of these New Testament texts.

[125] See H. Windisch, *Der zweite Korintherbrief* (KEK 6), Göttingen: Vandenhoeck & Ruprecht ⁹1924, pp. 23-26; C.K. Barrett, "Paul's Opponents in 2 Corinthians", in *Essays on Paul*, London: SPCK 1982, 60-86 (= *NTS* 17 (1970-71) 233-54), who believes these Judaizers "had their roots in Jerusalem" (80). Cf. the earlier study by E. Käsemann, "Die Legimität des Apostels", *ZNW* 41 (1942) 33-71.

[126] See, e.g., W. Schmithals, *Gnosticism in Corinth: An Investigation of the Letters to the Corinthians* ET, Nashville: Abingdon 1971.

[127] Georgi, *Gegner*.

(12.12).[128] This reconstruction whilst appearing perfectly reasonable may not be entirely correct in view of its speculative nature; but it does show that it is possible to combine more than one view regarding the identity of Paul's opponents and I believe it is quite plausible that these opponents were Judaizers or had a Judaizing theology as a major part of their polemic.

Paul attacks these opponents for preaching a different gospel (11.4). They are "false apostles" (ψευδαπόστολοι), "deceitful workmen" (ἐργάται δόλιοι) (11.13). Paul can also boast with them: "Are they Hebrews? So am I. Are they Israelites? So am I. Are they descendants of Abraham? So am I" (11.22). All these attributes have a positive significance. Yet despite this polemic against Judaizers, Paul does not seem to make any comment to suggest that Israel has been replaced by the Church of Jews and Gentiles.

2 Corinthians, like Philippians, does not seem to put forward an explicit substitution model. And, as we shall see in a later discussion, it is in 2 Cor. 3.16 that we see the first hope of the salvation of Israel.[129]

4.2. The Generation in the Wilderness (1 Corinthians 10.1-13)

As far as 1 Corinthians is concerned I consider here 1 Cor. 10.1-13 and in the next section 10.14-22. These texts are placed in the context of 8.1-11.1 where Paul is discussing questions of the eating of meat offered to idols and the participation in cultic meals.[130] 10.1-13 functions as a warning to Christians and in part addresses those who had a view that partaking in the

---

[128] J. Murphy-O'Connor, *The Theology of the Second Letter to the Corinthians*, Cambridge: CUP 1991, p. 15. He points out that his view is a development of that of Barrett, "Paul's Opponents in II Corinthians", 80. So although the intruders were "Jerusalem Jews, Judaizing Jews" they were prepared "to accept the criteria proposed by the Corinthians, and thus to adopt a measure of hellenization–one might almost say, of Corinthianization". Barrett suggests that this accommodation of Judaizing Christian Jews to hellenistic criteria may have contributed to the growth of gnosticism (86 n. 84). However, it is difficult to find any evidence of gnostic thought or groups before 70 AD (cf. M. Hengel, "Die Ursprünge der Gnosis und das Urchristentum", in J. Ådna, S.J. Hafemann and O. Hofius (ed.), *Evangelium – Schriftauslegung – Kirche. Festschrift für Peter Stuhlmacher zum 65. Geburtstag*, Göttingen: Vandenhoeck & Ruprecht 1997, 223 (190-223).

[129] See chapter 6 below.

[130] Cf. the heading given by W. Schrage, *Der erste Brief an die Korinther: 2. Teilband 1Kor 6,12-11,16* (KEK 7.2), Solothurn/ Düsseldorf: Benziger Verlag/Neukirchen-Vluyn: Neukirchener Verlag 1995, p. 211.

"sacraments" could offer them protection. So in 10.1 Paul refers to "our fathers" who "were all under the cloud, and all passed through the sea, 2 and all were baptized into Moses in the cloud and in the sea, and all ate the same supernatural food (πνευματικὸν βρῶμα) 4 and all drank the same supernatural drink (πνευματικὸν πόμα)". He adds: "They drank from the supernatural Rock which followed them, and the Rock was Christ".[131] Yet despite this "baptism" and partaking of supernatural food and drink, "God was not pleased with most of them, and they were struck down in the wilderness" (v. 5). Then in vv. 6-13 Paul moves from narrative to paraenesis (v. 6: "Now these things occurred as examples for us, so that we might not desire evil as they did"). Paul warns the Corinthians of idolatry, for their "fathers" succumbed to this. He recounts the idolatry of Israel in the wilderness. So he alludes to the Golden Calf (1 Cor. 10.7; Ex. 32), the yoking of Israel to Ba'al of Pe'or (1 Cor. 10.8; Num. 25.1-18), Israel's testing of God and the plague of serpents (1 Cor. 10.9; Num. 21.5-6), and the murmuring against Moses and the punishments by the plague (1 Cor. 10.10; Num. 16.41-49).

This text, 1 Cor. 10.1-13, suggests a number of key theological points regarding Israel as the people of God. First, Israel as well as Christians as the people of God cannot rely on "sacraments". This text, like many in the Corinthian correspondence, issues a stark warning, and it reflects Paul's serious concern with the activities of the Corinthian Christians. Put in dogmatic terms, the idea of "perseverance of the Saints" is not at its strongest in these letters (either for the Christian Church or for Israel).

But the theological issue I wish to focus on here is that this text relates the Church to the history of Israel and to what appears to be the "pre-existence" of Christ. There has been extensive discussion regarding Paul's statement: "and the rock was Christ" (ἡ πέτρα δὲ ἦν ὁ Χριστός).[132] Some commentators do indeed believe that here the pre-existent Christ accompanied

---

[131] The idea of the rock which followed them developed from the view that on two occasions (and in two different places) Moses struck a rock which gave water (Ex. 17.1-7; Num. 20.1-11; see also Num. 21.16-18). The tradition of the following rock is found in Ps. Philo (LAB 10.7; cf. 11.15) and in Rabbinic sources (see Billerbeck, *Kommentar*, 3:406-8).

[132] A useful overview (particularly of the anglo-saxon discussion) is given by Thiselton, *First Epistle to the Corinthians*, pp. 727-30.

Israel in the wilderness[133] and therefore see an identity of the rock with Christ. Somewhat different is the view of Schrage and others. Schrage argues "Christus war kein Wesen in der Gestalt eines Felsens";[134] but neither, he argues, does ἦν simply mean *significabat*.[135] For Paul does not downplay "die pneumatische Gegenwart und Realität des präexistenten Christus im wasserspendenden Felsen beim alten Bundesvolk".[136] This has to be the case for Paul's argument to stand. So in v. 9 he writes: "We must not put Christ to the test, *as some of them did*, and were destroyed by serpents". Therefore "[i]m Alten wie im Neuen Bund geben die geistliche Speise und der geistliche Trank realiter und nicht nur gleichnishaft und symbolisch Anteil am Christus".[137]

A somewhat different approach is to argue that as in Jude 5, Christ is portrayed as "pre-existent", but is so portrayed in order that this story has typological significance for Christians.[138] I believe 1 Cor. 10.1-13 does have some typological significance but any typology is a by-product of something more fundamental: myth.[139] Myth is often understood as related to narrative concerned with things happening *in illo tempore*. However, myth does not have to be confined to that category. As Sellin argues, certain Old Testament "Schlüsselszenen" fall into the category of myth and 1 Cor. 10.1-13

---

[133] Hanson has argued extensively for this position. So, e.g, he writes: "In 1 Cor. 10 we have an instance of the real presence of Christ in Israel's history of old" ("Birth with Promise", 100). See also *Jesus Christ in the Old Testament*, London: SPCK 1965, pp. 10-25, for a discussion of 1 Cor. 10.1-11. Hanson rejects the idea here of allegory or typology (p. 13).

[134] Schrage, *Korinther*, 2:395. See also C. Wolff, *Der erste Brief des Paulus and die Korinther* (ThHK 7), Leipzig: Evangelische Verlagsanstalt ²2000, (¹1996), p. 217.

[135] Schrage, *Korinther*, 2:395. Such was the view of Augustine (Ep. 179.9).

[136] Schrage, *Korinther*, 2:395.

[137] Schrage, *Korinther*, 2:395-96.

[138] See W. Kraus, *Das Volk Gottes: Zur Grundlegung der Ekklesiologie bei Paulus* (WUNT 85), Tübingen: J.C.B. Mohr (Paul Siebeck) 1996, p. 186. Cf. R. Bauckham's analysis of Jude 5 (*Jude, 2 Peter* (WBC 50), Waco: Word Books 1983, p. 49). Note, however, that Schrage does not exclude typology (*Korinther*, 2:383).

[139] Here one may compare Rom. 5.12-21. Adam is a type of the one to come (5.14) but the passage has to be understood as mythical (see R.H. Bell, "The Myth of Adam and the Myth of Christ", in A. Christofersen, C. Claussen, J. Frey and B. Longenecker (ed.), *Paul, Luke and the Graeco-Roman World: Essays in Honour of Alexander J.M. Wedderburn* (JSNTSup 217), Sheffield: Sheffield Academic Press 2002, 21-36).

functions as such a "Schlüsselszene". Although it is "kein schöpfungs-ursprüngliches Geschehen . . . handelt es sich um einen hervorgehobenen Abschnitt der Geschichte, die Wüstenzeit, die zu einer Art Urzeit mythifiziert wird".[140] And the narrative in 1 Cor. 10.1-13, as in all myth, is something distinctive. For in narratives other than myth, for example novels, parables, legends, there is a distinction between the time of the narrator and the time of the narrated events.[141] Likewise there is a distinction between the situation of the narrator and his hearers or readers and the fictional situation of the narrated world (the 'erzählte Welt'). Further, we can say that the narrated world is integrated into the world of the narrator.[142] The distinctive characteristic of myth is that the distinction between the time of the narrator and the narrated time and the world of the narrator and the narrated world *does not have to exist*. Here the world of the narrated is not integrated into the world of the narrator. Instead, myth builds on its side the framework for reality and then all further narrative or statements.[143] We are embedded into the reality of myth.[144]

---

[140] G. Sellin, "Mythologeme und mythische Züge in der paulinischen Theologie", in H.H. Schmid, *Mythos und Rationalität*, Gütersloh: Gütersloher Verlagshaus Gerd Mohn 1988, 219 (209-23).

[141] H. Weinrich, *Tempus: Besprochene und erzählte Welt*, Stuttgart: W. Kohlhammer ²1971, (¹1964).

[142] See Sellin, "Mythologeme", 211: "Die 'erzählte Welt' ist jeweils in die Welt des Erzählers eingebettet".

[143] See Sellin, "Mythogeme", 211: "Die 'Welt des Erzählten' ist hier nicht eingebettet in die Wirklichkeit, sondern es ist eher umgekehrt: Der Mythos bildet seinerseits überhaupt erst den Rahmen für die Wirklichkeit und dann alles weitere Erzählen". See also his comment that myths build "den Referenzrahmen aller weiteren Aussagen, d.h. aller Prädikationen" (222).

[144] But, of course, myth does not necessary operate in this way and this is why I wrote that the distinction between the time of the narrator and the narrated time and the world of the narrator and the narrated world *does not have to exist*. For myth can be received in one of two ways: it can be received either mythically or mythologically (cf. E. Jüngel, "Die Wahrheit des Mythos und die Notwendigkeit der Entmythologisierung", in *Indikative der Gnade – Imperative der Freiheit*, Tübingen: J.C.B. Mohr (Paul Siebeck) 2000, 42 (40-57)). So myth can be received and respected as a 'holy narrative' or it can be received critically whereby one distances oneself from the myth. It is only in the mythical reception that one can speak of the myth forming and building a reality into which we are embedded. In the mythological reception, the myth-critical reception, myth becomes like other narrative.

Paul's reference to "our fathers" is a means of making present to Christians the history of Israel. Kraus[145] compares Dt. 5.2-5:

The LORD our God made a covenant with us in Horeb. 3 Not with our fathers did the LORD make this covenant, but with us, who are all of us here alive today. 4 The LORD spoke with you face to face at the mountain, out of the midst of the fire, 5 while I stood between the LORD and you at that time to declare to you the word of the LORD; for you were afraid because of the fire, and you did not go up into the mountain.

Those addressed were not literally present at Horeb (according to Dt. 2.14ff. the generation who were physically present had died out).[146] But the author is portraying the covenant made at Horeb as real for this second generation[147] so much so that he writes "not with our fathers did the LORD make this covenant".[148] And one reason he does this is to make the covenant concrete to the addressees of the seventh century BC. And in such cases "fallen erzählte Zeit und Erzählzeit in eins".[149]

One of the remarkable aspects of 1 Cor. 10.1-13 is that Paul seems to make the history of Israel "concrete" by relating it to Christ. So Christ is the rock which followed Israel in the wilderness. Only by having Christ, the "supernatural Rock", present can one speak of "the same supernatural food" (τὸ αὐτὸ πνευματικὸν βρῶμα) (v. 3) and "the same supernatural drink" (τὸ αὐτὸ πνευματικὸν πόμα) (v. 4).[150] The "sacraments" of the wilderness generation are real and πνευματικόν because they are *Christian* sacraments.[151] I

---

[145] Kraus, *Volk Gottes*, p. 186 n. 209.

[146] See A.D.H. Mayes, *Deuteronomy* (NCB), London: Oliphants 1979, p. 165.

[147] So G. von Rad, *Deuteronomy* (OTL) ET, London: SCM 1966, p. 55, writes: "[The speaker] wants to bring the event of the covenant-making which already belongs to the past vividly before the eyes of his contemporaries . . . These are the words of a generation which must begin by providing itself with an explanation of its relation to the 'saving event' (*Heilsereignis*)". Von Rad's reference to "the speaker" is ambiguous (also in the original German, *Das fünfte Buch Mose: Deuteronomium* (ATD 8), Göttingen: Vandenhoeck & Ruprecht 1964, p. 40). The "speaker" ("Sprecher") could be either Moses or the author. Von Rad's sentence happens to be valid for both "speakers"!

[148] I take the reference to be the immediately preceding generation.

[149] Kraus, *Volk Gottes*, p. 186 n. 209.

[150] Cf. Kraus, *Volk Gottes*, p. 186, who refers to Luz, *Geschichtsverständnis*, p. 119.

[151] Although Conzelmann, *Der erste Brief an die Korinther*, p. 203, is not making quite the point I am, his remarks are pertinent: "Es ist zu beachten, daß von der gegenwärtigen Gegebenheit, der Taufe, ins Alte Testament zurückgedacht wird, nicht etwa umgekehrt die Taufe aus dem Alten Testament abgeleitet und gedeutet wird".

think one can make the general point in Paul that the history of Israel is only a reality in the light of Christ. Without Christ there is no "history of Israel". Likewise, without Christ Abraham's faith is really a non-entity. This may sound like a rather Lutheran[152] or Barthian reading of Paul but I suggest that the very seeds for their thought are to be found in the writings of Paul.[153]

4.3. Israel according to the Flesh (1 Corinthians 10.18)

Paul continues to warn the Corinthians about idolatry in vv. 14-22. In v. 18a he raises the question of Israel: βλέπετε τὸν Ἰσραὴλ κατὰ σάρκα. How is this to be translated? Harris translates it "observe the carnal Israel".[154] He then understands vv. 18b-19 to refer to the idolatrous practices of Israel (as described in Dt. 32) and takes the subject of v. 20 to be Israel: "I imply that what (the Jews) sacrifice they offer to demons and not to God". Elsewhere I have questioned in some detail such a view.[155] Here I simply emphasize the point that κατὰ σάρκα is be understood in a neutral sense and refers to the earthly Israel. V. 18b ("are not those who eat the sacrifices partners in the altar?") refers to the eating of sacrifices by the priests (Lev. 7.6, 15; 10.12-15; Dt. 18.1-4)[156] and not to the idolatrous practices of Israel in Dt. 32. Paul does not have a negative view here of Israel's sacrificial system.[157] Further, Paul is not implying that the Church is the Ἰσραὴλ κατὰ πνεῦμα as Robertson and Plummer suggest: "Christians are a new Israel, Israel after the Spirit, τὸν Ἰσραὴλ τοῦ θεοῦ (Gal. vi.16, iii.29; Phil. iii.3), whether Jews or Gentiles by birth".[158] That sort of idea is indeed, as we have argued, present

---

[152] Cf. Luther, *De servo arbitrio* (*WA* 606; H.-U. Delius (ed.), *Martin Luther: Studienausgabe Band 3*, Berlin: Evangelische Verlagsanstalt 1983, 185.3-4 (177-356)): *Tolle Christum e scripturis, quid amplius in illis inuenies?*

[153] One may compare this to the argument about a Trinitarian reading of Paul. Is such a reading so inappropriate when the letters of Paul themselves led the Church to formulate ideas about the Trinity? See N. Richardson, *Paul's Language about God* (JSNTSup 99), Sheffield: Sheffield Academic Press 1994, pp. 314-15.

[154] J.R. Harris, "A Factor of Old Testament Influence in the New Testament", *ExpT* 37 (1925-26) 8 (6-11).

[155] See Bell, *Provoked to Jealousy*, pp. 251-55.

[156] It could also possibly refer to the people of Israel eating of the sacrifices (see 1 Sam. 9.13).

[157] Cf. ἡ λατρεία of Rom. 9.4 (discussed below).

[158] Robertson and Plummer, *First Epistle of St. Paul to the Corinthians*, p. 215. See also Weiß, *Der erste Korintherbrief*, p. 260.

in Gal. 6.16. But it is not to be found in either the Corinthian correspondence or in Philippians.

5. Substitution Models in Romans?

5.1. Romans 2.25-29

Rom. 2.25-29 has been seen as supporting a substitution model in Romans.
However, I believe a close examination of the text reveals something different. Paul discusses the issue of circumcision. He argues in Rom. 2.25 that
circumcision is only of value if the Jew obeys the law: "Circumcision indeed
is of value if you obey the law; but if you break the law, your circumcision
becomes uncircumcision" (Περιτομὴ μὲν γὰρ ὠφελεῖ ἐὰν νόμον πράσσῃς·
ἐὰν δὲ παραβάτης νόμου ᾖς, ἡ περιτομή σου ἀκροβυστία γέγονεν). He
makes the radical point that if the Jew breaks the law his circumcision is not
only worthless, but it is as if he were uncircumcised.[159] The point of interest
for Paul is that circumcision by itself will not save. It will not shield the Jew
from the wrath of God.[160] Paul seems to assume that a perfect obedience of
the law is necessary in order to be saved.[161] As Gal. 5.3 makes clear, the
circumcised man has to obey the whole law.[162]

　　In Rom. 2.26 he takes the argument a stage further: "So, if a man who is
uncircumcised keeps the precepts of the law, will not his uncircumcision be
regarded as circumcision?" (ἐὰν οὖν ἡ ἀκροβυστία τὰ δικαιώματα τοῦ
νόμου φυλάσσῃ, οὐχ ἡ ἀκροβυστία αὐτοῦ εἰς περιτομὴν λογισθήσεται;)
The future λογισθήσεται could be merely a logical future, but it is more
likely that it refers to the future judgement.[163] Many commentators believe

---

[159] P. Althaus, *Der Brief an die Römer* (NTD 6), Göttingen: Vandenhoeck &
Ruprecht [10]1966, p. 27.

[160] See Moo, *Romans*, p. 167.

[161] See the discussion in chapter 1 section 2 above.

[162] Gal. 5.3: I testify again to every man who receives circumcision that he is bound to
keep the whole law (μαρτύρομαι δὲ πάλιν παντὶ ἀνθρώπῳ περιτεμνομένῳ ὅτι ὀφειλέτης
ἐστὶν ὅλον τὸν νόμον ποιῆσαι).

[163] See J. Denney, "St. Paul's Epistle to the Romans", in W. Robertson Nicoll, *The
Expositor's Greek Testament*, Grand Rapids: Eerdmans 1976 (repr), 2:601 (555-725),
who points to the use of the futures in 2.12-16 which refer to the final judgement. See
also E. Lohse, *Der Brief an die Römer* (KEK 4), Göttingen: Vandenhoeck & Ruprecht
[15]2003, p. 113.

that the Gentile who keeps the precepts of the law (τὰ δικαιώματα τοῦ νόμου) is the Gentile Christian.[164] It is, however, extremely unlikely that Paul is referring to the Gentile Christian in v. 26.[165] There are no clear indications here that Paul is speaking of Gentile Christians in v. 26 or in vv. 27-29. In fact to bring in a discussion of Gentile Christians would go largely against the whole context of Rom. 1.18-3.20.[166] I therefore come to a much simpler explanation: Paul speaks in v. 26 of the pious Gentile who keeps "the precepts of the law". This expression, τὰ δικαιώματα τοῦ νόμου, refers to the whole law[167] and it may be claimed that Paul's argument is incoherent since a Gentile is uncircumcised and circumcision itself was a commandment of the law. However, Paul seemed to believe that the law had been manifest in different ways to Jews and Gentiles. The law, God's condemning word, is manifest to Jews through the commandments of Moses. For Gentiles it is written on their hearts.[168] And one reason Paul was able to argue that Gentiles as well as Jews can be judged by the law is because Paul shared the view of Sir. 24.23 that wisdom had become identified with law. The whole creation therefore was in a certain sense under the law of God.

Paul then argues in v. 27 that this pious Gentile who keeps the law (ἡ ἐκ φύσεως ἀκροβυστία τὸν νόμον τελοῦσα) will judge the Jew who, although having the written code (γράμμα, i.e. the law)[169] and circumcision, is a transgressor of the law.[170] The Gentile will not take on the rôle of a judge as

---

[164] Barrett, *Romans*, p. 58; Cranfield, *Romans*, 1:173.

[165] Although Paul speaks in Rom. 8.4 of the Christian in whom τὸ δικαίωμα τοῦ νόμου is fulfilled, Paul in Rom. 2.26-27 is making a quite different point.

[166] A number of significant commentators have also seen a reference to Gentile Christians in Rom. 2.14. See Ambrosiaster, *In epistolam ad Romanos* (*CSEL* 81.1:74-75); Augustine, *De spiritu et littera* 26.43-28.49 (*CSEL* 60.196-204); Barth, *Shorter Commentary*, p. 36; Cranfield, *Romans*, 1:156. For my criticism of this view see *No one seeks for God*, pp. 151-53.

[167] Käsemann, *Romans*, p. 73.

[168] For a discussion of the law of the Gentiles, see Bell, *No one seeks for God*, pp. 153-57.

[169] On the meaning of γράμμα, see the discussion below on Rom. 2.29.

[170] I take διά in the expression διὰ γράμματος καὶ περιτομῆς not to be instrumental but to describe the "accompanying circumstances" (see Käsemann, *Romans*, p. 74; "Geist und Buchstabe", in *Paulinische Perspektiven*, Tübingen: J.C.B. Mohr (Paul Siebeck) ²1972, (¹1969), 246 (237-85)). Contrast A. Schlatter, *Gottes Gerechtigkeit: Ein Kommentar zum Römerbrief*, Stuttgart: Calwer Verlag ⁵1975, (¹1935), p. 110; G. Schrenk, γράφω κτλ, *TDNT* 1:765 (742-73).

in 1 Cor. 6.2 (a view which would perhaps be more plausible if Paul were referring to the Gentile Christian); rather the Gentile by his deeds will expose the deeds of the Jew.[171] The idea of a pious Gentile who keeps the law would seem to contradict Paul's view as expressed in Rom. 5.12ff., that all are in Adam. And even before that, in Rom. 3.9-20, Paul makes it clear that there are in fact no pious Gentiles or pious Jews. One has therefore to conclude that the Gentile Paul describes in Rom. 2.25-26 simply does not exist. In fact one of the main points in Rom. 1.18-3.20 is that no one will be justified by works of the law.[172]

The section 2.25-29 comes to a climax in 2.28-29: "For he is not a real Jew who is one outwardly, nor is true circumcision something external and physical. 29 He is a Jew who is one inwardly, and real circumcision is a matter of the heart, spiritual and not literal. His praise is not from men but from God".[173] Paul makes a distinction between the person who is out-wardly a Jew (ὁ ἐν φανερῷ Ἰουδαῖος) and the one who is inwardly a Jew (ὁ ἐν τῷ κρυπτῷ Ἰουδαῖος). Not all outward Jews are Jews in the special sense and not all Jews in the special sense are outward Jews. The Jew who is one inwardly (ἐν τῷ κρυπτῷ) has circumcision of heart (περιτομὴ καρδίας) but the Jew who is one outwardly (ἐν τῷ φανερῷ) has circumcision in flesh (ἐν σαρκί). It is widely assumed that Paul also speaks of Gentile Christians is vv. 28-29.[174] In fact Schreiner, who takes 2.26-29 to refer to Gentile Christians, writes that "the 'for' (γάρ) introducing verses 28-29 is decisive for the Gentile Christian interpretation", and the expression "by the Spirit not the letter" (ἐν πνεύματι οὐ γράμματι) of v. 29 is "the primary reason we know

---

[171] G.P. Carras, "Romans 2,1-29: A Dialogue on Jewish Ideals", *Bib* 73 (1992) 205 (183-207). On Gentiles exposing the sins of Jews, see Mt. 12.41 and Lk. 11.31.

[172] See Bell, *No one seeks for God*.

[173] In order to make sense of this one must add supplements as does Cranfield, *Romans*, 1:175: οὐ γὰρ ὁ ἐν φανερῷ (Ἰουδαῖος) Ἰουδαῖός ἐστιν, οὐδὲ ἡ ἐν τῷ φανερῷ ἐν σαρκὶ (περιτομὴ) περιτομὴ (ἐστιν)· (29) ἀλλ᾽ ὁ ἐν τῷ κρυπτῷ Ἰουδαῖος (Ἰουδαῖός ἐστιν), καὶ περιτομὴ καρδίας ἐν πνεύματι οὐ γράμματι (περιτομὴ ἐστιν), οὗ ὁ ἔπαινος οὐχ ἐξ ἀνθρώπων (ἐστὶν) ἀλλ᾽ ἐκ τοῦ θεοῦ.

[174] This is apparent as early as Justin Martyr. See the probable allusion to Rom. 2.29 in his discussion of Gentile Christians in *Dialogue* 92.4: "And we, therefore, in the uncircumcision of our flesh, believing God through Christ, and having that circumcision which is of advantage to us who have acquired it—namely that of the heart—we hope to appear righteous before and well-pleasing to God . . ." (*ANF* 1:245). Justin's exegesis of Paul can be accounted for by the fact that he wished to disinherit Israel.

that verses 26-27 speaks of Gentile Christians".[175] The view that Paul refers to Christians in Rom. 2.29 has a long and distinguished history.[176] However, there are a number of problems with this interpretation.

First, I consider the antithesis γράμμα/πνεῦμα, which occurs in the New Testament only in Rom. 2.29; 7.6 and 2 Cor. 3.6, and is completely lacking in the Old Testament. There are two basic interpretations of the terms.[177] The first is the "formalistic" interpretation, where γράμμα is the literal sense and πνεῦμα the spiritual sense of any document. The originator of this was Origen and it was characteristic of the Alexandrian school.[178] The second is the "realistic" interpretation, where γράμμα refers to the Mosaic law itself and πνεῦμα refers to the Holy Spirit. This view is found in Marcion[179] and became characteristic of the Antiochene school.[180] Many who argue for the realistic interpretation of Rom. 2.29 do so because of a realistic interpretation of Rom. 7.6 and 2 Cor. 3.6. But it is instructive to note that regarding the realistic and formalistic interpretations these γράμμα/πνεῦμα texts can be arranged in the following spectrum: 2 Cor. 3.6 (generally taken as realistic); Rom. 7.6 (often taken as realistic); Rom. 2.29 (usually taken as formalistic).[181] Now there may be some "realistic" elements in Rom. 2.29: γράμμα could refer to the Mosaic law[182] (note this use in Rom. 2.27) and πνεῦμα *may possibly* refer to the Holy Spirit. But even if that is the case, a reference to Christians is unlikely. For Paul and his hearers it was obvious that the Christian does the good and as pointed out above, the whole context goes

---

[175] T.R. Schreiner, *The Law and its Fulfillment: A Pauline Theology of Law*, Grand Rapids: Wm B. Eerdmans 1993, p. 198.

[176] For examples see Bell, *No one seeks for God*, p. 196.

[177] See B. Schneider, "The Meaning of St. Paul's Antithesis: 'The Letter and the Spirit'", *CBQ* 15 (1953) 164 (163-207).

[178] See Bell, *No one seeks for God*, p. 196.

[179] See the discussion of Rom. 2.29 in Tertullian, *Adversus Marcionem* 5.13 (*CSEL* 47:620). As Schneider points out, Tertullian does not object to Marcion's realistic interpretation ("The Letter and the Spirit", 166).

[180] See Bell, *No one seeks for God*, p. 197.

[181] See Schneider, "The Letter and the Spirit", 184-85.

[182] See especially Schrenk, γράφω, 765-66, and Hofius, "Gesetz und Evangelium nach 2. Korinther 3", 82. Note expressions such as ποιεῖν πάντα τὰ ῥήματα τοῦ νόμου τούτου τὰ γεγραμμένα ἐν τῷ βιβλίῳ τούτῳ (Dt. 28.58, used in Gal. 3.10) and ποιεῖν πάντα τὰ γεγραμμένα ἐν τῷ βιβλίῳ τοῦ νόμου Μωυσῆ (Jos. 23.6).

against a reference to Christians.[183] Further there are "formalistic" elements in Rom. 2.29 which would tend to go against a Gentile Christian interpretation. So the expression "in Spirit" (ἐν πνεύματι) has the general sense "in a spiritual way"[184] although I would not necessarily want to rule out completely a reference to the Holy Spirit.[185]

So according to Rom. 2.29 the circumcision that counts is that of the heart.[186] Such circumcision is not from the written law, but exists in a spiritual sense[187] and Paul envisages the situation where pious Gentiles are circumcised in this spiritual sense.[188] It is therefore unnecessary to bring in Gentile Christians (or Jewish Christians) at this point. In fact to do so would go against the context of Rom. 1.18-3.20, where Paul is arguing that no one, Jew nor Gentile, will be justified by works of law.

---

[183] Schreiner, *Law*, p. 199, points to the "remarkable similarity" between Phil. 3.3 (ἡμεῖς γὰρ ἐσμεν ἡ περιτομή, οἱ πνεύματι θεοῦ λατρεύοντες καὶ καυχώμενοι ἐν Χριστῷ Ἰησοῦ καὶ οὐκ ἐν σαρκὶ πεποιθότες) and Rom. 2.29. I take the point that Paul refers to the Holy Spirit in Phil. 3.3 (there is a text critical problem but θεοῦ rather than θεῷ is the most likely reading), but in Phil. 3.3 the context makes it absolutely clear that Paul is talking of Christians. I see no evidence from the context that Paul is speaking of Christians in Rom. 2.29.

[184] See Barrett, *Romans*, p. 58.

[185] The possible allusions to Jer. 31.31-34; Ezek. 11.19; 36.25-29 and Jub. 1.20-21, 23, may suggest the Holy Spirit in Rom. 2.29.

[186] See Dt. 30.6: "And the LORD your God will circumcise your heart and the heart of your offspring, so that you will love the LORD your God with all your heart and with all your soul, that you may live". Cf. Dt. 10.16; Jer. 4.4; 9.25.

[187] Cf. Althaus, *Römer*, p. 28.

[188] It is interesting to note that Jub. 1.16, 20-21 and 23 form a useful background to aspects of Rom. 2.25-29. In Jub. 1.20-21 Moses says: "O Lord, let your mercy be lifted up upon your people, and create for them an *upright spirit*. And do not let the spirit of Beliar rule over them to accuse them before you and ensnare them from every path of righteousness so that they might be destroyed from before your face. 21 But they are your people and your inheritance, whom you saved by your great might from the hand of the Egyptians. Create a *pure heart* and a *holy spirit* for them. And do not let them be ensnared by their sin henceforth and forever" (O.S. Wintermute's translation in *OTP*, 2:53-54, my emphasis). God then replies to Moses in vv. 22-26 and in v. 23 we read: "But after this they will return to me in all uprighteousness and with all (their) *heart* and soul. And I shall *cut off the foreskin of their heart* and the *foreskin of the heart* of their descendants. And I shall create for them a *holy spirit*, and I shall purify them so that they will not turn away from following me from that day and forever" (Wintermute, in *OTP*, 2:54, my emphasis). Wintermute dates Jubilees in the period 161-140 BC. If such terms can be used for pious Jews, why cannot Paul use similar ones for pious Gentiles.

There are in fact a number of other factors which support the idea that Paul is referring simply to pious Jews or Gentiles and not to Christians in vv. 28-29. First, there are a number of expressions here which are unusual for Paul.[189] This is the only text in Paul where there is the positive use of κρυπτόν, where Paul speaks of the circumcision of the heart, and where the heart is placed in opposition to the flesh.[190] This unusual use of these words suggests that Paul here is referring to an unusual situation, pious Jews and Gentiles; nowhere else does he refer to such hypothetical figures, although in many other passages he does speak about Christian existence. Further terms like "hidden" and "heart" are highly suitable for speaking of a pious person.[191]

The second factor which support a pious Gentile/Jew interpretation is that there are a number of parallels between Rom. 2.28-29 and Rom. 2.12-16. In 2.16 Jesus Christ will judge "the secrets of men" (τὰ κρυπτὰ τῶν ἀνθρώπων) (note also the reference in v. 14 to Gentiles, and to their *hearts* in v. 15 (τὸ ἔργον τοῦ νόμου γραπτὸν ἐν ταῖς καρδίαις αὐτῶν)). If Rom. 2.12-16 concerns the judgement according to works whereby pious persons will be acquitted (cf. Rom. 2.13), it would seem that Rom. 2.28-29 concerns such pious persons also and not Christians.

---

[189] See E. Schweizer, "'Der Jude im Verborgenen . . ., dessen Lob nicht von Menschen, sondern von Gott kommt'. Zu Röm 2,28f und Mt 6,1-18", in J. Gnilka (ed.), *Neues Testament und Kirche: Für Rudolf Schnackenburg*, Freiburg/Basel/Wien: Herder 1974, 115-16 (115-24). Note that although I draw on this article here and below, Schweizer himself does not make it clear whether he thinks Paul refers to Christians in Rom. 2.28-29.

[190] Schweizer, "Jude", 116 n. 4, highlights the unusual nature of the opposition of heart and flesh by pointing to 2 Cor. 3.3, where heart and flesh (as an adjective σάρκινος) are placed *together* in opposition to the tablets of stone. Note that σάρκινος has a neutral sense in 2 Cor. 3.3 (as noted by Schweizer in E. Schweizer and R. Meyer, σάρξ κτλ, *TDNT* 7:143-44 (98-151)). But also σάρξ in Rom. 2.28 is essentially neutral, for it is "in the first instance no more than the bodily member on which circumcision takes place" (σάρξ, 129). The expression ἐν σαρκί only takes on a negative connotation in that one can boast since such circumcision is outward (ἐν τῷ φανερῷ) rather than inward (ἐν τῷ κρυπτῷ).

[191] See 1 Sam. 16.7b: "man looks on the outward appearance, but the LORD looks on the heart".

Thirdly, Rom. 2.28-29 has a number of parallels with Mt. 6.1-6, 16-18.[192] Although the teaching in Matthew is clearly directed at the Christian Church, this teaching and that found in Rom. 2.28-29 can be traced back simply to the Old Testament and Judaism[193] and there is nothing to suggest that the teaching in Mt. 6.1-6, 16-18 is distinctively Christian.[194] So such a text could just as well apply to pious Jews and pious Gentiles as well as Christians.

I therefore conclude that in Rom. 2.28-29, as in 2.25-27, Paul is not concerned with Christians but with pious Jews and Gentiles. Paul argues in Rom. 2.25-29 that circumcision by itself will not save. What matters is keeping the law. Paul does not relativize the election of Israel in Rom. 2.25-29. This, however, has been argued by Dunn who writes that in Romans 2 "it becomes progressively clearer that Paul is seeking to undermine a Jewish assumption of national distinctiveness and privilege . . .".[195] Neither is he arguing that the Christian is a spiritual Jew. His point is that circumcision will not shield the Jew from the wrath of God.

5.2. Romans 3.1-4

In view of what Paul has said in 2.25-29 about the Jew and circumcision, the question is raised in 3.1 whether there is any advantage in being a Jew and in circumcision: "Then what advantage has the Jew? Or what is the value of circumcision?" (Τί οὖν τὸ περισσὸν τοῦ Ἰουδαίου ἢ τίς ἡ ὠφέλεια τῆς περιτομῆς;) According to Dodd, the logical answer to this question, based on Paul's argument, is: "None whatever!"[196] Paul's answer, however, is

---

[192] See A. Fridrichsen, "Der wahre Jude und sein Lob", *Symbolae Arctoae* 1 (1927) 46 (39-49); Schweizer, "Jude"; W.D. Davies and D.C. Allison, *A Critical and Exegetical Commentary on the Epistle to the Gospel According to Saint Matthew* (ICC), vol. 1, Edinburgh: T. & T. Clark 1988, pp. 576-77.

[193] See Schweizer, "Jude".

[194] See Davies and Allison, *Matthew I*, pp. 576-77.

[195] J.D.G. Dunn, "What was the Issue between Paul and 'Those of the Circumcision'?", in M. Hengel and U. Heckel (ed.), *Paulus und das antike Judentum: Tübingen-Durham-Symposium im Gedenken an den 50. Todestag Adolf Schlatters* (WUNT 58), Tübingen: J.C.B. Mohr (Paul Siebeck) 1991, 311 (295-313). See also Longenecker, *Eschatology*, p. 194, who argues that Paul wished "to discredit an ethnocentric understanding of God's ways".

[196] C.H. Dodd, *The Epistle of Paul to the Romans* (MNTC), London: Hodder and Stoughton 1949 (repr.), ([1]1932), p. 43.

"much in every way" (πολὺ κατὰ πάντα τρόπον). His reply is not as illogical as Dodd would suggest. There is, according to Paul, a clear advantage in being a Jew. Jews are entrusted with "the oracles of God" (τὰ λόγια τοῦ θεοῦ, 3.2). There are various ways of understanding τὰ λόγια τοῦ θεοῦ. The possibilities include: "the commandments of God";[197] the law as given on Sinai together with the promises relating to the Messiah;[198] the whole salvation history of the Old and New Covenants.[199] A reference to the commandments seems a little too narrow[200] and a reference to the whole salvation history up to and including Christ seems too wide. It is probably right to take the expression to mean words of revelation in the scriptures.[201] Paul then continues in 3.3: "But what if some did not believe? Does their unbelief nullify the faithfulness of God?" (τί γάρ; εἰ ἠπίστησάν τινες, μὴ ἡ ἀπιστία αὐτῶν τὴν πίστιν τοῦ θεοῦ καταργήσει;)[202] Paul is here probably referring to not believing in God (and because for Paul Christ was fully divine, this by implication would mean not believing in Christ).[203] Paul answers the question of 3.3 with "By no means" (μὴ γένοιτο). Hence it is absolutely clear that Paul is affirming that God's promises to Israel are irrevocable.[204] He continues in 3.4: "Let God be true though every man be false, as it is written, 'That thou mayest be justified in thy words, and prevail when thou art

---

[197] P. Stuhlmacher, *Der Brief an die Römer* (NTD 6), Göttingen: Vandenhoeck & Ruprecht 1989, pp. 47-48 (cf. P. Stuhlmacher, *Gerechtigkeit Gottes bei Paulus* (FRLANT 87), Göttingen: Vandenhoeck & Ruprecht ²1966, (¹1965), p. 85).

[198] W. Sanday and A.C. Headlam, *Romans*, Edinburgh: T. & T. Clark ²1896, p. 70.

[199] G. Kittel on λέγω κτλ, *TDNT* 4:138 (77-143). See also Barth, *Shorter Commentary*, p. 39: "The Jews are and remain the nation entrusted with the words, the revelations of God up to and including the person of Jesus Christ".

[200] Wilckens, *Römer*, 1:164 n. 433, rightly makes this point.

[201] Cf. Wilckens, *Römer*, 1:164, who writes: "τὰ λόγια (τοῦ θεοῦ) ist in LXX, bei Philon und Apg 7,38 eine pauschale Bezeichnung der Offenbarungsworte in der Schrift und dürfte hier entsprechend gebraucht sein". In Acts 7.38 Stephen speaks of the "living oracles" (λόγια ζῶντα) which were given by an angel to Moses which he handed on.

[202] Note that my translation differs from the RSV. In v. 3, there is the question about the meaning of ἀπιστεῖν and ἀπιστία. In view of the use of ἐπιστεύθησαν in 3.2, it may be thought that ἀπιστεῖν and ἀπιστία mean "be unfaithful" and "unfaithfulness" respectively. However, they most likely refer to unbelief, and not so much to unfaithfulness (cf. Sanday and Headlam, *Romans*, p. 71).

[203] Cf. Bell, *No one seeks for God*, p. 204.

[204] Cf. Bell, *No one seeks for God*, p. 205.

judged'" (γινέσθω δὲ ὁ θεὸς ἀληθής, πᾶς δὲ ἄνθρωπος ψεύστης, καθὼς γέγραπται· ὅπως ἄν δικαιωθῇς ἐν τοῖς λόγοις σου καὶ νικήσεις ἐν τῷ κρίνεσθαί σε). The train of thought in 3.3-4 is therefore that God has remained faithful even though Israel herself has not believed.

The section 2.25-3.4 therefore suggests that the Jew's election has not been annulled. There is value in being a Jew, and God has remained faithful even though Israel has not believed. Paul therefore does not hold to a substitution model here. God's election of Israel is unshakable.

5.3. Romans 9.1-5

These remarkable verses should make us seriously question the view that the Church has substituted Israel.

> 1 I am speaking the truth in Christ, I am not lying; my conscience bears me witness in the Holy Spirit, 2 that I have great sorrow and unceasing anguish in my heart. 3 For I could wish that I myself were accursed and cut off from Christ for the sake of my brethren, my kinsmen by race. 4 They are Israelites, and to them belong the sonship, the glory, the covenants, the giving of the law, the worship, and the promises; 5 to them belong the patriarchs, and of their race, according to the flesh, is the Christ, who is God over all, blessed for ever. Amen.[205]

The first section, Rom. 9.1-3, describes the plight of Paul's unbelieving kinsmen. The celebration at the end of chapter 8 abruptly changes (without any connecting particle) to this lament over Israel. Although laments concerning Israel were traditional motifs in the Old Testament and in Apocalyptic literature,[206] Paul expresses his *personal anguish* over the failure of Israel to believe the gospel[207] and he emphasizes this anguish by swearing that this is the case (v. 1). Then he implies in v. 3 that the unbelieving Jews are cut off from Christ, for he says that he would pray[208] that he might be

---

[205] On my understanding of the punctuation of v.5, see the discussion in chapter 2 above.

[206] E.g. Ex. 32.30ff.; 4 Ezr. 8.15-18; 10.6-8, 21-22; 2 Bar. 35.3; Test. Jud. 23.1.

[207] Luz, *Geschichtsverständnis*, p. 26.

[208] The other possible translation of εὔχεσθαι is to "wish". However, the parallel with Moses (Ex. 32.31-32) and with Rom. 10.1 would suggest "pray" (G.P. Wiles, *Paul's Intercessory Prayers: The Significance of the Intercessory Prayer Passages in the Letters of St Paul* (SNTSMS 24), Cambridge: CUP 1974, p. 256). There are six other occurrences of εὔχεσθαι in the NT: in three the verb certainly takes the meaning "to pray" (Acts 26.29; 2 Cor. 13.7; Jas 5.16); in two the verb probably takes the meaning "pray" (2 Cor. 13.9; 3 Jn 2); this leaves only one occurrence (Acts 27.29) where it is more natural to understand the verb as "to wish".

accursed (ἀνάθεμα) and cut off from Christ for the sake of his fellow kinsmen.[209] The expression "to be accursed" (ἀνάθεμα εἶναι) means to be delivered over to divine wrath, the consequence here being to forfeit final salvation,[210] and the prayer that he be separated from Christ (ηὐχόμην γὰρ ἀνάθεμα εἶναι αὐτὸς ἐγὼ ἀπὸ τοῦ Χριστοῦ) is startling in view of 8.35-39, where he argues that nothing can separate us from the love of Christ.[211] Paul's agonizing prayer deserves serious reflection especially in view of the position held by many prominent theologians and church leaders that Israel does not really need the gospel.[212]

Therefore, in Rom. 9.1-3, Paul points to the plight of Israel; but then in the second section, Rom. 9.4-5, he speaks of their privileges. Paul says that his kinsmen according to the flesh (συγγενεῖς κατὰ σάρκα) are Israelites (οἵτινές εἰσιν Ἰσραηλῖται). The use of the word Israelites is significant. In

---

[209] Paul uses a euphemism. Cf. 2 Sam. 18.32: "The king said to the Cushite, 'Is it well with the young man Absalom?' And the Cushite answered, 'May the enemies of my lord the king, and all who rise up against you for evil, be like that young man'".

[210] Cranfield, *Romans*, 2:457. Michel, *Römer*, p. 293, writes: "Selbstverständlich denkt Paulus auch hier an das eschatologische Gericht, nicht an die Übernahme zeitlicher Leiden oder an einen Akt der Kirchenzucht . . ."

[211] Luz, *Geschichtsverständnis*, p. 21. H.D. Betz, "Geschichte und Selbstopfer: Zur Interpretation von Römer 9,1-5", in C. Auffarth and J. Rüpke (ed.), *Epitome tes oikoumenes. Studien zur römischen Religion in Antike und Neuzeit für Hubert Cancik und Hildegard Cancik-Lindemaier* (PAB 6), Stuttgart: Steiner Verlag 2002, 75-87, believes that Rom. 9.3 is a real prayer of Paul and is to be understood as a vow: "Der Kontext und die religionsgeschichtlichen Zusammenhänge von Eid und Opfer sprechen für den vorgenommenen Opferakt eines Gelübdes (εὐχή), den Paulus im vorliegenden Text schriftlich dokumentiert" (81). Further, "Das Imperfekt ηὐχόμην deutet darauf hin, dass ein Opfer mit einem Bittgebet um Annahme verbunden ist. Ob und in welcher Weise Gott ein solches Bittgebet erfüllt, bleibt seinem Willen überlassen. Es handelt sich mithin nicht um einen sogenannten frommen Wunsch, wie ernst auch immer gemeint. Die Frage nach dem Realitätsgrund des Opfers beantwortet sich daher durch den Hinweis auf das erfolgte Bittgebet als Teil eines irreversiblen Opferritus". If Betz is correct, it clearly adds to the seriousness of this passage. Michel, *Römer*, p. 293, points to the way Luther took ηὐχόμην with the utmost seriousness (see Pauck (ed.), *Luther: Lectures on Romans*, pp. 260-65, for Luther's extensive discussion). However, Luther writes that those who "submit freely to the will of God whatever it may be, even for hell and eternal death . . . cannot possibly remain in hell" (p. 262). Many take the imperfect ηὐχόμην to signify a wish (C.F.D. Moule, *An Idiom Book of New Testament Greek*, Cambridge: CUP ²1977, (¹1953), p. 9, considers it to be a "desiderative imperfect") and hence soften the impact of these words (see also Barrett, *Romans*, p. 165).

[212] I will return to this in chapter 10 below.

early times (e.g., in the Song of Deborah, Judg. 5.2, 7), "Israel" was a sacred term denoting the chosen community of God. Later it became the designation of the Northern Kingdom (1 Kgs 12ff.) but after the Assyrian attack on the North and subsequent deportation, the term was applied to Judah.[213] After the exile "it became the self-designation of the Jewish people aware of its status as the holy and chosen people of God".[214] Von Rad believes that "faith in a greater Israel was still maintained as a theological postulate", something seen in the genealogical derivation of the twelve tribes in the books of Chronicles and that after the exile "Israel increasingly becomes the object of a hope that God will perform an eschatological act of salvation".[215] In later Palestinian Judaism, "Israel" was the self-designation of the Jews expressing their consciousness of being the people of God, and in the New Testament, 'Israel' and 'Israelite' continue to have a salvation-historical significance.[216] Therefore, in using the word Israelites in Rom. 9.4, Paul would seem to be asserting that the Jews are the chosen people of God.[217]

Paul's assertion "they are Israelites" (οἵτινές εἰσιν Ἰσραηλῖται) is followed by three relative clauses (ὧν ... ὧν ... ἐξ ὧν) having "Israelites" (Ἰσραηλῖται) as their antecedent. Within the first relative clause, Paul lists

---

[213] This view was suggested by L. Rost, *Israel bei den Propheten* (BWANT 71) Stuttgart: W. Kohlhammer Verlag 1937, pp. 54ff. See also von Rad, Ἰσραήλ, 357 n. 12. There is some disagreement on this question. Just to take one example, does Israel in Is. 5.7 refer to the Southern Kingdom? H. Wildberger, *Jesaja, 1. Teilband: Jesaja 1-12* (BKAT 10/1), Neukirchen-Vluyn: Neukirchener Verlag 1972, p. 172, thinks it does; but contrast R.E. Clements, *Isaiah 1-39* (NCB), London: Marshall, Morgan & Scott/Grand Rapids: Wm B. Eerdmans 1980, p. 16. Rost's theory has been criticized by R. Albertz, "Jer 2-6 und die Frühzeitverkündigung Jeremias", *ZAW* 94 (1982) 30-31 (20-47).

[214] J.A. Fitzmyer, *Romans* (AB 33), New York: Doubleday 1993, p. 545.

[215] Von Rad, Ἰσραήλ, 358.

[216] See, e.g., the occurrences in John: 1.31, 47, 49; 3.10; 12.13.

[217] Paul uses the word "Israel" in Rom. 9-11 in Rom. 9.6, 27; 10.19, 21; 11.2, 7, 25-26 (whereas he only uses Ἰουδαῖος in Rom. 9-11 in 9.24 and 10.12). The word Israelite(s) only occurs in Rom. 9.4; 11.1; 2 Cor. 11.22 in the Pauline letters. Israel is used by Paul in other letters but the usage there does not stress the election of Israel as it does in Rom. 9-11. So in 1 Cor. 10.18 the term is used in a neutral sense and refers to the earthly Israel, Ἰσραὴλ κατὰ σάρκα; in 2 Cor. 3.7, 13, Paul refers primarily to past Israel, i.e. the story of Ex. 34.29-35; in Gal. 6.16 the term is used for the Church of Jews and Gentiles; in Phil. 3.5 Paul refers to his own origins.

six privileges of Israel, with the first and fourth, second and fifth and third
and sixth having corresponding endings:

ἡ υἱο<u>θεσία</u> καὶ ἡ   δό<u>ξα</u> καὶ αἱ   δια<u>θῆκαι</u>
καὶ ἡ νομο<u>θεσία</u> καὶ ἡ λατρ<u>εία</u>   καὶ αἱ ἐπαγγελ<u>ίαι</u>

to them belong the sonship, the glory, the covenants,
the giving of the law, the worship, and the promises

There is also a correspondence in the significance of the words: sonship
(υἱοθεσία) and giving of the law (νομοθεσία) are related to the exodus from
Egypt; glory (δόξα) and worship (λατρεία) are related to the temple service;
covenants (διαθῆκαι) and promises (ἐπαγγελίαι) are related to the promises
to the fathers. It is striking that no parallels have been found in the Jewish
literature of a list of Israel's privileges that approximate to this form or
selection. So Luz writes writes concerning this list in 9.4-5: "Vor allem . . .
fehlen entsprechende Äußerungen im jüdischen Raum fast völlig. . . Das
zeitgenössische Judentum hat m. W. nie in derart indikativisch-präsentischer
Weise von seinen Prärogativen gesprochen wie Pls. von den Privilegien
Israels".[218] This list was probably Paul's own composition.[219]

To understand the significance of Paul's list of privileges a decision has to
be made whether these privileges are "theocratic" privileges[220] or whether
the privileges are to be given full soteriological significance, i.e. whether
these privileges are to be seen as naturally leading to Israel's salvation.
Those who support a theocratic understanding view these privileges as
belonging *solely* to Israel's past.[221] However, a number of general points
about Rom. 9.4-5 suggest that these privileges are to be given, where possible, full soteriological significance. The first obvious point is that if the
privileges are theocratic and belong to Israel's past, why does Paul then
write the whole section Romans 9-11 and, in particular, why does he feel it
necessary to struggle with the issue as to whether the word of God had

---

[218] Luz, *Geschichtsverständnis*, p. 270 n. 13.

[219] Lohse, *Römer*, p. 267.

[220] F.W. Maier, *Israel in der Heilsgeschichte nach Röm. 9-11*, in *Biblische Zeitfragen*
12 (11/12), Münster: Aschendorff 1929, p. 11, for example, writes that Rom. 9.4-5
refers to "die theokratische Sonderstellung Israels".

[221] E.g. J. Munck, *Christus und Israel: Eine Auslegung von Röm 9-11* (Acta Jutlandica, Aarsskrift for Aarhus Universitet 28.3, Teologisk Serie 7), Aarhus: Univer-
sitetsforlaget/Kφbenhavn: Ejnar Munksgaard 1956, p. 28.

failed (Rom. 9.6)? If, for example, the δόξα is understood as theocratic, it could be argued that the δόξα of God in Israel (Rom. 9.4), like the δόξα of God manifested in the law, is fading and is nothing compared to the δόξα of the gospel (cf. 2 Cor. 3.7-11).[222] But if the glory Paul writes about in Rom. 9.4 is fading, why is he then so perplexed about Israel's damnation? However, if the glory, like the other privileges, is to be given full saving significance, it is easy to understand Paul's dilemma in Rom. 9.1-5. Israel is cut off from Christ, is in danger of being damned, yet she has these privileges which have saving significance. Paul clearly had the view that if God had made a covenant with Israel, then Israel should be saved. His view is to be clearly distinguished from the general Rabbinic view that even if Israel is chosen, salvation is nevertheless by works.[223]

The second argument against a simple theocratic understanding is that the privileges listed, although given in the past, still belong to Israel.[224] It is therefore wrong to understand Rom. 9.4-5 in this way: there was in Israel's history the adoption as son, there was in Israel's history the glory, there was in Israel's history the giving of the law, etc. I now examine each of the six privileges and investigate whether, in fact, these privileges are to be understood as theocratic or not.

I turn first to the privilege of adoption.[225] In the New Testament υἱοθεσία is only used by Paul and the author of Ephesians (Rom. 8.15, 23; 9.4; Gal. 4.5; Eph. 1.5). It does not occur in the LXX and has virtually no history with a religious meaning before Paul.[226] The most natural meaning of υἱοθεσία in Rom. 9.4 would be the meaning as found in Rom 8.15, 23.[227] However, I

---

[222] On the terms παλαιὰ διαθήκη in 2 Cor 3.14 (signifying law) and καινὴ διαθήκη in 2 Cor. 3.6 (signifying gospel) see Hofius, "Gesetz des Mose", 273; "Gesetz und Evangelium nach 2. Korinther 3", 81-86.

[223] See chapter 3 above.

[224] J. Piper, *The Justification of God. An Exegetical and Theological Study of Romans 9:1-23*, Grand Rapids: Baker Book House 1983, p. 213 n. 17, points out that after the εἰσιν of 9.4a, the three modifying relative clauses are without verbs, and in such cases, the time of the subordinate clause is always determined by the time of the main verb. So Luther, for example, rightly translates vv. 4-5 as present.

[225] Following Scott, *Adoption*, pp. xiv, 55-57, I understand υἱοθεσία to mean "adoption as son(s)" rather than simply "sonship".

[226] Piper, *Justification*, p. 17; Scott, *Adoption*, chapters 1 and 2.

[227] Note, however, that Lohse, *Römer*, pp. 267-68, argues that Rom. 9.4 refers to sonship whereas 8.15, 23 refers to adoption.

take the point made by many commentators that the adoption of which Paul speaks in Rom. 9.4 is not the same as that which Christians enjoy in Rom. 8.15, 23. So Barrett argues rightly that in Rom. 9.4 Paul speaks of the sonship "conferred upon Israel at the Exodus"[228] has a different sense to that in Rom. 8.15, 23.[229] Similarly I can agree with these words of Murray:

'Adoption' is the filial relation to God constituted by God's grace (cf. Exod. 4:22, 23; Deut. 14:1, 2; Isa. 63:16; 64:8; Hos. 11:1; Mal. 1:6; 2:10). This adoption of Israel is to be distinguished from that spoken of as the apex of New Testament privilege ([Rom.] 8:15; Gal. 4:5; Eph. 1:5; cf. John 1:12; I John 3:1).[230]

However, I am a little uneasy when Murray continues in the following way:

This is apparent from Galatians 4:5, for here the adoption is contrasted with the tutelary discipline of the Mosaic economy. Israel under the Old Testament were indeed children of God but they were as children under age (cf. Gal. 3:23; 4:1-3). The adoption secured by Christ in the fulness of the time (Gal. 4:4) is the mature full-fledged sonship in contrast with the pupilage of Israel under the ceremonial institution. The difference comports with the distinction between the Old Testament and the New. The Old was preparatory, the New is consummatory.[231]

I am uneasy because although it is the case that Israel's sonship does not have the full meaning that Christian sonship has (Israel is cut off from Christ!) I do not think that in *Romans* Israel's sonship is simply concerned with "the tutelary discipline of the Mosaic economy" and neither is Israel's sonship simply related to a "ceremonial institution". The sonship of Israel in Romans has a fuller sense and is related to God's abiding election of Israel. Whereas in other texts, notably in Rom. 11.28, the election of Israel is related to God's choice of Abraham, here the choice of Israel is made in the exodus from Egypt (Ex. 4.22; Hos. 11.1).[232] The sonship or adoption which Paul speaks of in 9.4 is a *present* possession.[233] It is a gift which Israel has retained whether she believes in Jesus or not.

---

[228] See my point above that the rhyming words "sonship" (υἱοθεσία) and "giving of the law" (νομοθεσία) are related to the exodus from Egypt.

[229] Barrett, *Romans*, p. 166.

[230] J. Murray, *The Epistle to the Romans: The English Text with Introduction, Exposition and Notes* (NICNT), 2 vols, Grand Rapids: Wm B. Eerdmans 1968 (one-volume edition), (1 ¹1959; 2 ¹1965), 2:4-5.

[231] Murray, *Romans*, 2:5.

[232] On the idea of the fatherhood of God in the Old Testament and in Ancient Judaism, see G. Quell and G. Schrenk, πατήρ κτλ, *TDNT* 5:959-82 (945-1022).

[233] Piper, *Justification*, p. 213 n. 17.

The "glory" is related to Old Testament idea of כָּבוֹד.[234] The natural way to understand this is as God's glory which dwells in Israel.[235] But many commentators understand this δόξα to be *restricted* to Israel's past. So Murray points to the glory that appeared on Sinai (Ex. 24.16-17), the glory that filled the tabernacle (Ex. 40.34-38), the glory that appeared on the mercy-seat (Lev. 16.2), and the glory that filled the temple (1 Kgs 8.10-11).[236] Paul may well be alluding to this glory and one may add that this is not a glory intrinsic to Israel; rather it is the brilliant glory (Shekinah) of Yahweh, "die strahlende Atmosphäre und Kraft seiner unmittelbaren Gegenwart".[237] This glory was certainly bestowed in the past, but there is no indication that it is a gift which has been withdrawn.[238]

The expression αἱ διαθῆκαι is commonly translated "the covenants" and is usually taken to refer to certain covenants that God made in the past.[239] It is striking that there is no plural form of בְּרִית in the Old Testament, even

---

[234] Fitzmyer, *Romans*, p. 546, points out that in the Patristic literature the δόξα is sometimes understood in the Hellenistic sense of "reputation" in the world. He points, e.g., to Apollinaris of Laodicea (K. Staab, *Pauluskommentare aus der griechischen Kirche*, Münster: Aschendorff 1933, p. 66).

[235] Note that δόξα is not here to be understood as "god-likeness" as is suggested by L.H. Brockington, "The Septuagintal Background to the New Testament use of ΔΟΞΑ", in D.E. Nineham (ed.), *Studies in the Gospels: Essays in Memory of R.H. Lightfoot*, Oxford: Basil Blackwell 1967, 8 (1-8). He writes: "δόξα immediately follows υἱοθεσία and belongs more to that word in sense than it does to διαθῆκαι which follows it". But as we argued above, glory is related structurally to λατρεία. Note also that according to Paul's pessimistic anthropology, even Israel has lost God's likeness. See Bell, *No one seeks for God*, pp. 130-31.

[236] Murray, *Romans*, 2:5.

[237] Wilckens, *Römer*, 2:188.

[238] It is worth adding that just as Paul does not here exclusively refer to the glory of the past, neither does he here use δόξα exclusively for the future, eschatological glory of Israel. The term δόξα does often refer to eschatological glory. This is seen in Rom. 2.7, 10; 8.18; 9.23; 2 Cor. 4.17 (see also Col. 1.27; 3.4; 2 Tim. 2.10). See also δόξα with a modifier in Rom. 5.2; 8.21; 9.23; 1 Cor. 2.7; Phil. 3.21; 1 Thes. 2.12 (see also Eph. 1.18; 2 Thes. 1.9; 2.14; Tit. 2.13). But 2 Cor. 3.18 shows that Paul can refer to a glory of the present (although here he speaks of a glory not of Israel but of *Christians* who are now being transformed as they behold (or see in a mirror) the glory of the Lord).

[239] Cranfield, *Romans*, 2:463, suggests that Paul had in mind the covenants with Israel at Sinai (Ex. 19.5; 24.1ff.) and in the plains of Moab (Dt. 29.1ff.) and at Mounts Ebal and Gerizim (Jos. 8.30ff.), the covenant with Abraham (Gen. 15.17ff.; 17.1ff.), and possibly the covenant with David (2 Sam. 23.5).

though there are several "covenants" described.[240] But the plural form διαθῆκαι (in connection with the idea of several covenants) is found in the later Septuagintal writings[241] and the plural בְּרִיתוֹת is found in Rabbinic literature.[242] In Rom. 9.4, the plural form is most likely the original reading since it is the *lectio difficilior*. The singular ἡ διαθήκη, despite its early attestation (P[46] B D F G vg[cl]), may have been written in order to make clear a reference to the covenant with Moses.[243] Ironically though, such a covenant was probably not uppermost in Paul's mind. If any covenant stood out for Paul it was the one made with Abraham. The word διαθῆκαι produces an assonance with ἐπαγγελίαι and could even be a synonym.[244] Paul probably has in mind the covenants that God made with Israel in the past. But it would be a grave mistake to imagine that these covenants are now obsolete. As I will argue in chapter 7, the covenant Paul mentions in Rom. 11.26-27 is not simply a "new" covenant which he makes with his people. It is the fulfilment of the covenant which God made long ago with Abraham; and the fulfilment is precisely that God "takes away their sins" (Rom. 11.27b).

The fourth privilege νομοθεσία is often taken to mean the "giving of the law".[245] However, it should be noted that in Hellenistic-Jewish literature,

---

[240] H.-D. Neef, "Aspekte alttestamentlicher Bundestheologie", in F. Avemarie and H. Lichtenberger (ed.), *Bund und Tora: Zur theologischen Begriffsgeschichte in alttestamentlicher, frühjüdischer und urchristlicher Tradition* (WUNT 92), Tübingen: J.C.B. Mohr (Paul Siebeck) 1996, 2 (1-23), comments that this point has been neglected in academic discussion.

[241] Sir. 44.12, 18; Wis. 18.22; 2 Mac. 8.15.

[242] See b. Ber. 48b (which speaks of the torah being given with three covenants, i.e. at Mount Sinai, Mount Gerizim, and in the plains of Moab) and b. Ber. 49a (which speaks of thirteen covenants related to Abraham, this word occurring thirteen times in Gen. 17.1-14). On the multiplicity of covenants in Rabbinic literature, see J. Behm, διαθήκη, *TDNT* 2:128-29 (124-34).

[243] Cranfield, *Romans*, 2:462; Lohse, *Römer*, p. 268.

[244] H. Lietzmann, *An die Römer* (HzNT 8), Tübingen: J.C.B. Mohr (Paul Siebeck) [4]1933, p. 89. J. Calvin, *The Epistles of Paul The Apostle to the Romans and to the Thessalonians*, translated by R. Mackenzie (CNTC 8), Grand Rapids: Wm B. Eerdmans 1976 (repr.) ([1]1960), pp. 194-95, distinguishes between the covenants and promises. Kutsch, *Neues Testament*, pp. 154-55, argues that αἱ διαθῆκαι are the promises made to Abraham, the Patriarchs, and the people of Israel, and that αἱ ἐπαγγελίαι are the promises not coming under the category of διαθῆκαι (e.g. those of Rom. 9.9; Gal. 3.16-18). Kutsch rightly rejects the theory of C. Roetzel, "Διαθῆκαι in Romans 9,4", *Bib* 51 (1970) 377-90, that αἱ διαθῆκαι refer to statutes, ordinances, or commandments.

[245] Luz, *Geschichtsverständnis*, p. 272; Käsemann, *Römer*, p. 249.

νομοθεσία is often a synonym for νόμος.[246] In Rom. 9.4, Paul probably used νομοθεσία and not νόμος because he wished to use a word rhyming with υἱοθεσία. It is clear from Rom. 2.20, for example, that the law was a special gift for Israel. Even though Galatians stresses the shadow side of the law, I believe this letter still asserts that the law is *God's* law.[247] Romans generally has a more positive view of the law and here it is certainly seen in a positive light. Paul is probably stressing that the Jewish people received this revelation of God. But nevertheless, in a sense this privilege could be viewed as slightly problematic. If Paul's focus on the law is the condemning function, how can one speak of it having a special non-theocratic significance? It certainly has no saving significance. I think the answer may lie in the fact that despite the condemning nature of the law, Israel is uniquely privileged to be the one nation which preserves the law and the law marks them out as God's special people.[248]

The term λατρεία, the fifth in Paul's list, is used in the LXX for the sacrificial service (Ex. 12.25, 26; 13.5; Jos. 22.27; 1 Chr. 28.13) or for religion (1 Mac. 1.43; 2.19, 22) or for compulsory labour (3 Mac. 4.14). Paul only uses λατρεία on one other occasion, in Rom. 12.1, where it refers to the spiritual service of Christians. However, the most natural way to take λατρεία in Rom. 9.4 is as a reference to the various sacrificial provisions in the Old Testament.[249] But the λατρεία refers not only to the past but also to the present sacrificial cult. Through the sacrificial cult Israel's sins had been dealt with. But this fifth privilege could perhaps also be seen as problematic in that such temple services had ceased to have any soteriological value for

---

[246] See 2 Mac. 6.23; 4 Mac. 5.35; 17.16; Aristeas 15, 176; Philo, *De Abrahamo* 5; *De cherubim* 87; Josephus, *Antiquitates* 6.93.

[247] So in Gal. 3.19 Paul says the law was added (προσετέθη) (by God!) on account of transgressions (τῶν παραβάσων χάριν), i.e. to imprison sinners (cf. Eckstein, *Verheißung und Gesetz*, pp. 192-93). Nevertheless it is still God's law. Further Paul's statement that the law "was ordained by angels through an intermediary" (διαταγεὶς δι' ἀγγέλων ἐν χειρὶ μεσίτου) (v. 19b) by no means questions that it is God's law. For διά here is to be understood as instrumental and is not to be understood as ὑπ' ἀγγέλων (Eckstein, *Verheißung und Gesetz*, p. 201). Contrast, Hübner, *Law*, p. 27, who believes that "the angels are authors of the Law". But Gal. 3.19 only speaks of an inferiority of the law in that it comes indirectly through angels (cf. Dt. 33.2) whereas God speaks his promise to Abraham directly.

[248] On the issue of the law and Jewish identity, see chapter 10 below.

[249] Where the Hebrew is available λατρεία always corresponds to עֲבֹדָה.

Paul because of the atoning death of Christ. How then can he have a positive assessment of them? There are, I believe, two answers. First, it could be argued that not all the sacrifices had an atoning significance. This point, however, has limited strength, since it is likely that the whole system had atoning significance.[250] The second answer is that although the sacrifices were a temporary measure (in that they were fulfilled in Christ), they nevertheless were a special gift to Israel.

The sixth privilege consists of αἱ ἐπαγγελίαι, the promises.[251] Cranfield points out that in view of Rom. 4.13-22 and Gal. 3.16-29, the promises Paul primarily had in mind were those made to Abraham (Gen. 12.7; 13.14-17; 17.4-8; 22.16-18) and repeated to Isaac (26.3-4) and to Jacob (Gen. 28.13-14); also, in view of 2 Cor. 1.20 and 7.1, Paul probably had in mind many other Old Testament promises, particularly eschatological and messianic promises (e.g., Is. 9.6-7; Jer. 31.31ff.).[252]

It is to be noted that all six privileges are present possessions of Israel and, with the exceptions of νομοθεσία and λατρεία, have a soteriological dimension. Also, even the νομοθεσία and λατρεία have a positive sig-

---

[250] Gese, "Sühne", 94, argues that in the Priestly writing, all the offerings have atoning significance: "Das gesamte Opferwesen dient der Sühne . . .". This point is taken up by J. Ådna, "Jesus' Symbolic Act in the Temple (Mark 11:15-17): The Replacement of the Sacrificial Cult by His Atoning Death", in B. Ego, A. Lange and P. Pilhofer (ed.), *Gemeinde ohne Tempel: Zur Substituierung und Transformation des Jerusalemer Tempels und seines Kults im Alten Testament, antiken Judentum und frühen Christentum*, Tübingen: J.C.B. Mohr (Paul Siebeck) 1999, 468 (461-75), who goes on to argue that the cleansing of the temple "zeigt . . . seine Bereitschaft und seinen messianischen Anspruch, durch seinen Tod – als Lösegeld und Sühnetod verstanden (vgl. Mk 10,45; 14,24) – die Tempelsteuer und den täglichen Sühnopferkult im Tempel zu ersetzen" (473). See also the older study of F.C.N. Hicks, *The Fullness of Sacrifice: An Essay in Reconciliation*, London: Macmillan and Co. 1930, pp. 20-21: "Before the exile, burnt-offerings and peace offerings were generally offered together (e.g. 1 Sam. x.8); and when the system was complete the three are found together (Ex. xxix.14, 18, 28; Lev. viii.14-17, 18-21, 22-32, etc.). There was always a burnt-offering with the sin-offering, and the two, or the three, always followed in the same order–first the atonement, then the offering, then the meal. Thus the complete action of sacrifice is constant". See also J. Pedersen, *Israel: Its Life and Culture, II-IV* ET, London: OUP/Copenhagen: Branner og Korch 1953 (repr.), (¹1940), pp. 358-59.

[251] Note the variant ἡ ἐπαγγελία in P⁴⁶ D F G a (cf. the variant ἡ διαθήκη earlier). Again the plural should no doubt be accepted.

[252] Cranfield, *Romans*, 2:464.

nificance. Paul is therefore not simply talking of the privileges of Israel's past.

Having discussed the first relative clause, I turn briefly to the second and third clauses. In the second relative clause, Paul writes "to them belong the patriarchs" (ὧν οἱ πατέρες), the reference probably being to Abraham, Isaac, and Jacob, in view of Rom. 9.6-13. In the third relative clause, Paul writes "of their race, according to the flesh, is the Christ" (ἐξ ὧν ὁ Χριστὸς τὸ κατὰ σάρκα). Whereas the first two relative clauses begin with ὧν, here the climactic character of Christ's coming is stressed by the opening words ἐξ ὧν. If Paul then is referring to Christ as "God over all" (ὁ ὢν ἐπὶ πάντων θεός), he is emphasizing the remarkable salvation historical importance of Israel.[253]

---

[253] On the controversy concerning the punctuation, see chapter 2 above. Some in the Unitarian tradition have adopted the conjectural emendation of ὁ ὤν to ὧν ὁ thereby making belonging to God the climax of the privileges. Such an emendation was mentioned by the Socinian Jonasz Schlichting (Jonae Slichtingii de Bukowiec, *Commentaria posthuma in plerosque Novi Testamenti libros*, Amsterdam 1665-68, p. 254, see Cranfield, *Romans*, 2:465 n. 2) although he himself did not accept it. According to O. Kuss, *Der Römerbrief*, 3 vols, Regensburg: Verlag Friedrich Pustet 1 1957; 2 1959; 3 1978, 3:691, it is found earlier in Johann Crell's commentary on the beginning John's gospel (Crell, who died in 1631, was also a Socinian). According to Cranfield, *Romans*, 2:466 n. 1, the emendation was enthusiastically accepted by the Socinian Samuel Crell (he adopted the pseudonym Lucius Mellerius Artemonius, see M. Wolter, "Pseudonymität II", *TRE* 27:668 (662-70)), in his work *Initium Evangelii S. Joannis Apostoli ex antiquitate ecclesiastica restitutum indidemque nova ratione illustratum*, Amsterdam 1726, pp. 223-38. The secondary literature can tend to be a little confusing in that reference tends to be made *either* to J. Crell (Kuss, *Römerbrief*, 3:691; "Zu Römer 9,5", in J. Friedrich, W. Pöhlmann, and P. Stuhlmacher (ed.), *Rechtfertigung: Festschrift für Ernst Käsemann zum 70. Geburtstag*, Tübingen: J.C.B. Mohr (Paul Siebeck)/Göttingen: Vandenhoeck & Ruprecht 1976, 298 (291-303); Wilckens, *Römer*, 2: 189 n. 833) *or* to S. Crell (Cranfield, *Romans*, 2:466 n. 1; E. Güting, "Amen, Eulogie, Doxologie. Eine textkritische Untersuchung", in D.-A. Koch and H. Lichtenberger (ed.), *Begegnungen zwischen Christentum und Judentum in Antike und Mittelalter. Festschrift für Heinz Schreckenberger* (SIJD 1), Göttingen: Vandenhoeck & Ruprecht 1993, 147 n. 44 (133-162)). But both figures are discussed in J.J. Herzog and O. Zöckler, "Socin und der Socinianismus", *RE* [3] 18:464-67 (459-80), S. Crell being the grandson of J. Crell (18:464). The conjectural emendation was later accepted, for example, by J. Weiß, *Das Urchristentum*, Göttingen: Vandenhoeck & Ruprecht 1917, p. 363, and has been recently supported by Güting, "Amen, Eulogie, Doxologie", 148-150. The problem with the emendation is, as Cranfield, *Romans*, 2:466, argues: "ὧν (without καί) would be intolerably harsh after the καὶ ἐξ ὧν which is appropriate for the introduction of the last item of the list".

Rom. 9.1-5 has therefore stated the problem. Piper puts this problem as follows: "Since Israel is the real heir of God's promises which include personal, eternal salvation (9:4, 5), how is it that most of the Israelites of Paul's day are accursed and cut off from Christ (9:3)?"[254] Israel has the privileges but at the same time is accursed and separated from Christ.

5.4. Romans 9.6-13

This text could be interpreted as an attempt by Paul to disinherit the majority of his fellow-Jews. For example Peterson believes that Rom. 9.6b implies that Israel has essentially lost her election. He writes: "Als die Apostel zu den Heiden gingen, nahmen sie aber auch die Erwählung Israel mit, und das ist es nun, was schon die letzten Worte von Vers 6 andeuten: 'Denn nicht alle, die aus Israel sind, sind Israel'".[255] We now enquire to see if such a view finds any basis in the text.

Paul begins the section by declaring that "the word of God" (ὁ λόγος τοῦ θεοῦ) has not failed. The expression ὁ λόγος τοῦ θεοῦ could be understood in the sense of covenant, promise and law (cf. 9.4-5) and the τὰ λόγια τοῦ θεοῦ (Rom. 3.2) which were entrusted to Israel.[256] Alternatively, it could mean "the declared purpose of God".[257] Whichever is the case (and I am now more inclined to follow the former), Paul's message is of crucial pastoral concern to the Christians in Rome. As Gutbrod writes: "Kann die neue Gemeinde dem Worte Gottes trauen, wenn doch das Wort Gottes an die Judenschaft hinfällig geworden zu sein scheint".[258] Paul grounds his case that the word of God has not failed by arguing "For all those from Israel,

---

[254] Piper, *Justification*, p. 31.

[255] E. Peterson, *Die Kirche aus Juden und Heiden* (BüSH 2), Salzburg: Verlag Anton Pustet 1933, p. 18.

[256] See Käsemann, *Romans*, p. 262; K. Haacker, *Der Brief des Paulus an die Römer* (ThHK 6), Leipzig: Evangelische Verlagsanstalt 1999, p. 190.

[257] Sanday and Headlam, *Romans*, p. 240. See also O. Michel, *Der Brief an die Römer* (KEK 4), Göttingen: Vandenhoeck & Ruprecht [14]1978, ([10]1955), p. 299, who believes ὁ λόγος τοῦ θεοῦ is an "Ausdruck für die Absicht und den Willen Gottes, der sein Ziel trotz des Unglaubens der Menschen erreichen will".

[258] W. Gutbrod, Ἰσραήλ, *ThWNT* 3:389. This volume of Kittel's Wörterbuch was published in 1938! Users of the English translation *TDNT* may not be aware that Gutbrod died on the Russian front in 1941 at the age of 39. See the dedication in *ThWNT* 4.

these are not Israel"[259] (οὐ γὰρ πάντες οἱ ἐξ Ἰσραὴλ οὗτοι Ἰσραήλ). The first reference to Israel is most likely to the people of Israel rather than the patriarch. For if the reference were to Jacob one would perhaps expect that Paul would first refer to Abraham (ie. that v. 7a comes before v. 6b).[260] The second use of Ἰσραήλ most likely refers to Jews who are Christians[261] and certainly does not imply that the Church of Jews and Gentiles is the "true Israel" as Peterson suggested.[262] Paul therefore argues for an Israel within Israel. Although Paul's thought seems rather convoluted here, we can find a parallel in Rom. 2.28-29 where he speaks of those who are true Jews and those who are Jews in appearance. And just as those who are Jews in appearance still have an advantage, so Paul believes that those who are not within the inner Israel are still children of God. They still have the adoption (Rom. 9.4) and are still referred to as the sons of Israel (Rom. 9.27).

His argument is clearer in v. 7a when he says that "not all are children of Abraham because they are his descendants". He demonstrates this clearly in vv. 7-13. In vv. 7b-9 he is demonstrating the election of Isaac and implying the rejection of Ishmael. Isaac is the child of the promise. And in case any-

---

[259] This is the translation of Piper, *Justification*, p. 47, who has taken οὐ to modify οὗτοι Ἰσραήλ, rather than πάντες, on the basis of the parallel in Rom. 7.15. In Rom. 7.15, οὐ modifies the second clause of the four clauses: οὐ γὰρ ὃ θέλω τοῦτο πράσσω, ἀλλ' ὃ μισῶ τοῦτο ποιῶ. If it were to modify the first, we would simply have a repetition in the two sections, which would make little sense ("I practice what I do not will, *but* what I hate this I do"). If, however, οὐ modifies the second clause, we have something which makes more sense: "What I want, this I do not do, but what I hate this I do". Piper's translation of 9.6b is supported by Moo, *Romans*, p. 573 n. 19, and Dunn, *Romans*, 2:539. Most commentators and translations, however, seem to take οὐ to modify πάντες,.

[260] Cf. Wilckens, *Römer*, 2:192 n. 850.

[261] P.-G. Klumbies, "Israels Vorzüge und das Evangelium von der Gottesgerechtig- keit in Römer 9-11", in H.-P. Stähli (ed.), *Wort und Dienst: Jahrbuch der Kirchlichen Hochschule Bethel*, Kirchliche Hochschule Bethel, Bielefeld NF 18 (1985), 142 (135- 157), writes: "Über die konkrete Bestimmung des zweiten Israelbegriffs herrscht Unsicherheit. Charakteristisch dafür ist das Schwanken E. Dinklers, der ursprünglich davon ausgeht, "daß mit dem zweiten 'Israel' alle gemeint sind, die zum eschatologi- schen Volk gehören, unabhängig von jeder ethnischen Herkunft", später jedoch seine Ansicht korrigiert und das zweite Israel auf die Juden bezogen sieht". Klumbies refers to E. Dinkler, "Prädestination bei Paulus: Exegetische Bemerkungen zum Römerbrief", in *Signum Crucis: Aufsätze zum Neuen Testament und zur christlichen Archäologie*, Tübingen: J.C.B. Mohr (Paul Siebeck) 1967, 249 nn. 19, 267 (241-69).

[262] Peterson, *Die Kirche aus Juden und Heiden*, p. 18.

one should think that Isaac was special in that he was the son of the free woman Sarah and not the son of the slave Hagar, Paul gives an even more striking example in the next generation. For here the two children have not only the same father but also the same mother, Rebecca.[263] She was told "The elder [Esau] shall serve the younger [Jacob]".

I have assumed that Paul is referring the election of individuals. However, some believe Paul is rather speaking of the election of nations and their historical tasks and not of individuals and their eternal destinies. So Leenhardt argues that:

> . . . the names mentioned certainly do not connote individuals so much as peoples who are thus named after their eponymous ancestors, according to Old Testament practice. It is best to understand the names in this way, since the argument which they are quoted to support concerns the destiny of Israel as a whole, and not the destiny of the individuals who compose Israel.[264]

So Leenhardt argues that Paul's quotation of Gen. 25.23 in Rom. 9.12 ("the elder will serve the younger") demonstrates that perdition is not in Paul's mind.[265] Further, Leenhardt argues, Mal. 1.2, quoted in Rom. 9.13, makes plain that Paul is concerned with the descendants of Jacob and Esau.[266]

There are two main problems with this approach. First, although in the Old Testament context Gen. 25.23 and Mal. 1.2 are referring to nations, Paul seems to interpret them as applying to the individuals Jacob and Esau. God's oracle to Rebecca in Gen. 25.23 is: "Two peoples are in your womb, and two peoples, born of you, shall be divided; the one shall be stronger than the other, the elder shall serve the younger". Paul has chosen to quote just the final clause and has probably deliberately omitted Gen. 25.23a precisely because it points to "two peoples".[267] The second problem with the

---

[263] Paul does not mention the fact that they were twins.

[264] F.J. Leenhardt, *The Epistle to the Romans: A Commentary* ET, London: Lutterworth 1961, p. 250. Cf. Lietzmann, *Römer*, p. 91.

[265] R.T. Forster and V.P. Marston, *God's Strategy in Human History*, Minneapolis: Bethany House Publishers 1973, p. 59, also make the point that according to the Old Testament narrative the individual Esau did not serve Jacob.

[266] Leenhardt, *Romans*, p. 250.

[267] Lietzmann, *Römer*, p. 91, argues that one should hold in mind "daß nicht eigentlich die Prädestination des einzelnen Menschen, sondern die ganzer Völker das Thema des Pls ist . . . " and seems to defend this position as follows: "Für die Art, wie Pls die Zitate verwertet, ist lehrreich, daß im Gen 25₂₃ ausdrücklich von den zwei Völkern, nicht den beiden Personen gesprochen wird". The implication is that because the original text

"nations" interpretation is that it fails to explain Paul's train of thought in Rom. 9.1-13. The problem posed in Rom. 9.1-5 is that many individual Israelites are cut off from Christ although Israel as a whole remains the people of God (for example in possessing the covenant privileges). So Israel, whilst remaining the people of God, are largely heading for damnation. Paul's answer to this problem is that God's word has not failed (9.6a: Οὐχ οἷον δὲ ὅτι ἐκπέπτωκεν ὁ λόγος τοῦ θεοῦ); in fact, God's expressed purpose remains firm (9.11c: ἵνα ἡ κατ᾽ ἐκλογὴν πρόθεσις τοῦ θεοῦ μένῃ). The reason God's word has not failed is twofold. First, God does not guarantee that every descendant of Abraham has a place in the people of God.[268] There has always been a process of election of certain individuals among the descendants of Abraham and the rejection of others. Paul in Rom. 9.6b-13 is not therefore proving that God freely elected the nation of Israel (although that may be true); rather he is establishing a principle by which he could explain how individual Israelites were accursed, and yet God's word has not failed.[269] The second reason God's word has not failed is because of the conclusion Paul comes to in Rom. 11.25-32.[270] For Rom. 9.6a can be understood as forming a heading not only for 9.6b-13 but also for the whole of Romans 9-11.[271]

Now to return to the main problem, i.e. whether Paul is disinheriting the majority of Jews, the answer according to this text is that he does not. Some may consider that Rom. 9.6b is a problem for this approach: "For all those from Israel, these are not Israel". But as argued above, Paul's logic is rather like that in Rom. 2.28-29. It is also important not to draw a strict parallel between v. 6b and v. 7a. In v. 7a he makes a distinction between the "seed" (σπέρμα) and "children" (τέκνα) of Abraham. Not all the physical seed are children.[272] Paul has primarily in mind the exclusion of Ishmael although the

---

of Gen. 25.23 speaks of two peoples, Paul must have meant also two peoples. However, it is precisely because Paul omits v. 23a which suggests that he was making the text refer to individual persons.

[268] See Rom. 9.7: οὐδ᾽ ὅτι εἰσὶν σπέρμα Ἀβραὰμ πάντες τέκνα, . . .

[269] Piper, *Justification*, p. 48.

[270] Discussed in chapters 6 and 7 below.

[271] Cranfield, *Romans*, 2:473; Wilckens, *Römer*, 2:191.

[272] The quotation from Gen. 21.12 slightly confuses the term "seed" since it is argued that in Isaac the seed will be called (Εν Ἰσαὰκ κληθήσεταί σοι σπέρμα). Nevertheless Paul's overall intention is clear.

six sons of Keturah (Gen. 25.2) were also excluded.[273] However, the exclusion of Ishmael and the exclusion of Esau in the next generation should not be likened to the exclusion of unbelieving Jews. For although Paul draws a distinction between οἱ ἐξ Ἰσραήλ and Ἰσραήλ in 9.6b, he is by no means disinheriting the majority of his fellow Jews or excluding them in the way Ishmael and Esau were excluded. He is still able to call the unbelieving Jews his brethren (τῶν ἀδελφῶν μου (Rom. 9.3)).[274] As I have argued, even in their unbelief they are Israelites to whom the covenant privileges belong. And even in Rom. 9.27, which could be taken as a "low point" in Israel's Heilsgeschichte in Rom. 9-11, they are still called "sons of Israel". It is perhaps significant that Paul stops his genealogical discussion with Jacob, for all his descendants were to form the elect of God, the twelve tribes of Israel.

5.5. Romans 2.11, 3.9, 3.22 and 10.12

These four texts are frequently taken to imply that the privileged position of the Jew has been abolished. So in Rom. 2.11 Paul concludes that there is no partiality with God (οὐ γάρ ἐστιν προσωπολημψία παρὰ τῷ θεῷ). Although his conclusion is made in respect of Jews and Gentiles (see vv. 9-10) the context regards the judgement according to works and is not relevant to the issue of the election of Israel.[275]

I have discussed Rom. 3.9 elsewhere in some detail[276] and I will here summarize my conclusions. The question in v. 9a is often understood as: "What then, do we (i.e. Jews) have an advantage?" (Τί οὖν; προεχόμεθα;)[277] The answer οὐ πάντως has then often been taken to mean "Certainly not".[278] However, it is unlikely that Paul is speaking of Israel's advantage; rather, he

---

[273] See Fitzmyer, *Romans*, p. 560.

[274] This use of ἀδελφός can be compared with the use of brother in Rom. 8.12, a term used for Christians. See O. Betz, "Die heilsgeschichtliche Rolle Israels bei Paulus", in *Jesus, Der Herr der Kirche: Aufsätze zur biblischen Theologie II* (WUNT 52), Tübingen: J.C.B. Mohr (Paul Siebeck) 1990, 322 (312-34).

[275] For a discussion of Rom. 2.7-11, see Bell, *No one seeks for God*, pp. 141-44.

[276] Bell, *No one seeks for God*, pp. 210-15.

[277] For a discussion of the text critical problems see *No one seeks for God*, pp. 210-11.

[278] Sanday and Headlam, *Romans*, p. 77; Barrett, *Romans*, p. 65; Murray, *Romans*, 1:102. The answer "certainly not" follows from the Vulgate *nequaquam*.

is asking the question: "Are we making excuses?"[279] Further, even if Paul
were speaking of Israel's advantage here they would not have one in the
sense that Jews and Greeks are all "under the power of sin".

In Rom. 3.22b Paul declares that there is no distinction between Jews and
Gentiles: οὐ γάρ ἐστιν διαστολή. However, one cannot argue on the basis of
this verse that the privileged position of Israel has been abolished.[280] The
clause "for there is no distinction" (οὐ γάρ ἐστιν διαστολή) is explained and
qualified by the following two verses: "For all have sinned and fall short of
the glory of God 24 being justified freely by his grace through the redemption which is in Christ Jesus" (πάντες γὰρ ἥμαρτον καὶ ὑστεροῦνται τῆς
δόξης τοῦ θεοῦ δικαιούμενοι δωρεὰν τῇ αὐτοῦ χάριτι διὰ τῆς ἀπολυτ-
ρώσεως τῆς ἐν Χριστῷ Ἰησοῦ). There is therefore no difference because all,
Jews and Gentiles alike, have sinned and fall short of the glory of God.
There is no distinction in respect of the "righteousness of God" (δικαιοσύνη
θεοῦ) since both Jew and Gentile can only be justified by faith.

The same word διαστολή occurs in Rom. 10.12 where Paul writes that
there is no distinction between Jew and Greek: (οὐ γάρ ἐστιν διαστολὴ
Ἰουδαίου τε καὶ Ἕλληνος). Here there is no distinction because, as
explained in 10.12b, the same Lord (Jesus Christ) is Lord of all and bestows
his riches upon all who call upon him.

5.6. Romans 4.11-12

Rom. 4.11-12, whilst not directly concerned with the issue of a substitution
model, is nevertheless quite instructive for it gives a somewhat different picture to that of Galatians 3 which we found above. The issue I wish to focus
on is whether Paul considers Abraham to be the father of all Jews whether
they are Christian or not. Many commentators believe that in Rom. 4.11-12
Paul says Abraham is father of two groups: Christian Gentiles (those who, in
a state of uncircumcision, believe) and Christian Jews (those who, being cir-

---

[279] See *BA* and *BAG*: ". . . if the 'we' in 9a must of necessity be the same as in 9b, i.e.
Paul himself, he is still dealing w. the opponents whom he has in mind in vss. 7,8, and
asks ironically: *am I protecting myself?, am I making excuses?*" Again for a more
detailed treatment see Bell, *No one seeks for God*, pp. 210-15.

[280] This is precisely what Michel, *Römer*, p. 148, argues: "Der Allgemeinheit der
Knechtschaft (Röm 3,9) tritt die Allgemeinheit des Glaubens gegenüber; aber in diesem
Fall bedeutet Allgemeinheit Aufhebung der Unterschiede, auch Aufhebung des Vorrechts
Israels".

cumcised, are not only circumcised but are also believers). Cranfield, for example, translates the verses as follows:

11 And he received the sign of circumcision as a seal of the righteousness by faith which he had while still uncircumcised, so that he might be the father of all those who, in a state of uncircumcision, believe, so that righteousness is reckoned to them, 12 and also the father of the circumcision for those who not only belong to the circumcision but also walk in the steps of the faith of our father Abraham which he had while he was still uncircumcised.

Cranfield admits that he has not translated the τοῖς before στοιχοῦσιν and I believe this is a possible weakness of his translation.[281] An alternative way of understanding of these verses is presented by Kraus.[282] He suggests that in v. 12 it is not one group referred to by means of two determinations (i.e. circumcision and faith) but rather two groups, one referred to by circumcision and the other by faith. A possible parallel can be seen in v. 16:

That is why it depends on faith, in order that the promise may rest on grace and be guaranteed to all his descendents–not only to the adherents of the law but also to those who share the faith of Abraham, for he is the father of us all.

So although Paul stresses the importance of faith, he seems to argue here that the promise to Abraham is still valid for Jews.[283] Therefore in v. 12 Paul could be referring to Jews who do not believe in Christ and then to Jewish Christians in which case sense can be made of the second occurrence of τοῖς. However, it could be objected that if Paul were referring to two groups one would expect not τοῖς οὐκ in v. 12a but rather οὐ τοῖς. If v. 12 is understood to refer to two groups we therefore have to understand an inver-

---

[281] Cranfield defends his position in *Romans* 1:237. See also Moo, *Romans*, pp. 270-71 (especially n. 25).

[282] Kraus, *Volk Gottes*, pp. 278-79.

[283] So Fitzmyer, whilst taking v.12 to refer to Christians only, nevertheless writes this on v. 16: "The divine promise still holds good for the Jewish people descended physically from Abraham, but now all those who imitate Abraham's faith, whether Jew or Gentile, may find a share in it" (*Romans*, p. 385). On v. 12 Fitzmyer follows the line of J. Swetnam, "The Curious Crux at Romans 4,12", *Bib* 61 (1980) 110-15. Here τοῖς is retained before στοιχοῦσιν but περιτομή is assumed to have two meanings. "In the first instance (πατέρα περιτομῆς) the word refers to spiritual circumcision, in the second (ἐκ περιτομῆς) it refers to physical circumcision" ("Crux", 114).

sion[284] and the theological consequence is that Abraham is still regarded as the father of Jews, even those who do not believe in Christ. Galatians, as we have seen, does not share this view. This difference between Galatians and Romans is further confirmed in Rom. 4.13 where the promise is to Abraham or his seed, seed (σπέρμα) here not being confined to Christians (as it is in Gal. 3.16).[285]

6. How does Paul relate Israel to the Church?

In view of the above discussion it seems that Galatians and Romans give quite different accounts as to how Israel is related to the Church. Galatians has a substitution model. Romans, however, clearly does not. The closest one gets to a substitution model in Romans is, ironically, in the olive tree parable in Rom. 11.17-24 which gives Israel a central position in salvation history. This text will be discussed in chapter 8 below. But it must be stressed that in this parable one hardly has the substitution model one finds in Galatians.

The difference in approach could be explained in one of two ways. First, it could be argued that Paul faced a particularly acute problem in Galatians. His Jewish Christian opponents were arguing that salvation was through Christ *and* the law. Therefore they were trying to compel Gentile Christians to be circumcised. This could account for Paul's extremely negative view towards the law and towards the Jewish people. In Romans, however, he was not facing Judaizers. Rather his opponents in the Church of Rome were Jewish Christians who were critical of Paul's gospel. They felt that Paul's gospel implied that one should do evil so that good may come (cf. Rom. 3.8, 6.1). And in relation to the Israel question they believed that his gospel smooths over the distinction between Jews and Gentiles from a salvation

---

[284] Kraus' translation of v. 12 is therefore: "und [damit er sei] Vater von Beschnittenen, nicht derer allein, die beschnitten sind, sondern auch derer, die den Weg des Glaubens gehen, den unser Vater Abraham als Unbeschnittener ging" (Kraus, *Volk Gottes*, p. 278).

[285] Kraus, *Volk Gottes*, pp. 280-81. Cf. E. Stauffer, *Die Theologie des Neuen Testaments*, Stuttgart: W. Kohlhammer Verlag [4]1948, ([1]1941), p. 170, who points out that whereas in Gal. 3.16 the promises to Abraham have their goal in Christ, in Rom. 9.7 the promises are for the children of Abraham.

historical perspective and believed that his Gentile mission had contributed to the failure of the mission to Israel. In addition Paul was having to address a Gentile Christian anti-Judaism in Rome.[286] Therefore the quite different approaches to the Israel question could be explained by such different contexts for Galatians and Romans. Such an approach in explaining Paul's different outlooks on Israel is similar to Räisänen's attempt to explain Paul's different approaches to the law.[287]

I wonder though whether this approach to the Israel question sufficiently accounts for the differences in Galatians and Romans. One factor which questions such an analysis is that in 2 Corinthians and Philippians Paul is also having to contend with Judaizers yet in these later letters he does not give such a clear substitution theory.[288] This leads me to suggest that a better approach is to assume a development in Paul's view between writing Galatians and Romans (with 1, 2 Corinthians and Philippians taking an intermediate position).[289] But into what view does it develop? One can certainly say that in Romans Israel remains the people of God. But in order to establish how Paul exactly relates Israel to the Church, one must investigate Paul's argument in Romans 9-11. These chapters form Paul's most significant and profound statement on Israel. They will dominate the discussion in the following three chapters, and one of the issues that will be addressed is precisely how Paul relates Israel to the Church.

---

[286] Concerning the occasion of Romans, see Bell, *Provoked to Jealousy*, pp. 63-79.

[287] Räisänen, *Paul and the Law*. For a critical response to Räisänen, see T.E. van Spanje, *Inconsistency in Paul? A Critique of the Work of Heikki Räisänen* (WUNT 2.110), Tübingen: J.C.B. Mohr (Paul Siebeck) 1999.

[288] This fact confirms my view (expressed in *No one seeks for God*, pp. 238-39, n. 2) that Philippians was actually written before Romans and that it was written from Ephesus.

[289] I take the order of the epistles to be 1 Thessalonians, Galatians, 1 Corinthians, 2 Corinthians, Philippians, Philemon, Romans. A confirmation of the order Galatians – 1 Corinthians – 2 Corinthians – Romans can be gained by considering the issue of the collection. Cf. A.J.M. Wedderburn, "Paul's Collection: Chronology and History", *NTS* 48 (2002) 95-110. Note, however, that Wedderburn dates Philippians to the Roman (or possibly Caesarean) imprisonment (102-3).

Chapter 5

The Hardening of Israel

1. Why does Israel not believe in Christ?

We now deal with one of the most perplexing of all theological problems: the hardening of Israel. Within Romans 9-11 this idea occurs in Rom. 9.14-29 and again in 11.1-10, 25. One of the key terms is the verb πωρόω (Rom. 11.7), first used by Paul in 2 Cor. 3.14;[1] also important is the cognate πώρωσις (Rom. 11.25) together with the verb σκληρύνω (Rom. 9.18).[2]

One of the most striking examples of the hardening of Israel in the Old Testament is Is. 6.9-10. Isaiah has just accepted God's call and he addresses Isaiah with this startling commission:

> And he [God] said, "Go, and say to this people:
>> 'Hear and hear, but do not understand;
>> see and see, but do not perceive.'
>> 10 Make the heart of this people fat,
>>> and their ears heavy,
>>> and shut their eyes;
>> lest they see with their eyes,
>>> and hear with their ears,
>>> and understand with their hearts,
>>> and turn and be healed".

Jesus alludes to these severe words in Mk 4.11-12 par.:

> And he [Jesus] said to them [disciples and others], 'To you has been given the secret of the kingdom of God, but for those outside everything is in parables; 12 so that they may indeed see but not perceive, and may indeed hear but not understand; lest they should turn again, and be forgiven.

---

[1] This text will be discussed in chapter 6, below.

[2] Note also Paul's use of σκληρότης in Rom. 2.5 ("by your hard and impenitent heart you are storing up wrath for yourself") and σκληροτράχηλος in Acts 7.51 at the end of Stephen's speech ("You stiff-necked people, uncircumcised in heart and ears, you always resist the Holy Spirit").

Isaiah 6, as I will argue, may well have influenced Paul's argument in Romans 9-11, even though he does not actually quote from it.

Another famous story of hardening from the Old Testament concerns a Gentile, Pharaoh. See, for example, Ex. 10.1:

> Then the LORD said to Moses, 'Go in to Pharaoh; for I have hardened his heart and the heart of his servants, that I may show these signs of mine among them . . .'

It is this story of hardening which is clearly central to Paul's argument in Rom. 9.14ff. It is striking that after Paul has used texts from Genesis in Rom. 9.6-13, he then turns to the next book of Moses, Exodus, in Rom. 9.14ff.[3] He quotes Ex. 33.19b in Rom. 9.15 ("I will have mercy on whom I have mercy, and I will have compassion on whom I have compassion"), and then turns to the example of Pharaoh in Rom. 9.17-18. He is an example of someone who did not receive mercy.

> For the scripture says to Pharaoh, 'I have raised you up for the very purpose of showing my power in you, so that my name may be proclaimed in all the earth.' 18 So then he has mercy upon whomever he wills, and he hardens the heart of whomever he wills.

Paul implies already that just as Pharaoh then was hardened, so Israel now is hardened,[4] and he mentions Israel's hardening explicitly in Rom. 11.7-10.

One of the key questions regarding this hardening of Israel, indeed a key question for Romans 9-11, is this: is Israel hardened by God because she has not believed the gospel? Putting it another way does God harden Israel as a punishment because Israel has hardened herself first? Or could it be that Israel does not believe because she has been hardened first by God? Many commentators accept the first alternative. For example, Leon Morris, commenting on Rom. 9.18, writes that "neither here nor anywhere else is God said to harden anyone who had not first hardened himself".[5] To support his argument Morris points out that in the Exodus narrative Pharaoh is said to

---

[3] B. Chilton and J. Neusner, *Judaism in the New Testament: Practices and Beliefs*, London/New York: Routledge 1995, pp. 64-65, point out that this "shift in scriptural foundation (at 9:14f.) corresponds precisely to the development of Paul's argument".

[4] On the parallelism between Pharaoh and Israel, see Moo, *Romans*, p. 595 n. 44.

[5] L. Morris, *The Epistle to the Romans*, Grand Rapids: Wm B. Eerdmans/Leicester: IVP 1988, p. 361.

harden himself.[6] Much earlier John Locke had suggested something similar.[7] It is therefore assumed that God's hardening is in response to Pharaoh hardening himself.[8] However, it is not clear from Exodus 4-14 that this is the case. Moo correctly points out: "Before Pharaoh is said to harden his own heart, God twice predicts that he would harden Pharaoh's heart (4:21 and 7:3), and there are also five references, in the passive voice, to Pharaoh's heart being hardened (7:13, 14, 22; 8:11, 15). The understood subject of these passive verbs is probably God".[9] One can also add that in the Hebrew of 4.21 and 7.3 the added personal pronoun serves not only as a rhetorical device but also serves to stress that God does the hardening.[10]

Ex. 4.21: וַאֲנִי אֲחַזֵּק אֶת־לִבּוֹ

Ex. 7.3: וַאֲנִי אַקְשֶׁה אֶת־לֵב פַּרְעֹה

The Exodus narrative itself therefore stresses God's rôle is hardening Pharaoh and that his will "could not in any sense be thwarted by the will of the pagan ruler".[11] Further, one has to ask how Paul himself made use of

---

[6] Morris, *Romans*, p. 361.

[7] See J. Locke, *A Paraphrase and Notes on the Epistles of St Paul*, ed. by A.W. Wainwright (The Clarendon Edition of the Works of John Locke), 2 vols, Oxford: Clarendon Press 1987, 2:567-68.

[8] See Leenhardt, *Romans*, p. 254: "The hardening of heart is not therefore the effect of an arbitrary decision which God takes to exclude any man from the possibility of salvation. It is a way of suggesting the indisputable fact that God plunges the sinner deeper into his sin when He offers His grace and it is refused". See also F.L. Godet, *Commentary on Romans* ET, Grand Rapids: Kregel Publications 1977 (repr.), ([1]1883), pp. 353-56; E. Brunner, *The Letter to the Romans: A Commentary* ET, London: Lutterworth 1959, p. 86; Fitzmyer, *Romans*, p. 568.

[9] Moo, *Romans*, p. 598 n. 53. By "subject", Moo obviously means "implied agent". Moo is here considering the canonical text of Exodus. A more complex picture emerges if a source critical approach is adopted. See the excursus on the "Hardening of Pharaoh" in Childs, *Exodus*, pp. 170-75. Childs stresses that the Exodus text has little to do with "free will and predestination" although he writes: "It is clear that the P Source extended the origin of hardening into the plan of God and thus went beyond J" (*Exodus*, p. 174).

[10] Cf. J.I. Durham, *Exodus* (WBC 3), Waco: Word Books 1987, p. 85. Concerning the different verbs used for hardening, see R. Wakely, חזק, *DOTTE* 2:70 (63-87); A.S. van der Woude, חזק, *THAT* 1:538-41; קשה, *THAT* 2:689-92; L. Walker and I. Swart, קשה, *DOTTE* 3:998 (997-99). Note also that in Ex. 14.17 God says he will harden the hearts of the Egyptians.

[11] J.P. Hyatt, *Exodus* (NCB), London: Marshall, Morgan & Scott/Grand Rapids: Wm B. Eerdmans [2]1980, ([1]1971), p. 102.

Exodus. The only thing Paul has explicitly taken over is God's hardening of Pharaoh. And Paul has in certain significant respects introduced changes so as to stress God's sovereignty. A good example of this is the quotation from Ex. 9.16 in Rom. 9.17.

Ex. 9.16 LXX: καὶ ἕνεκεν τούτου διετηρήθης, ἵνα ἐνδείξωμαι ἐν σοὶ τὴν ἰσχύν μου, καὶ ὅπως διαγγελῇ τὸ ὄνομά μου ἐν πάσῃ τῇ γῇ.

Ex. 9.16 LXX translated: and on account of this have I let you live, that I might display in you my strength, and that my name might be published in all the earth.

Rom. 9.17: λέγει γὰρ ἡ γραφὴ τῷ Φαραὼ ὅτι 'Εἰς αὐτὸ τοῦτο ἐξήγειρά σε ὅπως ἐνδείξωμαι ἐν σοὶ τὴν δύναμίν μου καὶ ὅπως διαγγελῇ τὸ ὄνομά μου ἐν πάσῃ τῇ γῇ'.

Rom. 9.17 RSV: For the scripture says to Pharaoh, 'I have raised you up for the very purpose of showing my power in you, so that my name may be proclaimed in all the earth'.

Paul has made four significant changes. First, the phrase καὶ ἕνεκεν τούτου ("and on account of this") is changed to the more forceful Εἰς αὐτὸ τοῦτο ("for the very purpose"). Secondly, διετηρήθης ("you have been preserved"), i.e. God has let Pharaoh live, is changed to ἐξήγειρά σε ("I have raised you"), not in the sense of Jas 5.15 (". . . and the prayer of faith will save the sick man, and the Lord will raise him up (ἐγερεῖ αὐτὸν ὁ κύριος); and if he has committed sins, he will be forgiven") but in the sense of causing Pharaoh to appear on the stage of history. Thirdly, Paul has a double use of ὅπως thereby stressing the divine intention.[12] Fourthly, Paul has replaced ἰσχύν "strength" with δύναμίν "power". This is probably done to refer to the power of the gospel (Rom. 1.16b). Cranfield comments that the changes Paul has introduced to the LXX "represent a bringing out more sharply of the sovereignty of the divine purpose".[13] It is also important to stress that Paul's concern is not simply with Pharaoh's historical rôle but with salvation, for in changing ἰσχύν to δύναμίν, Paul has introduced a soteriological dimension to the story of Pharaoh.[14]

---

[12] See Michel, *Römer*, p. 11.

[13] Cranfield, *Romans*, 2:487.

[14] Note the following important Pauline uses of δύναμις in relation to salvation: Rom. 1.16b-17 where the gospel is the "power of God unto salvation" (see below); 1 Cor. 1.18 where the "word of the cross" is the "power of God" to those who are being saved; 1 Cor. 1.24 where Christ is the "power of God and wisdom of God" to those who are called. See also 1 Cor. 2.5; 4.20; 6.14; 2 Cor. 4.7; 6.7; 13.4.

It is therefore difficult to soft-pedal or deny the predestinarian aspect to the hardening of Pharaoh's heart in Rom. 9.14-29 by appealing to Exodus 4-14. But other approaches have been taken to argue that the initiative in hardening does not lie with God. I mention just two. First, Morris, whose view I have already mentioned, points to the fact that "God does not harden people who do not go astray first" and compares Jas 1.13.[15] However this hardly gives any support for this being *Paul's* view especially since there are good grounds for understanding the letter of James as anti-Pauline polemic. In fact Jas 1.13-14 may precisely be opposing Paul's view in Rom. 9.17-18; 11.8.[16]

A second argument which could be employed to argue that Israel is hardened because she has first hardened herself is that Paul believes Israel is responsible for her unbelief. In fact some take the next major section Rom. 9.30-10.21 to be concerned with "Israel's responsibility".[17] So it is often argued that having discussed predestination in Rom. 9.6-29, Paul now presents "the other side of the coin". I have argued elsewhere that this section is not concerned primarily with Israel's responsibility.[18] If a major theme can be found, it is the contrast between the belief of the Gentiles in the gospel and the unbelief of the Jews. This exchange of roles can be clearly seen throughout 9.30-10.21 and particularly in 9.30-33 and 10.19-21 (which form an inclusio). Now I do not deny that Rom. 9.30-10.21 (and other passages in Romans) may imply something of Israel's responsibility. See Rom. 10.21: "But of Israel he says, 'All day long I have held out my hands to a dis-

---

[15] Morris, *Romans*, p. 361.

[16] See Hengel, "Jakobusbrief", 528, who writes on Jas 1.13ff.: "So könnte möglicherweise bereits in der 1,13ff. beginnenden Polemik, die ältere weisheitliche Parallelen besitzt (Sir 15,11-20 . . .), ein antipaulinischer Ton anklingen. Während Jakobus jeden Gedanken daran, daß Gott den Menschen versuche, zurückweist, alle Versuchung auf die eigene sündige Begierde im Menschen zurückführt und im Anschluß daran bekennt, daß nur gute, vollkommene Gabe von Gott komme und es bei diesem 'keine Veränderung oder Verfinsterung durch Wechsel gibt' (1,17), konnte Paulus davon sprechen, daß Gott den Pharao verhärtet habe (Röm 9,17f.), daß er 'Gefäße des Zorns, bestimmt zum Verderben' schaffe, ja daß er Israel einen 'Geist der Betäubung' (Röm 11,8 . . .) gab". I will return to Rom. 11.7-8 shortly.

[17] Sanday and Headlam, *Romans*, p. 342; C.K. Barrett, "Romans 9.30-10.21: Fall and Responsibility of Israel", in *Essays on Paul*, London: SPCK 1982, 132-53; Dinkler, "Prädestination", 254; Dodd, *Romans*, p. 173; Käsemann, *Römer*, p. 276; Schlatter, *Gottes Gerechtigkeit*, p. 307; Cranfield, *Romans*, 2:505.

[18] See Bell, *Provoked to Jealousy*, pp. 81-106.

obedient and contrary people'". But Israel's responsibility for her unbelief can cohere with the view that her unbelief is caused by God first hardening her heart. Although a court of law would speak of diminished responsibility, a New Testament theologian should have no problem in holding together God's sovereignty and human responsibility.[19]

We could investigate this a little further by asking whether we can say anything about the internal workings of this hardening? According to Theobald's reading of Romans, the hardening of Israel has come about because God himself has placed a stone of offence in Zion (Rom. 9.33 = Is. 28.16; 8.14). This image of the stone of offence is applied to the Christ of the gospel, "freilich nicht auf den *irdischen* Jesus und sein Auftreten in Israel, sondern auf ihn als den an Ostern inthronisierten Kyrios (vgl. Röm 1,4f.; 10.9-13), den Gott selbst im Evangelium durch seine Boten als den 'Herrn aller' proklamieren läßt".[20] The way Theobald develops this is to argue that the "No" of Israel to the gospel is provoked because salvation by grace comes to the Gentiles. My problem with this is that things are not really that way round? According to Rom. 11.11-12 Israel is first "falls" and "trespasses" as a result of the hardening by God (cf. 11.7-10) *and then* salvation goes to the Gentiles. I think that Theobald mixes up two motifs which are really separate: hardening and provocation to jealousy. Regarding his treatment of Rom. 9.30-33 I would suggest a change of emphasis. If a reason is to be found here for Israel's hardening it is that Israel assumed salvation had to be by works and they could not grasp the idea that salvation is actually through grace (and hence they stumbled). The hardening of Israel is a blindness to the gospel; Israel is ignorant of the righteousness of God (Rom. 10.3) and has not understood the gospel.[21] There is, therefore, something rather irrational about the unbelief of Israel (just as there is something

---

[19] This is a vast area which I hope to address in a future work. Concerning the way in which divine sovereignty and human responsibility relate in the area of myth, see Bell, "The Myth of Adam and the Myth of Christ", 27-29. What I write there is not applicable to the case of Pharaoh in Rom. 9.14ff.

[20] Theobald, "Mit verbundenen Augen?", 376 n. 29 (Theobald's emphasis).

[21] Sometimes Rom. 10.19 is taken to imply that Israel "understood" the gospel. In this case the question is taken to mean: "Did Israel not understand" (μὴ Ἰσραὴλ οὐκ ἔγνω;) and "gospel" is taken as the object. The implied answer is of course "yes". However, this is a mistaken understanding of the question. See the discussion in chapter 6 below and see the detailed discussion in Bell, *Provoked to Jealousy*, pp. 95-104.

irrational in a Gentile who does not believe the gospel as is clear in 2 Cor. 4.4). Therefore regarding the internal mechanism of the hardening I would say that God had instilled in Israel the belief that she was to be saved by her works: she pursued the law οὐκ ἐκ πίστεως ἀλλ' ὡς ἐξ ἔργων (Rom. 9.32a) and she strove to build up her own righteousness (Rom. 10.3).[22] Because of this attitude of works-righteousness, so ingrained in the consciousness of Israel, she stumbled over the stone of offence (Rom. 9.32; cf. 1 Cor. 1.23). Because of this blindness, the preached word which creates faith (cf. τὸ ῥῆμα τῆς πίστεως, Rom. 10.8) cannot create faith in those Jews whose blindness has not been removed by God (cf. 2 Cor. 3.14-16).

To return to our main point, then, no support can be found for the view that God hardens Israel because Israel has hardened herself. In fact the texts suggest the very opposite. See Rom. 11.7-8:

> What then? Israel failed to obtain what it sought. The elect obtained it, but the rest were hardened, 8 as it is written,
>   'God gave them a spirit of stupor,
>   eyes that should not see and ears that should not hear,
>   down to this very day.'

The elect (literally the "election", ἐκλογή) to which Paul refers are the elect of Israel (i.e. the remnant of Rom. 9.27) which is, of course, a small minority. The rest were hardened. The quotation (from Is. 29.10 and Dt. 29.3 LXX)[23] makes abundantly clear that it is God who is the cause of the hardening and this is why Israel has failed to believe the gospel. And just as faith is the *mode* of salvation, so unbelief is the *mode* of damnation.[24]

We therefore find in Romans 9-11, as elsewhere in Paul, a strict predestinarian theology. Not only does God choose certain people for salvation, but also he chooses others for damnation. This is made clear throughout Rom. 9.6-29. But many commentators have struggled with these verses, attempting to get them to say something else. I give three examples.

---

[22] Note also that Paul emphasizes the crucial nature of grace as opposed to works in Rom. 11.6 just before he speaks of Israel's hardening in 11.7-10 (see below).

[23] See Dt. 29.3: καὶ οὐκ ἔδωκεν κύριος ὁ θεὸς ὑμῖν καρδίαν εἰδέναι καὶ ὀφθαλμοὺς βλέπειν καὶ ὦτα ἀκούειν ἕως τῆς ἡμέρας ταύτης. From Is. 29.10 he has taken πνεῦμα κατανύξεως. There may also be an allusion to Is. 6.10: μήποτε ἴδωσιν τοῖς ὀφθαλμοῖς καὶ τοῖς ὠσὶν ἀκούσωσιν.

[24] O. Hofius, "Das Evangelium und Israel: Erwägungen zu Römer 9-11", *Paulus-studien* (WUNT 51), Tübingen: J.C.B. Mohr (Paul Siebeck) 1989, 182 (175-202).

First the impact of Rom. 9.13 ("As it is written, 'Jacob I loved, but Esau I hated'", a quotation from Mal. 1.2-3) has been lessened by arguing that Paul means by the quotation "I preferred Jacob to Esau". So Fitzmyer compares Gen. 29.30-31: "So Jacob went in to Rachel also, and he loved Rachel more than Leah, and served Laban for another seven years. 31 When the LORD saw that Leah was hated, he opened her womb; but Rachel was barren".[25] However, in the context of Rom. 9.6-29 the idea is not that God preferred Jacob to Esau but that God chose Jacob and rejected Esau. As Moo writes: "If God's love of Jacob consists in his choosing Jacob to be the 'seed' who would inherit the blessings promised to Abraham, then God's hatred of Esau is best understood to refer to God's decision not to bestow this privilege on Esau. It might best be translated 'reject'".[26]

A second example where commentators have struggled to force the text to say something other than it clearly does say is the denial of the deterministic outlook of Romans 9. Such an outlook is found for example in Paul's analogy of the potter and the clay. See Rom. 9.19-21:

You will say to me then, 'Why does he still find fault? For who can resist his will?' 20 But who are you, a man, to answer back to God? Will what is moulded say to its moulder, 'Why have you made me thus?' 21 Has the potter no right over the clay, to make out of the same lump one vessel for beauty and another for menial use?

Many have tried to soften what Paul here writes.[27] So reference is made to the background in Jeremiah 18[28] and Paul, it is argued, is simply saying that "the unrepentant portion of Israel has become a 'vessel unto dishonor', and the faithful part a 'vessel unto honor'".[29] So as in the case of "hardening", God's action is a response to a prior human decision. Again, nothing could be further from the truth. The text of Romans 9 makes it absolutely clear that Israelites (or Pharaoh) have been made vessels of wrath because of God's decision. At least someone like Dodd recognized what Paul was saying even though he had to distance himself from Paul's argument. He speaks of

---

[25] Fitzmyer, *Romans*, p. 563.

[26] Moo, *Romans*, p. 587.

[27] E.g. Forster and Marston, *God's Strategy*, pp. 81-86.

[28] Forster and Marston, *God's Strategy*, p. 82: "The basic lump that forms a nation will either be built up or broken down by the Lord, *depending on their own moral response*".

[29] Forster and Marston, *God's Strategy*, p. 82.

Paul's "unethical determinism" in 9.17-18 and on 9.19 writes that "a mechanical determinism annihilates morality".[30] On 9.21 ("Has the potter no right over the clay?") Dodd writes: "It is a well-worn illustration. But the trouble is that a man is not a pot; he *will* ask, 'Why did you make me like this?' and he will not be bludgeoned into silence. It is the weakest point in the whole epistle".[31]

A third way of making Romans 9 more palatable is to adopt a Barthian understanding of election. Barth, although standing in the reformed tradition, was highly critical of Calvin's view of election or double predestination. For Calvin's view, see for example his comment on Rom. 9.18:

> Paul's purpose is to make us accept the fact that it has seemed good to God to enlighten some in order that they may be saved, and blind others in order that they may be destroyed, so that we may be satisfied in our minds with the difference which is evident between the elect and the reprobate, and not inquire for any cause higher than His will.[32]

Barth, believing that Calvin was not sufficiently Christocentric, argued that Christ is the electing God, the Word of God who existed with God at the very beginning. But at the same time he is the elected Man. He is chosen "before all created reality, before all being and becoming in time, before time itself" (*CD* 2.2:116).[33] Therefore Jesus is the electing God and the elected man. See *CD* 2.2:76:

> . . the doctrine of election must not begin *in abstracto* either with the concept of an electing God or with that of elected man. It must begin concretely with the acknowledgement of Jesus Christ as both the electing God and the elected man.

Barth then criticizes Calvin for tearing God and Jesus Christ asunder (*CD* 2.2:111). Barth argues that we are chosen in Christ and through Christ and double predestination is worked out in Christ. *Some* Barthian ideas on elec-

---

[30] Dodd, *Romans*, p. 158.

[31] Dodd, *Romans*, p. 159.

[32] Calvin, *Romans*, p. 207.

[33] E. Brunner, *Die Christliche Lehre von Gott: Dogmatik I*, Zürich: Theologischer Verlag [4]1972, ([1]1946), pp. 353-54, comments: "Es bedarf keines besonderen Nachweises, daß eine solche Lehre nirgends in der Bibel zu finden ist . . . Lehrt man die ewige Präexistenz des Gottmenschen, so ist die Inkarnation kein *Ereignis* mehr; sie ist nicht mehr das große Weihnachtswunder. . . . Die Idee von der präexistenten Gott*menschheit* ist eine ad-hoc-Konstruktion des theologischen Denkers, der nur mit Hilfe dieser Theorie seine These durchführen kann, daß der Mensch Jesus der einzig Erwählte sei" (Brunner's emphasis).

tion may *to some degree* be applicable to certain predestinarian texts such as Rom. 5.18-19 or 11.32 and aspects of Romans 9,[34] but often the use of Barth's ideas has been more eisegesis than exegesis.[35] For example, it is far from clear that the "vessel of mercy" (cf. Rom. 9.23) "is primarily the Lord Jesus Christ risen from the dead".[36] Barrett's commentary on Rom. 9.6-29 is I believe an example of someone with a pastoral (and Barthian!) heart struggling to get the text to say something more "palatable". So, for example, he argues that for Paul election takes place in Christ.[37] But Paul is not arguing this in Romans 9 and Barrett's argument that the "seed" of Abraham is Christ[38] is a point Paul makes in Gal. 3.16 *but not in Rom. 9.7*. In Rom. 9.7 the promises are for the children of Abraham (Rom. 9.6b-7: "For not all who are descended from Israel belong to Israel, 7 and not all are children of Abraham because they are his descendants; but 'Through Isaac shall your descendants be named'").[39] I believe Barrett therefore wrongly speaks of an "*apparent* double predestination".[40]

---

[34] Someone who has used Barth very sensitively in the exegesis of Romans 9-11 is Cranfield. See his appreciation of Barth in *Romans*, 2:450.

[35] But Barth himself implies that he is one of those who "were bound to labour with Paul" and could not "remain spectators in his presence" (K. Barth, *The Epistle to the Romans* ET (translated from the sixth edition by E.C. Hoskyns), London/Oxford/New York: OUP 1968 (repr.), (¹1933), p. 1). See also E. Jüngel, *Karl Barth: A Theological Legacy* ET, Philadelphia: Westminster Press 1986, p. 71. I do not dispute the fact that Barth's ideas on election are extremely fruitful in systematic theology. But they are a *radical redevelopment* of the view found in Rom. 9.6-29.

[36] K. Barth, *CD* 2.2:228.

[37] Barrett, *Romans*, p. 171.

[38] See Barrett, *Romans*, pp. 169, 72.

[39] I agree with C. Landmesser, *Wahrheit als Grundbegriff neutestamentlicher Wissenschaft* (WUNT 113), Tübingen: J.C.B. Mohr (Paul Siebeck) 1999, pp. 480-91, that a text can have an "open semantic worth" as well as a "direct semantic worth". The example he gives is that that of the reports of the easter events. "Die Osterberichte haben neben dem für unser Erkenntnisvermögen zugänglichen direkten semantischen Wert einen offenen semantischen Wert, der über das geschichtliche Ereignis, das den Traditionen vom leeren Grab und der Erscheinung Jesu vor seinen Jüngern zugrunde liegt, hinausgeht und seinerseits einen direkten semantischen Wert intendiert, der aber nicht vollständig dem menschlichen Erkenntnisvermögen zugänglich ist" (482). But I really wonder whether Rom. 9.7 can have such an open semantic worth such that we can draw the conclusions that Barrett does.

[40] See Barrett, *Romans*, p. 175 (my emphasis).

I therefore accept the predestinarian character of Romans 9. In reply to the question "Why does Israel not believe in Christ?" one has to say that God in his purposes decided to reject his people Israel. But already in Rom. 9.22-23 there is a hint that Israel was not simply rejected for the sake of being rejected. There are three reasons for this rejection and in order to discern these it is necessary to consider Rom. 9.22-23.[41] There have been a number of ways of understanding these difficult verses, but the one which I believe carries most conviction is the following:

But (what) if God,
> *because* he wishes
>> (1) to manifest his wrath and
>> (2) make known his power,
> bore with much patience the vessels of wrath prepared for destruction,
>> (3) (doing this because he wished) also (καί) to make known the riches of
> his glory to vessels of mercy that he prepared beforehand for glory . . .[42]

According to such an understanding the participial clause (θέλων . . . ἐνδείξασθαι τὴν ὀργὴν καὶ γνωρίσαι τὸ δυνατὸν αὐτοῦ) is taken as causal[43] rather than concessive[44] ("But (what) if God, *although* he wished . . ."). With the causal understanding there is a parallel with the idea put forward in 9.17-18. So in the case of Pharaoh and the vessels of wrath, God first manifests his wrath, secondly makes known his power, and thirdly makes known his riches for the vessels of mercy. This third point (together with v. 24)[45] hints at what is to come in Rom. 11. Israel has been rejected for the sake of the Gentiles.

The idea of hardening does not surface again explicitly until Rom. 11.7-10. I have already mentioned vv. 7-8, so I will now turn to 11.9-10:

---

[41] Rom. 9.22-23: εἰ δὲ θέλων ὁ θεὸς ἐνδείξασθαι τὴν ὀργὴν καὶ γνωρίσαι τὸ δυνατὸν αὐτοῦ ἤνεγκεν ἐν πολλῇ μακροθυμίᾳ σκεύη ὀργῆς κατηρτισμένα εἰς ἀπώλειαν, 23 καὶ ἵνα γνωρίσῃ τὸν πλοῦτον τῆς δόξης αὐτοῦ ἐπὶ σκεύη ἐλέους ἃ προητοίμασεν εἰς δόξαν;

[42] See Moo, *Romans*, p. 605.

[43] See Cranfield, *Romans*, 2:493-97; B.J. Byrne, *Romans* (SPS 6), Collegeville: Liturgical Press 1996, 305; Wilckens, *Römer*, 2:204-5.

[44] See R.C.H. Lenski, *The Interpretation of St. Paul's Epistle to the Romans*, Minneapolis: Augsburg Publishing House 1961 (repr.), ([1]1936), pp. 621-22; Fitzmyer, *Romans*, p. 569.

[45] Rom. 9.24: "even us whom he has called, not from the Jews only but also from the Gentiles?"

And David says, 'Let their table become a snare and a trap,
> a pitfall and a retribution for them;
> 10 let their eyes be darkened so that they cannot see,
> and bend their backs for ever'.

This is a quotation from Ps. 69.22-23 (68.23-24 LXX).[46] Psalm 69, a key text in the early Church for understanding Christ's passion, is here applied to the opponents of Christ, i.e., Jews who do not believe. The crucial phrase is "let their eyes be darkened".[47] Again it is made clear that it is God who is the cause of Israel's hardening: he darkens their eyes such that they fail to believe the gospel.

Paul's view of Israel's rejection is therefore fully predestinarian. Rom. 9.6-29 does not stand on its own. Elsewhere Paul evinces double predestination. See, for example, 1 Cor. 1.18: "For the word of the cross is folly to those who are perishing, but to us who are being saved it is the power of God". Conzelmann in his commentary rightly emphasizes that it is "the word itself which creates the division of the two groups".[48] Paul is more explicit in 2 Cor. 2.15-16: "For we are the aroma of Christ to God among those who are being saved and among those who are perishing, to one a fragrance from death to death, to the other a fragrance from life to life". Both these texts suggest that double predestination is integrally related to "word

---

[46] On Paul's use of Ps. 68.23-24 LXX, see Stanley, *Language*, pp. 163-66.

[47] So Cranfield, *Romans*, 2:551, and Moo, *Romans*, p. 683, rightly argue that Paul did not intend to apply the details of the Psalm quotation to Israel (i.e. the "table" or "bend their backs"). Contrast Käsemann, *Romans*, p. 302, who understands "table" (τράπεζα) to refer to the Jewish cult (he compares 1 Cor. 10.21): "Precisely the cultus which represents Jewish piety causes the blinding and fall of Israel, and keeps its back under the yoke from which it cannot escape. . . . Not sins, but pious works prevent Judaism from obtaining the salvation held out to it, and keep it in bondage". Wilckens, *Römer*, 2:239, whilst also seeing a cultic reference in τράπεζα believes that Paul uses the Psalm as a curse on the temple, whose atoning function has come to an end, being replaced by the cross of Christ.

[48] H. Conzelmann, *Der erste Brief an die Korinther* (KEK 5), Göttingen: Vandenhoeck & Ruprecht ²1981, (¹1969), p. 56: "Es ist das Wort selbst, das die Scheidung der beiden Gruppen schafft".

of God".[49] As already indicated, the word of God creates faith.[50] Rom. 10.8 makes it clear that the gospel produces faith in the hearers. The ῥῆμα τῆς πίστεως, the word of faith, the gospel, must in this context mean the word which *produces* faith.[51] The word therefore has creative power. It brings faith into being out of nothing (*creatio ex nihilo*). The *creatio ex nihilo* is also clearly to be seen in 2 Cor. 4.4-6:

> In their case the god of this world has blinded the minds of the unbelievers, to keep them from seeing the light of the gospel of the glory of Christ, who is the likeness of God. 5 For what we preach is not ourselves, but Jesus Christ as Lord, with ourselves as your servants for Jesus' sake. 6 For it is the God who said, 'Let light shine out of darkness', who has shone in our hearts to give the light of the knowledge of the glory of God in the face of Christ.

---

[49] "Gospel" is a synonym for "word of God". It is God's own word and is *not* identical with the apostolic preaching (contra Bultmann, *Theologie*, ⁴1961, p. 89). The gospel is signified by the synonyms τὸ εὐαγγέλιον (the gospel) and ὁ λόγος (the word) and sometimes a genitivus auctoris is used also: τὸ εὐαγγέλιον τοῦ θεοῦ, the gospel from God (Rom. 1.1; 15.16) and ὁ λόγος τοῦ θεοῦ, the word from God (1 Thes. 2.13). The gospel or its synonyms can appear as the object of proclamation (εὐαγγελίζεσθαι (1 Cor. 15.1), κηρύσσειν (Gal. 2.2) . . . .) as well as the object of the negative verbs μεταστρέφειν (pervert, Gal. 1.7), καπηλεύειν (peddle, 2 Cor. 2.17). Obviously it makes no sense to equate the gospel with the preaching if Paul speaks not only of the preaching of the gospel but also of the perversion of the gospel. See Hofius, "Wort Gottes", 151-52, and section 4.2 in chapter 2 above (on 1 Thes. 2.13).

[50] According to Rom 1.16-17 the gospel is "the power of God unto salvation to all those who believe". The gospel has this power simply because it is God's word. Some think that the παντὶ τῷ πιστεύοντι (to all who believe) places a condition on this power. B. Weiß wrote: "Faith is a condition on the side of men and women, without which the gospel has no power to save" (B. Weiß, *Der Brief an die Römer* (KEK 4), Göttingen: Vandenhoeck & Ruprecht ⁹1899, (⁶1881), p. 70: "Der Glaube ist auf Seiten des Menschen die Bedingung, ohne welche ihm das Evangelium jene Kraft nicht sein kann"). I agree with Hofius, "Wort Gottes", 158, in rejecting this view which, if correct, would paralyse the power of the gospel for salvation. Schlatter understood it correctly: the person who hears the gospel is made a believer through the gospel and as this believer is saved. See Schlatter, *Gottes Gerechtigkeit*, p. 33: "Es ist aber nicht möglich, Paulus eine synergistische Theologie zuzuschreiben, nach der der Mensch Gott wirksam macht. Bei Paulus wirkt Gott und der Mensch wird gewirkt. Er wird durch die Botschaft zu einem Glaubenden gemacht und deshalb, weil er dies geworden ist, gerettet".

[51] See Hofius, "Wort Gottes", 160. For this understanding of the genitive Hofius compares Phil. 2.16 where the genitive λόγος ζωῆς is again understood as gift and effect, i.e. "word which brings life". Hofius rightly rejects Bultmann's understanding of ῥῆμα τῆς πίστεως as "the message which demands faith" (πιστεύω κτλ, *TDNT*, 6:213 (174-228)).

There is in v.6 a clear allusion to the first day of creation of Gen 1.3: "Let there be light". God has likewise shone in the heart of Paul giving him the light of the knowledge of God in the face of Christ. So the word of God, the gospel, has creative power.[52] But not only does the word have this creative power. The Spirit has creative power to bring faith into being.[53] See, for example, 1 Cor. 2.4-5: "and my speech and my message were not in plausible words of wisdom, but in demonstration of the Spirit and of power, that your faith might not rest in the wisdom of men but in the power of God".

Another way of viewing the coming to faith is the image of the resurrection of a corpse. In fact this image is brought together with *creatio ex nihilo* in Rom. 4.17. Paul writes that Abraham believed God "who gives life to the dead and calls into existence the things that do not exist" (τοῦ ζωοποιοῦντος τοὺς νεκροὺς καὶ καλοῦντος τὰ μὴ ὄντα ὡς ὄντα). The primary reference to giving "life to the dead" is to God quickening the body of Abraham and the

---

[52] This idea of course goes back to the Old Testament. Note the creative power of the word in Gen. 1 with the repeated phrase "And God said . . .". E.g. 1.3: "And God said, 'Let there be light'; and there was light". See also Ps. 33.6: "By the word of the Lord the heavens were made, and all their host by the breath of his mouth".

[53] Again see the Old Testament. So for example in Job 33.4: "The Spirit of God has made me, and the breath of the Almighty gives me life". There is a remarkable passage in *Joseph and Aseneth* which points to the creative and renewing power of the spirit. *Joseph and Aseneth* is a wonderful tale written sometime between the first century BC and the second century AD. It tells of how the Egyptian Aseneth is converted to the faith of Joseph and marries him. The prayer of Joseph is for Aseneth's conversion (*Joseph and Aseneth* 8.9):
"Lord God of my father Israel,
the Most high, the Powerful One of Jacob,
who gave life to all (things)
and called (them) from the darkness to the light,
and from error to the truth,
and from the death to the life;
you, Lord, bless this virgin,
and renew her by your spirit,
and form her anew by your hidden hand,
and make her alive again by your life" (C. Burchard, *OTP*, 2:213).
By the way, if one is to find grace in Judaism as E.P. Sanders wishes, this is where it can be found. In fact the prayer is so remarkable and unusual in Judaism that I think there may well be Christian interpolations (see the discussion in chapter 3 above).

womb of Sarah[54] and the primary reference in "calls into existence the things that do not exist"[55] is the unborn Isaac. However, the chapter concerns the faith of Abraham and one of Paul's major points is that Abraham has no grounds for boasting.[56] If Abraham has no reason to boast his faith must surely be the work of God. And Paul suggests this by writing that "Abraham was strengthened in faith (ἐνεδυναμώθη τῇ πίστει), giving glory to God and being fully persuaded that he had the power to do what he had promised" (Rom. 4.20b-21). Abraham was not strengthened by means of faith (i.e. understanding τῇ πίστει as instrumental[57]) but with respect to faith and he was so strengthened *by God*.[58] Returning to Rom. 4.17, it could be the case that a secondary reference to the giving of life to the dead and the *creatio ex nihilo* is faith itself. But even if Paul is not making this point in Rom. 4.17 it is sufficiently clear in Romans 4 that Abraham's faith was in fact a gift of God.

Faith therefore is the work and gift of God.[59] Only God can bring it about and in Rom. 9.6-29 Paul shows that God has decided to reject Israel, hardening her so she does not come to faith in Christ. Whether this is a final rejection is something we will investigate later.

But we can perhaps anticipate our later findings by highlighting two points made already about Paul's view of predestination. The first is that in Paul the emphasis in predestination is in the preaching of the gospel.[60] The

---

[54] Cf. Rom. 4.19b: τὸ ἑαυτοῦ σῶμα νενεκρωμένον, ἑκατονταέτης που ὑπάρχων, καὶ τὴν νέκρωσιν τῆς μήτρας Σάρρας.

[55] Concerning the translation of ὡς ὄντα, see Cranfield, *Romans*, 1:244.

[56] In fact Cranfield, *Romans*, 1:244, entitles the whole chapter "The case of Abraham as confirmation that glorying has been excluded".

[57] Cf. Sanday and Headlam, *Romans*, p. 115.

[58] See Cranfield, *Romans*, 1:248-49.

[59] Cf. Schwabacher Artikel 6 (*BSELK* 59,16ff) "Daß solcher Glaube sei nicht ein menschlich Werk noch aus unsern Kräften muglich, sondern es ist ein Gotteswerk und Gabe, die der heilige Geist durch Christum gegeben in uns wirket". On the "Schwabacher Artikel", see T. Kolde, *RE*[3] 18.1-2.

[60] C. Müller, *Gottes Gerechtigkeit und Gottes Volk: Eine Untersuchung zu Römer 9-11* (FRLANT 86), Göttingen: Vandenhoeck & Ruprecht 1964, p. 78, writes that "Prädestination in der Wortverkündigung geschieht". This point seems clear from the texts discussed above (e.g. Rom. 10.8; 1 Cor. 1.18; 2 Cor. 2.15-16). It is in Eph. 1.4 that the idea occurs of election "before the foundation of the world". Such an idea of prior election is not foreign to Paul. So vessels of wrath are "made for destruction" (Rom. 9.22) and vessels of mercy are "prepared beforehand for glory" (Rom. 9.23). Note that

second is that predestination is related to the creative power of the word.[61] In the light of this, it is perhaps mistaken to believe that Israel's rejection is a definitive and irrevocable situation.[62] For the creator God who is constantly upholding the world can easily reverse a decision to reject Israel. However, I believe it is a mistake to adopt the position of Müller that *both* rejection *and* election are not definitive states. Müller argues that just as God can reverse rejection to election, so he can reverse election to rejection.[63] But do we find such a simple symmetry in Paul? Does not Paul emphasize the assurance of salvation (including that of Israel, Rom. 11.29)? And although God is the sovereign creator, is there not a sense in which he limits himself when he promises salvation?

2. Theological Reflection on the "Hardening" of Israel

Israel then in the purposes of God has been hardened. The picture of Rom. 9.1-29 is one of the utmost seriousness, pointing to the salvation of a mere remnant. Rom. 9.27-29:

And Isaiah cries out concerning Israel: 'Though the number of the sons of Israel be as the sand of the sea, only a remnant of them will be saved; 28 for the Lord will execute his sentence upon the earth with rigour and despatch'. 29 And as Isaiah predicted,
> 'If the Lord of hosts had not left us children,
> we would have fared like Sodom and been made like
> Gomorrah.'

Müller himself (*Gottes Volk*, p. 79 n. 25) grants that Paul can also relate predestination to a decree made before the foundation of the world as in 1 Cor. 2.7. This, he claims, has nothing to do with determinism as in apocalytic. Rather πρὸ τῶν αἰώνων is an expression for the *creatio ex nihilo*.

[61] Müller, *Gottes Volk*, p. 78: "Die paulinische Prädestinationslehre überhaupt ist sinnvoll nur als äußerste Radikalisierung des *Schöpfungsgedankens* zu verstehen" (Müller's emphasis).

[62] Müller, *Gottes Volk*, p. 79.

[63] Müller, *Gottes Volk*, p. 79: "Wegen der Verbindung von Wortverkündigung und Schöpfungsgedanken in der Prädestination ist es ausgeschlossen, daß Erwählung und Verwerfung definitive Zustände sind". Concerning the Gentiles, for example, he writes that they are not protected from falling back into rejection (see Rom. 11.17-23).

Of course there is mercy, for there is a remnant which will be saved.[64] But the message that *only* a remnant will be saved causes Paul great heartache (Rom. 9.1-3; 10.1). In the course of the discussion we have mentioned the hardening of Pharaoh. But there is another striking case of hardening, the hardened Israel, to which Isaiah after his call is sent (Isaiah 6).[65] This text, quoted at the beginning of this chapter, was probably of particular interest for Paul because he too was sent to a hardened Israel.[66] In fact Paul may have elicited Israel's hardening by seeing his own call in the light of Isaiah 6.[67]

One of the most striking things in Romans 9-11 is that *God* hardens Israel. In contrast, 2 Cor. 4.4 speaks of Satan blinding the minds of the unbelievers (among whom were Jews).[68] See 2 Cor. 4.3-4:

And even if our gospel is veiled, it is veiled only to those who are perishing. 4 In their case the god of this world has blinded the minds of the unbelievers, to keep them from seeing the light of the gospel of the glory of Christ, who is the likeness of God.

The term "god of this world" could of course refer to the one true God. But in fact the reference is most likely to Satan. The language Paul uses is dualistic "but only superficially so"[69] and a real dualism is excluded.[70]

---

[64] J.R. Wagner, *Heralds of the Good News: Isaiah and Paul "In Concert" in the Letter to the Romans* (NovTSup 101), Leiden/Boston/Köln: Brill 2002, emphasizes the positive message of Is. 10.22-23 LXX (pp. 100-6) and of Is. 1.9 (110-16) within Isaiah, and that this comes through in Paul's use of the texts (pp. 106-110).

[65] Childs, *Exodus*, p. 170, considers the problem of hardening to be unique to Exodus. But surely Is. 6 is just as problematic.

[66] Note the possible allusion to Is. 6.10 in Rom. 11.8 mentioned above.

[67] See O. Betz, "Die Vision des Paulus im Tempel von Jerusalem: Apg 22,17-21 als Beitrag zur Deutung des Damaskuserlebnisses", in *Jesus, Der Herr der Kirche: Aufsätze zur biblischen Theologie II* (WUNT 52), Tübingen: J.C.B. Mohr (Paul Siebeck) 1990, 97 (91-102); Bell, *Provoked to Jealousy*, pp. 329-30.

[68] According to R.P. Martin, *2 Corinthians* (WBC 40), Dallas, Texas: Word Books 1986, p. 78, the "unbelievers" is "a designation ordinarily used for unbelievers outside the church (see 1 Cor 14:23), but here slanted to those who were false brothers intent on doing Satan's work by undermining Paul's ([2 Cor.] 11:13-15)". But it is by no means clear that this is the case. The text does in fact suggest those outside the Church. The term ἄπιστος occurs 12 times in 1 Corinthians and 3 times in 2 Corinthians and nowhere else in Paul.

[69] Barrett, *Second Epistle to the Corinthians*, p. 131.

[70] H. Lietzmann, *An die Korinther I/II* (HzNT 9), Tübingen: J.C.B. Mohr (Paul Siebeck) [5]1969 (supplemented by W.G. Kümmel), p. 115.

Therefore the difference between Rom. 9.14-29 where God is described as hardening Israel (and also Rom. 11.8, where God gives Israel "a spirit of stupor" and "eyes that should not see and ears that should not hear") and 2 Cor. 4.3-4 does not present an insuperable difficulty. But the difference is nevertheless significant. It seems that in 2 Corinthians Paul had not yet worked out the purpose of Israel's unbelief and perhaps that is why he was satisfied to say Satan blinded the eyes of the unbelievers. In Romans, however, the hardening of Israel has a profound purpose and it is this that we consider in the next chapter.

But before doing this (and I have of course already anticipated the answer – i.e. Israel is hardened so that salvation goes to the Gentiles), how do we today understand the hardening now that salvation is with the Gentiles? For since the Church is now predominantly Gentile, what possible purpose can Israel's hardening now have? One route is to take the hardening to be relevant to *Gentile Christian* hardening. So Merklein writes: "Vielleicht muß man . . . die Rede von der 'Verstockung' Israels in eine Rede von der Verschuldung der Kirche überführen".[71] Theobald actually applies the hardening motif of Romans 9-11 to the Church in its attitude to Israel and refers to the prayer ascribed to Pope John XXIII:

Wir sind uns heute bewusst,
dass viele Jahrhunderte der Blindheit uns die Augen verhüllt haben,
so dass wir die Schönheit deines auserwählten Volkes nicht mehr zu sehen
und in ihren Gesichtern die Züge unserer bevorzugten Brüder nicht mehr zu erkennen
vermögen.
Wir verstehen, dass uns ein Kainsmal auf die Stirn geschrieben steht.
Im Laufe der Jahrhunderte hat unser Bruder Abel in dem Blut gelegen,
das wir vergossen,
oder er hat Tränen geweint, die wir verursacht haben,
weil wir deine Liebe vergaßen.
Vergib uns den Fluch,
den wir zu Unrecht an ihren Namen Jude hefteten.
Vergib uns,
dass wir dich in ihrem Fleisch zum zweitenmal ans Kreuz schlugen.

---

[71] H. Merklein, "Der (neue) Bund als Thema der paulinischen Theologie", in *Studien zu Jesus und Paulus II* (WUNT 105), Tübingen: J.C.B. Mohr (Paul Siebeck) 1998, 375 (357-76).

Denn wir wussten nicht,
was wir taten . . .[72]

I imagine it is legitimate to speak of the "hardening" of Gentile Christians. Very few Gentile Christians throughout the history of the Church have realized the theological significance of a passage such as Rom. 11.17-24.[73] However, can one really say that Paul's message of Israel's hardening is now no longer relevant?[74] According to Theobald, the theocentric core of the πώρωσις motif is: 'Gott hat seine Hand auf die Synagoge gelegt . . . und führt sie ihren eigenen Weg, hin zur Begegnung mit dem Messias, der den Name Jesus tragen wird'.[75] However, is this not simply making Paul's stern words concerning Israel more palatable? Do not Paul's words on the hardening of Israel speak more directly than Theobald allows? And although Israel's hardening was for a purpose, a purpose which one can say has been achieved in that salvation has passed to the Gentiles, and although Israel does have a great future in store, the text is impoverished if the seriousness of these words in Rom. 9.14-29 is in any way downplayed. Further, according to Paul, this hardening of Israel will last until a particular point in time is reached, namely that the full number of the Gentiles will have come in (Rom. 11.25).

The text is also impoverished (and Christian theology is impoverished) if one adopts a view such as that of Mußner who writes of a "gottgewollte und durch die Zeiten dauernde Sonderexistenz Israels neben die Kirche".[76] The

---

[72] Theobald, "Mit verbundenen Augen?", 394-95. Pope John XXIII is said to have written this prayer shortly before his death but there are doubts as to whether it is in fact authentic. An English translation is: "We are today conscious that for many centuries our eyes were blinded, so that we could no longer see the beauty of your chosen people or recognize in your people's countenance the features of our favoured brother. We understand that the mark of Cain has been written on our forehead. For centuries, Abel was lying prostrate in blood that we shed or he shed tears which we caused, because we had forgotten your love. Forgive us that we wrongly ascribed a curse upon the name of the Jew. Forgive us, that we crucified you again in their flesh. For we knew not what we were doing . . . "

[73] This will be discussed in chapter 8 below.

[74] In chapter 9 below I give an example from the Church of England where a prayer to remove the hardening of Israel has now been transformed into a prayer to remove the hardness of heart of Christians.

[75] Theobald, "Mit verbundenen Augen?", 393.

[76] Mußner, *Traktat*, p. 72.

impression is given that since Israel is hardened by God for a purpose, Christians can just accept the fact of Jewish unbelief. That cannot be done. The fact that Israel had been divided into a believing and unbelieving part deeply troubled Paul. How can God's people be so divided? That God's people is so divided should be a cause of deep distress for every Christian. Sadly, one of the results of Jewish-Christian dialogue is that many Christians actually lose any sense of distress caused by Jewish unbelief.[77] Paul never lost that sense of anguish. He speaks in Rom. 9.2 about his great sorrow and unceasing anguish in his heart. One can almost sense his tears as he quotes Isaiah in Rom. 10.21: "But of Israel he says, 'All day long I have held out my hands to a disobedient and contrary people'".

---

[77] I will return to this theme in chapter 10 section 4 below.

Chapter 6

Paul and the Salvation of Israel

1. The First Glimmer of Hope: 2 Corinthians 3.16

The first positive indication of Israel's salvation is to be found in 2 Cor.
3.16. In most translations, however, there is no clear indication that Paul has
Israel in mind. So in the RSV we read: "but when a man turns to the Lord
the veil is removed". However, in view of 2 Cor. 3.14b-15 the subject is
almost certainly Israel. 2 Cor. 3.12-18 is carefully structured and I render it
as follows:

12 Since we have such a hope, we are very bold,

> 13 not like Moses, who put a veil over his face
> so that the Israelites might not see the end of the fading splendour.
> 14 But their minds (i.e. of the Israelites) were hardened;

> for to this day, when they read the 'old covenant'
> (ἐπὶ τῇ ἀναγνώσει τῆς παλαιᾶς διαθήκης),
> that same veil remains unlifted (κάλυμμα ἐπὶ τὴν καρδίαν αὐτῶν κεῖται),
> because only through Christ is it taken away.

> 15 Yes, to this day whenever Moses is read a veil lies over their minds;

> 16 but when an Israelite/Israel turns to the Lord the veil is removed.
> 17 Now the Lord is the Spirit,
> and where the Spirit of the Lord is, there is freedom.

18 And we all, with unveiled face,
beholding the glory of the Lord,
are being changed into his likeness from one degree of glory to another;
for this comes from the Lord who is the Spirit.

The overall structure is chiastic.[1] So v. 12 speaks of the ministry of Paul,
and 13-14a about the ministry of Moses; then 14b-17 speaks of the

---

[1] Hofius, "Gesetz und Evangelium nach 2. Korinther 3", 114.

synagogue congregation, and v. 18 of the Christian congregation. In the section 14b-17, 14b-15 describe the current negative situation in the synagogue. So what happened in the case of Moses (v. 13) and the exodus generation (v. 14a) is a type of what is happening now in the synagogue. So to this day a veil lies over the eyes of the Jews in the reading of the torah. The expression ἡ παλαιὰ διαθήκη is often rendered "old covenant", a rather misleading translation. Paul actually means the 'torah' given to Moses, found in Exodus 20 and following.[2] So in v. 14b he speaks of Jews reading ἡ παλαιὰ διαθήκη (ἐπὶ τῇ ἀναγνώσει τῆς παλαιᾶς διαθήκης) and then in v. 15 speaks of "Moses" being read (ἀλλ᾽ ἕως σήμερον ἡνίκα ἂν ἀναγινώσκηται Μωϋσῆς). "Moses" here stands by metonymy for "the torah of Moses" (ὁ νόμος Μωϋσέως).[3] And Paul continues in v. 15 that to this day whenever Moses is read a veil lies over their minds. This veil prevents the Israelites from seeing that the torah, the "written thing" (γράμμα), kills (3.6) in that it condemns the sinner.[4] The torah can never bring salvation (and Israel has failed to appreciate this since she tried to find salvation through observing the torah). And it is only in Christ that it is realized that the function of the law is in fact to condemn. We then come to v. 16 which is central for our inquiry. Paul alludes to Ex. 34.34a:

2 Cor. 3.16: ἡνίκα δὲ ἐὰν ἐπιστρέψῃ πρὸς κύριον, περιαιρεῖται τὸ κάλυμμα.

Ex. 34.34a: ἡνίκα δ᾽ ἂν εἰσεπορεύετο Μωυσῆς ἔναντι κυρίου λαλεῖν αὐτῷ, περιῃρεῖτο τὸ κάλυμμα . . . .

Before discussing Paul's use of this text, I need to address the question of the subject of the verb ἐπιστρέψῃ and the sense of that verb. The sense of the verb ἐπιστρέφω is often taken to be "to convert", corresponding to the Hebrew שׁוּב.[5] Hofius, however, believes that Paul has Ex. 34.31 LXX in mind: καὶ ἐκάλεσεν αὐτοὺς Μωυσῆς, καὶ ἐπεστράφησαν πρὸς αὐτὸν Ααρων

---

[2] Hofius, "Gesetz und Evangelium nach 2. Korinther 3", 76. Likewise, the καινὴ διαθήκη (2 Cor. 3.6) is the "gospel" (see Hofius, "Gesetz und Evangelium", 78), not the "new covenant".

[3] Hofius, "Gesetz und Evangelium nach 2. Korinther 3", 76, points to 1 Cor. 9.9 as an example where Paul means the legal material of the Pentateuch.

[4] It is striking how often the idea of the law being God's condemning word is ignored by those who today write on the subject of Paul and the law.

[5] On the use of ἐπιστρέφω and μετανοέω in the LXX, see Bell, "Teshubah", 27.

καὶ πάντες οἱ ἄρχοντες τῆς συναγωγῆς, καὶ ἐλάλησεν αὐτοῖς Μωυσῆς. So Aaron and all the leaders "turn" to Moses, and in Ex. 34.32, so do all the people of Israel. This "turning" to Moses repeats itself whenever the law is read in the synagogue. The wording of 2 Cor. 3.15 is indeed striking (. . . ἡνίκα ἂν ἀναγινώσκηται Μωϋσῆς . . .)⁶ and Hofius may be right that in 3.16 Paul is saying they should turn to *Christ* rather than to *Moses*. "Israel soll und wird sich aber – das will Paulus sagen – zum *Kyrios* hinwenden, und *dann* wird die Hülle, die bei der Hinwendung zu *Mose* auf der verlesenen Tora wie auf den Herzen der Hörer bleibt, weggenommen werden".⁷ However, I wonder whether one can exclude the idea of "conversion". The verb ἐπιστρέφω is widely used in the Old Testament for turning to God⁸ and it is significant that in Is. 6.10 the verb ἐπιστρέφω is used.⁹ Further, Paul uses the verb in the context of Gentiles turning to God in 1 Thes. 1.9 (καὶ πῶς ἐπεστρέψατε πρὸς τὸν θεόν). I therefore conclude that the verb ἐπιστρέφω can take on these two aspects in 2 Cor. 3.16: turning to Christ as opposed to Moses, and conversion.

But what of the subject of the verb? Many translations simply take a generalized subject, "someone" (τις).¹⁰ However the subject is surely related

---

⁶ Hofius, "Gesetz und Evangelium nach 2. Korinther 3", 119 n. 256.

⁷ Hofius, "Gesetz und Evangelium nach 2. Korinther 3", 119 (Hofius' emphasis).

⁸ Windisch, *Der zweite Korintherbrief*, p. 123, points especially to Jer. 4.1; Neh. 1.9; Dt. 4.30.

⁹ Is. 6.10: ἐπαχύνθη γὰρ ἡ καρδία τοῦ λαοῦ τούτου, καὶ τοῖς ὠσὶν αὐτῶν βαρέως ἤκουσαν καὶ τοὺς ὀφθαλμοὺς αὐτῶν ἐκάμμυσαν, μήποτε ἴδωσιν τοῖς ὀφθαλμοῖς καὶ τοῖς ὠσὶν ἀκούσωσιν καὶ τῇ καρδίᾳ συνῶσιν καὶ ἐπιστρέψωσιν καὶ ἰάσομαι αὐτούς. Isaiah 6 was probably important for Paul's argument in Romans 9-11 and was of importance for the gospels (Mk 4.12; Mt. 13.13-15) and Acts (Acts 28.27, commenting on Paul's preaching to the Jews of Rome).

¹⁰ See A. Plummer, *A Critical and Exegetical Commentary on the Second Epistle of St Paul to the Corinthians* (ICC), Edinburgh: T. & T. Clark 1985 (repr.), (¹1915), p. 101; V.P. Furnish, *II Corinthians* (AB 32A), New York: Doubleday 1984, p. 210; Martin, *2 Corinthians*, p. 70.

to the Jews. So the subject could be Israel,[11] or Israelite[12] or possibly "their heart" of v. 15 (ἡ καρδία αὐτῶν).[13] Another possibility is Moses himself[14] or Moses in the sense of being a type.[15] So Hafemann understands "Moses' experience in the tent of meeting as a *type* of the one whose heart has been changed by the power of the Spirit under the ministry of the new covenant".[16] Moses is therefore likened to Abraham in Romans 4.[17] But this does not seem to be the natural way to read the text. Further, Hofius rightly criticizes those who claim that Moses encountered Christ according to 2 Cor. 3.16.[18] The subject of the verb ἐπιστρέφω is most likely Israel or the

---

[11] W. Bousset, "Der zweite Brief an die Korinther", in O. Baumgarten et al. (ed.), *Die Schriften des Neuen Testaments, Zweiter Band*, Göttingen: Vandenhoeck & Ruprecht 1917, 183-84 (167-223); J.H. Bernard, "The Second Epistle to the Corinthians", in W. Robertson Nicoll (ed.), *The Expositor's Greek Testament*, Grand Rapids: Eerdmans 1976 (repr), 3:57 (1-119); Lietzmann, *Korinther*, pp. 113; R. Bultmann, *Der zweite Brief an die Korinther* (KEK 6), Göttingen: Vandenhoeck & Ruprecht 1976, p. 92; Lang, *Korinther*, p. 275; J. Munck, *Paul and the Salvation of Mankind* ET, London: SCM 1959, p. 59.

[12] C. Wolff, *Der zweite Brief des Paulus an die Korinther* (ThHK 8), Berlin: Evangelische Verlagsanstalt 1989, p. 75. W. Rees, "1 and 2 Corinthians", *CCHS* 1104 (1081-1111), although translating v. 16a "But when a man turns to the Lord", comments: "When a Jew accepts the Gospel, he sees the real meaning of the Law".

[13] P.E. Hughes, *The Second Epistle to the Corinthians* (NICNT), Grand Rapids: Wm B. Eerdmans 1962, p. 113 n. 10, and Barrett, *Second Epistle to the Corinthians*, p. 122, think this the likely subject although they do not rule out other possibilities. See also Kümmel, in Lietzmann, *Korinther*, p. 200, who thinks the subject could either be Israel (Lietzmann's own view, *Korinther*, p. 113), or their heart.

[14] This is a possibility put forward by D.A. Clines, "The Second Letter to the Corinthians", in *BCFT*, 1469 (1462-88).

[15] J. Calvin, *The Second Epistle of Paul to the Corinthians, and the Epistles to Timothy, Titus and Philemon*, translated by T.A. Smail (CNTC 10), Grand Rapids: Wm B. Eerdmans 1991 (repr.), ([1]1964), p. 48, is critical of Latin and Greek writers for understanding Israel as the subject. Calvin thinks the subject is "Moses" but in the sense of "law" and translates: "But whensoever it shall turn to the Lord". His understanding of the law turning to Christ is later illumined. "And what is said of the Law applies to the whole of Scripture, for when it is not taken as referring to Christ, its one aim and centre[,] it is distorted and perverted" (p. 48).

[16] S. Hafemann, *Paul, Moses, and the History of Israel: The Letter/Spirit Contrast and the Argument from Scripture in 2 Corinthians 3*, Peabody: Hendrickson 1996 (repr.), ([1]1995), p. 388.

[17] Hafemann, *Moses*, p. 388 n. 171.

[18] See Hofius, "Gesetz und Evangelium nach 2. Korinther 3", 119 n. 257.

Israelite. One of the key issues in trying to work out the options is the meaning of the expression ἡνίκα δὲ ἐάν in v. 16. Here, when used with the aorist
subjunctive, it probably means "when", "then, when" or "as soon as".[19] In
this sense, the phrase could be translated "So soon as Israel/the Israelite
turns to the Lord". The use of ἡνίκα δὲ ἐάν is to be contrasted with its use in
v. 15 (ἀλλ᾽ ἕως σήμερον ἡνίκα ἂν ἀναγινώσκηται Μωϋσῆς, κάλυμμα ἐπὶ
τὴν καρδίαν αὐτῶν κεῖται) where ἡνίκα ἂν, here used with the present subjunctive, means "whenever". If in v. 16 ἡνίκα δὲ ἐάν is translated as "then,
when" or "as soon as", it opens the possibility that Paul is referring to the
mass turning of Israel: "the, when Israel turns to the Lord". "Israel" (as well
as "Israelite") therefore could be taken as the subject. If, on the other hand,
ἡνίκα δὲ ἐάν in v. 16 is translated "whenever", Israel cannot be the subject.
For by using "whenever" Paul could not be speaking of the mass conversion
of Israel (as in Rom. 11.26) but more in terms of Rom. 11.14 and 1 Cor.
9.19-20.[20] However, whilst preferring ἡνίκα δὲ ἐάν to be translated "as soon
as", it would be quite remarkable if Paul were *here* to refer to the mass conversion of Israel. It would be such a radical departure from his earlier views
as expressed in 1 Thessalonians and Galatians. It is much more likely that
Paul is referring to the "turning" or "converting" of individual Israelities[21]
and I therefore take "Israelite" as the subject. Therefore when Paul speaks
of the veil being removed (v. 16b) he is thinking of the veil over the heart of
the individual Israelite being removed.

---

[19] Hofius, "Gesetz und Evangelium nach 2. Korinther 3", 118 n. 250 compares Gen.
24.41; 27.40; Ex. 13.5; 33.22; Dt. 25.19; 27.3; Jos. 24.20; Ezek. 33.33. So, taking the
example of Ex. 13.5, we read: "And when (not whenever) the Lord your God brings you
into the land of the Canaanites, the Chettites, the Evites, the Gergesites, the Amorites,
the Pherezites, and the Jebusites which he swore to your fathers to give you, a land flow-
ing with milk and honey, you shall perform this service this month" (καὶ ἔσται ἡνίκα ἐὰν
εἰσαγάγῃ σε κύριος ὁ θεός σου εἰς τὴν γῆν τῶν Χαναναίων καὶ Χετταίων καὶ Εὐαίων
καὶ Γεργεσαίων καὶ Ἀμορραίων καὶ Φερεζαίων καὶ Ἰεβουσαίων, ἣν ὤμοσεν τοῖς
πατράσιν σου δοῦναί σοι, γῆν ῥέουσαν γάλα καὶ μέλι, καὶ ποιήσεις τὴν λατρείαν
ταύτην ἐν τῷ μηνὶ τούτῳ). So it refers to a once for all action.

[20] See Barrett, *Second Epistle to the Corinthians*, p. 122.

[21] Cf. Wolff, *Der zweite Brief des Paulus an die Korinther*, p. 75.

Paul has radically changed the sense of Ex. 34.34.[22] So instead of Moses going in before the Lord and removing the veil himself,[23] Paul refers to an Israelite turning to the Lord and the Lord removing the veil. Further, by turning the verb of the LXX (περιῃρεῖτο) into the present (περιαιρεῖται) Paul relates the passage to the future conversion of an Israelite[24] and therefore gives a *hint* of Israel's conversion. But it is only in Romans 11 that there is the unequivocal statement about Israel's conversion and it is to this chapter (and the end of Romans 10) that we now turn.

2. Provoked to Jealousy: Romans 10.19; Romans 11.11-15

In Rom. 10.19 Paul asks: "Did Israel not know (that God's purposes for salvation were universal)?"[25] In reply Paul quotes from Dt. 32.21:

First Moses says,
'I will make you jealous of those who are not a nation;
with a foolish nation I will make you angry'.

The idea of jealousy here is negative. Israel is to be provoked to jealous anger by means of a no-people, i.e. the Gentile Christians. Paul then sums up the strange situation of the belief of the Gentiles and the unbelief of Israel by quoting from Is. 65.1a, 2a. See Rom. 10.20-21:

Then Isaiah is so bold as to say,
'I have been found by those who did not seek me;
I have shown myself to those who did not ask for me'.
21 But of Israel he says,
'All day long I have held out my hands to a disobedient and contrary people'.

---

[22] Windisch, *Der zweite Korintherbrief*, p. 123, remarks that Paul's use of Ex. 34.34a, appears unbelievably arbitrary ("scheint unglaublich willkürlich"). Contrast Hafemann, *Moses*, p. 389, who believes that "Paul has remained true to the sense of the original text".

[23] Barrett, *Second Epistle to the Corinthians*, p. 122, points out that the verb περιῃρεῖτο in Ex. 34.34a is middle with Moses as subject.

[24] Lang, *Korinther*, p. 275.

[25] Note that there are various ways of understanding this question which in Greek is just "Did Israel not know" (μὴ Ἰσραὴλ οὐκ ἔγνω;). For a thorough discussion of this question and how one can understand the answer, see Bell, *Provoked to Jealousy*, pp. 95-104.

The situation concerning Israel's salvation at the end of Rom. 10 is therefore negative. But the tone changes very much in Rom. 11.11ff. Here the provoking to jealousy is taken up again by Paul but this time is used for a positive purpose.

In Rom. 11.11 Paul picks up the earlier theme of stumbling (cf. 9.33; 11.9) in asking: "Have they (Israel) stumbled so as to fall?"[26] It is over Christ, the exalted and preached Christ, that Israel has stumbled. And Paul goes on to reject the idea that Israel has fallen irrevocably with the expression "by no means" (μὴ γένοιτο). In fact Israel's fall has been providential. He continues in 11.11b:

But through their trespass salvation has come to the Gentiles, so as to make Israel jealous.

ἀλλὰ τῷ αὐτῶν παραπτώματι ἡ σωτηρία τοῖς ἔθνεσιν εἰς τὸ παραζηλῶσαι αὐτούς.

Paul picks up the terms "nation" (ἔθνος) and "provoke to jealousy" (παραζηλοῦν) from Rom. 10.19 where he has quoted Dt. 32.21.[27] But before I look at this jealousy motif I want to focus on Paul's idea that Israel's trespass[28] led to the salvation of the Gentiles. A similar idea is expressed in two nearby texts. First, there is Rom. 11.12:

Now if their trespass means riches for the world, and if their failure means riches for the Gentiles, how much more will their full inclusion mean!?

εἰ δὲ τὸ παράπτωμα αὐτῶν πλοῦτος κόσμου καὶ τὸ ἥττημα αὐτῶν πλοῦτος ἐθνῶν, πόσῳ μᾶλλον τὸ πλήρωμα αὐτῶν.

Second, there is Rom. 11.15:

---

[26] Λέγω οὖν, μὴ ἔπταισαν ἵνα πέσωσιν; The term πταίειν here means stumble (see K.L. Schmidt, πταίω, *TDNT* 6:883-84). πίπτειν, on the other hand, here means to fall irrevocably, although it can be used to describe a fall that is not final. πίπτειν is used to describe an irrevocable fall in the LXX: Is. 24.20, Ps. Sol. 3.10 (13). Compare also Heb. 4.11. Cranfield, *Romans*, 2:554, argues that ἵνα is here not final but means "so as to".

[27] Cf. J.W. Aageson, "Scripture and Structure in the Development of the Argument in Romans 9-11", *CBQ* 48 (1986) 279 (265-89).

[28] Concerning the translation of παράπτωμα as trespass, see Bell, *Provoked to Jealousy*, pp. 108-110.

For if their rejection means the reconciliation of the world, what will their acceptance mean but life from the dead?

εἰ γὰρ ἡ ἀποβολὴ αὐτῶν καταλλαγὴ κόσμου, τίς ἡ πρόσλημψις εἰ μὴ ζωὴ ἐκ νεκρῶν;

How then, especially in 11.11a and 12a, is Israel's trespass related to the salvation of the Gentiles? I consider six explanations.

1. The rejection of the gospel by the Jews compelled the messengers to turn to the Gentiles. One can compare the parable of the Great Supper as found in Lk. 14.15-24 and Mt. 22.1-14. So in Mt. 22.10, the reader is no doubt meant to have the Gentile mission in mind (cf. Mt. 21.43) when the servants "went out into the streets and gathered all whom they found, both bad and good; so the wedding hall was filled with guests" after those who had initially been invited had declined.[29] More importantly, this same pattern can be clearly discerned in the apostolic mission as recorded in Acts (Acts 8.1ff.; 13.45-48; 18.6; 28.24-28).[30] Sanday and Headlam comment on Rom. 11.11 as follows: "St Paul is here stating an historical fact. His own preaching to the Gentiles had been caused definitely by the rejection of his message on the part of the Jews".[31] There is surely some truth in this, but, as Ellison argues, it is inadequate. He writes that such a view "seems to ignore Paul's consciousness of having been called as a missionary to the Gentiles (Acts 9.15, 22.21) . . . After all, the beginning of the mission to the Gentiles had really taken place in Antioch before there could be any question of a definite refusal by the *diaspora* Jews . . ."[32]

2. Ellison's own theory is that the putting aside of the Jew was necessary for the salvation of the Gentile for otherwise the Jew would stand in the way of faith. The Jew would say, "You must come to God through me".[33] Ellison writes: "God had to harden Israel, put him to one side, cease to use him as

---

[29] So Luz, *Matthäus 3*, pp. 243-44: "Die Leser/innen sind durch ihre bisherige Lektüre des Evangeliums immer wieder auf die künftige Heidenmission vorbereitet worden und werden darum selbstverständlich an sie denken".

[30] Dodd, *Romans*, p. 176; P. Benoit, in L. de Lorenzi (ed.), *Die Israelfrage nach Röm 9-11* (MRvB.BÖA 3), Rom: Abtei von St Paul vor den Mauern 1977, 288; cf. F. Dreyfus, "Le passé et le présent d'Israël (Rom., 9,1-5; 11,1-24)", in de Lorenzi (ed.), *Israelfrage*, 149 (131-51). See also Moo, *Romans*, p. 687.

[31] Sanday and Headlam, *Romans*, p. 321.

[32] Ellison, *Mystery*, pp. 80-81 (Ellison's emphasis).

[33] Ellison, *Mystery*, p. 81.

the channel of revelation and blessing, for only so would the nations know that there were no obstacles in the way to God, which had been opened wide by Christ's death".[34] Similar thinking seems to underlie the suggestion of Lagrange that if the Jews had accepted the gospel, they may not have allowed the Church to attain freedom from Jewish customs.[35] One can also add that if every Jew were to have become a Christian, it is unlikely from a human perspective that a Gentile would ever consider joining a Church which is not only thoroughly Jewish but is identical in extent to the Jewish people.[36] Such views certainly make theological sense but it is perhaps not so clear that Paul is actually writing about this here.[37]

3. A third view is that Israel's hardening "relates to Gentile salvation somewhat as Pharaoh's hardening relates to the exodus (9:17)".[38] We saw in the previous chapter that Paul implies in Rom. 9.17-18 that just as Pharaoh was hardened, so Israel is now hardened. Further in Rom. 9.22-23 Paul argues that God "*because* he wishes (1) to manifest his wrath and (2) make known his power, bore with much patience the vessels of wrath prepared for destruction, (3) (doing this because he wished) also (καί) to make known the riches of his glory (τὸν πλοῦτον τῆς δόξης αὐτοῦ) to vessels of mercy that he prepared beforehand for glory". As Wright points out, the term "riches" of 9.23 is echoed in 11.12. Note also how Paul moves in Rom. 9.24: "even us whom he has called, not from the Jews only but also from the Gentiles?" There is little doubt in my mind that there is this link between Rom. 9.17-18, 22-23 and Rom. 11.11-12, 15.

---

[34] Ellison, *Mystery*, p. 82. Note his use of "put him to one side". Ellison does not accept the translation of ἀποβολή in 11.15 as rejection, for Paul has earlier said that God has not rejected his people (11.1). Hence Ellison suggests the meaning "put to one side" (*Mystery*, p. 81).

[35] M.-J. Lagrange, *Saint Paul: Épître aux Romains* (Étbib 13), Paris: J. Gabalda ²1922, (¹1915), p. 275.

[36] This was a point I remember Professor George B. Caird making in his lectures on Romans at Oxford (Hilary term, 1980). It is of course striking that today we have roughly the opposite problem in that many Jews are put off "joining" a Church which is now predominantly Gentile.

[37] I also have some reservations about some of Ellison's understanding of Rom. 11.11-12. So he does not take seriously enough the word παράπτωμα. Ellison believes that the translation "trespass" is too strong and adopts the literal meaning "false step" (Ellison, *Mystery*, p. 80).

[38] N.T. Wright, "The Letter to the Romans", in *NIB* 10 (2002) 680 (393-770).

4. Karl Barth suggests that it was the Jews' rejection of Jesus himself and their delivering him to the Gentiles (Mk 15.1) which led to his death and hence to the redemption of the world. So he writes:

As the Jews delivered up their rejected Messiah to the Gentiles for crucifixion, the latter became with them the instruments of the divine work of atonement completed by the death of Jesus Christ. . . . It is not the seven thousand elect but the blinded rest, Judas Iscariot to be precise, who managed to break open in this way the door between the Israelite and the non-Israelite world, to effect the solidarity both of sin and of grace between Israel and the Gentiles".[39]

Cranfield accepts Barth's solution and points to the use of the term "reconciliation" (καταλλαγή) in 11.15: "For if their rejection means the reconciliation of the world . . ." (εἰ γὰρ ἡ ἀποβολὴ αὐτῶν καταλλαγὴ κόσμου . . .).[40] It is the case, as Cranfield points out,[41] that the only other reference to reconciliation in Romans is the reference to the "reconciliation" to God "through the death of his Son" (διὰ τοῦ θανάτου τοῦ υἱοῦ αὐτοῦ (Rom. 5.10)). However, reconciliation in Paul involves two inextricably intertwined aspects of God's activity: the reconciling act and the reconciling word. As Hofius writes, both "Heils*tat*" and "Heils*wort*" "gehören für Paulus unlöslich zusammen".[42] Therefore "reconciliation" (καταλλαγή) in Rom. 11.15 does not have to refer exclusively to the reconciling act of Christ's death. But the main weakness of the solutions of Barth and Cranfield is that it is doubtful whether Paul was actually writing about Jewish rejection of the

---

[39] Barth, *CD* 2.2:279. Cf. Barth, *Shorter Commentary*, p. 139. See also Althaus, *Römer*, p. 104: "Er denkt vielleicht auch daran, daß Israels Unglaube Jesus an das Kreuz gebracht und so zu seinem Versöhnerwerk für die ganze Welt gewirkt hat". Note that Barth also accepts to some extent point 1 above. So he writes: "It is unmistakeably the case that when Paul bases his own approach to the Gentiles on his repulse by the Jews, which is so much emphasised in Acts (13[46], 18[6], 28[28]), he sees a parallel and illustration of the greater event which came on Jesus Christ Himself" (*CD* 2.2:279).

[40] The idea here is Israel's rejection by God and not Israel's rejection of God.

[41] Cranfield, *Romans*, 2:556.

[42] Hofius, "Wort Gottes", 148 (Hofius' emphasis). Commenting on 2 Cor. 5.18-21, he writes: "Mit der Versöhnungs*tat* sieht Paulus dann ganz unmittelbar das Versöhnungs*wort* verbunden" ("Wort Gottes", 149, Hofius' emphasis). The close relation of the reconciling act and reconciling word (λόγος τῆς καταλλαγῆς (2 Cor. 5.19c)) is seen not only in 2 Cor. 5.18-20 but also, for example, in Rom. 3.25 (the ἔνδειξις of God's δικαιοσύνη (referring to the sacrificial death of Christ)) and Rom. 1.17 (God's revelation of his δικαιοσύνη in the gospel).

historical Jesus in Rom. 11.11-15. In 11.15, Paul speaks of Israel's being cast aside, not her rôle in delivering the Messiah to the Gentiles.

5. N.T. Wright rightly stresses that the casting aside of Israel is the *means* through which salvation goes to the Gentiles (Rom. 11.11) and the world is reconciled to God (Rom. 11.15).[43] Although he suggests the link between Rom. 9.17-18, 22-24 and Rom. 11.11-12 "at one level",[44] he suggests that at another level something else is going on. He goes to the point of saying that Israel acts out not only the fall of Adam but also the death and resurrection of the Messiah. He draws attention to the parallels between Rom. 11.11-15 (Israel's casting aside and later acceptance) and Rom. 5 (the fall of Adam and the death and resurrection of the Messiah).[45] Interesting and significant though these parallels are, it is going beyond the evidence of the texts to say that Israel acts out the death and resurrection of the Messiah. Israel's casting aside is quite different to the casting aside of the Messiah.[46] The redemptive effects of Israel's casting aside are due to her disobedience, her παράπτωμα. The Messiah on the other hand works redemption through his obedience (Rom. 5.18).[47]

6. My own suggestion is that Paul understood the link between the "trespass" (παράπτωμα) of Israel and the salvation going to the Gentiles on the basis of his reading of Dt. 32. In order that the Gentiles should come to faith, it was necessary for Israel to disobey God. In Dt. 32, such disobedience was idolatry.[48] For Paul, the disobedience was failure to believe the gospel. This was Israel's "trespass" (παράπτωμα). It was not just a

---

[43] Wright, *Messiah*, p. 180.

[44] Wright, "Romans", 680.

[45] Wright, *Messiah*, pp. 181-82; *Climax of the Covenant*, p. 248.

[46] Wright, "Romans", 682-83, recognizes this: "Paul does not envisage Israel actually 'dying' for the sake of the world, as the Messiah himself has done; the Messiah's work is unique, standing over against Jew and Gentile alike. But the hardening that has come upon Israel, as in 9:14-24, was the necessary context for the Messiah's death, and as such has become part of the saving plan".

[47] The obedience of Christ in Rom. 5.18 is his sacrificial death. See Bell, "Universal Salvation".

[48] See, for example, Dt. 32.15-17. For a thorough discussion of Dt. 32, see Bell, *Provoked to Jealousy*, chapter 7.

"false step" as some have understood παράπτωμα.[49] It was trespass and disobedience.[50] On the basis of the scripture, Paul argued that it was necessary for Israel to disobey the gospel. Only in that way can the Gentiles be included in the people of God. Paul sees a reference to the inclusion of the Gentiles in Dt. 32.21 (quoted in Rom. 10.19 and alluded to here in 11.11, 14) and in Dt. 32.43 (quoted by Paul in Rom. 15.10). For Paul the disobedience of Israel, the inclusion of the Gentiles, the provoking to jealousy of Israel, and the final salvation of Israel all belong together. They belong together because the themes are linked in Dt. 32.[51]

However, although my own solution is to understand the logic of the rejection of Israel and salvation going to the Gentiles on the basis of Dt. 32.1-43, I do not want to see this as the only explanation. As pointed out above, there is some strength in solutions 2 and 3.

I now move on to Rom. 11.11b, where Paul explains that salvation passed to the Gentiles "to make them (Israel) jealous" (εἰς τὸ παραζηλῶσαι). The divine intention lies behind these words. The term παραζηλοῦν here takes on a positive meaning in the sense of provoke to emulation,[52] for through this provocation to jealousy, Israel will be saved (Rom. 11.14). Israel will come to see that the Gentiles have a closer relationship to God than they enjoy. This would naturally displease Jews since there was a widespread view that Gentiles are to be held in contempt. Jeremias' words are still worth quoting:

---

[49] See Sanday and Headlam, *Romans*, p. 321; Michel, *Römer*, p. 344; Barrett, *Romans*, p. 197; Ellison, *Mystery*, p. 80; J.M. Oesterreicher, "Israel's Misstep and her Rise: The Dialectic of God's Saving Design in Romans 9-11", in *Studiorum Paulinorum Congressus Internationalis Catholicus 1961* (AnBib 17-18), 2 vols, Rome: E Pontificio Instituto Biblico 1963, 1:322 (317-27). Note also the way the English versions translate παράπτωμα: RSV has "trespass", but AV and RV have "fall", Moffatt "lapse", Phillips "failure", and NEB "because they offended".

[50] Note that Paul speaks in 10.16 of Israel not *obeying* the gospel: Ἀλλ᾽ οὐ πάντες ὑπήκουσαν τῷ εὐαγγελίῳ. Note also the use of ἀπείθεια (11.30) and ἀπειθεῖν (11.31).

[51] Again see Bell, *Provoked to Jealousy*, chapter 7, for a detailed discussion of Paul's use of Dt. 32.

[52] See, e.g., Dreyfus, "Le passé et le présent d'Israël (Rom., 9,1-5; 11,1-24)", 151. P. Benoit, "Conclusion par mode de synthèse", in L. de Lorenzi (ed.), *Die Israelfrage nach Röm 9-11* (MRvB.BÖA 3), Rom: Abtei von St Paul vor den Mauern 1977, 230 (217-36), is, however, not completely right in understanding παραζηλοῦν in *both* 10.19 and in 11.11, 14 to mean "provoke to emulation". In 10.19, the verb, as I have argued, rather means "provoke to jealous anger".

The attitude of late Judaism towards non-Jews was uncompromisingly severe. In addition to their abhorrence of idolatry, their attitude was largely determined by the oppression which they had undergone at the hands of foreign nations, and by their fear of the increasing prevalence of mixed marriages. Thus it is easy to understand why to them the Gentiles were godless, rejected by God as worthless in his eyes as chaff and refuse; they were steeped in vice; they were given over to every form of uncleanness, violence, and wickedness.[53]

This was not, of course, the whole picture since, as we saw in chapter 3 above, there was the view that the righteous Gentile could enter the world to come. But there can be no doubt that extremely negative views were held about the Gentiles.[54] In addition to the points made in the quotation, one may add, for example, the Temple inscription banning Gentiles on pain of death from the inner temple and the view that the condemnation of the Gentiles will act as a ransom for Israel.[55] Perhaps the objections to Jeremias' views have more to do with political correctness than an examination of the sources (and a careful reading of what Jeremias actually wrote).[56]

---

[53] J. Jeremias, *Jesus' Promise to the Nations* ET (SBT 24), London: SCM 1958, p. 40.

[54] See the texts quoted in Billerbeck, *Kommentar*, 1:360. So in Mek. Ex. 14.7 we read: מכאן היה רבי שמעון בן יוחשי אמור היפה שבגוים הרוג which is translated by Lauterbach, *Mekilta*, 1:201, as "In this connection R. Simon the son of Yohai said: 'The nicest among the idolaters,–kill!'" (compare Billerbeck, *Kommentar*, 1:360: "Der Beste unter den Gojim verdient den Tod"). The context of this remark would, of course, be clear to both Jews and Christians of Billerbeck's generation. I say this in view of the claim that in Billerbeck's work, texts are taken out of context. Billerbeck also quotes b. Bab. Met. 114b, b. Yeb. 60b-61a. The latter text is translated as follows in the Soncino edition: "And so did R. Simeon b. Yohai state that the graves of idolaters do not impart levitical uncleanness by an *ohel*, for it is said, *And ye My sheep of My pasture, are men*; you are called *men* but the idolaters are not called *men*". "R. Schimeon b. Jochai sagte: Die Gräber der Gojim verunreinigen nicht; denn es heißt: 'Ihr aber, meine Schafe, Schafe meiner Weide: Menschen seid ihr' Ez 34,31; ihr (Israeliten) werdet Menschen genannt; aber die Völker der Welt werden nicht Menschen, sondern Vieh genannt"). See also Billerbeck, *Kommentar*, 4:722 (e.g. b. Yeb. 60b: "Ihr (Israeliten) heißet Menschen, aber nicht heißen die Nichtjuden Menschen") and 4:1067 (Pes. R. 10.5 (36b): "R. Levi hat gesagt: . . . Wie viele Völker gibt es in der Welt, wie viele Haufen von Völkern, u. Gott kümmert sich nicht um sie").

[55] Jeremias mentions the latter in *Nations*, p. 41. In *Provoked to Jealousy*, pp. 268-69, I discuss in particular Sifre Dt 333, a view corrected by Jesus in Mk 10.45.

[56] Jeremias was attacked in an article of E.P. Sanders, "Jesus and the Kingdom: The Restoration of Israel and the New People of God", published in a Festschrift edited by Sanders himself (*Jesus, the Gospels, and the Church. Essays in Honor of William R. Farmer*, Macon: Mercer University Press 1987, 225-239). A defence of Jeremias was

In 11.12, Paul then uses an *a fortiori* argument:

11.12: Now if their trespass means riches for the world, and if their defeat means riches for the Gentiles, how much more will their full inclusion mean!

11.12: εἰ δὲ τὸ παράπτωμα αὐτῶν πλοῦτος κόσμου καὶ τὸ ἥττημα αὐτῶν πλοῦτος ἐθνῶν, πόσῳ μᾶλλον τὸ πλήρωμα αὐτῶν.

Paul's logic is that if Israel's disobedience means riches for the world (the expression πλοῦτος κόσμου referring to riches for the Gentiles[57]) and if Israel's defeat[58] means riches for the Gentiles, then how much more their full inclusion. The expression πλήρωμα αὐτῶν refers to the full and complete number of Israelites. Further, the three uses of αὐτῶν in 11.12 refer most likely to the whole of Israel. In Paul's eyes virtually the whole of Israel

---

mounted by B.F. Meyer, "A Caricature of Joachim Jeremias and His Scholarly Work", *JBL* 110 (1991) 451-62, who pointed out that Jeremias' view of Jewish attitudes to the Gentiles were more nuanced than Sanders allowed. For Sanders' counter-attack, see "Defending the Indefensible", *JBL* 110 (1991) 463-77.

[57] See H. Sasse, κοσμέω, κόσμος κτλ., *TDNT* 3:892 (867-98). For the use of πλοῦτος, see Rom. 9.23 and 10.12.

[58] The word ἥττημα does not occur in classical or pagan-hellenistic literature and occurs only once in the LXX (Is. 31.8) and twice in the NT (here and in 1 Cor. 6.7). The verb ἡττάομαι, however, occurs in Is. 8.9; 13.15; 19.1; 20.5; 30.31; 31.4; 31.9; 33.1; 51.7; 54.17 and in 2 Pet. 2.19, 20 as well as in classical literature, and can take the meanings "be less", "be inferior (to someone)", or "be defeated". ἥττημα must mean defeat in Is. 31.8. In 1 Cor. 6.7, the word takes the meaning defeat in the sense of moral defeat (Barrett, *First Epistle to the Corinthians*, p. 138). The most natural meaning of ἥττημα in 11.12 is "defeat" (see Sanday and Headlam, *Romans*, p. 322; Murray, *Romans*, 2:78). However, many commentators, both ancient and modern, take the meaning of ἥττημα to be "fewness" or "diminution" in order to have a neat antithesis to πλήρωμα. But as Cranfield points out, the arguments for the meaning "fewness" are not strong. Cranfield, *Romans*, 2:557, argues that there is no strong reason for expecting a word in parallel to πλήρωμα. There is just as much reason for expecting a word in parallel to παράπτωμα. Paul may have used the word "defeat" because in Dt. 32, the disobedience of Israel actually leads to her defeat at the hands of a foolish people, i.e., the Gentiles. It is widely recognized by modern commentators that the provoking of Israel to jealousy through a no-people in Dt. 32.21b refers to a defeat Israel suffered from a Gentile nation. Paul could also have known of this interpretation although in Rom. 10.19, 11.11, 14 he applies the text to the situation facing him: Gentiles who believe in the messiah and Jews who do not. Because of Israel's disobedience (Israel is in a state whereby her members are no longer fit to be called God's children (Dt. 32.5)), she is deprived of her heritage by a foolish nation.

was disobedient, the whole was "defeated" and he now suggests the idea that the whole of Israel will be saved.[59]

In 11.13a, Paul directly addresses the Gentiles: "Now I am speaking to you Gentiles" (Ὑμῖν δὲ λέγω τοῖς ἔθνεσιν) and continues to address them up to 11.32. He continues in Rom. 11.13b-14:

Inasmuch then as I am an apostle to the Gentiles, I magnify my ministry 14 in order to make my fellow Jews jealous, and thus save some of them.

ἐφ' ὅσον μὲν οὖν εἰμι ἐγὼ ἐθνῶν ἀπόστολος, τὴν διακονίαν μου δοξάζω, εἴ πως παραζηλώσω μου τὴν σάρκα καὶ σώσω τινὰς ἐξ αὐτῶν.

Insofar as Paul is an apostle to the Gentiles,[60] he hopes to save some of his fellow Jews. There is no δέ to answer the μέν, and no δέ clause can be plausibly supplied. Cranfield suggests that the expression μὲν οὖν be taken as a single expression,[61] paraphrasing it as "contrary to what you may be inclined to think". Paul, far from turning his back on Israel in his mission to the Gentiles, is actually working for the salvation of Israel. He magnifies his ministry in order to provoke Israel to jealousy and so save some of them.

Paul's glorifying his ministry can be understood in quite a natural sense (i.e. Paul is not referring to something like a prayer of thankgiving as suggested by Michel).[62] So Paul honours his ministry and fulfils it with all his strength that it may lead Israel to jealousy. Whereas in 10.19, *God* provokes Israel to jealousy, here it appears that it is *Paul himself* who will provoke Israel to jealousy (i.e., to emulation) and so save some. However, two points need to be borne in mind. First, it is true that σῴζειν τινά is a "terminus der Missionssprache".[63] But the idea is not that the missionary himself saves; rather it is the word of God (witnessed to and mediated in the preaching) that creates faith in the hearer (cf. the word which creates faith, τὸ ῥῆμα τῆς πίστεως (Rom. 10.8)). The second point concerns the verbs παραζηλώσω and σώσω. They could be taken either as futures or as aorist subjunctives.

---

[59] For more detailed exegesis of Rom. 11.12, see Bell, *Provoked to Jealousy*, pp. 113-15.

[60] I translate ἐφ' ὅσον with "in so far as", and not with "as long as" as in the Vulgate and Old Latin *quamdiu*. Paul nowhere else speaks of his apostleship as something temporary (Cranfield, *Romans*, 2:559).

[61] See the use of μενοῦνγε in 10.18 (which means "indeed").

[62] See Michel, *Römer*, p. 347.

[63] Wilckens, *Römer*, 2:244, who points to 1 Cor. 7.16; 9.22 (n. 1096).

They are dependent on εἴ πως which indicates an expression of expectation.[64] By analogy with Rom. 1.10 (πάντοτε ἐπὶ τῶν προσευχῶν μου δεόμενος εἴ πως ἤδη ποτὲ εὐοδωθήσομαι ἐν τῷ θελήματι τοῦ θεοῦ ἐλθεῖν πρὸς ὑμᾶς) I would take the verbs to be future.[65] Paul believes that by provoking Israel to jealousy part of Israel will come to be saved. The expression εἴ πως in both these texts "express an expectation whose fulfillment comes from God, not one whose fulfillment is in doubt".[66] Therefore although Paul appears as subject of these two verbs παραζηλώσω and σώσω, *God's activity* is the crucial aspect.

What effect did Paul expect this provocation to jealousy to have? The expression σώσω τινὰς ἐξ αὐτῶν need not mean only a small number would be saved. Certainly τινές when used of Jewish unbelief does not refer to a small number (see Rom. 11.17a; 3.3). Further, he can use τινές as an understatement of the saved (as can be seen by comparing 1 Cor. 9.22 with 9.19). But two difficult issues need to be addressed and they are related to this issue of the τινές. First, what is the relationship between the provocation to emulation and the salvation of Israel in Rom. 11.14 (εἴ πως παραζηλώσω μου τὴν σάρκα καὶ σώσω τινὰς ἐξ αὐτῶν)? Secondly, what is the relationship of the salvation Paul speaks of in 11.11-15 and that of the final salvation of Israel in 11.26? Regarding the first point, it needs to be stressed that no Jewish person is going to be converted by simply being provoked to jealousy. It can only act as a preparation for someone's salvation. Someone can only come to faith through hearing the gospel.[67] This brings me to the second question. Provocation to jealousy functions as a preparation for the salvation of Israel when she receives the gospel either in the apostolic mission or when she receives the gospel directly from the coming Christ at his parousia.

That a sharp distinction is not to be drawn between the salvation of Israel through jealousy and the final salvation can be seen in Rom. 11.15. As in 11.12, there is an *a fortiori* argument:

---

[64] See *BDF* § 375.

[65] Cf. E. Kühl, *Der Brief des Paulus an die Römer*, Leipzig: Quelle & Meyer 1913, p. 381: "Die Verben παραζηλώσω und σώσω sind nach Analogie von 1,10 als futurische Formen zu fassen".

[66] Gundry Volf, *Paul and Perseverance*, p. 257. She also rightly argues that the same goes for Phil. 3.11: εἴ πως καταντήσω εἰς τὴν ἐξανάστασιν τὴν ἐκ νεκρῶν.

[67] I will return to this issue in the discussion of mission to Israel in chapter 10 below.

For if their rejection means the reconciliation of the world, what will their acceptance mean but life from the dead?

εἰ γὰρ ἡ ἀποβολὴ αὐτῶν καταλλαγὴ κόσμου, τίς ἡ πρόσλημψις εἰ μὴ ζωὴ ἐκ νεκρῶν;

"For" (γάρ) links 11.15 with vv. 13-14.[68] Rom. 11.15 therefore explains why Paul is especially eager as apostle to the Gentiles to provoke the Jews to jealousy. If the casting aside of Israel (ἀποβολή)[69] means reconciliation for the world, what will their acceptance (πρόσλημψις)[70] by God mean but life from the dead (ζωὴ ἐκ νεκρῶν)? Paul's apostolic mission together with the provoking to jealousy are therefore integrally related to Israel's "acceptance" and "life from the dead". This expression ζωὴ ἐκ νεκρῶν has been understood in a number of ways. The first is as the general resurrection of the dead.[71] But if Paul wished to refer to the resurrection, why did he not use ἀνάστασις?[72] The second possibility is the general resurrection of the dead and the everlasting life in fellowship with God and Christ.[73] This would be a natural way to understand "life from the dead" and there is much to commend this solution. A third solution is the general resurrection as a sign of the inauguration of the messianic kingdom.[74] This is a possibility. Although the idea of a messianic kingdom has been frequently rejected[75] the

---

[68] Cranfield, *Romans*, 2:561. The alternatives are that 11.15 is linked with v. 12, vv. 13-14 being regarded as parenthetical, or that there is a connection with both v. 12 and vv. 13-14 (Sanday and Headlam, *Romans*, p. 325).

[69] I assume Paul is using the expression ἡ ἀποβολὴ αὐτῶν as an objective genitive (cf. Murray, *Romans*, 2:81). Fitzmyer, *Romans*, p. 612 (followed by Lohse, *Römer*, p. 313), objects to this, preferring the subjective genitive. He argues that the idea of God's rejection of Israel is not to be found in the text; indeed Rom. 11.1 declares that God has not rejected his people. However, it is undeniable that Rom. 9.6-29 speaks of God rejecting unbelieving Israel. The idea of God's rejection of Israel is certainly seen in much of Rom. 9-11, even though it turns out to be a temporary rejection.

[70] This is a hapax legomenon in the New Testament, but its meaning is clear from the contrast with ἀποβολή and from Paul's use of the cognate verb προσλαμβάνειν (Rom. 14.1, 3; 15.7; Phlm 17).

[71] Cranfield, *Romans*, 2:562-63; Käsemann, *Romans*, p. 307.

[72] Used in Rom. 1.4; 6.5; 1 Cor. 15.12, 13, 21, 42; Phil. 3.10.

[73] Maier, *Heilsgeschichte*, p. 127.

[74] Sanday and Headlam, *Romans*, p. 325.

[75] See Davies, *Paul and Rabbinic Judaism*, p. 297, who writes that Paul's eschatology "contains no reference to a Messianic Kingdom such as is contemplated in Baruch, 4 Ezra, and Revelation and can be briefly summarized as the early expectation of the Parousia when there would be a final judgement, a general resurrection of the righteous

idea has recently found more acceptance.[76] However, even if Paul did conceive of a messianic kingdom (and I will examine such a possibility in chapter 10 below), such a ζωὴ ἐκ νεκρῶν could occur at the *end* of such a messianic kingdom.[77] A fourth solution is that Paul refers to resurrection understood in a figurative sense either for the whole world[78] or for Israel.[79] This is possible if, with Luz, it is stressed that Paul is not so much interested in an event in the linear course of salvation history or in the "when" question but more in the "what" question.[80] But if with Murray the ζωὴ ἐκ νεκρῶν is considered as something occurring in history, "an unprecedented quickening for the world in the expansion and success of the gospel",[81] there is a contradiction with 11.25-26, where the conversion of τὸ πλήρωμα τῶν ἐθνῶν takes place before the salvation of πᾶς Ἰσραήλ.[82]

Of the above possibilities I think solution 2 is the strongest (and I have supported this view in the past). But another possible view is that Paul has in mind the resurrection of Israel. If this is taken to include the life and fellowship with God and Christ, we have a variation on solution 2. This view

---

dead (and possibly of all dead), the transformation of the righteous living and ensuing upon all this the final consummation, the perfected kingdom of God when God would be all in all".

[76] For an overview see H. Räisänen, "Did Paul Expect an Earthly Kingdom?", in A. Christofersen, C. Claussen, J. Frey and B. Longenecker (ed.), *Paul, Luke and the Graeco-Roman World: Essays in Honour of Alexander J.M. Wedderburn* (JSNTSup 217), Sheffield: Sheffield Academic Press 2002, 2-20. See also L.J. Kreitzer, *Jesus and God in Paul's Eschatology* (JSNTSup 19), Sheffield: JSOT Press 1987, pp. 136-39, who criticizes Davies' objections to the idea of a messianic kingdom.

[77] Again, for a discussion as to the possible distinction between "from the dead" (resurrection of those who believe) and "of the dead" (a general resurrection) see chapter 10 section 2 below.

[78] Murray, *Romans*, 2:82-84; Morris, *Romans*, p. 411. E. Gaugler, *Der Brief an die Römer* (P.SBG), 2 vols, Zürich: Zwingli Verlag 1 1958; 2 1952, 2:187, writes: "Am Ausdruck 'Leben aus den Toten' haftet mehr das Merkmal eines allgemeinen Prinzips als eines bestimmten Ereignisses".

[79] Wright, *Climax of the Covenant*, p. 248: "when a Gentile comes into the family of Christ, it is as it were a *creatio ex nihilo*, but when a Jew comes in it is like a resurrection (compare [Rom.] 4.17, in context)".

[80] Luz, *Geschichtsverständnis*, p. 394; Luz attempts to underplay the Heilsgeschichte in Rom. 11.25-32 also. See Bell, *Provoked to Jealousy*, pp. 59-60, for criticism of Luz.

[81] Murray, *Romans*, 2:84.

[82] Cranfield, *Romans*, 2:563.

finds some support in Rom. 11.25-27. For if Israel's redemption is at the parousia when she comes to faith in Christ and if it is for "all Israel" throughout the ages,[83] the only possibility for Jews who have died before the parousia to receive the gospel from Christ is by a resurrection from the dead. Then her ζωή begins. But I have jumped ahead and we now need to examine Paul's argument in Rom. 11.25-27 in some detail.

3. The Final Salvation of Israel: Romans 11.25-27

These three verses together with vv. 28-32 form one of the most profound passages of the New Testament and without doubt are central for our theme of Paul and Israel. First I give my own translation:

For I want you to know this mystery, brethren, so that you may not be wise in your own eyes, that a partial hardening has come upon Israel until the goal is reached, that the fulness of the Gentiles will have come in, 26 and so all Israel will be saved, as it is written,
'The deliverer will come from Zion,
he will turn away ungodliness from Jacob,
27 and this is my covenant for them
when I take away their sins'.

25a Οὐ γὰρ θέλω ὑμᾶς ἀγνοεῖν, ἀδελφοί, τὸ μυστήριον τοῦτο, ἵνα μὴ ἦτε [παρ᾽] ἑαυτοῖς φρόνιμοι,
25b ὅτι πώρωσις ἀπὸ μέρους τῷ Ἰσραὴλ γέγονεν
     ἄχρι οὗ τὸ πλήρωμα τῶν ἐθνῶν εἰσέλθη
26   καὶ οὕτως πᾶς Ἰσραὴλ σωθήσεται,
     καθὼς γέγραπται·
     Ἥξει ἐκ Σιὼν ὁ ῥυόμενος,
     ἀποστρέψει ἀσεβείας ἀπὸ Ἰακώβ.
27   καὶ αὕτη αὐτοῖς ἡ παρ᾽ ἐμοῦ διαθήκη,
     ὅταν ἀφέλωμαι τὰς ἁμαρτίας αὐτῶν.

The central idea here is the remarkable phrase "all Israel will be saved". But before studying these words I need to make some preliminary points. First, the phrase is part of what Paul calls a mystery (μυστήριον, v. 25a), the content of the mystery being found in vv. 25b-27. The word μυστήριον corresponds to the Hebrew רז which is employed in the Dead Sea Scrolls to

---

[83] Paul's assumption is that those Jews who believe in Christ are already redeemed.

mean a mystery discovered through the study of scripture.[84] So Paul's mystery I believe came not through some vision or apocalyptic revelation (as in 2 Cor. 12.1ff.) but rather through a study of the scriptures.

The second preliminary point is that these words are addressed to Gentiles (see Rom. 11.13). Paul wishes to tell of this mystery so that they may not be wise in their own eyes. Many Gentiles probably thought that God had written off Israel. True, God had made promises to Israel, but did not their disobedience (i.e. not believing in Christ) effectively disinherit them? This, as we saw in chapter 2 above, was probably Paul's own view in 1 Thes. 2.12-16 and he was perhaps painfully aware here of his past arrogance towards Israel, God's chosen people. He therefore wishes to correct the misconceptions of the Gentile Christians in Rome by telling them of this mystery.[85]

What about the content of the mystery? The first point in the mystery is that a partial hardening (πώρωσις ἀπὸ μέρους) has come upon Israel. This could either be understood to mean that the hardening has come upon a certain number (a quantitative understanding) or that the hardening has come upon Israel for a certain period of time (a temporal understanding). In fact both understandings would fit the context and I believe the scales are evenly balanced. Therefore I leave the question open (and hence my translation "partial hardening"). Paul then goes on to say that this hardening will only be in effect until a certain goal is reached, namely that the full number of the Gentiles "will have come in".[86] The "full number of the Gentiles" refers to the number of Gentiles God intends to save and does not refer to a universal salvation of Gentiles. Jülicher argued for a universal salvation of Gentile partly on the basis that in 11.12b Paul speaks of the πλήρωμα of Israel.[87] He

---

[84] See 1QpHab 7.4-5: "Its interpretation concerns the Teacher of Righteousness, to whom God has disclosed all the mysteries of the words of his servants, the prophets (כול רָזֵי דִּבְרֵי עֲבָדָיו הַנְּבָאִים)" (Martínez, *Dead Sea Scrolls*, p. 200).

[85] On the history of anti-Judaism in Rome see W. Wiefel, "The Jewish Community in Ancient Rome and the Origins of Romans Christianity" in K.P. Donfried (ed.), *The Romans Debate: Revised and Expanded Edition*, Peabody: Hendrickson 1991, 85-101.

[86] For the translation using this future perfect see Bell, *Provoked to Jealousy*, p. 129.

[87] A. Jülicher, "Der Brief an die Römer", in O. Baumgarten et al. (ed.), *Die Schriften des Neuen Testaments, Zweiter Band*, Göttingen: Vandenhoeck & Ruprecht 1917, 307 (223-335). His universal salvation though seems to apply to those Gentiles alive during the preaching of the gospel. So referring to the point in time when the hardening of Israel comes to an end, he writes: "Dieser Zeitpunkt wird gekommen sein, wenn die Vollzahl

also argues that Paul's statement about the fulness of the Gentiles would be an "unworthy phrase" if he did not have in mind the universal salvation of Gentiles.[88] Jülicher works with a symmetry between Gentiles and Israel.[89] But there is no reason why the fulness of the Gentiles should correspond to the fulness of Israel. Paul's hope regarding the Gentiles was probably that once the Spanish mission had been completed their full number would have "come in".[90] He clearly works with the idea that the Gentiles have to receive the "word of God" and they do so through the apostolic mission.[91]

The words which have more significance than anything else for our understanding of Paul's idea of the salvation of Israel are those at the beginning of 11.26: "and so all Israel will be saved" (καὶ οὕτως πᾶς Ἰσραὴλ σωθήσεται). The exegesis is so crucial that I will spend some time examining the two expressions καὶ οὕτως and πᾶς Ἰσραήλ. For καὶ οὕτως there are four possible interpretations.

1. καὶ οὕτως has been understood temporally in the sense καὶ τότε, "and then".[92] However, there has been some debate as to whether καὶ οὕτως can mean this in the New Testament.[93]

2. καὶ οὕτως has been understood as modal, referring to that which precedes, i.e., referring back to the first two lines of the μυστήριον in

---

(vgl. V. 12b: vollzähliges Eintreffen) der Heiden in die Gemeinde Gottes eingetreten, zum Heil gelangt ist, wenn also die Erde keinen ungläubigen Heiden mehr birgt".

[88] So Jülicher, "Römer", 307, writes: "'die Fülle der Heiden' wäre eine des Paulus unwürdige Phrase, wenn er darunter nur Vertreter jeder heidnischen Nation oder die Völker im Ganzen oder die von Gott zum Heil vorherbestimmten Heiden verstünde".

[89] Jülicher, "Römer", 307: "Jede Einschränkung wird durch V. 26 verboten, wo 'ganz Israel' den deutlichsten Gegensatz zu dem teilweise verstockten Israel bildet, im Sinne von 'ausnahmslos'".

[90] The verb εἰσέρχομαι is rare in Paul and may be used to express the idea of Gentiles entering the community of the saved.

[91] See further the discussion on Rom. 11.32 in chapter 7 below.

[92] Käsemann, *Römer*, p. 303. Barrett, *Romans*, p. 206, also sees a temporal element.

[93] Käsemann, *Romans*, p. 303, writes that οὕτως has a temporal sense in Acts 17.33 and 20.11. But Hofius, "Evangelium und Israel", 192, rightly points out that the sense of οὕτως in Acts 17.33 is logical, not temporal (see Acts 17.32-33: "Now when they heard of the resurrection of the dead, some mocked; but others said, 'We will hear you again about this'. 33 So (οὕτως) Paul went out from among them".

11.25b. Thus καὶ οὕτως is translated as "and in this way" or "and in such a way".[94] This solution is certainly a possibility.

3. The third interpretation is that καὶ οὕτως is modal but refers to that which follows and so is translated "and in the following way". The terms οὕτως and καθώς are therefore understood correlatively.[95] However, this does not fit with Paul's usage elsewhere of οὕτως.[96]

4. The fourth possibility is to understand καὶ οὕτως in a logical sense following on from ἄχρι οὗ τὸ πλήρωμα τῶν ἐθνῶν εἰσέλθῃ. Although καὶ οὕτως is here understood as logical, it will also inevitably carry a temporal sense.[97] This use of καὶ οὕτως is attested in the "intertestamental literature".[98]

---

[94] See Barth, *CD* 2.2:300; Jeremias, "Beobachtungen", 198-99; Wilckens, *Römer*, 2:255; Cranfield, *Romans*, 2:576; F. Mußner, "Ganz Israel", 243-44, 248-49; Luz, *Geschichtsverständnis*, pp. 293-94; Wright, *Messiah*, pp. 196-97; *Climax of the Covenant*, p. 249.

[95] *BAG*, ⁴1952, p. 602 (οὕτως §2); P. Stuhlmacher, "Zur Interpretation von Römer 11₂₅₋₃₂", in H.W. Wolff (ed.), *Probleme biblischer Theologie: G. von Rad zum 70. Geburtstag*, München: Chr. Kaiser Verlag 1971, 560 (555-70); Benoit, "Conclusion par mode de synthèse", 232.

[96] Jeremias points out that Paul uses οὕτως correlatively 36 times (and once in the Pastorals). But in 27 of these 36 occurrences, οὕτως occurs in the following clause. Of the cases where οὕτως is in the first clause, on only one occasion do we find the order οὕτως . . . καθώς (Phil. 3.17) (Jeremias, "Beobachtungen", 198, 207). In addition, the formula καθώς/καθάπερ γέγραπται is never a correlation formula but always a citation formula in all 18 occurrences (Jeremias, "Beobachtungen", 208). Also if Paul had wished to use οὕτως . . . καθώς correlatively, οὕτως would have come in another position, viz., πᾶς Ἰσραὴλ οὕτως σωθήσεται (Mußner, "Ganz Israel", 243; Hofius, "Evangelium und Israel", 193).

[97] Note, however, that καὶ οὕτως is not taken here to mean καὶ τότε as in solution 1 above.

[98] See Ch.A. Wahl, *Clavis librorum Veteris Testamenti Apocryphorum philologica: Indicem verborum in libris pseudepigraphis usurpatorum* (J.B. Bauer (ed.)), 1972 (repr.), (Leipzig ¹1853), p. 371, who, commenting on καὶ οὕτως, writes: "ibi ponitur, ubi de re post aliam actam vel perpetrata vel perpetranda agitur = *rebus ita comparatis, i.e. quo facto*" (quoted in Hofius, "Evangelium und Israel", 193). Such a use of καὶ οὕτως (or καὶ οὕτω) can be seen in Sir. 32.1; 33.4; 1 Mac. 13.47; 4 Mac. 1.12 (given by Wahl); Test. Job 5.3; Apoc. Mos. 37; Barn. 7.8 (given by Hofius). Hofius also mentions the use of καὶ οὕτως in Philogelos, *Der Lachfreund*, §§ 57, 243 (in A. Thierfelder (ed.), *Philogelos der Lachfreund von Hierokles und Philagrios*, München: Heimeran Verlag 1968, pp. 50, 118). For the logical use of καὶ οὕτως in Paul, see 1 Cor. 11.28 and 1 Thes. 4.17.

Of the four solutions, 2 and 4 are the best, and of these, 4 would seem the most plausible.[99] The reason why solution 4 is to be preferred to solution 2 will become clear in the following discussion.

The next question is the meaning of πᾶς Ἰσραήλ in 11.26, a crucial question for the exegesis of the whole chapter. The term here and in the LXX is a semitism in view of the missing article[100] and corresponds to the Hebrew כָּל־יִשְׂרָאֵל. In the LXX it can refer to all twelve tribes (e.g. Dt. 27.9), to the northern kingdom (e.g. 1 Sam. 18.16) or the southern kingdom of Judah and Benjamin (e.g. 2 Chron. 11.3). Then in certain instances it can refer to every Israelite or Israel as a whole (see below).

Turning to its use in Rom. 11.26, there are four possible interpretations.
1. πᾶς Ἰσραήλ means all the elect, both Jews and Gentiles.[101] Calvin appeals to the use of Ἰσραήλ in Gal. 6.16.[102] Jeremias supports this interpretation partly on the basis of καὶ οὕτως. He understands οὕτως as "in this way" ("auf diese Weise", "solcherart"). Israel is therefore made up of (1) the remnant of 11.5, (2) the "fulness of the Gentiles" (πλήρωμα τῶν ἐθνῶν) of 11.25, and (3) those of Israel now under a temporary hardening but who will be freed from this hardening.[103] Jeremias' understanding could be plausible if it were not for the fact that the context so strongly points to Ἰσραήλ being the nation Israel. In Rom. 11.25 Paul has used Ἰσραήλ for the Jews. His whole argument in 11.11-32 consists of a contrast between the rôles of Jews (for whom he uses the term Ἰσραήλ) and Gentiles. Rom. 11.11-15 points in particular to the glorious future awaiting Israel. Further, 11.28-29 (God's

---

[99] W. Keller, *Gottes Treue – Israels Heil. Röm 11,25-27 – Die These vom 'Sonderweg' in der Diskussion* (SBB 40), Stuttgart: Katholisches Bibelwerk 1998, p. 218, misrepresents the position I argued for in *Provoked to Jealousy*, p. 136, when he writes: "Nach *R.H. Bell* ist die temporale Deutung von καὶ οὕτως die plausibelste".

[100] See Hofius, "Evangelium und Israel", 194. J.M. Scott, "'And then all Israel will be saved' (Rom 11:26)", in J.M. Scott (ed.), *Restoration: Old Testament, Jewish, and Christian Perspectives* (JSJSup 72), Leiden/Boston/Köln: Brill 2001, 498 n. 26 (489-527), points out that in Greek Patristic literature the terms πᾶς ὁ Ἰσραήλ and ὁ πᾶς Ἰσραήλ are used instead.

[101] Calvin, *Romans*, p. 255; Barth, *Kirchliche Dogmatik*, 2.2:330; Jeremias, "Beobachtungen", 200. Chilton and Neusner, *Judaism in the New Testament*, p. 67, believes Paul means "forgiven Jews and gentiles".

[102] Calvin, *Romans*, p. 255. Paul probably does have in mind the Church of Jews and Gentiles in Gal. 6.16. See my discussion in chapter 4, section 3.2.

[103] Jeremias, "Beobachtungen", 200.

love for and faithfulness to Israel) would be almost meaningless if Paul were not here referring to the Jews.[104]

2. The second interpretation is that πᾶς Ἰσραήλ refers to the elect of the nation Israel.[105] However, this renders Paul's declaration πᾶς Ἰσραήλ σωθήσεται "all Israel will be saved" an anticlimax. Paul's use of τὸ πλήρωμα (11.12) and ἡ πρόσλημψις (11.15), and his expectation that the broken-off branches will be grafted in again (11.23-24) point to something far greater than the salvation of a mere remnant.[106]

3. πᾶς Ἰσραήλ means the whole nation, including every single member.[107] Paul's assumption is that those Jews who already believe are saved, so Paul is clearly thinking of the vast majority of Jews, who have been hardened and have not yet been saved by Christ. One key strength of this solution is that Ἰσραήλ refers to the nation. Also there are Old Testament texts where the term "all Israel" refers to every member. So in Dt. 27.9 Moses and the Levitical priests speak to "all Israel". In Jos. 3.17 "all Israel" pass over the miraculously formed dry ground of the river Jordan. In Jos. 8.33 all Israel stand on opposites sides of the ark, half of them in front of Mount Gerizim and half in front of Ebal. However, it is often pointed out that there are Old Testament and Rabbinic texts where the expression πᾶς Ἰσραήλ (כל ישראל) was not used to refer to every single Israelite. As far as the Old Testament is concerned, the term "all Israel" could refer to a representative part of Israel. So in 1 Kgs 12.1, it is unlikely that every Israelite came to Shechem to make

---

[104] Note that this view that πᾶς Ἰσραήλ means the Church is found in patristic writers. Fitzmyer, *Romans*, p. 624, points to this understanding in Irenaeus, *Adversus haereses* 4.2.7; Clement of Alexandria, *Excerpta ex Theodoto* 56.4-5; Theodore of Mopsuestia, *In ep. ad Romanos* 11.26; Theodoret of Cyrrhus, *Interpretatio ep. ad Romanos* 11.26-27. It is interesting that Origen and Augustine are not consistent in their understanding of the verse. So, e.g., Origen in his *Commentarius in ep. ad Romanos* 8.13 believes that ethnic Israel is meant; however in his *Commentarius in Matthaeum* 17.5, he thinks of spiritual Israel.

[105] See, e.g., J.A. Bengel, *Gnomon Novi Testamenti*, Berlin: Gust. Schlawitz 1855 (³1773), p. 382, who compares Mic. 2.12: "I will surely gather all of you, O Jacob, I will gather the remnant (שארית) of Israel".

[106] See Cranfield, *Romans*, 2:576-77.

[107] Jülicher, "Römer", 307; E. Kühl, *Der Brief des Paulus an die Römer*, Leipzig: Quelle & Meyer 1913, pp. 392-93; K.L. Schmidt, *Die Judenfrage im Lichte der Kap. 9-11 des Römerbriefes* (ThSt 13), Zollikon-Zürich: Evangelischer Verlag 1943, p. 40 (3-72).

Rehoboam king. Further there are texts where "all Israel" means Israel as a whole but not necessarily including every member. So Daniel confesses that "all Israel has transgressed thy law and turned aside, refusing to obey thy voice" (Dan. 9.11). Likewise the Chronicler writes that "when the rule of Rehoboam was established and was strong, he forsook the law of the LORD, and all Israel with him" (2 Chron. 12.1). It is quite conceivable that there were a number of exceptions (and we know that Daniel, Hananiah, Mishael and Azariah, Dan. 1.6, and Shemaiah, 2 Chron. 12.5, were faithful). Then Mishnah Sanh. 10.1 is a striking example. This text could be especially important since it relates to Israel's salvation. It opens with the words: "All Israelites have a share in the world to come".[108] But this is then followed by a long list of exceptions.

> And these are they that have no share in the world to come: he that says that there is no resurrection of the dead prescribed in the Law, and [he that says] that the Law is not from Heaven, and an Epicurean. . . . Three kings and four commoners have no share in the world to come. The three kings are Jeroboam and Ahab and Manasseh. . . . The four commoners are Balaam and Doeg and Ahithophel and Gehazi. The generation of the flood have no share in the world to come. . . . The men of Sodom have no share in the world to come . . .[109]

And so the list continues.

4. This then leads to the fourth solution which I consider: πᾶς Ἰσραήλ means Israel as a whole but does *not necessarily* include every individual member.[110] This meaning of πᾶς Ἰσραήλ is found in the LXX and on *linguis-*

---

[108] Danby, *Mishnah*, p. 397. Danby's translation "All Israelites" is misleading. The Hebrew is כָּל־יִשְׂרָאֵל, i.e., "All Israel". Note that the words כל ישראל יש להם חלק לעולם הבא together with the quotation from Is. 60.21 are missing from the Kaufmann Manuscript (G. Beer (ed.), *Faksimile-Ausgabe des Mischna-codex Kaufmann A50*, Den Haag: Martinus Mijhoff 1929, p. 302-3) and the manuscript preserved in the University Library of Cambridge, Add. 470.1 (W.H. Lowe (ed.), *The Mishnah on which the Palestinian Talmud Rests*, Cambridge: CUP 1883, p. 128a). For a summary of the textual variants, see S. Krauss (ed.), *Die Mischna: Text, Übersetzung und ausführliche Erklärung: Sanhedrin, Makkot*, Gießen: Verlag von Alfred Töpelmann 1933, and for a helpful discussion of Sanh. 10.1, see Sjöberg, *Gott und die Sünder*, pp. 117-24.

[109] Danby, *Mishnah*, p. 397.

[110] E.g. T. Zahn, *Der Brief des Paulus an die Römer* (KzNT 6), Leipzig: A. Deichertsche Verlagsbuchhandlung ³1925, p. 524; Barrett, *Romans*, p. 206; Käsemann, *Römer*, p. 300; Cranfield, *Romans*, 2:577; Wilckens, *Römer*, 2:255-56; L. Goppelt, "Israel und die Kirche, heute und bei Paulus", in *Christologie und Ethik: Aufsätze zum Neuen Testament*, Göttingen: Vandenhoeck & Ruprecht 1968, 185 (165-89).

tic grounds, this solution is certainly possible. However, on *theological* grounds, there are strong reasons for believing *every* Jew will be saved, and so solution 3, a special case of solution 4, is to be preferred. In view of Rom. 11.29 and Paul's general view of perseverance in Romans,[111] it seems unthinkable that an Israelite could be excluded from final salvation. Paul's theology of "staying in" is very much different to that of m. Sanh. 10.1: for Paul, "staying in" was by faith (Rom. 11.20); for Judaism, "staying in" was by works.

Paul would seem to be using πᾶς Ἰσραήλ σωθήσεται ("all Israel will be saved") in contrast to τὸ ὑπόλειμμα σωθήσεται ("the remnant will be saved", Rom. 9.27, where Is. 10.22 is cited). Such contrasting pictures of Israel's salvation have perplexed some to such an extent that they have suggested that 11.25-27 is an interpolation[112] or that there is in Rom. 9-11 a plain contradiction.[113] Others have tried to smooth over the seeming contradiction.[114] Plag's suggestion that Rom. 11.25-27 is an interpolation because the content is at variance with the rest of Rom. 11 does not convince me. On the basis of textual considerations, there is no hint of an interpolation. Further, the salvation of "all Israel" (πᾶς Ἰσραήλ) is suggested earlier in Rom. 11.12 (τὸ πλήρωμα ("the fulness") of Israel), 11.15 (ἡ πρόσλημψις ("the receiving") of Israel), and 11.23-24 (God has the power to graft in the broken-off branches). There is, if we judge Paul's argument by modern western standards (as Bultmann did), a contradiction between Rom. 9 and 11. But Paul was not writing systematic theology. He is not setting out a careful static doctrine of the salvation of Israel. Rather he is telling a story about Israel, telling a history of salvation. Paul stood firmly in the traditions of the Old Testament and of the Pharisees.[115] However much he may have reacted against some of these traditions after his conversion, certain traditions continued to shape his thinking. The Song of Moses (Dt.

---

[111] This is discussed in detail in chapter 7 below.

[112] See C. Plag, *Israels Wege zum Heil: Eine Untersuchung zu Römer 9 bis 11* (AzTh 1.40), Stuttgart: Calwer Verlag 1969, pp. 41, 45.

[113] See, e.g., R. Bultmann, "Geschichte und Eschatologie im Neuen Testament", in *Glauben und Verstehen: Gesammelte Aufsätze, Bd 3*, Tübingen: J.C.B. Mohr (Paul Siebeck) ²1962, (¹1960), 101 (91-106); Dinkler, "Prädestination", 252.

[114] See, for example, those who take πᾶς Ἰσραήλ in 11.26 to refer to a remnant of Israel or the Church of Jews and Gentiles.

[115] See chapter 1 above.

32.1-43) was a decisive influence on Paul's consideration of Israel's role in God's plan for the world.[116] This Song influenced Paul in his thinking about the election and salvation of Israel and salvation of the Gentiles. This Song shows exactly these "contradictions" that are seen in Rom. 9-11: it speaks of God's judgement on a disobedient Israel with the salvation of a remnant *and* of the salvation of Israel as a whole.[117]

Therefore, I take Paul's statement in Rom. 11.26a to mean that "all Israel" (including every single member) will be saved. This raises the question of who is a member of Israel and I shall return to this question in chapter 10 below.

I shall argue below that this salvation takes place at the parousia, but for now I raise the question whether Paul understood πᾶς Ἰσραήλ to refer to every Jew alive at the time of the parousia or whether it referred to every Jew from every age. In other words, did he understand πᾶς Ἰσραήλ synchronically or diachronically? I have mentioned above the contradiction between Rom. 9.6-29 and 11.1-32. Dinkler has argued that this contradiction can be mollified if πᾶς Ἰσραήλ is understood synchronically (although he does not use this term). He argues that the phrase "all Israel will be saved" could refer just to only those Jews alive at the end of time and not to the whole people throughout history.[118]

Another factor in favour of a synchronic interpretation is that in the LXX πᾶς Ἰσραήλ is always used synchronically, and only on one occasion is the Hebrew equivalent possibly used diachronically.[119] However, a number of

---

[116] See the detailed discussion in Bell, *Provoked to Jealousy*, chapter 7.

[117] See, for example, Dt. 32.23-24a, which speaks of the destruction of Israel: "I will heap evils upon Israel; I will spend my arrows upon them; they shall be wasted with hunger and devoured with burning heat and poisonous pestilence . . ." Then, in 32.36, we have a completely different picture: "For the LORD will vindicate his people and have compassion on his servants . . ." Attempts to harmonize Rom. 11.26 (salvation of "all Israel") with Rom. 9.27 (salvation of a remnant) are to be rejected and impoverish the dynamic nature of the text. Such a harmonisation is given by F. Refoulé, *"...et ainsi tout Israël sera sauvé": Romains 11,25-32* (LD 117), Paris: Les éditions du Cerf 1984. As a result of his exegesis he writes (p. 143): "La contradiction majeure: 'C'est le Reste qui sera sauvé' et 'Tout Israël sera sauvé' disparait, puisque tout Israël est identique au Reste".

[118] Dinkler, "Prädestination", 252.

[119] Mal. 3.22 (MT), mentioned by Hofius, "Evangelium und Israel", 194. The LXX diverges considerably from the MT here, and the phrase πᾶς Ἰσραήλ is not used.

important factors support a diachronic understanding of "all Israel". First, there are a number of Jewish texts where "all Israel" is used diachronically in relation to Israel's salvation:

1. m. Sanh. 10.1: "All Israel (כל ישראל) has a share in the world to come . . .";
2. Test. Ben. 10.11: "If ye therefore, my children, walk in holiness according to the commandments of the Lord, ye shall again dwell securely with me, and all Israel shall be gathered unto the Lord" (καὶ συναχθήσεται πρὸς Κύριον πᾶς Ἰσραήλ).[120]
3. Midr. Ps. 21: "All Israel (כל ישראל) will be taught precepts of Torah by the Holy One Himself".[121]
4. Leq. t. Num. 24.17 (103a): ". . . in our days and in the days of all Israel (כל ישראל)".[122]
5. Targ. Yer. II to Ex. 12.42 ("The Song of the Four Nights"), which begins: "A night of vigil: It is a night that is preserved and prepared for salvation before the Lord (ליל נטיר ומזומן לפורקנ הוא קדם יי), when the Israelites went forth redeemed from the land of Egypt". The four nights are then described and reach a climax in the fourth when "Moses will go forth from the midst of the wilderness and the King Messiah, from the midst of Rome". "This is the Passover night before the Lord (ליל פיסחא קודם יי); it is preserved and prepared for all the sons of Israel, according to their generations (נטיר ומזומן לכל בני ישראל לדריהון)".[123]

Secondly, if the gifts and call of God are irrevocable (Rom. 11.29), it would seem natural to take πᾶς Ἰσραήλ in 11.26 as diachronic. As we shall shortly see, Rom. 11.26-27 suggests that Israelites from every age will believe in the Christ when they see him coming again in his glory.

Having declared that "all Israel will be saved" Paul gives information about *how* "all Israel will be saved" and *when* she will be saved. He does this by quoting from Is. 59.20-21 and Is. 27.9:

---

[120] Charles, *APOT*, 2:360. Test. Ben. 10.10 is also of interest: "And He shall convict Israel through the chosen (ones of the (texts c,ß,S¹)) Gentiles . . ." (*APOT*, 2:359). Cf. Rom. 10.19. This appears in what is most likely a Christian interpolation.

[121] Hebrew in S. Buber (ed.), *Midrash Tehillim*, Jerusalem 1966 (repr.), (¹1891, Wilna), p. 177.

[122] Hebrew in A.M. Katzenellenbogen von Padua (ed.), *Leqach tob to Leviticus - Deuteronomy*, Wilna 1880, p. 257.

[123] The Aramaic can be found in M.L. Klein (ed.), *The Fragment Targums of the Pentateuch According to their Extant Sources* (AnBib 76), 2 vols, Rome: Biblical Institute Press 1980, 1:167. I have altered Klein's translation, which can be found in *Fragment Targums*, 2:126. Note the inclusio in this section (נטיר ומזומן).

The deliverer will come from Zion,
he will turn away ungodliness from Jacob,
and this is my covenant
when I take away their sins.

The first three lines are taken from Is. 59.20-21 and the last line from Is. 27.9. One question which is crucial for the Christological (or non-Christological) understanding of this passage is the reference of ὁ ῥυόμενος ("the deliverer"). Some have taken this to refer to God as the deliverer.[124] However, the reference is almost certainly to Christ[125] and not God for the following reasons.

1. In 1 Thes. 1.10, "the deliverer" (ὁ ῥυόμενος) is used for Christ at his parousia.[126]

2. The expression ἐκ Σιών[127] would make good sense if ῥυόμενος referred to Christ and less sense if it referred to God.[128]

3. The change from the third person ἥξει ἐκ Σιὼν ὁ ῥυόμενος ("The deliverer will come from Zion"), to the first person καὶ αὕτη αὐτοῖς ἡ παρ᾽ ἐμοῦ διαθήκη ("when I take away their sins") shows that Paul does not take God to be ὁ ῥυόμενος.

4. Is. 59.20 was used in a messianic sense in Rabbinic tradition.[129]

Paul in 11.26-27 therefore refers to Israel's salvation and deliverance which takes place at the parousia of Christ.[130] He speaks of the salvation in 11.26a

---

[124] L. Gaston, *Paul and the Torah*, Vancouver: University of British Columbia Press, 1987, p. 143.

[125] See, e.g., Kuss, *Römerbrief*, 3:816; Sanday and Headlam, *Romans*, p. 337; D. Zeller, *Juden und Heiden in der Mission des Paulus: Studien zum Römerbrief* (FzB 8), Stuttgart: Verlag Katholisches Bibelwerk ²1976, (¹1973), p. 259.

[126] See below for further discussion of 1 Thes.1.10.

[127] Whereas Paul has ἐκ Σιών, the MT has לְצִיּוֹן, and the LXX ἕνεκεν Σιών (Paul has most likely been influenced by Ps. 49.2: ἐκ Σιων ἡ εὐπρέπεια τῆς ὡραιότητος αὐτοῦ, ὁ θεὸς ἐμφανῶς ἥξει).

[128] M. Theobald, *Die überströmende Gnade: Studien zu einem paulinischen Motivfeld* (FzB 22), Würzburg: Echter Verlag 1982, p. 165 n. 203. Dt. 33.2 does speak of Yahweh coming from Sinai. But such a usage (e.g. God coming from Sinai, Zion etc) seems non-Pauline.

[129] See b. Sanh. 98a, quoted in Billerbeck, *Kommentar*, 4.2:981.

[130] For two other views, see Luz, *Geschichtsverständnis*, p. 295, who concludes that Paul "an das Christusgeschehen als ganzes denkt", and Wright, *Messiah*, pp. 205-8, who argues that Paul does not refer to the parousia but to the first coming and thinks it better "to see the passage as *inaugurated* eschatology" (p. 207, Wright's emphasis; see also

and the deliverance in 26b. Note that the verb ῥύεσθαι is not as common as σῴζειν but when used it refers to being rescued from something.[131] So in 1 Thes. 1.10 Christ rescues us from ἐκ τῆς ὀργῆς τῆς ἐρχομένης. In Rom. 7.24 there is a deliverance ἐκ τοῦ σώματος τοῦ θανάτου τούτου. Cf. Col. 1.13, where there is a deliverance ἐκ τῆς ἐξουσίας τοῦ σκότους. In Rom. 11.26b I assume Paul has in mind a deliverance from ungodliness and sins in view of v. 27 (although one must bear in mind that Paul is to some extent constrained by his quotation from the Old Testament).

If Paul does have in mind a salvation and deliverance of Israel at the parousia, he certainly does not envisage a situation whereby after the fulness of the Gentiles has come in, the gospel is preached to Israel, and Israel comes to believe in Christ. But it is equally mistaken to believe that Paul viewed the salvation of Israel taking place independently of faith in Christ.[132] Israel will not be saved independently of the gospel and independently of faith in Christ. Salvation for Israel, as for Gentiles, is through faith.[133] This is shown clearly by 11.23: "if they do not persist in their unbelief, they will be grafted in" (ἐὰν μὴ ἐπιμένωσιν τῇ ἀπιστίᾳ, ἐγκεντρισθήσονται).[134] Faith (πίστις) and salvation (σωτηρία) in Romans are inextricably intertwined.[135] This is made absolutely clear at the begin-

---

Wright, *Climax*, pp. 250-51). Fitzmyer, *Romans*, p. 625, also argues against a reference to the parousia. He points out that although the verb ῥύεσθαι is used in 1 Thes. 1.10 for Christ at his parousia, the verb is used more generically in Rom. 15.31 and 2 Cor. 1.10 (for God) and in Rom. 7.24 (for Christ). But is it not significant that the same participle form occurs in both 1 Thes. 1.10 and Rom. 11.26?

[131] Wanamaker, *Thessalonians*, p. 88.

[132] Those who argue for a "special way" ("Sonderweg") of salvation for Israel include Schmidt, *Judenfrage*, p. 33; Mußner, "Ganz Israel", 250-51 and *Traktat*, p. 60; B. Klappert, "Traktat für Israel (Römer 9-11)", in M. Stöhr (ed.), *Jüdische Existenz und die Erneuerung der christlichen Theologie: Versuch der Bilanz des christlich-jüdischen Dialogs für die Systematische Theologie* (ACJD 11), München: Chr. Kaiser Verlag 1981, 90 (58-137).

[133] Faith, it should be noted, is not the condition for salvation but the mode of salvation: i.e., salvation is not *propter fidem* but *per fidem*. See Hofius, "Wort Gottes", 172-73.

[134] F. Hahn, "Zum Verständnis von Römer 11.26a: '... und so wird ganz Israel gerettet werden'", in M.D. Hooker and S.G. Wilson (ed.), *Paul and Paulinism: Essays in honour of C.K. Barrett*, London: SPCK 1982, 228 (221-34). I return to this verse below in relation to questions of "believing" and "seeing".

[135] D. Sänger, "Rettung der Heiden und Erwählung Israels", *KuD* 32 (1986) 117 (99-119).

ning of Romans in 1.16-17. As Theobald argues, "die Selbst-Bindung Gottes im Evangelium ausschließlich an die πίστις" is in fact "der '*strittige* Punkt' der *propositio*" (i.e. of Rom. 1.16-17).[136] This can be seen from the three fold use of πίστις /πιστεύειν in each of the clauses in 1.16-17.[137]

Israel must come to faith in Christ in order to be saved.[138] How then does Israel come to faith? Israel comes to faith through the gospel, which she receives from the coming Christ. In encountering the coming Christ, Israel encounters the gospel. This gospel is not identical with the apostolic preaching. This is a point I made earlier in considering 1 Thes. 2.13.[139] As Käsemann comments on Rom. 1.16: "The gospel is more than the message actualized in the church. It is God's declaration of salvation to the world, which is outside human control, which is independent even of the church and its ministers, and which constantly becomes a reality itself in proclamation in the power of the Spirit".[140]

It would seem therefore that Israel comes to faith by receiving the gospel. Some, however, have objected to this. Moltmann makes a distinction between "Glauben" and "Schauen". So he writes that Paul directs his hope for his people:

---

[136] M. Theobald, "Der 'strittige Punkt' (Rhet. a. Her. I,26) im Diskurs des Römerbriefs: Die propositio 1,16f und das Mysterium der Errettung ganz Israels", in *Studien zum Römerbrief* (WUNT 136), Tübingen: J.C.B. Mohr (Paul Siebeck) 2001, 292 (278-323).

[137] Appealing to A. Fridrichsen, "Aus Glauben zu Glauben: Röm 1,17" (*ConNeo* 12), Lund: Gleerup 1948, 54, he argues that ἐκ πίστεως εἰς πίστιν is a semitic usage (cf. Jer. 9.2: ἐκ κακῶν εἰς κακά; Ps 83.8: ἐκ δυνάμεως εἰς δύναμιν) and quotes from H. Schlier, *Der Römerbrief* (HThKNT 6), Freiburg/Basel/Wien: Herder 1977, p. 45: "das Geschehen der Gerechtigkeit Gottes [ereignet] sich im Evangelium dort, wo der Glaube Anfang und Ende ist".

[138] Hahn, "Verständnis", 228. G. Klein, "'Christlicher Antijudaismus': Bemerkungen zu einem semantischen Einschüchterungsversuch", *ZThK* 79 (1982) 450 (411-50), is in agreement with Hahn. See also E. Gräßer, "Zwei Heilswege? Zum theologischen Verhältnis von Israel und Kirche", in P.-G. Müller and W. Stenger (ed.), *Kontinuität und Einheit: Für Franz Mußner*, Freiburg/Basel/Wien: Herder 1981, 427 (411-29), who writes that in view of the context, there can be no doubt "that the complete conversion of Israel is expected" ("daß die *Gesamtbekehrung* Israels erwartet wird" (Gräßer's emphasis)).

[139] See chapter 2 section 4.2 above.

[140] Käsemann, *Romans*, p. 22 (*Römer*, p. 19).

. . . auf den in sichtbarer Herrlichkeit kommenden Erlöser 'aus Zion'. Von ihm erwartet er keine Bekehrung der Juden und daß sie zum christlichen Glauben kommen, sondern Israels Erlösung und Auferweckung von den Toten: 'Was wird ihre Annahme anderes sein als Leben aus den Toten?' (11,15). Die Erlösung Israels durch das Schauen der Herrlichkeit geschieht nicht nur der letzten überlebenden Generation, sondern quer durch die Zeiten der Geschichte allen Toten zugleich 'in einem Augenblick'.[141]

This distinction between "believing" and "seeing", made earlier by Peter von der Osten-Sacken,[142] is made on the basis of 2 Cor. 5.7. This is often translated as "for we walk by faith, not by sight" (NRSV).[143] This verse, however, as Theobald argues, is not a piece of dogma but is rather "eine kontextuell bedingte Behauptung einer Opposition, die hier anti-enthusiastisch den eschatologischen Vorbehalt anbringen will".[144] In fact, as Wolff argues, εἶδος cannot be translated by the active "Schauen". Rather, Paul is saying that we walk by faith, not by what one is able to see (i.e. the coming new bodily existence).[145] It is true that Paul makes a distinction in 1 Cor. 13 between "seeing in a glass darkly" and "seeing from face to face" but this is in respect of prophecy, speaking in tongues and knowledge. It is not in respect to faith.[146] Faith, together with hope and love remains (1 Cor. 13.13).

Israel therefore comes to faith in Christ. Rom. 11.23 has been interpreted to mean that Israel's unbelief comes to an end not because they come to believe but because they come to see.[147] This opposition between seeing and

---

[141] J. Moltmann, *Der Weg Jesu Christi: Christologie in messianischen Dimensionen*, München: Chr. Kaiser Verlag 1989, p. 53.

[142] See P. von der Osten-Sacken, "Antijudaismus um Christi willen?", in *Evangelium und Tora. Aufsätze zu Paulus* (ThBü 77), München 1987, 245 (239-55).

[143] Cf. Luther, *Die gantze Heilige Schrift Deudsch (Wittenberg 1945)*: "Denn wir wandeln im glauben vnd nicht im schawen".

[144] Theobald, "Der 'strittige Punkt'", 309.

[145] See Wolff, *Der zweite Brief des Paulus an die Korinther*, pp. 112-13. "εἶδος bezeichnet die 'äußere Erscheinung, sichtbare Gestalt' (vgl. Luk. 3,22; 9,29; Joh. 5,37); für den aktiven Sinn 'Schauen' gibt es keine eindeutigen Belege. Mit εἶδος ist die kommende neue Leiblichkeit gemeint".

[146] Regarding faith, it may be necessary to make a distinction between the faith to move mountains (13.2) and what I understand as justifying faith (13.13).

[147] See Keller, *Gottes Treue – Israels Heil*, pp. 210-11: "Die Volloffenbarung bei der Parusie Christi wird den Unglauben der Juden beseitigen, aber sie nicht mehr zum Glauben bringen, sondern zur Schau führen".

believing is, as I have argued, untenable, and Paul clearly thinks that just as he came to "faith", so "all Israel" will come to faith. This will happen for Israel through a direct meeting with the risen Christ, just as it did for Paul. Rom. 11.1 then takes on a new meaning: God has by no means cast off his people, for Paul himself is also an Israelite, a descendant of Abraham, a member of the tribe of Benjamin.[148] Paul, like Israel, had been hardened in unbelief and like Israel had a zeal for God but not according to knowledge (Rom. 10.2). Yet he as a member of the chosen people of God was the object of God's grace. And it is to the theme of God's irrevocable promises to his people Israel that I now turn.

---

[148] Cf. Hofius, "Evangelium und Israel", 198.

Chapter 7

Israel and the Irrevocable Call of God

1. Romans 11.1-7

In considering the irrevocable call of God I first return to the beginning of Romans 11 where Paul asks: " . . . has God rejected his people?" He responds: "By no means! I myself am an Israelite, a descendant of Abraham, a member of the tribe of Benjamin" (Rom. 11.1). Paul's logic is that God cannot have rejected his people since Paul himself is an Israelite, a descendant of Abraham, "a full-blooded Jew".[1] Luther believes that Paul is arguing *a minori ad maius*: "For if God had cast away his people, then above all he would have cast away the apostle Paul who fought against him with all his strength".[2] Then Paul writes in 11.2a: "God has not rejected his people whom he foreknew". Paul's language in v. 2aα οὐκ ἀπώσατο ὁ θεὸς τὸν λαὸν αὐτοῦ reflects 1 Sam 12.22 and Ps. 93.14 LXX.[3] Both these Septuagintal texts have interesting contexts which relate them to Paul's thought and language in Romans 9-11.[4] So in 1 Sam. 12.23, Samuel says "far be it from me that I should sin against the LORD by ceasing to pray for you" (cf.

---

[1] Lenski, *Romans*, p. 678.

[2] Luther, *Romans*, p. 305.

[3] Both these Old Testament texts have ὅτι οὐκ ἀπώσεται κύριος τὸν λαὸν αὐτοῦ. Ps. 93.14b continues: καὶ τὴν κληρονομίαν αὐτοῦ οὐκ ἐγκαταλείψει. Moo, *Romans*, p. 674 n. 16, believes that Paul's allusion to these texts accounts for his use of the verb ἀπωθέω which is unusual in the New Testament. Paul has changed the future ἀπώσεται to an aorist ἀπώσατο, making his statement more definitive. He has changed κύριος to θεός since he has God rather than Christ in mind. Cf. Rom. 3.30, where, in his allusion to the shema, Paul has changed κύριος to θεός.

[4] See R.B. Hays, *Echoes of Scripture in the Letters of Paul*, New Haven/London: Yale University Press 1989, pp. 69-70.

Rom. 9.3; 10.1).[5] Then Ps. 93.14 has a number of words significant for
Paul's argument.[6]

Turning to Rom. 11.2bβ "whom he foreknew" (ὃν προέγνω), there are
two issues to clarify. The first is the meaning of "foreknow" (προγινώσκω).
This verb occurs earlier in Rom. 8.29a: "For those whom he foreknew he
also predestined to be conformed to the image of his Son . . . ". Some in the
Arminian tradition have taken this foreknowing to mean that God saw in
advance who would become a Christian.[7] However, in view of the Old
Testament use of "to know" (Gen. 18.19; Jer. 1.5; Am. 3.2) and Paul's own
use of "know" (e.g. Gal. 4.9) Paul is most likely referring to God's electing
grace both in Rom. 8.29 and 11.2.[8] The second issue to clarify in 11.2 is
whether the clause "whom he foreknew" has a restrictive sense, limiting the

---

[5] Hays, *Echoes*, p. 69.

[6] See Hays, *Echoes*, p. 69-70. Ps. 93.14-15: ὅτι οὐκ ἀπώσεται κύριος τὸν λαὸν
αὐτοῦ καὶ τὴν κληρονομίαν αὐτοῦ οὐκ ἐγκαταλείψει, 15 ἕως οὗ δικαιοσύνη ἐπιστρέψῃ
εἰς κρίσιν καὶ ἐχόμενοι αὐτῆς πάντες οἱ εὐθεῖς τῇ καρδίᾳ. διάψαλμα. Hays points to the
verb ἐγκαταλείπω (v. 14) which is used in Rom. 9.29 (Is. 1.9) and the related words
καταλείπω (used in Rom. 11.4) and λεῖμμα (used in 11.5). Clearly δικαιοσύνη is a central word for Paul. The sense of Ps. 93.15 LXX is not entirely clear but however it is
understood, it is not really conducive to Paul's theology: "until righteousness turn to
judgement, and all the upright in heart shall follow it". The MT is much more interesting
כִּי־עַד־צֶדֶק יָשׁוּב מִשְׁפָּט וְאַחֲרָיו כָּל־יִשְׁרֵי־לֵב׃. This can be translated: "For judgement turns to
righteousness, and all the upright in heart will follow it". However, A. Weiser, *The
Psalms* (OTL) ET, London: SCM 1962, p. 622, although giving such a literal translation
of v. 15a in his footnote, translates it in the main text as: "For justice will return to the
righteous". Most commentators take v. 15a in this sense. So H.-J. Kraus, *Psalms 60-
150: A Continental Commentary*, Minneapolis: Fortress Press 1993, p. 238, following
Symmachus and the Syriac, reads צדיק (see also the apparatus in *BHS*).

[7] See J.A. Beet, *A Commentary on St. Paul's Epistle to the Romans*, London: Hodder
and Stoughton [10]1902, p. 243, who supports the meaning "to know beforehand". He
writes: "In the everlasting past, we, our circumstances, disposition, and conduct, stood
before the mind of God". On "foreordained" or "predestined" he writes (p. 244): "A
parent who, before his child is old enough for a trade, chooses one for him predestines
the boy (sic). He marks out beforehand a path in which he would have him go. This purpose, whether accomplished or not, is predestination". See also A. Barnes, *Notes on the
New Testament Vol. IV.—Romans*, London: Blackie & Son 1842, p. 191, and the
Patristic view that Paul is concerned with foreknowing "future moral fitness" (referred to
in Cranfield, *Romans*, 2:431 n. 1).

[8] Calvin, *Institutes* 3.22.8, points to Augustine's change in mind on this issue of
"foreknowledge".

reference of "his people" to those within Israel whom he has elected.[9] In favour of such a position is that in 11.4-7 Paul does in fact refer to the elect remnant and the rest who were hardened. However, there is the problem that in 11.1a "his people" refers to the whole of Israel and in 10.21 Paul writes "But of Israel he says, 'All day long I have held out my hands to a disobedient and contrary people'". This suggests that Paul is referring to the whole of Israel whether they believe in Christ or not.[10]

Paul continues in vv.2b-6:

Do you not know what the scripture says of Eli'jah, how he pleads with God against Israel? 3 'Lord, they have killed thy prophets, they have demolished thy altars, and I alone am left, and they seek my life'. 4 But what is God's reply to him? 'I have kept for myself seven thousand men who have not bowed the knee to Ba'al'. 5 So too at the present time there is a remnant, chosen by grace. 6 But if it is by grace, it is no longer on the basis of works; otherwise grace would no longer be grace.

Elijah was zealous for the Lord and despaired of the Israel he was facing. Paul was also zealous for God (his Christian zeal being quite different to his zeal as a Pharisee) and no doubt he also despaired of Israel (Rom. 9.1-3). But here he introduces a note of hope. For just as in Elijah's day there were 7000 who had not bowed down to Baal,[11] so in Paul's day there was the remnant, chosen by grace. However, this remnant anticipates a much greater salvation.

2. Romans 11.16

In Rom. 11.16 Paul argues "If the dough offered as first fruits is holy, so is the whole lump; and if the root is holy, so are the branches". In v. 16a he alludes to the offering of a cake from the first of the dough in Num. 15.17-21 LXX:

---

[9] Calvin, *Romans*, p. 239.

[10] See Cranfield, *Romans*, 2:545.

[11] The number 7000 is clearly of symbolic significance. The number cannot be deduced from the Elijah narrative in 1 Kings. In the Bible the number seven and its multiples refers to perfection and completeness (cf. K.H. Rengstorf, ἑπτά κτλ, *TDNT* 2:627-35).

The Lord said to Moses, 'Say to the sons of Israel, and you shall say to them: When you enter the land into which I bring you 19 and it will come to pass when you eat of the bread of the land, you shall present an offering to the LORD. 20 Of the first of your dough you shall present a cake as an offering (ἀπαρχὴν φυράματος ὑμῶν ἄρτον ἀφαίρεμα ἀφοριεῖτε αὐτό); as an offering from the threshing floor, so shall you present it. 21 Of the first of your dough (ἀπαρχὴν φυράματος ὑμῶν) you shall give to the LORD an offering throughout your generations.

Both the LXX and MT are obscure at certain points here. The LXX renders the Hebrew רֵאשִׁית ("first") with ἀπαρχή which has a sacrificial connotation and is usually translated "first fruits". The obscure עֲרִיסָה is translated by the RSV as "coarse meal" but the NEB renders the term as "dough", corresponding to φύραμα in the LXX. But in any event it is clear in the MT that because the offering was presented as a חַלָּה ("cake") "some product of household cookery was here intended".[12] Paul adds to the obscurity of the text by arguing that since the first fruits are holy, so is the whole lump (εἰ δὲ ἡ ἀπαρχὴ ἁγία, καὶ τὸ φύραμα). But his logic is clear: since the first fruits (ἀπαρχή) are holy and consecrated to God, so the whole is. But who are the "first fruits" and the "lump of dough" (φύραμα)? There are three theories.

1. The "first fruits" (ἀπαρχή) refers to Abraham or the patriarchs and the dough to the Jews, a view adopted by many commentators.[13] It is argued that ἡ ῥίζα in 11.16b refers to the patriarchs and that ἀπαρχή and ῥίζα must have the same reference. However, it is by no means compelling that ῥίζα and ἀπαρχή must have the same reference.[14]

2. The "first fruits" (ἀπαρχή) refers to the first converts among the Jews and the "lump of dough" (φύραμα) to Israel as a whole, the πλήρωμα of 11.12. This is a much more natural way to understand the terms, for Paul has shortly before been speaking of a "remnant" (λεῖμμα, 11.5) or "the elect" (ἡ ἐκλογή, 11.7) on the one hand and "the rest" (οἱ λοιποί, 11.7) on the other. The believing Jewish Christians serve to sanctify the unbelieving majority

---

[12] E.W. Davies, *Numbers* (NCB), Grand Rapids: Wm B. Eerdmans 1995, p. 155.

[13] See Chrysostom, *In epistulam ad Romanos*, homily 19 (in *MPG* 60:588 (394-682)), who relates "first fruits" to the patriarchs, the prophets and all the other Old Testament saints. See also Calvin, *Romans*, p. 249; Sanday and Headlam, *Romans*, p. 326; Lagrange, *Romains*, p. 279; Michel, *Römer*, p. 274; Murray, *Romans*, 2:85; Käsemann, *Römer*, p. 294; Schlier, *Römerbrief*, p. 322.

[14] F.F. Bruce, *The Epistle of Paul to the Romans: An Introduction and Commentary* (TNTC), London: IVP 1976 (repr.), (¹1963), p. 217, and Cranfield, *Romans*, 2:564, for example, understand the ἀπαρχή as the believing Jews and the ῥίζα as the patriarchs.

rather as the believing marriage partner sanctifies the unbelieving partner and the children (1 Cor. 7.14). The use of ἀπαρχή to describe the believing Jews would be natural in view of Rom. 16.5 and 1 Cor. 16.15 (cf. 2 Thes. 2.13).

3. A third solution is that "first fruits" (ἀπαρχή) refers to Christ and "lump of dough" (φύραμα) to those in Christ.[15] Such a view is supported by some of the early Fathers[16] and by K. Barth[17] and A.T. Hanson.[18] An argument in favour of this is that Christ is described as the ἀπαρχή in 1 Cor. 15.20, 23. Furthermore, in 1 Cor. 15.20, he is described as the first fruits in the context of resurrection (cf. the idea of resurrection in Rom. 11.15). Paul's argument then, according to this solution, is that if Christ (the first fruits) is holy, then so is the whole lump, i.e., those who are in Christ, Jews and Gentiles.[19] However, this does not seem to fit into the flow of Paul's argument in Rom. 11.11-15.

Of these views solution 2 seems the most natural and fits the flow of Paul's argument. So the first Jewish converts are the first of the harvest; they are an offering to God and they serve to sanctify the whole harvest. However, as Barrett writes, "it is not impossible that behind the Jewish Christians Paul sees the figure of Christ himself, whom he actually describes as the 'first-fruit' in 1 Cor. xv.20".[20] Barrett also mentions the Rabbinic

---

[15] The term φύραμα is used for Christians in 1 Cor. 5.7.

[16] See K.H. Schelkle, *Paulus Lehrer der Väter: Die altkirchliche Auslegung von Römer 1-11*, Düsseldorf: Patmos Verlag ²1959, (¹1956), pp. 394-95. See the quotation, for example, from Gregory of Nyssa (*Contra Eunomium* 3.2.54): "Christus ist die Erstlingsgabe aller, damit er über die Toten und Lebenden herrsche und er durch seine Erstlingsgabe den ganzen Sauerteig heilige".

[17] Barth, *CD*, 2.2:285.

[18] A.T. Hanson, "Christ the First Fruits, Christ the Tree", in *Studies in Paul's Technique and Theology*, London: SPCK 1974, 110-17 (104-25).

[19] An alternative understanding is to argue that the lump refers to Israel alone. If Jesus, the first Jew to rise from the dead, is holy, so then is the whole lump, i.e., Israel. Such a view is found in Wright, *Messiah*, p. 186. However, he has changed his understanding of Rom. 11.16a to solution 2 above (see Wright, "Romans", 683-84).

[20] Barrett, *Romans*, p. 200.

understanding of Adam as the "first-fruit loaf".[21] As Adam was the head of the old humanity, so is Christ the head of the new (Rom. 5.12-21; 1 Cor. 15.21ff., 48-49).

I turn now to Rom. 11.16b: "and if the root is holy, so are the branches" (καὶ εἰ ἡ ῥίζα ἁγία, καὶ οἱ κλάδοι). Those who take Christ as the first fruits also take Christ as the root in 11.16b.[22] A case can certainly be made for this understanding. In the only other place where Paul uses "root" (ῥίζα), the quotation of Is. 11.10 in Rom. 15.12, he refers to Jesus as messiah. In Is. 11.1-10, ῥίζα is used to translate not only שֹׁרֶשׁ ("root") but also גֵּזַע ("stock", "stem").[23] In Is. 53.2, ῥίζα is again used for שֹׁרֶשׁ not only in the LXX but also in Aquila, Symmachus, and Theodotion.[24] It is therefore highly likely that this is what Paul's Greek text would have contained.[25] Paul certainly understood Is. 11.10 in a messianic sense.[26] As Is. 52.13-53.12 was also important for Paul,[27] he may well have understood the reference to ῥίζα in Is. 53.2 also in a messianic sense.[28] The word ῥίζα in Rom. 11.16 was com-

---

[21] See Billerbeck, *Kommentar*, 4:667-68. See also K.H. Rengstorf, "Das Ölbaum-Gleichnis in Röm 11,16f: Versuch einer weiterführenden Deutung", in C.K. Barrett, E. Bammel, W.D. Davies (ed.), *Donum Gentilicium: New Testament Studies in honour of David Daube*, Oxford: Clarendon Press 1978 1978, 128-35 (127-64). Rengstorf goes to the point of arguing that ἀπαρχή refers to Adam. However, it is difficult to see how this would fit Paul's argument in Romans 11.

[22] Also there are those like Wright, "Romans", 684, who do not take Christ as first fruit in 11.16a but nevertheless take Christ as the root in 11.16b.

[23] C. Maurer, ῥίζα κτλ, *TDNT* 6:987 (985-991), suggests that ῥίζα can mean both "remnant" and "possibility of new beginning".

[24] K.F. Euler, *Die Verkündigung vom Leidenden Gottesknecht aus Jes 53 in der Griechischen Bibel*, Stuttgart/Berlin: W. Kohlhammer Verlag 1934, pp. 12, 29, 33, 37.

[25] Hanson, "Christ the First Fruits", 119.

[26] Note also the messianic interpretation of Is. 11.1, 10 in the Targum of Isaiah (Hanson, *Studies*, p. 118). Mauer, ῥίζα, 987, suggests that ἡ ῥίζα τοῦ Ἰεσσαι was considered by the LXX translators as a messianic title. Note also the messianic understanding of ῥίζα in Rev. 5.5 (Jesus is ἡ ῥίζα Δαυίδ) and Rev. 22.16 (Jesus as ἡ ῥίζα καὶ τὸ γένος Δαυίδ).

[27] See Bell, *Provoked to Jealousy*, pp. 89-92.

[28] Cf. W. Zimmerli, in W. Zimmerli and J. Jeremias, παῖς θεοῦ, *TDNT* 5:676 (654-717). Note also the messianic use of ῥίζα in Test. Jud. 24.5-6 (clearly a Christian interpolation):
"Then the sceptre of my kingdom will shine,
And from your root a stem will arise;

monly held to refer to Jesus in the Patristic exegesis.[29] If this is applied to Rom. 11.16b, Jesus' messianic rôle would be stressed. The septuagintal use of ῥίζα for "root" and "stem" would also allow Paul to develop his thinking in Rom. 11.17ff. that Christ was not only the root but also the stem, the stock.

However, I again wonder whether such an interpretation fits the flow of Paul's argument. A more natural reference for the root is the patriarchs, especially Abraham.[30] Texts used to support Abraham as the root are Jub. 16.26,[31] 1 En. 93.8[32] and Philo, *Quis rerum divinarum heres* 279.[33] Further, the verses following 11.16 would suggest that the root is to be taken as Abraham and not as Christ.[34] Paul's point therefore in Rom. 11.16b is that since the patriarchs are "holy" in that God chose them, so are all the branches, i.e. the Jewish people who were descended from the patriarchs. Paul is not emphasizing Abraham's rôle as father of all believers (Jews and Gentiles) as he does in Romans 4. He has the Jewish people primarily in view.

---

6 And in it a rod of righteousness will arise to the nations
to judge and save all who call upon the Lord".
This translation is that of H.W. Hollander and M. de Jonge, *The Testaments of the Twelve Patriarchs: A Commentary* (SVTP 8), Leiden: E.J. Brill 1985, p. 227. They also points to parallels in early Christian literature (e.g. Justin, *Dialogue* 86.4; 87.2, both of which relate Christ to Is. 11.1).

[29] See Clement of Alexandria, *Stromata* 6.1.2.4; 6.15.117.1-2; 6.15.120.1; Cyril of Jerusalem, *Catecheses mystagogicae* 2. Origen in his *Commentarius in ep. ad Romanos* 8.11 (*MPG* 14:1193) writes: *Radicem vero hanc alii Abraham nominant, alii Seth, alii aliquem unum ex patribus bene meritis ponunt. Ego autem radicem aliam quae sancta sit, et sanctas primitias nescio nisi Dominum nostrum Jesum Christum.*

[30] Most commentators take this view. See, for example, Wilckens, *Römer*, 2:246; Cranfield, *Romans*, 2:565; Rengstorf, "Ölbaum", 138ff.

[31] "And he [Abraham] blessed his Creator who created him in his generation because by his will he created him for he knew and he perceived that from him there would be a righteous planting for eternal generations" (Wintermute, *OTP*, 2:89). On the term "righteous planting" ("plant of righteousness", R.H. Charles, *APOT*, 2:38), see also 1 En. 10.16; 84.6.

[32] ". . . and therein the whole clan of the chosen root shall be dispersed" (E. Isaac, *OTP*, 1:74). In view of the context, especially 93.5, 10, the root is most likely Abraham.

[33] "Surely he (Abraham) is indeed the founder of the nation and the race, since from him as root sprung the young plant called Israel . . ." (*Philo* (LCL), 4:427).

[34] See chapter 8 section 2 below for a further discussion of the "olive tree parable", Rom. 11.17-24.

3. Romans 11.26b-27

I argued in the last chapter that Paul asserts the salvation of "all Israel" in Rom. 11.26a, a salvation which takes place at the parousia. But what is one to make of the passage 11.26b-27 in regard to God's call of Israel?

The deliverer will come from Zion,
he will turn away ungodliness from Jacob,
27 and this is my covenant for them
when I take away their sins.

By διαθήκη Paul probably means by metonymy the fulfilment.[35] Paul therefore is speaking of Israel's election and the fulfilment of this election. As Theobald puts it: "Nicht an eine *neue* Setzung, die eine *alte* ablöst, sondern an die 'Setzung' der Erwählung ist gedacht, die Gott Israel in seinen Vätern einst hat zuteil werden lassen".[36] Therefore this covenant is not an added covenant to those made earlier with Israel. It is the fulfilment of the covenant made with Abraham.

Theobald also makes the point that although there is a certain affinity between the covenant made with Abraham in Romans 4 and that of 11.27, they are not simply exchangable. For the promise of Romans 4 regards the universal incorporation of Gentiles in God's blessing. However, in 11.27 the stress is on God's faithfulness to the people of Israel. So Paul writes with a *dativus commodi*: "my covenant *for them* (αὐτοῖς)".[37]

4. Romans 11.28-29

We saw in the last chapter that Paul argues for the salvation of "all Israel". In turning now to Rom. 11.28-29 it will become clear why Paul felt compelled to come to this remarkable conclusion. Although there is an asyndeton between 11.25-27 and 11.28, the passage 11.28-32 is linked with

---

[35] See Hofius, "Evangelium und Israel", 197 n. 86: "Im Sinne des Paulus meint διαθήκη 11,27 die Abraham gegebene 'Bundeszusage', und das Wort steht metonymisch für deren *Erfüllung* . . ."

[36] Theobald, "Der 'strittige Punkt'", 319-20.

[37] Theobald, "Der 'strittige Punkt'", 320.

that which precedes.[38] Rom. 11.28 consists of two contrasting parallel statements:

κατὰ μὲν τὸ εὐαγγέλιον ἐχθροὶ δι' ὑμᾶς,
κατὰ δὲ τὴν ἐκλογὴν ἀγαπητοὶ διὰ τοὺς πατέρας·

Jeremias correctly points out that there is an incongruence in the use of the prepositions κατά and διά.[39] A suitable translation would be:

As regards the progress of the gospel
they (i.e. Israel) are enemies for your sake,
but on the basis of election
they are beloved because of the patriarchs.[40]

Israelites are enemies of God so that the gospel goes to the Gentiles.[41] But in what sense are Israelites enemies of God? Cranfield and Lohse argue that in view of the carefully worked out parallelism between the two halves of the verse, "enemies" (ἐχθροί) should be understood in a passive sense in correspondence with "beloved" (ἀγαπητοί).[42] However, the two halves are not perfectly parallel anyway (as has been noted in Paul's use of the prepositions κατά and διά) and the context could just as well suggest an active meaning as in the above translation.[43]

---

[38] Compare the asyndeton between Rom. 9.33 and 10.1. Nevertheless, the argument in 10.1ff. continues that of 9.30-33. On the asyndeton, see *BDF* § 463.

[39] Jeremias, "Beobachtungen", 202: "κατὰ μὲν τὸ εὐαγγέλιον = κατά zur Angabe der Norm 'hinsichtlich ihrer Einstellung gegenüber dem Evangelium'/κατὰ δὲ τὴν ἐκλογήν = κατά mit kausaler Nuance 'auf Grund ihrer Erwählung', sowie δι' ὑμᾶς = διά mit finaler Nuance/διὰ τοὺς πατέρας = διά mit kausaler Nuance".

[40] Cf. the translation of Jeremias, "Beobachtungen", 202: "hinsichtlich ihrer Einstellung gegenüber dem Evangelium sind sie Feinde um euretwillen, auf Grund ihrer Erwählung sind sie (Gott-) Geliebte um der Väter willen".

[41] Dinkler, "Prädestination", 268, writes: "Die Erwählung hat nicht einen Zweck in sich selbst, im positiv Betroffenen, sondern geschieht 'für andere'!"

[42] Cranfield, *Romans*, 2:580; Lohse, *Römer*, p. 322.

[43] The "passive idea" that Israel is rejected by God so that salvation comes to the Gentiles is of course not lacking in Romans 11. But the idea of salvation coming to the Gentiles because of Israel's disobedience is also here in Romans 11 (note 11.30b, 31a as well as 11.11, 12). Note that if a passive meaning is adopted, this is the only place in Paul where God is said to be an enemy of human beings. In all other cases it is human beings who are enemies of God (Rom. 5.8-10a). That is why in the atonement human beings are reconciled to God (2 Cor. 5.19) and not vice versa. See Bell, "Sacrifice and Christology".

Rom. 11.28b then gives the contrasting statement: "but on the basis of election they are beloved because of the patriarchs". Why is Israel beloved for the sake of the patriarchs? The answer is given in Rom. 11.29:

for irrevocable are the gifts and call of God.
ἀμεταμέλητα γὰρ τὰ χαρίσματα καὶ ἡ κλῆσις τοῦ θεοῦ.

God's "gracious gifts" (τὰ χαρίσματα) are most likely the election of and promise to Abraham and his descendants κατὰ χάριν (Rom. 4.4, 16).[44] This promise to Abraham implies not only "salvation" but also land and seed, an argument I will pursue in chapter 10 below. And these gracious gifts together with God's call are "irrevocable" (ἀμεταμέλητα).[45] The irrevocable nature of the gifts and call is stressed by placing the word ἀμεταμέλητα at the beginning of the sentence.[46] In view of the argument in 11.28-29, it is unthinkable that πᾶς Ἰσραήλ in 11.26 refers to the elect of Jews and Gentiles or the remnant of Israel. This assertion that God's gifts and call are irrevocable has enormous implications not only for Israel but also for the Church. In fact I believe one of the difficult questions facing the Christians in Rome was that if God had gone back on his promises to Israel could he not do the same for Christians? The salvation of Israel is therefore a special case of the "perseverance of the saints".[47] It is significant that although Calvin believed πᾶς Ἰσραήλ in 11.26 referred to the Church, he could not escape the significance of Rom. 11.29 (expressed more graphically in the *Institutes* than in his Romans commentary):

Therefore, that they might not be defrauded of their privilege, the gospel had to be announced to them first. For they are, so to speak, like the first-born in God's household. Accordingly, this honor was to be given them until they refused what was offered, and by their ungratefulness caused it to be transferred to the Gentiles. Yet, despite the great obstinacy with which they continue to wage war against the gospel, we must not despise them, while we consider that, for the sake of the promise, God's bless-

---

[44] O. Hofius, "Die Unabänderlichkeit des göttlichen Heilsratschlußes", *ZNW* 64 (1973) 144 (135-45)).

[45] C. Spicq, "ΑΜΕΤΑΜΕΛΗΤΟΣ dans Rom., XI,29", *RB* 67 (1960) 215 (210-19), argues that ἀμεταμέλητα is a juridical term meaning "irrevocable" (see also Spicq, *Theological Lexicon of the New Testament* ET, 3 vols, Peabody: Hendrickson 1994, 1:94).

[46] See Michel, *Römer*, p. 357.

[47] Cf. Müller, *Gottes Volk*, p. 100: "Die Rettung Israels verbürgt der Kirche die Gewißheit, daß ihre κλῆσις und χαρίσματα ἀμεταμέλητα sind".

ing still rests among them. For the apostle indeed testifies that it will never be completely taken way: 'For the gifts and the calling of God are without repentance'".[48]

Also, paragraph four of the declaration *nostra aetate* from the Second Vatican Council asserts that "the Jews still remain most dear to God because of their fathers, for He does not repent of the gifts He makes nor of the calls He issues (cf. Rom. 11:28-29)".[49]

5. Romans 11.30-31

Rom. 11.30-31 takes up 11.28. The structure of these verses is complex and I give first my translation:

For as you (i.e. Gentiles) were disobedient to God
but now have received mercy
because of their (i.e. Israel's) disobedience,
31 so they have now been disobedient
in order that they also may (now) receive mercy
because of the mercy shown to you.

The careful balance between the protasis (v. 30) and the apodosis (v. 31) may be set out as follows:[50]

11.30	11.31
ὑμεῖς	οὗτοι
ποτε	νῦν
ἠπειθήσατε	ἠπείθησαν
νῦν	νῦν
ἠλεήθητε	ἐλεηθῶσιν
τῇ τούτων ἀπειθείᾳ	τῷ ὑμετέρῳ ἐλέει

In v. 30 the dative τῇ τούτων ἀπειθείᾳ can be taken as either a *dativus causae*[51] (Gentiles have received mercy because of Israel's disobedience) or a *dativus instrumentalis*[52] (Gentiles have received mercy through Israel's

---

[48] Calvin, *Institutes* 4.16.14 (J.T. McNeill, (ed.), *Calvin: Institutes of the Christian Religion* (LCC 20-21), 2 vols, Philadelphia: Westminster Press 1960, 2:1337).

[49] W.M. Abbott (ed.), *The Documents of Vatican II*, London/Dublin: Geoffrey Chapman 1966, p. 664.

[50] Cranfield, *Romans*, 2:582.

[51] Jeremias, "Beobachtungen", 203.

[52] Hofius, "Evangelium und Israel", 199.

disobedience). The understanding of the datives in v. 31 is not so clear. For it is disputed whether τῷ ὑμετέρῳ ἐλέει (which I have translated as "because of the mercy shown to you") should be connected to ἠπείθησαν ("they have been disobedient")[53] or ἐλεηθῶσιν ("they may receive mercy").[54] If τῷ ὑμετέρῳ ἐλέει is taken with ἠπείθησαν, a *dativus causae* or a *dativus instrumentalis* (possibilities for v. 30) does not make sense. So Jeremias takes the dative in v. 31 with a final sense: the Israelites were disobedient so that the Gentiles receive mercy.[55] Wilckens takes the dative as a *dativus commodi*: the Israelites are disobedient for the sake of the mercy you receive.[56] But if τῷ ὑμετέρῳ ἐλέει is taken with ἐλεηθῶσιν, both datives can take on an identical or nearly identical meaning, that is, *dativus causae* (because of) or *dativus instrumentalis* (by means of). The fact that the two datives can take similar or identical meanings is not the main advantage of this solution. There are two much stronger reasons for taking τῷ ὑμετέρῳ ἐλέει with ἐλεηθῶσιν. The first regards the structure of 11.30-31. Commenting on the two parallel columns for v. 30 and v. 31 (see above), Cranfield writes:

The correspondence between six elements of the protasis and six elements of the apodosis is so carefully balanced that it is most unlikely that there is not also a correspondence between the two clauses of the protasis and the two clauses of the apodosis. If τῷ ὑμετέρῳ ἐλέει is taken with ἐλεηθῶσιν there is, in fact, an exact correspondence between them - the corresponding elements being equally distributed between the two clauses in both the protasis and apodosis in the form 3-3: 3-3; but, if τῷ ὑμετέρῳ ἐλέει is taken with ἠπείθησαν, the balance is destroyed, and we get an arrangement of 3-3: 4-2. This consideration is by itself, in our judgement, almost certainly decisive.[57]

The second reason regards the whole argument in 11.11-32. The clause of v. 30b νῦν δὲ ἠλεήθητε τῇ τούτων ἀπειθείᾳ looks back to 11.11-12. The

---

[53] E.g., Jeremias, "Beobachtungen", 203; Wilckens, *Römer*, 2:260-61; Hofius, "Evangelium und Israel", 199-200.

[54] E.g., Sanday and Headlam, *Romans*, p. 388; Munck, *Christus und Israel*, p. 105; Cranfield, *Romans*, 2:583-84.

[55] Jeremias, "Beobachtungen", 203: "genauso waren diese (die Israeliten) jetzt ungehorsam, damit Euch (den Heidenchristen) Erbarmen widerführe".

[56] Wilckens, *Römer*, 2:261: "so sind auch sie ungehorsam zugunsten eurer Erbarmung".

[57] Cranfield, *Romans*, 2:584. The ZB also takes τῷ ὑμετέρῳ ἐλέει with ἐλεηθῶσιν: "so sind auch diese jetzt ungehorsam gewesen, damit infolge der Barmherzigkeit gegen euch auch sie Barmherzigkeit erlangen".

Gentiles have been able to receive mercy because Israel has been disobedient. According to my interpretation of τῷ ὑμετέρῳ ἐλέει ἵνα καὶ αὐτοὶ νῦν ἐλεηθῶσιν, Israel now receives mercy because of the mercy shown to the Gentiles. In fact, because τῷ ὑμετέρῳ ἐλέει precedes the ἵνα clause, it is stressed that it is because of or by means of the mercy shown to the *Gentiles* that Israel has received mercy.[58] Paul here clearly looks back to 11.11, 14. The mission to the Gentiles will serve to bring Israel to salvation in that it will provoke Israel to jealousy and prepare for her salvation when she receives the gospel. Paul is also clearly looking back to 11.25-28. For Paul, the salvation of Israel comes through the salvation of the Gentiles. The mission of Paul to the Gentiles is an integral part of the salvation of πᾶς Ἰσραήλ as described in 11.25-27.[59]

This now brings me to the question whether we should read νῦν in 11.31b. There are three readings:

1. now   νῦν: B ℵ D* 1506 pc bo;
2. later   ὕστερον: 33 365 pc sa;
3.   – :   p⁴⁶ A D² F G Ψ M latt sy.

The harder reading is clearly νῦν and, with most commentators, I accept this reading.[60] It is easy to understand why this νῦν was either changed to ὕστερον or left out altogether. However, Barth rightly points out: "The whole passage is controlled by an almost intolerable eschatological tension.

---

[58] Lagrange, *Romains*, p. 287, argues that to take τῷ ὑμετέρῳ ἐλέει with the following ἵνα is to attribute to Paul a bizarre construction. But see *LSJ* p. 830 under ἵνα B: "mostly first word in the clause, but sometimes preceded by an emphatic word". *BDF* § 475.1, comments: "As in classical Greek, there are some exceptions (especially in Paul) to the obvious rule that the *subordinating* conjunctions stand at the beginning of the dependent clause. In such cases elements belonging to the subordinate clause which are to be emphasized precede the conjuction: 2 C 2:4 τὴν ἀγάπην ἵνα γνῶτε" (italics of *BDF*). Cranfield, *Romans*, 2:584, also points to Plato, *Charmides* 169d (κἀγὼ ἡμῖν ἵνα ὁ λόγος προΐοι, εἶπον . . .); Gal. 2.10; Col. 4.16; Acts 19.4. See also the placing of emphatic words before the relative pronoun (1 Cor. 15.35; 1 Jn 2.24) and before the interrogative pronoun (Rom. 11.2) or before ὅτι (Rom. 7.21). Wilckens, *Römer*, 2:260, although not accepting our solution, finds no grammatical objection. He points also to 1 Cor. 6.4; 11.14; 14.9, where ἐάν does not stand at the beginning of the clause.

[59] Against Luz, *Geschichtsverständnis*, p. 393. See Stuhlmacher's criticisms of Luz in "Interpretation", 567.

[60] Note, however, that Zahn, *Römer*, p. 528; Plag, *Wege*, p. 40; Wilckens, *Römer*, 2:261-62, accept reading 3.

The νῦν is therefore entirely congruous".[61] Now there are four possible ways to understand this νῦν.

1. The first is to view νῦν simply as present.[62] This has the advantage that all three occurrences of νῦν in 11.30-31 would carry the same meaning. However, Wilckens rightly objects that such an understanding is impossible, for the salvation of Israel according to 11.25ff. so clearly lies at the end of time.

2. A variation of solution 1 is that νῦν means in this age. Paul then wishes to stress that the salvation of Israel is in this age and not in the age to come. It is in the concrete now that Israel is saved.[63]

3. A third view is that νῦν refers to the near future when Israel will be saved, the assumption being that Paul expected the parousia in the near future.[64] In spite of the criticisms of Cranfield,[65] the view that Paul expected that the parousia would occur soon seems very well founded. This "Naherwartung" ("near expectation") is to be found from the very early letters (e.g., 1 Thessalonians) through to the later letters (Romans, Philippians) and was clearly a central driving force behind Paul's mission.[66] Wilckens argues that there is no evidence that νῦν can be used for the immediate future.[67] However, Jn 12.31[68] and Ezek. 39.25[69] have νῦν with a future tense, and νῦν in these texts, I believe, is used to point to the immediate future.

---

[61] Barth, *Epistle to the Romans*, p. 417.

[62] E.g. Lietzmann, *Römer*, p. 106; J. Munck, *Christus und Israel: Eine Auslegung von Röm 9-11* (Acta Jutlandica, Aarsskrift for Aarhus Universitet 28.3, Teologisk Serie 7), Aarhus: Universitetsforlaget/København: Ejnar Munksgaard 1956, p. 105; Schlier, *Römer*, p. 343.

[63] Barrett, *Romans*, p. 209.

[64] Michel, *Römer*, p. 358; Käsemann, *Römer*, p. 306; Stuhlmacher, "Interpretation", 567 n. 49.

[65] Cranfield, *Romans*, 2:586, 683-84.

[66] See W. Wrede, "Paulus", in K.H. Rengstorf (ed.), *Das Paulusbild in der neueren deutschen Forschung* (WdF 24), Darmstadt: Wissenschaftliche Buchgesellschaft 1982, 27-28 (1-97), and P. Wernle, *Paulus als Heidenmissionar*, Tübingen: J.C.B. Mohr (Paul Siebeck) ²1909, (¹1899), pp. 13-14.

[67] Wilckens, *Römer*, 2:261.

[68] Mentioned by F. Siegert, *Argumentation bei Paulus gezeigt an Röm 9-11* (WUNT 34), Tübingen: J.C.B. Mohr (Paul Siebeck) 1985, p. 174.

[69] Mentioned by Hofius, "Evangelium und Israel", 200.

4. A fourth interpretation is to view νῦν as a prophetic νῦν.[70] According to this view Paul is so certain that this salvation will take place that he can speak of it occurring in the present.

Of these 4 possibilities, I consider solutions 3 and 4 the most credible. Since it seems likely that the νῦν in texts like Jn 12.31 and Ezek. 39.25 points to the immediate future and since this fits Paul's thinking so well, I prefer solution 3.

Therefore, Israel now is disobedient and in the near future will receive mercy. The clue to this double predestination is found in 11.32.

6. Romans 11.32

Rom. 11.32 states: "For God has consigned all to disobedience, that he may have mercy upon all" (συνέκλεισεν γὰρ ὁ θεὸς τοὺς πάντας εἰς ἀπείθειαν, ἵνα τοὺς πάντας ἐλεήσῃ). Barrett comments: "God has predestined *all men* to wrath and he has predestined *all men* to mercy. If they were not predestined to the former they could not be predestined to the latter".[71] A crucial issue in understanding this verse is whether Paul espouses universalism in the sense that every individual will be saved. Michaelis argues that as the πάντας in 11.32a must refer to every single individual, the πάντας in 11.32b must be "precisely so universal" ("genauso universal").[72] Although there are texts in Paul that suggest a universal salvation (e.g., Rom. 5.18-19; Phil. 2.9-11), two points should make us cautious in drawing a universalist conclusion from Rom. 11.32. First, Paul's use of the article in τοὺς πάντας suggests that Paul is referring to groups, i.e. Jews and Gentiles, and not referring to every single individual.[73] The parallel in Gal. 3.22 also tends to suggest that Paul is referring to groups in Rom. 11.32[74]: "But the scripture

---

[70] Jeremias, "Beobachtungen", 203. Hofius, "Evangelium und Israel", 200, follows Jeremias and compares Ezek. 39.25.

[71] Barrett, *Romans*, p. 210 (Barrett's emphasis).

[72] W. Michaelis, *Versöhnung des Alls: Die frohe Botschaft von der Gnade Gottes*, Gümligen bei Bern: Verlag Siloah 1950, p. 129. A similar argument could be used for 1 Cor. 15.22.

[73] *BDF* § 275.7.

[74] See Luz, *Geschichtsverständnis*, p. 299: "πάντες ist nach Gl. 3,22 und R. 11,25f. nicht individualistisch, sondern kollektiv zu fassen und meint hier zunächst nur: Juden und Heiden". However, Stauffer, *Theologie*, p. 203, writes: "Einst hatte Paulus ge-

consigned (συνέκλεισεν) all things (τὰ πάντα) to sin, that what was promised to faith in Jesus Christ might be given to those who believe". Second, although on theological grounds (but not necessarily on linguistic grounds) πᾶς Ἰσραήλ most likely refers to every single Jew from every age, τὸ πλήρωμα τῶν ἐθνῶν cannot refer to every single Gentile who ever lived. Those Gentiles of the "fullness of the Gentiles" are those who have heard and believed the gospel. This would exclude large numbers of Gentiles who had never heard the gospel. Such excluded Gentiles would not only be those who never had a chance to hear to gospel in the apostolic mission but also those who, like Pharaoh (Rom. 9.17), had lived before the reconciling event of the cross and the reconciling word of the gospel.[75]

Paul's point is therefore that God has predestined Jews and Gentiles to damnation in order that he may have mercy on both Jews and Gentiles. In

---

schrieben: 'Die Schrift hat alles unter die Sünde beschlossen, auf daß die Verheißung auf Grund des Glaubens an Jesus Christus geschenkt werde denen, die da glauben' (Gl 3,22). Jetzt fällt der letzte Vorbehalt: 'Gott hat sie alle unter den Unglauben beschlossen, auf daß er sich ihrer aller erbarme' ([R] 11,32)". G. Eichholz, *Die Theologie des Paulus im Umriß*, Neukirchen-Vluyn: Neukirchener Verlag [5]1985, ([1]1972), pp. 288-89, rightly comments: "Diese These Stauffers ist unhaltbar, weil sie sowohl dem Zusammenhang von Röm 9-11 wie dem ganzen Römerbrief widerspricht. Israel und aller Völker Rettung besteht darin, daß der Mensch zum Glauben an Christus kommt, ob er der Herkunft nach Jude oder Glied der Völkerwelt ist".

[75] A third argument against a universal salvation is often given. It is argued that in view of Paul's ideas of judgement, a universalism is impossible. For a discussion of Paul's doctrine of judgement, see L. Mattern, *Das Verständnis des Gerichtes bei Paulus* (AThANT 47), Zürich/Stuttgart: Zwingli Verlag 1966. See also Luz, *Geschichtsverständnis*, p. 299, who writes: "Bei Annahme einer Allversöhnung würde der Widerspruch zu den fundamentalen Aussagen des Apostels über das Gericht unerträglich". There are texts in earlier letters which speak clearly of a judgement and double exit (i.e., 1 Cor. 1.18; 2 Cor. 2.15; 4.3). However, in Romans, which I take to be Paul's last letter, matters are more complex. There is a discussion of the final judgement and double exit in Rom. 1.18-3.20 (see, e.g., 2.7-10), but it must be kept in mind that this section functions as a preparation for 3.21ff. by proving that no one can be justified by works of law. Paul's understanding of the final judgement cannot be simply read off from Romans 2; this chapter must be seen in the context of 1.18-3.20 (see Bell, *No one seeks for God*). In Romans Paul never says that some will ultimately be damned on the day of judgement. In fact, Rom. 5.18-19 speaks of the universal effects of Christ's death (see the discussion below).

this sense, God treats Jews and Gentiles alike.[76] In another respect, however, God clearly does show favouritism towards Israel. This may be seen by comparing "all Israel" (πᾶς Ἰσραήλ) and "the fullness of the Gentiles" (τὸ πλήρωμα τῶν ἐθνῶν). If my exegesis above is correct, then all Jews will be saved but only a tiny fraction of Gentiles will be saved.[77] But how can this be reconciled with Paul's frequent assertion throughout Romans that there is no distinction between Jews and Gentiles? One way of solving the problem is to assume that Paul was a universalist or that his theology points towards universalism. For example, Dodd considers Paul's premises (the most important being "all Israel will be saved" (Rom. 11.26) and that "no distinctions are drawn" (Rom. 3.22)) and concludes: "Whether or not, therefore, Paul himself drew the 'universalist' conclusion, it seems that we must draw it from his premises".[78] Two things need to be said in response to this.

First, we have seen that when Paul asserts there is no distinction between Jew and Gentile he is making a specific point either about the universality of sin (Rom. 3.22-23) or that Jesus Christ is Lord of all and bestows his riches upon all who call upon him (Rom. 10.12). But as far as election is concerned Israel's privileged position remains[79] and I do not think Dodd's argument has much weight. After all the gospel is for the Jew *first* (Rom. 1.16b). Rom. 11.25-32 points to a gross inequality concerning the percentages of Jews and Gentiles who are saved and this may seem "unfair". But Paul like many other early Christians believed that human beings are in no position to point a finger of accusation at God. All deserve condemnation and God, if he is God, is in a position to give grace to those he wishes. According to the parable of the labourers in the vineyard, no one should begrudge God's generosity (Mt. 20.16).

---

[76] G. Schrenk, *Die Weissagung über Israel im Neuen Testament*, Zürich: Gotthelf-Verlag 1951, p. 37, asserts that for Paul, the main point is "daß Gott sein Heilsziel mit Israel erreicht, und daß es mit der Heidenwelt zusammen aus gleicher Schuld in gleiches Erbarmen eingeht".

[77] Cf. Hahn, "Römer 11.26a", 229, who comments that the πᾶς of πᾶς Ἰσραήλ "steht insofern dem Begriff πλήρωμα (τῶν ἐθνῶν) nahe, aber dem Apostel geht es in Röm. 11.26a darum, dass Israel am Ende der Geschichte die Heiden prozentual hinsichtlich der Vielzahl der zum Heil eingehenden Glieder noch übertreffen wird".

[78] Dodd, *Romans*, p. 184.

[79] See chapter 4 above.

Secondly, there are other texts where Paul seems to point to a universal salvation. This is a vast area but I briefly consider two texts, Rom. 5.18-19 and Phil. 2.9-11. Rom. 5.18-19 points to the universal effects of Adam's disobedience and Christ's obedience:

Then as one man's trespass led to condemnation for all, so one man's act of righteousness leads to acquittal and life for all. 19 For as by one man's disobedience many were made sinners, so by one man's obedience many will be made righteous.

First of all it must be stressed that the "many" in v. 19 does not qualify the "all" in v. 18. "Many" is a well known semitic way of saying "all".[80] One way of understanding these verses is to say "all those on Adam's side will be condemned, all on Christ's side will be acquitted". However I find this a rather unnatural way to understand the verse. A better understanding is that there are two ways of viewing human beings, "in Adam" and "in Christ". "In Adam" all will be condemned but "in Christ" all will be acquitted. We have a type of double predestination rather different from that in Rom. 9.6-29 or 1 Cor. 1.18 and 2 Cor. 2.15. The double predestination in Rom. 5.18-19 is that all are damned in that they are in Adam, but all are acquitted in that they are in Christ. Although I do not think Rom. 11.32 points to a universalist conclusion the idea of double predestination found there is nevertheless rather similar. I therefore believe that Rom. 5.18-19 points to the universal effects of the trespass of Adam and the obedience of Christ.[81]

I turn now to Phil. 2.9-11.

Therefore God has highly exalted him and bestowed on him the name above every name, 10 that at the name of Jesus every knee shall bow, in heaven and on earth and under the earth, 11 and every tongue shall confess that Jesus Christ is Lord, to the glory of the Father.[82]

---

[80] See J. Jeremias, πολλοί, *TDNT* 6:536-45. He points out that whereas in Greek usage πολλοί has an exclusive sense (i.e. "many (but not all)") in Greek Jewish usage it it has an inclusive sense (i.e. "all") corresponding to the Hebrew רבים and Aramaic סַגִּיאִין. According to Jeremias, this inclusive use occurs because Hebrew has no word for "all" (πολλοί, 536). There is the word כֹּל (Hebrew)/כָּלְּא (Aramaic) but this expresses totality and not "all" which expresses sum as well as totality.

[81] See my article "Universal Salvation".

[82] Note that the future indicative ἐξομολογήσεται is read in A C D F* G K L P (instead of the aorist subjunctive ἐξομολογήσηται). As O'Brien, *Philippians*, p. 203, points out, this change could have been unintentional or could have occurred in order to bring the text into line with Is. 45.23. If the latter is the case, then v. 11 is understood as a clause independent of v. 10 and asserts what will certainly happen in the future: every tongue will confess.

Some have disputed that there is a universal salvation here. O'Brien points to Is. 45.24: "All who have raged against him will come to him and be put to shame". The significance of this verse is that Paul alludes to the previous verse (Is. 45.23) in Phil. 2.10-11. Applying Is. 45.23-24 to Phil. 2.10-11 implies, according to O'Brien, that all including the enemies of Christ (unbelievers and demons) will have to bow the knee.[83] Christians will bow the knee willingly, unbelievers unwillingly. Not only will every knee bow but also every tongue will confess that Jesus is Lord. But what does confessing here mean? Does it imply faith in Christ and therefore salvation for all? Or does it simply mean acknowledgement? If it simply means acknowledgement then it could be understood that unbelievers will acknowledge that Jesus is Lord unwillingly and be forced to bow the knee. But there are strong reasons for preferring the universalist view that all will confess Christ in the sense of having a saving faith. For to confess Christ is to believe in him. This is clearly seen in Rom. 10.9 ("because, if you confess with your lips that Jesus is Lord and believe in your heart that God raised him from the dead, you will be saved") and 1 Cor. 12.3 ("Therefore I want you to understand that no one speaking by the Spirit of God ever says 'Jesus be cursed!' and no one can say 'Jesus is Lord' except by the Holy Spirit").[84] For Paul the sign of salvation is confession of faith.

But to return to Rom. 11.32, the main point in Paul's argument is not about universal salvation but that God will justify both Jews and Gentiles *sola gratia, sola fide,* and *propter Christum.*[85] The depth of God's plan to save the world is expressed in the final hymn of praise (Rom. 11.33-36).

7. Romans 15.8-9

These verses are in the context of Paul's discussion of the weak and the strong in 14.1-15.13. I have argued elsewhere that the weak are mainly to be

---

[83] O'Brien, *Philippians,* p. 243.

[84] See Hofius, *Christushymnus,* p. 38.

[85] Cf. Müller, *Gottes Volk,* p. 107: "Das Israelproblem wird schließlich Röm.11 mit Hilfe der Rechtfertigungslehre gelöst. . . . Die Bekehrung Israels wird justificatio impii sein. Nichts anderes ist auch der Sinn von 11,30-32".

identified with Jewish Christians and the strong with Gentile Christians.[86] Our text can be translated:

Welcome one another, therefore, as Christ has welcomed you, for the glory of God. 8 For I tell you that Christ has become a servant of the circumcision for the sake of God's truthfulness/faithfulness, in order to confirm the promises made to the patriarchs; 9 but the Gentiles should glorify God for his mercy, as it is written . . .

This translation is based on the following structure of vv. 8-9a:

λέγω γὰρ
    Χριστὸν διάκονον γεγενῆσθαι περιτομῆς ὑπὲρ ἀληθείας θεοῦ,
        εἰς τὸ βεβαιῶσαι τὰς ἐπαγγελίας τῶν πατέρων,
    τὰ δὲ ἔθνη ὑπὲρ ἐλέους δοξάσαι τὸν θεόν,
        καθὼς γέγραπται, . . .

The sense is therefore that Christ has become a servant of Israel (and remains so!)[87] for the sake of the truth of God (ὑπὲρ ἀληθείας θεοῦ), that is for the sake of God's covenant faithfulness to Israel. And the purpose of this was to confirm the promises made to the fathers. There is some dispute as to how v. 9 is related to v. 8. Many take it such that the infinitives βεβαιῶσαι and δοξάσαι stand in parallel. So Christ's becoming a servant of the circumcision has two purposes: 1. to confirm the promises to the patriarchs; 2. so that the Gentiles might glorify God.[88] This is then based on the following structure:

λέγω γὰρ
    Χριστὸν διάκονον γεγενῆσθαι περιτομῆς ὑπὲρ ἀληθείας θεοῦ,
        εἰς τὸ βεβαιῶσαι τὰς ἐπαγγελίας τῶν πατέρων,
    τὰ δὲ ἔθνη ὑπὲρ ἐλέους δοξάσαι τὸν θεόν,

However, it is to be noted that 8b and 9a are not in fact grammatically parallel.[89] Further, this second structure destroys the correspondence between

---

[86] See Bell, *Provoked to Jealousy*, pp. 72-73, 77-78.

[87] Wilckens, *Römer*, 3:105 n. 510, points out that the reading γενέσθαι (B C* D* F G etc) weakens the sense of the perfect γεγενῆσθαι (א A C² D¹ 048 etc).

[88] This is the prefered option of L.E. Keck, "Christology, Soteriology, and the Praise of God (Romans 15:7-13)", in R.T. Fortuna and B.R. Gaventa (ed.), *The Conversation Continues: Studies in Paul and John in Honor of J. Louis Martyn*, Nashville: Abingdon 1990, 90 (85-97).

[89] Wilckens, *Römer*, 3:106, points out that the *accusativus cum infinitivo* in 9a has its own subject τὰ ἔθνη whereas the infinitive in 8b takes its subject Χριστόν from the main clause.

ὑπὲρ ἀληθείας and ὑπὲρ ἐλέους.[90] I therefore stay with the first structure and take 9a to be dependent on λέγω and so v. 9a stands opposite v. 8. The praising of God by the Gentiles is therefore related to the series of quotations in vv. 9b-12.[91]

The essential point for this enquiry is the idea of Christ becoming a servant of Israel for the sake of his abiding covenant with Israel so confirming the promise to the patriarchs. By means of λέγω γάρ Paul "introduces a solemn doctrinal declaration".[92] The idea of Christ confirming the promises made to the patriarchs has a parallel in Christ making concrete the history of Israel. We saw that without Christ one can hardly speak of a "history of Israel".[93] Just as Christ makes the history of Israel concrete, so he makes the promises God made to Israel concrete. This theme will be taken up in chapter 10 below.

---

[90] See Cranfield, *Romans*, 2:743.

[91] I have discussed the quotation in Rom. 15.10 in *Provoked to Jealousy*, pp. 259-62. The quotations may refer either to 9a (they all concern the Gentiles) or may possibly be related to 8-9a.

[92] Cranfield, *Romans*, 2:740.

[93] See the discussion above in chapter 4 on 1 Cor. 10.1-13.

Chapter 8

Towards a Coherent Theology of Israel

1. The Development of Paul's View of Israel

It should now be abundantly clear from the discussions in chapters 4, 6 and 7 that Romans presents a different view of Israel to that in Galatians and 1 Thessalonians. Further, having studied 1 Thes. 2.14-16 and Rom. 11.25-32 in some detail it would seem that the central ideas expressed in these two texts are irreconcilable. In 1 Thes. 2.16 there is no hope for those Jews who do not now believe in Jesus Christ ("God's judgement has come upon them forever"). Rom. 11.26 on the other hand affirms that at the parousia every Jew from every age will be saved. The only ways in which the two texts could be reconciled are as follows.

1. If "all Israel" of Rom. 11.26 is understood to mean either the remnant of Israel or the Church of Jews and Gentiles then it could be reconciled to 1 Thes. 2.16. But I have shown that there are compelling arguments to reject both these understandings of "all Israel".

2. If "all Israel" is taken to mean Israel as a whole or even all Israel including every single member and if these are understood synchronically (i.e. referring only to those Jews alive at the second coming) then a reconciliation with 1 Thes. 2.16 may appear to be possible. But if Paul expected an imminent parousia then this reconciliation is unlikely. If God's judgement has come upon Israel is it likely that God's salvation will come upon the same people at the parousia which is going to occur within a generation of Jesus' death? For surely there would be Jews who had hindered Paul's mission to the Gentiles who would be alive at the time of the parousia.

3. If it is claimed that 1 Thes. 2.14-16 has nothing to do with eschatology a reconciliation may be possible with Rom. 11.25-32. So εἰς τέλος could be translated as "fully" (giving "God's judgement has come upon them fully") or "until the end" (giving "God's judgement has come upon them until the end"). I rejected both these understandings of εἰς τέλος in chapter 2 above.

In such an attempted reconciliation one suspects that the exegesis of 1 Thes. 2.16 is carried out in a forced way so as to be in harmony with Rom 11.[1]

It is true that there are key theological principles which 1 Thes. 2.14-16 and Romans 9-11 have in common. Both texts speak of the wrath of God which comes upon those Jews who do not believe in Christ (1 Thes. 2.16; Rom. 9.22). Further, I can agree with Holtz, when he writes: "nicht nur 1. Thess 2,16, sondern auch Röm 9-11 läßt nicht den mindesten Zweifel daran erkennen, daß die Angehörigen der das Evangelium von Jesus Christus ablehnenden Synagoge dem Gericht verfallen sind".[2] But the point about Rom. 11.26 is that all Jews will come to believe in Christ. There clearly has been a development in Paul's view regarding Israel. We see this both in terms of salvation (by comparing 1 Thes. 2.14-16 and Rom. 11.25-32) and also by considering Paul's view of Israel as the people of God in Galatians and Romans (discussed above, chapter 4).

The question now arises that if Paul's view on Israel developed, into what view did it develop? Further what was his view on the relationship between Israel and the Church in Romans? This was the question which remained unanswered at the end of chapter 4 above.

2. Paul's View of Israel's Relationship to the Church in Romans

Paul in Romans clearly believed that Israel remains the people of God, that the election is firm and that God's call of Israel is irrevocable. Paul stresses that if God has chosen Israel then Israel has to come through to final salvation. Less easy to tackle though is the precise relationship of Israel to the

---

[1] This is I believe the case of M. Meinertz, *Theologie des Neuen Testamentes (Die Heilige Schrift des Neuen Testamentes Ergänzungsband II)*, 2 vols, Bonn: Peter Hanstein Verlag 1950, 2:34.

[2] T. Holtz, "Das Gericht über die Juden und die Rettung ganz Israels. 1. Thess 2,15f. und Röm 11,25f.", *Geschichte und Theologie des Urchristentums. Gesammelte Aufsätze* (WUNT 57), Tübingen: J.C.B. Mohr (Paul Siebeck) 1991, 324 (313-25). Holtz believes there are differences between the texts: "Röm 9-11 ringt in engagiertester Weise um die Frage des eschatologischen Geschickes des Volkes der Verheißung, Israel; 1. Thess 2,15f. spricht geprägt und scharf den zeitgenössischen Juden als den aktiven Gegnern des Evangeliums das Urteil zu" (324). But he does not believe that between the two texts Paul had radically changed his mind about Israel.

Church. One of the most telling passages in Romans is the parable of the olive tree in Rom. 11.17-24.

But if some of the branches were broken off, and you, a wild olive shoot, were grafted among them to share the richness of the olive tree, 18 do not boast over the branches. If you do boast, remember it is not you that support the root, but the root that supports you. 19 You will say, 'Branches were broken off so that I might be grafted in'. 20 That is true. They were broken off because of their unbelief, but you stand fast only through faith. So do not become proud, but stand in awe. 21 For if God did not spare the natural branches, neither will he spare you. 22 Note then the kindness and the severity of God: severity toward those who have fallen, but God's kindness to you, provided you continue in his kindness; otherwise you too will be cut off. 23 And even the others, if they do not persist in their unbelief, will be grafted in, for God has the power to graft them in again. 24 For if you have been cut from what is by nature a wild olive tree, and grafted, contrary to nature, into a cultivated olive tree, how much more will these natural branches be grafted back into their own olive tree.

Just as Abraham is the root in Rom. 11.16, so in 11.17 he is the "rich root" (ἡ ῥίζα τῆς πιότητος) in which the Gentiles (i.e. Gentile Christians) share.[3] Paul's sense is that the Gentiles are participating in the blessing and promises made to Abraham. Therefore the Gentile Christians have no reason to look down on Jews. Further, he argues in v. 18b that, Abraham, the root, supports the Gentile Christians.[4] There are, however, two alternative views which I must now consider.

The first is that it is not only Abraham who supports Gentile Christians, but also Israel. Such a view is supported by Mußner, who claims that Paul is thinking not only of the root supporting Gentile Christians but also the

---

[3] Note the textual variants: τῆς ῥίζης is omitted in p[46] D* F G bo[ms]; Ir[lat], and καί is inserted between τῆς ῥίζη and τῆς πιότητος in א[2] A D[2] Gothic M vg sy.

[4] Hofius, "Evangelium und Israel", 187 n. 43, writes that the words οὐ σὺ τὴν ῥίζαν βαστάζεις ἀλλὰ ἡ ῥίζα σέ (v. 18b), mean "daß die Heidenchristen aufgrund der freien Gnadenwahl Gottes Anteil haben an der Abraham und seinem σπέρμα gegebenen und in Christus erfüllten Heilsverheißung (vgl. V. 17b), und sie weisen zugleich im Sinne von V. 20b.21 nachdrücklich darauf hin, daß die Heidenchristen von ihren eigenen Voraussetzungen her nicht den geringsten Anspruch auf den ihnen damit gewährten Heilsstand (V. 20a) haben".

trunk.[5] Mußner's view is sharpened further by Klappert who stresses that the Israel which supports the Gentile Christians includes the majority who have refused to believe the gospel.[6] But, as Hofius points out, such ideas go completely against the context.[7] A similar misuse of 11.18b is to be found in the highly influential "Synod resolution for the renewing of the relationship of Christians and Jews" of the Rhineland Church.[8]

The second alternative is to say that Christ is the root and he supports the Gentile Christians. Theologically this is of course true and would be more congenial to Gentile-Christian ears than saying that Abraham supports them. But it would not make much sense in this context where Paul is arguing against anti-Judaism.

I therefore take the root in Rom. 11.17-18, as in Rom. 11.16, to be Abraham. But what about the olive tree itself? This has been understood as either Israel or Christ. There are a number of arguments for taking this tree, from which unbelieving Jews have been cut off and in which believing Gentiles are ingrafted, as Israel. The olive tree was used for Israel in Hos. 14.6. Referring to Israel, the author writes: "his shoots shall spread out; his

---

[5] See F. Mußner, *Traktat über die Juden*, München: Kösel-Verlag 1979, pp. 69-70: "Wenn er also formuliert: 'die Wurzel trägt dich', so denkt er dabei den 'Stamm' mit, der ja in Wirklichkeit die Zweige 'trägt'. Das bedeutet aber, daß mit der 'Wurzel' (ῥίζα) in Röm 11,16.18 nicht bloß der 'Wurzelstock', die Väter Israels, gemeint ist, sondern auch der Stamm, der aus dem Wurzelstock emporgewachsen ist und der identisch ist mit Israel. Nicht bloß die Väter 'tragen' die Kirche, sondern Israel als Ganzes 'trägt' die Kirche".

[6] B. Klappert, "Traktat für Israel (Römer 9-11)", in M. Stöhr (ed.), *Jüdische Existenz und die Erneuerung der christlichen Theologie: Versuch der Bilanz des christlich-jüdischen Dialogs für die Systematische Theologie* (ACJD 11), München: Chr. Kaiser Verlag 1981, 92 (58-137), picks up Mußner's point, taking it to a further extreme: "Dabei kommt der Beobachtung F. Mußners entscheidende Bedeutung zu, daß mit der Wurzel von Röm 11,16.18 nicht - wie z.B. Käsemann will - nur die Erzväter Israels gemeint sind, 'sondern auch der Stamm, der aus dem Wurzelstock emporgewachsen ist' und der das sich dem Evangelium verweigernde Mehrheits-Israel mit umschließt".

[7] Hofius, "Evangelium und Israel", 187.

[8] "Synodalbeschluß zur Erneuerung des Verhältnisses von Christen und Juden" of the Rheinischen Landessynode, 11.1.1980. The text may be found in B. Klappert and H. Starck (ed.), *Umkehr und Erneuerung: Erläuterungen zum Synodalbeschluß der Rheinischen Landessynode 1980 "Zur Erneuerung des Verhältnisses von Christen und Juden"*, Neukirchen-Vluyn: Neukirchener Verlag 1980, pp. 264-66. This misuse in identifying Israel with the root is pointed out by N. Walter, "Zur Interpretation von Römer 9-11", *ZThK* 81 (1984) 180-81 (172-95).

beauty shall be like the olive, and his fragrance like Lebanon". Jer. 11.16 also likens Israel to an olive tree, and is quoted in b. Men. 53b: "'The Lord called thy name a leafy olive-tree, fair with goodly fruit': as the olive tree produces its best only at the very end, so Israel will flourish at the end of time".[9] It is also significant for Rom. 11.16b-24 that in Jub. 16.26 and Philo, *Quis rerum divinarum heres* 279, the plant Israel is said to arise out of the root Abraham. Paul most likely understands the olive tree in Rom. 11.17-24 to be Israel.[10] However, just as Paul may have seen the figure of Christ behind the first fruits in 11.16 (the first converts among the Jews), it could also be the case that he sees Christ behind the olive tree (Israel) also. In Patristic exegesis the tree was understood to be Christ.[11] There is an interesting parallel to Rom. 11.17-24 in Jn 15.1-11 (Jesus is the vine; Christians are the branches). As in Rom. 11.17-24, there is also a reference in Jn 15.1-11 to cutting out branches. The image of the vine was used for Israel in Is. 5.1-7,[12] but nevertheless, the Johannine author has no problem in using this image for Christ. Likewise, although the olive tree was used in Jer. 11.16 and Hos. 14.6 for Israel, Paul could perhaps understand Christ behind

---

[9] See Billerbeck, *Kommentar*, 3:290-92, for ancient Jewish texts regarding the olive tree.

[10] See N.A. Dahl, *Das Volk Gottes: Eine Untersuchung zum Kirchenbewußtsein des Urchristentums*, Darmstadt: Wissenschaftliche Buchgesellschaft [2]1963, ([1]1941), p. 243; Stuhlmacher, *Römer*, p. 152. N. Walter, "Zur Interpretation von Römer 9-11", *ZThK* 81 (1984) 180 (172-95), questions such an interpretation: "M.E. 'ist' der Ölbaum, oder der Stamm, und insbesondere die Wurzel *nicht* = Israel, trotz Jer 11,16f. Denn 'Israel' ist die Bezweigung des Ölbaumes, . . ." He is right to deny that Israel is the root. But I wonder whether it makes much sense to identify Israel with the branches. Haacker, *Römer*, p. 233, makes the point that although we speak of a tree consisting of roots, trunk and branches, this is not necessarily how a tree (especially an olive tree) was understood in first century Palestine. Olive trees have a short "Wurzelstock" and branches grow thickly over the surface of the ground.

[11] See, for example, Cyril of Jerusalem, *Catecheses mystagogicae* 2.3 (Catechetical Lectures 20, on the mysteries 2). In the context of a discussion of Rom. 6.3-14, he says: "Then, when ye were stripped, ye were anointed with exorcised oil, from the very hairs of your head to your feet, and were made partakers of the good olive-tree, Jesus Christ. For ye were cut off from the wild olive-tree, and grafted into the good one, and were made to share the fatness of the true olive-tree" (*NPNF2* 7:147). For further examples, see Schelkle, *Paulus Lehrer der Väter*, p. 395.

[12] See also the detailed comparison of Israel with the vine in Lev. R. 36 (133a) quoted in Billerbeck, *Kommentar*, 2:563-64.

this image of the olive tree in Rom. 11.17-24, especially in view of the symbolism of the olive tree for the anointed one.[13] But the primary reference of the olive tree has to be Israel.

It is into the olive tree of Israel that Gentile Christians have been grafted. Although I argued above (against Mußner and Klappert) that it is Abraham and not Israel who supports the Gentile Christians, one can still say that Gentiles are grafted into Israel. The view of Walter, supported by Lohse, that Paul is simply saying that Gentiles participate in the blessings promised to the patriarchs is inadequate.[14] There is no denying that Paul is using the noble image of the olive tree for Israel. It is worth recalling the rich imagery in the Old Testament: the olive, first mentioned in Gen. 8.11, is a symbol of righteousness (Ps. 52.8), fruitfulness (Ps. 128.3) and beauty (Hos 14.6; Jer. 11.16), and perhaps most importantly, a symbol of the anointed ones (Zech. 4.3, 11-14). Israel, the olive tree, which has grown out of the rich root of the fathers, has incorporated Gentiles. They have the privilege of being supported and fed by the patriarchs.

Although Paul was a town-bred man, he was probably aware that the arboricultural process he describes, grafting wild shoots into the cultivated olive, is exactly the opposite of what is usually done. Hence he uses the phrase κατὰ φύσιν in 11.24. And it may be that he was aware of the fact that the wild olive by itself never produces oil.[15] W.D. Davies writes:

The Gentiles in being engrafted into the root contribute nothing. Perhaps it is the necessity of bringing this out forcefully that explains Paul's use of the symbol of the olive rather than the more customary one of the vine.[16]

Note that Paul is clearly not arguing that the incoming of the Gentiles has given new life to Israel. Such a view could possibly be argued in view of the fact that wild olive branches could be ingrafted into an unproductive cultivated tree in order to invigorate it;[17] but it is extremely unlikely that this

---

[13] See Zechariah 4, which speaks of the two olive trees or the two branches of the olive trees as "the two anointed who stand by the Lord of the whole earth" (Zech. 4.14). The reference is most likely to Joshua and Zerubbabel.

[14] Walter, "Interpretation", 185; Lohse, *Römer*, pp. 314-15.

[15] G. H. Dalman, *Arbeit und Sitte in Palästina* (BFCTh 2.33), 7 vols, Gütersloh: Verlag von C. Bertelmann 1928-42, 3:153-54.

[16] W.D. Davies, "Paul and the Gentiles: A Suggestion Concerning Romans 11:13-24", in *Jewish and Pauline Studies*, London: SPCK 1984, 155 (153-63).

[17] See Columella, *De re rustica* 5.9.16; Palladius, *De insitione* 53-54.

is what Paul wishes to argue in view of his reference to the "rich root" in v. 17.[18]

Gentiles have only being ingrafted because of the lopping off of Jews from the tree. It is important to stress that Paul does not argue in 11.17 that Gentiles have been grafted in "in place of" those who have been cut off.[19] The antecedent of ἐν αὐτοῖς is not the branches that have been cut off. Rather, Paul has in mind that the wild branches have been grafted in among the branches that still remain. Käsemann is therefore correct to say: "ἐν αὐτοῖς means 'among them,' not 'in place of them'".[20] Then, in v. 20, Paul admits the truth that Jews were broken off in order that the Gentiles be grafted in,[21] although, as Paul goes on to explain, this is only half the truth. Jews were broken off because of their disobedience. However, Paul does not say that the Church has replaced Israel. Again we see that Paul does not support a substitution theory in Romans. The logic of the cutting off of unbelieving Israelites and the ingrafting of believing Gentiles is most likely to be understood as in Rom. 11.11: Israel is disobedient so that salvation goes to the Gentiles; therefore the Gentiles are not to boast over the branches (11.18a, 20b), the Jews.[22] If God did not spare the natural branches, neither will he spare the wild branches if they fall from his kindness.

We come here to a most serious issue. Paul speaks in v. 22 in terms of the ἀποτομία ("severity") of God which contrast to his χρηστότης ("kindness"). The picture of God here is that of father[23] although God may also appear here as judge. The term ἀποτομία is only found here in the New Testament (but note the use of the cognate ἀποτόμως in 2 Cor. 13.10; Tit. 1.13). It is true that the cognate terms ἀποτόμως and ἀπότομος are used in Wisdom of Solomon to refer to God's judgement (Wis. 5.20, 22; 6.5; 11.10; 12.9; 18.15). But is Rom. 11.22 to be understood exclusively in terms of God as judge? Such a view is put forward by Köster.[24] He writes: "Those who do

---

[18] See Rengstorf, "Ölbaum", 156.

[19] See the translation of Ziesler, *Romans*, p. 279.

[20] Käsemann, *Romans*, p. 308. See also Moo, *Romans*, p. 701 n. 25.

[21] Paul's καλῶς in v. 20 admits the truth of v. 19.

[22] It is not immediately clear to which branches Paul is referring: those broken off or the natural branches generally. As οἱ κλάδοι in 11.17 has the inclusive sense, Paul is most likely referring to natural branches generally.

[23] See Rengstorf, "Ölbaum", 158.

[24] H. Köster, τέμνω κτλ, *TDNT* 8:107-8 (106-12).

not cleave to God's goodness are threatened by the 'inflexible hardness and severity' of the Judge as the only alternative. The severity of the divine judgement is thus described here by an expression which was used already in Greek for the pitiless severity of the law . . . and which was applied by Paul to God's judicial work under the influence of the usage of Wis.".[25] Is this really the nature of Paul's thought in Rom. 11.22? Note that in Wisdom the adjective ἀπότομος qualifies not only the judgement (κρίσις, 6.5) but also wrath (ὀργή, 5.20), king (βασιλεύς, 11.10), word (λόγος, 12.9) and warrior (πολεμιστής, 18.15). I see no reason why the word ἀποτομία in Rom. 11.22 has to refer primarily to God's rôle as judge. In fact Rengstorf makes a case that Paul's primary image in 11.22 is that of father. He relates ἀποτομία to קצצה, the exclusion of someone from the family. So if cutting off corresponds to exclusion from the family, ingrafting corresponds to adoption. An interesting confirmation that Paul is thinking along these lines can be found in Philo, *De agricultura* 6, who remarks that a wild tree can be brought under cultivation by grafting in other branches. He writes that one can improve trees "such as yield poor crops by inserting grafts into the stem near the roots and joining them with it so that they grow together as one. The same thing happens, I may remark, in the case of men, when adopted sons become by reason of their native qualities congenial to those who by birth are aliens from them, and so become firmly fitted into the family".[26] Note also that in Rom. 11.21 Paul writes of God not sparing the natural branches or the wild branches and uses the verb φείδεσθαι. Paul's only other use of this verb with God as subject is Rom. 8.32, where Paul writes that the Father did not spare his own son.[27] The severity of which Paul speaks in Rom. 11.22 therefore may include both the ideas of judge and father. The fact that the fatherly rôle of God is stressed has terrifying and humbling theological implications. For if Paul speaks of the "cutting off" he is in effect saying that God disinherits those Jews who do not believe. Yet how is this to be reconciled to Rom. 9.4? Perhaps it can only be reconciled since Paul believed that these natural branches which had been cut off will in fact be grafted in again. Ultimately Israel's sonship must depend on her relationship to Christ. Christ makes concrete Israel's sonship, just as he makes concrete

---

[25] Köster, τέμνω, 108.

[26] *Philo* (LCL), 3:110-111. See Scott, *Adoption*, pp. 80-81.

[27] See Gundry Volf, *Paul and Perseverance*, p. 200.

Israel's history. This again highlights Paul's dilemma in Rom. 9.1-5. Israel has the adoption as sons. The scriptures assert this. Yet Israel is cut off from Christ. He needs three whole chapters to wrestle with this baffling question.

Paul therefore writes as though the sonship of Israel is in jeopardy. God's relationship to his people is ultimately to be seen in fatherly terms. As Barth writes, "God's fatherly disposition to his people is the prime and ultimate meaning of its history".[28] So "even the intention of the divine warning and punishment that dominate so powerfully the portrait presented by this history is fatherly".[29] But Paul is perhaps more radical in that he conceives of the situation that some Jews are being disinherited. For in 11.17-24, Paul speaks of the Jews who have not believed in Christ as being cut off from the family whereas the Gentile Christians have been adopted into the family. And this is why I said in chapter 4 that the closest Paul gets to a substitution model in Romans is in this passage. Paul contemplates the disinheriting of Jews who do not believe. However, Paul does not have the view here that the Church is the "new Israel". For the wild olive branches have not been grafted "in place of" of the unbelieving Jews but rather "among" the branches that remain in the tree.[30]

It has been claimed that Paul speaks of the people of God being extended. Earlier it was Israel; now it is Israel and the Christian Church. So Mußner writes that the Church represents "das erweiterte Volk Gottes . . . , das zusammen mit Israel das eine Volk Gottes bildet".[31] But is it simply a case of extending the people of God? Gräßer rightly gives a resounding "Nein", since the Church is a creation of the resurrected Christ.[32] Great care therefore has to be taken in using this image of the olive tree. It is just one image and has to be balanced with others. Since the Church is the creation of the resurrected Christ, we have to ask how the people of God are to be understood. The answer according to Galatians is the Church of Jews and Gentiles. The answer according to Romans is something more complex. Both Israel and the Church constitute the people of God, but the Church, as we have seen, is the creation of the resurrected one. Further, it is a new

---

[28] Barth, *CD* 2.2:266.

[29] Barth, *CD* 2.2:266.

[30] See the discussion above.

[31] Mußner, *Traktat*, p. 24.

[32] Gräßer, "Zwei Heilswege", 221-22.

creation[33] and a resurrected entity. The Church has union with the resurrected Christ. Those of Israel who do not believe in Christ have been cut off from him (cf. Rom. 9.3).

It has sometimes been argued that if the Church is related to the resurrected Christ, Israel must be related to the crucified Christ. If Israel has been cut off from the resurrected Christ and if Israel is under the judgement of God, it may indeed suggest that Israel represents the people of God in her rejection. Just as those who have faith are represented by the resurrected Christ, so those members of the people of God who do not have faith (i.e. Jews who do not believe in Christ) are represented by the crucified Christ.

This is the sort of view one finds in Barth's *Church Dogmatics* 2.2 (§ 34.2). So he writes:

> The Church form of the community stands in the same relation to its Israelite form as the resurrection of Jesus to His crucifixion, as God's mercy to God's judgement.[34]

Such views have come in for some criticism. So Klappert argues that based on Barth's statements in *CD* 2.2 and 4.1:

> Der gekreuzigte Messias Israel ist der auferweckte Messias Israels und als solcher auch der offenbarte Herr der Kirche und der Welt. Noch umfassender formuliert: Jesus Christus ist der gekreuzigte, auferweckte und kommende Messias Israels und als solcher auch der gekreuzigte, auferweckte und kommende Herr der Kirche und der Völkerwelt.[35]

Barth's analysis may be at times inconsistent[36] and I would not wish to defend every point he makes. But his analysis does take seriously both the idea that Israel remains the people of God and the fact that the Church is a resurrected entity (whereas Israel, although remaining the people of God, is not). Further, his view does rightly stress that Israel is the people of God under the judgement of God. But if it is pursued as the only image, a distorted picture is going to emerge. I suggest that alongside this view one should also hold the view that just as the Church is related to the *exalted* Christ, so Israel is related to the *earthly* Jesus. Such a view is seen in Rom.

---

[33] This is a point Dinkler, "Prädestination", 252, makes in the context of a discussion about Rom. 11.11b-24.

[34] Barth, *CD* 2.2:211.

[35] Klappert, *Israel und die Kirche*, p. 53.

[36] So he writes that Israel does not cease to be "das Volk des auferstandenen Christus" (*KD* 2.2:289).

9.5, where from Israel comes the Christ *according to the flesh*. But Israel is
cut off from the exalted Christ (cf. Rom. 9.3) whereas nothing can separate
Christians from the exalted Christ (Rom. 8.39) who is at the right hand of
God and intercedes for them (Rom. 8.34). Further textual support can be
found in Rom. 1.3-4. Theobald is critical of an interpretation simply in terms
of a 'Zweistufenchristologie' whereby Rom. 1.3 is related to Jesus' humility
and 1.4 to his exaltation as Son of God in power.[37] Such a view, he believes,
comes about partly by reading Phil. 2.6-11 into Rom. 1.3-4. Rom. 1.3-4
does not describe the pathway of the redeemer (pre-existence – humility –
exaltation). Rather, Rom. 1.4 is concerned with Jesus as κύριος in relation
to the Gentile world (cf. 10.9, 12) and 1.3 the Davidic origin of Jesus as
messiah of Israel. Paul emphasises 'die *gleichzeitige* Gültigkeit beider
Aspekte, der Einbindung Jesu in den jüdischen Erwartungshorizont und
seiner universalen, eschatologischen Bedeutung im Geist . . . '.[38] The
priority of Israel expressed in Rom. 1.16b ('Ιουδαίῳ τε πρῶτον καὶ "Ελληνι)
"ist nicht nur der Reflex einer missionsgeschichtlichen Gegebenheit, sondern
vor allem ein christologisch begründeter Sachverhalt: Weil Christus
zunächst Israels Messias ist, gilt auch das Evangelium 'zunächst dem
Juden'".[39] Theobald believes such an interpretation of Rom. 1.3-4 finds
some confirmation in Rom. 15.8-9. He may well be correct to believe that
Rom. 1.3-4 is not simply about a two-level Christology. If he is corrrect then
with a slight modification, it gives further confirmation to the view that
Israel is related to the earthly Jesus as the Church of Gentiles and Jews is
related to the exalted Christ. Just as Jesus was confined to live as a Jew and
keep the law, so Israel lives under the same constraints.

I therefore believe a balance has to be kept between these two views,
namely first that the Church is related to Israel as God's mercy is related to
his judgement and as the resurrected Christ is related to the crucified Jesus;
and secondly that the Church is related to Israel as the exalted Christ is
related to the earthly Jesus. It should also be stressed at this point that Israel
in reflecting their rejected status, that of the crucified messiah, should in no

---

[37] M. Theobald, "'Dem Juden zuerst und auch dem Heiden'. Die paulinische Auslegung der Glaubensformel Röm 1,3f.", in *Studien zum Römerbrief* (WUNT 136),
Tübingen: J.C.B. Mohr (Paul Siebeck) 2001, 111-12 (102-18).

[38] Theobald, "Juden", 113 (Theobald's emphasis).

[39] Theobald, "Juden", 114.

sense be used to legitimate the suffering of the Jewish people (just as the Church being the people of the resurrected Christ should not legitimate Christian earthly rule).

3. Israel according to Jesus and Paul

At various points in the present work I have mentioned how Paul's view in Romans towards Israel is quite different to that put forward in the gospels. Of the gospels Matthew and John have the strongest "antisemitic" sentiments. The most "antisemitic" sections (Jn 8.41-47; Mt. 27.25) are probably redactional material from the evangelists.[40] But there seems little doubt that some of the "negative" material about Israel comes from Jesus himself.

I have employed quotation marks in the preceding paragraph partly because words like "antisemitic" are perhaps employed a little too easily in relation to the gospels. Jesus' view of Israel is a vast topic which can only be covered here with broad brush strokes. But I will outline what I believe his view was and ask how this can be related to the teaching of Paul.

The first point to make is that Jesus brought a radical message of judgement to Israel, a message which was anticipated by John the Baptist. John preached of the coming wrath which is coming upon the entire people (Lk. 3.7-9).[41] It may be, as Meyer suggests, that John was "[b]ent on confronting the whole of Israel with his proclamation"[42] and that his "summons to baptism in the wilderness was . . . directed not simply to all Israelites but to all Israel, i.e. to the nation as an ecclesial entity or to Israel as people of God".[43] He does not call upon them to keep the law and neither does he teach a new Halacha. Again, as Meyer argues:

---

[40] On Mt. 27.25, see the discussion about the Jewish responsibility for Jesus' death in chapter 2 above.

[41] According to Luke, John addresses the multitudes. However, Mt. 3.7-10 has John address these words to the Pharisees and Saduccees. The tone of John's words, however, suggest that they are relevant for the whole people. See also P. Sacchi, "Das Problem des 'wahren Israel' im Lichte der universalistischen Auffassungen des Alten Orients", *Jahrbuch für Biblische Theologie Band 7: Volk Gottes, Gemeinde und Gesellschaft*, Neukirchen-Vluyn: Neukirchener Verlag 1992, 96-97 (77-100).

[42] B.F. Meyer, *The Aims of Jesus*, London: SCM 1979, p. 116.

[43] Meyer, *Aims*, p. 118.

The last hour had come,[sic] the blade of the axe was already sunk in the root of the tree. There was no time, no need, no place for long study of the Torah, for priestly robes, for isolation in *élite* groups, for a massively detailed *halaka* to guide the conduct of life. Indeed there was no point in any of this. God's demand was radical and urgent.[44]

John tells them that appealing to their father Abraham will be of no help (Mt. 3.9a/Lk. 3.8a). The only way to escape this imminent wrath is to make a decisive break with sin by repenting[45] and by being baptized. As Becker argues, "God will remain true to his promises to Abraham, because God can, with an extravagant miracle, raise up children to Abraham from stones, the deadest material of the wilderness".[46] For Jesus, John was the greatest person ever to have lived up until that time (Mt. 11.11)[47] and it is no surprise to discover that Jesus' teaching on judgement shares much with John's. Like John he believed that all Israel was under God's judgement. It is true that some of his polemic is directed against particular groups. So in Mt. 23.1-39 he speaks against the leaders and in Lk. 6.24-25 against the rich. But the thrust of Jesus' teaching is that all Israel was under judgement. So a passage such as Lk. 13.1-5 parallels the message of John. A passage such as Mk 2.17, which speaks of only those who are sick as needing a physician, does not have to imply that there were some in Israel who did not need redemption.[48]

Against the backdrop of this judgement Jesus announced the kingdom of God. This was God's way of restoring Israel. Part of his message was, like John's, a call to repentance.[49] His call was what one could term a "pure prophetic version of repentance" rather than a "prophetic-legal version" as found in normative Judaism.[50] But there are additional key elements in

---

[44] Meyer, *Aims*, p. 120.

[45] On repentance see Bell, "Teshubah" and the brief discussion below on Jesus' call to repentance.

[46] Becker, *Jesus*, p. 41.

[47] Such a saying is likely to be authentic since it goes against the grain of Matthew which, if anything, wished to downplay the importance of the Baptist.

[48] See Becker, *Jesus*, p. 50-51.

[49] On this, see my brief discussion in "Teshubah", 45-46.

[50] Such a distinction is made by E.K. Dietrich, *Die Umkehr (Bekehrung und Buße) im Alten Testament und im Judentum*, Stuttgart: W. Kohlhammer 1936, pp. 212-13. He distinguishes between the "rein prophetische Fassung der Umkehr" (212-13) as found in Hosea, Isaiah, Jeremiah, Deutero-Isaiah and some Psalms and the "prophetisch-gesetzliche" version (213-14) as found in Ezekiel, the Deuteronomists, some Psalms and

Jesus' restoration of Israel:[51]

1. Jesus preached salvation to the poor.[52]
2. He had table fellowship with the tax collectors and sinners.[53]
3. He chose 12 disciples to lead the eschatological 12 tribes of Israel.[54]
4. He conducted a ministry of healing and exorcism.[55]

---

ancient Judaism. In the former we have "die radikale Umgestaltung des menschlichen inneren Seins" resulting in a καινὴ κτίσις (p. 213). In the latter "[d]as Objekt der Ab- und Zukehr wird nicht vom Wesen Gottes her belichtet, sondern vom geschriebenen Gesetz" with an increasing stress on individual commandments (p. 213). I think this is a fair distinction provided one bears in mind that earlier prophets refer to law and elements of the "pure prophetic version" are found in later prophets. See Bell, "Teshubah", 24-25.

[51] On the relationship of these elements to Jesus' messiahship, see P. Stuhlmacher, "Der messianische Gottesknecht", in *Biblische Theologie und Evangelium. Gesammelte Aufsätze* (WUNT 146), Tübingen: J.C.B. Mohr (Paul Siebeck) 2002, 128-32 (119-40).

[52] A key text here is Is. 61.1-2 which begins "The Spirit of the Lord God is upon me, because the LORD has anointed me to bring good tidings to the afflicted . . .". This became an important early Jewish messianic text (4Q521: "And as for the wonders that are not the work of the Lord, when he (i.e. the Messiah) [comes] then he will heal the sick, resurrect the dead, and to the poor announce glad tidings") and is quoted in Lk. 4.16-21. The striking thing about this quotation is that Jesus omits the final words of Is. 61.1-2, about proclaiming the day of vengeance of God. Jeremias makes the point that in Is. 61.1-2 the term "poor" refers to those who are oppressed in a quite general sense, the word "poor" being explained by the parallel expressions "the broken hearted", "captives", "those who are bound", "those who mourn" and "those who are of a faint spirit" (J. Jeremias, *Theology of the New Testament, Volume One: The Proclamation of Jesus* ET, London: SCM 1971, p. 113). 1:108-121. On the poor see also Lk. 6.20 ("Blessed are you poor, for yours is the kingdom of God"); Lk. 7.22-23/Mt. 11.5-6.

[53] See Mk 2.15-17 par. The stress on eating points to the messianic banquet (cf. Is. 25.6-9); but whereas in a text such as 1 En. 62.13-15 "the righteous shall eat and rest with that Son of Man for ever and ever", i.e. sinners are excluded in this messianic banquet, Jesus specifically eats with sinners.

[54] See Lk. 22.28-30. Compare this to Ps. Sol. 17.26, 44:

He will gather a holy people
whom he will lead in righteousness;
and he will judge the tribes of the people
that have been made holy by the Lord their God.

....

44 Blessed are those born in those days
to see the good fortune of Israel
which God will bring to pass in the assembly of the tribes (Wright, *OTP* 2:667, 669).

[55] I do not have space here to discuss this fundamental aspect of Jesus' ministry. I assume that Jesus was in fact a healer and an exorcist. Among the large volume of literature I mention two studies I have found particularly helpful: A.E. Harvey, "The Intel-

But there are also texts which point to a judgement coming upon Israelites because they failed to respond to Jesus' preaching and mighty works. So Jesus upbraids the cities of Chorazin, Bethsaida and Capernaum (Mt. 11.20-24/Lk. 10.13-15) for not responding.[56] Reiser believes that Luke is close to the original logion in Q which he gives as:

Woe to you, Chorazin! Woe to you, Bethsaida!
For if the deeds of power done in you
    had been done in Tyre and Sidon,
they would have repented long ago, sitting in sackcloth and ashes.
But at the judgement
    it will be more tolerable for Tyre and Sidon than for you.
And you, Capernaum,
    will you be exalted to heaven?
No, you will be brought down to Sheol![57]

Jesus issues a similar threat of judgement to his generation (Mt. 12.41-42/Lk. 11.31-32). Reiser's reconstruction of Q is:

The queen of the South will rise
    at the judgment with the people of this generation
    and condemn them,
because she came from the ends of the earth
    to listen to the wisdom of Solomon,
and see, something greater than Solomon is here!

The men of Nineveh will rise up
    at the judgment with this generation
    and condemn it,

---

ligibility of Miracle", *Jesus and the Constraints of History: The Bampton Lectures, 1980*, London: Duckworth 1982, 98-119, and G.H. Twelftree, *Jesus the Exorcist: A Contribution to the Study of the Historical Jesus* (WUNT 2.54), Tübingen: J.C.B. Mohr (Paul Siebeck) 1993.

[56] Becker, *Jesus*, p. 64, believes that there are arguments for the authenticity of this saying since Chorazin and Bethsaida have no importance in early Christianity. "It is easier to assume that, since Jesus had condemned these places so harshly, there was no post-easter mission at all in them than to argue the opposite position, viz., that the saying was attributed to Jesus, because Christian missionaries had no success in the villages".

[57] M. Reiser, *Jesus and Judgment: The Eschatological Proclamation in Its Jewish Context* ET, Minneapolis: Fortress Press 1997, pp. 223-24.

because they repented at the proclamation of Jonah,
and see, something greater than Jonah is here![58]

Mt. 8.11-12, paralleling Lk. 13.28-29, was discussed in chapter 4 above in relation to the "substitution model". Reiser reconstructs the Q version as:

Many will come from east and west
  and will eat with Abraham, Isaac, and Jacob
  in the kingdom of God,
while the heirs of the kingdom will be thrown out
where there will be weeping and gnashing of teeth.[59]

This functions as a stark warning to Israel.

As a final example of Jesus' judgement on Israel for not responding, I take one of Jesus' most serious parables, that of Mk 12.1-12.[60] As Hooker writes, the clear meaning of the parable is that "those who have rejected God's messengers will themselves be rejected; others will inherit the promises".[61] The parable appears to be an attack on the leaders of Israel (see Mk 12.12); such an interpretation would certainly cohere with the fact that Jesus had a rapturous reception at his entry into Jerusalem (Mk 11.8-10) and that the chiefs priests and scribes feared Jesus "because all the multitude was astonished at his teaching" (Mk 11.18). However, it could also be that the parable originally had a wider reference (cf. Is. 5.1-7; Mk 11.12-14) and "was intended as an indictment of Israel in general for her failure to produce fruit".[62] Then, as we saw in chapter 4, Matthew has sayings (8.11-12; 21.43) which speak not only of the rejection of those in Israel who do not respond to Jesus (this being the vast majority) but also of the inclusion of the Gentiles. Mt. 8.11-12 may well be early in view of the Jewish mode of

---

[58] Reiser, *Judgment*, p. 208. Becker, *Jesus*, pp. 65-66, argues for the authenticity of this logion. Among other things he points to the lack of interest in the Queen of Sheba in primitive Christianity. He also believes the original is semitic (see also Reiser, *Judgment*, p. 208). T.W. Manson, *The Teaching of Jesus: Studies in its Form and Content*, Cambridge: CUP ²1935, (¹1931), p. 56, considered the "strophic parallelism", evident in this text and elsewhere in Jesus' teaching, to be Jesus' "special contribution to the forms of poetry in general".

[59] Reiser, *Judgment*, p. 233.

[60] Reiser, *Judgment*, p. 303, gives this parable in his list of texts which he considers to be authentic "at least at the core".

[61] M.D. Hooker, *The Gospel according to Mark* (BNTC), London: A. & C. Black 1991, p. 274.

[62] Hooker, *Mark*, p. 274.

thought,[63] the semitic style[64] and the "semitisms".[65] Jesus therefore may well have worked with a substitution model as one later finds in most of the rest of the New Testament.[66]

I therefore think it likely that Jesus, like John the Baptist, brought a stern message of judgement to Israel. An opportunity had been given to repent. An invitation had been issued to the banquet (Mt. 22.1-14/Lk. 14.16-24). But many in Israel were to refuse and as a whole Israel had become the corrupt and apostate generation of Dt. 32.5.[67] Only a remnant, it appears, was to be "restored"[68] and Gentiles were promised a share in the kingdom of God in place of apostate Jews.

How then is this teaching of Jesus to be related to that of Paul? Many studies aim to emphasize the disparities between the teachings of Jesus and Paul. But in view of the quite different situations facing Jesus and Paul the degree of agreement is remarkable. Paul, like Jesus, speaks of the judgement of God coming upon Israel. Like Jesus he also speaks (using different terms) of the new way open for Israel. There is also agreement that Israel, by not responding, is going to be judged. In fact we noted in chapter 2 above the similarities between 1 Thes. 2.13-16 and Mk 12.1-9; Mt. 23.29-38. Further, Jesus in Mt. 8.11-12 implies some sort of substitution model which we found in Galatians. But do we find anything in the teaching of Jesus which approaches Paul's view expressed in Romans that Israel's election remains firm or that Israel will be saved at the parousia? The answer would appear to be "No". However, I must consider one possible exception.

In Mt. 23.39 (Lk. 13.35b) Jesus says "For I tell you, you will not see me again, until you say, 'Blessed is he who comes in the name of the Lord'".

---

[63] E.g. the messianic banquet with the Patriarchs.

[64] So we have the antithetic parallelism in 8.12 by means of the verbs ἔρχεσθαι and ἐκβάλλεσθαι. See Jeremias, *Nations*, p. 56.

[65] E.g. οἱ υἱοὶ τῆς βασιλείας. Again, see Jeremias, *Nations*, p. 56.

[66] According to Jeremias, *Nations*, p. 55, Jesus limited his activity to Israel but at the same time "expressly promised the Gentiles a share in the Kingdom of God, and even warned his Jewish hearers that their own place might be taken by the Gentiles".

[67] See also my discussion of the allusions to Dt. 32.5 and 32.20 in Mt. 17.17 and Lk. 9.41 in *Provoked to Jealousy*, pp. 266-67. See also S.M. Bryan, *Jesus and Israel's Traditions of Judgement and Restoration* (SNTSMS 117), Cambridge: CUP 2002, pp. 84-85.

[68] Bryan, *Restoration*, pp. 128-29.

Some have taken this to mean that Jesus envisaged a future conversion of Israel at the parousia. Luther in fact mentions Rom. 11.25-26 in relation to Mt. 23.39 in a sermon for St Stephens Day 1521.[69] However, there are two other interpretations. One is that Jesus speaks a conditional prophecy in the sense that "when his people bless him, the Messiah will come".[70] The other is that Jesus speaks a word of judgement. Such an understanding is widepread and can be found, for example, in Calvin,[71] T.W. Manson[72] and Luz.[73] In view of the context, this is the most likely understanding. As Luz writes:

Nach der schroffen Weherede, nach der Gerichtsankündigung über 'diese Generation' (V 35f), nach der Ankündigung des Auszugs Gottes aus dem Tempel und unmittelbar, bevor Jesus diesen engültig verläßt, wäre die Ankündigung einer Möglichkeit oder gar der Wirklichkeit der kommenden Umkehr Israels überraschend, rhetorisch sehr ungeschickt und sprengte den Kontext. Eine solche Aussage wäre außerdem im Matthäusevangelium völlig vereinzelt.[74]

Further, the section Mt. 24.29-25.46 makes clear that the Son of man will not come when Israel converts, but rather then, "wenn die Drangsal und die Verwirrung am größten ist, unerwartet und plötzlich, wie der Blitz vom Himmel (24,27-31)".[75]

So what could have been a saying of Jesus which supports Paul's view in Rom. 11.25-27 turns out to be saying something quite different: Jesus affirms the judgement which will come upon Israel. They will bless him, but it will be too late. It seems therefore that Paul's statement in Romans that all

---

[69] See J.N. Lenker (ed.), *Sermons of Martin Luther: The Church Postils*, 8 vols, Grand Rapids: Baker Books 1995 (repr.), [1]1905-9, 1:238.

[70] See D.C. Allison Jr., "Matt. 23:39 – Luke 13:35b as a Conditional Prophecy", *JSNT* 18 (1983) 77 (75-84).

[71] J. Calvin, *A Harmony of the Gospels: Matthew, Mark and Luke vol. III; James and Jude*, translated by A.W. Morrison (CNTC 3), Grand Rapids: Wm B. Eerdmans 1989 (repr.), ([1]1972), p. 71: "[Jesus] says that He will not come to them until they cry out in fear–too late–at the sight of His terrible majesty, 'truly He is the Son of God'".

[72] T.W. Manson, *The Sayings of Jesus*, London: SCM 1950 (repr.), ([1]1937), p. 128.

[73] Luz, *Matthäus (Mt 18-25)*, p. 384.

[74] Luz, *Matthäus (Mt 18-25)*, p. 384.

[75] Luz, *Matthäus (Mt 18-25)*, p. 384. Therefore the Jewish "parallels" which Allison, "Conditional Prophecy", 79, puts forward to support his view, are not parallels at all. E.g., b. Sanh. 98a: "The Son of David will not come until there are no conceited men in Israel".

Israel will be saved at the parousia stands alone (as does his view that the election of Israel is irrevocable).

This now leads me to ask the uncomfortable question of where the truth concerning Israel is to be found. Is it to be found in the teaching of Jesus (whose view is reflected in most of the New Testament including Galatians)? Or is it to be found in Paul's views expressed in Romans? One answer I offer is that the most profound truth concerning Israel's salvation is actually in Romans. Jesus' teaching is not the last "word" for Israel (just as Rom. 9.27 is not the last "word").[76] And it is not the last "word" for two main reasons.

First, although it can be declared in faith that Jesus was the divine Son of God, a good case can be made that he was fallible. He was fallible with regard to his second coming.[77] He was fallible regarding biblical criticism.[78] Why could he not also have been fallible regarding Israel? Being the Son of God does not mean that he could not have made any mistakes.[79] I would fur-

---

[76] The reason for employing quotations marks will become clear shortly.

[77] Although according to Mk 13.32 only the Father knows the time of the parousia, Jesus and the early Church seemed to believe that the second coming would occur within a generation. See Mk 9.1 ("Truly, I say to you, there are some standing here who will not taste death before they see the kingdom of God has come with power"). A.L. Moore, *The Parousia in the New Testament* (NovTSup 13), Leiden: E.J. Brill 1966, pp. 125-31, argues that the reference is to the transfiguration. However, Mk 9.1 would more naturally belong to Mk 8.38 (which concerns the Son of man who "comes in the glory of his Father with the holy angels" at the judgement) than to Mk 9.2-8 (which concerns the transfiguration). So J. Gnilka, *Das Evangelium nach Markus* (EKK 2), 2 vols, Zürich/Einsiedeln/ Köln: Benziger Verlag/Neukirchen-Vluyn: Neukirchener Verlag 1 [5]1998, ([1]1978); 2 [4]1994, ([1]1978), 2:26-27, sees 9.1 as a continuation of 8.38. But although Gnilka understands "taste death" as a semitism, he believes 9.1 comes from the Palestinian Church after the resurrection and not from Jesus.

[78] For example, he assumed Moses wrote the Pentateuch and that David wrote Psalm 110. For an attempt to defend Jesus' views regarding the second coming and biblical criticism, see J.W. Wenham, *Christ and the Bible*, London: Tyndale Press 1972, pp. 62-81.

[79] I am here going beyond the position of R.E. Brown, "How much did Jesus know?–A Survey of the Biblical Evidence", *CBQ* 29 (1967) 38 (9-39). He argues that there are areas "in which Jesus' views do *seem* to have been the limited views of his time" (Brown's emphasis). But adds: "Perhaps these were areas in which he brought no new revelation to man". He writes that there is an area "where his views were not at all those of his time, namely, the area of belief and behaviour called for by the coming of the kingdom. And in this area, in my personal opinion, his authority is supreme for every century, because in this area he spoke for God". One could argue that his views on Israel

ther say that an infallible Christ is a docetic Christ. According to Phil. 2.6-7a Jesus Christ "who, though he was in the form of God, did not count the equality with God as something to be used for his own advantage (usually translated 'as something to be grasped'), 7 but made himself poor (usually translated 'emptied himself') . . . ". Jesus Christ therefore voluntarily laid aside his "omniscience", did not take advantage of his equality with God,[80] but rather made himself poor.[81] If one takes the incarnation seriously, if one believes that God assumed human form, then I believe this must entail the view that "omniscience" (together with "omnipotence" and "omnipresence") were renounced.[82]

The second reason why Jesus' "word" on Israel is not the last "word" is simply because Jesus' "words" issued in his ministry preceded his atoning death and resurrection.[83] It is true that he proclaimed the kingdom of God

---

belonged to the "area of belief". But I agree with Brown's view that Jesus' limitation of knowledge does not contradict his divinity. He quotes Cyril of Alexandria who says of Christ: "We have admired his goodness in that for love of us he has not refused to descend to such a low position as to bear all that belongs to our nature, INCLUDED IN WHICH IS IGNORANCE" (39, Brown's emphasis).

[80] For this understanding see R.W. Hoover, "The Harpagmos Enigma: A Philological Solution", *HTR* 64 (1971) 95-119.

[81] See Hofius, *Christushymnus*, p. 60. He argues that the idea in Phil. 2.6-7a corresponds to 2 Cor. 8.9: "though he was rich, yet for our sake he became poor".

[82] I may be accused here of using rigid systematic categories and simply restating the kenotic Christology of G. Thomasius, *Christi Person und Werk*, 1852-61. There is, I believe, much value in the approach of Thomasius, one which takes seriously Phil. 2.6-7. However, I appreciate the problems of working with concepts such as "divine attributes". In fact I would maintain that one cannot define God by defining his attributes (cf. Bell, *No one seeks for God*, pp. 90-102). Further, I would want to avoid a sharp distinction between "relative" attributes (omniscience, omnipotence and omnipresence) and "immanent" attributes (power, truth, holiness and love). Nevertheless, the approach of Thomasius still has value for those who wish to adopt a lutheran understanding of the word made flesh and who reject the *extra Calvinisticum*. On kenosis see P. Althaus, "Kenosis", *RGG*[3] 3:1243-46; J. Macquarrie, "Jesus Christus VI", *TRE* 17:26-27 (16-42). On Thomasius, see C. Brown, *Jesus in European Protestant Thought 1778-1860*, Grand Rapids: Baker 1985, pp. 248-54; K. Beyschlag, *Die Erlanger Theologie* (EKGB 67), Erlangen: Martin-Luther-Verlag 1993, pp. 93-98.

[83] Bultmann's comments at the very beginning of his Theology of the New Testament are still important, even if one does not accept his anthropological approach: "*The message of Jesus* is a presupposition for the theology of the New Testament rather than a part of that theology itself. . . . Christian faith did not exist until there was a Christian kerygma; i.e. a kerygma proclaiming Jesus Christ–specifically Jesus Christ the Crucified

and in this proclamation he actually brings to humanity the kingdom of God. Using this approach it is perhaps possible to bring together Jesus' preaching and Paul's teaching on justification.[84] But, one has also to bear in mind the future dimension of Jesus' proclamation. As Jüngel points out:

> In der Verkündigung Jesu hat sich die Gottesherrschaft in unserer Zeit ihre Zeit gezeitigt; aber sie hat sich ihre Zeit *als Zukunft* gezeigt, und zwar so, daß sie in Jesu Wort als Zukunft angesagt werden kann. Insofern ist Jesu Verkündigung eschatologische Zeitansage; Ansage der als Zukunft schon gezeitigten Gottesherrschaft.[85]

Further, Paul, like many of the early Christians, was more concerned about what Jesus did than what he taught. In fact Paul was so overwhelmed by what Christ did for him in the cross and resurrection that the teaching of Jesus took a secondary place and explains why there are relatively few quotations from and allusions to the teaching of Jesus in his letters.[86] It is for

---

and Risen One–to be God's eschatological act of salvation. He was so proclaimed in the kerygma of the earliest Church, not in the message of the historical Jesus . . . But the fact that Jesus had appeared and the message which he had proclaimed were, of course, among its historical presuppositions; and for this reason Jesus' message cannot be omitted from the delineation of New Testament theology" (*Theology*, 1:3).

[84] E. Jüngel, *Paulus und Jesus. Eine Untersuchung zur Präzisierung der Frage nach dem Ursprung der Christologie* (HUTh 2), Tübingen: J.C.B. Mohr (Paul Siebeck) ⁶1986. In his discussion of how Paul's understanding of justification and Jesus' proclamation is to be related, he writes: "Man kann . . . miteinander vergleichen, *was* in der Verkündigung Jesu und in der paulinischen Rechtfertigungslehre jeweils zur Sprache gekommen ist, und von da her dann auch den Unterschied im Wie beider Sprachereignisse zu erklären versuchen. In diesem Sinne vergleichen wollen heißt: zwei einander folgende Sprachereignisse als Ereignisse einer Sprachgeschichte zu erklären versuchen" (p. 263, Jüngel's emphasis).

[85] E. Jüngel, "Jesu Wort und Jesus als Wort Gottes. Ein hermeneutischer Beitrag zum christologischen Problem", in *Unterwegs zur Sache. Theologische Bemerkungen* (BEvTh 61), München: Chr. Kaiser Verlag 1988, 131 (126-44) (Jüngel's emphasis).

[86] An extremely helpful case study is that of M.B. Thompson, *Clothed with Christ: The Example and Teaching of Jesus in Romans 12.1-15.13* (JSNTSup 59), Sheffield: Sheffield Academic Press 1991. See his sixth conclusion: "In rarely citing J[esus] T[radition] Paul does not represent a special case, but is typical of what we find in early Christianity. . . . The proper question is not why does Paul not quote or directly refer to J[esus] T[radition] more often, but why he does so at all" (p. 239).

this reason that attempts (largely by conservative scholars) to harmonize the teaching of Jesus and Paul are somewhat beside the point.[87]

If my analysis of Jesus' teaching is correct, it means that the letter to the Romans is all the more outstanding among the New Testament books. Only in this book does a view of Israel's unconditional election clearly emerge. Most of the New Testament seems to support a substitution model and it is this model which has been the dominant one throughout the history of the Church. Most of the major theologians throughout the history of the Church have denied Israel's unconditional election.[88]

However, I do not wish to dismiss Jesus' teaching on Israel. Two reasons for not doing so are as follows. First, there are dangers inherent in an approach whereby the "words" of Jesus and Paul concerning Israel are abstracted and set against each other. I am not simply making a point about the historical context of their "words". I am saying something much more fundamental. "Words" have to be seen not only as describing or depicting. "Words", as is well known, can operate as a speech-act. It is therefore a mistake simply to abstract "teaching about Israel" from Jesus' words. The parables in particular can operate as a "Sprachereignis".[89] Through these

---

[87] See the attempts made to demonstrate Paul was a "disciple" of Jesus rather than the "founder of Christianity" by showing that Paul's teaching did not contradict that of Jesus. M. Rese, *TLZ* 121 (1996) 674 (672-74), in his review of D. Wenham, *Paul: Follower of Jesus or Founder of Christianity?*, Grand Rapids: Wm B. Eerdmans 1995, rightly points out: "Was aber die Frage nach dem Verhältnis des Paulus zu Jesus betrifft, so greift schon die von W[enham] in den Vordergrund gerückte Alternative zu kurz. Auch wenn Paulus kein Jünger des irdischen Jesus gewesen ist, so hat nie jemand bestritten, daß er selbst sich als Jünger Jesu verstand. Zu bestreiten ist aber auch nicht – wenigstens nicht von dem, der die uns überlieferten Texte des Paulus, d.h. seine Briefe, ernster nimmt als subjektive Vermutungen und Behauptungen über mögliche Anspielungen des Paul auf Worte des irdischen Jesus: Im theologischen Denken des Paulus steht nicht das, was der irdische Jesus gelehrt hat, im Mittelpunkt, sondern das, was Gott in Kreuz und Auferstehung Jesu für die gottlosen Menschen getan hat".

[88] One of the notable exceptions is, of course, Karl Barth. See, for example, "The Jewish Problem and the Christian Answer", in *Against the Stream: Shorter Post-War Writings 1946-52*, London: SCM 1954, 200 (195-201), a radio address given on 13th December 1949: "Without any doubt the Jews are to this very day the chosen people of God in the same sense as they have been so from the beginning, according to the Old and New Testaments".

[89] See E. Fuchs, *Studies of the Historical Jesus* (SBT 42) ET, London: SCM 1964, p. 220: "I understand Jesus' proclamation as a 'language-event'. That is not to say that Jesus created new concepts. . . . [The] parables certainly contain the same proclamation

parables God's kingdom comes to us.[90] Interpretation of the New Testament cannot always operate in a "Cartesian" manner. One must take into account the way the text can change the reader (or rather the way God through the text transforms the reader).

A second reason for not wanting to dismiss Jesus' teaching on Israel is that the "truth" of scripture is not simply found in isolated statements. The "truth" of scripture can be discerned also in the developments of thought. Such developments can take place in three ways. The first is the type of development found in a text like Romans 9-11. Elsewhere I have argued in some detail that the "shape" of Romans 9-11 is similar to that of the second Song of Moses, Dt. 32.1-43.[91] This great song contains the same sorts of "contradictions" one finds in Romans 9-11. It speaks of Israel's election, fall, judgement and salvation. To some extent the Song provides a "bridge" between the judgement on Israel and the salvation of Israel (see Dt. 32.36).[92] Likewise, a bridge can be found in Romans 9-11 which links the negative statements on Israel (e.g. Rom. 9.27 that a remnant will be saved) to the positive idea in Rom. 11.26 that all Israel will be saved.[93] In fact this

---

as the 'logia' . . . [b]ut they go further than the 'logia' in this respect at least, that in the parables Jesus' understanding of his situation 'enters language' in a special way".

[90] Fuchs, *Historical Jesus*, 221, writes that the "decisive achievement of the parables of Jesus" is that "whoever understands and goes this way moves already in a new context, in being before God. He can then relate God to himself in a relationship like that of the prodigal son to his loving father, and like that of the labourer who actually came too late to the generous lord of the vineyard".

[91] See Bell, *Provoked to Jealousy*, pp. 200-85.

[92] Such a "bridge" is not, of course, unique to Dt. 32.1-43. The same pattern of judgement/salvation can be found in many Old Testament texts (e.g. Hosea 1).

[93] In my review of C. Landmesser, *Wahrheit als Grundbegriff neutestamentlicher Wissenschaft*, *JTS* 51 (2000) 636 (631-37), I raised some questions about taking "consistency" as a criterion of truth, which in turn led to questions regarding Sachkritik. I pointed out in chapter 6 above that according to modern western standards, a contradiction between Romans 9 and 11 can be found and therefore in a sense Bultmann was correct to describe Paul's view of the salvation of Israel as "widerspruchsvoll" (Bultmann, "Geschichte und Eschatologie", 101). But is simple consistency the right criterion to employ here? The truth of Romans 9-11, as in many other biblical texts, is to be found in the dynamic of the text and in the dialectic of judgement and salvation. I therefore questioned Weder's comments on Sachkritik where he argues that God is *either* loving and creative (1 Jn 4.8) *or* judging and destructive (Rev. 19.11-16). "Von Gott kann nicht gleichzeitig wahr sein, dass er *kreativ und destruktiv* ist" (H. Weder, "Die Externität der Mitte. Überlegungen zum hermeneutischen Problem des Kriteriums der Sachkritik am

bridge turns out to be a much more compelling one than that found in Dt. 32.1-43. In the Song of Moses the link is simply that God will vindicate his people "when he sees that their power is gone" (v. 36). In Romans 9-11 the bridge is that Israel's hardening was predestined by God in order that salvation comes to the Gentiles, thus leading to the jealousy of Israel for the Gentile Christians which prepares for the salvation of Israel at the parousia.[94]

The second type of development is that found in Paul's letters from 1 Thessalonians to Galatians and then to Romans. It is difficult to discern any "bridge" here. In this case Paul seems to have changed his mind, moving, as we have seen in chapter 4 above, from a substitution model to one where Israel's election remains firm. This change of mind though, rather than shaming Paul as someone who was "inconsistent", actually demonstrates that Paul, struggling over the question of Israel, was brave enough to change his theological position concerning Israel. His words in Rom. 11.25 "lest you be wise in your own conceits" may even refer back to his own position he held earlier in 1 Thes. 2.13-16: in his own conceits he had believed that God had cast off Israel.[95] I would maintain that texts like 1 Thes. 2.13-16 and Galatians 3-4 actually serve to highlight Paul's position in Romans 9-11. Paul's teaching on Israel would be impoverished if we did not have these earlier works, even though they "contradict" his mature position as found in Romans 9-11.

The third development is that which one finds on the "larger canvas". It is the development which is found thoughout the whole tradition history which is now embedded in the Old and New Testaments. To trace this third type of

---

Neuen Testament", in C. Landmesser, H.-J. Eckstein and H. Lichtenberger (ed.), *Jesus Christus als die Mitte der Schrift* (BZNW 86), Berlin/New York: Walter de Gruyter 1997, 310 (291-320), Weder's emphasis). Note, however, that below I do give an important rôle to Sachkritik. But I do have reservations in applying "consistency" as a criterion of truth in the case of a text like Romans 9-11.

[94] B. Lindars, "The Old Testament and Universalism in Paul", *BJRL* 69 (1986-87) 526 (511-27), describes the jealousy motif as a "master stroke".

[95] Hofius, "Evangelium und Israel", 189, comments on ἵνα μὴ ἦτε ἑατοῖς φρόνιμοι: "Dieser Satz will m.E. dahingehend verstanden sein, daß Paulus die römischen Heidenchristen vor eben jenem Urteil warnen möchte, das er selbst im 1. Thessalonicherbrief gefällt hatte: 'Das Zorngericht Gottes wird jetzt endgültig über sie hereinbrechen' (1Thess 2,16)".

development one has to engage in a careful historical critical approach to the scriptures. Material has to be dated and changes in the tradition history have to be determined. One of the key figures here is Hartmut Gese whose work I believe has proved enormously fruitful. Because of its importance I will spend a little time on his ideas of revelation and tradition history. One of the strengths of his approach is that he is able to give weight to all biblical traditions and to avoid the idea of a canon within the canon. According to Gese one has to consider the whole sweep of the tradition history and revelation is seen to occur in the *mutations* in the *tradition history*.[96] Tradition history corresponds to a revelation history.[97] Further:

> . . . die Offenbarung ging in Lebensvorgänge ein. Und daß die Bibel nicht ein Lehrbuch, sondern ein Lebensbuch ist, Zeugnis gibt und verkündigt, hängt mit dieser Wahrnehmung der Wahrheit im gelebten Leben, im Lebensvollzug zusammen.[98]

So the revelation history is not "jene statische Wahrheit einer zeitlosen Doktrin, sondern die den Menschen ergreifende und ihn wandelnde, die Sein schaffende Wahrheit".[99] Gese takes the example of eternal life: this is only found in certain Psalms (e.g. Psalms 49 and 73) but seemingly denied in earlier ones. Gese writes that the discovery of eternal life does not come about by reception of information but can only be found in an existential struggle.[100] If Paul were familiar with Jesus' teaching on Israel, perhaps he came to his new conclusion in Romans similarly through an "existential struggle". The converse of this is that for the reader the truth of Romans 9-11 can only be appreciated in the light of the teaching of Jesus on Israel. And just as Gese writes that the earlier Psalms which denied eternal life

---

[96] See the MTh dissertation of F.-P. Bock, *Biblical Theology: The Programme of Hartmut Gese and Peter Stuhlmacher*, Aberdeen MTh thesis 1999. Bock rightly points to the influence of G.W.F. Hegel and G. von Rad upon Gese.

[97] So, in the context of a discussion of Psalms 2 and 110 (whereby the idea of the king in Zion as son of God develops into the idea of the messianic king), Gese writes: "Der traditionsgeschichtliche Prozeß entspricht einem offenbarungsgeschichtlichen Prozeß" ("Schriftverständnis", 16).

[98] Gese, "Schriftverständnis", 15.

[99] Gese, "Schriftverständnis", 17.

[100] Gese, "Schriftverständnis", 17: "Erkenntnisse dieser Tiefe sind keine Informationen, die einfach vermittelt werden, sondern gleichsam Einweihungen, Durchgänge, ja Durchbrüche, die vom Menschen vollzogen werden müssen, Akte, in denen er sich selbst wandelt".

were not removed precisely because they were not considered to be "untrue",[101] so Jesus' teaching on Israel cannot be removed on the basis that it contradicts the new insights of Romans 9-11.

However, there are problems with this approach, and I consider just one, returning to more general problems at the end of this chapter. Taking the specific issue of Israel, one can see an intelligible development say from Jesus' judgement on Israel through to Paul's early teaching and then on to Romans 9-11. But after Romans the tradition history "degenerates". So Ephesians is clearly a development of Pauline theology[102] and such that it has been described in an earlier generation as "the crown of St Paul's writings".[103] In certain respects one can certainly find a positive development of themes found in the "genuine seven letters".[104] But on the Israel question there appears to be a regression.[105] Ephesians has no positive theological view of Jews who do not believe in Christ.[106] This omission is striking in view of the fact that Eph. 2.11-22 precisely concerns Israel and the Church. For the author the elect are simply Christians. Then in the

---

[101] Gese, "Schriftverständnis", 17.

[102] This can be understood as a creative systematizing of Paul's thought. See M. Gese, *Das Vermächtnis des Apostels: Die Rezeption der paulinischen Theologie im Epheserbrief* (WUNT 2.99), Tübingen: J.C.B. Mohr (Paul Siebeck) 1997, pp. 271-72: "Aus seiner Kenntnis der paulinischen Briefe heraus gelingt dem Verfasser eine *umfassende Gesamtschau* der paulinischen Theologie. . . . Mit der neu ordnenden Zusammenstellung paulinischer Aussagen beginnt eine *theologische Systematisierung*; der erste Schritt zur Ausbildung eines dogmatischen Systems der paulinischen Theologie ist getan. Dies hat nichts mit einer Erstarrung zu dogmatischen Formeln zu tun, vielmehr konnten wir hinter einer solchen Neustrukturierung einen lebendigen Interpretationsprozeß entdecken" (Gese's emphasis).

[103] J.A. Robinson, *St Paul's Epistle to the Ephesians*, London: Macmillan ²1904, (¹1903), vii.

[104] An example may be the highly exalted view of Christian marriage (Eph. 5.22-33) compared to Paul's view in 1 Cor. 7.8-9.

[105] This is a point which does not seem to be made in Michael Gese's study (cf. *Vermächtnis*, pp. 113-14).

[106] I return to the issue of the "Christologie der Völkerwallfahrt zum Zion" in chapter 11 below. But for now note that Eph. 2.12 speaks of the privileges of Israel *before* Christ. M. Rese, "Die Vorzüge Israels in Röm. 9,4f. und Eph. 2,12", *ThZ* 31 (1975) 221 (211-22) rightly argues: "nach Christus gibt es keine Besonderheit Israels mehr, und deshalb ist es nicht erstaunlich, dass im Epheserbrief im Gegensatz zu Röm. 9-11 weder vom gegenwärtigen noch vom zukünftigen Schicksal Israels die Rede ist und dass allein das Schicksal der Kirche interessiert".

Pastoral Epistles, Jews who do not believe in Christ are portrayed as rather ridiculous people.[107] Such "regression" is a possible problem for this approach of Gese.[108]

This then is a possible way to apply Gese's tradition history to the New Testament. One ought perhaps to highlight that Gese views the "New Testament" as "das apostolische Zeugnis des offenbarungsgeschichtlichen Telos".[109] The idea of "Apostel" assumes "das Endereignis der Auferstehung" such that the apostle is the witness to the resurrection.[110] Biblical tradition history reaches its end with the apostles because the revelation history reaches its goal in the death and resurrection of Jesus.[111]

A variation on this tradition historical approach is that revelation is to be found in the "mutations" in the biblical canon (i.e. in moving from the promises to the fathers, to the exile and return, to the ministry, death and resurrection of Jesus and then to the letters of the "apostles"). Therefore the truth concerning the destiny of Israel is to be found in all biblical tradition in the light of the mutations. But the mutations are not taken in relation to tradition history but in relation to the "position" in the canon. One obvious apparent problem in this approach is that the order of works in the canons of both Old and New Testaments is somewhat arbitrary. Indeed some canons have different orders.[112] However, the broad order of the works according to what

---

[107] Cf. M. Rese, "Church and Israel in the Deuteropauline Letters", *SJT* 43 (1990) 19-32. He concludes: "Historically it seems to be incredible, that one and the same person, Paul, should have changed his mind so drastically with regard to the relationship of church and Israel, that he could be made responsible for the different points of view in Romans 9-11 on the one side and Ephesians and the rest of the Deuteropaulines on the other side". It is perhaps necessary to add that the problem is even more serious. Paul has struggled with his thinking on Israel from 1 Thessalonians to Galatians to his mature thought in Romans. But then if he did write the deutero-Paulines he then regresses back to a view which resembles his earlier view. This seems highly implausible.

[108] It may be objected that exactly the same problem is found in certain interpretations of post-exilic Israel, whereby after the exile Israel's religion became less spontaneous and more fossilized and legalistic, a view I supported in chapter 3 above. However, although Israel's religion degenerated, there are rich theological traditions to be found in the Priestly writing (e.g. concerning sacrifice).

[109] Gese, "Schriftverständnis", 28.

[110] Gese, "Schriftverständnis", 28.

[111] Gese, "Schriftverständnis", 29.

[112] The most obvious examples being MT and LXX.

they purport to portray (primeval history, patriarchs, Sinai, conquest, kings, exile and return, ministry, death and resurrection of Jesus, letters of the "apostles" and the apocalypse) does seem to be a natural progression (and it happens to be the order which the vast majority of "bible-reading Christians" work with). Concerning Paul's epistles, the usual canonical order seems to be based on descending order of length.[113] So Romans appears first. Note, however, that the earliest canon, the Muratorian Canon, gives the historical sequence of letters to Churches as Corinthians, Ephesians, Philippians, Colossians, Galatians, Thessalonians, Romans.[114] If such a canonical approach is adopted, then one could argue that Paul's teaching in Romans is the high point (following the Gospels and Acts). However, one is still left with the problem we noted earlier of the "degeneration" of the teaching concerning Israel.

There are no doubt strengths in some of the above views of the "development of thought". Certainly, the idea that the "truth" regarding Israel is to be found in the movement of thought in Romans 9-11 is one which I adhere to. And there are strengths in Gese's tradition historical approach. However, as I indicated in chapter 3 above, the approach of Gese can result in an over-emphasis of the continuities in the tradition history and a downplaying of the Old Testament/New Testament dialectic. So he maintains:

... daß der Traditionsprozeß ja das Alte beibehält, daß auf der neuen Stufe das Alte verdrängt wird. Das Alte gehört zur Aussage des Neuen. Es wird durch die spätere Stufe nicht überholt, vielmehr entsteht auf diese Weise erst ein mehr oder weniger kontinuierlicher Kanonisierungsprozeß.[115]

Further, he gives a priority to the tradition historical process over the actual content:

Verdrängt die Aneignung der Tradition im Prozeß nicht den eigentlichen Inhalt einer Überlieferung? Die Aussage der Einzelstoffe wird doch relativiert, d.h. in Beziehung gesetzt zur späteren Aussage. Dagegen ist zu sagen: Es soll nicht herausdestilliert wer-

---

[113] F.F. Bruce, *The Canon of Scripture*, Glasgow: Chapter House 1988, p. 130. This order is set by P[46] (although this included Hebrews between Romans and 1 Corinthians and excluded the Pastoral Epistles).

[114] In fact C. Buck, "The Early Order of the Pauline Corpus", *JBL* 68 (1949) 351-57, argued that the early Pauline corpus began with 1 Corinthians and ended with Romans. See, however, the critical comments of G.M. Hahneman, *The Muratorian Fragment and the Development of the Canon* (OTM), Oxford: Clarendon 1992, pp. 86-90.

[115] Gese, "Einheit der biblischen Theologie", 20.

den ein hinter dem Prozeß stehendes Allgemeines und Absolutes, das sich in dem Prozeß verwirklicht. Nicht ein solches postuliertes Absolutes, nämlich, die Offenbarung schlechthin, nicht etwas Zeitloses verwirklicht sich, sondern im Gegenteil, das Entscheidende liegt im Prozeß, im procedere auf ein Zukünftiges hin. Gerade der tiefste Zusammenhang von Tradition und Geschichte weist auf das Ziel der Vollendung.[116]

But if this is the case, is it at all possible to say anything definitive regarding fundamental issues of theology? So what is one to say regarding Israel's election and salvation? What is one to say regarding some of the controversial issues which will be faced in chapters 9 and 10 (e.g. the promise of the land)? Can one say that two conflicting views of Israel are "true"; can one say both that God's election of Israel is conditional and that it is unconditional? King Lear complained of those who said "ay" and "no" to everything he said. He added: "'Ay' and 'no' too was no good divinity".[117] Because of this some form of *Sachkritik* (theological criticism) is going to be inevitable. I therefore turn to the question whether it is at all possible to combine the strengths of Gese's approach with *Sachkritik*. In the course of doing this I will ask some more fundamental questions about the nature of truth.

4. Sachkritik

4.1. Introduction

King Lear's words alert one to the need for Sachkritik. But there are two further reasons for this. The first regards the specific problem of studying the tradition history. I argued above that by considering the mutations in the tradition history one can to some extent give a positive rôle to a text such as 1 Thes. 2.13-16. Further, one can argue that Paul's words in 1 Thes. 2.13-16 serve to highlight his remarkable statements in Rom. 11.25-32 (just as Psalm 88 serves to highlight the "life after death" one finds in Psalm 73). Therefore to some extent I think one can appeal to this sort of tradition-historical approach. However, I noted that if this approach is applied to the whole of the "Pauline corpus" (i.e. including those works which are generally not considered genuine) the problem of the degeneration of the tradition arises.

---

[116] Gese, "Einheit der biblischen Theologie", 20.

[117] Shakespeare, King Lear, Act IV scene vi. The significance of this text was brought to my attention by Otfried Hofius.

This can be seen in the change from Paul to the deutero-Pauline epistles regarding Israel. Also if one were to take the wider canon and consider the issue of justification, there is what I would call a "degeneration" as we move from Paul to James.[118] If we had a simple progressive "revelation" one could perhaps just read off from the final "omega point" and all the preceding revelation could simply serve to highlight that final "revelation". The biblical witnesses are however not so accommodating and this problem of degeneration points to the inevitability of Sachkritik.

But there is also a second and more fundamental reason why the use of Sachkritik is inevitable. This is because the word of God, even though it is understood as coming about because "God has spoken", is only accessible according to the reception of human beings.[119] I now engage in a short examination of the theology of the "word of God" and of "truth" to help clarify the issue of Sachkritik and how it is to be carried out in the case of the diverse teachings found in the New Testament concerning Israel.

4.2. The Word of God

The first point to clarify is that for Paul the "word of God" is equivalent to the term "gospel" and is not to be equated with the apostolic preaching.[120] For John this "word", this λόγος, is of course the word which became flesh and can be said to be a development of Paul's idea that Christ is the content of the word of God, the gospel.[121] The Pauline word of God is the life giving word as opposed to the "law", the word which brings death.[122] The "word

---

[118] I am assuming that Jas 2.14-26 is a response to Paul's teaching on justification in Galatians and Romans rather than vice versa.

[119] Jüngel, "Die Wahrheit des Mythos", 41, writes that protestant theology has not renounced "das immer nur secundum recipientem hominem zugängliche verbum divinum nun doch secundum dicentem deum zu verstehen und auszulegen". He adds: "Nur unter dieser Prämisse ist ja die für die reformatorische Theologie kennzeichnende Rede vom 'Kanon im Kanon' und die auch gegenüber den Texten der Heiligen Schrift erhobene Forderung theologischer 'Sachkritik' überhaupt sinnvoll".

[120] See the discussion in chapter 2 above on 1 Thes. 2.13.

[121] Cf. C.K. Barrett, *The Gospel acording to John*, London: SPCK ²1978, (¹1955), p. 154.

[122] Note, however, that just as the gospel is not equated with the apostolic preaching, so the law in the sense of God's condemning word is not simply equated with the law of Moses. God's condemning word is manifest for Jews in the commandments given to Moses and for Gentiles it is written on their heart (Rom. 2.14-16). See R.H. Bell, *"Extra ecclesiam nulla salus*? Is there a salvation other than through faith in Christ according to

of God" must be distinguished from the "word of theology". Using Jüngel's terminology, I understand the "word of God" as God's own word and I call Jesus Christ the *event* of the word of God in person.[123] Theology is essentially the encounter with this word of God.[124] The word of God cannot be found *in the bible* but can be perceived *through the bible*. The word of God is to be found in the event of the word of God around which the biblical texts are written.[125]

The bible, then, is not itself the word of God. But it is an example of the "word of theology" (of *fundamental and foundational* importance).[126] Further, the bible can be considered as a construct of "theoretical knowing". J. Fischer considers "theoretical knowing" ("theoretische Erkenntnis") to be "scientific knowing" ("wissenschaftliche Erkenntnis"). This is the sort of "knowing" employed in a science such as classical physics.[127] On the other hand "practical knowing" ("praktische Erkenntnis") is the knowing of faith (faith in the Pauline sense). Fischer helpfully distinguishes between these two types of knowing by speaking in terms of "localisation". He writes:

Die wissenschaftliche Erkenntnis lokalisiert das Erkannte im Zusammenhang der Wirklichkeit des Erkennenden, unter den Bedingungen seiner ontologischen Prämissen. *Die*

Romans 2.12-16?", in O. Hofius, S. Hafeman and J. Ådna (ed.), *Evangelium - Schriftauslegung - Kirche*, Göttingen: Vandenhoeck & Ruprecht 1997, 31-43.

[123] E. Jüngel, "Die Freiheit der Theologie", in *Entsprechungen: Gott – Wahrheit – Mensch. Theologische Erörterungen*, München: Chr. Kaiser Verlag 1986, 16 (11-36), identifies Jesus Christ with the "Ereignis des Wortes Gottes in Person". Further, he writes: "Die Sache der Theologie ist Gottes Wort, genauer: das Ereignis des Wortes Gottes" (13).

[124] Cf. Jüngel, "Freiheit", 15: "Geht man davon aus, daß die Theologie vom Worte Gottes herausgefordertes Denken ist, so legt es sich nahe, der Theologie ihren Ort in einem unaufhebbaren *Gegenüber* zum Worte Gottes anzuweisen" (Jüngel's emphasis).

[125] Jüngel, "Freiheit", 16 (who refers to his teacher, Ernst Fuchs).

[126] Clearly in the creator-creation divide, scripture is part of the created order. Luther, *De Servo arbitrio: Duae res sunt Deus et Scriptura Dei, non minus quam duae res sunt, Creator et creatura Dei* (H.-U. Delius, *Martin Luther: Studienausgabe, Band 3*, Berlin: Evangelische Verlagsanstalt 1983, 184.8-9).

[127] Fischer seems to assume that *all science* works with this cartesian system. This, however, is not the case as I argued in "Myths, Metaphors and Models: An Enquiry into the Role of the Person as Subject in Natural Science and Theology", *Studies in Science and Theology* 7 (1999-2000) 115-36.

Erkenntnis des Glaubens dagegen lokalisiert den Erkennenden im Zusammenhang der Wirklichkeit des Erkannten [128]

His comments on the "Erkenntnis des Glaubens" bear a strong resemblance to these words of Bultmann on Jn 17.3 (eternal life being knowledge of the one true God and the one he sent, Jesus Christ):

Diese doppelte d.h. im Grunde einheitliche Erkenntnis – denn Gott wird ja nur durch den Offenbarer erkannt, und dieser ist nur erkannt, wenn in ihm Gott erkannt wird – ist aber identisch mit der dem Glauben verheißenen Erkenntnis der ἀλήθεια ([Jn] 8,32) d.h. mit der Erkenntnis, die Gott als die einzige Wirklichkeit erfaßt und die Wirklichkeit der Welt als Schein durchschaut . . . Das Erkennen aber ist als ein glaubendes . . . kein Distanz nehmendes theoretisches Erkennen, sondern ein sich Bestimmenlassen durch das Erkannte, ein Sein im Erkannten, so daß das Verhältnis zum Offenbarer und zu Gott auch durch das εἶναι ἐν bezeichnet werden kann ([Jn] 15,3 ff.; 17,21). [129]

The biblical witness is therefore an encounter with the word of God and an interpretation of the word of God. [131] The task of the theologian is to study the bible such that one searches for the *verbum dei*. This is what Fischer calls a practical hermeneutic. [132] Fischer writes: "Wirklich *theologische* Hermeneutik müßte daher, statt theoretische Hermeneutik der biblischen Texte, praktische Hermeneutik des vom biblischen Text zu unterscheiden-den Wortes Gottes sein". [133] And it is a practical hermeneutic which requires "Sachkritik" (theological criticism) and historical-critical work. For the word of God although understood *secundum dicentem deum* is given only

---

[128] J. Fischer, *Glaube als Erkenntnis*, München: Chr. Kaiser Verlag 1989, p. 25 (Fischer's emphasis).

[129] Bultmann, *Theologie*, p. 431. I will return to Bultmann's idea of "theoretisches Erkennen".

[130] W.D. Davies, "Paul and the Gentiles: A Suggestion Concerning Romans 11:13-24", in *Jewish and Pauline Studies*, London: SPCK 1984, 155 (153-63).

[131] Cf. Jüngel, "Freiheit", 19: "Das Wort der Theologie ist auslegendes Wort, ein die Ausgelegtheit des Wortes Gottes im Wort der Theologie von einst auslegendes und so nach dem *Ereignis* des Wortes Gottes fragendes Wort".

[132] J. Fischer, "Über die Beziehung von Glaube und Mythos", *ZThK* 85 (1988) 326 (303-28). Fischer believes P. Stuhlmacher, *Vom Verstehen des Neuen Testaments: Eine Hermeneutik*, Göttingen: Vandenhoeck & Ruprecht 1979, is wrong in arguing for an "Einverständnis" *with the biblical texts*.

[133] Fischer, "Glaube und Mythos", 326 (Fischer's emphasis).

secundum recipientem hominem. The theologian therefore needs to engage in "Sachkritik" of the biblical texts in order to seek after the word of God.[134]

There is much value in Fischer's approach. However, the way in which he develops his thought in relation to the question of truth poses some problems and needs to be modified. The fundamental problem for our purposes is: can one actually say anything *about* God and the things of God? Fischer's view displays what Dalferth and Stoellger call "eine veritative und ontologische Inkommensurabilität von Theologie und Glaube".[135] For he builds upon the following idea of Mildenberger:

> Die Wahrheit, der sie [die Theologie] verpflichtet ist, ist ihr äußerlich, verwirklicht sich in anderen Lebenszusammenhängen als denen der theologischen Reflexion. Diese kann den Lebenszusammenhängen nur zudienen, die hier als einfache Gottesrede bezeichnet werden".[136]

Fischer argues that such truth is therefore to be found in "einfache Gottes-rede" rather than in the realm of theological reflective discussion. He stresses that the key is not talking *about* God but rather talking *to* him. The God in the bible is "als *Handelnder*". Faith is concerned with communication between God and man. "An dieser kommunikativen Perspektive des Glaubens hat der theologische Diskurs nicht teil. Er bleibt auf die Ebene der menschlichen Intersubjektivität beschränkt, auf der Gott in der Weise des Redens *über* Gott zur Sprache kommt".[137] Dalferth and Stoellger rightly ask whether "die Wahrheit des Glaubens der Theologie nicht völlig entzogen ist resp. werden kann?"[138] They believe that it is too strong to assert as Fischer does "daß die Wahrheit *nur* im Glaubensleben und *gar nicht* in der Theo-

---

[134] Cf. Jüngel, "Freiheit", 19: "Das Wort der Theologie hat also die Funktion, das immer nur secundum recipientem hominem vernehmbare Wort Gottes secundum dicentem deum zu verantworten. Sie kann diese assertorische Aufgabe jedoch nur wahrnehmen, wenn sie in historisch-kritischer Arbeit die secundum recipientes homines vollzogene Ausgelegtheit des Wortes Gottes analysiert".

[135] I.U. Dalferth and P. Stoellger, "Wahrheit, Glaube und Theologie. Zur theologischen Rezeption zeitgenössischer wahrheitstheoretischer Diskussionen", *ThR* 66 (2001) 43 (36-102).

[136] F. Mildenberger, *Biblische Dogmatik. Eine Biblische Theologie in dogmatischer Perspektive, Band 1. Prolegomena: Verstehen und Geltung der Bibel*, Stuttgart/Berlin/Köln: W. Kohlhammer 1991, p. 15.

[137] J. Fischer, "Zum Wahrheitsanspruch der Theologie", *ThZ* 50 (1994) 100-1 (93-107) (Fischer's emphasis).

[138] Dalferth and Stoellger, "Wahrheit, Glaube und Theologie", 43.

logie präsent und thematisch sei".[139] They continue: "Vielmehr *lebt* auch die Theologie von dieser Wahrheit, die ihr zutiefst *innerlich* ist und von ihr *aufgewiesen* wird, wenn sie das entsprechende Wirklichkeitsverständnis voraussetzt und von ihm her argumentiert".[140] Theology can participate in the life of faith and Fischer's own theology indeed contradicts his own thesis of non-participation.

4.3. Truth

Truth therefore is related to two aspects: faith and theology. In faith one speaks *to* God; in the discourse of theology one speaks *about* God. There is a duality and in both cases one can speak of "truth", the "einfache Gottesrede" being the more fundamental. But as we shall see in the following discussion, to be able to speak of "truth" in relation to "theology" is essential if one is to make any public declaration about the theological status of Israel.

In many circles there has been a reticence to make theological declarations. In England this has something to do with an innate feeling that it is arrogant to make assertions. It is also related to "a kind of relativism which reveals extreme pessimism about questions of truth".[141] In Germany it has something to do with a continental theological tradition which is suspicious of "concepts" and "propositions". To some extent this is found in the work of Bultmann and I want to examine this briefly.

Just as we saw a certain duality in the idea of truth as speaking *to* God and speaking *about* God so in Heidegger and Bultmann we find another kind of duality: truth in the sense of "Aufgedecktheit" and truth in terms of propositions. One of Heidegger's key discussions of his idea of truth is in *Sein und Zeit* § 44.[142] He speaks of two aspects to his understanding of "Wahrheit". The original fundamental idea of truth is "die Erschlossenheit des Daseins".[143] He believes: "Die Wahrheit (Entdecktheit) muß dem

---

[139] Dalferth and Stoellger, "Wahrheit, Glaube und Theologie", 44 (emphasis of Dalferth and Stoellger). They go on to quote Fischer, "Wahrheitsanspruch", 101: "diese Wahrheit ist der Theologie äusserlich und in ihrer Perspektive nicht aufweisbar".

[140] Dalferth and Stoellger, "Wahrheit, Glaube und Theologie", 44 (emphasis of Dalferth and Stoellger).

[141] A.C. Thiselton, "Truth", *NIDNTT* 3:899 (874-902).

[142] M. Heidegger, *Sein und Zeit*, Tübingen: Max Niemeyer [18]2001, pp. 212-30.

[143] Heidegger, *Sein und Zeit*, p. 223. A fundamental point for the uninitiated is that "die Erschlossenheit des Daseins" is a *subjective* genitive. See Landmesser, *Wahrheit*, p. 150 n. 276.

Seienden immer erst abgerungen werden. Das Seiende wird der Verborgenheit entrissen. Die jeweilige faktische Entdecktheit ist gleichsam immer ein
Raub."[144] He suggests that it is no coincidence that the Greeks expressed
the essence of truth in a word having a privative prefix (ά-λήθεια).[145] He
then establishes these two fundamental points regarding his existential-
ontological interpretation of the phenomenon of truth: "1. Wahrheit im
ursprünglichen Sinne ist die Erschlossenheit des Daseins, zu der die Entdecktheit des innerweltlichen Seienden gehört. 2. Das Dasein ist gleichursprünglich in der Wahrheit und Unwahrheit".[146] The reason this understanding of truth is so essential for the basis of our theological enquiry into
"truth" is that it takes seriously the fact that coming to a knowledge of the
truth involves an existential change in the subject.[147] According to Heidegger, "[t]ruth, in effect, is almost synonymous with revelation".[148] Truth is
essentially practical.[149]

But "die Erschlossenheit des Daseins" is related to "die Rede".[150]
"Dasein spricht sich aus; *sich* – als entdeckendes Sein zu Seiendem. Und es
spricht sich als solches über entdecktes Seiendes aus in der Aussage".[151]
This is a fundamental point which a Christian theologian can develop. For
through the expression of credal propositions the "Dasein spricht sich aus".
Therefore although there is a duality in relation to the concept of "truth",

---

[144] Heidegger, *Sein und Zeit*, p. 222 (Heidegger's emphasis).

[145] Heidegger, *Sein und Zeit*, p. 222. The possible problem here of course is whether
the etymology played any part in the Greek understanding of the word (see Thiselton,
"Truth", 875). The word άλήθεια is etymologically related to λήθω, λανθάνω. See LSJ,
p. 64 on άληθής, who quote *EM* 62.51.

[146] Heidegger, *Sein und Zeit*, p. 223.

[147] Cf. E. Jüngel, "Gottesgewißheit", in *Entsprechungen: Gott – Wahrheit – Mensch.
Theologische Erörterungen*, München: Chr. Kaiser Verlag 1986, 264 (252-64): "*Im
Wort des Evangeliums* redet Gott so mit uns, daß er uns unbedingt angeht. Und indem er
uns unbedingt angeht, unterbricht Gott unseren jeweiligen Lebenszusammenhang derart
elementar, daß wir uns selber verlassen, um uns extra nos neu und definitiv zu finden"
(Jüngel's emphasis).

[148] Thiselton, "Truth", 898.

[149] Cf. J. Macquarrie, *An Existentialist Theology. A Comparison of Heidegger and
Bultmann*, London: SCM 1955, pp. 54-55.

[150] Heidegger, *Sein und Zeit*, p. 223.

[151] Heidegger, *Sein und Zeit*, p. 223-24 (Heidegger's emphasis).

"Aufgedecktheit" on the one hand and "statements" and "concepts" on the other, the two can be related.

Landmesser writes that for Bultmann, as for Heidegger, there is the original truth seen as "Enthülltheit oder Aufgedecktheit"[152] and then derived truth which is found in sentences. So there are two related but distinct ideas of truth: "die Enthülltheit des Gegenstandes und die Wahrheit des Satzes".[153] For Bultmann, as in Heidegger, the former is the primary truth, and Landmesser speaks of "einen doppelten Wahrheitsbegriff"[154] or, using an expression of Gethmann, of "zwei äquivoken Wahrheitsbegriffen".[155] Bultmann writes that the primary sense of truth is *"Enthülltheit, Aufgedeckt- heit, der wahre Sachverhalt, der wirkliche Tatbestand. . . . In abgeleiteter Weise wird nun auch eine Rede, ein Satz als wahr* bezeichnet; dann nämlich, wenn sie einen Tatbestand aufdeckt, wenn sie ihn in seiner Wahrheit enthüllt, ihn so darstellt, wie er wirklich ist".[156] Landmesser finds this existential-ontological idea of truth wanting. His key criticism is that Bultmann and the early Heidegger work with two ideas of truth. Landmesser gives Heidegger credit for later realising the problem with his view of truth in *Sein und Zeit*. In his address "Das Ende der Philosophie und die Aufgabe des Denkens" (1964) Heidegger related "Wahrheit" to the "Aussage- wahrheit" whereas "die Erschlossenheit des Daseins wird von ihm terminologisch als Unverborgenheit bestimmt, wobei letzteres dann die ein- zig angemessene Übersetzung von ἀλήθεια sei".[157]

However, despite what Landmesser calls "Martin Heideggers Selbstkor- rektur"[158] it seems that there is something fundamentally right about "zwei äquivoken Wahrheitsbegriffen" and rather than being a problem may actually point to something fundamental. For it could be argued that the New Testament itself has these two ideas of truth. So the first type of truth can

---

[152] Landmesser, *Wahrheit*, p. 192.

[153] Landmesser, *Wahrheit*, p. 193.

[154] Landmesser, *Wahrheit*, p. 159.

[155] Landmesser, *Wahrheit*, p. 161, referring to C.F. Gethmann, "Zu Heideggers Wahrheitsbegriff", *KantSt* 65 (1974) 192 (186-200).

[156] R. Bultmann, "Wahrheit und Gewißheit" (Vortrag gehalten am 2. Oktober 1929), in *Theologische Enzyklopädie* (ed. by E. Jüngel and K.W. Müller), Tübingen: J.C.B. Mohr (Paul Siebeck) 1984, 183 (183-205) (Bultmann's emphasis).

[157] Landmesser, *Wahrheit*, p. 159. See also Gethmann, "Wahrheitsbegriff", 192.

[158] This forms the heading 1.3.6.1 in Landmesser, *Wahrheit*, p. 159.

relate to a number of New Testament texts. In Rom. 1.18 I think Bultmann is correct to understand ἀλήθεια as *"die erschlossene Wirklichkeit (Gottes)"*[159] (*"the revealed reality* (of God)").[160] This truth is not a rationalistic truth.[161] It is not truth in the sense of sentences. Likewise in John, ἀλήθεια takes on various nuances. Jesus Christ is the truth "because he embodies the supreme revelation of God" and is "God's gracious self-disclosure".[162] Bultmann understood ἀλήθεια in John as "die sich offenbarende göttliche Wirklichkeit"[163] which Schnackenburg considers "hat für viele Texte etwas Bestechendes".[164] But although Bultmann may be mistaken in seeing the Gnostic myth as the clue he may still nevertheless be right for some texts.[165] In Jn 14.6 he considers ἀλήθεια to be "die offenbare Wirklichkeit Gottes".[166] Although Schnackenburg disagrees with Bultmann's existential approach, he nevertheless argues that ἀλήθεια has an ontological emphasis.[167] Bultmann rightly emphasizes the personal nature of this "truth":

---

[159] R. Bultmann, ἀλήθεια κτλ, *ThWNT* 1:244 (239-51).

[160] R. Bultmann, ἀλήθεια κτλ, *TDNT* 1:243 (238-51).

[161] Cf. M. Lackmann, *Vom Geheimnis der Schöpfung*, Stuttgart: Evangelisches Verlagswerk 1952, p. 183-84, who is critical of the many who have understood ἀλήθεια here in a rationalistic sense: "Im Munde des Israeliten und Apostels wird er aber nur in Anlehnung an die Schöpfungsvorstellung des Alten Bundes verwandt worden sein, so daß 'Wahrheit' hier gleichbedeutend der sich selbst erschließenden Wirklichkeit Gottes, kein Abstraktum sondern das Konkretum Gottes selbst sein wird" (p. 183).

[162] D.A. Carson, *The Gospel according to John*, Leicester: IVP/Grand Rapids: Wm B. Eerdmans 1995 (repr.), (¹1991), p. 491.

[163] Bultmann, ἀλήθεια, 246.

[164] R. Schnackenburg, *Das Johannesevangelium, II Teil: Kommentar zu Kap. 5-12* (HThKNT 4.2), Freiburg/Basel/Wien: Herder ⁴1985, (¹1971), p. 267.

[165] Schnackenburg, *Johannesevangelium, II*, p. 267, appears to dismiss Bultmann's view for this reason.

[166] R. Bultmann, *Das Evangelium des Johannes* (KEK 2), Göttingen: Vandenhoeck & Ruprecht ¹⁸1964, (¹⁰1941), p. 468. Note that a frequent modern interpretation is that "truth" and "life" serve to explain the term "way". See Schnackenburg, *Johannesevangelium III*, p. 73: "Ich bin der Weg, nämlich die Wahrheit und das Leben". See also Barrett, *John*, p. 458.

[167] R. Schnackenburg, *Das Johannesevangelium, I Teil: Einleitung und Kommentar zu Kap. 1-4* (HThKNT 4.1), Freiburg/Basel/Wien: Herder ⁷1992, (¹1965), p. 248, sees the emphasis on "göttliche Wirklichkeit" in Jn 1.14, 17; 4.23-24; 8.44; 14.6; 17.17; 18.37d.

Die Entdeckung dieser ἀλήθεια ist nicht ein für allemal gesichert und verfügbar und dann 'verkürzt' mitzuteilen wie die Wahrheit der Wissenschaft, sondern jeder muß den Weg zu ihr selber gehen; denn nur im Gehen erschließt sie sich. So ist Jesus die Wahrheit, nicht *sagt* er sie einfach. Man kommt nicht zu ihm, ihn um Wahrheit zu befragen, sondern als zur Wahrheit".[168]

Therefore truth in the New Testament has this personal existential aspect.[169]

But at the same time truth can be expressed in propositions. In order to demonstate this I consider Paul's use of the term "truth of the gospel". Hofius believes that Paul's expression ἡ ἀλήθεια τοῦ εὐαγγελίου (Gal. 2.5, 14) relates not only and not primarily to the *consequences* of the gospel but to the *content* of the gospel. And this content is the person and work of Jesus Christ.[170] Likewise, according to 2 Cor. 4.1-6, the content of Paul's gospel is "der gekreuzigte und auferstandene Herr Jesus Christus in seiner göttlichen Macht und Herrlichkeit".[171] An essential implication of this content is salvation *sola gratia* and *sola fide*. So according to Galatians, salvation through Christ is through grace alone (1.6; 2.21; 5.4) and through faith alone (2.16).[172] Paul is opposing those who claim that salvation is through Christ and the law and is affirming *solus Christus*.[173]

But although the gospel itself cannot be equated with the apostolic preaching the *truth* of the gospel *can* be expressed in human language through assertions. Hofius rightly argues:

Da die von Gott geoffenbarte 'Wahrheit des Evangeliums' inhaltlich klar bestimmt ist, läßt sie sich in menschlicher Sprache *aussagen*. Sie wird in jenen christologischen und

---

[168] Bultmann, *Johannes*, pp. 468-49 (Bultmann's emphasis).

[169] See also E. Jüngel, "Wertlose Wahrheit. Christliche Wahrheitserfahrung im Streit gegen die 'Tyrannei der Werte'", in *Wertlose Wahrheit. Zur Identität und Relevanz des christlichen Glaubens. Theologische Erörterungen III* (BevTh 107), München: Chr. Kaiser Verlag 1990, 100 (90-109), who argues that Jn 14.6 suggests that truth, far from being *adequatio intellectus et rei*, is actually a "Unterbrechung des menschlichen Lebenszusammenhanges". For the idea of interruption in relation to the "Holy Spirit", "love" and "faith", see Jüngel, "Gottesgewißheit", 260, 262, 264.

[170] O. Hofius, "'Die Wahrheit des Evangeliums': Exegetische und theologische Erwägungen zum Wahrheitsanspruch der paulinischen Verkündigung", in *Paulusstudien II* (WUNT 143), Tübingen: J.C.B. Mohr (Paul Siebeck) 2002, 23 (17-37).

[171] Hofius, "Wahrheit", 26.

[172] Hofius, "Wahrheit", 27.

[173] Hofius, "Wahrheit", 27: "Eine notwendige Konsequenz der 'Wahrheit des Evangeliums' – des *solus Christus* – ist das grundsätzliche Nein zur Heilsrelevanz der Tora und somit zur Heilsnotwendigkeit von Tora-Observanz und Beschneidung".

soteriologischen Sätzen laut, die für Paulus zweifellos den Charakter von Assertionen, d.h. von verbindlichen theologischen Ausagen haben.[174]

He then points to 1 Cor. 15.1-2[175] and the "Credo" in 15.3b-5. Such assertions are essential for the Christian faith. One may compare Luther's famous declaration in opposition to the scepticism of Erasmus: "Tolle assertiones, (et) Christianismum tulisti".[176]

So in Paul there is this "equivocation" in respect to truth. There is truth in the sense of revealed reality and truth which can be expressed in the form of propositions. But such "equivocation", rather than being a problem, may well be the clue to "truth". If I may give an everyday example, there are many Christians who have encountered the "truth" in a fundamental way. They have been grasped by the reality of Christ. Yet at the same time they have real problems in formulating "true" propositions.[177] The equivocal nature of truth parallels the equivocal nature of faith. One can say that faith in Paul's theology has two aspects. In one sense faith is related to union with Christ. One participates in the Christ event through faith.[178] But at the same time faith is a rational activity and concerned with propositions. A Christian believes certain things to be true. A Christian believes "that Jesus died and rose again" (1 Thes. 4.14), "that God raised him from the dead" (Rom. 10.9). So faith as union with Christ parallels the existential nature of truth. Faith as believing certain things to be true corresponds to truth as expressed in propositions. Another way of describing the equivocal nature of faith is by the traditional distinction between *fides qua creditur* and *fides quae creditur*.

I therefore wish to give full weight to both aspects of truth, the existential and the propositional. In doing this, it is possible to avoid the weaknesses of

---

[174] Hofius, "Wahrheit", 29 (Hofius' emphasis).

[175] Note Hofius' translation of these difficult verses (Hofius, "Wahrheit", 29): "Ich stelle euch . . . im Blick auf das Evangelium – das ich euch verkündigt habe, das ihr auch empfangen habt, in dem ihr auch euer Fundament habt, durch das ihr auch die Rettung erlangt – nachdrücklich vor Augen, mit welcher *Aussage* ich es euch verkündigt habe . . ." (Hofius' emphasis).

[176] *WA* 18:603 (in Delius (ed.), *Martin Luther: Studienausgabe Band 3*, p. 181).

[177] I hope it is not irreverent to suggest that James, the brother of Jesus, although encountering the truth in the fact that Christ appeared to him, nevertheless had problems with the idea of justification.

[178] See, for example, Bell, "Sacrifice and Christology", 8-9.

Bultmann who relativizes the propositional nature of the Christian faith. Bultmann writes:

> . . . there can be no normative Christian dogmatics, in other words, . . . it is not possible to accomplish the theological task once for all . . . Theology's continuity through the centuries consists not in holding fast to once formulated propositions but in the constant vitality with which faith, fed by its origin, understandably masters its constantly new historical situation. It is of decisive importance that *the theological thoughts be conceived and explicated as thoughts of faith,* that is: *as thoughts in which faith's understanding of God, the world, and man is unfolding itself* . . . *Theological propositions*–even those of the New Testament–can never be the *object* of faith; they can only be the *explication* of the understanding which is inherent in faith itself. Being such explications, they are determined by the believer's situation and hence are necessarily incomplete.[179]

Bultmann is right to affirm that theological statements cannot be the objects of faith.[180] And, I would add, neither can they create faith; for although such theological propositions witness to the word of God, it is this word itself which creates faith and not the theological statements themselves. But I wonder whether the "once formulated propositions" are to be relativized as Bultmann appears to do. To repeat a point Heidegger made: "Dasein spricht sich aus; *sich* – als entdeckendes Sein zu Seiendem. Und es spricht sich als solches über entdecktes Seiendes aus in der Aussage".[181] The truth of theological propositions is related to the primary truth, "die Erschlossenheit des Daseins", but is not to be relativized as Bultmann does.[182]

---

[179] Bultmann, *Theology*, 2:237-38 (Bultmann's emphasis).

[180] Note that although Bultmann equated the gospel with the apostolic preaching, he did make a distinction between kerygma and statements of theology. To some extent this corresponds to the distinction I made above between "word of God" and "word of Theology". But Bultmann's programme differs very much from the one being proposed here.

[181] Heidegger, *Sein und Zeit*, p. 223-24 (Heidegger's emphasis).

[182] E. Jüngel concludes his study of Bultmann's "Theologiebegriff" by putting some "Kritische Rückfragen" ("Glauben und Verstehen. Zum Theologiebegriff Rudolf Bultmanns", in *Wertlose Wahrheit. Zur Identität und Relevanz des christlichen Glaubens. Theologische Erörterungen III* (BevTh 107), München: Chr. Kaiser Verlag 1990, 68-77 (16-77). One of his criticisms of Bultmann is that he should have drawn the conclusion "daß dem theologischen Wissen durchweg ein theoretisches Moment eignet, das zwar niemals vom praktischen Charakter dieses Wissens isoliert werden kann, aber ebensowenig von diesem absorbiert werden darf. Gott wird in der Theologie niemals nur in der Weise der Gegenstände praktischen Wissens Gegenstand des Glaubenswissens. Er bleibt immer der *für* dieses Wissen gegebene Gegenstand, obwohl er niemals nur in der Weise der Gegenstände theoretischen Wissens Gegenstand des Glaubenswissens ist. Und so darf denn die Theologie, wenn sie sachgemäß von Gott reden will, diesen niemals nur

Regarding the nature of truth I want to do justice to the dual nature of truth, truth as disclosure and truth in the form of propositions. But for the purpose of our enquiry about the truth concerning Israel, I focus now on the propositional aspect of truth.[183]

4.4. Sachkritik and Criteria for Truth

When engaging in Sachkritik, some sort of criterion of truth is required. So Landmesser, who largely supports Nicholas Rescher's coherence theory of truth, argues for a "Christologisches Präferenzkriterium".[184] Although I do not think such a coherence theory of truth does full justice to the New Testament, there are nevertheless positive aspects one can utilize.[185] Some sort of "Präferenzkriterium" is necessary since it is possible to have many different groups of coherent propositions. For natural sciences, the "Präferenz-kriterium" is the theoretical explanation of nature and practical prediction and control. For Landmesser such a "Präferenzkriterium" is unsuitable for theology:

Die theologische Wissenschaft hat – kurz gesagt – als Aufgabe die Explikation der christlichen Glaubensinhalte sowie aufgrund dieser Glaubensinhalte die Bereitstellung eines Orientierungs- und Handlungswissens, das es ermöglicht, unter den Bedingungen des christlichen Glaubens verstehend mit der Welt umzugehen.[186]

Pointing to the many texts of the New Testament which concentrate on the person and work of Christ, Landmesser therefore chooses a "Christologi-

---

wie einen Gegenstand theoretischen Wissens oder nur wie einen Gegenstand praktischen Wissens behandeln. Gott ist in der Theologie vielmehr Gegenstand eines Wissens sui generis, das man sich als ein gleichursprünglich theoretisches und praktisches Wissen zu denken hat" (77, Jüngel's emphasis).

[183] In my next project I shall among other things be exploring the truth of myth in relation to the defeat of Satan in New Testament theology. This will deal these two aspects of truth.

[184] One aspect of "coherence" for Landmesser is "consistency", i.e. freedom from contradiction (*Wahrheit*, pp. 458-59). Note some of my reservations above about a rigid application of a criterion of "consistency".

[185] There are two respects in which a simple coherence theory of truth falls short. First, it neglects the existential aspect of truth discussed above. Secondly, a desire for coherence in the sense of consistency is not always helpful for understanding biblical texts such as Romans 9-11. See the discussion in chapter 6 above and see my criticism of Weder's Sachkritik in the present chapter.

[186] Landmesser, *Wahrheit*, p. 461.

sches Präferenzkriterium". He suggests: "Innerhalb des neutestamentlichen Kanons wäre diejenige kohärente Menge von (komplexen) Sätzen vorzuziehen, welche Person und Werk Jesu Christi adäquat – oder wenigstens am ehesten adäquat – zur Geltung bringen können".[187] Although there are indicators in the New Testament itself that this is a suitable "Präferenzkriterium", Landmesser stresses: "Dieses christologische Präferenzkriterium ist – wie jedes andere Präferenzkriterium auch – logisch weder begründbar noch zu bestreiten".[188] This "Präferenzkriterium" is related to the metaphor of "Mitte der Schrift",[189] Jesus Christ being the centre, and implies a "Sachkritik".[190]

Since Christ is the content of the gospel/word of God I agree that this "Christologisches Präferenzkriterium" is entirely appropriate, even if it is not, as Landmesser points out, "logisch . . . begründbar". Such a criterion is of course related to that of Luther: "What urges Christ" ("was Christum treibet").[191] And a good case can be made that Christ comes to be glorified in the *sola gratia, sola fide* theology. For, as we have seen, this is the implication of a *solus Christus* theology.[192]

4.5. *Conclusions concerning the "Truth" about Israel*
When therefore dealing with Paul's assertions about Israel, I suggest that this criterion, "what urges Christ", is entirely appropriate. Therefore 1 Thes.

---

[187] Landmesser, *Wahrheit*, p. 464.

[188] Landmesser, *Wahrheit*, p. 464.

[189] Landmesser, *Wahrheit*, p. 469.

[190] Landmesser, *Wahrheit*, p. 472.

[191] Luther wrote: "Whatever does not teach Christ is not apostolic, even though St. Peter or St. Paul does the teaching. Again, whatever preaches Christ would be apostolic, even if Judas, Annas, Pilate, and Herod were doing it". The German can be found in Bornkamm, *Luthers Vorreden*, pp. 216-17 (in the preface to the epistles of James and Jude): "Was Christum nicht lehret, das ist nicht apostolisch, wenn's gleich S. Petrus oder S. Paulus lehrete. Wiederum, was Christum predigt, das ist apostolisch, wenn's gleich Judas, Hannas, Pilatus und Herodes täte".

[192] A case could perhaps be made that Christ is "urged" when salvation is not simply by grace alone and through faith alone. So Christ could be urged in the letter of James. Does not much of this letter reflect the teaching of Jesus himself (for a useful analysis, see Bauckham, *James*, pp. 93-108)? However, one has to reckon with the fact that James reflects very much the earthly Jesus and has not taken into full consideration the implications of the glorified Jesus.

2.13-16 comes to be criticized not because it is considered "antisemitic"[193] but because Christ is not urged. The truth of Paul's message ultimately depends on whether Christ is glorified through it. And if Jews are singled out as guilty of deicide (as Paul explicitly does in 1 Thes. 2.15) and if their election is denied (which is implied in 1 Thessalonians and made more explicit in Galatians[194]), Christ ultimately is not "urged". The reasons for this are as follows. Regarding deicide, I argued in chapter 2 above that although *historically* the Jews were responsible, *theologically* Jesus was delivered over by God (Rom. 8.32). The central significance of Jesus' death is that he was given up by his Father, Jesus' death being a sacrifice for sin. Blaming any human being for Jesus' death misses the whole point of his atoning death.[195] As regards Israel's election, I believe that by going back on his promises, God would not be honoured and therefore Christ would not be glorified. By going back on his election of Israel the basis for a *sola gratia*, *sola fide* theology is essentially destroyed. Further it undermines the central idea that Christ confirms the promises made to the patriarchs (Rom. 15.8). I therefore believe that a *Sachkritik* ("theological criticism") of Paul's views on Israel in Galatians and 1 Thessalonians is justified.

In the light of Paul's earlier statements in Galatians and 1 Thessalonians, one has to say that Paul's theology of Israel in Romans 9-11 is remarkable. It is true that there are element there which may correspond to what Paul writes in Galatians but, as argued above, Paul provides a bridge between these statements of judgement and the salvation of a remnant (Rom. 9.27) and the positive message of the salvation of all Israel (Rom. 11.25-27). He stresses God's irrevocable call of Israel (Rom. 11.29). Israel's election remains firm and Israel will ultimately be saved.

But I now wish to ask whether the above approach can be combined with Gese's tradition history which was discussed above. His approach has

---

[193] This is a frequent reason given for the rejection of this section.

[194] In view of this one has to say that Galatians, fine though it is in stressing salvation *sola fide* and *sola gratia*, is inconsistent in that the abiding election of Israel is denied.

[195] In this regard it could be said that Paul has a more profound view of Jesus' death than Luke. Luke does emphasize the responsibility of the Jews for Jesus' death (even though, as J.A. Weatherly, *Jewish Responsibility for the Death of Jesus in Luke-Acts* (JSNTSup 106), Sheffield: Sheffield Academic Press 1994, p. 271, rightly concludes: "among Jews Luke regards only the leaders of Jerusalem and the people of Jerusalem as responsible for the crucifixion of Jesus").

certainly been attacked by those who share a "Lutheran" or "Barthian" view of revelation, notably H.-J. Kraus. So Kraus argues that according to Gese's approach, "'Theologie als Traditionsbildung' wird Theologie in eine Phänomenologie der Überlieferungsgeschichte verwandelt".[196] He believes Gese's approach suggests "die entscheidende Einleitungsformel biblischer Aussagen laute nicht, 'So hat Jahwe gesprochen', sondern 'Ich habe es von den Vätern empfangen'. M.a.W. 'Wort Gottes' wird als Kerygma-Phänomen der Tradition verstanden. . . . Statt Theo-Logie – Logo-Paradosie".[197]

Kraus' critique has had some influence.[198] However, Gese feels he has been misrepresented: "Die Traditionsgeschichte ist keine historische Konstruktion, geschweige denn eine an die Texte herangetragene religiöse Phänomenologie".[199] Further, Mildenberger has argued that according to Gese the "Anredecharakter des Wortes Gottes" which Kraus rightly emphasizes does not contradict Gese's approach.[200] For Kraus mistakenly assumes that for Gese the "Traditionsbildung" is "ein verfügendes historisches Rekonstruieren".[201] Mildenberger believes:

> Geses Ausführungen in ihrer, zugegeben schwierigen ontologischen Terminologie zielen aber gerade auf Wirklichkeit, über die das Erkennen nicht verfügt, die sich vielmehr solchem Erkennen, dem die Offenbarung erfahrenden Bewußtsein, selbst zu erkennen gibt".[202]

---

[196] H.-J. Kraus, "Theologie als Traditionsbildung? Zu Hartmut Gese, 'Vom Sinai zum Zion'", *EvTh* 36 (1976) 502 (498-507).

[197] Kraus, "Theologie als Traditionsbildung?", 502.

[198] His critique is adopted by B.S. Childs, *Introduction to the Old Testament as Scripture*, London: SCM 1979, p. 699.

[199] H. Gese, "Der auszulegende Text", in *Alttestamentliche Studien*, Tübingen: J.C.B. Mohr (Paul Siebeck) 1991, 277 (266-82).

[200] F. Mildenberger, "Systematisch-theologische Randbemerkungen zur Diskussion um eine Biblische Theologie", in F. Mildenberger and J. Track (ed.), *Zugang zur Theologie. Fundamentaltheologische Beiträge. Wilfried Joest zum 65. Geburtstag*, Göttingen: Vandenhoeck & Ruprecht 1979, 15 (11-32). Kraus, "Theologie als Traditionsbildung?", 503, writes: "Was Gese mit dem 'tiefsten Zusammenhang von Tradition und Geschichte meint, bleibt unbestimmt. Überhaupt ist es eigenartig, wie beharrlich in unseren Tagen, sei es in der überlieferungsgeschichtlichen Perspektive, sei es in der 'Theologie der Hoffnung', Wort Gottes in die Horizontale eingeordnet wird. Der Anrede-Charakter dieses Wortes wird abgebogen in die Richtung eines Prozesses".

[201] Mildenberger, "Randbemerkungen", 15.

[202] Mildenberger, "Randbemerkungen", 15.

I think Gese's approach can be positively used if the traditions are seen as a representation of how Israel responded to God's self-disclosure. So consider these words of Gese:

The Bible does not teach us revealed truth in doctrinal form. Revelation comes in the form of truth experienced in Israel's life processes–and even at that, this life is almost immeasurably diverse and even seemingly contradictory. This fact, of course, is connected with the very nature of revelation. It is not revelation of the deity as such. It is the revelation of God as Self, in a self-disclosure to his personal counterpart, Israel. It is the revelation of God as the divine 'I' in association with the 'Thou.' It is revelation in an exclusive relation, in an ultimate union between God and humanity: 'I am YHWH, your God.' Revelation in this exclusive personal relationship therefore enters into the very life of this Israel and is rooted in Israel's life processes.[203]

The tradition therefore can be seen as the *response* to this self-disclosure of God (just as above I spoke of the biblical witness as a construct of "theoretical knowing"). Likewise, Mildenberger considers these words of Gese: "Die Geschichte der Traditionsbildung ist in gewisser Weise eine Geschichte des die Offenbarung erfahrenden Bewußtseins, an dem sich eine ungeheure Aufweitung des Wirklichkeitsfeldes vollzieht".[204] Mildenberger believes that one cannot speak of "Theologie als Traditionsbildung". But he thinks one can adopt Gese's "Beschreibung des Traditionsprozesses als Beschreibung dessen zu nehmen, was der Glaube wahrnimmt".[205] So the traditions are not themselves revelation but, as Fischer argues, constructs of theoretical knowing. The traditions show how Israel responded to the "Word of God" but are not to be identified with the "Word of God" itself. Rather they belong to the category of "word of Theology". The word of God is something transcendent. But nevertheless, the *truth* of the word of God can be expressed in assertions as Hofius argues.

These two approaches could be brought together by simply viewing tradition history as a horizontal axis upon which we see the precipitate of revelation. The mutations of tradition history then simply witness rather indirectly

---

[203] H. Gese, "Tradition and Biblical Theology", in D.A. Knight (ed.), *Tradition and Theology in the Old Testament*, London: SPCK 1977, 310 (301-26).

[204] Gese, "Einheit der biblischen Theologie", 23.

[205] Mildenberger, "Randbemerkungen", 14. There may be a terminological problem here. Surely theology is what faith perceives ("was der Glaube wahrnimmt"). What Mildenberger is objecting to is not "Theologie als Traditionsbildung" but rather "Offenbarung als Traditionsbildung".

to the revelation events. But revelation itself is to be seen as occurring on a vertical axis. And Sachkritik can be employed to determine where the focal point of the truth of the revelation is to be found. These two approaches of tradition history and Sachkritik therefore do not have to be set against each other.[206]

---

[206] One may compare also the issue of Heilsgeschichte and justification. These also correspond to a horizontal and vertical axis. As I argued in *Provoked to Jealousy*, p. 61, these two approaches do not have to be set against one another.

Chapter 9

Pauline Perspectives on Israel I

1. Introduction

So far I have been considering Paul's theological understanding of Israel. In this chapter and the next I will consider what relevance Paul has for some central theological questions concerning Israel.

2. Do Jews worship the same God as Christians?

In the Patristic period the Jews were accused by Christians of idolatry.[1] However, it needs to be noted that this was usually because Jews had deserted the one God of the Old Testament and gone after idols. So Tertullian, commenting on Gen. 25.21-23 that two nations are in the womb of Rebecca, identifies the older with the Jews and the younger with Christians. He explains that Israel abandoned the Divinity and worshipped idols:

For, withal, according to the memorial records of the divine Scriptures, the people of the Jews–that is, the more ancient–quite forsook God, and did degrading service to idols, and, abandoning the Divinity, was surrendered to images. . . For thus in the later times in which kings were governing them, did they again, in conjunction with Jeroboam, worship golden kine, and groves, and enslave themselves to Baal. Whence is proved that they have ever been depicted, out of the volume of the divine Scripture, as guilty of the crime

---

[1] For examples of such texts see, for example, P.M. Casey, *From Jewish Prophet to Gentile God: The Origins and Development of New Testament Christology*, Cambridge: James Clarke 1991, pp. 174-75; D. Cohn-Sherbok, *The Crucified Jew: Twenty Centuries of Christian Anti-Semitism*, London: Harper Collins 1992, pp. 26-28. See also the detailed discussion in K.H. Rengstorf and S. von Kortzfleisch (ed.), *Kirche und Synagoge: Handbuch zur Geschichte von Christen und Juden. Darstellung mit Quellen*, 2 vols, München: DTV 1988 (repr.), ([1]1968-70), 1:84-209 (B. Blumenkranz, "Die Entwicklung im Westen zwischen 200 und 1200", 84-135; B. Kötting, "Die Entwicklung im Osten bis Justinian", 136-175; W. Cramer, "Die Entwicklung im Bereich der orientalischen Kirchen", 176-209).

of idolatry; whereas our 'less'–that is, posterior–people, quitting the idols which formerly it used slavishly to serve, has been converted to the same God from whom Israel, as we have above related, had departed. For thus has the 'less'–that is posterior–people overcome the 'greater people,' while it attains the grace of divine favour, from which Israel has been divorced.[2]

Likewise Ephraim Syrus writes: "But Israel crucified our Lord, on the plea that verily He was seducing us from the One God. But they themselves used constantly to wander away from the One God through their many idols".[3] The assumption then seems to be that Jews have left the worship of the One God (identified with the God of Christians) and worshipped idols. The position of John Chrysostom seems much more radical. He seems to believe that in principle it is impossible for a non Christian Jew to worship the true God.

Jeremiah said . . . 'I have abandoned my house, I have cast off my inheritance.' But when God forsakes a people, what hope of salvation is left? When God forsakes a place, that place becomes the dwelling of demons. (2) But at any rate the Jews say that they, too, adore God. God forbid that I say that. No Jew adores God! Who says so? The Son of God says so. For he said: 'If you were to know my Father, you would also know me. But you neither know me nor do you know my Father'. Could I produce a witness more trustworthy than the Son of God? (3) If, then, the Jews fail to know the Father, if they crucified the Son, if they thrust off the help of the Spirit, who should not make bold to declare plainly that the synagogue is a dwelling of demons? God is not worshipped there. Heaven forbid! From now on it remains a place of idolatry.[4]

A central part of his argument, based on a misquotation from Jn 8.19,[5] is that since the Jews do not *know* God then they do not *worship* God. Whilst it is true generally that worship of God has to be intelligent worship, it must be stressed that Paul, as we shall see, has a somewhat different perspective. Chrysostom further argues that even though there are no images in the synagogues, they are the homes of idolatry and devils.[6] Chrysostom

---

[2] Tertullian, "An Answer to the Jews" 1, *ANF* 3:151-52.

[3] Ephraim Syrus, Homily "On our Lord" 6, *NPNF2* 13:307.

[4] Chrysostom, Discourses 1.3.1-3 (Harkins, *Discourses against Judaizing Christians*, p. 11).

[5] Jn 8.19 is actually: "You know neither me nor my Father. If you knew me, you would know my Father also". There are no significant textual variants.

[6] Chrysostom, Discourses 1.6.3: "For, tell me, is not the dwelling place of demons a place of impiety even if no god's statue stands there? Here the slayers of Christ gather together, here the cross is driven out, here God is blasphemed, here the Father is ignored, here the Son is outraged, here the grace of the Spirit is rejected. Does not greater harm come from this place since the Jews themselves are demons?" (Harkins, *Discourses*, p. 23).

delivered his eight sermons against the Jews in Antioch in 387, the occasion being that Christians were attending synagogue services. As was pointed out in chapter 4 above, he actually directed his sermons against the *Christians* who were attending the services. Chrysostom claims that attending a synagogue is effectively blasphemy.[7] Further, if Christians attempt to justify themselves through the law, they must be prepared for the verdict "Depart, I know you not". "You made common cause with those who crucified me. You . . . started up again the festivals to which I had put an end".[8] Chrysostom propagates the view that the destruction of Jerusalem and its temple was an act of God's wrath.[9] He admits that there are holy books in the synagogue. But these books do not serve to sanctify the synagogue;[10] the Jews do not honour these books but rather they disbelieve them and reject their witness.[11] Note, however, that Chrysostom never goes to the point of saying that the Old Testament God is a different God to that of the New Testament.[12]

The Gnostics, however, went a stage further in claiming that the God of the Old Testament (whom the Jews worship) is not the same as the Father of Jesus Christ. Therefore they developed the idea of the demiurge, the creator God. Such a view goes well beyond what the New Testament teaches. It is true that the Johannine Jesus says the Jews do not know the Father (Jn 5.37-38; 7.28; 8.19, 54-55; 15.21; 16.3). In fact the Father had not been known by the world before Christ revealed him (Jn 15.21; 17.25) and Christ reveals the name of the Father (Jn 17.6, 26). But this does not imply that the Father is to be distinguished from "Yahweh". It is true that Yahweh, according to the Old Testament, was already known to the people of Israel. But the Johannine Jesus works with the assumption that such a God is only known

---

[7] Cf. Chrysostom, Discourses 1.7.11.

[8] Chrysostom, Discourses 6.7.4 (Harkins, *Discourses*, p. 174).

[9] Chryostom, Discourses 6.3.6 (Harkins, *Discourses*, p. 157)

[10] Chryostom, Discourses 1.5.2 (Harkins, *Discourses*, p. 18-19); Discourses 6.7.1 (Harkins, *Discourses*, p. 172).

[11] Chryostom, Discourses 1.5.2 (Harkins, *Discourses*, p. 19); cf. Discourses 6.6.8-11 (Harkins, *Discourses*, pp. 170-72).

[12] Chrysostom has been sharply criticized for his views on the Jews. So J. Parkes, *The Conflict of the Church and the Synagogue: A study in the origins of antisemitism*, London: Soncino 1934, p. 163 writes: "In these discourses there is no sneer too mean, no gibe too bitter for him to fling at the Jewish people".

through himself. Such a God is not known through Judaism. This view finds a parallel in Paul that Christ makes the history of Israel concrete. It must be stressed that although Paul and John were often appealed to by the Gnostics and may in fact have given rise to Gnosticism, the Gnostic separation of Gods is going beyond what John and Paul teach.[13]

Marcion also posited the idea of separate Gods.[14] It can be maintained that the roots of Marcion's system are to be found in Paul. So Harnack writes:

Wie immer M[arcion] den Gegensatz von Glaube und Werken, Evangelium und Gesetz aufgefaßt und welche Folgerungen er aus ihm für die Religionslehre gezogen hat – er war das wirklich, was er sein wollte, ein Jünger des Paulus, der das Werk und den Kampf des Apostels wiederaufgenommen hat als ein wirklicher Reformator.[15]

Therefore the possibility arises that Paul himself believed that Jews and Christians worship different Gods. This may at first appear to receive some support. It could be argued that since Paul held to a trinitarian[16] (or at least binitarian) view of God, he assumed Jews do not worship the same God as Christians. However, nowhere in Paul is there a suggestion that Jews worship a different God.[17] So in Rom. 10.2 he says Jews have a "zeal for God but not according to knowledge". They may be misguided but their God is

---

[13] S. Pétrement, *A Separate God: The Origins and Teachings of Gnosticism* ET, San Francisco: Harper 1990, p. 211, writes: "It is true that the Gnostics diverge from Paul and John in considering that the God of the Old Testament is not the Father spoken of by the Savior". Pétrement then argues that this questioning of the Old Testament, prepared for by Paul's criticism of the law and John's anti-Jewish polemic, might be explained by the growing tension between Christianity and Judaism at the end of the first and beginning of the second century.

[14] For Marcion's view of the Jewish God see A. von Harnack, *Marcion: Das Evangelium vom fremden Gott* (BKT), Darmstadt: Wissenschaftliche Buchgesellschaft 1996 (repr.), (²1924), pp. 106-118. Harnack stresses that although Gnosticism and Marcion had common elements, the two are in fact quite different (see *Marcion*, pp. 196-97 n. 1).

[15] See Harnack, *Marcion*, p. 198.

[16] See F. Watson, "The Triune Divine Identity: Reflections on Pauline God-Language, in Disagreement with J.D.G. Dunn", *JSNT* 80 (2000) 99-124.

[17] Also Harnack, *Marcion*, p. 199, writes that Paul would have been shocked by Marcion's teaching. Nevertheless Harnack claims that the step which Marcion took (based on Paulinism) was actually smaller than the step Paul himself took. But Harnack, as is well known, took a radical view of Paul's understanding of the Old Testament (see, e.g., *Marcion*, pp. 202-3).

the same as the God Paul worships. Jews may have wrong ideas about the one true God, but they are referring to the one same reality. In this discussion, it is essential to make a clear distinction between reference and description. Although Christian and Jewish *descriptions* of God may differ, the *reference* is the same.[18] For example, in Rom. 10.2 Paul does not dispute that Jews worship the same God as Christians do. Tertullian in fact appealed to Rom. 10.2-4 in his treatise against Marcion. After quoting these verses he writes:

> Hereupon we shall be confronted with an argument of the heretic, that the Jews were ignorant of the superior God, since, in opposition to him, they set up their own righteousness–that is, the righteousness of their law–not receiving Christ, the end (or finisher) of the law. But how then is it that he bears testimony to their zeal for their own God, if it is not in respect of the same God that he upbraids them for their ignorance? They were affected indeed with zeal for God, but it was not an intelligent zeal; they were, in fact, ignorant of Him, because they were ignorant of His dispensations by Christ, who was to bring about the consummation of the law; and in this way did they maintain their own righteousness in opposition to Him.[19]

Tertullian also points to 1 Thes. 2.15. He quotes it as "Who killed the Lord Jesus and their own prophets" but adds "although (the pronoun) *their own* be an addition of the heretics". He then asks:

> Now, what was there so very acrimonious in their killing Christ the proclaimer of the new god, after they had put to death also the prophets of their own god? The fact, however, of their having slain the Lord and His servants, is put as a case of climax. Now, if it were the Christ of one god and the prophets of another god whom they slew, he would certainly have placed the impious crimes on the same level, instead of mentioning them in the way of a climax; but they did not admit of being put on the same level; the climax therefore was only possible by the sin having been in fact committed against one and the same Lord in the two respective circumstances. To one and the same Lord, then, belonged Christ and the prophets.[20]

This text, although it counters Marcion's view, does not necessarily prove that Paul believed the Jews of his time worshipped the same God as he did. Rom. 10.2, however, does demonstrate this.

Paul's attitude to pagans, however, was quite different. For Paul, their "god" was a different entity. In fact Paul argues in 1 Cor. 10.19-20 that

---

[18] See Bell, *No one seeks for God*, p. 112 n. 227.

[19] Tertullian, Against Marcion 5.14, *ANF* 3:460 (271-474).

[20] Tertullian, Against Marcion 5.15, *ANF* 3:462.

pagans sacrifice not to a "god" but to demons.[21] Paul seems to be saying that as far as pagan gods are concerned, the *reference* as well as the *description* are quite different. Outside these two covenant peoples of Israel and the Church, all speech about "God" refers to something other than the true God. It is therefore essential to appreciate the point that reference to the same God depends on the covenant God has made exclusively with Jews and with Christians. And this God who has made a covenant with Jews and Christians is "Christlike". For just as "God is light and in him is no darkness at all" (1 Jn 1.5), so, as a former Archbishop of Canterbury put it, one can say "God is Christlike and in him there is no unChristlikeness at all".[22] Further, "The Christlikeness of God means that his passion and resurrection are the key to the very meaning of God's own deity".[23]

From a Pauline perspective it can be affirmed that non-Christian Jews worship the same God as Christians. But any other religion apart from Judaism and Christianity involves some other god. It is therefore regrettable that Judaism is often bracketed with other non-Christian religions. And for this reason I find the third collect for Good Friday in the Book of Common Prayer questionable in that it puts Jews together with Turks and Infidels and Heretics:[24]

---

[21] See, for example, the comments of Lang, *Korinther*, p. 128, and Schrage, *Korinther 2*, p. 444.

[22] A.M. Ramsey, *God, Christ and the World: A Study in Contemporary Theology*, London: SCM 1969, p. 98.

[23] Ramsey, *God, Christ and the World*, p. 99.

[24] However, I do not have any problems about the reference in the prayer that their hardness of heart be taken away. A new Christian prayer for the Jews is that the blindness of *Christians* be taken away and that there be greater understanding between Jews and Christians. So see the new "politically correct" prayer of the Church of England (*Lent, Holy Week, Easter: Services and Prayers*, London: Church House Publishing/SPCK/ Cambridge: CUP 1986, pp. 213-14):

Let us pray for God's ancient people, the Jews,
the first to hear his word–
for greater understanding between Christian and Jew
for the removal of our blindness and bitterness of heart
that God will grant us grace to be faithful to his covenant
and to grow in love of his name.

The beginning of this prayer is similar to that found in H. Winstone (ed.), *The Sunday Missal*, London: Collins [2]1977, ([1]1975), p. 197:

Let us pray
for the Jewish people,

. . . Have mercy upon all Jews, Turks, Infidels, and Hereticks, and take from them all ignorance, hardness of heart, and contempt for thy word . . . [25]

Although the Jew stands first in the list,[26] he is essentially lumped together with all other unbelievers. The same thing happens in Luther's Large Catechism, where he writes that belief in a "holy, Christian Church" separates "us Christians from all other peoples on earth . . . be they heathens, Turks, Jews, or false Christians and hypocrites".[27] It is also unfortunate that Jews are put together with other non-Christians (Hindus, Buddhists, Muslims) in the "Declaration on the Relationship of the Church to Non-Christian Religions" (*Nostra aetate*) of the Second Vatican Council.[28]

---

the first to hear the word of God,
that they may continue to grow in the love of his name
and in faithfulness to his covenant.

Both prayers are woefully inadequate. They give no indication that Israel is cut off from Christ and needs to believe in him. I am grateful to Revd Dr John Darch of St John's College, Bramcote, Nottingham, for locating the first prayer and to my colleague Mr Ed Ball at Nottingham University for locating the second.

[25] *Book of Common Prayer*, Cambridge: CUP (no date), p. 121.

[26] A point raised by J. Jocz, *The Jewish People and Jesus Christ: A Study in the Relationship between the Jewish People and Jesus Christ*, London: SPCK 1949, pp. 314-15. Jocz (interestingly as a Jewish Christian) describes the collect as "beautiful". The beauty of the collect is seen for example in the prayer "fetch them home, blessed Lord, to thy flock". Note, however, the implied substitution model in that "they may be saved among the remnant of the true Israelites", these "true Israelites" being Christians (predominantly Gentile).

[27] See H.A. Oberman, *The Roots of Anti-semitism in the Age of Renaissance and Reformation* ET, Philadelphia: Fortress Press 1984, p. 103.

[28] For the Latin text (with German translation) see H. Denzinger, *Enchiridion symbolorum definitionum et declarationum de rebus fidei et morum* (ed. P. Hünermann), Freiburg: Herder 1991, pp. 1245-49. For an English translation see W.M. Abbott (ed.), *The Documents of Vatican II*, London/Dublin: Geoffrey Chapman 1966, pp. 660-68. Originally the council planned a document concerning the Church and the Jews. This was initiated by John XXIII, written under Cardinal Bea and submitted to the central commission in June 1962. However, it had to be withdrawn due to a protest by the Arab world (see Denzinger/Hünermann, *Enchiridion*, p. 1245; Abbott, *Vatican II*, 656-57). The section on the Jewish people (article 4) makes up about 40% of the declaration.

3. The Witness of Israel to God and the World

The first sense in which Israel witnesses to God is, as Paul emphasizes, that they are entrusted with the "oracles of God", that is God's revelation in the scriptures.[29] Also to them belong the Patriarchs and from them comes the Christ "according to the flesh" (Rom. 9.4-5). They are the tree into which the wild olive branches have been grafted (Rom. 11.17-24).

But Israel also represents humanity in relationship to God. There have been two sides to this. The first is that Israel represents the human being under God's judgement and in rebellion against God. The second is that Israel represents the human being receiving the promises of God. I will now expand on these two aspects.

Israel throughout her history has been seen as in rebellion against God. This is found in the Old Testament and for the Christian this rebellion finds its culmination in Israel's rejection of Jesus and rejection of the Gospel. Israel represents the "No" of humanity to God. Also for Paul Israel represents the religious person who by his good works tries to make a claim upon God.[30]

The consequence of this rebellion is that Israel is placed under the curse of God. Israel again is representative of the whole of humanity. The law as the condemning word of God accuses both Jews and Gentiles.[31] For not only is Israel under this curse of the law but the whole of humanity is also under this curse (Gal. 3.12-13). I imagine that many theologians who have been shaped by Paul's theology would accept such an understanding of the curse upon Israel as a representative curse. But in much of Christian tradition the Jew has been understood to live under a special curse, a curse which has not come upon other peoples. This has largely come about because of their part in the death of Jesus. Such a view can even be found (perhaps rather surprisingly) in the writings of Bonhoeffer. "The church of Christ has never lost sight of the thought that the 'chosen people', who nailed the redeemer of the world to the cross, must bear the curse for its action through

---

[29] See the discussion of Rom. 3.2 in chapter 4 above.

[30] See chapter 3 above.

[31] It is of course true that only Jews possess the law in the sense that they have the law of Moses. But Paul views Gentiles also as condemned by the law since they have the "work of the law" i.e. the demand of the law written on their hearts (Rom. 2.15). See Bell, *No one seeks for God*, p. 157.

a long history of suffering".[32] He speaks of the "consciousness on the part of
the church of the curse that bears down upon this people".[33]

Can such a view be defended by Paul? Certainly he does speak of God's
judgement coming upon the Jews (1 Thes. 2.16) which is related to their
"killing Jesus". But even here, despite the theological problems involved, it
is unlikely that Paul is relating God's judgement upon Israel to some historical calamity.[34] In fact nowhere does Paul relate Israel's curse to a historical
event or a series of historical events. What Paul would have made of 70 AD
we can hardly guess. Had he lived to know of it, perhaps he would have
shared the view of the synoptic gospels that this was a judgement of God
upon Israel. But moving on to Romans 9-11, we find here a quite different
sort of "curse": Israel is hardened by God (Rom. 9.18; 11.7-10). But this
"curse" is not a *reaction* of God to Israel's disobedience. Rather, Israel's
rejection of Christ is a *consequence* of this hardening. He may even be
saying that God has made himself an enemy of Israel (see the exegesis of
Rom. 11.28 in chapter 7 above). In view of this I think that there is no
escaping the fact that Israel is under a special curse of God. For Israel has
been hardened precisely in order that the gospel goes out to the nations
(Rom. 11.11). Israel is under a curse *for our sake*.

So Israel is under a special judgement in that she is hardened for the sake
of the Gentiles; but she also represents the human being under God's judgement. At the same time, however, Israel is in receipt of God's special promises. She is under God's special protection and God's promises to Israel still
stand. I will turn to this issue below. But as well as being in receipt of God's

---

[32] D. Bonhoeffer, *No Rusty Swords*, London/New York 1965, p. 226. This is followed by a quotation from Luther's Table Talk. Bonhoeffer does, however, qualify this
by adding: "But the history of the suffering of this people, loved and punished by God,
stands under the sign of the final home-coming of the people of Israel to its God".

[33] Bonhoeffer, *No Rusty Swords*, p. 227. Three things should be noted. First, the
above two quotations come from a text from 1933 where Bonhoeffer attacks the "Aryan
Clauses" which disqualified those of Jewish origin from holding office in the state. Secondly, Bonhoeffer changed his mind. According to B. Klappert, *Miterben der Verheißung: Beiträge zum jüdisch-christlichen Dialog* (NBST 25), Neukirchen-Vluyn:
Neukirchener 2000, pp. 72-80, Bonhoeffer moved away from this position (Klappert
calls it a "theologische[s] Antijudaismus"), the events of 1938 (Reichskristallnacht) and
1940 (expulsions) being decisive. Thirdly, even in 1933 Bonhoeffer affirmed the abiding
election of Israel (Klappert, *Miterben*, pp. 75-76).

[34] See the discussion on 1 Thes. 2.16 in chapter 2 above.

promises, Israel also represents humanity as a whole. Just as the Jew represents the human being receiving the promises of God,[35] so Israel represents the faithfulness of God to humanity. Zimmermann, physician to Frederick the Great, told him that the continued existence of the Jews was a proof of God's existence.[36] Barth sees the Jewish people and the Christian Church as miraculously sustained people. "By all analogies of world history, the Jews as a race should no longer have existed after the Fall of Jerusalem in A.D. 70. . . . The Christian community exists in the same way as the Jews; miraculously sustained throughout the years . . .".[37] Although I do not believe that God's existence can be "proved" by such observations, the continued existence of Israel through a traumatic history does witness to God's faithfulness. During the biblical period Israel was broken up by the Assyrians, Babylonians, Greeks and Romans. Various attempts were made to wipe out Israel. This was done in a variety of ways: destroying Israel's cities (by Assyria), taking Israel into exile (by Babylon), trying to destroy her faith (by the Greeks), destroying her capital city (by Rome), scattering the Jews throughout the world (by Rome). After the biblical period, Israel faced persecution, expulsion, and the end of the second millenium witnessed a systematic attempt to obliterate them. Yet Israel has continued as a distinct people. Erik Peterson commented: "No power in the world will be able to extirpate Judaism. Indeed not even the Jews themselves will be able to extirpate themselves so long as God's long-suffering endures this year also (Lk. 13.8) the vessels of wrath".[38]

---

[35] See the discussion in chapter 3 above.

[36] See D.W. Torrance, "The witness of the Jews to God (their purpose in history)", in D.W. Torrance (ed.), *The Witness of the Jews to God*, Edinburgh: Handsel Press 1982, 1 (1-12). It is also worth noting that the continued existence of the Jewish people and of Judaism was an enigma for G.W.F. Hegel. See H. Graetz, *Geschichte der Juden*, 11 vols, Darmstadt: Wissenschaftliche Buchgesellschaft 1998 (repr.), 11:409-13; *History of the Jews* ET, 6 vols, Philadelphia: JPS 1891-98, 5:583-86. Graetz quotes from Edward Gans, someone whom Graetz believed had been led astray by Hegel's philosophy: "Die Juden können weder untergehen, noch kann sich das Judentum auflösen. Aber in der großen Bewegung des Ganzen soll es untergegangen scheinen und dennoch fortleben, wie der Strom fortlebt in dem Ozean" (*Geschichte*, 11:412).

[37] K. Barth, "The Jewish Problem and the Christian Answer", in *Against the Stream: Shorter Post-War Writings 1946-52*, London: SCM 1954, 196, 200 (195-201).

[38] Peterson, *Kirche*, p. 226, quoted in Barth, *CD* 2.2:226.

There is, I believe, a certain symmetry in that Israel is under a special judgement yet also represents humanity under the judgement of God; and at the same time is in receipt of special promises and yet also represents humanity receiving the promises of God. Israel is under a special curse but is also the apple of God's eye (Dt. 32.10). And whoever touches Israel touches the apple of God's eye (Zech. 2.8).

This brings me to the final witness of Israel to God, her suffering. And I now turn to the most traumatic period of Israel's history of suffering, the Holocaust.

4. The Holocaust

The Holocaust[39] is perhaps the most theologically perplexing of all acts of cruelty.[40] Other genocides have been appalling. One thinks of the massacre of Armenian Christians by the Turks last century (which the Turks until today virtually deny). But the Holocaust was not simply an act of genocide. It was the attempt by an avowedly "Christian" culture to wipe out the people of God. In this sense it stands way beyond events in Armenia or Bosnia, terrible though they have been. Further, many Christians either acquiesced (by opposing any resistance to Hitler) or took part in the extermination of Jews. Dare anyone claim that no genuinely believing Christians took part in the mass extermination? How then could genuinely believing Christians either take part in or allow such an atrocious act?

This brings me to the uncomfortable issue whether Paul's teaching on Israel directly or indirectly influenced the Holocaust. There are four significant points to make.

---

[39] The term Holocaust (whole offering or burnt offering) was introduced by Elie Wiesel, an American Jewish writer and a survivor of Auschwitz. The term will be used here although, as H. Küng, *Judaism: The Religious Situation of our Time* ET, London: SCM 1992, p. 239, points out, it is not without its problems. The Jews wanted to live, not die, and those who exterminated them did not want them to be a sacrifice. Therefore the term Shoah (disaster, castatrophe) is employed by many Jews. Küng, *Judaism*, p. 239, points out that the term as used in Is. 47.11 is applied to Bablyon and therefore is also not an ideal term. Other biblical uses of the term also seem inappropriate (e.g. in Zeph. 1.15 the word is used in connection with the day of the Lord, i.e. the day of judgement).

[40] Cf. the address by V. Drehsen in Katz, *Antisemitismus*, p. 108, who says that at the heart of Steven Katz's work lies his "respect for the singularity of the Holocaust".

4.1. Paul and the Persecution of the Jews

First, it has been claimed that the New Testament teaching on Judaism is to some extent responsible for the Holocaust. For example, James Parkes, a Christian expert on antisemitism, writes:

> More than six million deliberate murders are the consequence of the teachings about Jews for which the Christian Church is ultimately responsible, and of an attitude to Judaism which is not only maintained by all the Christian churches, but has its ultimate resting place in the teaching of the New Testament itself.[41]

However, when one reads the reasons for the "Final Solution" ("Endlö-sung"),[42] the New Testament view of Judaism does not appear to figure.[43] It would be extremely difficult to argue that the New Testament view of Jewish responsibility for the death of Jesus or Paul's critique of Judaism had any influence.[44] It is true that Hitler when questioned by two bishops about his racial policy said that he was only putting into practice what the Church had taught for 2000 years. But, as Saperstein argues, he was clearly scoring a debating point rather than explaining his own motivation.[45] And it needs stressing again that the New Testament itself, even in its most antisemitic sections, never argues that Jews should be persecuted.[46] But what is one to

---

[41] Quoted in Saperstein, *Moments of Crisis*, p. 74 n. 2.

[42] In 1941 Göring gave Heydrich the task of carrying out a "final solution" or "total solution" to the Jewish question. The Wannsee conference convened on 20 January 1942 discussed the means of implementing the "final solution".

[43] It is true that in the earlier years appeal was made to antisemitism in Christian tradition. See, e.g., Dietrich Eckart, *Der Bolschewismus von Moses bis Lenin. Zwiegespräch zwischen Adolf Hitler und mir*, München 1924 (discussed in K. Scholder, *Requiem*, p. 173).

[44] Perhaps one of the most uncomfortable passages for a Christian reading the *Table-Talk* is where Hitler argues that the Passion Play at Oberammergau be continued "for never has the menace of Jewry been so convincingly portrayed as in this presentation of what happened in the times of the Romans. There one sees in Pontius Pilate a Roman racially and intellectually so superior, that he stands out like a firm, clean rock in the middle of the whole muck and mire of Jewry" (H. Trevor-Roper (ed.), *Hitler's Table-Talk, 1941-44*, Oxford: OUP 1988 (repr.), ([1]1953), p. 563, 5 July 1942). However, note that Hitler does not so much criticize the Jews for killing Jesus. Rather, he reads his racial theories into the Passion Play.

[45] See Saperstein, *Moments of Crisis*, p. 40.

[46] Note, the rather odd speech of Hitler's given to a catholic audience in April 1922: "I tell you that my Christian feelings point me to the man who once in solitude, surrounded by only a few supporters, recognized these Jews and summoned people to fight against them . . . But today, after two thousand years, I can recognize his tremendous

say to the passages in *Mein Kampf* where Hitler calls upon divine sanction for his views about the Jews? He writes "I believe that I am acting in accordance with the will of the Almighty Creator: by defending myself against the Jew, I am fighting for the work of the Lord".[47] But the context clearly shows that Hitler's "Lord" is far from being the one true God of the bible.[48]

4.2. Paul's Influence via Luther

My second point is that it is hard to make a case that Paul via Luther contributed to the Holocaust.[49] Paul was of course the fundamental influence on Luther and Luther's bitter words about the Jews were appealed to in nazi Germany.[50] It is significant that "On the Jews and their Lies" was included in the second Munich edition of Luther's selected works (1936)[51] but had not been included in the first edition (1922ff.) or third edition (1948ff.).[52] Also a pamphlet containing excerpts of Luther's work, including his programme of persecution, was printed separately by the nazis and distributed in Germany and Sweden.[53] Although Luther does appeal to Paul for some of his points, his understanding of Paul is often either flawed or he draws a

---

battle for this world against the Jewish poison, and be most deeply and powerfully moved by the fact that he had to shed his blood for it on the cross" (quoted in Scholder, *Requiem*, pp. 172-73).

[47] Quoted in Saperstein, *Moments of Crisis*, p. 40.

[48] On Hitler's relationship to Christinaity, see Scholder, *Requiem*, pp. 172-75. One of the remarkable stories which highlights Hitler's religion concerns his speech at the funeral celebration of President Hindenburg (7 August 1934). After the Protestant Bishop of the Wehrmacht had given what one could call a biblical sermon, Hitler gave his speech which ended: "Departed General, go now to Valhalla" (K. Scholder, *The Churches and the Third Reich, Volume 2: The Year of Disillusionment: 1934 Barmen and Rome* ET, London: SCM 1988, p. 210).

[49] The literature on Luther and the Jews is vast. On Luther against the Jews see H.J. Hillerbrand, "Martin Luther and the Jews", in J.H. Charlesworth (ed.), *Jews and Christians: Exploring the Past, Present, and Future*, New York: Crossroad 1990, 127-45; W. Maurer, in Rengstorf and von Kortzfleisch (ed.), *Kirche und Synagoge*, 1:375-452; G. Müller, "Antisemitismus VI", TRE 3:146-49 (143-55); H. Oberman, *The Impact of the Reformation*, Grand Rapids: Wm B. Eerdmans 1994, pp. 110-16; *Roots*, pp. 94-124.

[50] See "On the Jews and Their Lies, 1543", in *LW* 47:137-306 (*WA* 53:417-552).

[51] See H.H. Borchert and G. Merz (ed.), *Martin Luther: Ausgewählte Werke*, Vol. III of the *Ergänzungsreihe*, München 1936, pp. 61-228.

[52] See M.H. Bertram's introduction to "On the Jews and Their Lies", *LW* 47:136.

[53] See Saperstein, *Moments of Crisis*, p. 41.

false premise.[54] Further, Paul is *not* used to back up his most notorious sections.[55] Luther's work against the Jews is a disgrace.[56] But three things need to be borne in mind. First, the roots of nazi antisemitism are not to be found in Martin Luther but rather in nineteenth century racial theories. Nazis were concerned to *eliminate* the Jews.[57] Luther's antisemitism, on the other hand,

---

[54] For example, he accuses the Jews of arrogance on the basis of Rom. 9.5 (and Jn 4.22)! Paul in Romans 9-11 is, as we have seen, attacking *Gentile* arrogance. A more valid point is made on the basis of Romans 11, that "Jews stand as a terrifying example of God's wrath" (253, 267). He is presumably thinking here of Rom. 11.22. But had Luther considered the text that follows (and he did in his *Lectures on Romans*, see Pauck (ed.), *Lectures on Romans*, pp. 314-18) his whole tract would have been invalidated. In fact in his Lectures, he writes on Rom. 11.25-26: "The Jews who are now fallen will return and be saved, after the Gentiles are come in, according to the fullness of the election. They will not stay outside forever, but they will return in their own time" (p. 315). On 11.29-32 he writes: "Hence the Jews will turn back and they will at last be led to the truth of faith" (p. 318). Note also the comment he makes on Rom. 9.5 in "That Jesus Christ was Born a Jew" (quoted below).

[55] The most despicable section runs as follows: "I wish and I ask that our rulers who have Jewish subjects exercise a sharp mercy toward these wretched people, as suggested above, to see whether this might not help (though it is doubtful). They must act like a good physician who, when gangrene has set in, proceeds without mercy to cut, saw, and burn flesh, veins, bone, and marrow. Such a procedure must also be followed in this instance. Burn down their synagogues, forbid all that I enumerated earlier, force them to work, and deal harshly with them, as Moses did in the wilderness, slaying three thousand lest the whole people perish" ("On the Jews the Their Lies", 292).

[56] I can echo Bainton's words: "One could wish that Luther had died before ever this tract was written" (R.H. Bainton, *Here I Stand: A Life of Martin Luther*, Nashville: Abingdon Press 1950, p. 297). Although Luther lived in an age of antisemitism, even his contemporary Protestants (e.g. Melanchthon, Ossiander, Bullinger) were dismayed by what he had written. Likewise, Bucer considered Luther's *Schem Hamphoras* (again from 1543) as "piggish" and "mucky". But we ought to remember that "[h]is remarks about Anabaptists or the pope were every bit as vitriolic–and obscene–as those against the Jews. The Jews were not a separate category in Luther's polemic; they were an integral part of those who misinterpreted or falsified the true gospel. And that included the Catholics, the pope, the Anabaptists, even the Turks" (Hillerbrand, "Martin Luther and the Jews", 131).

[57] See for example this statement from the *Table-Talk* (22 February 1942): "The discovery of the Jewish virus is one of the greatest revolutions that have taken place in the world. The battle in which we are engaged to-day is the same sort as the battle waged, during the last century, by Pasteur and Koch. How many diseases have their own origin in the Jewish virus! . . . We shall regain our health only by eliminating the Jew" (Trevor-Roper (ed.), *Hitler's Table-Talk*, p. 332).

was a "coarse manifestation of the medieval *Adversus Iudaeos* tradition"[58]
and not something new.[59] He stood in the tradition of Augustine who
believed that the *survival* of Jews was essential for they witness to the truth
of Christianity. They wander the earth as proof of their rejected status. They
bear the mark of Cain and therefore are to be *protected*.[60] And in God's
good time they will return to him.[61] Luther stood in this tradition. It is worth
emphasizing that even in his most bitter discourse *On the Jews and their
Lies*, he prays: "May Christ, our dear Lord, convert them mercifully".[62] And
although in this discourse he does advocate violence against Jewish institu-

---

[58] Katz, *Antisemitismus*, p. 54.

[59] If there was a novel element it is that his hostility to the Jews is related to his
apocalyptic expectation (see Oberman, *Roots*, p. 117).

[60] See Augustine, *Contra Faustum* 12.12. See also *De civitate Dei* 18.46, which
brings together an interesting series of verses. He quotes Rom. 9.27 (Is. 10.22) and then
11.9-10 (Ps. 69.22-23). He then goes on to quote Ps. 59.10-11 and Rom. 11.11: "'My
God, His mercy shall prevent me. My God hath shown me concerning mine enemies, that
Thou shalt not slay them, lest they should at last forget Thy law: disperse them in Thy
might.' Therefore God has shown the Church in her enemies the Jews the grace of His
compassion, since, as saith the apostle, 'their offence is the salvation of the Gentiles.'
And therefore He has not slain them, that is, He has not let the knowledge that they are
Jews be lost in them, although they have been conquered by the Romans, lest they should
forget the law of God, and their testimony should be of no avail in this matter of which
we treat. But it was not enough that he should say, 'Slay them not, lest they should at
last forget Thy law,' unless he had also added, 'Disperse them'" (*NFNF1* 2:389).

[61] Augustine, *De civitate Dei*, 20.29. Commenting on the very end of the book of
Malachi (Mal. 4.5-6) he writes that "in the last days before the judgment the Jews shall
believe in the true Christ, that is, our Christ, by means of this great and admirable
prophet Elias who shall expound the law to them. For not without reason do we hope
that before the coming of our Judge and Saviour Elias shall come, because we have good
reason to believe that he is now alive" (*NPNF1* 2:448).

[62] *LW* 47:306. This prayer is at the very end of this discourse. Contrast this to the
opening where he writes: "It is not my purpose to quarrel with the Jews, nor to learn
from them how they interpret or understand scripture; I know all of that very well
already. Much less do I propose to convert the Jews, for that is impossible" (*LW*
47:137). Perhaps these seemingly contrasting views can be reconciled in that Luther
hopes that on the last day Christ will convert the Jews (compare his lectures on Rom.
11.25-26, Pauck (ed.), *Lectures on Romans*, p. 316, quoted below).

tions[63] and books,[64] he does not generally support or condone violence against Jewish people.[65] The most that can be claimed concerning any influence Luther or other any other Christian theologian had is that they contributed to a long history of antisemitism and that without this long history the nazi antisemitism could not have taken hold. See the statement "dabru emet"[66] which declares that "Nazism was not a Christian phenomenon". This is qualified by the further statement: "Without the long history of Christian anti-Judaism and Christian violence against Jews, Nazi ideology could not have taken hold nor could it have been carried out". But it further adds that "Nazism itself was not an inevitable outcome of Christianity". Although nazis did appeal to Luther I suggest that they had about as much understanding of his ideas as they did about the music dramas of Richard Wagner.[67] For Julius Streicher to claim at the Nuremberg Trials that Luther ought to be in the dock since he said the same things but much more sharply is outrageous.[68]

The second point to bear in mind is that Luther in his lectures on Romans sharply criticizes those who call the Jews "dogs" or "accursed", referring to the Cologne theologians (e.g. Arnold von Tungern).[69] Commenting on Rom.

---

[63] So, for example, he advises that synagogues and schools be set on fire (*LW* 47:268). He also advises that houses "be razed and destroyed" but for the reason that "they pursue in them the same aims as in their synagogues" (269). They are not to be left homeless and he suggests they live "under a roof or in a barn" (269).

[64] He advises that "all their prayer books and Talmudic writings, in which such idolatry lies, cursing, and blasphemy are taught, be taken from them" (269).

[65] If there is any violence advocated it is that if the Jews fail to "reform", "we must drive them out like mad dogs, so that we do not become partakers of their abominable blasphemy and all their other vices and thus merit God's wrath and be damned with them" (*LW* 47:292).

[66] Many Jews, though, would not agree with this statement. The whole statement together with a number of other key statments on Jewish-Christian relations is available at www.jcrelations.net.

[67] This is a theme I wish to consider in detail at some later date. But examples abound to demonstrate that Hitler often fundamentally misunderstood Wagner.

[68] See Gutteridge, *Open thy Mouth for the Dumb*, p. 315. Gutteridge also adds that the city of Nuremberg presented Streicher in 1937 with a copy of the rare first edition of Luther's *Von den Juden und ihren Lügen*. In March of that year *Der Stürmer* described it as the most radical anti-semitic tract ever published (*Open thy Mouth for the Dumb*, p. 323 n. 2).

[69] Unfortunately, Luther himself, as we have seen, advocated driving Jews out "like mad dogs".

11.22 ("Behold, then, the goodness and severity of God: to them that fall, severity, but toward you, God's goodness, if you continue in his goodness, otherwise you also shall be cut off"), he says that "many display an amazing stupidity when they are so presumptuous as to call the Jews 'dogs' or accursed or whatever they choose to name them . . . They should feel compassion for them fearing that they themselves may have to take similar punishment . . . Today the theologians of Cologne are this kind of people".[70] Further in these lectures he gives the view that the Jews will in fact come to God in the last days.[71]

The third point is that Luther's positive statements towards the Jews in his earlier work "That Jesus Christ was Born a Jew" (1523),[72] which was well received by Jews at that time, were an embarrassment to nazi historians and propagandists.[73] I take an example where Luther appeals to Paul to make positive comments on the Jews:

When we are inclined to boast of our position we should remember that we are but Gentiles, while the Jews are of the lineage of Christ. We are aliens and in-laws; they are blood relatives, cousins, and brothers of our Lord. Therefore, if one is to boast of flesh and blood, the Jews are actually nearer to Christ than we are, as St. Paul says in Romans 9[:5]. God also demonstrated this by his acts, for to no nation among the Gentiles has he granted so high an honor as he has to the Jews. For from among the Gentiles there have been raised up no patriarchs, no apostles, no prophets, indeed, very few genuine Christians either. And although the gospel has been proclaimed to all the world, yet He committed the Holy Scriptures, that is, the law and the prophets, to no nation except the Jews, as Paul says in Romans 3[:2] and Psalm 147[:19-20], 'He declares his word to Jacob, his statues and ordinances to Israel. He has not dealt with any other nation; nor revealed his ordinances to them.'[74]

Although there is the view that such an attitude is to be understood as "a temporary modification" of his otherwise consistent negative attitude to the Jews,[75] the most likely view is that there is a general shift in Luther's views.

---

[70] Pauck (ed.), *Lectures on Romans*, p. 314.

[71] See Pauck (ed.), *Lectures on Romans*, p. 315: ". . . the Jews who expelled Christ to the Gentiles, where he now reigns, will come to him in the end"; p. 316: "Christ, therefore, has not yet come to the Jews, but he will come to them, namely, in the Last Day . . . ." In view of this I find it difficult to understand Oberman's claim that Luther did not expect any great conversion of the Jews (*Roots*, pp. 110-11).

[72] See *LW* 45:199-229.

[73] See Oberman, *Roots*, p. 128 n. 26.

[74] Luther, "That Jesus Christ was Born a Jew", *LW* 45:201.

[75] See Bertram's "Introduction" to "On the Jews and Their Lies", *LW* 47:127.

Luther held out hope for the conversion of the Jews, a hope probably linked to his apocalyptic expectation of the end of the world. But there was no sign of such a conversion and indeed some Christians in Bohemia and Moravia had become "Sabbatarians". They were keeping the Jewish Sabbath and indeed there were reports that some in Moravia were getting circumcised.[76] In his treatise "Against the Sabbatarians" Luther assumed that Jewish proselytization lay at the root of this movement. Luther's bitterness therefore came about largely because the Jews failed to convert despite the reforms in the Church (indeed matters were even worse since he believed that Jews were converting Christians in some cases) and despite Luther's earlier kind words to the Jews. Nevertheless, even in the later Luther positive things are said about the Jewish people.[77]

So my conclusion of this section is that Paul via Luther did little to contribute to the negative attitude of the nazis to the Jewish people.

4.3. Reception of Paul during the Third Reich

I now come to my third point as to why Paul's teachings had little to do with the policies which led to the holocaust. It regards the fact that during the Third Reich Paul was seen as having a strongly Jewish bias. For some this may be a surprising point because Paul is often taken to have a pro-Gentile and anti-Jewish bias. So although the Hellenists were probably the first to take the gospel to the Gentiles, it is Paul who is credited with opening up the gospel to Gentiles and insisting that Gentiles did not have to keep the Jewish law. Further, as we have seen, in Galatians a very negative view of Judaism

---

[76] The first clear evidence of the shift in Luther's attitude towards the Jews is found in his response to a letter from Josel Rosheim (1537), asking that permission be obtained from the elector to grant him safe passage through the principality. Luther asks: "Why should these rascals, who injure people in body and property and who withdraw many Christians to their superstitions, be given permission? In Moravia they have circumcised many Christians and call them by the name of Sabbatarians" (see Table Talk recorded by A. Lauterbach and J. Weller, no. 3597, in *LW* 54:239).

[77] See for example Table Talk (4425) recorded by Lauterbach (March 20, 1539). After speaking of the genius of David as author of the Psalter, he comments: "In like fashion the New Testament was written by real Jews, for the apostles were Jews. Thus God indicates that we should honor the Word of God in the synagogue. We Gentile Christians have no book that has such authority in the church–except Augustine, who is the only doctor in the church of the Gentiles who stands out above all others" (T.G. Tappert (ed.), *Table Talk* (*LW* 54:340)).

emerges and 1 Thes. 2.14-16 can be understood as antisemitic. Yet during the Third Reich and earlier in nineteenth century Germany, Paul was accused by many of making Christianity Jewish. So some "German Christians" (those supporting the nazis) set Jesus against Paul, Paul being seen as the corrupter of Christianity.[78] The origins of this view are to be found in the late eighteenth century where Reimarus considered Paul (and other apostles) to be the architect and founder of the whole of Christianity.[79] But in this case Jesus stood wholly within Judaism (even though he opposed teaching of the Saduccees and the Pharisees).[80] Then Fichte made Paul responsible for the "degeneration of Christianity" ("Ausartung des Christenthums").[81] In an effort to de-Judaize Christianity, Fichte took John as the authentic non-Jewish gospel, seeing it as representing an entirely different form of Christianity to that of Paul: "Es giebt nach unserem Erachten zwei höchst verschiedene Gestalten des Christenthums: die im Evangelium Johannis und die beim Apostel Paulus".[82] According to John, it remains wholly doubtful whether or not Jesus was of Jewish origin at all.[83] Paul, on the other hand, affirmed Jesus' Jewish origins in an effort to combine two systems,

---

[78] For example, R. Krause in a speech delivered at the Berlin Sports Palace (13 November, 1933) demanded the "Befreiung von jüdischer Lohnmoral" and from the "Sündenbock- und Minderwertigkeitstheologie des Rabbiners Paulus" (quoted in G. Theißen, "Theologie und Exegese in den neutestamentlichen Arbeiten von Günther Bornkamm", *EvTh* 51 (1991) 314 n. 20 (308-322)). On this meeting at the "Sportpalast", see E.C. Helmreich, *The German Churches Under Hitler: Background, Struggle, and Epilogue*, Detroit: Wayne State University Press 1979, pp. 149-50.

[79] See H.S. Reimarus, "Von dem Zwecke Jesu und seiner Jünger", in H. Göbel (ed.), *Gotthold Ephraim Lessing Werke, Siebenter Band: Theologiekritische Schriften I und II*, Darmstadt: Wissenschaftliche Buchgesellschaft 1996 (repr.), (¹1976), 492-604.

[80] As Brown, *Jesus in European Protestant Thought*, p. 3, summarizes: "In contrast with the Sadducees and what Reimarus took to be the teaching of the Old Testament, Jesus preached a gospel of personal immortality. In contrast with the pettifogging legalism of the Pharisees, Jesus strove for the moral elevation of mankind".

[81] See J.G. Fichte's 13th lecture in "Die Grundzüge des gegenwärtigen Zeitalters", in I.H. Fichte (ed.), *Fichtes Werke Band VII: Zur Politik, Moral ind Philosophie der Geschichte*, Berlin: Walter de Gruyter 1971 (repr.), 190 (3-256).

[82] Fichte's 7th lecture in "Die Grundzüge des gegenwärtigen Zeitalters", 98.

[83] Fichte's 7th lecture in "Die Grundzüge des gegenwärtigen Zeitalters", 99: "Es bleibt . . . bei diesem Evangelisten immer zweifelhaft, ob Jesus aus jüdischem Stamme sey, oder fals er es doch etwas wäre, wie es mit seiner Abstammung sich eigentlich verhalte".

"Judaism" and "Christianity".[84] Further, that Judaism was once the true religion is wholly denied by John, but asserted by Paul.[85] As Scholder points out, "Fichte was convinced that Christianity, Jesus, the truth and the Germans belonged together in the same way as Judaism, Paul and error".[86] Fichte thereby was a key impetus to the idea of a German national religion which was further developed by the famous orientalist Paul Anton de Lagarde whose polemic against Paul was to become influential.[87] So he writes:

> Paulus hat uns das Alte Testament in die Kirche gebracht, an dessen Einflusse das Evangelium, soweit dies möglich, zugrunde gegangen ist: Paulus hat uns mit der pharisäischen Exegese beglückt, die alles aus allem beweist, den Inhalt, der im Texte gefunden werden soll, fertig in der Tasche mitbringt und dann sich rühmt, nur dem Worte zu folgen: Paulus hat uns die jüdische Opfertheorie und alles, was daran hängt, in das Haus getragen: die ganze unten noch mit einigen Worten zu besprechende jüdische Ansicht von der Geschichte ist uns von ihm aufgebunden. Er hat das getan unter dem lebhaften Widerspruche der Urgemeinde, die, so jüdisch sie war, weniger jüdisch dachte als Paulus, die wenigstens nicht raffinierten Israelitismus für ein von Gott gesandtes Evangelium hielt. Paulus hat sich endlich gegen alle Einwürfe gepanzert mit der aus dem zweiten Buche des Gesetzes herübergeholten Verstockungstheorie, die es freilich so leicht macht zu disputieren, wie leicht ist, einen Menschen, der Gründe bringt und Gegengründe hören will, damit abzufertigen, daß man ihn für verhärtet erklärt.[88]

Also standing in this tradition of Fichte was Alfred Rosenberg whose work *Der Mythus des 20. Jahrhunderts*, first published in 1930, was the National

---

[84] Fichte's 7th lecture in "Die Grundzüge des gegenwärtigen Zeitalters", 99-100.

[85] Fichte's 7th lecture in "Die Grundzüge des gegenwärtigen Zeitalters", 100: Paul believed that "das Judenthum irgend einmal wahre Religion gewesen sey, die der Johanneische Jesus rund abläugnete".

[86] K. Scholder, *The Churches and the Third Reich, Volume 1: 1918-1934* ET, London: SCM 1987, p. 82, who refers to F. Regner, *Paulus und Jesus im 19. Jahrhundert. Beiträge zur Geschichte des Themas Paulus und Jesus in der neutestamentlichen Theologie von der Aufklärung bis zur Religionsgeschichtlichen Schule*, Tübingen: Protestant Faculty dissertation 1975, p. 163.

[87] On de Lagarde, see R. Heiligenthal, "Lagarde, Paul Anton de", *TRE* 20: 375-78.

[88] P.A. de Lagarde, "Über das Verhältnis des deutschen Staates zu Theologie, Kirche und Religion. Ein Versuch, Nicht-Theologen zu orientieren" (1873), in K. Fischer (ed.), *Deutsche Schriften*, München: J.K. Lehrmann 1934, 68 (45-90). The *Deutsche Schriften* were first published in 1878; they were a collection of articles of Paul de Lagarde in which he expressed his vision for a spiritually renewed Germany based on a Christianity "cleansed" of Jewish influence (see Gutteridge, *Open thy Mouth for the Dumb*, pp. 19-20).

Socialist book second only to Hitler's *Mein Kampf* in terms of distribution.[89] Rosenberg attacked Paul partly because of his view that God had called those who were not of noble birth.[90] He was also appalled by Paul's positive statements about Israel in Romans:

> Daß Paulus sich (trotz gelegentlicher Kritik des Jüdischen) bewußt gewesen ist, doch eine jüdische Sache zu vertreten, geht aus einigen gar zu offenherzigen Stellen seiner Briefe hervor: 'Verstockung ist zu einem Teil über Israel gekommen, bis dahin, wo die Fülle der Heiden wird eingegangen sein, und alsdann wird ganz Israel gerettet werden, sie, der Erwählung und Lieblinge um der Väter willen. Die da sind von Israel, denen die Kindschaft gehört, und die Herrlichkeit, die Bündnisse, die Gesetzgebung, die Gottesdienste, die Verheißungen, aus denen der Christos stammt nach dem Fleisch . . . . . Wenn der Heide aus dem von Natur wilden Ölbaume ausgeschnitten, und gegen die Natur auf den edlen gepfropft wurde, wieviel eher werden diese, deren Natur es entspricht, auf ihren ursprünglichen Baum gepfropft werden.' Gegen diese gesamte Verbastardierung, Verorientalisierung und Verjudung des Christentums wehrte sich bereits das durchaus noch aristokratischen Geist atmende Johannesevangelium.[91]

Christianity therefore had to be cleansed of any Jewishness which entailed cleansing it of Paul. Another work calling for this was by Oskar Michel, *Vorwärts zu Christus! Fort mit Paulus! Deutsche Religion!*, published in 1905. He argued that Paul was the "poisoner of the religious sources and the false teacher" and the "arch-enemy of Jesus, his Volk, and humanity".[92]

---

[89] Scholder, *Churches and the Third Reich*, p. 190. Hitler made it plain that he rejected *Der Mythus des 20. Jahrhundert*, "written by a Protestant" and which was "not a party book", when he received Bishop Wilhelm Berning of Osnabrück and Vicar General Prelate Johannes Steinmann (Helmreich, *German Churches*, p. 241). See also *Table Talk*, p. 422. Rosenberg's book was put on the Roman Catholic "index".

[90] A. Rosenberg, *Der Mythus des 20. Jahrhunderts: Eine Wertung der seelisch-geistigen Gestaltenkämpfe unserer Zeit*. München: Hoheneichen-Verlag 1944 (repr.), ([1]1930), p. 606: "Paulus hat ganz bewußt alles staatliche und geistig Aussätzige in den Ländern seines Erdkreises gesammelt, um eine Erhebung des Minder-Wertigen zu entfesseln. Das erste Kapitel des 1. Briefes an die Korinther ist ein einziger Lobgesang auf die 'Törichten vor der Welt' und zugleich die Beteuerung, das 'Unedle vor der Welt und das Verachtete' habe Gott erwählt, um dann den Christen die Richterherrschaft zu versprechen. . . ". He then quotes 1 Cor. 6.2-3.

[91] Rosenberg, *Mythus*, p. 75. After the quotations from Romans (incompletely referenced as "Römer 11,25; 9,4; 11,24"), he adds in a footnote: "Das ist das gleiche, was heute die bastardische Sekte der 'Ernsten Bibelforscher' lehrt". On the Jehovah's Witnesses ("Ernste Bibelforscher") in the Third Reich, see Helmreich, *German Churches*, pp. 392-97.

[92] I have not been able to see this work but Scholder, *Churches and the Third Reich*, 1:82, writes that the book includes a long section "Pauline poison in the history of the people".

An influential exponent of "Aryan Christianity" was Artur Dinter, a science teacher who then became an author, dramatist and theatre director. He was to become a driving force behind the NSDAP[93] but was expelled from the party in 1928.[94] One of his key works was a "Romantrilogie", *Die Sünden der Zeit*, the third volume being *Die Sünde wider die Liebe* (1922). In this story apears the teacher Dr Helmut Schwertfeger who demonstrates that the Old Testament is rejected, Paul is the Anti-Christ, and Jesus is a Gentile. Some of the basic elements of the main theological section of the novel is as follows. Through the fall of pre-existent spirits the material world came into being,[95] Jews being "verstockte Geister in Menschengestalt".[96] The "Judenfrage" cannot be solved by physical force but through spiritual power.[97] He goes on to argue that Jesus opposed Judaism; indeed the Gospel of John "ist die gewaltigste antisemitische Schrift, die jemals geschrieben worden ist".[98] Jesus, coming from Galilee of the Gentiles (Mt. 4.15),[99] was mistakenly portrayed as a Jew in the pious legendary birth narratives.[100] Jesus does not fulfil the Old Testament prophecies[101] and neither is he to be seen as the Old Testament messiah.[102] Although Dinter was a Roman Catholic, he accuses Winfried Bonifazius of bringing to the German people a false Christianity, "dieses römisch-jüdische Gift",[103] the ultimate source of this poison being a Jew called Paul, the Antichrist, "der die Heilandslehre in ihr Gegenteil verkehrt, sie materialistisch verfälscht hat".[104]

---

[93] Scholder, *Churches and the Third Reich*, p. 94.

[94] Scholder, *Churches and the Third Reich*, pp. 94-98.

[95] A. Dinter, *Die Sünde wider die Liebe*, Leipzig/Hartenstein im Erzgebirge: Matthes und Thost 1922, p. 77.

[96] Dinter, *Sünde*, p. 79.

[97] Dinter, *Sünde*, p. 79.

[98] Dinter, *Sünde*, p. 92. But he has to argue that Jn 4.22 has been mistranslated. He claims it should read "weil das Heil außerhalb' der Juden (d.h. 'nicht bei' den Juden) ist" (p. 92). For his more detailed discussion see *Sünde*, pp. 289-90.

[99] Dinter, *Sünde*, p. 93.

[100] Dinter, *Sünde*, pp. 94-95.

[101] Dinter, *Sünde*, pp. 103-114.

[102] Dinter, *Sünde*, pp. 114-19.

[103] Dinter, *Sünde*, p. 102. Dinter discusses his relationship to the Catholic Church in the "Nachwort", *Sünde*, p. 327.

[104] Dinter, *Sünde*, p. 103.

Luther had not recognized this and Dinter calls for a second Luther to free Christianity from its Jewishness.[105] Paul was "der Antichrist, der reißende Wolf im Schlafkleide, der erste jener falschen Propheten, vor denen der Heiland seine Jünger gewarnt hatte".[106] Paul's idea of God offering his Son as a sacrifice (Rom. 5.6ff.) is "eine barbarische Vorstellung" born "aus dem jüdischen Materialismus des alten Testamentes, aus der despotischen Will-kür und Grausamkeit des Judengottes Jahwe".[107] Paul's theological logic for example in Rom. 9.10ff.[108] or in the "Rabbinerkunststück" Rom. 3.1-10[109] is considered "Unsinn, Wirrsinn und Irrsinn" on which theologians write "dickbändige Bücher voll ehrfürchtiger Bewunderung des Tiefsinnes und der Unergründlichkeit paulinischer Weisheit!"[110] To his refrain "Fort mit dem alten Testamente!"[111] is added "Fort mit Paulus!"[112] and then "Zurück zu Christus!"[113] And so he ends his "Nachwort":

Das Geistchristentum wird unsichtbar seine überirdische Macht ausbreiten, wenn jeder deutsche Christ nur der Wahrheit seines Herzens folgt:
> *Fort mit dem alten Testamente!*
> *Fort mit Paulus!*
> *Zurück zu Christus!*[114]

Dinter's writings against Paul were to have considerable influence.[115]

Therefore Paul, far from giving any support to nazi antisemitism, was seen as the one who had infected Christianity with Judaism. Hitler was con-sistently negative about Paul.[116] Therefore the picture given by Harnack that

---

[105] Dinter, *Sünde*, p. 103.

[106] Dinter, *Sünde*, p. 224.

[107] Dinter, *Sünde*, p. 226.

[108] Dinter, *Sünde*, p. 227-29.

[109] Dinter, *Sünde*, p. 232-33.

[110] Dinter, *Sünde*, p. 233.

[111] Dinter, *Sünde*, p. 202.

[112] Dinter, *Sünde*, p. 234.

[113] Dinter, *Sünde*, p. 263.

[114] Dinter, *Sünde*, p. 330 (Dinter's emphasis).

[115] Dinter's book, *Die Sünde wider die Liebe*, is dedicated to Paul de Lagarde and he expresses his debt not only to de Lagarde but also to H.S. Chamberlain (*Sünde*, pp. 327-38). But, as we shall see, in many respects Chamberlain was an admirer of Paul.

[116] Consider these statements from the *Table-Talk*: "Christ was an Aryan, and St. Paul used his doctrine to mobilise the criminal underworld and thus organise a proto-Bolshevism" (p. 143, 13 December 1941); "the very market-place itself in Athens shook

Jesus was solely concerned with Israel[117] and that Paul "tore the gospel from its Jewish soil and rooted it in the soil of humanity"[118] has been reversed. Likewise the view of Paul's theology as a hellenized Christianity put forward by Reitzenstein and Bousset was reversed.[119]

---

with laughter when St. Paul spoke there in favour of the Jews" (p. 563, 5 July 1942); "Jesus was most certainly not a Jew . . . St. Paul distorted with diabolical cunning the Christian idea. Out of this idea, which was a declaration of war on the golden calf, on the egotism and the materialism of the Jews, he created a rallying point for slaves of all kinds against the élite, the masters and those in dominant authority. The religion fabricated by Paul of Tarsus, which was later called Christianity, is nothing but the Communism of today" (pp. 721-22, 29-30 November 1944). Martin Bormann, who recorded the conversations, adds that "any doctrine which is anti-Communist, any doctrine which is anti-Christian must, ipso facto, be anti-Jewish as well" (p. 722).

[117] See A. von Harnack, *The Expansion of Christianity in the First Three Centuries* (TTL 19-20) ET, 2 vols, London: Williams & Norgate/New York: G.P. Putnam's 1904-5, 1:40-45.

[118] Harnack, *Expansion*, 1:64-65 (see also *What is Christianity?* ET, London: Ernest Benn ⁵1958, pp. 130-32). Harnack argues that Paul "dethroned the people and the religion of Israel" (64) and suggests that it is no surprise that the Ebionites thought Paul was a "pagan in disguise" (64 n. 1). See Epiphanius, *Panarion* 30.16: "They say that he was a pagan, with a pagan mother and father, that he went up to Jerusalem and stayed there a while, that he desired to marry the priest's daughter and therefore became a proselyte and was circumcised, but then did not obtain the girl, who was of such high station, and in his anger wrote against circumcision, the Sabbath, and the law . . ." (P.R. Amidon (ed.), *The Panarion of St. Epiphanius, Bishop of Salamis*, Oxford/New York: OUP 1990, pp. 103-4).

[119] One exception of a Christian antisemite whose views to some extent touch on those of Reitzenstein and Bousset is the Englishman H.S. Chamberlain. In his *Die Grundlagen des 19. Jahrhunderts*, 2 vols, München: F. Bruckmann, ⁹1909, (¹1899), 2:580-81 (page numbers, as is customary, are from the "grosse Ausgabe"), he suggests that although Paul's father came from the tribe of Benjamin, his mother was Greek and converted to Judaism. This mixed blood, he believes, accounts to some extent for "das Zwitterwesen dieses merkwürdigen Mannes". Therefore: "In dieser Brust wohnen zwei Seelen: eine jüdische und eine unjüdische, oder vielmehr: eine unjüdische beflügelte Seele angekettet an eine jüdische Denkmaschine" (588). Chamberlain's work was widely read and influential among the German educated middle classes, including many churchmen (Gutteridge, *Open thy Mouth for the Dumb*, p. 22). Although he is said to have influenced Hitler, Chamberlain was criticized by him for "regarding Christianity as a reality upon the spiritual level" (*Table-Talk*, p. 144); further, Hitler obviously did not share Chamberlain's admiration for Paul. It should also be noted that in 1936 the journal of the confessing Church, *Junge Kirche*, affirmed that Chamberlain was outstanding among the ardent confessors of Jesus Christ at the turn of the century (see Gutteridge, *Open thy Mouth for the Dumb*, p. 25). Chamberlain's later work, *Mensch und Gott. Betrachtungen über Religion und Christentum*, München: F. Bruckmann 1921, develops

4.4. Use of Romans 9-11 during the Third Reich

My fourth point in support of Paul is that had the Church taken more seriously his words in, for example, Rom. 9.4-5; 11.24; 11.25-26, 28 (which Rosenberg quoted in his attack on Paul), there may have been much more support for the Jewish people if not serious opposition to Hitler. I may be accused of wishful thinking here. I am under no illusion that a Christian living in the Third Reich reading Romans 9-11 and taking the message seriously is not necessarily going to give support to the Jewish people which we today expect in a modern democracy. Neither can we assume it would inevitably lead them to oppose Hitler publicly. It is also the case that there is no simple correlation between a respect for Romans 9-11 and a positive view of the Jewish people. One reason for this is that there are so many theological variables. But nevertheless it is indeed striking that those theologians who took the message of Romans 9-11 seriously generally were much more sympathetic to the Jewish people even though some had short-comings. This is even the case for theologians such as Paul Althaus and Ger-hard Kittel who one wishes had adopted a different attitude to Hitler. So Althaus welcomed Hitler's coming to power in 1933;[120] but he did become

---

the theological views of *Die Grundlagen des 19. Jahrhunderts.* H. Windisch, *Paulus und das Judentum*, Stuttgart: W. Kohlhammer 1935, pp. 1-10, gives a fascinating portrait of some of the research carried out on Paul and Judaism up to 1934. Windisch himself is critical of those who see Paul's theology as thoroughly Jewish. He comments: "Diejenigen, die Paulus für einen unverfälschten Juden erklären und von ihm nicht viel mehr zu sagen wissen, als daß er das Evangelium verfälscht und verjudet habe, können nicht erklären, warum Paulus mit solchem Haß von den Juden verfolgt worden ist und warum er selbst so leidenschaftlich gegen die Juden eifert, ja warum er gerade von Judenchristen beargwöhnt und verfolgt worden ist, schließlich warum sein Evangelium als Ganzes nicht aus dem Judentum und auch nicht aus dem Alten Testament erklärt wer-den kann" (p. 7).

[120] Althaus opposed the Barmen Declaration in the Ansbacher Ratschlag, 11 June 1934. Beyschlag, *Die Erlanger Theologie*, pp. 167-69, argues that the Ansbacher Ratschlag did not simply oppose the Barmer Bekenntnissynode as such. Indeed Althaus wrote: "Daß in der Erklärung viele Sätze stehen, zu denen wir . . . vorbehaltlos Ja sagen, bedarf keines Wortes" (Beyschlag, *Die Erlanger Theologie*, p. 168). The key issue the Ansbacher Ratschlag attacked was the issue of "revelatio generalis" or "Schöpfungs-ordnung". And as Beyschlag comments, "Seit Harleß hatten die 'natürlichen Ordnungen', zumal von Volk und Staat', in Erlangen einen selbstverständlichen theologischen Platz innegehabt" (*Die Erlanger Theologie*, p. 169). Beyschlag asks whether even Bonhoeffer may have gone beyond the Barmen declaration in writing that God himself has spoken through the Barmen declaration and: "wer sich wissentlich von

critical later on although the extent of this criticism is a matter of dispute.[121] Any support he offered to National Socialism seemed to be based on his ideas such as "Volk", "Ur-Offenbarung"[122] and a conservative Lutheran view of the state based on Rom. 13.1-7. But Althaus always understood Rom. 11.26 to mean that the whole of Israel will come to final salvation.[123] Further he believed that "Israel bleibt das Volk der Wahl und des Segens".[124] Perhaps such theological ideas tempered Althaus' views.

The figure of Gerhard Kittel has appeared a number of times in this study. The two sides of his approach are summed up by Siegele-Wenschkewitz:

Kittel fordert, daß die staatlichen Maßnahmen sich streng im gesetzlichen Rahmen zu halten hätten. Nicht wilde Aktionen dürften erlaubt sein, aber Gesetze der Apartheid. Zugleich fordert er die Christen auf, verfolgten Juden als barmherzige Samariter beizustehen. Damit zielt er ausschließlich auf individuelle Hilfsaktionen gegenüber einzelnen. Denn er gibt dem Staat das Recht zu seiner Judenpolitik, indem er ihn gleichsam als Werkzeug für Gottes Gericht über die Juden ansieht. Eine Erlösung Israels sei nach Röm 9-11 erst Gott in der Endzeit vorbehalten. Einstweilen verlange es der Gehorsam gegenüber dem von Gott in dieser geschichtlichen Situation bekundeten Willen, die nationalsozialistische Judenpolitik zu unterstützen, die die gottgewollte Unheilsgeschichte an den Juden vollstrecken hilft, die sich letztlich aber den Juden als Heilsgeschichte erweisen wird".[125]

Again I stress that one wishes Kittel had not seen the state as an instrument of God's judgement on the Jewish people. But again his view of the salva-

---

der BK in Deutschland trennt, trennt sich vom Heil" (*Die Erlanger Theologie*, p. 169 n. 332).

[121] R.P. Ericksen, *Theologians under Hitler: Gerhard Kittel, Paul Althaus and Emanuel Hirsch*, New Haven/London: Yale University Press 1985, p. 111, writes that according to Helmut Thielicke's defence of Althaus after the war, when the true picture of National Socialism became apparent, Althaus became an opponent. Ericksen, however, believes this to be an exaggeration.

[122] I have discussed Althaus' controversial view of "Ur-Offenbarung" in *No one seeks for God*, pp. 105-9, 112-13.

[123] See Meiser, *Althaus*, p. 237 n. 263. This view of Althaus can be found from the first edition of his Romans commentary (1932) to the last edition, the tenth (1966).

[124] Althaus, *Römer*, p. 118. For further details on Althaus, see Meiser, *Althaus*, and R.H. Bell, Review of M. Meiser, *Paul Althaus als Neutestamentler*, SEÅ 61 (1996) 53-55.

[125] L. Siegele-Wenschkewitz, *Neutestamentliche Wissenschaft vor der Judenfrage: Gerhard Kittels theologische Arbeit im Wandel deutscher Geschichte* (ThExH 208), München: Chr. Kaiser Verlag 1980, p. 26-27.

tion of Israel and his view that they remain the people of God tempered his attitude to the Jewish people. On the other hand some of those who despised Paul's words in Romans 9-11 (like Rosenberg) were in a completely different category.

4.5. Paul and the State

I believe therefore that the terrible suffering endured by Jews during the years of 1933-45 is not a consequence of Paul's theology of Israel. However, Paul's teaching on the state in Rom. 13.1-7 has had tragic consequences, something I have already alluded to. It begins: "Let every person be subject to the governing authorities. For there is no authority except from God, and those that exist have been instituted by God". It is first worth reflecting that although Daniel emphasizes that God gives power to the king (Dan. 1.2; 2.37ff.; 5.18) and the letter of Aristeas affirms that God "prospers the kingdom" (15), "[t]he consequence . . . that the whole pyramidal system of governmental organs is divinely ordained is rarely drawn".[126] Various attempts have been made to mollify the problems in this text, some of which are more convincing than others.[127] Another approach is to suggest that Rom. 13.1-7 is an interpolation;[128] however, there are no text critical indica-

---

[126] E. Bammel, "Romans 13", in E. Bammel and C.F.D. Moule (ed.), *Jesus and the Politics of his Day*, Cambridge: CUP 1992 (repr.), (¹1984), 373 (365-83).

[127] One such attempt is to argue that the term "authorities" (ἐξουσίαι) refers not to human governing authorities but to "invisible angelic powers which stand behind the state government" (Cullmann, quoted in Fitzmyer, *Romans*, p. 666). Another attempt, one which I find more convincing, it that of O. Wischmeyer, "Staat und Christen nach Röm 13,1-7. Ein hermeneutischer Zugang", in M. Karrer, W. Kraus and O. Merk (ed.), *Kirche und Volk Gottes: Festschrift für Jürgen Roloff zum 70. Geburtstag*, Neukirchen-Vluyn: Neukirchener 2000, 149-62. She believes Paul *is* speaking about political authorities but that Paul, despite the imperatives, is actually describing what is the case: "Die Beschreibung der Lebenswelt der Christen ist notwendig, wenn Paulus deutlich machen will, daß er ihre Situation kennt, ernst nimmt und ihnen diese von Gott her verständlich machen kann" (160). She argues that the advice to pay taxes, not to resort to "Selbstjustiz" and to be subject to the authorities, is "trivial". "Welcher Bürger einer Stadt, welchen Rechts auch immer, oder gar welcher Inhaber des römischen Bürgerrechtes, der Christ war, hätte sich zu der Zeit anders verhalten? (159)".

[128] See E. Barnikol, "Römer 13: Der nichtpaulinische Ursprung der absoluten Obrigkeitsbejahung von Römer 13,1-7", in *Studien zum Neuen Testament und zur Patristik* (TU 77), Berlin: Akademie-Verlag 1961, 65-133; J. Kallas, "Romans xiii.1-7: An Interpretation", *NTS* 11 (1964-65) 365-74; W. Munro, "Romans 13:1-7: Apartheid's Last Biblical Refuge", *BTB* 20 (1990) 161-68; W. Schmithals, *Der Römerbrief als histori-*

tions that it is an interpolation,[129] and indeed there are good reasons to believe that this text belongs precisely where it is now found.[130] But I believe the text contains certain theological problems that some measure of *Sachkritik* is the only satisfactory way to deal with the text.

Note that Paul is saying that the powers that be, not some ideal government, receives authority from God.[131] But if the powers have been instituted by God, one does not necessarily have to conclude, as Paul does, that "every person be subject to the governing authorities" (just as one does not accept suffering but seeks to allieviate it). And there are very good reasons for not taking Paul's line of argument. How can one support the idea that the ruler "does not bear the sword in vain" (Rom. 13.4)? The reference, as many commentaters recognize, is to the death penalty.[132] Paul's argument that the state is a minister of God to execute his wrath on the wrongdoer presents profound theological problems. For in the case of the state there is not the direct and immediate presence of God which was present in the community of Sinai whereby if an offender was put to death it was God himself who was acting.[133] By enacting the death penalty the state is usurping the divine prerogative.[134] Although Paul was writing before the first state persecution of Christians under Nero, he surely knew of the injustices of the Roman

---

sches Problem (StNT 9), Gütersloh: Gütersloher Verlagshaus Gerd Mohn 1975, pp. 185-97.

[129] Cf. the discussion above on 1 Thes. 2.13-16. Also, Fitzmyer, *Romans*, p. 664, points out that it is quoted at the end of the second century by Irenaeus (*Adversus haereses* 5.24.1).

[130] See Fitzmyer, *Romans*, p. 664.

[131] W. Schrage, *The Ethics of the New Testament* ET, Edinburgh: T. & T. Clark 1988, p. 237.

[132] So Michel, *Römer*, p. 401, points to the importance of the fear motif in Rom. 13.3-4: "Wenn der Böse die staatliche Gewalt fürchten muß (V 4: beachte den Imperativ!) und der Rechtschaffene sie nicht zu fürchten braucht (V 3), dann handelt es sich um die Furcht vor Strafe. In diesem Sinn ist auch der Hinweis auf das Schwert zu verstehen: es ist nicht das Zeichen des Krieges, sondern des Rechtes . . .".

[133] Cf. O. O'Donovan, *Measure for Measure: Justice in Punishment and the Sentence of Death* (Grove Booklet on Ethics 19), Bramcote, Notts: Grove Books 1977, pp. 6-7.

[134] As Barth, *CD* 3.4:445, writes: ". . . in capital punishment the state leaves the human level and acts with usurped divinity". The text of Rom. 13.4 remains a problem even if one takes the line that the death penalty is not mandatory (as does Stott, *Romans*, p. 345).

empire and the miscarriages of justice, the supreme example being that Jesus Christ had been executed under the Roman procurator Pontius Pilate.[135] In view of this, how can Paul write that every person should be subject to the governing authorities?

In one sense it is understandable why Paul should have such a conservative view of the state. He was a Roman citizen[136] and the Roman empire and

---

[135] So J. Moltmann, *The Crucified God: The Cross of Christ as the Foundation and Criticism of Christian Theology* ET, London: SCM 1974, p. 328, although not explicitly mentioning Rom. 13.1-7, writes: "If the Christ of God was executed in the name of the politico-religious authorities of his time, then for the believer the higher justification of these and similar authorities is removed. In that case political rule can only be justified 'from below'".

[136] Paul's Roman citizenship (explicitly referred to only in Acts) has been questioned by W. Stegemann an article which has been frequently appealed to, "War der Apostel Paulus ein römischer Bürger?", *ZNW* 78 (1987) 200-29. He puts forward four arguments: 1. Luke as a free novelist portrayed Paul as a Roman citizen as it suited his theological-political inclination ("Bürger", 205, 212). But why would Luke invent this as he has a rather negative view of the state (see Lk. 4.5-6, where the Roman empire is portrayed as subject to Satan)? Further, if Paul were not a Roman citizen, the whole narrative of Paul's arrest and trial (Acts 21-28) would make no sense. 2. Stegemann, "Bürger", 213, argues that the Roman procurators sent Jewish rebels to Rome for trial, although they were not Roman citizens. But these rebels (Eleazar ben Deinaeus of Judea (Josephus, *Bellum* 2.253) and the σικάριος Jonathan of Cyrene (*Bellum* 7.437-50)) were violent guerilla leaders. 3. Stegemann, "Bürger", 223, points out that according to 2 Cor. 11.25, Paul was beaten with rods three times, but Roman citizens may not be beaten (Acts 16.37). But Acts 16.23, 37-39 also shows that Paul sometimes remained silent about his citizenship and wished to suffer for Christ (Gal. 6.17; 2 Cor. 4.10, cf. Acts 5.41). Also, there are examples of Roman citizens being beaten: according to Josephus, *Bellum* 2.308, Florus had Jews of equestrian rank scourged and crucified. 4. Stegemann, "Bürger", 220-21, argues that it was very difficult for a Jew to receive Roman citizenship (that it was bestowed because of the military service of Paul and his ancestors is very unlikely). Stegemann, however, passes too quickly over the most important source for the bestowal of citizenship on Jews ("Bürger", 214), namely, on emancipated slaves (Philo, *De legatione ad Gaium* 155-58, 285-87). It is probable that Paul was descended from Galilean Jews who had been freed by a Roman citizen (Jerome, *Ad Philemonem* 5.23 (*MPL* 26:653) writes: *Aiunt parentes apostoli Pauli de Giscalis regione fuisse Judaeae: et eos, cum tota provincia Romana vastaretur manu, et dispergerentur in orbem Judaei, in Tharsum urbem Ciliciae fuisse translatos: parentum conditionem adolescentulum Paulum secutum* (cf. *De viris illustribus* 5, *MPL* 23:645-46)). On the above points, see Hengel, *Pre-Christian Paul*, pp. 6-15. Two recent studies that have affirmed Paul's Roman citizenship are H.W. Tajra, *The Trial of St. Paul: A Juridical Exegesis of the Second Half of the Acts of the Apostles* (WUNT 2.35), Tübingen: J.C.B. Mohr (Paul Siebeck) 1989, pp. 86-89, and Riesner, *Early Period*, pp. 147-56.

the system of transportation had enabled him to carry out his missions. Further, it would be naive to assume that Paul himself would always be subject to the governing authorities. So he evaded imprisonment by the ethnarch King Aretas (2 Cor. 11.32-33)[137] and clearly relativizes the earthly law courts in 1 Cor. 6.1-11.[138] Paul clearly knew that obedience to the state has its limits. As Schrage writes: "He would never have obeyed an order to cease preaching Christ (cf. Acts 16:19ff.), nor would he have allowed 'Ceasar is Lord' to pass his lips".[139] One also needs reminding of the simple hermeneutical fact that "[t]he *same word* can be said to another time only by being said differently".[140] Paul's words addressed to a tiny powerless minority cannot simply be said identically to times such as ours when the Church has much greater power. Despite the problem that Rom. 13.1-7 raises, it can be employed positively, as is seen in the fifth thesis of the Barmen Declaration. After quoting 1 Pet. 2.17 ("Fürchtet Gott, ehret den König"), there is a statement which alludes to 1 Pet. 2.13-17 and Rom. 13.1-7:

Die Schrift sagt uns, daß der Staat nach göttlicher Anordnung die Aufgabe hat, in der noch nicht erlösten Welt, in der auch die Kirche steht, nach dem Maß menschlicher Einsicht und menschlichen Vermögens unter Androhung und Ausübung von Gewalt für Recht und Frieden zu sorgen. Die Kirche erkennt in Dank und Ehrfurcht gegen Gott die Wohltat dieser seiner Anordnung an. Sie erinnert an Gottes Reich, an Gottes Gebot und Gerechtigkeit und damit an die Verantwortung der Regierenden und Regierten. Sie vertraut und gehorcht der Kraft des Wortes, durch das Gott alle Dinge trägt.[141]

This is then followed by an attack on the totalitarian claim of the state.[142] As was indicated earlier, the Barmen Declaration was criticized in the Ansbacher Ratschlag, formulated by a group of Franconian theologians and subscribed to by two prominent theologians from Erlangen: Werner Elert and Paul Althaus.[143] Here it is affirmed that the "law", "namely the unchange-

---

[137] Schrage, *Ethics*, p. 238.

[138] Cf. Stuhlmacher, *Romans*, p. 183.

[139] Schrage, *Ethics*, p. 238.

[140] G. Ebeling, quoted by A.C. Thiselton, "The New Hermeneutic", in I. H. Marshall (ed.), *New Testament Intrepretation: Essays on Principles and Methods*, Exeter: Paternoster [2]1979, ([1]1977), 309 (308-333).

[141] Quoted in Stuhlmacher, *Romans*, p. 185.

[142] On the history of the formulation of this fifth thesis, see Scholder, *Churches and the Third Reich*, 2:152-54.

[143] On the Ansbacher Ratschlag, see Scholder, *Churches and the Third Reich*, 2:163-64.

able will of God . . . encounters us in the total reality of our life". "As believing Christians we thank . . . God the Lord that he has given to our people in its need the Führer as 'pious and faithful overlord' and wills to prepare in the National Socialist state order good government, a government with 'discipline and honour'".[144]

It is an obvious point to make but Paul could have little idea of the use or misuse of Rom. 13.1-7;[145] and because of this one should perhaps avoid the use of the word "Wirkungsgeschichte" and replace it with "Auslegungsgeschichte"[146] or "application history". Rom. 13.1-7 has had an influential "application history".[147] This text more than any other in the New Testament was to influence the way that Christians think about the state,[148] including the attitude of Christians during the Third Reich.

Before I leave the issue of the Church in the Third Reich, I ought to stress that it is very easy for a British theologian to point an accusing finger at the German Church. Too often, British Christians have not enough understanding as to why Hitler did receive such support (even from Christians). It was all too easy for a German patriot to be impressed by the political and economic success of Hitler, not to mention his "successes" in foreign policy,[149]

---

[144] Quoted in Scholder, *Churches and the Third Reich*, 2:163-64 ("Ansbacher Ratschlag", *AELKZ* 67 (1934), no 25 of 2 June, col. 586).

[145] Rom. 13.1-7 exercised its influence either directly or via theologians. For example, Rom. 13.1-7 was a central text for Luther's idea of the state (see G. Rupp, *The Righteousness of God: Luther Studies*, London: Hodder and Stoughton 1953, pp. 301-9) and was to influence thinking decisively during the Third Reich.

[146] Kampling, "Auslegungsgeschichtliche Skizze", 189, points out that in "Wirkungsgeschichte" the text is so to speak the subject whereas in "Auslegungsgeschichte" (reception history) the recipients are the subjects.

[147] See Wilckens, *Römer*, 3:43-66. See also E. Käsemann, "Römer 13,1-7 in unserer Generation", *ZThK* 56 (1959) 316-76.

[148] However, it needs stressing that many Christians down the ages have made a serious attempt to follow the theologically satisfying views of the state as found in Revelation 13 and Acts 5.29.

[149] Hengel, "Wilderness", 71, tells of how on the morning after the Munich meeting, his schoolmaster, "a highly cultivated son of a pastor, and by no means a Nazi", "entered the classroom, deeply moved, with the words: 'Wir danken unserem Führer' (We thank our Fuhrer)".

especially in view of the elaborate nazi propaganda.[150] After the chaos of Weimar, many Christians clearly did think that in Hitler they had a "pious and faithful overlord". It is to the credit of Barth and others that they acted so quickly and decisively to Hitler's totalitarian claims.

4.6. Pauline Perspectives on the Holocaust

But can Paul shine any light on the darkness of those years? I believe five fundamental points can be made in the light of Paul's theology.

The first is that God remains faithful to Israel. It may seem of little import but there were many Jews who did not go to concentration camps and among those who did go to the camps, some did survive. This point is often neglected in the Holocaust debate.[151] Rom. 9.29, although addressing a different context, seems apposite: "And as Isaiah predicted, 'If the Lord of hosts had not left us children, we would have fared like Sodom and been made like Gomorrah'". Israel had not been totally destroyed as had Sodom and Gomorrah.

The second point is that despite the appalling events of the holocaust, God remained sovereign. Some, however, have disputed this. Hans Jonas has argued that after Auschwitz one cannot reconcile God's omnipotence, goodness and comprehensibility.[152] Jonas maintains God's goodness and comprehensibility, but his omnipotence is rejected. Against the omnipotence of God Jonas sets the impotence of God, who in Auschwitz and elsewhere kept silent and "did not intervene, not because he did not want to, but because he could not".[153] This solution to the holocaust is incompatible with

---

[150] The "propaganda" is not only to be seen in terms of publications or film but also crucial events such as the "Day of Potsdam" when Hindenburg officially greeted the newly elected "Reichstag" and Hitler's first cabinet. As J.A. Moses writes: "It was virtual confirmation for the German people that National Socialism was a legitimate expression of the spirit of Prussian-German history. This explains in part why there was so little effective resistance to Nazism. It appeared to represent the resurrection and continuation of a political culture that distinguished Prussia-Germany from the barbarous East (communism) and the decadent West (liberalism)" ("Bonhoeffer's Germany: the political context", in J.W. de Gruchy, *The Cambridge Companion to Dietrich Bonhoeffer*, Cambridge: CUP 1999, 17 (3-21)).

[151] It is, however, a point emphasized in Spielberg's film "Schindler's List".

[152] H. Jonas, "Der Gottesbegriff nach Auschwitz: Eine jüdische Stimme", in O. Hofius (ed.), *Reflexionen finsterer Zeit*, Tübingen: J.C.B. Mohr (Paul Siebeck) 1984, 61-86.

[153] See Jonas, "Der Gottesbegriff nach Auschwitz", 82: ". . . nicht weil er nicht wollte, sondern weil er nicht konnte, griff er nicht ein".

a theology based on Paul. And even if such a theodicy appears "to let God off the hook", there are two fundamental problems. First, why did God create a universe he could not control?[154] Secondly, if God is not sovereign, one has no assurance that evil will be overcome.

This is an appropriate point at which to discuss another theodicy, that of the crucified God. The execution of two Jewish men and a young boy in Auschwitz as told by Elie Wiesel, himself a survivor of Auschwitz, has frequently been quoted. I make no apology for citing it again:

> The three victims mounted together on to the chairs.
> The three necks were placed at the same moment within the nooses.
> 'Long live liberty!' cried the two adults.
> But the child was silent.
> 'Where is God? Where is He?' someone behind me asked.
> At a sign from the head of the camp, the three chairs tipped over.
> Total silence throughout the camp. On the horizon, the sun was setting.
> ....

---

[154] The article of E. Jüngel, "Gottes ursprüngliches Anfangen als Schöpferische Selbstbegrenzung", in *Wertlose Wahrheit. Zur Identität und Relevanz des christlichen Glaubens. Theologische Erörterungen III* (BevTh 107), München: Chr. Kaiser Verlag 1990, 151-62, has the subtitle "Ein Beitrag zum Gespräch mit Hans Jonas über den 'Gottesbegriff nach Auschwitz'", and speaks of God's self-limitation through the creation of the universe. "Ist die creation ex nihilo Ausdruck der Gottheit Gottes, dann ist die schöpferische Selbstbegrenzung Gottes, die mit dem Anfang eines Anderen dem ursprünglich Anfangenden selber ein Gegenüber gibt, ein zum Wesen Gottes gehörender Akt" (154). Therefore, he argues, the traditional metaphysical idea of God's limitlessness must be corrected by his self-limitation. "Es ist Gott keineswegs fremd, es ist ihm vielmehr wesentlich, sich selbst begrenzen zu können". God's very nature is love and the essence of love is "daß der Liebende sich selbst zurücknimmt zugunsten des geliebten Anderen. . . . Es ist Au[s]druck der Gottheit Gottes, wenn Gott sich zugunsten seines Geschöpfes im Akt des Schaffens selber zurücknimmt: wohlgemerkt, nicht *als Gott zurücknimmt*, sondern in dem Sinne, daß er einem anderen neben sich, neben seinem göttlichen Sein und Wesen Dasein und Wesen gewährt, Raum einräumt, Zeit gibt" (154, Jüngel's emphasis). I wonder though how satisfactory this really is? Has not God through his self-limitation precisely made a universe which he cannot control (as long as the universe as we know it is in existence)? Further, although human love gives space and takes great risks, can the same be said for the love of God? Is not the love of God a sovereign love? This seems to be the implication of Paul's theology. He can speak of God's love yet also of a predestination to salvation (i.e. he precisely does not give his creatures room and space!). His love is a power over creation (Rom. 8.31-39). Note that just as there are fundamental differences between God's wrath (according to Paul) and human wrath, so there are fundamental differences between God's love and our love.

Then the march past began. The two adults were no longer alive. Their tongues hung swollen, blue-tinged.
But the third rope was still moving; being so light the child was still alive...
For more than half an hour he stayed there, struggling between life and death, dying in slow agony under our eyes. And we had to look him full in the face. He was still alive when I passed in front of him. His tongue was still red, his eyes were not yet glazed.
Behind me I heard the same man asking:
'Where is God now?'
And I heard a voice within me answer him:
'Where is He? Here He is—He is hanging here on this gallows . . .'[155]

Moltmann comments: "Any other answer would be blasphemy. There cannot be any other Christian answer to the question of this torment".[156] Whatever Wiesel himself meant by "Here He is—He is hanging here on this gallows"[157], Moltmann's comment has some theological weight. In the light of Pauline theology one can affirm that God participates in the depth of human misery. Christ suffers as man and God (!) on the cross. Also the Father suffers the death of his Son (Rom. 8.32).[158] "The Fatherlessness of the Son is matched by the Sonlessness of the Father . ."[159] Jesus' death was not so much a death of God but a death *in* God.[160] Further, not only does the Father hand over the Son (Rom. 8.32), but the Son also hands over himself (Gal. 2.20).[161] There is a unity of action.[162]

Küng raises some questions about such an approach. He argues that if one identifies human suffering with God's suffering, does not human sin (i.e. the crimes of SS butchers) become God's sin?[163] This may be a legitimate point. But if it has been maintained in much theological discussion that there is a

---

[155] E. Wiesel, *Night*, Harmondsworth: Penguin 1969, pp. 76-77.

[156] Moltmann, *Crucified God*, p. 274.

[157] On this question see R. Bauckham, *The Theology of Jürgen Moltmann*, Edinburgh: T. & T. Clark 1995, p. 78, who writes that "within the book the story marks the final, crucial step in Wiesel's loss of faith in God. God hangs on the gallows because the possibility of faith in him is dying with every moment the dying child suffers and the God of Israel fails to deliver him".

[158] Cf. Moltmann, *Crucified God*, p. 243.

[159] Cf. Moltmann, *Crucified God*, p. 243.

[160] Moltmann, *Crucified God*, p. 207.

[161] Cf. Moltmann, *Crucified God*, p. 243.

[162] This is to be found also in Paul's view of the atonement. See my article "Sacrifice and Christology".

[163] Küng, *Judaism*, p. 601.

certain asymmetry in the way God stands behind good and evil,[164] can one not also maintain that there is also an asymmetry in the way God is related to suffering and sin. Nevertheless, Küng's point may have some validity. Less legitimate is his following point: "it is not 'God' hanging there on the cross, but God's anointed, his 'Christ', the 'Son of Man'".[165] In view of Paul's high christology, I believe one has to say that God died on the cross, something which can only be said in faith.[166] Jüngel points out that for Luther, the death of God was not only *possible* as a logical consequence of the *communicatio idiomatum*, but was in fact necessary. So Luther writes:

Denn wenn ich das gleube
das allein die menschliche natur für mich gelidden hat
so ist mir der Christus ein schlechter heiland
so bedarff er wol selbs eines heilands.[167]

The Good Friday hymn of Johann Rist is therefore quite appropriate:

O große Not, Gott selbst liegt todt,
am Kreuz ist er gestorben,
hat dadurch das Himmelreich
uns aus Lieb erworben.[168]

---

[164] See, for example, Carson, *Divine Sovereignty*, p. 212.

[165] Küng, *Judaism*, p. 601.

[166] On the relationship between Jesus' divinity and humanity, see Bell, "Sacrifice and Christology".

[167] Quoted in E. Jüngel, "Vom Tod des lebendigen Gottes. Ein Plakat", in *Unterwegs zur Sache. Theologische Bemerkungen* (BEvTh 61), München: Chr. Kaiser Verlag 1988, 115 (105-25).

[168] Quoted in J. Moltmann, *Der gekreuzigte Gott: Das Kreuz Christi als Grund und Kritik christlicher Theologie*, München: Chr. Kaiser Verlag ⁵1987, (¹1972), p. 221. He gives the original reference as J. Porst, *Geistliche und liebliche Lieder*, Berlin 1796, Nr. 114. For an English translation, see *Crucified God*, p. 233:
   O great distress, God himself lies dead,
   He died upon the cross,
   In this he won the kingdom of heaven
   For love of us.

But which God lies dead? It is the one who voluntarily renounced omnipotence.[169] This is therefore a variation, but a radical variation, of Jonas' view.[170]

I come now to my third point. Although I believe there is some power in Moltmann's concept of the crucified God, Paul does not in fact give a theoretical explanation of suffering. Suffering cannot be comprehended. But that is not to say that God himself is totally incompehensible. Jonas writes "Göttliche Allmacht kann mit göttlicher Güte nur zusammenbestehen um den Preis gänzlicher göttlicher Unerforschlichkeit, d.h. Rätselhaftigkeit".[171] But he then rightly comments: "Der deus absconditus, der verborgene Gott (nicht zu reden vom absurden Gott), ist eine zutiefst unjüdische Vorstellung".[172] "Ein gänzlich verborgener, unverständlicher Gott ist ein unannehmbarer Begriff nach jüdischer Norm".[173] And it is not only unacceptable according to Jewish theology but also according to the gospel.[174] As Jüngel writes, "Wir haben aber gerade zu der Behauptung, daß *Gott selbst* verborgen und unverständlich sei, dann nicht den geringsten Grund, wenn Gott sich in Tod und Auferstehung Jesus Christi als Liebe definiert hat".[175] It is not *God himself* who is the *deus absconditus*; rather his work is the work of a hidden God. Further,

Es ist deshalb zwischen Gott selbst und *einem* seiner Werke – eben seinem concurrere mit dem entstehenden Bösen in der Welt – so zu unterscheiden, daß wir zwar auf keinen Fall Gott selbst als deus absconditus, wohl aber dieses sein Werk als opus dei absconditum und damit nur eben dessen Unverständlichkeit zu verstehen haben.

---

[169] See the discussion in chapter 8 concerning Phil. 2.6-7.

[170] For the ontological implications of the death of Jesus for God's being, see Jüngel, "Vom Tod des lebendigen Gottes", 119-20: ". . . wenn Gott sich im Tode Jesu *als* Gott definiert hat, dann hat der Tod *ontologische Relevanz* für das Sein Gottes und also für das Leben Jesu Christi. Gott nämlich definiert sich nicht mit Sätzen, sondern mit seinem eigenen Sein. Und er tut es, indem er den toten Jesus als lebendigen Gottessohn definiert. . . . Im Ereignis des Todes Jesu treffen Gottes Wesen und des Todes Wesen so aufeinander, daß das Wesen des Einen am Wesen des Anderen das eigene Wesen in Frage stellt. . . . Was der Tod *aus sich selbst heraus* noch zu verwirklichen vermag, ist nicht mehr Wesen, sondern nur noch Unwesen" (Jüngel's emphasis).

[171] Jonas, "Der Gottesbegriff nach Auschwitz", 79.

[172] Jonas, "Der Gottesbegriff nach Auschwitz", 80.

[173] Jonas, "Der Gottesbegriff nach Auschwitz", 80.

[174] Jüngel, "Gottes ursprüngliches Anfangen", 161.

[175] Jüngel, "Gottes ursprüngliches Anfangen", 161 (Jüngel's emphasis).

Angesichts dieses verborgenen Wirkens Gottes wendet sich deshalb das Gotteslob, das für die Rede von der Schöpfung kennzeichend ist, zur Gottesklage. Nicht nur Gott zu loben, sondern auch Gott zu klagen – was uns an seinem Wirken grauenhaft dunkel bleibt, Gott zu klagen – ist unser Amt.[176]

My fourth point is that despite my earlier reservations concerning Küng's approach to the suffering God, there is some force in his argument that "*meaningless suffering*—both individual and collective—*cannot be understood theoretically, but can only be lived through*".[177] Küng points to words of Paul which come from his own experience of suffering (Rom. 8.31, 38-39):

Today he could write them even above Auschwitz, Hiroshima and the Gulag Archipelago: 'If God is for us, who is against us . . . ? For I am sure that neither death, nor life, nor angels, nor principalities, nor things present, nor things to come, nor powers, nor height, nor depth, nor anything else in all creation will be able to separate us from the love of God in Christ Jesus our Lord'.[178]

It may be objected that a text such as Rom. 8.31-39 is relevant to the suffering of Christians but not of Jews. But Jesus Christ is for Jews just as he is for Christians. It is true that Jews are temporarily separated from Christ (Rom. 9.3!) but their conversion at the parousia is, as Bonhoeffer put it, "the final home-coming of the people of Israel to its God".[179] "The conversion of Israel, that is to be the end of the people's period of suffering".[180]

My fifth and final point is that the horrors of the Holocaust should not, from a Pauline perspective, be used to attack God. Paul experienced suffering and the suffering of others. Yet he never uses this to attack God in any way. He does not question God's goodness nor his sovereignty. We do find in Paul a positive "theology of glory". So in Rom. 15.18-19 he writes of what Christ has accomplished through Paul "to win obedience from the Gentiles, by word and deed, 19 by the power of signs and wonders, by the power of the Spirit of God, so that from Jerusalem and as far around as Illyricum I have fully proclaimed the good news of Christ". Paul and his co-workers changed the face of Asia Minor and Europe. The gospel of Christ

---

[176] Jüngel, "Gottes ursprüngliches Anfangen", 161 (Jüngel's emphasis).

[177] Küng, *Judaism*, p. 605 (Küng's emphasis).

[178] Küng, *Judaism*, p. 609. See also my comments on Rom. 8.31-39 above in the discussion of Jüngel's response to Jonas.

[179] Bonhoeffer, *No Rusty Swords*, p. 226.

[180] Bonhoeffer, *No Rusty Swords*, p. 226.

was destroying the evils of that world. I therefore think it is a legitimate development of Paul's theology to argue that rather than using the "problem of evil" to attack God as in some Philosophy of Religion, we through God's power should "attack" and "destroy" evil in the world and so contribute to bringing the problem of evil to an end.[181]

---

[181] Note that Moltmann's *Crucified God* ends on the positive note of "Ways towards the Political Liberation of Mankind" (pp. 317-40).

Chapter 10

Pauline Perspectives on Israel II

1. The Promise of the Land

There can be little doubt that the Holocaust precipitated the foundation of the state of Israel in 1948. Zionism had been a major issue since the end of the nineteenth century. But the horrific events of the Holocaust pointed to the need for a homeland for Jews where they could be safe from persecution.[1] What can one say about the promise of the land in view of Pauline theology?

In the discussion of Rom. 9.4-5 I pointed out that the land is missing from the list of privileges. However, a number of other fairly self-evident privileges are also missing. The list therefore should not be considered exhaustive. Also, although there is no explicit mention of the land, the city of Jerusalem and Mount Zion in particular were at least required to perform the "worship" (λατρεία).[2] One should also add that the list of privileges is, as I noted in chapter 4, expressed in a form which involves corresponding endings (e.g. υἱοθεσία . . . νομοθεσία etc.). Therefore one is perhaps asking too much that the land should be explicitly mentioned in the list. Further, the promise of the land is probably included in the ἐπαγγελίαι, and this promise

---

[1] On the biblical support for this idea of being safe from persecution, see below.

[2] In the LXX "λατρεύειν means more precisely to serve or worship cultically, especially by sacrifice" (H. Strathmann, λατρεύω, λατρεία, *TDNT* 4:60 (58-65)) and λατρεία always has a cultic use except in 3 Mac. 4.14. In the five occurrences of λατρεία in the New Testament, three refer to sacrificial ministry (Rom. 9.4; Heb. 9.1, 6) and two refer to sacrifice in a metaphorical sense (Jn 16.2; Rom. 12.1). This cultic meaning of λατρεία therefore underlines the importance of Mount Zion. It is unlikely that Paul has in mind worship in the synagogue (which of course can be carried out anywhere). It is of course true that the cognate verb λατρεύω can be used in a non-cultic sense in the New Testament (see Strathmann, λατρεύω, λατρεία, 62-63) but at least in Paul one can say that even though the verb may be applied in a non-cultic way (Rom. 1.9, 25; Phil. 3.3), the metaphor of sacrifice is nevertheless employed.

of the land together with "seed" was one of the fundamental promises of the Old Testament.[3]

But there are some who argue that the land of Israel is now simply irrelevant. W.D. Davies has written the standard academic text on the New Testament and the land. He writes:

. . . in the last resort this study drives us to one point: the person of a Jew, Jesus of Nazareth, who proclaimed the acceptable year of the Lord only to die accursed on a cross and so to pollute the land, and by that act and its consequences to shatter the geographical dimension of the religion of his fathers. Like everything else, the land also in the New Testament drives us to ponder the mystery of Jesus, the Christ, who by his cross and resurrection broke not only the bonds of death for early Christians but also the bonds of the land.[4]

Note also the position of Knight who believes that the resurrection of Jesus is the fulfilment of the promise of the land. He writes:

I felt empty of God's promise of *The Land* when I discovered, on my visit to Palestine, that Tel Aviv could have been built in Utah, or Jaffa in southern France. This to me was no longer the Holy Land. And then it all came home to me why this was so. 'He is not here; he is risen!' And *in* him, I saw clearly, as I reviewed in my mind the on-going work of God, there had risen, not just the will and purpose of God, but also, in epitome and in a representative capacity, *The Land* itself, to become the first-fruits of the new heaven and the new *earth*, wherein dwelleth righteousness. And so I realised that the Risen Christ *is* the eschatological significance and ultimate outcome of God's ancient promise of *The Land*.[5]

I take the point that the significance of the land of Israel has been radically changed in view of the Christ event. So in chapter 4 above it was noted that the language of "inheritance" in Gal. 3.18 and Rom. 4.13 is now applied to the promise to Abraham which finds its fulfilment in Christ.[6] Further, I can give qualified support to N.T. Wright's view that "the whole world is now seen as God's holy land, to be redeemed in the new creation".[7] But is the

---

[3] This promise of the land was, for example, more fundamental than say that of Israel having a king.

[4] W.D. Davies, *The Gospel and the Land: Early Christianity and Jewish Territorial Doctrine*, Sheffield: Sheffield Academic Press 1994 (repr.), [1]1974, p. 375.

[5] G.A.F. Knight, "Israel - the land and resurrection", in D.W. Torrance (ed.), *The Witness of the Jews to God*, Edinburgh: Handsel Press 1982, 41 (32-41) (Knight's emphasis).

[6] See chapter 4, section 3.1 above.

[7] Wright, "Romans", 680. He refers not only to Rom. 4.13 but also to 8.18-27.

extreme view of Davies, who seems to find the land almost completely irrelevant, tenable? From a Pauline perspective, I do not think it is. Apart from the significance of Rom. 9.4-5 (which I have already discussed), I give these two further reasons for opposing Davies' view.

First, Jesus the stone of offence laid in Zion will also come from Zion according to Rom. 11.26. There has been a debate whether Paul here is thinking of the redeemer coming from the earthly Jerusalem or from the heavenly Jerusalem. The latter could be supported by Gal. 4.26. Davies, supporting the idea of "heavenly Jerusalem", writes:

This interpretation becomes even more persuasive if there were among Paul's opponents in Galatia, Corinth, and Rome those who emphasized the role of Jerusalem in the present and future: there is some evidence that there were such.[8]

However, the situation Paul faced in Rome was, as I have argued, quite different to that which he faced in Galatia (and also that which he faced in Corinth). Paul does not seem to be concerned with Judaizers in Romans. And in fact Paul is concerned to counter a Christian anti-Jewish attitude. And we have seen that in Rom. 11.13ff. Paul is in fact concerned with Gentile Christian arrogance towards non-Christian Jews (see especially Rom. 11.17-24) and/or towards Christian Jews (cf. Rom. 14.1-15.6). Far from downplaying Jerusalem, it could be that Paul was wishing to stress the *abiding theological importance* of the city. It also needs stressing that the question whether Paul refers to the earthly or heavenly Jerusalem is in fact a false antithesis. For on the last day the heavenly Jerusalem will come down upon the raised earthly Jerusalem.[9] We find this idea in part in Is. 2.2-4, a text which was of some importance for Paul.[10] So Is. 2.2 speaks of Mount Zion being "established as the highest of the mountains" in the "latter days". Views of the earthly/heavenly Jerusalem are also reflected in Rev. 21.10. Here we have a vision of a "great, high mountain" of "the holy city Jerusa-

---

[8] Davies, *The Gospel and the Land*, p. 198.

[9] P. Stuhlmacher, "Die Stellung Jesu und des Paulus zu Jerusalem", *ZThK* 86 (1989) 155 (140-56), commenting on "out of Zion" in Rom. 11.26 rightly points out: "Der Erlöser wird kommen aus dem himmlischen Jerusalem, das sich am Ende der Tage auf den zum Gottesberg erhöhten Zion herabsenken wird".

[10] Paul seems to have reversed the imagery; i.e. rather than the nations coming to the glory of Israel, Israel through jealousy comes to the glory of the Church.

lem coming down out of heaven from God".[11] The earthly Jerusalem (which would merge with the heavenly Jerusalem) did therefore have abiding significance for Paul.[12]

The second point which goes against Davies is that in Rom. 11.29 Paul claims that the gifts and call of God are irrevocable. The term τὰ χαρίσματα refers most likely to the election of and promise to Abraham and his descendants κατὰ χάριν (Rom. 4.4, 16). Although Paul's argument is primarily concerned with salvation I wonder whether one can exclude the concrete promise of the land (and of "seed").[13] Further, one should add that the promise of the land is made more concrete through Jesus Christ. For by becoming a servant of the circumcision, he has confirmed the promises made to the patriarchs.[14] Jesus Christ does not make the promises to Israel less concrete; he makes them more concrete. As I argued in chapter 7, he makes the sonship of Israel more concrete. And, as I argued in chapter 4, he makes the history of Israel concrete. We have here what can be termed a form of theological Platonism.[15]

---

[11] On the Rabbinic texts concerning the elevation of Mount Zion and the descent from heaven, see B. Ego, *Im Himmel wie auf Erden: Studien zum Verhältnis von himmlischer und irdischer Welt im rabbinischen Judentum* (WUNT 2.34), Tübingen: J.C.B. Mohr (Paul Siebeck) 1989, pp. 102-3.

[12] Contrast the view of P.W.L. Walker, *Jesus and the Holy City: New Testament Perspectives on Jerusalem*, Grand Rapids/Cambridge U.K.: Wm B. Eerdmans 1996, p. 142: "Neither Jerusalem nor the Temple located there retained in the thought of Paul any significance in the realization of God's eschatological promises". But he can only write this because he follows N.T. Wright in understanding "the deliverer will come from Zion" (Rom. 11.26) as a reference to the *first* coming of Christ. And even if there is a reference to the parousia, he thinks Paul has in mind the heavenly Jerusalem (p. 143 n. 109).

[13] This link between Rom. 11.29 and the land is suggested by Jostein Ådna in an address "Landverheißung für Israel in der Bibel und Nahostkonflikt heute" given at a conference "Christen, Juden, 'Judenchristen' – eine spannungsreiche Beziehung" held in Schloß Reichenberg. Ådna himself, though, is unsure whether the promise of the land is contained within Rom. 11.29.

[14] Rom. 15.8. Cf. 2 Cor. 1.20.

[15] Cf. I.U. Dalferth, "Karl Barth's eschatological realism", in S.W. Sykes (ed.), *Karl Barth: Centenary Essays*, Cambridge: CUP 1989, 14-45. The basis for such a "theological Platonism" can be found in Paul (although this does not necessarily mean that Paul was directly influenced by Plato). In addition to the points made in chapters 4 and 7 about Christ making the sonship and history of Israel "concrete", compare also the contrast (or contradiction) between σκιά and σῶμα in Col. 2.17. As H. Hübner, *An Philemon/An die Kolosser/An die Epheser* (HzNT 12), Tübingen: J.C.B. Mohr (Paul Siebeck) 1997, p. 87, writes, "Volle Realität kommt nur dem σῶμα zu, wobei dieses

I therefore conclude that from a Pauline perspective God's promise to Israel of the land still stands.[16] It is the gift of the electing God to his elected people.[17] And although the Old Testament can speak of Israel possessing the land,[18] ultimately it belongs to God.[19] But does "possessing the land" mean that Israel must have overall political control? In Old Testament texts, the implication does certainly seem to be that "possessing the land" includes having political control (Gen. 22.17; Dt. 1.8; Jos. 1.11). The Babylonian exile was to change this and for Jeremiah it introduced a radical change. In fact Knight's view that the resurrection Jesus fulfils the promise of the Land[20] is partly built upon the idea that Jeremiah points to a new covenant in the heart. He "recognised that the ancient covenant must, in God's good time, find a new place from which to operate, and that place, he believed, would be the individual human heart (Jer. 31:31-3)".[21] Knight can therefore write that "The Land of Israel had now by 587 B.C. served its purpose in the plan of God".[22] He therefore deduces that "[t]he fall of Jerusalem with all that went with it was thus the first step towards the winding up of the Old Covenant in the form it took when Israel was necessarily constituted as a political state".[23]

But is this the whole story? What about the restoration? The return of the exiles under Cyrus, God's anointed (Is. 45.1), was seen as a fulfilment of

---

Wort als Inbegriff für die *volle und eigentliche Wirklichkeit* erscheint" and this σῶμα refers to the "Heils-*Raum* des Christus als Raum der vollen Heilswirklichkeit" (Hübner's emphasis).

[16] For a useful summary of the significance of the land for Judaism see J. Parkes, *Whose Land? A History of the Peoples of Palestine*, Harmondsworth: Penguin ²1970, (¹1949), pp. 135-47.

[17] Cf. H.D. Preuß, *Theologie des Alten Testaments*, 2 vols, Stuttgart/Berlin/Köln: W. Kohlhammer Verlag 1991-92, 1:132.

[18] E.g. Lev. 20.24; Dt. 4.1. On the verb ירשׁ see H.H. Schmid, ירשׁ, *THAT* 1:778-81. Commenting on the deuteronomic use, he writes: "Obgleich in der Regel grammatikalisch im Qal Israel als Subjekt zu *jrš* erscheint, ist doch deutlich, daß es letztlich Jahwe ist, er Israel das Land zum (Erb-)Besitz gibt" (781).

[19] Lev. 25.23.

[20] See the quotation above.

[21] Knight, "Israel – the land and resurrection", 39.

[22] Knight, "Israel – the land and resurrection", 39.

[23] Knight, "Israel – the land and resurrection", 39.

God's covenant faithfulness. Also in the time of Jesus and Paul, Israel was not considered to be still in exile.[24]

In Paul's time the land of Israel was largely under Roman direct rule. But Jews were still living there and Paul does not seem to give any indication that God's promise of the land to Israel had failed because they did not have ultimate political control. Had he written his letter to the Romans eighty years later the tone of his letter may well have been different. For at that time not only would Israel have no temple (and therefore no λατρεία) but also would have no Jerusalem; for at the end of the Bar Kochba revolt Jews were excluded from their holy city. Siegfried Herrmann points out that "Israel's history is inextricably bound up with the land, indeed the lands, in which it took place".[25] Martin Noth heads the final section of his *History of Israel*, "The Insurrections against Rome and the End of Israel".[26] Describing what happened to Jerusalem at the end of the Bar Kochba revolt he writes:

> The Jews were . . . excluded from their own ancient holy city, which had for so long formed the centre of their ancestors' lives. The province now probably exchanged its former name of Judaea for the new name of Palestine, which it bore henceforth and which derived from the older description of the coastal area as 'the land of the Philistines' . . . And so the descendants of the Isarel of old had become strangers in their own former homeland just as they were in the Diaspora; and their holy city was prohibited to them. Thus ended the ghastly epilogue of Israel's history.[27]

Noth therefore views the end of Israel as 135 AD. The end of Israel corresponds to the time when Jews could no longer live in the holy city.[28]

When we come to apply Paul's theology of the land to the present problem in the middle east, a distinction therefore needs to be made. It is one

---

[24] I expressed some reservations about this view in chapter 1 above. See also Bryan, *Restoration*, pp. 12-20. Interestingly, the idea of Israel still being in exile has been used by some Jews to argue against Israel having the land.

[25] S. Herrmann, *A History of Israel in Old Testament Times* ET, London: SCM 1975, p. 3.

[26] M. Noth, *The History of Israel* ET, London: A. & C. Black ²1960, (¹1958), p. 432.

[27] Noth, *History of Israel*, p. 454.

[28] Note, however, that there was always a Jewish presence after the Bar Kochba revolt. So Schäfer, *History of the Jews*, p. 164, points out that after the revolt relations with the Romans slowly improved. So Hadrian's successor, Antoninus Pius (138-61 AD), relaxed the ban on circumcision and the ban on entering Jerusalem itself was also relaxed. See also M. Gilbert, who points to the presence of Jews near Safed, Tiberias, Hebron and even Jerusalem during the first six centuries AD (*The Routledge Atlas of the Arab-Israeli Conflict*, London/New York ⁷2002, (¹1974), p. 1).

thing to say that Jews have a right to live in the land. It is another to say that Jews should have overall political control or that "Israel" should be a "Jewish" state. From a Pauline perspective, Israel certainly has a right to live in the land. If one were to argue that Israel should have overall political control or that it should be a "Jewish" state, further arguments would have to be advanced. One would have to point to the fact that simply living in the land without political control could be, or would be, disastrous for the Jewish people.[29] For whereas in Paul's time there was a Roman empire which in a real sense gave some protection to Jews, today Israel is surrounded by undemocratic and largely Muslim/Arab countries and some of the Arab and Muslim leaders have an attitude to the Jews which approaches that of Haman in the book of Esther.[30] Bauckham, I believe, is correct to plea for a political realism, a view he finds in the book of Esther.[31] He writes that the book of Esther:

. . . recognizes that a threatened minority like the Jews cannot be safe from the hostility of their neighbours without access to political control. . . . Just as in Mordecai's time Jewish survival seemed to require Jewish participation in the power-structure of the Persian Empire, so in the modern world of nation states Jewish survival seemed to require the power of self-determination in the form of a Jewish nation state.[32]

This brings me to the question whether one can discern God's providential hand in the foundation of the state of Israel in 1948?[33] Torrance writes:

---

[29] Here one has to recognize not only the virulent anti-Jewish sentiments of Arab Muslims but also of many Arab Christians. I consider it unfortunate that in Israel/Palestine the Jews are on one side and Arab Muslims and Christians are on the other. Muslim antisemitism and the long history of antisemitism in the Eastern Church are unfortunately yoked.

[30] Some countries are quite explicit about wishing to see Israel extinguished. Others are more prudent in their view of Israel. But it is worth stressing that what one hears from Arab leaders in the Western media often does not correspond to statements made to fellow Arabs or Muslims.

[31] One could also add that Paul was a political realist. Despite the problems of Rom. 13.1-7, it does show that Paul was aware of the political realies of the Roman empire. If Christians as a small minority were to oppose the Roman state, they would be taking incredible risks.

[32] R.J. Bauckham, *The Bible in Politics: How to read the Bible politically* (TWB), London: SPCK 1989, pp. 127-28.

[33] Note that the book of Esther never speaks explicitly about God's providential care (and, famously, of course, never mentions God) but invites the readers to discern God's providence (cf. Bauckham, *Bible in Politics*, pp. 123-24).

The establishment of the new State of Israel, following hard upon the most harrowing ordeal of suffering the Jews have known, is surely the most significant sign given by God in his providential dealings with his covenanted People since the destruction of Jerusalem in A.D. 70, for now Israel as a complete entity has been openly thrust into the very centre of world history where it must bear witness to the sovereign rule of the living God and give an account of its divine vocation among the nations and peoples of mankind.[34]

It may be objected that had the foundation of the state of Israel been an act of God, it would not be necessary to found a state through human activity. God would simply establish it. Also, in the case of the establishing of the state of Israel, there were serious acts of violence which must never be overlooked.[35] But human acts, sometimes done with the worst motives, can nevertheless be interpreted as God's acts. This is seen dramatically in the cross of Christ. But a more appropriate parallel would be the return of the exiles from Babylon. It has been pointed out that Cyrus's motives for allowing the return were not entirely pure.[36]

Before responding to Torrance's comments, it is worth considering the "Jewish" nature of the state of Israel. It is appropriate that the state is not simply a secular and political entity.[37] But, at the same time, it is not a "theocracy". Theodor Herzl rightly rejected this option:

Shall we end by having a theocracy? No indeed. . . . We shall . . . prevent any theocractic tendencies from coming to the fore on the part of our priesthood. We shall keep our

---

[34] T.F. Torrance, "The divine vocation and destiny of Israel in world history", in D.W. Torrance (ed.), *The Witness of the Jews to God*, Edinburgh: Handsel Press 1982, 94-95 (85-104).

[35] The event that stands out in the British mind is the bombing of the King David Hotel in Jerusalem on 22 July 1946 by the Irgun, led by Menahem Begin. See also the story of what happened to the village of Lydda on July 13 1948. See G.M. Burge, *Whose Land? Whose Promise? What Christians Are Not Being Told about Israel and the Palestinians*, Paternoster 2003, pp. 145-46. This work is partly intended to bring uncomfortable truths to Americans (especially Christians) who support Israel. My own experience is that the British media take a pro-Palestinian bias. In the events leading up to the foundation of the state of Israel, atrocities, of course, were committed on all sides.

[36] It has been suggested that Cyrus "shrewdly calculated that a tribute-paying subject nation would be more profitable than an unproductive desert" (J.K.S. Reid, "Israel – people, nation, state", in D.W. Torrance (ed.), *The Witness of the Jews to God*, Edinburgh: Handsel Press 1982, 49 (42-57), who refers to M.I. Dimont, *Jews, God and History*, London: W.H. Allen 1964, p. 199).

[37] K. Stendahl, "Judaism and Christianity II: A Plea for a New Relationship", in *Meanings: The Bible as Document and as Guide*, Philadelphia: Fortress Press 1984, 226-27 (217-32).

priests within the confines of their temples, in the same way as we shall keep our professional army within the confines of their barracks. Army and priesthood shall receive honours high as their valuable functions deserve. But they must not interfere in the administration of the State, which confers distinctions upon them, else they will conjure up difficulties without and within.[38]

It is therefore appropriate that Israel be a *Jewish* state even though it is also a *pluralist* state (just as England can in a certain respect be called a "Christian" country even though it allows freedoms to non-Christian religions). Israel is the land promised to the patriarchs and it is fitting that it reflects "Jewish" values.

So what do we say to Torrance's remarks that the establishing of the state of Israel "is surely the most significant sign given by God in his providential dealings with his covenanted People since the destruction of Jerusalem in A.D. 70"? I essentially agree with him. The Jewish people need a land where they will be free from persecution. It could be argued that they did not necessarily have to settle in Israel to be free from persecution (and being surrounded by Arab/Muslim countries they are rather vulnerable as events have demonstrated). They had been offered land in Argentina and Uganda.[39] But for theological reasons, I think it essential that they did in fact settle in the land of Israel. This, after all, was the land promised to them. Also, the Jewish people and the land of Israel are inextricably intertwined. But now that Israel is established, they must, in Torrance's words, "bear witness to the sovereign rule of the living God". This must have implications for the treatment of the Palestinian people in the occupied territories, some of whom, of course, are Christians.[40]

---

[38] Quoted in Küng, *Judaism*, p. 525.

[39] See H. Wilson, *The Chariot of Israel: Britain, America and the State of Israel*, London: George Weidenfeld & Nicholson/Michael Joseph 1981, pp. 17-18 (on Argentina) and pp. 13, 25-26, 31-32, 34-35, 53 (on Uganda). In 1903 Herzl reluctantly accepted Chamberlain's proposal for a Jewish state in Uganda but the idea was abandoned after opposition from both the Zionist movement and the British public. See the entries on Joseph Chamberlain and Theodor Herzl in J. Comay and L. Cohn-Sherbok (ed.), *Who's Who in Jewish History after the period of the Old Testament*, London/New York: Routledge [2]1995, ([1]1974), pp. 80-81 and pp. 167-68 (162-69), and see also Cohn-Sherbok, *Crucified Jew*, p. 172.

[40] One of the problems though in speaking of a "viable Palestinian state" with East Jerusalem as capital is that if any part of Israel is filled with theological significance it is the temple mount.

But is the establishment of the state of Israel (or the return of Jews to the land) to be seen as a sign of God's *faithfulness* to Israel?[41] Some have objected to this pointing out that the converse is that there not being a return to Israel or the existence of the state of Israel is a sign of God's unfaithfulness to Israel.[42] But I am not at all sure that this argument stands theologically and I will return to this shortly. In this connection it is interesting to note that "dabru emet" affirms: "Christians can respect the claim of the Jewish people upon the land of Israel. . . . Christians appreciate that Israel was promised – and given – to Jews as the physical center of the covenant between them and God".

Before leaving this issue I want to reflect on the Holocaust and the establishing of the state of Israel. I argued above that not only is Israel representative of humanity under God's judgement and humanity receiving the promises of God. She also stands under her special curse and still enjoys her special privileges. I argued that Paul did not relate this curse to historical occurrences. And I believe it would be a serious mistake to imagine that God's judgement was expressed in the historical events we call the Holocaust just as it would be a mistake to relate Israel's suffering to this curse.[43] But must

---

[41] See, e.g., M.A. MacLeod, "The witness of the church to the Jewish People", in D.W. Torrance (ed.), *The Witness of the Jews to God*, Edinburgh: Handsel Press 1982, 76 (71-80): "It is . . . our Christian duty to recognise in the restoration of the people of Israel to the land of Israel the faithfulness of God to His own promises".

[42] W. Kraus, "'Eretz Jisrael'. Die territoriale Dimension in der jüdischen Tradition als Anfrage an die christliche Theologie", in M. Karrer, W. Kraus and O. Merk (ed.), *Kirche und Volk Gottes: Festschrift für Jürgen Roloff zum 70. Geburtstag*, Neukirchen-Vluyn: Neukirchener 2000, 40 (19-41).

[43] Gottfried Maltusch reported on a discussion which took place in Bonhoeffer's Seminar of the Confessing Church when news reached them of the destruction of the synagogues in nearby Köslin: "Unter uns entstand nun eine große Diskussion, wie diese Tat zu werten sei . . . Einige sprachen von dem Fluch, der seit dem Kreuzestod Jesu Christi auf dem Volk der Juden läge. Hiergegen wandte sich Bonhoeffer auf das allerschärfste . . . Bonhoeffer lehnte die Auslegung, daß sich in der Zerstörung der Synagogen durch die Nazis der Fluch über die Juden erfülle, auf das schärfste ab. Hier sei reine Gewalt geschehen . . . Mit dieser Tat habe sich aufs Neue die gottlose Gewalt des Nationalsozialismus gezeigt" (Klappert, *Miterben*, p. 73, quoting W.-D. Zimmermann, *Begegnung mit Dietrich Bonhoeffer*, [4]1969, p. 142). Contrast the view of Gerhard Kittel. According to Siegele-Wenschkewitz, *Judenfrage*, p. 97, who writes that in 1933 he introduced the new idea of "Unheilsgeschichte", "unter die er das jüdische Volk gestellt sieht, mit der aktuellen Politik verknüpft, ja sie geradezu der nationalsozialistischen Politik zur Verfügung stellt. Der Gehorsam gegen die Geschichte Gottes

one argue by symmetry that it is equally mistaken to say the establishment of the state of Israel is a sign of God's blessing? I think not. As argued above (chapter 9), God stands behind good in a different way to how he stands behind evil. And just as one can refrain from relating illness to a curse yet at the same time praise God for healing, so one can refrain from seeing the Holocaust as a curse yet at the same time view the homecoming and the establishment of the State of Israel as an expression of God's blessing.

2. The Question of the Millennium

A discussion about the State of Israel and questions of fulfilment of prophecy leads to the question as to whether Paul envisaged a "millennium" where Israel played a central part. The question of the millennium was raised in chapter 6 above when I considered the meaning of "life from the dead" in Rom. 11.15. One way in which a millennial reign of Christ with his saints has been argued for on a Pauline basis is by understanding the expressions "life *from the dead*" (ζωὴ ἐκ νεκρῶν, Rom. 11.15) or "resurrection *from the dead*" (ἐξανάστασις ἐκ νεκρῶν, Phil. 3.11) in a specific way. The preposition ἐκ, it is claimed, points to a resurrection of the righteous *from among* the dead. The general resurrection *of the dead*, on the other hand, is referred to precisely by ἡ ἀνάστασις τῶν νεκρῶν.[44] So 1 Cor. 15.42 is given as an example of such a general resurrection.[45] In addition, 1 Cor. 15.20-28 is given as support for a millennial reign of Christ.[46] Let me take just vv. 22-24:

For as in Adam all die, so also in Christ shall all be made alive. 23 But each in his own order: Christ the first fruits, then at his coming (παρουσία) those who belong to Christ. 24 Then comes the end (τέλος), when he delivers the kingdom to God the Father, after destroying every rule and every authority and power.

---

gebiete dem christlichen Staat, Jesu Fluch über das jüdische Volk zu vollstrecken; dessen Erlösung sei allein Gott vorbehalten. Der Gehorsam gegenüber Gott verlange, die Juden in ihrem Unglück zu lassen".

[44] So J.B. Lightfoot, *St. Paul's Epistle to the Philippians*, Peabody: Hendrickson 1993 (repr.), ([1]1868), p. 151, makes this distinction.

[45] Lightfoot, *Philippians*, p. 151.

[46] For a helpful survey of the debate regarding this passage, see L.J. Kreitzer, *Jesus and God in Paul's Eschatology* (JSNTSup 19), Sheffield: JSOT Press 1987, pp. 131-64.

If support for a messianic kingdom is to be found, then it has to be placed between the parousia (v. 23) and the τέλος (v. 24). But the sense of v. 24 is this: Christ begins destroying the evil powers from the time of his exaltation.[47] Then, when the destruction is complete, the end comes. 1 Cor. 15.20-28 does not speak of a messianic kingdom. Further, care has to be taken about the distinction made between resurrection *from the dead* and *of the dead* which I discussed above. It is true that Paul makes a distinction between Jesus being raised ἐκ νεκρῶν (i.e out from among the dead) and the resurrection of the dead (ἀνάστασις νεκρῶν) in 1 Cor. 15.12. But it is not clear that ἀνάστασις νεκρῶν refers to the general resurrection. In fact in its context it would tend to refer to the resurrection of believers.[48] It may be that in 1 Corinthians 15 Paul distinguishes between the resurrection of believers in vv. 12, 21 by using the expression ἀνάστασις νεκρῶν which lacks the article and the general resurrection by using the articular expression ἡ ἀνάστασις τῶν νεκρῶν in v. 42.[49] But it is dangerous to systematize on the resurrection by analysing the Greek expressions.[50] I myself find the arguments for Paul having an idea of a millennium unconvincing and if it were not for Rev. 20.1-10 I wonder whether the idea would ever be entertained. If one is to speak of an *interregnum Christi* then it is between his resurrection and the τέλος which is related to his parousia.[51]

By associative reasoning, Moltmann argues in this way:

---

[47] Conzelmann, *Der erste Brief an die Korinther*, p. 332: "Die Vernichtung beginnt mit der Erhöhung; das ist ja der Zweck seiner Inthronisation".

[48] R. Bauckham, in R. Bauckham (ed.), *God will be All in All: The Eschatology of Jürgen Moltmann*. Edinburgh: T. & T. Clark 1999, pp. 144-45, argues that for Paul resurrection is a soteriological concept.

[49] See M. Bachmann, "Zur Gedankenführung in 1. Kor. 15,12ff", *ThZ* 34 (1978) 270 (265-76). Note, however, the sceptical comments of W. Schrage, *Der erste Brief an die Korinther: 4. Teilband 1Kor 15,1-16.24* (KEK 7.4), Zürich/Düsseldorf: Benziger Verlag/Neukirchen-Vluyn: Neukirchener Verlag 2001, p. 128 n. 574.

[50] Cf. M. Bockmuehl, *The Epistle to the Philippians* (BNTC), London: A. & C. Black 1997, p. 218, who, commenting on Phil. 3.11, warns against systematizing Paul unduly in regard to resurrection "of the dead" or "from the dead".

[51] See Schrage, *Korinther (1 Kor 15,1-16,24)*, pp. 170-71.

Right down to the present day, Christian millenarianism has had a clearly detectable affinity to Israel. It is only here that the theological recognition of Israel's enduring vocation, and the hope for Israel's future, are really preserved . . . Up to now I have seen no positive Israel theology on the Christian side which fails to integrate Christ's chiliastic kingdom of peace into the eschatology.[52]

However, there can be a positive theology of Israel (and I hope I have presented one in the present work) which does not go with a Christian millenarianism. It is perhaps rather unfair of Moltmann to give Paul Althaus as an example of someone who disregarded such a chiliastic kingdom since the opinion he expresses is an extreme one.[53] It is possible to affirm the establishment of the state of Israel as an act of the providential activity of God without having to take the view that in this modern state the prophecies of the Old Testament, which hitherto have not been fulfilled, are now being fulfilled (or will be fulfilled in the millennium).[54]

In relation to this issue of the fulfilment of prophecy, it is instructive to consider how someone like Paul would understand Jesus' fulfilment of the Old Testament prophecies. It is striking that Paul's understanding of Jesus as suffering servant differs in certain crucial respects from that put forward in Is. 52.13-53.12; indeed, it can be argued that the fourth servant song as it stands in the Old Testament is theologically wanting.[55] So in relation to

---

[52] J. Moltmann, in Bauckham (ed.), *God will be All in All*, p. 151.

[53] He quotes from the seventh edition of *Die letzten Dinge* (Gütersloh 1957): "Israel no longer has any special position in the church and for the church, nor has it any special 'salvific vocation' for 'Christ is also the end of the Messiah'" (Moltmann, in Bauckham (ed.), *God will be All in All*, p. 151).

[54] Although I have been critical of Althaus, he is rightly critical of scholars such as K.A. Auberlen. So Auberlen, for example, writes concerning the promise of Dan. 7.18, 27 that the Saints of the Most High will possess the kingdom and that all dominions shall serve and obey them: "Diese Verheißung ist aber an Israel bis auf diesen Tag noch nicht erfüllt, sondern wird sich erst im Reiche der tausend Jahre erfüllen" (*Der Prophet Daniel und die Offenbarung Johannis*, Basel 1854, p. 221, quoted in P. Althaus, *Die letzten Dinge: Entwurf einer christlichen Eschatologie* (SAS 9), Gütersloh: C. Bertelsmann ³1926, p. 109)

[55] See O. Hofius, "Das vierte Gottesknechtlied in den Briefen des Neuen Testaments", *NTS* 39 (1993) 422 (414-37): "Was dieses Lied von dem stellvertretenden Sterben des Gottesknechts sagt, das ist so, wie es da zu lesen steht und auch gemeint ist, theologisch nicht nachvollziehbar. Diese Feststellung gilt ganz unabhängig von der Beantwortung jener recht umstrittenen Frage, *wer* denn dem alttestamentlichen Text zufolge mit dem Gottesknecht gemeint sei. Denn ob es sich nun um den Propheten Deuterojesaja selbst handelt oder – kollektiv – um das jahwetreue Israel oder auch um

Jesus fulfilling messianic prophecies of the Old Testament, I can agree with these theses of Hofius in respect to *Paul*:[56]

Hinsichtlich der Frage, ob Jesus der 'Messias' ist, bedeutet das:
Wenn unter 'Messias' der Messias Israels im Sinne der aus bestimmten alttestament-lichen Texten erwachsenen frühjüdischen Messiaserwartung verstanden wird, so ist die Antwort eindeutig eine negative: Dieser Messias Israel ist der im Neuen Testament bezeugte Jesus Christus nicht.[57]

If, therefore, one cannot *read off* from the Old Testament what the messiah is to be like, I wonder likewise whether one can point to "unfulfilled prophecies" in the Old Testament and say they are going to be fulfilled in the millennium. But can one say that Old Testament prophecies are being fulfilled in the return of Jews to the land and the establishment of the state of Israel? In relation to the return of Jews to the land of Israel, a passage like Is. 11.10-11, stands out:

On that day the root of Jesse shall stand as a signal to the peoples; the nations shall inquire of him, and his dwelling shall be glorious. On that day the Lord will extend his hand yet a second time to recover the remnant that is left of his people, from Assyria, from Egypt, from Pathros, from Ethiopia, from Elam, from Shinar, from Hamath, and from the coastlands of the sea.

One commentator writes:

. . . the primary focus of the passage seems to be upon the historical nation of Israel, so that one is led to believe that it points to some great final ingathering of the Jewish people such as that referred to by Paul in Rom. 11. If that has begun with the Zionist movement, as many believe, we may look forward with anticipation to its ultimate completion in a turning to God in Christ by the Jewish nation.[58]

---

eine messianische Gestalt der Zukunft, – in jedem Fall ist zu sagen: Befreiung von Sünde und Schuld durch *menschliche* Stellvertretung ist theologisch schlechterdings undenkbar" (Hofius' emphasis).

[56] There are, I believe, problems if these words are applied to all the New Testament witnesses. See Stuhlmacher's criticisms of Hofius in "Der messianische Gottesknecht", 139-40. See also the discussion above regarding Jesus' restoration of Israel (chapter 8). Certainly on a *historical level*, Jesus put himself forward as the messiah of Israel, even though he radically changed the concept of messiahship (e.g. Mk 8.27-33).

[57] O. Hofius, "Ist Jesus der Messias? Thesen", in *Jahrbuch für Biblische Theologie Band 8: Der Messias*, Neukirchen-Vluyn: Neukirchener Verlag 1993, 128 (103-29).

[58] See J.N. Oswalt, *The Book of Isaiah: Chapter 1-39* (NICOT), Grand Rapids: Wm B. Eerdmans 1986, p. 286.

Although I have some reservations about the wording of this (e.g. the "ingathering of the Jewish people", something which Paul does not say in Romans 9-11), it is nevertheless a serious attempt to read the Old Testament as a Christian. But he writes, correctly, with some caution.[59] Perhaps rather than speaking in terms of the fulfilment of prophecy one should say that a text such as Is. 11.10-11 "speaks" to us in the light of the return of Jews to the land of Israel. One may compare the way in which the fall of tyrants spoken of in the Old Testament speaks to situations where today's tyrants fall from power.[60]

3. Election, Law and Identity

One of the most difficult current issues regarding Israel is the question "Who is a Jew?" This is not, of course, a new problem.[61] But the issue is of fundamental importance when discussing "All Israel will be saved" (Rom. 11.26a).

In Paul's time, the definition of who was a Jew was relatively straightforward. Although the various Jewish groups (Pharisees, Sadducees, Essenes, Zealots) disagreed on fundamental issues, "no sect ever claimed that the others were not Jews".[62] The traditional halakhic answer is that one is a Jew through matrilinear descent or conversion.[63] The idea of matrilinear descent goes back as far as the mid-fifth century.[64] The whole thinking of "who was a Jew" was changed as a result of the Babylonian exile. For in the first temple period "it seems that apart from Ammon and Moab, with whom

---

[59] One may contrast some of the statements by dispensationalists.

[60] C. Michalson, "Bultmann against Marcion", in B.W. Anderson (ed.), *The Old Testament and Christian Faith*, New York: Harper & Row 1963, 57 (49-63), tells of how towards the end of the war, when news circulated of Hitler's death, Ebeling read to his "entirely nonchurchly comrades" Isaiah 14, the song of triumph on the fall of the king of Babylon. Ebeling commented on the power of this text to speak to this situation in 1945. Likewise, it could "speak" to the fall of a modern tyrant such as Saddam Hussein.

[61] L.H. Schiffman, *Who was a Jew? Rabbinic and Halakhic Perspectives on the Jewish Christian Schism*, Hoboken, NJ: Ktav 1985, p. ix.

[62] Schiffman, *Who was a Jew?*, p. 3.

[63] See b. Yeb. 47b; b. Kid. 68b.

[64] Schiffman, *Who was a Jew?*, p. 16.

intermarriage was eternally prohibited, Israelites might marry those who sought to become part of the people of Israel".[65] Israel was a land-related national entity so no formal conversion was necessary. However, all this changed with the Babylonian exile. After the exile the people of Israel were not simply defined by attachment to the land and therefore the issue of genealogy became important.[66] Some texts in Ezra-Nehemiah forbid inter-marriage whether the partner is male or female (Neh. 13.25) but the main issue is that of non-Jewish wives (Ezr. 9.2; 10.2, 10-11); because of mar-riage to non-Jewish wives, "the holy race has mixed itself with the peoples of the lands" (Ezr. 9.2).

By the time of Jesus the principle of matrilinear descent was fairly well established. So according to Josephus, when Herod surrounded Jerusalem in 39 BC, Antigonus responded saying that Herod could not rule as king since he was a commoner and an Idumaean, that is a "half-Jew" (ἡμιϊουδαῖος).[67] He could not be considered a full-Jew since although his father Antipater was a descendant of Idumeans converted to Judaism by John Hyrcanus, his mother was of a Nabatean family.[68] The Rabbinic material regarding matrilinear descent is harder to date. But m. Kid. 3.12 ("[If] any [woman] is disqualified from marrying not only this [man] but also any other [Jew], [then her] child is equal in status to her . . . ")[69] would seem to be dated 125 at the latest (and possibly before 70 AD).[70] Also t. Kid. 4.16 ("If a non-Jew or a slave had intercourse with a Jewish woman, and she gave birth to a child, the offspring is a *mamzer* . . . "),[71] which would also seem to be dated to 125AD at the latest.

One could also be defined a Jew by conversion. This idea of "conversion" helps to define someone as a Jew not only for Gentiles who convert to Judaism but also in those cases where one has Jewish blood but there is a

---

[65] Schiffman, *Who was a Jew?*, p. 16.

[66] Schiffman, *Who was a Jew?*, p. 16. See also Jeremias, *Jerusalem*, p. 270, who points out that genealogies became so important because "the promises of the age to come were valid for the pure seed".

[67] Josephus, *Antiquitates* 14.403 (Josephus (LCL), 7:660).

[68] See Schiffman, *Who was a Jew?*, p. 12.

[69] Translation of Schiffman, *Who was a Jew?*, p. 9.

[70] Schiffman, *Who was a Jew?*, p. 10.

[71] Translation of Schiffman, *Who was a Jew?*, p. 12. The *mamzer* is a full-Jew (except in respect to marriage law).

missing or several missing matrilinear links. The four basic requirements since second temple times were acceptance of the torah, circumcision for males, immersion and sacrifice. This is reflected in the saying attributed to Rabbi Judah ha Nasi: "Rabbi says: Just as Israel did not enter the covenant except by means of three things–circumcision, immersion, and the acceptance of a sacrifice–so it is the same with the proselytes".[72] The actual conversion procedure and ceremony is described in b. Yeb. 47a-b. This text does not reflects the situation before 70 AD (since sacrifice is not mentioned); rather it represents the situation after the first or second Jewish revolt in view of the reference to the persecution of Israel.

Schiffman's conclusion is that the halakhot regarding both the identity of the Jew by birth and by conversion were in force "before the rise of Christianity".[73] It is highly significant that a Jew was defined in this way since even those who are heretics and apostates remain Jews.[74] So according to Rabbinic understanding, even those who will be excluded from the world to come would still belong to the people of Israel.[75] One could make a case that Paul understood the term "Israel" in the same way. "Israel" therefore was defined in Paul's mind as someone who had a Jewish mother or someone who converted to Judaism. It includes even heretics and apostates. And I see no reason why these "Jewish people" should not come under Paul's definition of "all Israel" in Rom. 11.26 in view of my exegesis of this passage in chapter 6 above. So according to Paul all Jews will be saved, even those who were apostates. But did Paul have an understanding of Israel which was simply defined by the *legal* understanding of matrilinear descent and conversion? Would he not have a more profound view? After all, anyone could make the free decision to convert to Judaism. Where is the electing activity of God here? To guide my thoughts on this I consider these questions put by a Jewish scholar on the election of Israel and its relation to "who is a Jew" and "what is a Jew":

(1) What is it about the Jewish mother that enables her to confer this Jewish identity on her child? (2) And what is it about a Jewish tribunal that enables it to confer Jewish

---

[72] Sifre Num. 108 (translation of Schiffman, *Who was a Jew?*, p. 19).

[73] See Schiffman, *Who was Jew?*, p. 39.

[74] Schiffman, *Who was a Jew?*, p. 49.

[75] As Schiffman, *Who was a Jew?*, p. 46, referring to m. Sanh. 10.3, points out, "[i]f a portion in the world to come went hand in hand with Jewish status, why even mention the men of Sodom?"

identity on someone who heretofore has not been considered to be a Jew? In both cases, whether of birth or of conversion, one can further ask: Does the law itself simply create this identity by fiat, or does the law recognize and structure a reality that is prior to its own workings? . . . For it would seem that the question of Jewish identity is not simply one that can be attributed to the workings of the law but, rather, one which the law itself recognizes as prior.[76]

Paul, I suspect, thought along similar lines. Israel is not simply *legally* defined (and certainly not legally created). Israel is chosen in God's heart. Using Novak's language, "the law recognizes a reality that must be constituted in a prelegal mode before the law can deal with it cogently".[77] In fact one wonders whether some Jewish views on Israel's election have been influenced to some extent by Christian views which have ultimately gone back to Paul.[78]

I now raise the question how the election of Israel is related to questions of identity. So Marshall argues:

The permanent election of Israel seems to require that the identifiable existence of the Jewish people also be permanent. Israel's election would be void if the biological descendants of Abraham indeed received God's promised blessing, but had ceased to be identifiable as Abraham's descendants, that is, as Jews.[79]

Marshall suggests that the obvious way to maintain the identity of Jews is by observance of the traditional Jewish law. There is *perhaps* some truth in this from a human perspective; but does God really require such "identity markers"? It is significant that even some Jewish theologians have argued that Jewish identity is not contingent upon keeping the law.[80]

In this connection it is interesting to note that Gerhard Kittel argued for Jews in nazi Germany to have the status of "Gastzustand"[81] and that they

---

[76] Novak, *Election*, p. 3.

[77] Novak, *Election*, p. 4.

[78] Novak, for example, acknowledges his debt to theologians such as Karl Barth.

[79] B.D. Marshall, "Christ and the cultures: Jewish people and Christian theology" in C.E. Guton (ed.), *The Cambridge Companion to Christian Doctrine*, Cambridge: CUP 1997, 91 (81-100).

[80] So M. Wyschogrod, *The Body of Faith: Judaism as Corporate Election*, Minneapolis: Seabury Press 1983, p. 174ff., argues that Israel's election is indeed *sola gratia* and Israel remains elected even if the commandments are rejected!

[81] See G. Kittel, *Die Judenfrage*, Stuttgart: W. Kohlhammer 1933, pp. 38-62.

retain their traditions and customs.[82] He argued this for he felt it was in the best interests not only of Germans but also of Jews. But his wish to have them so identified seems on first appearance to be largely negative, i.e., so it would be clear that God's curse had come down upon them.[83] So he writes:

Die einzige für die abendländischen Völker und für das echte Judentum selbst tragbare und sinnvolle Form des Judentums ist darum *das in seiner Stellung als nicht assimilierter Gast verbleibende Judentum*. Für das echte Judentum ist dieser Zustand eine *von Gott gewollte* und darum bejahte und anerkannte Tragik. Es nimmt nämlich diesen Zustand als Gericht Gottes über den Ungehorsam Israels. Die 'Zerstreuung' heute mit politischen und kulturellen Maßnahmen aufheben und beseitigen wollen, heißt für den echten Juden dem von Gott verhängten Gericht widerstreben. So bleibt dem frommen Juden tatsächlich nur der eine Weg: die entschlossene, fromme Bejahung eines Lebens in der 'Zerstreuung' und in der 'Fremdlingschaft'.[84]

Hence, according to Kittel, the "solutions" of "assimilation" and "Zionism" are to be rejected. However, I wonder whether he may have had a more positive view that the people of Israel need to be clearly identified for God to have mercy on them on the last day! For it should not be forgotten that Kittel stressed that according to the bible Israel is the chosen people of God.[85] And even though they have been rejected by Jesus, Israel is to be res-

---

[82] Kittel, *Judenfrage*, p. 40-41: "Jedoch sollte dem echten, frommen Juden, der sich als anständiger Gast führt, mit Achtung und Freiheit seines jüdischen Lebens, seiner Lebensformen und seiner Sitten begegnet werden, soweit das irgend erträglich erscheint. . . . Deshalb sind Synagoge, Beschneidung, Sabbat, Feste, Ritualformen, wie alle echten religiösen Bekenntnisse, zu schützen". In view of these positive words, it is understandable that it led to outrage among some nazis (see below).

[83] Siegele-Wenschkewitz, *Judenfrage*, pp. 97-98.

[84] Kittel, *Judenfrage*, p. 38 (Kittel's emphasis).

[85] G. Kittel, "Die Judenfrage im Lichte der Bibel", *Glaube und Volk* 2 (1933) 153 (152-55): "Die Bibel weiß davon, daß Gott der Herr mit diesem seinem erwählten Volk eine Geschichte des Heils und der Gnade gelebt hat. . . Keiner, der mit dem Worte Gottes Ernst macht, darf vergessen, wenn er von diesem Volke redet, was für ein Volk das ist! Auch die Christenheit müßte zu allen Zeiten etwas spüren von jener Traurigkeit und Betrübnis über dieses Schicksal; sie müßte, wenn sie von 'Juden' redet, sich erinnern des hohen und hehren Bildes, das dieses Judentum in Wirklichkeit bedeutet".

pected[86] and there is the eschatological hope for Israel.[87] Balance is required in assessing the controversial figure of Gerhard Kittel.[88]

4. The Church's Mission to Israel

I now come to the issue of a mission to Israel. "Mission" can of course have a broad meaning. But for the early Christians the centre of the Church's mission was "evangelism", the preaching of the good news, and it is this issue which I now consider.[89] Evangelism does not of course mean the winning of

---

[86] See, e.g, G. Kittel, "Die Stellung des Jakobus zu Judentum und Heidenchristentum", *ZNW* 30 (1931) 156 n. 1 (145-57): "Auch in Rm 9-11 ist die Tendenz des Paulus durchaus, den Heidenchristen vor vorschnellen Urteilen über den Juden, d.h. aber auch: über den Judenchristen, zu bewahren (11_{11}ff.)". See also "Neutestamentliche Gedanken zur Judenfrage", *AELKZ* 66 (1933) 905-6 (903-7).

[87] Kittel, "Neutestamentliche Gedanken zur Judenfrage", 906.

[88] G. Kittel has been somewhat unfairly condemned by Albright, "Gerhard Kittel and the Jewish question in antiquity". See also the very one-sided view of C. Klein, *Anti-Judaism in Christian Theology* ET, London: SPCK 1978, pp. 12-13. Deines, *Pharisäer*, p. 414 n. 24, referring to the German original (*Theologie und Anti-Judaismus*, München, Chr. Kaiser Verlag 1975), even suggests that she has not read any of Kittel's books. For a more sympathetic view of Kittel, see Porter, "The Case of Gerhard Kittel" and Gutteridge (who studied under Kittel), *Open thy Mouth for the Dumb*, p. 143 n. 61. Gutteridge points to the outrage of the local nazi "Neues Tübinger Tagblatt" (2 June 1933) following Kittel's lecture on the Judenfrage, complaining that "he did not merely advocate tolerance of believing Jewry, but went so far as to demand for its representatives the most extensive 'guest' privileges. . . . The culmination of his anti-volkish argument was his description of mission to the Jews as one of the principal obligations of the German Christian Church". Gutteridge also points to the tribute paid to Kittel after the war. For example, "Richard Fischer . . . relates how Kittel gave proof of real brotherliness on Jewish Boycott Day, when in Tübingen he spent a long time going up and down in company with Hugo Löwenstein, a baptised Jew, in front of the latter's wall-paper shop in the Wilhelmstrasse, in order to protect him from acts of hooliganism". See also the balanced assessments of R.P. Ericksen, "Theologian in the Third Reich: The Case of Gerhard Kittel", *JCH* 12 (1977) 595-622; *Theologians under Hitler: Gerhard Kittel, Paul Althaus and Emanuel Hirsch*, New Haven/London: Yale University Press 1985, pp. 28-78, and of G. Friedrich and J. Friedrich, "Kittel, Gerhard", *TRE* 19:221-25. A list of Kittel's works is given by G. Reyher in G. Friedrich and G. Reyher, "Bibliographie Gerhard Kittel", *TLZ* 74 (1949) 171-75.

[89] For a study which rightly emphasizes the centrality of evangelism for the Pauline Churches, see J.P. Dickson, *Mission-Commitment in Ancient Judaism and in the Pauline Communities: The shape, extent and background of early Christian mission* (WUNT 2.159), Tübingen: J.C.B. Mohr (Paul Siebeck) 2003.

converts. It entails the preaching of the good news whether converts are made or not. It entails presenting Jesus Christ to sinful men and women in order that, through the power of the Holy Spirit, they may come to faith in Christ.[90] Alongside this central aspect of evangelism there was also healing the sick and casting out demons (Mt. 10.5-15; Mk 6.6b-13; Lk. 9.1-6; Lk. 10.1-12). This original mission was carried out to Jewish people. In view of this, it is quite remarkable that a Bishop of the Church of England can write that the Church's mission to Israel is to encourage them to practice their own religion. Richard Harries, Bishop of Oxford, writes that:

. . . in the light of the Church's appalling record towards Jews it would seem more appropriate to show love of the Jewish people, a mission toward the Jewish people, not by trying to convert them to the Christian faith but by supporting them in the practice of their own religion.[91]

I do not deny that evangelizing Jewish people is a sensitive issue, something which has been seen as threatening the very identity of the Jewish people. But before considering this, I look at a number of reasons Christians have given for not evangelizing Jews. They are as follows:

1. God in Christ will intervene to save Israel as is clear in Rom. 11.26. It is necessary therefore to make a clear distinction between the mission of God and the mission of human beings.

2. Israel is the elect people of God and his promises to Israel are irrevocable.

3. The Church's role is to be a witness to Israel in provoking Israel to jealousy. This the Church achieves by her life of holiness and glory.

4. Since Auschwitz Christians have absolutely no right to evangelize Jews.

Lothar Steiger therefore sums up many people's view on a mission to Israel when he argues that "since Paul a mission to Israel is theologically impossible and since Auschwitz ethically impossible. In the case of Israel a

---

[90] See J.I. Packer, *Evangelism and the Sovereignty of God*, London: IVP 1961, p. 40, who rightly makes a crucial theological change to the Archbishop's Committee in its report on evangelism in 1918 in order to stress that whereas evangelism is a human work, the gift of faith is God's work.

[91] R. Harries, *After the Evil: Christianity and Judaism in the Shadow of the Holocaust*, Oxford: OUP 2003, p. 131.

mission of God and mission of human beings is to be clearly distinguished".[92] I now address these four objections to a mission to Jewish people.

1. Concerning the first point (i.e. Israel's salvation at the parousia), it is important to stress that Paul himself did not share this objection to Jewish mission. Paul was engaged in Jewish mission for almost the whole of his Christian career. Even after his theology of Israel was most developed (i.e., in Romans 9-11), it is most likely that Paul continued, wherever possible, to evangelize Jews. In the letter to the Romans itself, a Jewish mission is supported, for Rom. 10.14-18 refers to a mission to Jews as well as Gentiles, although Paul was painfully aware that it had failed (Rom. 10.16).[93] Also Acts 28.17-31, especially vv. 23-28, depicts Paul preaching to the Jews in Rome.[94] It is also necessary to stress that if one objects to a mission to Israel on the grounds that we can simply wait for the parousia when God will save Israel anyway, one has shown that one has not understood Paul's concept of mission. Mission for Paul was not simply to save people from the wrath to

---

[92] L. Steiger, "Schutzrede für Israel. Römer 9-11", in T. Sundermeier (ed.), *Fides pro mundi vita: Missionstheologie heute. Hans-Werner Gensichen zum 65. Geburtstag* (Missionswissenschaftliche Forschungen 14), Gütersloh: Gütersloher Verlaghaus Gerd Mohn 1980, 57 (44-58): "Die christliche Kirche hat an Israel darüber hinaus keine Mission. Eine christliche Missionierung Israels ist seit Paulus theologisch und seit Auschwitz allgemein ethisch (kategorisch) unmöglich. Im Fall Israels ist zwischen missio Dei und missio hominum *streng* zu unterscheiden" (Steiger's emphasis).

[93] For a detailed exegesis of this passage, see Bell, *Provoked to Jealousy*, pp. 83-95.

[94] Haenchen, *Acts*, pp. 726-32, questions the historicity of these verses. According to Roloff, *Apostelgeschichte*, p. 370, Luke has created this scene "frei und ohne Traditionsgrundlage". On the other hand, Pesch, *Apostelgeschichte*, 2:307, argues that the narrative could go back to traditions of the Roman Church. If Paul did give up preaching to Jews (as Acts 28.28 suggests), this refers only to his work in Rome. If released, Paul would in his future journeys most likely continue preaching to Jews (on Paul's probable release, see Tajra, *Trial of St. Paul*, p. 196). It is the case that Acts 28.17-31 implies that the Jewish mission not only in Rome but also as a whole is now ended and that this signals the final turning to the Gentiles (Pesch, *Apostelgeschichte*, 2:306 writes: "Lukas nutzt die wuchtige, dreiteilige (17-22.23-28.30-31) Schlußszene seines Doppelwerkes dazu, das Ende der Epoche der Judenmission zu markieren und die nun endgültige Wendung der urchristlichen Mission zu den Heiden zu signalisieren, für die er in seiner Zeit im Römischen Reich eine weitere ungehinderte Entfaltung erwartet"). However, this picture may reflect more the situation at the time of the writing of Acts and not Paul's situation in Rome. It must also be added that when Paul turns away from preaching to Jews in Acts, it is clearly not because he, like Steiger, felt the Jews did not need evangelizing, but because of their hardness of heart.

come. It was also related to seeing God's glory and righteousness manifest in the world,[95] and this is one reason why he continued preaching to Jews even after writing Rom. 11.26. If the benefits of being a Christian are glorious (and Jewish Christians acknowledge that!) and if the conversion of a single Jewish person rebounds to God's glory, why wait until the parousia?

One of the striking uses of Rom. 11.25-26 is in fact by a Jewish scholar, Jacob Bernays (1824-81). Christian Josias Karl Freiherr von Bunsen (1791-1860), amateur theologian and Prussian ambassador to London 1845-54, wrote to his friend Bernays (November 7, 1852) appealing to him to become a Christian. "Should it not be that you *as a son of Israel* find an even greater blessedness in the religion of love and humanity than *I* do as a pagan Teuton".[96] Bernays replied (November 22, 1852) that according to Rom. 11.25-26 Jews have a right and duty "to continue as Jews ἄχρις οὗ τὸ πλήρωμα τῶν ἐθνῶν εἰσέλθῃ".[97] He understood Paul's argument to mean "*as long as* not all Gentiles have become Christians, because of that μυστήριον, the Jews should remain Jews". Bernays mistakenly assumes that τὸ πλήρωμα τῶν ἐθνῶν means every Gentile. But even if it did, his argument that Jews have a right and duty to continue as (non-Christian) Jews simply does not follow.

2. The second view that there is no point in evangelizing Israel since they are the elect people of God is found, for example, in Barth. He writes:

The Gentile Christian community of every age and land is a guest in the house of Israel. It assumes the election and calling of Israel. It lives in fellowship with the King of Israel. How, then, can we try to hold missions to Israel? It is not the Swiss or the German or the Indian or the Japanese awakened to faith in Jesus Christ, but the Jew, even the

---

[95] It would be interesting to know what Paul would have made of Hab. 2.14 ("For the earth will be filled with the glory of God as the waters cover the sea"; LXX: ὅτι πλησθήσεται ἡ γῆ τοῦ γνῶναι τὴν δόξαν κυρίου, ὡς ὕδωρ κατακαλύψαι αὐτούς). Paul never quoted from or alluded to Hab. 2.14 but he did quote from Hab. 2.4b on two occasions (Rom. 1.17; Gal. 3.11) and may well have alluded to Hab. 2.18-19 in 1 Cor. 12.2 (see Conzelmann, *Der erste Brief an die Korinther*, p. 125 n. 16).

[96] See H.D. Betz, "Practicality or Principle? A Memorable Exchange of Letters", in I. Gruenwald, S. Shaked and G.G. Stroumsa (ed.), *Messiah and Christos: Studies in the Jewish Origins of Christianity Presented to David Flusser on the Occasion of his Seventy-Fifth Birthday* (TSAJ 32), Tübingen: J.C.B. Mohr (Paul Siebeck) 1992, 212 (207-17).

[97] Betz, "Memorable Exchange", 216.

unbelieving Jew, so miraculaously preserved, as we must say, through the many calamities of his history, who as such is the natural historical monument to the love and faithfulness of God, who in concrete form is the epitome of the man freely chosen and blessed by God, who as a living commentary on the Old Testament is the only convincing proof of God outside the Bible. What have we to teach him that he does not already know, that we have not rather to learn from him?[98]

The Christian does have something to learn from the Jew for, as I argued above, the Jew witnesses to God. But does the Jew have nothing to learn from the Christian, even the Gentile Christian? But Barth then adds that "at the decisive moment the same Israel denied its election and calling". The Jew "who is uniquely blessed offers the picture of an existence which, characterised by the rejection of its Messiah and therefore of its salvation and mission, is dreadfully empty of grace and blessing".[99] How can the Gospel which is proclaimed by human beings be of any help "when already it has been repudiated, not just accidentally or incidentally, but in principle"? The only hope, Barth argues, is through the eschatological action of God (Rom. 11.15, 25-26).[100] I have two problems with this approach. First, as mentioned above, Paul himself continued to evangelize Jews even after writing Romans 11. Secondly, Barth's whole approach here appears to devalue the Church's proclamation of the gospel. Here the gospel is admittedly mediated by "earthen vessels" (cf. 2 Cor. 4.7) but the power of the gospel, even when mediated by human beings, can nevertheless transform even the most hardened heart.

3. The view that the Church's *only* witness to Israel is to lead a life of holiness and so provoke Israel to jealousy is mistaken.[101] As a Christian one can only rejoice if the life of the Church were such that Israel is provoked to emulate the Church.[102] But jealousy alone will not convert anyone. Provoking Israel to jealousy is no replacement for mission. It is just one possible precursor for mission (or for the parousia). *No Jew can be saved simply by being provoked to jealousy*. The gospel must be preached for it is only the

---

[98] Barth, *CD* 4.3.2:877.

[99] Barth, *CD* 4.3.2:877.

[100] Barth, *CD* 4.3.2:878.

[101] Barth, *CD* 4.3.2:878, stresses the importance of this ministry of witness to the Jews but adds that the Church has failed in this witness.

[102] This is the meaning of "provoke to jealousy" in Rom. 11.11, 14. See "emulation" in the index of Bell, *Provoked to Jealousy*, p 464.

gospel, God's reconciling word, which can make someone a Christian (Rom. 10.17). According to Paul, jealousy alone can make no one a Christian for faith is not derivable from the lives or faith of others.[103]

So far I have dealt with possible theological objections (based on Paul's thinking) to a mission to Jews. But there are cases where Paul did not see the true consequences of his own gospel.[104] Could this be the case in the question of Jewish mission? I think not. The Pauline gospel of the justification and recreation of an ungodly humanity of Jews and Gentiles *sola gratia, sola fide, propter Christum* can in no way be used to argue against a mission to Jewish people. In fact, Paul's theology *demands* a mission to the Jewish people. Someone will only come to faith by means of the preached word.

4. The fourth objection is more a moral objection. Since Auschwitz Christians have absolutely no right to evangelize Jews. But is a renunciation of mission to the Jews really the most loving response to this ancient and persecuted people? Mission can, of course, be carried out in a way contrary to the spirit of Christ. A document formulated at Sigtuna in 1988 rightly declares that "coercive proselytism directed towards Jews is incompatible with Christian faith".[105] It is not made clear in the document what "coercive proselytism" exactly means. Presumably it means any physical, social, or economic pressure brought to bear on Jews to make them become Christians. Such "coercive proselytism" towards the Jews or towards any group is

---

[103] See Bell, *Provoked to Jealousy*, p. 158. Theobald, who rejects a mission of the Church to Israel, refers to Mt. 5.14-16 ("Mit verbundenen Augen?", 393). Christians are to be a light on a hill, an idea corresponding to Paul's idea of provoking to jealousy (in the sense of emulation) in Rom. 11.11-14. Although according to the Matthean Jesus those who see the good works of the Christian will "give glory to your Father in heaven", this is hardly a view Paul could share (partly in view of his pessimistic anthropology).

[104] One of the most well-known examples is Paul's attitude to women in the Church. There is a good case for arguing that Paul's teaching on the rôle of women in the Church (1 Cor. 11.2-16) actually contradicts his own gospel (see Gal. 3.28). Paul has mistakenly expounded Gen. 1.27 as though ἀνήρ stood in the LXX and not ἄνθρωπος (see, e.g., 1 Cor. 11.7).

[105] "The Churches and the Jewish People: Towards a New Understanding", (adopted at Sigtuna, Sweden, by the Consultation on the Church and the Jewish People, World Council of Churches, 4 November 1988) (see *International Bulletin of Missionary Research* 13 (1989) 153 (152-54)).

un-Christian. But does this have to rule out a mission to Jews altogether? Are there not ways of evangelizing other than through "coercive proselytism"?[106] It is often claimed that evangelizing Jews, however it is carried out, is antisemitic. However, I would maintain that evangelism to Jews is not antisemitism; rather to renounce preaching the liberating gospel to Jewish people is antisemitism. The "Willowbank Declaration on the Christian Gospel and the Jewish People", affirms that:

> . . . it is unchristian, unloving, and discriminatory, to propose a moratorium on the evangelizing of any part of the human race, and that failure to preach the Gospel to the Jewish people would be a form of anti-Semitism, depriving this particular community of its right to hear the Gospel.[107]

Further, not to preach the gospel to Jewish people would be to disobey Christ's commission. The great commission to make disciples of all nations (Mt. 28.19-20) can hardly exclude Jewish people[108] and in fact this mission is to begin in Jerusalem (Lk. 24.47).[109] Paul also affirms that the gospel is for the Jews first (Rom. 1.16). So Macleod writes:

---

[106] So back in the seventeenth century Philip Jacob Spener advocated a mission, but a gentle mission, to Jewish people. So Gutteridge, *Open thy Mouth for the Dumb*, p. 326, writes that according to Spener "[m]issionary endeavour among the Jews . . . should show understanding for their obedience to the Law and the peculiarity of their traditions, avoid all compulsion and respect their freedom of conscience. Harsh and insensitive treatment of them was contrary to the instructions of Jesus". Gutteridge points out that the evidence of such an approach is found in the decree of 1703 of King Frederick of Prussia "which admonished the clergy to exercise gentile persuasion upon Jewish unbelievers" (p. 327).

[107] "Willowbank Declaration on the Christian Gospel and the Jewish People", Article IV.23 (in *International Bulletin of Missionary Research* 13 (1989) 163 (161-64).

[108] J.P. Meier, "Nations or Gentiles in Matthew 28:19", *CBQ* 39 (1977) 94-102. There are of course problems concerning the historicity of this commission. Nevertheless it is to be taken seriously theologically. But note that any doubts about its historicity concern the mission to the Gentiles. A mission to Israel seems to be assumed in the early Church. On this see Bell, *Provoked to Jealousy*, pp. 346-50.

[109] On the expression "beginning in Jerusalem" (ἀρξάμενοι ἀπὸ Ἰερουσαλήμ) and the variants, see I.H. Marshall, *The Gospel of Luke: A Commentary on the Greek Text* (NIGTC), Exeter: Paternoster 1978, p. 906, who writes that "it is loosely added and has adverbial force".

Before His ascension, when He commissioned His disciples, Christ charged them to begin the preaching of the gospel at Jerusalem. If the church were to disobey this command to preach Jesus Christ to the Jewish people, she would be guilty of infidelity to her Lord and of a most virulent anti-semitism. To withhold the gospel, the good news, from the Jewish people would be most culpable.[110]

It is also worthwhile considering that many involved in Christian mission to Israel have had a positive attitude to the Jewish people. For example in nineteenth century Germany there was alongside the pernicious antisemitism of people like Paul de Lagarde (1827-91), the philosemitism of Johann Christian Konrad von Hofmann (1810-77),[111] Christoph Ernst Luthardt (1823-1902),[112] the Lutheran theologian Johann Konrad Wilhelm Löhe (1808-72)[113] and Franz Delitzsch (1813-90).[114] They all supported a mission to Israel and at the same time were philosemites.[115]

---

[110] MacLeod, "The witness of the church to the Jewish People", 71-72 (see also 74).

[111] See F. Mildenberger, "Hofmann, Johann Christian Konrad v.", *TRE* 15:477-79 and Beyschlag, *Die Erlanger Theologie*, pp. 58-82. As Professor in Rostock (1842-45) he taught Old and New Testament and then in Erlangen (where he had studied) he taught "Enzyclopädie", New Testament and Ethics. Von Hofmann was concerned with the unity of the bible, "the integrating principle being defined in terms of a divinely guided history of redemption, a *Heilsgeschichte*, which had as its ultimate goal the establishment of the kingdom of God" (J.H. Hayes and F.C. Prussner, *Old Testament Theology*, London: SCM 1985, p. 82). On von Hofmann's philosemitism, see F.-H. Philipp, "Protestantismus nach 1848", in Rengstorf and von Kortzfleisch, *Kirche und Synagoge*, 2:285-86 (280-357).

[112] Luthardt was a pupil of von Hofmann and was Professor of Systematics and New Testament in Leipzig from 1856-95. See Philipp, "Protestantismus nach 1848", 286-87.

[113] Löhe was a Lutheran theologian and was pastor in Neuendettelsau and founded the "Neuendettelsauer Missionsanstalt". See Philipp, "Protestantismus nach 1848", 287-88.

[114] Delitzsch was, of course, one of the most influential Old Testament scholars in the nineteenth century and taught at Leipzig. See Philipp, "Protestantismus nach 1848", 288-90. One of his great legacies was his translation of the New Testament into Hebrew (first published in 1877 by the British and Foreign Bible Society, London, and later revised by Gustav Dalman).

[115] So Delitzsch, although not directly active as a missionary to Jews, held addresses in the context of mission to Jews, wrote on the subject (see *Missionsvorträge*, Leipzig 1892) and in 1863 founded the journal *Saat auf Hoffnung. Zeitschrift für die Mission der Kirche an Israel*. In 1870/71 the "evangelisch-lutherischen Centralverein für die Mission unter Israel" was founded on his initiative. Then in 1886 he founded the "Institutum Judaicum" in Leipzig which was to function both as a centre of learning and as a base for educating missionaries to Jews (E. Plümacher, "Delitzsch, Franz Julius", *TRE* 8:432 (431-33)). Shortly before his death in 1890 he wrote that he considered it a disgrace that

Having questioned the three objections commonly employed against a mission to Jews I examine an objection which is hardly ever mentioned but which practically is perhaps the most influential of all objections: many Christians at least in the West have lost their confidence in the Christian gospel. The widespread belief that Jews (and those of other religions) do not need the gospel is, I believe, a major heresy in the Church today. I find it quite remarkable that the Bishop of Oxford not only opposes evangelism for Jews but does not even think a Christian should pray for Jewish friends. He writes:

Can I pray that my Jewish friends are converted to Christianity? My honest answer is no.[116]

The bishop can be commended for his candour. Perhaps the same cannot be said for the theological weight of his argument. For he continues:

I am happy if they are trying to be faithful Jews as I am trying to be a faithful Christian. They have insights as Jews whose loss would make the world a poorer place. They have spiritual riches which it is essential that Christianity keeps in contact with and is strengthened by. Their Jewish identity is part of their identity as the person whose friendship I appreciate. To pray for their conversion would be to ask God to make them betray their deepest convictions and lose what is most fundamental to their identity.[117]

When I read such words I wonder whether we are members of the same religion never mind the same denomination. Where is the New Testament warning about Israel standing under the judgement of God? Where is the good news of salvation in Christ which sets us free from sin, death and the devil? More specifically, what the bishop writes bears little resemblance to Paul's "great sorrow and unceasing anguish" in his heart. He was prepared to be cut off from Christ thereby forfeiting his own salvation for the sake of his Jewish kinsmen. Without the gospel Jewish people are heading for damnation (Rom. 9.3; 10.1). In Johannine terms, they are *not* already with the

---

Christians should subscribe to "the orthodox anti-semitic view that the Election of Israel, though a fact of past history, has become no longer tenable, and is without present relevance or future promise" (*Sind die Juden wirklich das auserwählte Volk?*, Leipzig 1889, p. 4, quoted in Gutteridge, *Open thy Mouth for the Dumb*, p. 328).

[116] Harries, *After the Evil*, p. 131.
[117] Harries, *After the Evil*, p. 131.

Father and so Jn 14.6 *does* apply to them (*pace* Franz Rosenzweig).[118] According to Paul they remain the people of God and their election still stands. Indeed, as we have seen in Rom. 9.4, they still have the sonship. But they are cut off from Christ and facing damnation (Rom. 9.1-3; Rom. 10.1-3) and need the gospel. The bishop of Oxford, however, seems to have little confidence in the Christian gospel for Jewish people.[119]

It is refreshing to speak to Christian Jews, a curiously neglected group in the Jewish mission debate, who rejoice in the forgiveness of their sins and in the new life they enjoy in Jesus the Messiah. It is also worth stressing that a Christian Jew according to Paul may continue to keep the Jewish law. This is clear from Romans 14 where Paul defends the Jewish Christians who wish to keep the food laws and holy days.[120] Although circumcision is not mentioned, I assume that Paul would have no problem with Jewish Christians circumcising their children.[121]

This now brings me to an issue which some may find quite remarkable. The general Jewish view today is that Jews who convert to Christianity are no longer Jews. This is certainly a radical departure from the time of Paul. It is also all the more remarkable that at the same time that Jewish Christians

---

[118] Commenting on Jn 14.6 in a letter to Rudolf Ehrenberg (1 November 1913), he writes: "No one *comes* to the Father – but it is different when one no longer needs to come to the Father, because he is already with him. And this is the case with the people of Israel" (see E.T. Oakes (ed.), *German Essays on Religion* (GL 54), New York: Continuum 1994, p. 191). Note also Rosenzweig's questionable understanding of 1 Cor. 15.28 that Jesus Christ will "cease to be the Lord" of the Church at the end of the world.

[119] Some of the documents issued by the Anglican Church make very depressing reading. Not only is there thinking about Judaism which I believe is highly misguided but the waters are further muddied by bringing in a religion which does not even worship the same God: "Jews, Muslims and Christians have a common mission. They share a mission to the world that God's name may be honoured: 'Hallowed be thy name'. . . . And in the dialogue there will be mutual witness. Through learning from one another they will enter more deeply into their own inheritance. Each will recall the other to God, to trust him more fully and obey him more profoundly" ("Jews, Christians and Muslims: The Way of Dialogue", appendix 6 of *The Truth Shall Make You Free*, the Lambeth Conference 1988 published by the Angican Consultative Council (quoted in Harries, *After the Evil*, pp. 121-22).

[120] See Bell, *Provoked to Jealousy*, p. 73.

[121] Cf. Acts 16.1. Note that Paul opposes circumcision of *Gentiles* in Galatians for the implication is that one is saved not only through faith in Christ but also in keeping the law.

are not recognized as Jews in the twenty-first century, Jews who do not even believe in God are recognized as such. But I need to address an issue which is clearly a central concern for Jewish people. If a Jew becomes a Christian it is quite clear that they have no obligation to keep the law, are free to marry a Gentile and thereby their identity as Jews is eroded. In fact keeping the law is simply a way of maintaining Jewish identity.[122] I appreciate that this is a legitimate concern for non-Christian Jewish people. And this is probably the main reason why Jewish people are usually angered by Christian missionary activity however sensitively it is carried out.[123] However, angering the Jewish community on this issue is a risk which I believe has to be taken. The gospel must be proclaimed. As Paul writes in 1 Cor. 9.16:

For compulsion presses upon me; it is agony for me if I do not proclaim the gospel.[124]

I believe, therefore, that at the end of the day there are no theological or ethical objections from a Christian perspective to a mission sensitively directed towards Jewish people. I would also go further and say there are no objections to a mission to Jewish people carried out by Gentiles. It has been argued that there is no text in the New Testament where a Gentile is encouraged to evangelize a Jew.[125] However, such an argument from silence is weak, especially when we know so little about how Gentiles evange-

---

[122] The Jewish perspective on this is put well by H. Maccoby: ". . . if Jews converted to Christianity were to continue to practice the Torah, this would be an empty observance, deprived of its inner drive and meaning. Such Jews would not really be remaining Jews in any meaningful sense. Christian mission to the Jews based on the idea of toleration of Jewish observances is based on a shallow and condescending attitude towards those observances as *mere identity-markers*" (quoted in Harries, *After the Evil*, p. 137). I have emphasized *"mere identity-markers"* in view of the debate regarding "works of law" in Paul.

[123] For the State of Israel's opposition to mission, see K. Kjaer-Hansen and O.Chr.M. Kvarme, *Messianische Juden: Judenchristen in Israel* (ET 67), Erlangen: Verlag der Ev.-Luth. Mission 1983, especially pp. 131-52.

[124] Translation of Thiselton, *First Epistle to the Corinthians*, p. 676.

[125] See H. Kremers, "Mission an Israel in heilsgeschichtlicher Sicht", in H. Kremers and E. Lubahn (ed.), *Mission an Israel in heilsgeschichtlicher Sicht*, Neukirchen-Vluyn: Neukirchener Verlag 1985, 82 (65-91), writes: "Nicht nur in Röm 9-11, sondern im ganzen Neuen Testament wird an *keiner* Stelle ein Heidenchrist aufgefordert, 'Judenmissionar' zu werden und den 'ungläubigen Juden' das Evangelium von Jesus Christus zu *sagen*" (Kremers' emphasis).

lized.[126] Further, certain New Testament texts suggest that Gentile Christians are expected to evangelize both Jews and Gentiles. So Christians are called upon to defend the gospel: "Always be prepared to make a defence to any one who calls you to account for the hope that is in you" (1 Pet. 3.15). Further, evangelists are encouraged to "preach the word" and to "be urgent in season and out of season" (2 Tim. 4.2).[127]

Therefore I see no objections to a mission to Jews. In fact there are very positive reasons for evangelizing Jewish people. Jews are not like any other non-Christian group. As I argued in chapters 4 and 7 above, Jews are and remain God's people. God has made promises to them and they are promises he will not revoke. Jesus Christ is the messiah of Israel. In him all God's promises find their "Yes" (2 Cor. 1.20). How important then that God's people, the Jews, should be made aware of the significance of Jesus Christ.

Although the Church is called to evangelize Jewish people, it may be that she wins few converts. The hardness that has come upon the Jewish people is still operative and indeed according to Paul it will not be lifted until "the full number of the Gentiles will have come in" (Rom. 11.25). Also, in conversation with Jewish people, the central objection to Christianity is that it is clear for all to see that the Messiah has not come: there is war, famine, and earthquake. There is violence between nations, violence on the streets, and even violence in the home. But when the Messiah comes, "the wolf shall dwell with the lamb, and the leopard shall lie down with the kid" (Is. 11.6). So David Flusser of the Hebrew University in Jerusalem writes:

The question to the Jews would be better expressed thus: Was Jesus the Messiah of the Jews or, rather, will he be the Messiah? For the Jews the question should be stated as

---

[126] Acts, for example, concentrates almost entirely on Jewish missionaries (the Hellenists, Peter, and Paul).

[127] J.P. Dickson, *Mission-Commitment in Ancient Judaism and in the Pauline Communities: The shape, extent and background of early Christian mission* (WUNT 2.159), Tübingen: J.C.B. Mohr (Paul Siebeck) 2003, rightly argues that Paul expected his converts not only to support his mission but also to engage in evangelising those in their own cities. This involves not just "living" the gospel but also by "verbal apologetic" (p. 293). He points to 1 Cor. 14.20-25 as a case of "mission-commitment as public worship" (pp. 293-302) and Col. 4.6 as individual verbal apologetic (pp. 302-7). Although the latter is probably deutero-Pauline it reflects, I believe, Paul's own view. On 2 Tim. 4.1-5 see Dickson, *Mission-Commitment*, pp. 322-26.

about the future, as I think Jesus also would have stated it. No one feels more strongly than the Jews that the world today is a world of brutal injustice and not the messianic kingdom. Jews expect the Messiah to save our people and, in this darkness[,] this is our hope for ourselves and for the world. . . . I do not think many Jews would object if the Messiah when he came again was the Jew Jesus.[128]

In short, it can be said that the second coming for Christians corresponds to the first coming for non-Christian Jews (Rom. 11.26-27). There have been Christians who have identified the Jewish messiah with the coming Christ.[129] But for there to be non-Christian Jews who can identify Jesus with their coming messiah is something previously unheard of.

---

[128] D. Flusser, "To What Extent is Jesus a Question for the Jews?", *Concilium: Theology in the Age of Renewal* 10.8 (1974) 164-65 (162-66). Cf. B. Klappert, "Der Verlust und die Wiedergewinnung der israelitischen Kontur der Leidensgeschichte Jesu (das Kreuz, das Leiden, das Paschamahl, der Prozeß Jesu)", in H.H. Henrix and M. Stöhr (ed.), *Exodus und Kreuz im ökumenischen Dialog zwischen Juden und Christen. Diskussionsbeiträge für Religionsunterricht und Erwachsenenbildung* (ABPB 8), Aachen: Einhard-Verlag 1978, 150-51 (107-53).

[129] So Paul Felgenhauer, like other philosemites, identified the two. See W. Philipp, "Spätbarock und frühe Aufklärung. Das Zeitalter des Philosemitismus", Rengstorf and von Kortzfleisch (ed.), *Kirche und Synagoge*, 2:58-61 (23-86), which refers to Felgenhauer's work *Bonum Nuncium Israeli quod offertur Populo Israel et Judae in hisce temporibus novissimis*, Amsterdam 1655, pp. 5-84. Felgenhauer in fact speaks of three comings of the messiah: a spiritual coming (Zech. 12.10, incorrectly given as Is. 12.10); a second coming in his birth (Is. 7.14), entry into Jerusalem (Zech. 9.9) and healing of the blind, deaf, lame and dumb (Is. 35.5-6); then a third coming. This third coming consists of three signs. First that the people of Judah and Israel will turn to God and the messiah and return to the land. The second is the coming of Elijah. Elijah comes in a threefold form, the third being the angel of Rev. 14.6-7 who brings the eternal gospel. The third sign is the preaching of the kingdom of God to Israel, including the ten tribes "which live in an unknown southern land".

Chapter 11

Paul: Antisemite or Philosemite?

1. Antisemitism and Anti-Judaism

Any Christian today writing on Paul and Israel cannot fail to be aware of the tragic events which befell the Jewish people in the last century. At various points in the present work the issue of antisemitism has been raised and in this final chapter I wish to clarify certain matters which remain and draw some of the threads together which relate to antisemitism.

In Jewish-Christian dialogue and in intra-Christian dialogue the term "antisemitism" is often used indiscriminately. For example, it is not unknown for a Christian who supports a mission to Jews to be accused of "antisemitism".[1] I wish to make it absolutely clear how I am using the term. Antisemitism, as I understand it, involves a negative attitude towards the Jewish people themselves and is irrational, indiscriminate and based on prejudice. Antisemitism could manifest itself in blatant persecution or it could take a more subtle approach such as accusing the Jewish people as a whole of deicide. But to be critical of Israel's religion and religious practices (as Paul was) is not, I believe, appropriately termed "antisemitism". It could be described as anti-Judaism, but not antisemitism. To highlight this distinction one could point to certain groups who have had a very positive attitude to the Jewish *people* but who have carried out mission to them (indicating that they believed the Jewish *religion* was either wrong or incomplete). For example, many of the Pietists of the 17th and 18th centuries believed Israel had a special place in God's plan, something seen especially clearly in the Jewish-German hymns of the Herrnhuter. Consider, for example, this beautiful hymn (1995 in the "Gesangbuch der Gemeinde in Herrnhut", 1731, vol. 2):

---

[1] See the discussion in chapter 10 above.

Gelobt seist du, Jesu Christ,
daß dein Jisrol geblieben ist
und hajom (heute) Purim feiern kann
wir achim (Brüder) nehmen chelek (Anteil) an.

Der schomer Jisrol (Wächter Israels) hat gewacht
und die gesere (Verfolgung) zunicht gemacht
sonst wär Maschiach (Messias) nicht geboren,
wir wären allzumal verloren.

Berucha (Gesegnet sei) Esther, die Königin!
sie wagte sich zum melech (König) hin
und fand vor seinen Augen Gnad'
als sie nur chaim (Leben) für ihr Volk bat.

Haman harosche (der gottlose Hamann) ward gefällt
und Mardochai zu Ehren gestellt,
dem Feinde gelang ihr Anschlag nicht,
Jisroel hatte Freud' und Licht.

Das hat haschem Jisborech getan (der Name Gottes, der gesegnete)
er nahm sich seines Volkes an:
des freuet sich Jisroel heut'.
Ach! Hätt es so am Tolah (Gekreuzigten) Freud'.

Das Volk Jisrol wird nicht vergehn,
sondern gewiß den Tolah sehn,
und die chabburah bezzido (Seiten-Wunde)
wird es machen reich und froh.[2]

Yet these Herrnhuter and the philosemites discussed in the previous chapter supported mission to the Jews.[3]

But what are we to say of Paul? Was he an antisemite? He cannot be accused of antisemitism on the basis of his wanting to convert the Jews to faith in Christ. This is a point I hope I have established in the previous chapter. Neither can he be accused of it on the basis of his critique of Judaism.

---

[2] See S. Riemer, *Philosemitismus im deutschen evangelischen Kirchenlied des Barock* (StDel 8), Stuttgart: W. Kohlhammer Verlag 1963, pp. 76-77. I have here quoted it (with a minor correction) in the form given by W. Philipp in Rengstorf and von Kortzfleisch, *Kirche und Synagoge*, 2:80.

[3] On Count Nikolaus von Zinzendorf, the founder of the Herrnhuter, and his attitudes to Jews and Judaism, see M. Schmidt in Rengstorf and von Kortzfleisch, *Kirche und Synagoge*, 2:118-21.

Paul came to critique Judaism in the light of his life changing experience on the road to Damascus. He came to see that salvation was only possible through the grace of God as revealed in Jesus Christ. He came to see that a salvation by works was impossible. This was one factor which led him to believe that "grace" was superior to "legalism", a point I will return to. But we did find some problems in 1 Thes. 2.14-16 in that he makes indiscriminate remarks about the Jewish people (hence such remarks could be described as "antisemitic"). However, this "antisemitism" in 1 Thes. 2.14-16 has often been exaggerated in the secondary literature. It is essential to bear in mind these three factors. First, as was argued in chapter 2 above, Paul seems to imply that the main reason the Jews "displease God" and "oppose all people" is that they prevent Paul and his fellow evangelists from preaching to the Gentiles. This, as Kampling has shown, was the understanding of the anti-Jewish sentiment in the passage by key Patristic authors.[4] Secondly, his comments are "inner-Jewish polemic". As was argued in chapter 2, the text would carry a quite different sense had it been written after the clear separation of Judaism and Christianity. Thirdly, it is perhaps unfair to judge Paul by standards of today. Compared to first century "anti-Jewish" polemic Paul's criticism of "the Jews" is mild. Nevertheless there are some "antisemitic" remarks in 1 Thes. 2.14-16 in that he does make indiscriminate and negative comments about the Jews. The comments of Simon that "[t]here is no shadow of anti-Semitism in St. Paul"[5] seems to be too simplistic.

But what about the implication of the idea in Galatians that God disinherits those Jews who do not now believe in Christ? Is this "antisemitic"? I think not. This is Paul's theological judgement about the Jewish people and since it has its own theological rationality it cannot be said to be "irrational". Further, one can hardly say it is built upon prejudice. He came to this position in Galatians in the light of the Christ event and he had clearly thought through the theological issue even though he was to change his mind when writing Romans. Paul's comments in Galatians cannot be described as antisemitic even though they do not represent his most profound view of

---

[4] Kampling, "Auslegungsgeschichtliche Skizze", 212.

[5] M. Simon, *Verus Israel: A Study of the relations between Christians and Jews in the Roman Empire (135-425)* (LLJC) ET, Oxford: OUP 1986, p. 207. He refers simply to Rom. 10.1 and 11.1-32 (p. 471 n. 20).

Israel. It is instructive to compare criticism made of Paul's view of the Jewish people in Galatians in say the last forty years with that levelled against certain Christian evangelical groups in Britain (and other "western" countries) today. The climate has become so hysterical that any theological judgement which implies criticism of a non-Christian religion is judged as "racist".[6]

I argued in chapter 8 above that the most profound view of Israel in the whole of the New Testament is to be found in Romans. In this letter Paul can certainly be described as a "philosemite". He affirms the abiding election of Israel and believes that Israel will ultimately be saved. Further, on a personal level he could hardly show more love for the Jewish people than he does in Rom. 9.1-3. He was prepared to be cut off from Christ and lose his salvation for the sake of his brethren. How could one be more philosemitic?

However, not all have been convinced that Paul is so positive towards the Jewish people in Romans 9-11. One such person is G. Baum. He writes:

All attempts of Christian theologians to derive a more positive conclusion from Paul's teaching in Romans 9-11 (and I have done this as much as others) are grounded in wishful thinking. What Paul and the entire Christian tradition taught is unmistakably negative: the religion of Israel is now superceded, the Torah abrogated, the promises fulfilled in the Christian Church, the Jews struck with blindness, and whatever remains of the election to Israel rests as a burden upon them in the present age.[7]

Clearly, it has to be acknowledged that Paul did believe that Judaism was superceded and that the torah was essentially abrogated, points I will discuss shortly. Further, God's promises to Israel can in a certain sense be said to be fulfilled in the Christian Church (although, as I have stressed throughout the present work, God's promises to Israel still stand). All these points are related to Paul's critique of Judaism. But when we move over to statements such as "Jews are struck with blindness" or their election "rests as a

---

[6] For example, I know a fine English Evangelical minister who was recently reported to the police by a race equality council for making negative comments about Islam. The British government is considering introducing legislation which makes "incitement to religious hatred" a criminal offence. The Home Office claims that this will still allow criticism of religions. However, in Victoria, Australia, where legislation concerning "incitement to religious hatred" is in force, a court has ruled against two Christian pastors (of Pakistani origin) for "vilifying" Islam.

[7] G. Baum in the introduction to R. Radford Ruether, *Faith and Fratricide: The Theological Roots of Anti-Semitism*, New York: Seabury Press 1974, p. 6.

burden upon them in the present age", then could we be moving over from an "anti-Judaism" to an "antisemitism"? Is Paul not only saying things against their religion but also against their person? There is no doubt that Paul considered the Jews to be struck with blindness. Although it is not complimentary to Jewish people to say they are "blind",[8] it is, as I argued above in chapter 5, an indispensible part of a Christian theology of Israel. Also, their election can to some extent be seen as a burden. For although they remain God's people those who do not believe in Christ do not reap the benefits of being God's people. Indeed they stand under the judgement and curse of God,[9] something not lifted until their final "home-coming" when they come to believe in Christ at the second coming.

So is Paul being "antisemitic" when he speaks of Israel's blindness and the burden of her election? Antisemitism, as I defined it above, is an attitude which is irrational, based on prejudice and is applied indiscriminately. I consider these three aspects. First, are his views irrational? Paul uses a theological logic and thereby makes a theological judgement. There is therefore a *rationality* about his comments about Israel's blindness. Secondly, are his views based on prejudice? I believe they are not since, as argued above, he came to his understanding of Israel's blindness in the light of the Christ event and his study of scripture. Thirdly, are his comments about the Jews indiscriminate? They are certainly not indiscriminate in that he believes that it is those Jews who do not believe in Christ that are blind and have a burdensome election. Further, one has to realise that Paul believed that *all* those who do not believe in Christ, Jew *and Gentile*, are blind, although he does attach special theological significance to the blindness of non-Christian Jews. I conclude, therefore, that on the basis of a Christian outlook Paul cannot be accused of antisemitism in Romans.

Although Paul's views about non-Christian Jews sound harsh, it must be stressed that they are *theological* judgements. Problems arise when these negative theological judgements are transposed into discrimination against

---

[8] Such a theme was frequently portrayed in Christian art. See the various representations of Ecclesia and Synagoga in H. Schreckenberg, *The Jews in Christian Art: An Illustrated History* ET, London: SCM 1996, pp. 31-74. One of the better known representation are the stone sculptures of Ecclesia and Synagoga of Strasbourg Cathedral (Schreckenberg, *Jews*, p. 47).

[9] See the discussion in chapter 9 above.

the Jewish people. So during the Third Reich certain theologians saw the burden of Israel's election and the curse upon them not simply as a theological judgement but misused such ideas to legitimate a degree of political oppression of the Jewish people. It is instructive again to consider the position of Gerhard Kittel. One of his articles from 1933 was "Neutestamentliche Gedanken zur Judenfrage".[10] He focusses on Romans 9-11 but one should add that the article is short so there is little chance for more than a brief discussion of some of the texts. Points of his exegesis could be criticized[11] but much of his biblical work would probably not differ from many other Christian theologians trying to discuss Romans 9-11 and relate it to other essential New Testament texts concerning Israel.[12] Although his discussion about Israel *is not racial but salvation historical*[13] problems do arise in the way he applies the New Testament to the then current political situation. So one can say that *theologically* the Jewish people are not "at home" since their final conversion is their "home-coming". But Kittel then develops this in the sense that Jewish people should not be assimilated into German society.[14] This, as I argued in the previous chapter, is a dangerous and theologically illegitimate conclusion. Kittel uses the idea of God's

---

[10] *AELKZ* 66 (1933) 903-7.

[11] For example, he thinks that the words "auf daß ihr nicht stolz seid" of Rom. 11.25 are addressed to *Jewish* Christians and goes on to compare Lk. 18.11 ("Neutestamentliche Gedanken zur Judenfrage", 906).

[12] His approach would differ from mine in that he does not emphasize the diverse nature of the New Testament teaching on Israel.

[13] So, after discussing a number of texts including Lk. 13.34-35, he comments: "Es ist merkwürdig, wie wenig auch von ernsten und bewußten Christen die Frage des Judentums als eine religiöse, als eine heilsgeschichtliche Frage gestellt worden ist und gestellt wird" ("Neutestamentliche Gedanken zur Judenfrage", 905, Kittel's emphasis).

[14] Kittel moves from God's election of Israel and then judgement on Israel to the idea that *"die Assimilation des Judentums den klaren und eindeutigen Willen Gottes über diesem Volk verneint"* ("Neutestamentliche Gedanken zur Judenfrage", (Kittel's emphasis). He then continues: "Bismarck hat einst in seiner berühmten Rede aus dem Jahr 1847 auf die christliche Grundsätze sich berufen und vor ihrer Übertretung gewarnt, als er mit Leidenschaft gegen die Zulassung der Juden zum Beamtentum sich wandte. Von Goethe gibt es ein Wort aus dem Jahr 1823: ein Generalsuperintendent solle lieber, wenn er Charakter habe, sein Amt niederlegen, als eine jüdisch-christliche Mischehe segnen. Viele Härten der Gegenwart wären unnötig und viele Ausbrüche unchristlicher Leidenschaft würden unterblieben sein, *wenn der klare Wille Gottes beachtet worden wäre*" (905-6, Kittel's emphasis).

judgement on Israel to legitimate a certain degree of oppression of the Jewish people.[15] The New Testament theology of Israel does not lead inevitably to an approach such as Kittel's. During his internment at Balingen Kittel is reported to have said: "My position in the Jewish question is based on Holy Scripture and the tradition of the primitive Christian Church".[16] To be fair to Kittel I think in many of his writings he did *try* to apply the New Testament teaching to his time. But he clearly made some grave mistakes in trying to do so.[17]

There are some who whilst believing that "antisemitic" is too strong a word for Paul's ideas in Romans 9-11, think he is condescending towards Jewish people in proclaiming in Rom. 11.26 that Jews will be saved at the second coming by believing in Jesus (which I believe is the correct inter-pretation).[18] Such critics claim that it is analogous to a Protestant saying that Roman Catholics will be saved on the last day when they will finally see the truth of Protestantism. In response to this it is necessary to stress that the truth of Paul's claims concerning Israel in Romans cannot be determined by considering whether they happen to be condescending (as in the case of Israel's salvation) or whether they are critical of Israel's religion or whether Israel is portrayed as being blind. The truth of Paul's message can only be considered in the light of Luther's criterion "What urges Christ". And in no way is Christ diminished in Paul's theology of Israel as found in Romans. Indeed Christ is exalted by insisting that Israel will only come to salvation by believing in him. This brings us to the next theme.

2. Compromising Christ

Although throughout this work I have generally adopted a philosemitic view, I am concerned about the many attempts made to "sell out" the Christian

---

[15] In previous chapters I have emphasized the way Kittel's views differed quite radi-cally from the mainstream nazi view.

[16] Porter, "Kittel", 401.

[17] As far as the issue of Jewish Christians and their relationship to Gentile Christians is concerned, one can agree with Porter, "Kittel", 405, that Kittel "raises up, rather than breaks down the 'middle wall of partition'".

[18] See my exegesis of Rom. 11.26 in chapter 6 above.

gospel. In each case the centrality of Christ has been compromised. I give three examples of this.

The first is the programme carried out by Rosemary Radford Ruether and supported by Gregory Baum. These theologians stress the incompleteness of the revelation and redemption found in Christ. So Ruether writes:

> The cross and Resurrection are a paradigm for Christians, not for 'all who would be a part of Israel' or necessarily for 'all men'. . . . Those who have not chosen to make it their paradigm, because they have other paradigms which are more compelling to them from their own histories, are not to be judged as false or unredeemed thereby. This contextual view of the significance of the cross and Resurrection takes seriously the diversity of peoples and their histories, out of which they hear God through the memory of different revelatory experiences.[19]

This approach though would require the rewriting of much of the New Testament (including much of Paul) and is motivated by a need to "Christianity so as to leave room for other religions, and in particular for Judaism, before God"?[20] The view of the New Testament and in particular of Paul is that there is no salvation outside Jesus Christ.[21] Paul's *general* view is that any attempt to find God outside of Christ leads to idolatry.[22] One may compare Luther's statement that "to seek God outside of Jesus is the devil".[23] Although Paul would be cautious in accusing his contemporary Jews of idolatry[24] (hence my qualification *general* view), he certainly thought that Jews have wrong *ideas* about the one true God. As argued in chapter 9, Christian and Jewish *descriptions* of God are different, even though the *reference* is the same.

A second example of "selling out" is when theologians minimize the significance of Christ for Israel. I give a number of examples. Stendahl believes in the peaceful coexistence of Jews and Christians according to Romans 11. He writes:

---

[19] Ruether, *Faith and Fratricide*, pp. 250-51.

[20] Baum in Ruether, *Faith and Fratricide*, p. 17.

[21] See, for example, Bell, "Extra ecclesiam nulla salus?".

[22] Cf. Bell, *No one seeks for God*, p. 100.

[23] See *WA* 40.3:337,11: *Extra Iesum quaerere deum est diabolus*. This can be interpreted to mean either that seeking God outside of Jesus leads to despair, hence the devil; or it could mean that if one seeks God outside of Jesus one finds the devil (cf. Althaus, *Die Theologie Martin Luthers*, p. 33).

[24] See my discussion of 1 Cor. 10.1-22 in *Provoked to Jealousy*, pp. 251-55.

Consciously or unconsciously, Paul writes this whole section in Romans (10:18-11:36) without mentioning the name of Jesus Christ, and his final doxology has no Christ-language—as do all his other doxologies. It is pure God-language (11:33-36). It is as if Paul did not want them to have the Christ-flag to wave, since it might fan their conceit.[25]

I believe such an interpretation is wrong since Israel comes to salvation through believing in Christ who is the "deliverer" in Rom. 11.26.[26] Another example of minimizing Christ is found in the work of Gaston. He believes that Jesus Christ is the saviour only for Gentiles. The Jews have the torah (which is not abrogated) and therefore do not need Jesus Christ as their saviour.[27] This is a view which has been adopted by Gager.[28] There are a number of problems with Gaston's approach, one of which is that although Paul believed that Jewish believers can keep the law if they wish (Romans 14), he believed that Christ by his death had superceded the law for Jew as well as for Gentile.[29] As I shall argue, Christian theology, if properly done, is going to be inevitably "supercessionist".

As a third example there are those who support a so-called "Christologie der Völkerwallfahrt zum Zion" ("Christology of pilgrimage to "), i.e. that through Christ's cross and resurrection the foundations are laid for the eschatological pilgrimage to Zion. So H.-J. Kraus and B. Klappert believe that Israel is already in the community of salvation and that Gentiles simply have to be brought near (Eph. 2.13ff.).[30] Such a view is rightly criticized by

---

[25] K. Stendahl, "Christ's Lordship and Religious Pluralism", in *Meanings: The Bible as Document and as Guide*, Philadelphia: Fortress Press 1984, 243 (233-44).

[26] See my exegesis of Rom. 11.26 above in chapter 6. Note that Stendahl himself has changed his mind, earlier believing that 11.26 pointed to Jews accepting Jesus as messiah. See K. Stendahl, "Judaism and Christianity I: Then and Now", in *Meanings: The Bible as Document and as Guide*, Philadelphia: Fortress Press 1984, 215 n. 1 (205-15).

[27] L. Gaston, "Paul and the Torah" in A.T. Davies (ed.), *Antisemitism and the Foundations of Christianity*, New York/Ramsey/Toronto: Paulist Press 1979, 48-71.

[28] J.G. Gager, *The Origins of Anti-Semitism: Attitudes Towards Judaism in Pagan and Christian Antiquity*, New York/Oxford: OUP 1983.

[29] A similar criticism is made by R.R. Ruether, "The *Faith and Fratricide* Discussion: Old Problems and New Dimensions" in A.T. Davies (ed.), *Antisemitism and the Foundations of Christianity*, New York/Ramsey/Toronto: Paulist Press 1979, 241-42 (230-56).

[30] H.-J. Kraus, *Systematische Theologie im Kontext biblischer Geschichte und Eschatologie*, Neukirchen-Vluyn: Neukirchener Verlag 1983, pp. 490-93; B. Klappert, "Miterben der Verheißung: Christologie und Ekklesiologie der Völkerwallfahrt zum Zion", in *Miterben der Verheißung: Beiträge zum jüdisch-christlichen Dialog* (NBST 25), Neukirchen-Vluyn: Neukirchener Verlag 2000, 223-34 (203-40).

Theobald when he comments that "nach dem Zeugnis des Neuen Testaments Sündenvergebung, Rechtfertigung, Neuschöpfung in der Taufe, Anwartschaft auf die σωτηρία unterschiedslos für Juden wie Heiden an den *einen* Herrn Jesus als den eschatologischen Repräsentanten Gottes gebunden sind".[31]

3. Christianity supercedes Judaism

I believe that to emphasize the centrality of Christ, as Paul does, is not "antisemitic" even though the implications of this may offend Jewish people (e.g. the relativizing of the law). Christian theology, properly done, is inevitably supercessionist. For if Christ is central to Christian theology it is inevitable that the law of Moses will be relativized and Christianity will supercede Judaism.[32] The Jewish people and the Church cannot be properly understood as having parallel histories. I therefore question what Brueggemann writes of the Church and Israel:

> It strikes me that for all the polemics that sustain supercessionism, the truth is that these two communities, because they face the same God, share the same reassuring, demanding life. It is perhaps with such realization that Franz Rosenzweig could dare to imagine that were both communities honest, they would recognize that they live parallel histories, with the same hopes to hope and the same obediences to obey.[33]

Brueggemann thereby loses the law-gospel dialectic.[34] In Christian theology one cannot escape the New Testament insight that Israel is the people of the

---

[31] Theobald, "Mit verbundenen Augen?", 391 (Theobald's emphasis). See also Haacker, *Römer*, p. 297 (on Rom. 15.8): "Eine Reduzierung der Mission Jesu auf die Hinführung der Völker zu dem Gott, bei dem Israel schon immer ist, würde den Grundbegriff der Christologie verleugnen".

[32] Likewise, Muslims consider Islam to have superceded Christianity. However, it is not necessary for a Christian to take this as a personal affront even though one would wish to refute the claim vigorously.

[33] W. Brueggemann, *Theology of the Old Testament: Testimony, Dispute, Advocacy*, Minneapolis: Fortress Press 1997, p. 449.

[34] Earlier in his work Brueggemann sees a theological problem in "setting at odds law and gospel". However, certainly in Paul it is difficult to avoid a law-gospel dialectic. On Paul's attitude to the obedience of the Christian see Hofius, "Das Gesetz des Mose und das Gesetz Christi", 66-74.

law and the Church is the people of the gospel. Even more significant is the fact that the Church is a resurrected community.[35]

If Christians have the courage of their convictions they can today boldly declare that they see their theology as one which is superior to a Jewish theology. Through God's grace in Christ, one is saved from the wrath to come. One is saved as "one who does not work" and as one who "trusts him who justifies the ungodly" (Rom. 4.5). One is saved "by grace" and "not on the basis of works" (Rom. 11.6). A Christian theologian finds grace superior to works. However, a Jewish theologian could argue the converse. He could argue that a merit theology is superior to one of salvation by grace. He could argue that it is superior to be one who works, who wages *are* reckoned as a due. Daniel Schwartz tells the story of Christians who posted a placard near Times Square in New York bearing the words "Jesus Saves". In response some Jewish entrepreneurs posted opposite a placard with the words "Moses Invests".[36]

One could also perhaps argue that Christianity is superior in that it can *in principle* be more humane.[37] The Christian can be rightly proud of the New Testament not only as a work which witnesses to the gospel of God but also for its remarkable "humanity" (despite some "hard sayings"[38]). Such a work together with its values has fashioned our western civilization. Sadly in my own country we are in danger of losing and forgetting our Christian heritage. Of course, Christians have plenty to be ashamed of in regard to their past *practices*. However, the dark episodes in Christian history are precisely

---

[35] See chapter 8 section 2 above.

[36] D.R. Schwartz, *Leben durch Jesus versus Leben durch die Torah: Zur Religionspolemik der ersten Jahrhunderte* (Franz-Delitzsch-Vorlesung 1991), Münster: Franz-Delitzsch-Gesellschaft 1993, p. 3.

[37] One of the controversies raging in British society is the question of cruelty to animals involved in the production of kosher meat. This practice has been defended as humane by orthodox Jews; my own judgement is that this is inhumane (as is the preparation of Halal meat in the Muslim community). I am grateful to Dr Nick Palmer, Member of Parliament for Broxtowe, for providing me information on this (e-mail of 15.5.04). The Farm Animal Welfare Council issued a report in June 2003 and recommended that religious slaughter without prior stunning should be banned in the UK. Unfortunately it appears that the government is not prepared to accept this recommendation.

[38] See, for example, the problem of Rom. 13.4 which seems to allow the death penalty (discussed in chapter 9, section 4.5 above).

those periods where Christians have not been faithful to the teachings of the New Testament.

So in criticizing Jewish theology, we are not necessarily saying anything against the *Jewish people*; rather it is making a theological point about their *religion*. Likewise, there has been plenty of criticism of Christianity; but the Christian does not have to take such criticisms as a personal affront.

Inevitably for Christian theology there is an "Old" Testament and a "New" Testament, and although terms such as "Hebrew Bible" or "Tanak" may be used for the former to avoid offending Jewish people, it is nevertheless an "*Old* Testament". There are crucial elements of discontinuity. But this position does not necessarily mean there is no rôle for Israel. So R. Kendall Soulen wrongly assumes that supercessionism (which he opposes) means the people of Israel no longer have any special role.[39] But is this really the case? Can one not have a supercessionist approach (i.e. salvation is found only in Christ and the law now has no rôle in salvation) and at the same time affirm God's abiding election of his people Israel? I have argued above that Paul held this position in Romans.[40]

4. Christian Critiques of Judaism

In chapter 3 above I argued that Judaism was a religion of works-righteousness and that Judaism exhibited some of the negative aspects of legalism. Further, I argued that this is how Paul himself viewed the Judaism of his day. I argued that there were those who interpreted Judaism and Paul in this traditional Protestant sense who were not in fact antisemitic (I gave the examples of H.L. Strack, Paul Billerbeck and Rudolf Bultmann). But I need briefly to revisit the issues. Certainly to criticize Judaism because it teaches salvation by works is not antisemitic. As pointed out above, Christian theologians believe that "grace" is superior to "works". Their criticism of Judaism for believing in salvation by works should simply be termed anti-*Judaism*. But what about the charge that Judaism in Paul's time was

---

[39] See R. Kendall Soulen, "Removing Anti-Judaism" in H.C. Kee and I.J. Borowsky (ed.), *Removing the Anti-Judaism from the New Testament*, Philadelphia: American Interfaith Institute 1998, 151-52 (149-56).

[40] Systematic theologians such as Karl Barth have also argued such a case.

legalistic in a negative sense? Here I am thinking of Jewish pride in achievement, casuistry and externalism. Are we not here criticizing the Jewish *person* and not simply the religion?[41] Is this then not antisemitic? It certainly is
antisemitic if it is based on prejudice and if it is an indiscriminate charge.
But if there is truth in it, then I would claim it is not antisemitic.

I do not think we do the Jewish people any favours by abandoning the traditional Protestant understanding of Paul's critique of Israel's religion and
by adopting the "new perspective". Indeed, it is striking that if the "new perspective" is adopted one is in danger of making even more serious negative
theological comments about the Jewish people (I refrain from using the term
"antisemitism"). For, with the exception of Stendahl, who believes that Paul
has no polemic against Judaism (and there may be other exceptions too),
most have accepted that if Paul did not attack Jews for works-righteousness,
he must have attacked them for something else. It is true that some interpretations of Paul's critique of Judaism are fairly lame. So Sanders' understanding of Paul's critique was that Judaism was not Christianity.[42] He later
changed this (or made it more precise) to Paul objecting to justification by
works since justification can only be through Christ.[43] But other understandings of Paul's critique are more serious. According to Dunn, Paul either
seems to deny or seriously relativize the election of Israel. So Dunn writes
that in Romans 2 "it becomes progressively clearer that Paul is seeking to

---

[41] However, it is worth noting that pride in doing good works is negative from a
Christian perspective but not necessarily from a Jewish one. Further, pride in Judaism did
not have the extremely negative connotation it had in Christianity as one of the seven
"deadly" sins (or more appropriately called "capital" or "root" sins (see K.E. Kirk, *Some
Principles of Moral Theology*, London: Longmans, Green and Co. 1920)). There is no
entry for "pride" in the *Jewish Encyclopedia*. For an overview of the idea of humility in
Judaism, see E. Schreiber, "Humility" *JE* 6:490-92.

[42] Sanders, *Paul and Palestinian Judaism*, p. 552.

[43] See Sanders, *Paul, the Law, and the Jewish People*, p. 27. Schreiner, *Law and its
Fulfillment*, p. 46, rightly argues that according to Sanders' interpretation Paul's argument in Galatians would not convince his opponents. For the Judaizers did not simply
argue that salvation was through the law; rather they argued that salvation was through
Christ *and the law*. And Paul provides an argument (e.g. in Gal. 3.10) as to why salvation cannot be achieved through works of law: those who rely on works of law are under
the curse of the law.

undermine a Jewish assumption of national distinctiveness and privilege".[44] In Galatians, Dunn believes that Paul was arguing against those who "were putting too much weight on the distinctiveness of Jews from Gentiles, and on the special laws which formed boundary markers between them, those who rested their confidence in Israel's 'favoured nation' status . . . ".[45] This is a fairly serious accusation against the Jew even though Dunn emphasizes that Judaism *as such* did not support such "national righteousness". So Barclay writes that "[i]n Dunn's analysis, the objects of Paul's critique were 'nationalistic presumption' and 'ethnic restrictiveness,' neither of which were in Paul's view, a proper interpretation of Jewish scriptures. And although these features may have been typical of the Judaism of his day, Dunn is careful to keep his discourse strictly historical and not to suggest that such features typify Judaism *as such*".[46]

The upshot of this is that Judaism is criticized for *something*: it can be for works-righteousness or national righteousness. Jews themselves are criticized for negative legalism or they are criticized for "ethnic restrictiveness". Bouncing around the term "antisemitism" does not help. One simply needs to ask which particular view corresponds to reality. I have tried to establish in chapter 3 above that Jews did believe in salvation by works and that there was some negative legalism. Regarding the approach of Wright and Dunn,[47] there may have been some "national righteousness" but I do not find it strongly represented in Paul's letters. In fact, as argued in chapter 4 above, Paul in his mature thought as reflected in the letter to the Romans does not relativize the election of Israel; on the contrary, he emphasizes the salvation historical priority of Israel and the abiding election of Israel.

---

[44] Dunn, "Issue between Paul and 'Those of the Circumcision'?", 311. This view was discussed in chapter 4 above in relation to Rom. 2.28-29. I also mentioned the view of Longenecker, *Eschatology*, p. 194, that Paul wished "to discredit an ethnocentric understanding of God's ways".

[45] Dunn, *Galatians*, p. 172.

[46] Barclay, "Multiculturalism and the New Perspective on Paul", 202 (Barclay's emphasis).

[47] It is perhaps worth noting that Dunn is not only indebted to N.T. Wright for the *term* "national righteousness" (see Dunn "New Perspective", 205 n. 36, who refers to Wright's Oxford D.Phil. thesis *The Messiah and the People of God: A Study in Pauline Theology with Particular Reference to the Argument of the Epistle to the Romans*, 1980) but also for much of his thought on "national righteousness".

5. Is Paul a Philosemite in Romans?

If therefore Paul cannot be described as an antisemite (even though he was critical of the religion of the Jewish people and some of the practices of the Jewish people) can he be positively described as a "philosemite" in Romans? If, as I have argued, he affirmed in this great epistle the abiding election of Israel and the ultimate salvation of Israel, then surely he can be described as a philosemite. And I believe we can share this philosemitism. It may be objected that as Paul wrote Romans, he believed that the would occur soon. He believed that all Israel would be saved once the Gentile mission was complete and that in all likelihood he would live to experience this himself. But he did not live to see it and we have had over two thousand years of Church history. Can the promises of salvation to Israel be stretched to include this extensive period of history (not to mention any future history)? I believe they can. A delay in the parousia, an important theological motif in the New Testament itself, does not change the fact that Israel remains the people of God and that the ultimate assurance of her salvation is grounded in the fact that "the gifts and call of God are irrevocable" (Rom. 11.29).

Bibliography

1. Primary Sources

1.1. *Bible*

Aland, Kurt, et al., (ed.), *The Greek New Testament*, Stuttgart: Deutsche Bibel-gesellschaft ⁴1993.

Die Bibel nach der Übersetzung Martin Luthers mit Apokryphen, Stuttgart: Deutsche Bibelgesellschaft 1984.

Biblia sacra iuxta vulgatam versionem, 2 vols, Stuttgart: Deutsche Bibelgesellschaft 1983.

Elliger, K. – Rudolph, W., et al., (ed.), *Biblia Hebraica Stuttgartensia*, Stuttgart: Deutsche Bibelstiftung 1967/77.

Die heilige Schrift des Alten und des Neuen Testaments, Zürich: Verlag der Zürcher Bibel 1987.

The Holy Bible: Revised Standard Version, New York/Glasgow/London/Toronto/ Sydney/Auckland: Collins 1973.

The Holy Bible: New Revised Standard Version, Anglicized Edition, Oxford: OUP 1995.

Luther, Martin, *Die gantze Heilige Schrift Deudsch (Wittenberg 1945)*, edited by Heinz Blanke and Hans Volz, 3 vols, München: Rogner & Bernhard 1972.

Menge, Hermann, (ed.), *Die heilige Schrift*, Stuttgart: Württembergische Bibelanstalt 1926.

Moffatt, James, (ed.), *The New Testament: A New Translation*, London: Hodder & Stoughton 1913.

Nestle, Eberhard – Aland, Kurt, et al., (ed.), *Novum Testamentum Graece*, Stuttgart: Deutsche Bibelgesellschaft ²⁷1993.

The New English Bible with Apocrypha, Oxford: OUP/Cambridge: CUP 1970.

Phillips, J.B., (ed.), *The New Testament in Modern English*, London: William Collins 1958.

Rahlfs, Alfred, (ed.), *Septuaginta: Id est Vetus Testamentum graece iuxta LXX interpretes*, 2 vols, Stuttgart: Württembergische Bibelanstalt 1935.

Wetstenius (Wettstein), J.J., (ed.), *Novum Testamentum Graecum*, 2 vols, Amsterdam 1752.

1.2. *Apocrypha, Pseudepigrapha and Hellenistic Jewish Literature*

Bogaert, P., (ed.), *L'Apocalypse syriaque de Baruch* (SC 144-45), 2 vols, Paris: Cerf 1969.

Box, G.H., (ed.), *The Apocalypse of Ezra (II Esdras II-XIV)* (Translations of Early Documents, Series I: Palestinian Jewish Texts), London: SPCK 1917.

Burchard, Christoph, (ed.), *Joseph und Aseneth* (JSHRZ 2.4), Gütersloh: Gütersloher Verlagshaus Gerd Mohn 1983.

Charles, R.H., (ed.), *The Apocrypha and Pseudepigrapha of the Old Testament in English*, 2 vols, Oxford: OUP 1977 (repr.), (^{1}1913).

Charles, R.H., *The Book of Enoch*, Oxford: Clarendon Press 1893.

Charles, R.H., (ed.), *The Greek Version of the Testaments of the Twelve Patriarchs*, Oxford: OUP/Darmstadt: Wissenschaftliche Buchgesellschaft ^{2}1960 (^{1}1908).

Charlesworth, James H., (ed.), *The Old Testament Pseudepigrapha*, 2 vols, London: Darton, Longman & Todd 1 1983; 2 1985.

Colson, F.H. – Whitaker, G.H. – Marcus, R. – Earp, J.W., (ed.), *Philo* (LCL), 10 vols with 2 supplements, London: William Heinemann/Cambridge, Mass.: Harvard University Press 1929-62.

Dietzfelbinger, Christian, (ed.), *Pseudo-Philo: Antiquitates Biblicae* (JSHRZ 2.2), Gütersloh: Gütersloher Verlagshaus Gerd Mohn ^{2}1979, (^{1}1975).

Georgi, Dieter, (ed.), *Weisheit Salomos* (JSHRZ 3.4), Gütersloh: Gütersloher Verlagshaus Gerd Mohn 1980.

Jacobson, Howard, *A Commentary on Pseudo-Philo's Liber Antiquitatum Biblicarum with Latin Text and English Translation* (AGAJU 31), 2 vols, Leiden/New York/Köln: E.J. Brill 1996.

James, M.R., *The Biblical Antiquities of Philo*, London: SPCK 1917.

de Jonge, M., (ed.), *The Testaments of the Twelve Patriarchs: A Critical Edition of the Greek Text* (PVTG 1.2), Leiden: E.J. Brill 1978.

Kautzsch, E., (ed.), *Die Apokryphen und Pseudepigraphen des Alten Testaments*, 2 vols, Tübingen/Freiburg/Leipzig: J.C.B. Mohr (Paul Siebeck) 1900.

Lévi, Israel, (ed.), *The Hebrew Text of the Book of Ecclesiasticus* (SSS 3), Leiden: E.J. Brill 1951 (repr.), (^{1}1904).

Sauer, Georg, (ed.), *Jesus Sirach (Ben Sira)* (JSHRZ 3.5), Gütersloh: Gütersloher Verlagshaus Gerd Mohn 1981.

Thackeray, H.St.J. – Marcus, Ralph – Wikgren, Allen – Feldman, Louis H., (ed.), *Josephus* (LCL), 9 vols, London: William Heinemann/Cambridge, Mass.: Harvard University Press 1926-65.

Violet, B., (ed.), *Die Apokalypsen des Esra und des Baruch in deutscher Gestalt* (GCS 18), Leipzig: J.C. Hinrichs'sche Buchhandlung 1924.

1.3. Qumran Literature

Lohse, Eduard, (ed.), *Die Texte aus Qumran, Hebräisch und Deutsch mit Masoretischer Punktation, Übersetzung, Einführung und Anmerkungen*, Darmstadt: Wissenschaftliche Buchgesellschaft ⁴1986, (¹1964).

Maier, Johann, (ed.), *The Temple Scroll: An Introduction, Translation and Commentary* (JSOTSup 34) ET, Sheffield: JSOT Press 1985.

Martínez, Florentino García, *The Dead Sea Scrolls Translated* ET, Leiden: E.J. Brill, 1994

Qimron, Elisha – Strugnell, John, (ed.), *Discoveries in the Judaean Desert X: Qumran Cave 4, V: Miqṣat Ma'aśe Ha-Torah* (DJD 10), Oxford: OUP 1994.

Steudel, Annette, (ed.), *Die Texte aus Qumran II, Hebräisch/Aramäisch und Deutsch mit Masoretischer Punktation, Übersetzung, Einführung und Anmerkungen*, Darmstadt: Wissenschaftliche Buchgesellschaft 2001.

Vermes, Geza, *The Complete Dead Sea Scrolls in English*, Harmondsworth: Penguin 1998.

1.4. Rabbinic Literature and Targumim

Beer, Georg, (ed.), *Faksimile-Ausgabe des Mischnacodex Kaufmann A50*, Haag: Martinus Mijhoff 1929.

Braude, William G., (ed.), *The Midrash on the Psalms* (YJS 13), 2 vols, New Haven: Yale University Press 1959.

Braude, William G., (ed.), *Pesikta Rabbati* (YJS 18), 2 vols, New Haven/London: Yale University Press 1968.

Buber, S., (ed.), *Midrasch Tanchuma*, 2 vols, Wilna 1885.

Buber, S., (ed.), *Midrash Tehillim*, Jerusalem 1966 (repr.), (¹1891, Wilna).

Clarke, E.G., et al., *Targum Pseudo-Jonathan of the Pentateuch: Text and Concordance*, Hoboken, N.J.: Ktav 1984.

Cohen, A., (ed.), *The Minor Tractates of the Talmud (Massekoth Ketannoth)*, London: Soncino 1 ²1971, (¹1965); 2 ²1971, (¹1965).

Danby, Herbert, (ed.), *The Mishnah*, Oxford: OUP 1985 (repr.), (¹1933).

Epstein, I., (ed.), *The Babylonian Talmud*, 35 vols, London: Soncino 1938-52.

Epstein, I., (ed.), *The Hebrew-English Edition of the Babylonian Talmud*, 30 vols, London: Soncino 1994 (repr.).

Etheridge, J.W., (ed.), *The Targums of Onkelos and Jonathan Ben Uzziel on the Pentateuch with the Fragments of the Jerusalem Targum (from the Chaldee)*, New York: Ktav 1968.

Finkelstein, Louis, (ed.), *Siphre ad Deuteronomium: H.S. Horovitzii schedis usus cum variis lectionibus et adnotationibus*, New York: Jüdischer Kulturverband in Deutschland 1939.

Freedman, H. - Simon, Maurice, (ed.), *Midrash Rabbah*, 10 vols, London/New York: Soncino ³1983.

Freedman, H., (ed.), *Midrash Rabbah: Genesis*, 2 vols, London/New York: Soncino ³1983.

Grossfeld, Bernard, (ed.), *The Targum Onqelos to Deuteronomy* (ArB 9), Edinburgh: T. & T. Clark 1988.

Grossfeld, Bernard, (ed.), *The Targum Onqelos to Exodus* (ArB 7), Edinburgh: T. & T. Clark 1988.

Grossfeld, Bernard, (ed.), *The Targum Onqelos to Genesis* (ArB 6), Edinburgh: T. & T. Clark 1988.

Grossfeld, Bernard, (ed.), *The Targum Onqelos to Leviticus and The Targum Onqelos to Numbers* (ArB 8), Edinburgh: T. & T. Clark 1988.

Hammer, Reuven, (ed.), *Sifre: A Tannaitic Commentary on the Book of Deuteronomy* (YJS 24), New Haven/London: Yale University Press 1986.

Hoffmann, D., (ed.), *Mechilta de-Rabbi Simon b. Jochai: Ein halachischer und haggadischer Midrasch zu Exodus*, Frankfurt am M.: J. Kauffmann 1905.

Horovitz, H.S., (ed.), *Siphre d'be Rab* (Corpus Tannaiticum, sectio tertia, pars tertia), Leipzig: Gustav Fock 1917.

Horovitz, H.S. - Rabin, I.A., (ed.), *Mechilta d'Rabbi Ismael* (Corpus Tannaiticum, sectio tertia, pars prima), Frankfurt am M.: J. Kauffmann 1931.

Israelstam, J. - Slotki, Judah J., (ed.), *Midrash Rabbah: Leviticus*, London/New York: Soncino ³1983.

Katzenellenbogen von Padua, Aaron Mose, (ed.), *Leqach tob to Leviticus - Deuteronomy*, Wilna 1880.

Klein, Michael L., (ed.), *The Fragment Targums of the Pentateuch According to their Extant Sources* (AnBib 76), 2 vols, Rome: Biblical Institute Press 1980.

Krauss, Samuel, (ed.), *Die Mischna: Text, Übersetzung und ausführliche Erklärung: Sanhedrin, Makkot*, Gießen: Verlag von Alfred Töpelmann 1933.

Kuhn, Karl Georg, (ed.), *Der tannaitische Midrasch: Sifre zu Numeri* (Rabbinische Texte 2. Reihe: Tannaitische Midraschim 3), 2 vols, Stuttgart: W. Kohlhammer Verlag 1959.

Lauterbach, Jacob Z., (ed.), *Mekilta de-Rabbi Ishmael* (SLJC), 3 vols, Philadelphia: JPS 1 ²1949, (¹1933); 2 ²1949, (¹1933); 3 ²1949, (¹1935).

Lehrman, S.M., (ed.), *Midrash Rabbah: Exodus*, London/New York: Soncino ³1983.

Lieberman, Saul, (ed.), *A Comprehensive Commentary on the Tosephta*, 11 vols, New York: Louis Rabinowitz Institute in Rabbinics/Jewish Theological Seminary of America 1955-88.

Lieberman, Saul, (ed.), *Midrash Debarim Rabbah*, Jerusalem: Wahrmann 1964.

Lieberman, Saul, (ed.), *The Tosephta According to Codex Vienna with Variants from Codices Erfurt, Genizah Mss. and Editio Princeps (Venice 1521)*, 5 vols, New York: Louis Rabinowitz Institute in Rabbinics/Jewish Theological Seminary of America 1955-88.

Lowe, W.H., (ed.), *The Mishnah on which the Palestinian Talmud Rests*, Cambridge: CUP 1883.

Midrash Rabbah, 3 vols, Jerusalem 1923 (repr.), (Wilna [1]1887).

Neusner, Jacob, (ed.), *Sifre to Deuteronomy: An Analytical Translation* (BJS 98 and 101), 2 vols, Atlanta: Scholars Press 1987.

Neusner, Jacob, (ed.), *Sifré to Numbers: An American Translation and Explanation* (BJS 118-19), 2 vols, Atlanta: Scholars Press 1986.

Neusner, Jacob, (ed.), *Talmud of the Land of Israel* (CSHJ), 35 vols, London/Chicago: University of Chicago Press 1983ff.

Neusner, Jacob, (ed.), *The Tosefta. Translated from the Hebrew*, 6 vols, New York: Ktav 1977-86.

Singer, Isidore, (ed.), *Jewish Encyclopedia*, 12 vols, London/New York: Funk and Wagnalls 1901-6.

Slotki, Judah J., (ed.), *Midrash Rabbah: Numbers*, 2 vols, London/New York: Soncino [3]1983.

Sperber, Alexander, (ed.), *The Bible in Aramaic*, 5 vols, Leiden: E.J. Brill 1959-73.

Stenning, J.F., (ed.), *The Targum of Isaiah*, Oxford: OUP 1949.

Taylor, Charles, *Sayings of the Jewish Fathers* (LJC), New York: Ktav [2]1969, ([1]1897).

Theodor, J. - Albeck, Ch., (ed.), *Midrash Bereshit Rabba: Critical Edition with Notes and Commentary*, 2 vols, Jerusalem: Wahrmann [2]1965, ([1]1912).

Zuckermandel, M.S., (ed.), *Tosephta based on the Erfurt and Vienna Codices*, Jerusalem: Wahrmann 1963.

1.5. Early Christian Literature

Amidon, Philip R., (ed.), *The Panarion of St. Epiphanius, Bishop of Salamis*, Oxford/New York: OUP 1990.

Elliott, J.K. (ed.), *The Apocryphal New Testament: A Collection of Apocryphal Christian Literature in English Translation based on M.R. James*, Oxford: Clarendon Press 1993.

Falls, Thomas B., (ed.), *Saint Justin Martyr* (The Fathers of the Church 6), Washington, D.C.: The Catholic University of America Press 1965 (repr.), ([1]1948).

Ferrar, W.J., (ed.), *Eusebius of Caesarea: The Proof of the Gospel being the Demonstratio Evangelica* (Translation of Christian Literature, Series I: Greek Texts), 2 vols, London: SPCK/New York: Macmillan 1920.

Gaisford, Thomas, (ed.), *Eusebii Pamphili episcopi Caesariensis eclogae propheticae*, Oxford: OUP 1842.

Glover, T.R., (ed.), *Tertullian* (LCL), London: William Heinemann/Cambridge, Mass.: Harvard University Press 1966.

Goodspeed, Edgar J., (ed.), *Die ältesten Apologeten: Texte mit kurzen Einleitungen*, Göttingen: Vandenhoeck & Ruprecht 1914.

Grant, Robert M., (ed.), *Ignatius of Antioch* (The Apostolic Fathers 4), London/Camden, N.J./Toronto: Thomas Nelson 1966.

Hall, Stuart George (ed.), *Melito of Sardis: On Pascha and Fragments* (OECT), Oxford: Clarendon Press 1979.

Hammond Bammel, Caroline P., (ed.), *Der Römerbriefkommentar des Origenes: Kritische Ausgabe der Übersetzung Rufins, Buch 1-3* (Vetus Latina 16), Freiburg: Herder 1990.

Harkins, P.W., (ed.), *Saint John Chrysostom: Discourses against Judaizing Christians* (FaCh 68), Washington: Catholic University of America Press 1977.

Heikel, I.A., (ed.), *Eusebius Werke, Band. 6: Die Demonstratio evangelica* (GCS), Leipzig: J.C. Hinrichs'sche Buchhandlung 1913.

Klostermann, Erich, (ed.), *Origenes Werke: Dritter Band* (GCS), Leipzig: J.C. Hinrichs'sche Buchhandlung 1961.

Holl, K., (ed.), *Epiphanius Band 1: Ancoratus und Panarion, Haer. 1-33* (GCS), Leipzig: J.C. Hinrichs'sche Buchhandlung 1915.

Lake, Kirsopp, (ed.), *Eusebius: The Ecclesiastical History* (LCL), 2 vols, London: William Heinemann/Cambridge, Mass.: Harvard University Press 1 1965; 2 1964.

Migne, Jacques-Paul, (ed.), *Patrologiae cursus completus*, Paris 1845ff.

Musurillo, H., (ed.), *The Acts of the Christian Martyrs*, Oxford: Clarendon Press 1972.

Robinson, J. Armitage, (ed.), *The Philocalia of Origen*, Cambridge: CUP 1893.

Schaff, Philip, (ed.), *The Confessions and Letters of St. Augustine* (NPNF 1), Grand Rapids: Wm B. Eerdmans 1974 (repr.).

Souter, Alexander, (ed.), *Pelagius's Exposition of Thirteen Epistles of St. Paul. II* (Texts and Studies 9, 2), Cambridge: CUP 1926.

Stählin, Otto, (ed.), *Clemens Alexandrinus, Bd 2* (GCS), Leipzig: J.C. Hinrichs'sche Buchhandlung 1906.

Stählin, Otto, (ed.), *Clemens Alexandrinus, Bd 3* (GCS), Leipzig: J.C. Hinrichs'sche Buchhandlung 1909.

Vogels, H.I., (ed.), *Ambrosiastri qui dicitur commentarius in epistulas Paulinas, pars 1: In epistulam ad Romanos* (CSEL 81.1), Vienna: Hoelder/Pichler/Tempsky 1961.

Welldon, J.E.C., (ed.), *S. Aurelii Augustini: De Civitate Dei*, 2 vols, London: SPCK 1924.

Williams, Frank, (ed.), *The Panarion of Epiphanius of Salamis Book I (sects 1-46)* (NHS 35), Leiden: E.J. Brill 1987.

de Zwaan, J., (ed.), *The Treatise of Dionysius Bar Ṣalibhi Against the Jews*, Leiden: E.J. Brill 1906.

1.6. *Gnostic Literature*

Robinson, James M., (ed.), *The Nag Hammadi Library in English*, Leiden/New York/
Kφbenhavn/Köln: E.J. Brill ³1988, (¹1977).

1.7. *Greek and Roman Literature*

Ash, Harrison Boyd – Forster, E.S. – Heffner, Edward H., (ed.), *Lucius Junius Moder-
atus Columella, On Agriculture* (LCL), 3 vols, London: William
Heinemann/Cambridge, Mass.: Harvard University Press 1941-55.

Heller, Erich, (ed.), *P. Cornelius Tacitus Annalen: Lateinisch und deutsch*,
München/Zürich: Artemis Verlag 1982.

Moore, Clifford H. – Jackson, John, (ed.), *Tacitus: The Histories, the Annals* (LCL), 4
vols, London: William Heinemann/Cambridge, Mass.: Harvard University Press
1986-94 (repr.).

Ramsey, G.G., (ed.), *Juvenal and Persius* (LCL), London: William Heinemann/Cam-
bridge, Mass.: Harvard University Press 1965 (repr.), (¹1918).

Schmitt, J.C., (ed.), *Palladii Rutilii Tauri Aemiliani, De insitione: liber ad Pasiphilum
virum doctissimum*, Wirceburgi 1876.

Thierfelder, Andreas, (ed.), *Philogelos der Lachfreund von Hierokles und Philagrios*,
München: Heimeran Verlag 1968.

Tredennick, Hugh (ed.), *Aristotle: Metaphysics, Books I-IX* (LCL), London/Cambridge
Mass.: Harvard University Press 1996 (repr.), (¹1933).

1.8. *Liturgical Works*

The Alternative Service Book, Cambridge: CUP/London: Clowes, SPCK 1980.

Book of Common Prayer, Cambridge: CUP (no date).

Common Worship: Services and Prayers for the Church of England, London: Church
House Publishing 2000.

Lent, Holy Week, Easter: Services and Prayers, London: Church House Publish-
ing/SPCK/Cambridge: CUP 1986.

Winstone, H., (ed.), *The Sunday Missal*, London: Collins ²1977, (¹1975).

2. Reference Works and Exegetical Aids

I give here the main reference works and exegetical aids used in the present work.

Allenbach, J., et al., *Biblia Patristica: Index des citations et allusions bibliques dans la
littérature patristique*, 4 vols with Supplement (Philon d'Alexandrie), Paris: Éditions du centre national de la recherche scientifique 1975-87.

Altaner, Berthold – Stuiber, Alfred, *Patrologie: Leben, Schriften und Lehre der Kirchenväter*, Freiburg/Basel/Wien: Herder [8]1978.

Ars Graeca: Griechische Sprachlehre, neu bearbeitet von R. Mehrlein, F. Richter, W. Seelbach and O. Leggewie, Paderborn: Ferdinand Schöningh [5]1981.

Bachmann, H. – Slaby, W.A., *Concordance to the Novum Testamentum Graece*, Berlin/New York: Walter de Gruyter [3]1987.

Balz, Horst – Schneider, Gerhard, (ed), *Exegetical Dictionary of the New Testament* ET, 3 vols, Grand Rapids: Wm. B. Eerdmans 1990-93.

Bauer, Walter, *Griechisch-deutsches Wörterbuch zu den Schriften des Neuen Testaments und der frühchristlichen Literatur*, Berlin: Walter de Gruyter [6]1988 (völlig neu bearbeitet von Kurt und Barbara Aland).

Bauer, W. – Arndt, W.F. – Gingrich, F.W., *Greek-English Lexicon of the New Testament and Other Early Christian Literature*, Chicago and London: University of Chicago Press 1961.

Di Berardino, Angelo (ed.), *Encylopedia of the Early Church* ET (with a foreword and bibliographic amendments by W.H.C. Frend), 2 vols, New York: OUP 1992.

Blass, F. – Debrunner, A., *A Greek Grammar of the New Testament*, translated and revised by R.W. Funk, Chicago/London: University of Chicago Press 1961.

Bornemann, Eduard – Risch, Ernst, *Griechische Grammatik*, Frankfurt/Berlin/München: Verlag Moritz Diesterweg [2]1978.

Botterweck, G. Johannes – Ringgren, Helmer, (ed.), *Theologisches Wörterbuch zum Alten Testament*, 8 vols, Stuttgart/Berlin/Köln/Mainz: W. Kohlhammer Verlag 1973-95.

Bromiley, Geoffrey W., (ed.), *The International Standard Bible Encyclopedia*, 4 vols, Grand Rapids: Wm B. Eerdmans 1979-88.

Brown, Colin, (ed.), *The New International Dictionary of New Testament Theology*, 3 vols, Exeter: Paternoster 1975-78.

Brown, F. – Driver, S.R. – Briggs, C.A., *A Hebrew and English Lexicon of the Old Testament based on the Lexicon of W. Gesenius*, Oxford: Clarendon Press 1978 (repr.).

Buttrick, George A., (ed.), *The Interpreter's Bible*, 12 vols, New York/Nashville: Abingdon-Cokesbury Press 1952-57.

Buttrick, George A., (ed.), *The Interpreter's Dictionary of the Bible*, 4 vols, New York/Nashville: Abingdon-Cokesbury Press 1962 (supplement 1976).

Comay, Joan – Cohn-Sherbok, Lavinia, (ed.), *Who's Who in Jewish History after the period of the Old Testament*, London/New York: Routledge [2]1995, ([1]1974).

Cremer, Hermann, *Biblico-Theological Lexicon of New Testament Greek* ET, Edinburgh: T. & T. Clark [4]1895.

Cross, F.L. – Livingstone, E.A., (ed.), *The Oxford Dictionary of the Christian Church*, Oxford: OUP [2]1978, ([1]1957).

Dalman, Gustaf H., *Grammatik des jüdisch-palästinischen Aramäisch und aramäische Dialektproben*, Darmstadt: Wissenschaftliche Buchgesellschaft 1981 (repr.), ([2]1905).

Dana, H.E., – Mantey, J.R., *A Manual Grammar of the Greek New Testament*, New York: Macmillan 1927.

Davies, W.D., et al., (ed.), *The Cambridge History of Judaism*, 3 vols, Cambridge: CUP 1984-99.

Denis, Albert-Marie, (ed.), *Concordance grecque des Pseudépigraphes d'Ancien Testament*, Louvain-la-Neuve: Université catholique de Louvain 1987.

Encyclopaedia Judaica, 16 vols, Jerusalem: Keter Publishing House 1978 (repr.), ([1]1971-72).

Galling, Kurt, (ed.), *Die Religion in Geschichte und Gegenwart: Handwörterbuch für Theologie und Religionswissenschaft*, 7 vols, Tübingen: J.C.B. Mohr (Paul Siebeck) [3]1957-65.

Gunkel, Hermann – Zscharnack, Leopold, (ed.), *Die Religion in Geschichte und Gegenwart: Handwörterbuch für Theologie und Religionswissenschaft*, 7 vols, Tübingen: J.C.B. Mohr (Paul Siebeck) [2]1927-32.

Goodblatt, David, "The Babylonian Talmud", *ANRW* 2.19.2 (1979) 257-336.

Hatch, Edwin - Redpath, Henry A., *A Concordance to the Septuagint*, 2 vols, Grand Rapids: Baker Book House 1983 (repr.), ([1]1897).

Hauck, Albert, (ed.), *Realencyklopädie für protestantische Theologie und Kirche*, 22 vols, Leipzig: J.C. Hinrichs'sche Buchhandlung [3]1896-1909.

Hawthorne, Gerald F. – Martin, Ralph P., (ed.), *Dictionary of Paul and his Letters*, Leicester: IVP 1993.

Höfer, J. - Rahner, K., (ed.), *Lexikon für Theologie und Kirche*, 11 vols, Freiburg: Herder [2]1957-67.

Hornblower, Simon – Spawforth, Antony, (ed.), *The Oxford Classical Dictionary*, Oxford: OUP [3]1996.

Jastrow, Marcus, *A Dictionary of the Targumim, the Talmud Babli and Yerushalmi, and the Midrashic Literature*, 2 vols, New York: Pardes Publishing House 1950.

Jenni, Ernst - Westermann, Claus, (ed.), *Theologisches Handwörterbuch zum Alten Testament*, 2 vols, München: Chr. Kaiser Verlag/Zürich: Theologischer Verlag 1 1971; 2 1976.

Kautzsch, E., (ed.), *Gesenius' Hebrew Grammar* ET, Oxford: Clarendon Press [2]1910 (revised by A.E. Cowley).

Keck, Leander E., et al., (ed.), *The New Interpreter's Bible*, 12 vols, Nashville: Abingdon Press 1994ff.

Kittel, G. – Friedrich, G., (ed.), *Theological Dictionary of the New Testament* ET, 10 vols, Grand Rapids: Wm B. Eerdmans 1964-76.

Kittel, G. – Friedrich, G., (ed.), *Theologisches Wörterbuch zum Neuen Testament*, 10 vols, Stuttgart: W. Kohlhammer Verlag 1933-78.

Koehler, L. – Baumgartner, W., *Lexicon in Veteris Testamenti libros*, Leiden: E.J. Brill 1953.

Koehler, L. – Baumgartner, W. - Stamm, J.J., *Hebräisches und Aramäisches Lexikon zum Alten Testament*, 3 vols, Leiden: E.J. Brill 1967-83.

Krause, G. – Müller, G., (ed.), *Theologische Realenzyklopädie*, 27 vols, Berlin/New York: Walter de Gruyter 1977-97.

Kuhn, Karl Georg, *Konkordanz zu den Qumrantexten*, Göttingen: Vandenhoeck & Ruprecht 1960.

Kuhn, Karl Georg, "Nachträge zur 'Konkordanz zu den Qumrantexten'", *RQ* 4 (1963-64) 163-234.

Lampe, G.W.H., (ed.), *Patristic Greek Lexicon*, Oxford: Clarendon Press 1961-68.

Leisegang, Joannes, *Indices ad Philonis Alexandrini opera* (Philonis Alexandrini: Opera quae supersunt 7), Berlin: Walter de Gruyter 1926.

Levy, Jacob, *Wörterbuch über die Talmudim und Midraschim*, 4 vols, Darmstadt: Wissenschaftliche Buchgesellschaft 1963.

Lewis, Charlton T. – Short, Charles, *A Latin Dictionary*, Oxford: Clarendon Press [2]1962 ([1]1879).

Liddell, H.G. – Scott, R., *Greek-English Lexicon*, Oxford: Clarendon Press 1985 ([1]1843) (revised by H.S. Jones and R. McKenzie with a Supplement 1968).

Lisowsky, Gerhard, *Kondordanz zum Hebräischen Alten Testament*, Stuttgart: Deutsche Bibelgesellschaft [2]1966, ([1]1958).

Lust, J. – Eynikel, E. – Hauspie, K. – Chamberlain, G., *A Greek-English Lexicon of the Septuagint: Part I, A-I*, Stuttgart: Deutsche Bibelgesellschaft 1992.

Metzger, Bruce M., *A Textual Commentary on the Greek New Testament*, London/New York: United Bible Societies 1971.

Morgenthaler, Robert, *Statistik des neutestamentlichen Wortschatzes*, Zürich/ Frankfurt am M.: Gotthelf-Verlag 1958.

Moule, C.F.D., *An Idiom Book of New Testament Greek*, Cambridge: CUP [2]1977, ([1]1953).

Moulton, James Hope – Turner, Nigel, – Howard, Wilbert Francis, *A Grammar of New Testament Greek*, 4 vols, Edinburgh: T. & T. Clark 1978-80 (repr.), ([1]1908-76).

Mulder, Martin Jan, (ed.), *Mikra: Text, Translation, Reading and Interpretation of the Hebrew Bible in Ancient Judaism and Early Christianity* (CRINT 2.1), Assen: Van Gorcum/Philadelphia: Fortress Press 1987.

Paulys Realencyclopädie der classischen Altertumswissenschaft, Neue Bearbeitung von Georg Wissowa, Wilhelm Kroll, Karl Mittelhaus et al., Stuttgart: Alfred Druckenmüller Verlag 1894ff., 2. Reihe 1914ff.

Rehkopf, Friedrich, *Septuaginta-Vokabular*, Göttingen: Vandenhoeck & Ruprecht 1989.

Rengstorf, Karl Heinrich, *A Complete Concordance to Flavius Josephus*, 4 vols, Leiden: E.J. Brill 1973-83.

Safrai, Shmuel, (ed.), *The Literature of the Sages. First Part: Oral Tora, Halakha, Mishna, Tosefta, Talmud, External Tractates* (CRINT 2.3.1), Assen: Van Gorcum/Philadelphia: Fortress Press 1987.

Schiele, Friedrich Michael – Zscharnack, Leopold, (ed.), *Die Religion in Geschichte und Gegenwart: Handwörterbuch in gemeinverständlicher Darstellung*, 5 vols, Tübingen: J.C.B. Mohr (Paul Siebeck) [1]1909-13.

Schwyzer, Eduard, *Griechische Grammatik* (Handbuch der Altertumswissenschaft, 2. Abteilung, 1. Teil), 4 vols, München: C.H. Beck'sche Verlagsbuchhandlung 1 1939; 2 1950; 3 1953; 4 1971.

Segal, M.H., *A Grammar of Mishnaic Hebrew*, Oxford: Clarendon Press 1927.

Sokoloff, Michael, *A Dictionary of Jewish Palestinian Aramaic of the Byzantine Period*, Ramat-Gan: Bar Ilan University Press 1990.

Souter, Alexander, *A Glossary of Later Latin to 600 A.D.*, Oxford: Clarendon Press 1949.

Spicq, Ceslas, *Theological Lexicon of the New Testament* ET, 3 vols, Peabody: Hendrickson 1994.

Stern, Menahem, *Greek and Latin Authors on Jews and Judaism*, 3 vols, Jerusalem: Israel Academy of Sciences 1974-84.

Stevenson, W.B., *Grammar of Palestinian Jewish Aramaic*, Oxford: Clarendon Press ²1962 (ed. by J.A. Emerton), (¹1924).

Stone, Michael E., *Jewish Writings of the the Second Temple Period* (CRINT 2.2), Assen: Van Gorcum/Philadelphia: Fortress Press 1984.

Temporini, H. - Haase, W., (ed.), *Aufstieg und Niedergang der römischen Welt*, Berlin/New York: Walter de Gruyter 1972ff.

Thesaurus Linguae Graecae (Data Bank); Theodore F. Brunner (Director), University of California, Irvine, CA 92717, USA.

Wahl, Ch.A., *Clavis librorum Veteris Testamenti Apocryphorum philologica: Indicem verborum in libris pseudepigraphis usurpatorum*, (ed. by Johannes Baptista Bauer), 1972 (repr.), (Leipzig ¹1853).

Weber, Otto, *Karl Barths Kirchliche Dogmatik: Ein einführender Bericht*, Neukirchen-Vluyn: Neukirchener Verlag ¹¹1989, (¹1950).

Weingreen, J., *A Practical Grammar for Classical Hebrew*, Oxford: Clarendon Press 1978 (repr.), (¹1939).

Whittaker, Molly, *Jews and Christians: Graeco-Roman Views* (CCWJCW 6), Cambridge: CUP 1984.

Würthwein, Ernst, *Der Text des Alten Testaments: Eine Einführung in die Biblia Hebraica*, Stuttgart: Deutsche Bibelgesellschaft ³1988, (¹1952).

van Zijl, J.B., *A Concordance to the Targum of Isaiah* (SBL Aramaic Studies 3), Missoula: Scholars Press 1979.

3. Secondary Literature

Aageson, James W., "Scripture and Structure in the Development of the Argument in Romans 9-11", *CBQ* 48 (1986) 265-89.

Abbott, Walter M., (ed.), *The Documents of Vatican II*, London/Dublin: Geoffrey Chapman 1966.

Abrahams, I, *Studies in Pharisaism and the Gospels, First Series*, Cambridge: CUP 1917.

Ådna, Jostein, "Jesus' Symbolic Act in the Temple (Mark 11:15-17): The Replacement of the Sacrificial Cult by His Atoning Death", in Beata Ego, Armin Lange and Peter Pilhofer (ed.), *Gemeinde ohne Tempel: Zur Substituierung und Transformation des Jerusalemer Tempels und seines Kults im Alten Testament, antiken Judentum und frühen Christentum*, Tübingen: J.C.B. Mohr (Paul Siebeck) 1999, 461-75.

Aland, Kurt and Barbara, *The Text of the New Testament: An Introduction to the Critical Editions and to the Theory and Practice of Modern Textual Criticism* ET, Grand Rapids: Eerdmans/Leiden: E.J. Brill 1987.

Albertz, Rainer, "Jer 2-6 und die Frühzeitverkündigung Jeremias", *ZAW* 94 (1982) 20-47.

Albright, W.F., "Gerhard Kittel and the Jewish question in antiquity", in *History, Archaeology and Christian Humanism*, London: A. & C. Black 1965, 229-40.

Alexander, Philip S., Review of E.P. Sanders, *Judaism: Practice and Belief, 63BCE-66CE, JJS* 37 (1986) 103-6.

Alexander, Philip S., "Torah and Salvation in Tannaitic Literature", in D.A. Carson, Peter T. O'Brien and Mark A. Seifrid (ed.), *Justification and Variegated Nomism, Volume I: The Complexities of Second Temple Judaism* (WUNT 2.140), Tübingen: J.C.B. Mohr (Paul Siebeck)/Grand Rapids: Baker 2001, 261-301.

Allison, Dale C., Jr., "Matt. 23:39 – Luke 13:35b as a Conditional Prophecy", *JSNT* 18 (1983) 75-84.

Althaus, Paul, *Der Brief an die Römer* (NTD 6), Göttingen: Vandenhoeck & Ruprecht [10]1966.

Althaus, Paul, "Kenosis", *RGG*[3] 3:1243-46.

Althaus, Paul, *Die letzten Dinge: Entwurf einer christlichen Eschatologie* (SAS 9), Gütersloh: C. Bertelsmann [3]1926.

Althaus, Paul, *Paulus und Luther über den Menschen* (SLA 14), Gütersloh: C. Bertelsmann [2]1951.

Althaus, Paul, *Die Theologie Martin Luthers*, Gütersloh: Güterloher Verlagshaus Gerd Mohn [6]1983 ([1]1962).

Althaus, Paul, *Die Wahrheit des kirchlichen Osterglaubens: Einspruch gegen E. Hirsch*, Gütersloh: C. Bertelsmann [2]1941, ([1]1940).

Arendt, Hannah, *The Origins of Totalitarianism*, Cleveland: World Publishing Company [2]1958, ([1]1951).

Ashcraft, Morris, *Rudolf Bultmann* (MMTM), Peabody: Hendrickson 1972.

Avemarie, Friedrich, "Bund als Gabe und Recht", in Friedrich Avemarie and Hermann Lichtenberger (ed.), *Bund und Tora: Zur theologischen Begriffsgeschichte in alttestamentlicher, frühjüdischer und urchristlicher Tradition* (WUNT 92), Tübingen: J.C.B. Mohr (Paul Siebeck) 1996, 163-216.

Avemarie, Friedrich, "Erwählung und Vergeltung. Zur optionalen Struktur rabbinischer Soteriologie", *NTS* 45 (1999) 108-26.

Avemarie, Friedrich, *Tora und Leben: Untersuchungen zur Heilsbedeutung der Tora in der frühen rabbinischen Literatur* (TSAJ 55), Tübingen: J.C.B. Mohr (Paul Siebeck) 1996.

Bachmann, Michael, "4QMMT und Galaterbrief, התורה מעשי und EΡΓA NOMOY", *ZNW* 89 (1998) 91-113.

Bachmann, Michael, "Zur Gedankenführung in 1. Kor. 15,12ff", *ThZ* 34 (1978) 265-76.

Bailey, Daniel P., *Jesus as the Mercy Seat: The Semantics and Theology of Paul's Use of Hilasterion in Romans 3:25*, Cambridge Ph.D. Dissertation 1999.

Bainton, Roland H., *Here I Stand: A Life of Martin Luther*, Nashville: Abingdon 1950.

Bammel, Ernst, "Gottes ΔIAΘHKH (Gal. III.15-17) und das jüdische Rechtsdenken", *NTS* 6 (1959-60) 313-19.

Bammel, Ernst, "Judenverfolgung und Naherwartung: Zur Eschatologie des Ersten Thessalonicherbriefs", *ZThK* 56 (1959) 294-315.

Bammel, Ernst, "Romans 13", in Ernst Bammel and C.F.D. Moule (ed.), *Jesus and the Politics of his Day*, Cambridge: CUP 1992 (repr.), ([1]1984), 365-83.

Barclay, J.M.G., "'Neither Jew nor Greek': Multiculturalism and the New Perspective on Paul", in M.G. Brett (ed.), *Ethnicity and the Bible* (BIS 19), Leiden/New York/Köln: E.J. Brill 1996, 197-214.

Barclay, J.M.G., *Obeying the Truth: A Study of Paul's Ethics in Galatians*, Edinburgh: T. & T. Clark 1988.

Barnes, Albert, *Notes on the New Testament Vol. IV.—Romans*, London: Blackie & Son 1842.

Barnikol, E., "Römer 13: Der nichtpaulinische Ursprung der absoluten Obrigkeitsbejahung von Römer 13,1-7", in *Studien zum Neuen Testament und zur Patristik* (TU 77), Berlin: Akademie-Verlag 1961, 65-133.

Barr, James, *The Semantics of Biblical Language*, Oxford: OUP 1961.

Barrett, C.K., *The Acts of the Apostles* (ICC), 2 vols, Edinburgh: T. &. T. Clark 1994-98.

Barrett, C.K., "The Allegory of Abraham, Sarah, and Hagar in the Argument of Galatians", in Johannes Friedrich, Wolfgang Pöhlmann, and Peter Stuhlmacher (ed.), *Rechtfertigung: Festschrift für Ernst Käsemann zum 70. Geburtstag*, Tübingen: J.C.B. Mohr (Paul Siebeck)/Göttingen: Vandenhoeck & Ruprecht 1976, 1-16.

Barrett, C.K., *A Commentary on the First Epistle to the Corinthians* (BNTC), London: A. & C. Black [2]1971, ([1]1968).

Barrett, C.K., *A Commentary on the Second Epistle to the Corinthians* (BNTC), London: A. & C. Black ²1979, (¹1973).

Barrett, C.K., *A Commentary on the Epistle to the Romans* (BNTC), London: A. & C. Black ²1991, (¹1957).

Barrett, C.K., *The Gospel according to St John*, London: SPCK ²1978, (¹1955).

Barrett, C.K., *Paul: An Introduction to His Thought* (OCT), London: Cassell 1994.

Barrett, C.K., "Paul and the Introspective Conscience", in W.P. Stevens (ed.), *The Bible, the Reformation and the Church: Essays in Honour of James Atkinson* (JSNTSup 105), Sheffield: Sheffield Academic Press 1995, 36-48.

Barrett, C.K., "Paul's Opponents in 2 Corinthians", in *Essays on Paul*, London: SPCK 1982, 60-86 (= *NTS* 17 (1970-71) 233-54).

Barrett, C.K., "Romans 9.30-10.21: Fall and Responsibility of Israel", in *Essays on Paul*, London: SPCK 1982, 132-53.

Barth, Karl, *Church Dogmatics* ET, 4 vols, Edinburgh: T. & T. Clark 1936-60.

Barth, Karl, *Church Dogmatics: Index Volume with Aids for the Preacher* ET, Edinburgh: T. & T. Clark 1977.

Barth, Karl, *Die Kirchliche Dogmatik*, 4 vols, Zürich: Evangelischer Verlag A.G. Zollikon 1932-1967.

Barth, Karl, *The Epistle to the Romans* ET (translated from the sixth edition by E.C. Hoskyns), London/Oxford/New York: OUP 1968 (repr.), (¹1933).

Barth, Karl, "The Jewish Problem and the Christian Answer", in *Against the Stream: Shorter Post-War Writings 1946-52*, London: SCM 1954, 195-201.

Barth, Karl, *A Shorter Commentary on Romans* ET, London: SCM 1959.

Bauckham, Richard J., *The Bible in Politics: How to read the Bible politically* (TWB), London: SPCK 1989.

Bauckham, Richard J., (ed.), *God will be All in All: The Eschatology of Jürgen Moltmann*. Edinburgh: T. & T. Clark 1999.

Bauckham, Richard J., "James and the Jerusalem Church", in Richard Bauckham (ed.), *The Book of Acts in Its Palestinian Setting* (The Book of Acts in its First Century Setting vol. 4), Grand Rapids: Wm B. Eerdmans/Carlisle: Paternoster, 415-80.

Bauckham, Richard J., *James: Wisdom of James, disciple of Jesus the sage* (NTR), London/New York: Routledge 1999.

Bauckham, Richard J., "James and Jesus", in Bruce Chilton and Jacob Neusner (ed.), *The Brother of Jesus: James the Just and His Mission*, Louisville: Westminster John Knox Press 2001, 100-135.

Bauckham, Richard J., *Jude, 2 Peter* (WBC 50), Waco: Word Books 1983.

Bauckham, Richard J., *The Theology of Jürgen Moltmann*, Edinburgh: T. & T. Clark 1995.

Bauer, Karl, "Holsten", *RGG*² 2:1998.

Baumgarten, A.I., "The Name of the Pharisees", *JBL* 102 (1983) 411-28.

Baumgarten, J.M., "Does tlh in the Temple Scroll refer to Crucifixion?", *JBL* 91 (1972) 472-81.

Baur, Ferdinand Christian, *Paulus, der Apostel Jesu Christi*, 2 vols, Leipzig: Fues's Verlag (L.W. Reisland) 1 ²1866, 2 ²1867.

Beale, G.K., "Peace and Mercy Upon the Israel of God: The Old Testament Background of Galatians 6,16b", *Bib* 80 (1999) 204-23.

Beare, F.W., *The Epistle to the Philippians* (BNTC), London: A. & C. Black 1959.

Becker, Jürgen, *Jesus of Nazareth* ET, New York/Berlin: Walter de Gruyter 1998.

Becker, Jürgen, *Paulus: Der Apostel der Völker*, Tübingen: J.C.B. Mohr (Paul Siebeck) 1989.

Beckwith, Roger T., *The Old Testament Canon of the New Testament Church*, London: SPCK 1985.

Beet, Joseph Agar, *A Commentary on St. Paul's Epistle to the Romans*, London: Hodder and Stoughton ¹⁰1902.

Behm, Johannes, διαθήκη, *TDNT* 2:124-34.

Beker, J. Christiaan, *Paul the Apostle: The Triumph of God in Life and Thought*, Edinburgh: T. & T. Clark 1980.

Bell, Richard H., "Extra ecclesiam nulla salus? Is there a salvation other than through faith in Christ according to Romans 2.14-16?", in Jostein Ådna, Scott J. Hafemann and Otfried Hofius (ed.), *Evangelium – Schriftauslegung – Kirche. Festschrift für Peter Stuhlmacher zum 65. Geburtstag*, Göttingen: Vandenhoeck & Ruprecht 1997, 31-43.

Bell, Richard H., "The Myth of Adam and the Myth of Christ", in Alf Christofersen, Carsten Claussen, Jörg Frey and Bruce Longenecker (ed.), *Paul, Luke and the Graeco-Roman World: Essays in Honour of Alexander J.M. Wedderburn* (JSNTSup 217), Sheffield: Sheffield Academic Press 2002, 21-36.

Bell, Richard H., *No one seeks for God: An Exegetical and Theological Study of Romans 1.18-3.20* (WUNT 106), Tübingen: J.C.B. Mohr (Paul Siebeck) 1998.

Bell, Richard H., "Origen, Eusebius and an -οω Verb", *JTS* 44 (1993) 157-62.

Bell, Richard H., *Provoked to Jealousy: The Origin and Purpose of the Jealousy Motif in Romans 9-11* (WUNT 2.63), Tübingen: J.C.B. Mohr (Paul Siebeck) 1994.

Bell, Richard H., "Rom. 5.18-19 and Universal Salvation", in *NTS* 48 (2002) 417-32.

Bell, Richard H., "Sacrifice and Christology in Paul", *JTS* 53 (2002) 1-27.

Bell, Richard H., "Sin Offerings and Sinning with a High Hand", *JPJ* 4 (1995) 25-59.

Bell, Richard H., "Teshubah: The Idea of Repentance in Ancient Judaism", *JPJ* 5 (1995) 22-52.

Bell, Richard H., Review of C. Landmesser, *Wahrheit als Grundbegriff neutestamentlicher Wissenschaft*, *JTS* 51 (2000) 631-37.

Bell, Richard H., Review of M. Meiser, *Paul Althaus als Neutestamentler: Eine Untersuchung der Werke, Briefe, unveröffentlichten Manuskripte und Randbemerkungen, SEÅ* 61 (1996) 53-55.

Bengel, Johann Albrecht, *Gnomon Novi Testamenti*, Berlin: Gust. Schlawitz 1855 (³1773).

Benoit, Pierre, "Conclusion par mode de synthèse", in Lorenzo de Lorenzi (ed.), *Die Israelfrage nach Röm 9-11* (MRvB.BÖA 3), Rom: Abtei von St Paul vor den Mauern 1977, 217-36.

Berger, Klaus, "Jesus als Pharisäer und frühe Christen als Pharisäer", *NovT* 30 (1988) 231-62.

Bernard, J.H., "The Second Epistle to the Corinthians", in W. Robertson Nicoll (ed.), *The Expositor's Greek Testament*, Grand Rapids: Eerdmans 1976 (repr), 3:1-119.

Bertram, Georg, ἔργον, *TDNT* 2:635-55.

Best, Ernest, *A Commentary on The First and Second Epistles to the Thessalonians* (BNTC), London: A. & C. Black ³1979, (¹1972).

Betz, Hans Dieter, *Galatians* (Hermeneia), Philadelphia: Fortress Press 1979.

Betz, Hans Dieter, "Geschichte und Selbstopfer: Zur Interpretation von Römer 9,1-5", in Christoph Auffarth and Jörg Rüpke (ed.), *Epitome tes oikoumenes. Studien zur römischen Religion in Antike und Neuzeit für Hubert Cancik und Hildegard Cancik-Lindemaier* (PAB 6), Stuttgart: Steiner Verlag 2002, 75-87.

Betz, Hans Dieter, "Practicality or Principle? A Memorable Exchange of Letters", in Ithamar Gruenwald, Shaul Shaked and Gedaliahu G. Stroumsa (ed.), *Messiah and Christos: Studies in the Jewish Origins of Christianity Presented to David Flusser on the Occasion of his Seventy-Fifth Birthday* (TSAJ 32), Tübingen: J.C.B. Mohr (Paul Siebeck) 1992, 207-17.

Betz, Otto, "Die heilsgeschichtliche Rolle Israels bei Paulus", in *Jesus, Der Herr der Kirche: Aufsätze zur biblischen Theologie II* (WUNT 52), Tübingen: J.C.B. Mohr (Paul Siebeck) 1990, 312-34 (original and shorter version appeared in *ThBei* 9 (1978) 1-21).

Betz, Otto, "Jesus and the Temple Scroll", in J.H. Charlesworth (ed.), *Jesus and the Dead Sea Scrolls*, New York: Doubleday 1992, 75-103.

Betz, Otto, "Die Vision des Paulus im Tempel von Jerusalem: Apg 22,17-21 als Beitrag zur Deutung des Damaskuserlebnisses", *Jesus, Der Herr der Kirche: Aufsätze zur biblischen Theologie II* (WUNT 52), Tübingen: J.C.B. Mohr (Paul Siebeck) 1990, 91-102 (= Otto Böcher and Klaus Haacker (ed.), *Verborum Veritas: FS für Gustav Stählin*, Wuppertal: Theologischer Verlag Rolf Brockhaus 1970, 113-23).

Betz, Otto, *Was wissen wir von Jesus?*, Wuppertal/Zürich: R. Brockhaus Verlag ²1991, (¹1965).

Beyschlag, Karlmann, *Die Erlanger Theologie* (EKGB 67), Erlangen: Martin-Luther-Verlag 1993.

Bickerman, E.J., "A propos de la phénoménologie religieuse" in *Studies in Jewish and Christian History III* (AGJU 9.3), Leiden: E.J. Brill 1986, 212-24.

Bickerman, E.J., "The Date of Fourth Maccabees" in *Studies in Jewish and Christian History I* (AGJU 9.1), Leiden: E.J. Brill 1986, 275-81.

Bickerman, E.J., "Syria and Cilicia", *AJP* 68 (1947) 353-62.

Bickerman, E.J., "The Warning Inscription of Herod's Temple", *JQR* 37 (1946-47) 387-405.

Bicknell, E.J., *The First and Second Epistles to the Thessalonians* (WC), London: Methuen & Co. 1932.

Bietenhard, Hans, *Caesarea, Origenes und die Juden* (Franz Delitzsch-Vorlesungen 1972), Stuttgart: W. Kohlhammer Verlag 1974.

Billerbeck, Paul, (Strack, Hermann L.), *Kommentar zum Neuen Testament aus Talmud und Midrasch*, 4 vols, München: C.H. Beck'sche Verlagsbuchhandlung 1-3 ³1961; 4 ²1956.

Blinzler, Josef, "The Jewish Punishment of Stoning in the New Testament Period", in Ernst Bammel (ed.), *The Trial of Jesus: Cambridge Studies in honour of C.F.D. Moule* (SBT 2.13), London: SCM 1970, 147-61.

Blinzler, Josef, *The Trial of Jesus* ET, Cork: Mercier Press 1959.

Blumenkranz, Bernhard, "Die Entwicklung im Westen zwischen 200 und 1200", in Karl Heinrich Rengstorf and Siegfried von Kortzfleisch (ed.), *Kirche und Synagoge: Handbuch zur Geschichte von Christen und Juden. Darstellung mit Quellen*, 2 vols, München: DTV 1988 (repr.), (¹1968-70), 1:84-135.

Boccaccini, Gabriele, *Middle Judaism: Jewish Thought 300 B.C.E. to 200 C.E.*, Minneapolis: Fortress Press 1991.

Bockmuehl, Markus, "1QS and Salvation at Qumran", in D.A. Carson, Peter T. O'Brien and Mark A. Seifrid (ed.), *Justification and Variegated Nomism, Volume I: The Complexities of Second Temple Judaism* (WUNT 2.140), Tübingen: J.C.B. Mohr (Paul Siebeck)/Grand Rapids: Baker 2001, 381-414.

Bockmuehl, Markus, *The Epistle to the Philippians* (BNTC), London: A. & C. Black 1997.

de Boer, Martinus C., "God-Fearers in Luke-Acts", in C.M. Tuckett (ed.), *Luke's Literary Achievement: Collected Essays* (JSNTSup 116), Sheffield: Sheffield Academic Press 1995, 50-71.

Boers, Hendrikus, "The Form Critical Study of Paul's Letters: 1 Thessalonians as a Case Study", *NTS* 22 (1976) 140-58.

Bonhoeffer, Dietrich, *No Rusty Swords* ET, London: Collins 1965.

Bonnard, Pierre, *L'épîtres de saint Paul aux Philippiens et l'épître aux Colossiens* (CNT), Neuchâtel: Delachaux et Nestle 1950.

Borchert, H.H. – Merz, G., (ed.), "Von den Jüden und jren Lügen", *Martin Luther: Ausgewählte Werke*, Vol. III of the *Ergänzungsreihe*, München 1936, pp. 61-228.

Bornkamm, Günther, "Paulus", [3]*RGG* 5:166-90.

Bornkamm, Günther, *Paul* ET, London: Hodder and Stoughton 1985 (repr.), ([1]1971).

Bornkamm, Günther, "The Letter to the Romans as Paul's Last Will and Testament", in Karl P. Donfried (ed.), *The Romans Debate*, Peabody: Hendrickson [2]1991 ([1]1977, Minneapolis: Augsburg Publishing House), 16-28.

Bornkamm, Günther, "Der Lohngedanke im Neuen Testament", in *Studien zu Antike und Urchristentum. Gesammelte Aufsätze Band II* (BevTh 28), München: Chr. Kaiser Verlag [3]1970, ([1]1959), 69-92.

Bornkamm, Günther, "The Missionary Stance of Paul in I Corinthians 9 and in Acts", in Leander E. Keck and J. Louis Martyn (ed.), *Studies in Luke-Acts: Essays presented in honor of Paul Schubert*, London: SPCK 1968, 194-207.

Bornkamm, Heinrich, (ed.), *Luthers Vorreden zur Bibel*, Göttingen: Vandenhoeck & Ruprecht [3]1989.

Bousset, Wilhelm, *Die Religion des Judentums im neutestamentlichen Zeitalter*, Berlin: Reuther & Reichard 1903.

Bousset, Wilhelm, "Der zweite Brief an die Korinther", in Otto Baumgarten et al. (ed.), *Die Schriften des Neuen Testaments, Zweiter Band*, Göttingen: Vandenhoeck & Ruprecht 1917, 167-223.

Bousset, Wilhelm – Greßmann, Hugo, *Die Religion des Judentums im späthellenistischen Zeitalter* (HzNT 21), Tübingen: J.C.B. Mohr (Paul Siebeck) [3]1926.

Bovon, François, *Das Evangelium nach Lukas: 1. Teilband Lk 1,1-9.50* (EKK 3.1), Zürich: Benziger Verlag/Neukirchen-Vluyn: Neukirchener Verlag 1989.

Brandenburger, E. *Die Verborgenheit Gottes im Weltgeschehen* (AThANT 68), Zürich: Theologischer Verlag 1981.

Brandon, S.G.F., *The Fall of Jerusalem and the Christian Church*, London: SPCK [2]1957, ([1]1951).

Braun, Herbert, "Vom Erbarmen Gottes über die Gerechten", in *Gesammelte Studien zum Neuen Testament und seiner Umwelt*, Tübingen: J.C.B. Mohr (Paul Siebeck) [2]1967, 8-69.

Braun, Roddy, *1 Chronicles* (WBC 14), Waco: Word Books 1986.

Bright, John, *A History of Israel* (OTL), London: SCM [2]1972, ([1]1960).

Brockington, L.H., "The Septuagintal Background to the New Testament use of ΔΟΞΑ", in D.E. Nineham (ed.), *Studies in the Gospels: Essays in Memory of R.H. Lightfoot*, Oxford: Basil Blackwell 1967, 1-8.

Broshi, M., "La Population de l'ancienne Jérusalem", *RB* 82 (1975) 5-14.

Brown, Colin, *Jesus in European Protestant Thought 1778-1860*, Grand Rapids: Baker 1985.

Brown, Raymond E., *The Death of the Messiah: A Commentary on the Passion Narratives in the Four Gospels* (ABRL), 2 vols, New York: Doubleday 1994.

Brown, Raymond E., "How much did Jesus know?–A Survey of the Biblical Evidence", *CBQ* 29 (1967) 9-39.

Bruce, F.F., *The Book of the Acts* (NICNT), Grand Rapids: Wm B. Eerdmans [2]1988, ([1]1954).

Bruce, F.F., *The Canon of Scripture*, Glasgow: Chapter House 1988.

Bruce, F.F., *1 and 2 Corinthians*, Grand Rapids: Wm B. Eerdmans 1996 (repr.), ([1]1971).

Bruce, F.F., *New Testament History*, Garden City, New York: Doubleday & Co. 1980 (repr.), ([1]1969).

Bruce, F.F., *The Epistle of Paul to the Galatians: A Commentary on the Greek Text* (NIGTC), Exeter: Paternoster 1982.

Bruce, F.F., *The Epistle of Paul to the Romans: An Introduction and Commentary* (TNTC), London: IVP 1976 (repr.), ([1]1963).

Bruce, F.F., *Paul: Apostle of the Free Spirit*, Exeter: Paternoster 1977.

Bruce, F.F., *1 & 2 Thessalonians* (WBC 45), Waco: Word Books 1982.

Brueggemann, Walter, *Theology of the Old Testament: Testimony, Dispute, Advocacy*, Minneapolis: Fortress Press 1997.

Brunner, Emil, *Die Christliche Lehre von Gott: Dogmatik I*, Zürich: Theologischer Verlag [4]1972, ([1]1946).

Brunner, Emil, *The Letter to the Romans: A Commentary* ET, London: Lutterworth 1959.

Bryan, Steven M., *Jesus and Israel's Traditions of Judgement and Restoration* (SNTSMS 117), Cambridge: CUP 2002.

Buchanan, George Wesley, "Judas Iscariot", *ISBE* 2:1151-53.

Buck, Charles, "The Early Order of the Pauline Corpus", *JBL* 68 (1949) 351-57.

Bultmann, Rudolf, "Adam und Christus nach Römer 5", in *Exegetica. Aufsätze zur Erforschung des Neuen Testaments*, Tübingen: J.C.B. Mohr (Paul Siebeck) 1967, 424-44.

Bultmann, Rudolf, *Das Evangelium des Johannes* (KEK 2), Göttingen: Vandenhoeck & Ruprecht [18]1964, ([10]1941).

Bultmann, Rudolf, "Geschichte und Eschatologie im Neuen Testament", in *Glauben und Verstehen: Gesammelte Aufsätze, Bd 3*, Tübingen: J.C.B. Mohr (Paul Siebeck) [2]1962, ([1]1960), 91-106.

Bultmann, Rudolf, *Primitive Christianity in its Contemporary Setting* ET, London: Collins 1960.

Bultmann, Rudolf, *Das Urchristentum im Rahmen der antiken Religionen*, Zürich: Artemis Verlag [5]1986, ([1]1949).

Bultmann, Rudolf, "Theologie als Wissenschaft", *ZThK* 81 (1984) 447-69.

Bultmann, Rudolf, *Theologie des Neuen Testaments* (UTB 630), Tübingen: J.C.B. Mohr (Paul Siebeck) [9]1984 (durchgesehen und ergänzt von Otto Merk), ([1]1948).

Bultmann, Rudolf, *Theology of the New Testament* ET, 2 vols, London: SCM 1 1952; 2 1955.

Bultmann, Rudolf, "Wahrheit und Gewißheit" (Vortrag gehalten am 2. Oktober 1929), in *Theologische Enzyklopädie* (ed. by Eberhard Jüngel and Klaus W. Müller), Tübingen: J.C.B. Mohr (Paul Siebeck) 1984, 183-205 (Anhang 3).

Bultmann, Rudolf, *Der zweite Brief an die Korinther* (KEK 6), Göttingen: Vandenhoeck & Ruprecht 1976.

Bultmann, Rudolf, ἀλήθεια κτλ, *TDNT* 1:238-51.

Bultmann, Rudolf, ἀλήθεια κτλ, *ThWNT* 1:239-51.

Bultmann, Rudolf, καυχάομαι κτλ, *TDNT* 3:645-54.

Bultmann, Rudolf, πιστεύω κτλ, *TDNT* 6:174-228.

Burchard, Christoph, *Der dreizehnte Zeuge: Traditions- und kompositionsgeschichtliche Untersuchungen zu Lukas' Darstellung der Frühzeit des Paulus* (FRLANT 103), Göttingen: Vandenhoeck & Ruprecht 1970.

Burchard, Christoph, "Fußnoten zum neutestamentlichen Griechisch", *ZNW* 61 (1970) 157-71.

Burge, G.M., *Whose Land? Whose Promise? What Christians Are Not Being Told about Israel and the Palestinians*, Paternoster 2003.

Burkill, T.A., "The Competence of the Sanhedrin", *VC* 10 (1956) 80-96.

Burkill, T.A., "Ecclesiasticus", *IDB* 2:13-21.

Burkill, T.A., "The Trial of Jesus", *VC* 12 (1958) 1-18.

Burton, Ernst De Witt, *The Epistle to the Galatians* (ICC), Edinburgh: T. & T. Clark 1988 (repr.).

Byrne, Brendan J., *Romans* (SPS 6), Collegeville: Liturgical Press 1996.

Cadbury, H.J., *The Book of Acts in History*, London: A. & C. Black 1955.

Caird, G.B., *Paul's Letters from Prison* (NClB), Oxford: OUP 1976.

Caird, G.B., *Principalities and Powers*, Oxford: Clarendon Press 1956.

Calvin, John, *The Epistles of Paul The Apostle to the Galatians, Ephesians, Philippians and Colossians*, translated by T.H.L. Parker (CNTC 11), Grand Rapids: Wm B. Eerdmans 1993 (repr.), (Edinburgh: Oliver and Boyd [1]1965).

Calvin, John, *The Epistles of Paul The Apostle to the Romans and to the Thessalonians*, translated by Ross Mackenzie (CNTC 8), Grand Rapids: Wm B. Eerdmans 1976 (repr.) (Edinburgh: Oliver and Boyd [1]1960).

Calvin, John, *A Harmony of the Gospels: Matthew, Mark and Luke vol. III; James and Jude*, translated by A.W. Morrison (CNTC 3), Grand Rapids: Wm B. Eerdmans 1989 (repr.), (Saint Andrew Press [1]1972).

Calvin, John, *The Second Epistle of Paul to the Corinthians, and the Epistles to Timothy, Titus and Philemon*, translated by T.A. Smail (CNTC 10), Grand Rapids: Wm B. Eerdmans 1991 (repr.) (Edinburgh: Oliver and Boyd [1]1964).

Capes, David B., *Old Testament Yahweh Texts in Paul's Christology* (WUNT 2.47), Tübingen: J.C.B. Mohr (Paul Siebeck) 1992.

Carras, George P., "Romans 2,1-29: A Dialogue on Jewish Ideals", *Bib* 73 (1992) 183-207.

Carroll, John T. – Green, Joel B., *The Death of Jesus in Early Christianity*, Peabody: Hendrickson 1995.

Carson, D.A., *Divine Sovereignty and Human Responsibility: Biblical Perspectives in Tension* (MTL), London: Marshall, Morgan & Scott 1981.

Carson, D.A., *The Gospel according to John*, Leicester: IVP/Grand Rapids: Wm B. Eerdmans 1995 (repr.), ([1]1991).

Casey, P.M., *Aramaic Sources of Mark's Gospel* (SNTSMS 102), Cambridge: CUP 1998.

Casey, P.M., *From Jewish Prophet to Gentile God: The Origins and Development of New Testament Christology*, Cambridge: James Clarke 1991.

Casey, P.M., "Some Anti-Semitic Assumptions in the *Theological Dictionary of the New Testament*", *NovT* 41 (1999) 280-91.

Catchpole, David R., "The Problem of the Historicity of the Sanhedrin Trial", in Ernst Bammel (ed.), *Trial of Jesus: Cambridge Studies in honour of C.F.D. Moule* (SBT 2.13), London: SCM 1970, 47-65.

Cerfaux, Lucien, "Le privilège d'Israël selon saint Paul", in *Recueil Lucien Cerfaux: Études d'Exégèse et d'Histoire Religieuse de Monseigneur Cerfaux réunies à l'occasion de son soixante-dixième anniversaire* (BEThL 6-7), 2 vols, Gembloux: Éditions J. Duculot 1954, 2:339-64.

Chamberlain, Houston Stewart, *Die Grundlagen des 19. Jahrhunderts*, 2 vols, München: F. Bruckmann, [9]1909, ([1]1899).

Chamberlain, Houston Stewart, *Mensch und Gott. Betrachtungen über Religion und Christentum*, München: F. Bruckmann 1921.

Charlesworth, James H., *Old Testament Pseudepigrapha and the New Testament* (SNTSMS 54), Cambridge: CUP 1985.

Childs, Brevard S., *Exodus* (OTL), London: SCM 1974.

Childs, Brevard S., *Introduction to the Old Testament as Scripture*, London: SCM 1979.

Chilton, Bruce, "Caiaphas", *ABD* 1:803-6.

Chilton, Bruce – Neusner, Jacob, *Judaism in the New Testament: Practices and Beliefs*, London/New York: Routledge 1995.

444 *Bibliography*

von Christ, Wilhelm, *Geschichte der griechischen Litteratur 2.2: Die nachklassische Periode der griechischen Litteratur von 100 bis 530 nach Christus* (umgearbeitet von Wilhelm Schmid u. Otto Stählin*)* (HAW 7.2.2), München: C.H. Beck [6]1924.

Clements, R.E., *Isaiah 1-39* (NCB), London: Marshall, Morgan & Scott/Grand Rapids: Wm B. Eerdmans 1980.

Clines, David A., "The Second Letter to the Corinthians", in *BCFT*, 1462-88.

Cohen, Shaye J.D., *Josephus in Galilee and Rome: His Vita and Development as a Historian* (CSCT 8), Leiden: E.J. Brill 1979.

Cohen, Shaye J.D., *From Maccabeees to the Mishnah* (LEC 7), Philadelphia: Westminster Press 1987.

Cohen, Shaye J.D., "The Significance of Yavneh: Pharisees, Rabbis, and the End of Jewish Sectarianism", *HUCA* 54 (1984) 27-53.

Cohn, Leopold, "An Apocryphal Work Ascribed to Philo of Alexandria", *JQR* 19 (1898) 277-332.

Cohn-Sherbok, Dan, *The Crucified Jew: Twenty Centuries of Christian Anti-Semitism*, London: Harper Collins 1992.

Collins, John J., *Apocalypticism in the Dead Sea Scrolls* (LDSS), London/New York: Routledge 1997.

Collins, John J., "Early Jewish Apocalypticism", *ABD* 1:282-88.

Collins, John J., "Genre, Ideology and Social Movements in Jewish Apocalypticism", in John J. Collins and James H. Charlesworth (ed.), *Mysteries and Revelations: Apocalyptic Studies since the Uppsala Colloquium* (JSPSup 9), Sheffield: JSOT Press 1991, 11-32.

Collins, N.L., review of S. Mason, *Flavius Josephus on the Pharisees: A Composition-Critical Study*, *NovT* 34 (1992) 303-7.

Conzelmann, Hans, *Die Apostelgeschichte* (HzNT 7), Tübingen: J.C.B. Mohr (Paul Siebeck) [2]1972, ([1]1963).

Conzelmann, Hans, *Der erste Brief an die Korinther* (KEK 5), Göttingen: Vandenhoeck & Ruprecht [2]1981, ([1]1969).

Conzelmann, Hans, *Geschichte des Urchristentums* (GNT 5), Göttingen: Vandenhoeck & Ruprecht [6]1989.

Conzelmann, Hans, *Grundriß der Theologie des Neuen Testaments* (UTB 1446), Tübingen: J.C.B. Mohr (Paul Siebeck) [4]1987 (revised by Andreas Lindemann), ([1]1967).

Conzelmann, Hans, *An Outline of the Theology of the New Testament* (NTL) ET, London: SCM 1969.

Cramer, Winfrid, "Die Entwicklung im Bereich der orientalischen Kirchen", in Karl Heinrich Rengstorf and Siegfried von Kortzfleisch (ed.), *Kirche und Synagoge:*

Handbuch zur Geschichte von Christen und Juden. Darstellung mit Quellen, 2 vols, München: DTV 1988 (repr.), (^{1}1968-70), 176-209.

Cranfield, C.E.B., *A Critical and Exegetical Commentary on the Epistle to the Romans* (ICC), 2 vols, Edinburgh: T. & T. Clark 1 ^{2}1977, (^{1}1975); 2 1979.

Cross, F.M., *The Ancient Library of Qumran and Modern Biblial Studies*, Garden City, New York: Doubleday ^{2}1961.

Crossan, John Dominic, *Who Killed Jesus? Exposing the Roots of Anti-Semitism in the Gospel Story of the Death of Jesus*, New York: Harper Collins 1995.

Crossley, James G., *How Understanding the Importance of the Law in the Teaching of Jesus and in Earliest Christianity Can Help Date the Second Gospel*, Nottingham Ph.D. Dissertation 2002.

Cullmann, Oscar, *Christ and Time: The Primitive Christian Conception of Time and History* ET, Philadelphia: Westminster Press 1964.

Cullmann, Oscar, *The Christology of the New Testament* ET, London: SCM ^{2}1963, (^{1}1959).

Dahl, Nils Alstrup, "Der Name Israel: Zur Auslegung von Gal. 6,16", *Jud* 6 (1950) 161-70.

Dalferth, Ingolf U., "Karl Barth's eschatological realism", in S.W. Sykes (ed.), *Karl Barth: Centenary Essays*, Cambridge: CUP 1989, 14-45.

Dalferth, Ingolf U. – Stoellger, Philipp, "Wahrheit, Glaube und Theologie. Zur theologischen Rezeption zeitgenössischer wahrheitstheoretischer Diskussionen", *ThR* 66 (2001) 36-102.

Dahl, Nils Alstrup, *Das Volk Gottes: Eine Untersuchung zum Kirchenbewußtsein des Urchristentums*, Darmstadt: Wissenschaftliche Buchgesellschaft ^{2}1963, (^{1}1941).

Dalman, Gustaf H., *Arbeit und Sitte in Palästina* (BFCTh 2.33), 7 vols, Gütersloh: Verlag von C. Bertelmann 1928-42.

Daly, Robert J., "The Soteriological Significance of the Sacrifice of Isaac", *CBQ* 39 (1977) 45-75.

Davies, Douglas James, *Studies in Pastoral Theology and Social Anthropology*, Birmingham: University of Birmingham ^{2}1990, (^{1}1986).

Davies, Eryl W., *Numbers* (NCB), Grand Rapids: Wm B. Eerdmans 1995.

Davies, P.R., "The social world of apocalyptic writings", in R.E. Clements (ed.), *The World of Ancient Israel*, Cambridge: CUP 1989, 251-71.

Davies, P.R. – Chilton, B.D., "The Aqedah: A Revised Tradition History", *CBQ* 40 (1978) 514-46.

Davies, W.D., "Apocalyptic and Pharisaism", in *Christian Origins and Judaism*, London: Darton, Longman & Todd 1972, 19-30.

Davies, W.D., *The Gospel and the Land: Early Christianity and Jewish Territorial Doctrine*, Sheffield: Sheffield Academic Press 1994 (repr.), ^{1}1974.

Davies, W.D., "Paul and the People of Israel", in *Jewish and Pauline Studies*, London: SPCK 1984, 123-152 (= *NTS* 24 (1978) 4-39).

Davies, W.D., *Paul and Rabbinic Judaism: Some Rabbinic Elements in Pauline Theology*, London: SPCK ²1955, (¹1948).

Davies, W.D., "Paul and the Gentiles: A Suggestion Concerning Romans 11:13-24", in *Jewish and Pauline Studies*, London: SPCK 1984, 153-163.

Davies, W.D. - Allison, D.C., *A Critical and Exegetical Commentary on the Epistle to the Gospel According to Saint Matthew* (ICC), vol. 1, Edinburgh: T. & T. Clark 1988.

Davies, W.D. - Allison, D.C., *A Critical and Exegetical Commentary on the Epistle to the Gospel According to Saint Matthew* (ICC), vol. II, Edinburgh: T. & T. Clark 1991.

Dean, Lester, "Paul's 'Erroneous' Description of Judaism", in Leonard Swidler, Lewis John Eron, Gerard Sloyan and Lester Dean (ed.), *Bursting the Bonds? A Jewish-Christian Dialogue on Jesus and Paul*, Maryknoll, New York: Orbis Books 1990, 136-42.

Deines, Roland, *Die Pharisäer: Ihr Verständnis im Spiegel der christlichen und jüdischen Forschung seit Wellhausen und Graetz* (WUNT 101), Tübingen: J.C.B. Mohr (Paul Siebeck) 1997.

Deißmann, Adolf, *Paulus: Eine kultur- und religionsgeschichtliche Skizze*, Tübingen: J.C.B. Mohr (Paul Siebeck) ²1925.

Delius, Hans-Ulrich, (ed.), *Martin Luther: Studienausgabe Band 3*, Berlin: Evangelische Verlagsanstalt 1983.

Delling, Gerhard, "Merkmale der Kirche nach dem Neuen Testament", 13 (1966-67) 297-316.

Delling, Gerhard, τάσσω κτλ, *TDNT* 8:27-48.

Denney, James, "St. Paul's Epistle to the Romans", in W. Robertson Nicoll, *The Expositor's Greek Testament*, Grand Rapids: Eerdmans 1976 (repr), 2:555-725.

Denzinger, Heinrich, *Enchiridion symbolorum definitionum et declarationum de rebus fidei et morum* (ed. P. Hünermann), Freiburg: Herder 1991.

Dibelius, Martin, *An die Thessalonicher I-II. An die Philipper* (HzNT 11), Tübingen: J.C.B. Mohr (Paul Siebeck) ³1937.

Dickson, John P., *Mission-Commitment in Ancient Judaism and in the Pauline Communities: The shape, extent and background of early Christian mission* (WUNT 2.159), Tübingen: J.C.B. Mohr (Paul Siebeck) 2003.

Dietrich, E.K., *Die Umkehr (Bekehrung und Buße) im Alten Testament und im Judentum*, Stuttgart: W. Kohlhammer Verlag 1936.

Dietzfelbinger, Christian, *Die Berufung des Paulus als Ursprung seiner Theologie* (WMANT 58), Neukirchen-Vluyn: Neukirchener Verlag 1985.

Dinkler, Erich, "Die christliche Wahrheitsfrage und die Unabgeschlossenheit der Theologie als Wissenschaft. Bemerkungen zum wissenschaftlichen Werk Rudolf Bultmanns", in Otto Kaiser (ed.), *Gedenken an Rudolf Bultmann*, Tübingen: J.B.C. Mohr (Paul Siebeck) 1977, 15-40.

Dinkler, Erich, "Prädestination bei Paulus: Exegetische Bemerkungen zum Römerbrief", in *Signum Crucis: Aufsätze zum Neuen Testament und zur christlichen Archäologie*, Tübingen: J.C.B. Mohr (Paul Siebeck) 1967, 241-69.

Dinter, Artur, *Die Sünde wider die Liebe*, Leipzig/Hartenstein im Erzgebirge: Matthes und Thost 1922.

Dodd, C.H., *The Epistle of Paul to the Romans* (MNTC), London: Hodder and Stoughton 1949 (repr.), ([1]1932).

Dodd, C.H., "Matthew and Paul", in *New Testament Studies*, Manchester: Manchester University Press 1953, 53-66.

Dodd, C.H., "The Mind of Paul: II", in *New Testament Studies*, Manchester: Manchester University Press 1953, 83-128.

Donaldson, T.L., "The 'Curse of the Law' and the Inclusion of the Gentiles", *NTS* 32 (1986) 94-112.

Dreyfus, François, "Le passé et le présent d'Israël (Rom., 9,1-5; 11,1-24)", in Lorenzo de Lorenzi (ed.), *Die Israelfrage nach Röm 9-11* (MRvB.BÖA 3), Rom: Abtei von St Paul vor den Mauern 1977, 131-51.

Driver, S.R., *A Critical and Exegetical Commentary on Deuteronomy* (ICC), Edinburgh: T. & T. Clark 1973 (repr. of [3]1901, [1]1895).

Dunn, J.D.G., "4QMMT and Galatians", *NTS* 43 (1997) 147-53.

Dunn, J.D.G., *Christology in the Making: An Inquiry into the Origins of the Doctrine of the Incarnation*, London: SCM [2]1989, ([1]1980).

Dunn, J.D.G., *The Epistle to the Galatians* (BNTC), London: A. & C. Black 1993.

Dunn, J.D.G., "How Controversial Was Paul's Christology?", in M.C. De Boer (ed.), *From Jesus to John: Essays on Jesus and New Testament Christology in Honour of Marinus de Jonge* (JSNTSup 84), Sheffield: JSOT Press 1993, 148-67.

Dunn, J.D.G., "The Justice of God: A Renewed Perspective on Justification by Faith", *JTS* 43 (1992) 1-22.

Dunn, J.D.G., "The New Perspective on Paul", *BJRL* 65 (1983) 95-122.

Dunn, J.D.G., *The Partings of the Ways Between Christianity and Judaism and their Significance for the Character of Christianity*, London: SCM 1991.

Dunn, J.D.G., "Rom. 7,14-25 in the theology of Paul", *ThZ* 31 (1975) 257-73.

Dunn, J.D.G., *Romans* (WBC 38), 2 vols, Dallas, Texas: Word Books 1988.

Dunn, J.D.G., *The Theology of Paul the Apostle*, London/New York: T. & T. Clark 2003 (repr.), ([1]1998).

Dunn, J.D.G., "Two Covenants or One? The Interdependence of Jewish and Christian Identity", in Hubert Cancik, Hermann Lichtenberger and Peter Schäfer (ed.), *Geschichte–Tradition–Reflexion. Festschift für Martin Hengel zum 70. Geburtstag. Band III: Frühes Christentum*, Tübingen: J.C.B. Mohr (Paul Siebeck) 1996, 97-122.

Dunn, J.D.G., "What was the Issue between Paul and 'Those of the Circumcision'?", in Martin Hengel and Ulrich Heckel (ed.), *Paulus und das antike Judentum: Tübingen-Durham-Symposium im Gedenken an den 50. Todestag Adolf Schlatters* (WUNT 58), Tübingen: J.C.B. Mohr (Paul Siebeck) 1991, 295-313.

Dunn, J.D.G., "The Works of the Law and the Curse of the Law (Galatians 3:10-14)", *NTS* 31 (1985) 523-42.

Dupont, Jaques, "The Conversion of Paul, and its Influence on His Understanding of Salvation by Faith", in W. Ward Gasque and R.P. Martin (ed.), *Apostolic History and the Gospel: Biblical and Historical Essays presented to F.F. Bruce on his 60th Birthday*, Exeter: Paternoster 1970, 176-94.

Dupont-Sommer, André, *The Essene Writings from Qumran* ET, Oxford: Basil Blackwell 1961.

Durham, John I., *Exodus* (WBC 3), Waco: Word Books 1987.

Eckstein, Hans-Joachim, *Verheißung und Gesetz: Eine exegetische Untersuchung zu Galater 2,15-4,7* (WUNT 86), Tübingen: J.C.B. Mohr (Paul Siebeck) 1996.

Edwards, Thomas Charles, *A Commentary on the First Epistle to the Corinthians*, London: Hodder and Stoughton 1897.

Ego, Beate, *Im Himmel wie auf Erden: Studien zum Verhältnis von himmlischer und irdischer Welt im rabbinischen Judentum* (WUNT 2.34), Tübingen: J.C.B. Mohr (Paul Siebeck) 1989.

Eichholz, Georg, *Die Theologie des Paulus im Umriß*, Neukirchen-Vluyn: Neukirchener Verlag [5]1985, ([1]1972).

Eichrodt, Walther, *Theologie des Alten Testaments*, 2 vols, Stuttgart: Ehrenfried Klotz Verlag/Göttingen: Vandenhoeck & Ruprecht 1 [7]1962; 2 [4]1961, (originally appeared as 3 vols, 1 [1]1933; 2 [1]1935; 3 [1]1939).

Eichrodt, Walther, *Theology of the Old Testament* (OTL) ET, 2 vols, London: SCM 1961-67.

Eißfeldt, Otto, *The Old Testament: An Introduction* ET, Oxford: Basil Blackwell 1966.

Ellis, E. Earle, *The Old Testament in Early Christianity*, Tübingen: J.C.B. Mohr (Paul Siebeck) 1991.

Ellis, E. Earle, *Paul's Use of the Old Testament*, London/Edinburgh: Oliver and Boyd 1957.

Ellison, H.L., *The Message of the Old Testament*, Grand Rapids: Wm B. Eerdmans 1969.

Ellison, H.L., *The Mystery of Israel*, Exeter: Paternoster ³1976, (¹1966).

Enslin, Mortin S. – Zeitlin, Solomon, *The Book of Judith* (JAL 7), Leiden: E.J. Brill/Philadelphia: Dropsie University 1972.

Epstein, Isidore, *Judaism: A Historical Presentation*, Harmondsworth: Penguin 1977 (repr.), (¹1959).

Ericksen, Robert P., "Theologian in the Third Reich: The Case of Gerhard Kittel", *JCH* 12 (1977) 595-622.

Ericksen, Robert P., *Theologians under Hitler: Gerhard Kittel, Paul Althaus and Emanuel Hirsch*, New Haven/London: Yale University Press 1985.

Espy, John M., "Paul's 'Robust Conscience' Re-examined", *NTS* 31 (1985) 161-88.

Euler, Karl Friedrich, *Die Verkündigung vom Leidenden Gottesknecht aus Jes 53 in der Griechischen Bibel*, Stuttgart/Berlin: W. Kohlhammer Verlag 1934.

Fee, Gordon D., *The First Epistle to the Corinthians* (NICNT), Grand Rapids: Wm B. Eerdmans 1987.

Fee, Gordon D., *God's Empowering Presence: The Holy Spirit in the Letters of Paul*, Peabody: Hendrickson 1994.

Fee, Gordon D., *Paul's Letter to the Philippians* (NICNT), Grand Rapids: Eerdmans 1995.

Feldman, Louis H., "Hengel's *Judaism and Hellenism* in Retrospect", *JBL* 96 (1977) 371-82.

Feldman, Louis H., "Josephus", *ABD* 3:981-998.

Feldman, Louis H., "*Josephus'* Jewish Antiquities *and Pseudo-Philo's* Biblical Antiquities", in Louis H. Feldman and Gohei Hata (ed.), *Josephus, the Bible and History*, Detroit: Wayne State University Press 1989, 59-80.

Felgenhauer, Paul, *Bonum Nuncium Israeli quod offertur Populo Israel et Judae in hisce temporibus novissimis. De messiah quod scilicet Redemptio Israelis ab omnibus inquitatibus suis et Liberatio a captivitate et Adventus Messias gloriosus iam nunc proxime instent*, Amsterdam 1655.

Fichte, Johann Gottlieb, "Die Grundzüge des gegenwärtigen Zeitalters", in Immanuel Hermann Fichte (ed.), *Fichtes Werke Band VII: Zur Politik, Moral und Philosophie der Geschichte*, Berlin: Walter de Gruyter 1971 (repr.), 3-256.

Fiensy, David, "The Composition of the Jerusalem Church", in Richard Bauckham (ed.), *The Book of Acts in Its Palestinian Setting* (The Book of Acts in its First Century Setting vol. 4), Grand Rapids: Wm B. Eerdmans/Carlisle: Paternoster, 213-36.

Filson, Floyd V., *A New Testament History* (NTL), London: SCM Press 1965.

Fischer, Johannes, *Glaube als Erkenntnis*, München: Chr. Kaiser Verlag 1989.

Fischer, Johannes, "Über die Beziehung von Glaube und Mythos", *ZThK* 85 (1988) 303-28.

Fischer, Johannes, "Zum Wahrheitsanspruch der Theologie", *ThZ* 50 (1994) 93-107.

Fitzmyer, Joseph A., "Crucifixion in Ancient Palestine, Qumran Literature and the New Testament", *CBQ* 40 (1978) 493-513.

Fitzmyer, Joseph A., *Romans* (AB 33), New York: Doubleday 1993.

Fleischner, Eva, (ed.), *Auschwitz: Beginning of a New Era? Reflections on the Holocaust*, New York: Ktav 1977.

Flusser, David, "To What Extent is Jesus a Question for the Jews?", *Concilium: Theology in the Age of Renewal* 10.8 (1974) 162-66.

Forster, Roger T. – Marston, V. Paul, *God's Strategy in Human History*, Minneapolis: Bethany House Publishers 1973.

France, R.T., "The Worship of Jesus: A Neglected Factor in Christological Debate", in Harold H. Rowdon (ed.), *Christ the Lord: Studies in Christology presented to Donald Guthrie*, Leicester: IVP 1982, 17-36.

Fridrichsen, Anton, "Aus Glauben zu Glauben: Röm 1,17", *(ConNeo* 12), Lund: Gleerup 1948, 54.

Fridrichsen, Anton, "Der wahre Jude und sein Lob", *Symbolae Arctoae* 1 (1927) 39-49.

Friedrich, G. – Friedrich, J., "Kittel, Gerhard", *TRE* 19:221-25.

Friedrich, G. – Reyher, G., "Bibliographie Gerhard Kittel", *TLZ* 74 (1949) 171-75.

Fuchs, Ernst, *Studies of the Historical Jesus* (SBT 42) ET, London: SCM 1964.

Fung, Ronald Y.K., *The Epistle to the Galatians* (NICNT), Grand Rapids: Eerdmans 1988.

Furnish, Victor Paul, *II Corinthians* (AB 32A), New York: Doubleday 1984.

Gager, John G., "Some Notes on Paul's Conversion", *NTS* 27 (1981) 697-703.

Gager, John G., *The Origins of Anti-Semitism: Attitudes Towards Judaism in Pagan and Christian Antiquity*, New York/Oxford: OUP 1983.

Garland, David E., "The Composition and Unity of Philippians: Some Neglected Factors", *NovT* 27 (1985) 141-73.

Gaston, Lloyd, "Israel's Enemies in Pauline Theology", *NTS* 28 (1982) 400-23.

Gaston, Lloyd, *Paul and the Torah*, Vancouver: University of British Columbia Press, 1987.

Gaston, Lloyd, "Paul and the Torah" in Alan T. Davies (ed.), *Antisemitism and the Foundations of Christianity*, New York/Ramsey/Toronto: Paulist Press 1979, 48-71.

Gathercole, Simon J., *Where is Boasting? Early Jewish Soteriology and Paul's Response in Romans 1-5*, Grand Rapids/Cambridge U.K.: Wm B. Eerdmanns 2002.

Gaugler, Ernst, *Der Brief an die Römer* (P.SBG), 2 vols, Zürich: Zwingli Verlag 1 1958; 2 1952.

Georgi, Dieter, *Die Gegner des Paulus im 2. Korintherbrief: Studien zur religiösen Propaganda in der Spätantike* (WMANT 11), Neukirchen-Vluyn: Neukirchener Verlag 1964.

Gese, Hartmut, "Der auszulegende Text", in *Alttestamentliche Studien*, Tübingen: J.C.B. Mohr (Paul Siebeck) 1991, 266-82.

Gese, Hartmut, "Das biblische Schriftverständnis", in *Zur biblischen Theologie: Alttestamentliche Vorträge*, Tübingen: J.C.B. Mohr (Paul Siebeck) [3]1989, ([1]1977), 9-30.

Gese, Hartmut, "Die dreifache Gestaltwerdung des Alten Testaments", in *Alttestamentliche Studien*, Tübingen: J.C.B. Mohr (Paul Siebeck) 1991, 1-28.

Gese, Hartmut, "Erwägungen zur Einheit der biblischen Theologie", in *Vom Sinai zum Zion: Alttestamentliche Beiträge zur biblischen Theologie* (BEvTh 64), München: Chr. Kaiser Verlag [3]1990, ([1]1974), 11-30.

Gese, Hartmut, "Das Gesetz", in *Zur biblischen Theologie: Alttestamentliche Vorträge*, Tübingen: J.C.B. Mohr (Paul Siebeck) [3]1989, ([1]1977), 55-84.

Gese, Hartmut, "Hermeneutische Grundsätze der Exegese biblischer Texte", in *Alttestamentliche Studien*, Tübingen: J.C.B. Mohr (Paul Siebeck) 1991, 249-65.

Gese, Hartmut, "Die Sühne", in *Zur biblischen Theologie: Alttestamentliche Vorträge*, Tübingen: J.C.B. Mohr (Paul Siebeck) [3]1989, ([1]1977), 85-106.

Gese, Hartmut, "Tradition and Biblical Theology", in Douglas A. Knight (ed.), *Tradition and Theology in the Old Testament*, London: SPCK 1977, 301-26.

Gese, Michael, *Das Vermächtnis des Apostels: Die Rezeption der paulinischen Theologie im Epheserbrief* (WUNT 2.99), Tübingen: J.C.B. Mohr (Paul Siebeck) 1997.

Gethmann, Carl Friedrich, "Zu Heideggers Wahrheitsbegriff", *KantSt* 65 (1974) 186-200.

Gilbert, Martin, *The Routledge Atlas of the Arab-Israeli Conflict*, London/New York [7]2002, ([1]1974).

Gilliard, Frank D., "The Problem of the Antisemitic Comma Between 1 Thessalonians 2.14 and 15", *NTS* 35 (1989) 481-502.

Gnilka, Joachim, *Das Evangelium nach Markus* (EKK 2), 2 vols, Zürich/Einsiedeln/ Köln: Benziger Verlag/Neukirchen-Vluyn: Neukirchener Verlag 1 [5]1998, ([1]1978); 2 [4]1994, ([1]1978).

Gnilka, Joachim, *Das Matthäusevangelium* (HThKNT 1), 2 vols, Freiburg/Basel/ Wien: Herder 1 1986, 2 1988.

Gnilka, Joachim, *Paulus von Tarsus. Zeuge und Apostel* (HThKNTSup 6), Freiburg/ Basel/ Wien: Herder 1996.

Gnilka, Joachim, *Der Philipperbrief* (HThKNT 10.3), Freiburg/Basel/Wien: Herder [4]1987, ([1]1968).

Godet, Frederic L., *Commentary on Romans* ET, Grand Rapids: Kregel Publications 1977 (repr.), (^{1}1883).

Goldstein, Jonathan A., *1 Maccabees* (AB 41), Garden City, New York: Doubleday & Co. 1976.

Goodenough, E.R., "Philo's Exposition of the Law and his De Vita Mosis", *HTR* 27 (1933) 109-25.

Goodman, Martin, "Jewish Proselytizing in the First Century", in Judith Lieu, John North and Tessa Rajak (ed.), *The Jews among Pagans and Christians in the Roman Empire*, London/New York: Routledge 1992, 53-78.

Goppelt, Leonhard, "Israel und die Kirche, heute und bei Paulus", in *Christologie und Ethik: Aufsätze zum Neuen Testament*, Göttingen: Vandenhoeck & Ruprecht 1968, 165-89.

Grabbe, Lester L., "Chronography in 4 Ezra and 2 Baruch", in K.H. Richards (ed.), *Society of Biblical Literature 1981 Seminar Papers*, Chico: Scholars Press 1981, 49-63.

Grabbe, Lester L., *Judaism from Cyrus to Hadrian*, 2 vols, Minneapolis: Fortress Press 1992.

Grabbe, Lester L., "The Social Setting of Early Jewish Apocalypticism", *JSP* 4 (1989) 27-47.

Grabbe, Lester L., *Wisdom of Solomon*, Sheffield: Sheffield Academic Press 1997.

Graetz, Heinrich, *Geschichte der Juden*, 11 vols, Darmstadt: Wissenschaftliche Buchgesellschaft 1998, (repr.).

Graetz, Heinrich, *History of the Jews* ET, 6 vols, Philadelphia: JPS 1891-98.

Gräßer, Erich, "Antijudaismus bei Bultmann? Eine Erwiderung", *Der Alte Bund im Neuen: Exegetische Studien zur Israelfrage im Neuen Testament* (WUNT 35), Tübingen: J.C.B. Mohr (Paul Siebeck) 1985, 201-11.

Gräßer, Erich, "Zwei Heilswege? Zum theologischen Verhältnis von Israel und Kirche", *Der Alte Bund im Neuen: Exegetische Studien zur Israelfrage im Neuen Testament* (WUNT 35), Tübingen: J.C.B. Mohr (Paul Siebeck) 1985, 212-30 (= Paul-Gerhard Müller and Werner Stenger (ed.), *Kontinuität und Einheit: Für Franz Mußner*, Freiburg/Basel/Wien: Herder 1981, 411-29).

Green, E.M.B., "Syria and Cilicia–A Note", *ExpT* 71 (1959-60) 52-53.

Greenberg, Irving, "Cloud of Smoke, Pillar of Fire: Judaism, Christianity, and Modernity after the Holocaust", in Eva Fleischner (ed.), *Auschwitz: Beginning of a New Era? Reflections on the Holocaust*, New York: Ktav 1977, 7-53, 441-46.

Grundmann, Walter, "Paulus, aus dem Volke Israel, Apostel der Völker", *NovT* 4 (1960) 267-91.

Güting, Eberhard, "Amen, Eulogie, Doxologie. Eine textkritische Untersuchung", in Dietrich-Alex Koch and Hermann Lichtenberger (ed.), *Begegnungen zwischen Christentum und Judentum in Antike und Mittelalter. Festschrift für Heinz Schreckenberger* (SIJD 1), Göttingen: Vandenhoeck & Ruprecht 1993, 133-162.

Gundry, Robert H., "Grace, Works and Staying Saved in Paul", *Bib* 66 (1985) 1-38.

Gundry, Robert H., *Mark: A Commentary on His Apology for the Cross*, Grand Rapids: Wm B. Eerdmans 1993.

Gundry, Robert H., "The Moral Frustration of Paul before his Conversion: Sexual Lust in Romans 7:7-25", in Donald A. Hagner and Murray J. Harris (ed.), *Pauline Studies: Essays presented to Professor F.F. Bruce on his 70th Birthday*, Exeter: Paternoster 1980, 228-45.

Gundry Volf, Judith, *Paul and Perseverance: Staying in and Falling Away* (WUNT 2.37), Tübingen: J.C.B. Mohr (Paul Siebeck) 1989.

Gutteridge, Richard, *Open thy Mouth for the Dumb! The German Evangelical Church and the Jews*, Oxford: Basil Blackwell 1976.

Haacker, Klaus, *Der Brief des Paulus an die Römer* (ThHK 6), Leipzig: Evangelische Verlagsanstalt 1999.

Haacker, Klaus, "Werdegang des Apostels Paulus", *ANRW* 2.26.2 (1995) 815-938.

Haenchen, Ernst, *The Acts of the Apostles* ET, Oxford: Basil Blackwell 1971.

Haenchen, Ernst, *Die Apostelgeschichte* (KEK 3), Göttingen: Vandenhoeck & Ruprecht [7]1977, ([1]1956).

Hafemann, Scott J., *Paul, Moses, and the History of Israel: The Letter/Spirit Contrast and the Argument from Scripture in 2 Corinthians 3*, Peabody: Hendrickson 1996 (repr.), ([1]1995).

Hagner, Donald A., *Matthew 1-13* (WBC 33A), Dallas: Word Books 1993.

Hagner, Donald A., *Matthew 14-28* (WBC 33B), Dallas: Word Books 1995.

Hagner, Donald A., "Paul & Judaism: Testing the New Perspective", in Peter Stuhlmacher, *Revisiting Paul's Doctrine of Justification: A Challenge to the New Perspective*, Downers Grove: IVP 2001, 75-105.

Hahn, Ferdinand, *Christologische Hoheitstitel: Ihre Geschichte im frühen Christentum* (FRLANT 83), Göttingen: Vandenhoeck & Ruprecht [2]1964, ([1]1963).

Hahn, Ferdinand, *Mission in the New Testament* (SBT 47) ET, London: SCM 1965.

Hahn, Ferdinand, *Der urchristliche Gottesdienst* (SBS 41), Stuttgart: Verlag katholisches Bibelwerk 1970

Hahn, Ferdinand, "Zum Verständnis von Römer 11.26a: '... und so wird ganz Israel gerettet werden'", in M.D. Hooker and S.G. Wilson (ed.), *Paul and Paulinism: Essays in honour of C.K. Barrett*, London: SPCK 1982, 221-34

Hahneman, Geoffrey Mark, *The Muratorian Fragment and the Development of the Canon* (OTM), Oxford: Clarendon Press 1992.

Hanson, Anthony Tyrrell, "Abraham the Justified Sinner", in *Studies in Paul's Technique and Theology*, London: SPCK 1974, 52-66.

Hanson, Anthony Tyrrell, "Birth with Promise", in *Studies in Paul's Technique and Theology*, London: SPCK 1974, 87-103.

Hanson, Anthony Tyrrell, "Christ the First Fruits, Christ the Tree", in *Studies in Paul's Technique and Theology*, London: SPCK 1974, 104-25.

Hanson, Anthony Tyrrell, *Jesus Christ in the Old Testament*, London: SPCK 1965.

Hanson, Paul D., "Apocalypticism", *IDBSup* 28-34.

von Harnack, Adolf, *The Expansion of Christianity in the First Three Centuries* (TTL 19-20) ET, 2 vols, London: Williams & Norgate/New York: G.P. Putnam's 1904-5.

von Harnack, Adolf, *Marcion: Das Evangelium vom fremden Gott* (BKT), Darmstadt: Wissenschaftliche Buchgesellschaft 1996 (repr.), (²1924).

von Harnack, Adolf, *What is Christianity?* ET, London: Ernest Benn ⁵1958.

Harries, Richard, *After the Evil: Christianity and Judaism in the Shadow of the Holocaust*, Oxford: OUP 2003.

Harris, J. Rendel, "A Factor of Old Testament Influence in the New Testament", *ExpT* 37 (1925-26) 6-11.

Harris, Murray J., *Jesus as God: The New Testament Use of Theos in Reference to Jesus*, Grand Rapids: Baker Book House 1992.

Harvey, A.E., "The Intelligibility of Miracle", *Jesus and the Constraints of History: The Bampton Lectures, 1980*, London: Duckworth 1982, 98-119.

Harvey, Graham, *The True Israel: Uses of the Names Jew, Hebrew and Israel in Ancient Jewish and Early Christian Literature* (AGAJU 35), Leiden/New York/Köln: E.J. Brill 1996.

Hasel, G.F., "Sabbath", *ABD* 5:849-56.

Hawthorne, Gerald F., *Philippians* (WBC 43), Waco: Word Books 1983.

Hayes, John H. - Prussner, Frederick C., *Old Testament Theology*, London: SCM 1985.

Hays, Richard B., *Echoes of Scripture in the Letters of Paul*, New Haven/London: Yale University Press 1989.

Hemer, Colin J., *The Book of Acts in the Setting of Hellenistic History* (ed. by Conrad H. Gempf) (WUNT 49), Tübingen: J.C.B. Mohr (Paul Siebeck) 1989.

Heidegger, Martin, *Sein und Zeit*, Tübingen: Max Niemeyer ¹⁸2001.

Heiligenthal, Roman, "Lagarde, Paul Anton de", *TRE* 20: 375-78.

Heirich, Max, "Change of Heart: A Test of Some Widely Held Theories of Religious Conversion", *AJS* 83 (1977) 653-680.

Helmreich, Ernst Christian, *The German Churches Under Hitler: Background, Struggle, and Epilogue*, Detroit: Wayne State University Press 1979.

Hengel, Martin, "Der alte und der neue 'Schürer'", *JSS* 35 (1990) 19-72.

Hengel, Martin, "Between Jesus and Paul", in *Between Jesus and Paul: Studies in the Earliest History of Christianity*, London: SCM 1983, 1-29 (= "Zwischen Jesus und Paulus", *ZThK* 72 (1975) 151-206).

Hengel, Martin, *The Charismatic Leader and his Followers* (SNTW) ET, Edinburgh: T. & T. Clark 1981.

Hengel, Martin, *The Cross of the Son of God*, London: SCM 1986.

Hengel, Martin, "A Gentile in the Wilderness: My Encounter with Jews and Judaism", in James H. Charlesworth (ed.), *Overcoming Fear between Jews and Christians*, New York: Crossroad 1992, 67-83.

Hengel, Martin, *The 'Hellenization' of Judaea in the First Century after Christ* (in collaboration with Christoph Markschies) ET, London: SCM/Philadelphia: TPI 1989.

Hengel, Martin, "Der Jakobusbrief als antipaulinische Polemik", in *Paulus und Jakobus. Kleine Schriften III* (WUNT 141), Tübingen: J.C.B. Mohr (Paul Siebeck) 2002, 511-48 (original and shorter version appeared in Gerald F. Hawthorne and Otto Betz (ed.), *Tradition and Interpretation in the New Testament*, Grand Rapids: Wm B. Eerdmans/Tübingen: J.C.B. Mohr (Paul Siebeck) 1987, 248-78).

Hengel, Martin, *Judaism and Hellenism: Studies in their Encounter in Palestine during the Early Hellenistic Period* ET, 2 vols, London: SCM 1974.

Hengel, Martin, *Judentum und Hellenismus* (WUNT 10), Tübingen: J.C.B. Mohr (Paul Siebeck) [2]1973, ([1]1969).

Hengel, Martin, "The Origins of the Christian Mission", in *Between Jesus and Paul*, London: SCM 1983, 48-64 (= "Die Ursprünge der christlichen Mission", *NTS* 18 (1971) 15-38).

Hengel, Martin, "Präexistenz bei Paulus?", in Christof Landmesser, Hans-Joachim Eckstein and Hermann Lichtenberger (ed.), *Jesus Christus als die Mitte der Schrift* (BZNW 86), Berlin/New York: Walter de Gruyter 1997, 479-518.

Hengel, Martin, *The Pre-Christian Paul*, London: SCM 1991.

Hengel, Martin, "The Scriptures in Second Temple Judaism", in D.R.G. Beattie and M.J. McNamara (ed.), *The Aramaic Bible: Targums in their Historical Context* (JSOTSup 166), Sheffield: JSOT Press 1994, 158-75.

Hengel, Martin, "Die Septuaginta als 'christliche Schriftensammlung', ihre Vorgeschichte und das Problem ihres Kanons" (unter Mitarbeit von Roland Deines), in Martin Hengel und Anna Maria Schwemer (ed.), *Die Septuaginta zwischen Judentum und Christentum* (WUNT 72), Tübingen: J.C.B. Mohr (Paul Siebeck) 1994, 182-284.

Hengel, Martin, *The Septuagint as Christian Scripture: Its Prehistory and the Problem of Its Canon* (with the assistance of Roland Deines; introduction by Robert Hanhart) ET, Edinburgh/New York: T. & T. Clark 2002.

Hengel, Martin, "Die Synagogeninschrift von Stobi", *ZNW* 57 (1966) 145-83.

Hengel, Martin, "Die Ursprünge der Gnosis und das Urchristentum", in Jostein Ådna, Scott J. Hafemann and Otfried Hofius (ed.), *Evangelium – Schriftauslegung – Kirche. Festschrift für Peter Stuhlmacher zum 65. Geburtstag*, Göttingen: Vandenhoeck & Ruprecht 1997, 190-223.

Hengel, Martin, "Der vorchristliche Paulus", *ThBei* 21 (1990) 174-95.

Hengel, Martin, *The Zealots: Investigations into the Jewish Freedom Movement in the Period from Herod I until 70 A.D.* ET, Edinburgh: T. & T. Clark 1989.

Hengel, Martin, *Die Zeloten: Untersuchungen zur jüdischen Freiheitsbewegung in der Zeit von Herodes I. bis 70 n. Chr.* (AGAJU 1), Leiden/Köln: E.J. Brill ²1976, (¹1961).

Hengel, Martin – Deines, Roland, "E.P. Sanders' 'Common Judaism', Jesus, and the Pharisees", *JTS* 46 (1995) 1-70.

Hengel, Martin – Heckel, Ulrich, (ed.), *Paulus und das antike Judentum: Tübingen-Durham-Symposium im Gedenken an den 50. Todestag Adolf Schlatters* (WUNT 58), Tübingen: J.C.B. Mohr (Paul Siebeck) 1991.

Hengel, Martin – Schwemer, Anna Maria, *Paulus zwischen Damaskus und Antiochien: Die unbekannten Jahre des Apostels* (WUNT 108), Tübingen: J.C.B. Mohr (Paul Siebeck) 1998.

Hengel, Martin – Schwemer, Anna Maria, *Paul Between Damascus and Antioch: The Unknown Years*, London: SCM 1997.

Hennecke, E. – Schneemelcher, W., (ed.), *New Testament Apocrypha* ET, 2 vols, London: SCM 1973-74, (¹1963-65).

Herrmann, Siegfried, *A History of Israel in Old Testament Times* ET, London: SCM 1975.

Herzog, J.J. – Zöckler, O., "Socin und der Socinianismus", *RE*³ 18:459-80.

Hicks, F.C.N., *The Fullness of Sacrifice: An Essay in Reconciliation*, London: Macmillan and Co. 1930.

Hill, Craig C., *Hellenists and Hebrews: Reappraising Division within the Earliest Church*, Minneapolis: Fortress Press 1992.

Hill, David, *The Gospel of Matthew* (NCB), London: Oliphants 1972.

Hillerbrand, Hans J., "Martin Luther and the Jews", in James H. Charlesworth (ed.), *Jews and Christians: Exploring the Past, Present, and Future*, New York: Crossroad 1990, 127-45.

Hofius, Otfried, "Die Adam-Christus-Antithese und das Gesetz", in *Paulusstudien II* (WUNT 143), Tübingen: J.C.B. Mohr (Paul Siebeck) 2002, 62-103 (= J.D.G. Dunn (ed.), *Paul and the Mosaic Law: The Third Durham-Tübingen Research Symposium on Earliest Christianity and Judaism* (WUNT 89), Tübingen: J.C.B. Mohr (Paul Siebeck) 1996, 165-206).

Hofius, Otfried, *Der Christushymnus Philipper 2,6-11* (WUNT 17), Tübingen: J.C.B. Mohr ²1991, ¹(1976).

Hofius, Otfried, "Das Evangelium und Israel: Erwägungen zu Römer 9-11", in *Paulusstudien* (WUNT 51), Tübingen: J.C.B. Mohr (Paul Siebeck) 1989, 175-120 (= *ZThK* 83 (1986) 297-324).

Hofius, Otfried, "Gesetz und Evangelium nach 2. Korinther 3", in *Paulusstudien* (WUNT 51), Tübingen: J.C.B. Mohr (Paul Siebeck) 1989, 75-120 (= *Jahrbuch für Biblische Theologie Band 4: "Gesetz" als Thema Biblischer Theologie*, Neukirchen-Vluyn: Neukirchener Verlag 1989, 105-50).

Hofius, Otfried, "Das Gesetz des Mose und das Gesetz Christi", in *Paulusstudien* (WUNT 51), Tübingen: J.C.B. Mohr (Paul Siebeck) 1989, 50-74 (= *ZThK* 80 (1983) 262-86).

Hofius, Otfried, "Ist Jesus der Messias? Thesen", in *Jahrbuch für Biblische Theologie Band 8: Der Messias*, Neukirchen-Vluyn: Neukirchener Verlag 1993, 103-29.

Hofius, Otfried, "Der Mensch im Schatten Adams. Römer 7,7-25a", in *Paulusstudien II* (WUNT 143), Tübingen: J.C.B. Mohr (Paul Siebeck) 2002, 104-54.

Hofius, Otfried, *Paulusstudien* (WUNT 51), Tübingen: J.C.B. Mohr (Paul Siebeck) 1989.

Hofius, Otfried, "'Rechtfertigung des Gottlosen' als Thema biblischer Theologie", in *Paulusstudien* (WUNT 51), Tübingen: J.C.B. Mohr (Paul Siebeck) 1989, 121-47.

Hofius, Otfried, "Die Unabänderlichkeit des göttlichen Heilsratschlusses", *ZNW* 64 (1973) 135-45.

Hofius, Otfried, "Das vierte Gottesknechtlied in den Briefen des Neuen Testaments", *NTS* 39 (1993) 414-37.

Hofius, Otfried, "'Die Wahrheit des Evangeliums': Exegetische und theologische Erwägungen zum Wahrheitsanspruch der paulinischen Verkündigung", in *Paulusstudien II* (WUNT 143), Tübingen: J.C.B. Mohr (Paul Siebeck) 2002, 17-37.

Hofius, Otfried, "Wort Gottes und Glaube bei Paulus", in *Paulusstudien* (WUNT 51), Tübingen: J.C.B. Mohr (Paul Siebeck) 1989, 148-74.

Hollander, H.W. – de Jonge, M., *The Testaments of the Twelve Patriarchs: A Commentary* (SVTP 8), Leiden: E.J. Brill 1985.

Holsten, Carl, *Zum Evangelium des Petrus und des Paulus*, Rostock: Rittersche Hofbuchhandlung 1868.

Holtz, Traugott, "Christliche Interpolationen in 'Joseph and Aseneth'", *NTS* 14 (1967-68) 482-97.

Holtz, Traugott, *Der erste Brief an die Thessalonicher* (EKK 13), Zürich/Einsiedeln/Köln: Benziger Verlag/Neukirchen-Vluyn: Neukirchener Verlag 1986.

Holtz, Traugott, "Das Gericht über die Juden und die Rettung ganz Israels. 1. Thess 2,15f. und Röm 11,25f.", *Geschichte und Theologie des Urchristentums. Gesammelte Aufsätze* (WUNT 57), Tübingen: J.C.B. Mohr (Paul Siebeck) 1991, 313-25.

Hooker, Morna D., *The Gospel according to Mark* (BNTC), London: A. & C. Black 1991.

Hooker, Morna D., "Paul and 'Covenantal Nomism'", in M.D. Hooker and S.G. Wilson (ed.), *Paul and Paulinism: Essays in honour of C.K. Barrett*, London: SPCK 1982, 47-56.

Hoover, R.W., "The Harpagmos Enigma: A Philological Solution", *HTR* 64 (1971) 95-119.

Hübner, Hans, *Das Gesetz bei Paulus: Ein Beitrag zum Werden der paulinischen Theologie* (FRLANT 119), Göttingen: Vandenhoeck & Ruprecht ³1982, (¹1978).

Hübner, Hans, *Law in Paul's Thought* (SNTW) ET, Edinburgh: T. & T. Clark 1984.

Hübner, Hans, *Nietzsche und das Neue Testament*, Tübingen: J.C.B. Mohr (Paul Siebeck) 2000.

Hübner, Hans, "Pauli theologiae proprium", *NTS* 26 (1980) 445-473.

Hübner, Hans, *An Philemon/An die Kolosser/An die Epheser* (HzNT 12), Tübingen: J.C.B. Mohr (Paul Siebeck) 1997.

Hughes, Philip Edgcumbe, *The Second Epistle to the Corinthians* (NICNT), Grand Rapids: Wm B. Eerdmans 1962.

Hultgren, Arland J., "Paul's Pre-Christian Persecutions of the Church: Their Purpose, Locale, and Nature", *JBL* 95 (1976) 97-111.

Hurd, John C., "Paul Ahead of His Time: 1 Thess. 2:13-16", in Peter Richardson (ed.), *Anti-Judaism in Early Christianity: Volume 1: Paul and the Gospels* (SCJ 2), Ontario: Wilfrid Laurier University Press 1986, 21-36.

Hurst, L.D., "Re-enter the Pre-existent Christ in Philippians 2.5-11?", *NTS* 32 (1986) 449-57.

Hyatt, J. Philip, *Exodus* (NCB), London: Marshall, Morgan & Scott/Grand Rapids: Wm B. Eerdmans ²1980, (¹1971).

Jacobson, Howard, *A Commentary on Pseudo-Philo's Liber Antiquitatum Biblicarum with Latin Text and English Translation* (AGAJU 31), 2 vols, Leiden/New York/Köln: E.J. Brill 1996.

Japhet, Sara, *I & II Chronicles* (OTL), London: SCM 1993.

Jeremias, Joachim, *Die Abendmahlsworte Jesu*, Göttingen: Vandenhoeck & Ruprecht ⁴1967, (¹1935).

Jeremias, Joachim, "Billerbeck, Paul", *TRE* 6:640-42.

Jeremias, Joachim, *The Eucharistic Words of Jesus* ET, London: SCM 1966.

Jeremias, Joachim, "Einige vorwiegend sprachliche Beobachtungen zu Röm 11,25-36", in Lorenzo de Lorenzi (ed.), *Die Israelfrage nach Röm 9-11* (MRvB.BÖA 3), Rom: Abtei von St Paul vor den Mauern 1977, 193-216.

Jeremias, Joachim, *Jerusalem in the Time of Jesus* ET, Philadelphia: Fortress Press 1969.

Jeremias, Joachim, *Jesu Verheißung für die Völker* (Franz Delitzsch-Vorlesungen 1953), Stuttgart: W. Kohlhammer Verlag 1956.

Jeremias, Joachim, *Jesus' Promise to the Nations* ET (SBT 24), London: SCM 1958.

Jeremias, Joachim, *Neutestamentliche Theologie I*, Gütersloh: Gütersloher Verlagshaus Gerd Mohn 1971.

Jeremias, Joachim, *The Parables of Jesus* ET, London: SCM [3]1972, ([1]1954).

Jeremias, Joachim, *Theology of the New Testament, Volume One: The Proclamation of Jesus* ET, London: SCM 1971.

Jeremias, Joachim, "Zur Geschichtlichkeit des Verhörs Jesu vor dem Hohen Rat", in *Abba: Studien zur neutestamentlichen Theologie und Zeitgeschichte*, Göttingen: Vandenhoeck & Ruprecht 1966, 139-44.

Jeremias, Joachim, πολλοί, *TDNT* 6:536-45

Jewett, Robert, "The Agitators and the Galatian Congregation", *NTS* 17 (1970-71) 198-212.

Jewett, Robert, *The Thessalonian Correspondence: Pauline Rhetoric and Millenarian Piety* (FFNT), Philadelphia: Fortress Press 1986.

Jocz, Jacób, *The Jewish People and Jesus Christ: A Study in the Relationship between the Jewish People and Jesus Christ*, London: SPCK 1949.

Johnson, Luke Timothy, "The New Testament's Anti-Jewish Slander and the Conventions of Ancient Polemic", *JBL* 108 (1989) 419-41.

Johnson, Marshall D., *The Purpose of the Biblical Genealogies* (SNTSMS 8), Cambridge: CUP 1969.

Jonas, Hans, "Der Gottesbegriff nach Auschwitz: Eine jüdische Stimme", in O. Hofius (ed.), *Reflexionen finsterer Zeit: Zwei Vorträge von Fritz Stern und Hans Jonas*, Tübingen: J.C.B. Mohr (Paul Siebeck) 1984, 61-86.

Jones, Gwilym. H., *1 and 2 Kings, Volume I* (NCB), Grand Rapids: Wm B. Eerdmans/London: Marshall, Morgan & Scott 1994 (repr.), ([1]1984).

Jülicher, Adolf, "Der Brief an die Römer", in Otto Baumgarten et al. (ed.), *Die Schriften des Neuen Testaments, Zweiter Band*, Göttingen: Vandenhoeck & Ruprecht 1917, 223-335.

Jüngel, Eberhard, *Karl Barth: A Theological Legacy* ET, Philadelphia: Westminster Press 1986.

Jüngel, Eberhard, "Die Freiheit der Theologie", in *Entsprechungen: Gott – Wahrheit – Mensch. Theologische Erörterungen*, München: Chr. Kaiser Verlag 1986, 11-36.

Jüngel, Eberhard, "Glauben und Verstehen. Zum Theologiebegriff Rudolf Bultmanns", in *Wertlose Wahrheit. Zur Identität und Relevanz des christlichen Glaubens. Theologische Erörterungen III* (BevTh 107), München: Chr. Kaiser Verlag 1990, 16-77.

Jüngel, Eberhard, "Gottesgewißheit", in *Entsprechungen: Gott – Wahrheit – Mensch. Theologische Erörterungen*, München: Chr. Kaiser Verlag 1986, 252-64.

Jüngel, Eberhard, "Gottes ursprüngliches Anfangen als Schöpferische Selbstbegrenzung", in *Wertlose Wahrheit. Zur Identität und Relevanz des christlichen Glaubens. Theologische Erörterungen III* (BevTh 107), München: Chr. Kaiser Verlag 1990, 151-62.

Jüngel, Eberhard, "Jesu Wort und Jesus als Wort Gottes. Ein hermeneutischer Beitrag zum christologischen Problem", in *Unterwegs zur Sache. Theologische Bemerkungen* (BEvTh 61), München: Chr. Kaiser Verlag 1988, 126-44.

Jüngel, Eberhard, *Paulus und Jesus. Eine Untersuchung zur Präzisierung der Frage nach dem Ursprung der Christologie* (HUTh 2), Tübingen: J.C.B. Mohr (Paul Siebeck) [6]1986.

Jüngel, Eberhard, "Vom Tod des lebendigen Gottes. Ein Plakat", in *Unterwegs zur Sache. Theologische Bemerkungen* (BEvTh 61), München: Chr. Kaiser Verlag 1988, 105-25.

Jüngel, Eberhard, "Die Wahrheit des Mythos und die Notwendigkeit der Entmythologisierung", in *Indikative der Gnade – Imperative der Freiheit*, Tübingen: J.C.B. Mohr (Paul Siebeck) 2000, 40-57.

Jüngel, Eberhard, "Wertlose Wahrheit. Christliche Wahrheitserfahrung im Streit gegen die 'Tyrannei der Werte'", in *Wertlose Wahrheit. Zur Identität und Relevanz des christlichen Glaubens. Theologische Erörterungen III* (BevTh 107), München: Chr. Kaiser Verlag 1990, 90-109.

Juster, Jean, *Les Juifs dans l'Empire romain*, 2 vols, Paris: Librairie Paul Geuthner 1914.

Kallas, J., "Romans xiii.1-7: An Interpretation", *NTS* 11 (1964-65) 365-74.

Kampling, Rainer, "Eine auslegungsgeschichtliche Skizze zu 1 Thess 2,14-16", in Dietrich-Alex Koch and Hermann Lichtenberger (ed.), *Begegnungen zwischen Christentum und Judentum in Antike und Mittelalter. Festschrift für Heinz Schreckenberger* (SIJD 1), Göttingen: Vandenhoeck & Ruprecht 1993, 183-213.

Käsemann, Ernst, *Exegetische Versuche und Besinnungen, Bd 2*, Göttingen: Vandenhoeck & Ruprecht [3]1970, ([1]1964).

Käsemann, Ernst, "Geist und Buchstabe", in *Paulinische Perspektiven*, Tübingen: J.C.B. Mohr (Paul Siebeck) [2]1972, ([1]1969), 237-85.

Käsemann, Ernst, "Die Legimität des Apostels", *ZNW* 41 (1942) 33-71.

Käsemann, Ernst, "Paul and Israel", in *New Testament Questions of Today* (NTL) ET, London: SCM 1969, 183-87 (= "Paulus und Israel", in *Exegetische Versuche und Besinnungen, Bd 2*, 194-97).

Käsemann, Ernst, "On the Subject of Primitive Christian Apocalyptic", in *New Testament Questions of Today* (NTL) ET, London: SCM 1969, 108-37 (= "Zum Thema der urchristlichen Apokalyptik", *ZThK* 59 (1962) 257-84 = *Exegetische Versuche und Besinnungen, Bd 2*, 105-31).

Käsemann, Ernst, *An die Römer* (HzNT 8a), Tübingen: J.C.B. Mohr (Paul Siebeck) ⁴1980, (¹1973).

Käsemann, Ernst, *Romans* ET, London: SCM 1980.

Käsemann, Ernst, "Römer 13,1-7 in unserer Generation", *ZThK* 56 (1959) 316-76.

Katz, Steven Theodore, *Kontinuität und Diskontinuität zwischen christlichem und nationalsozialistischem Antisemitismus*, Tübingen: J.C.B. Mohr (Paul Siebeck) 2001.

Keck, Leander E., "Christology, Soteriology, and the Praise of God (Romans 15:7-13)", in Robert T. Fortuna and Beverly R. Gaventa (ed.), *The Conversation Continues: Studies in Paul and John in Honor of J. Louis Martyn*, Nashville: Abingdon 1990, 85-97.

Keller, W., *Gottes Treue – Israels Heil. Röm 11,25-27 – Die These vom 'Sonderweg' in der Diskussion* (SBB 40), Stuttgart: Katholisches Bibelwerk 1998.

Kilpatrick, George D., "BΛΕΠΕΤΕ, Philippians 3:2", in Matthew Black and Georg Fohrer (ed.), *In Memoriam Paul Kahle* (BZAW 103), Berlin: A. Töpelmann 1968.

Kim, Seyoon, *The Origin of Paul's Gospel* (WUNT 2.4), Tübingen: J.C.B. Mohr (Paul Siebeck) 1981.

Kim, Seyoon, *Paul and the New Perspective: Second Thoughts on the Origin of Paul's Gospel*, Grand Rapids/Cambridge: Wm B. Eerdmans 2002.

Kirk, Kenneth E., *Some Principles of Moral Theology*, London: Longmans, Green and Co. 1920.

Kittel, Gerhard, *Die Judenfrage*, Stuttgart: W. Kohlhammer Verlag 1933.

Kittel, Gerhard, "Die Judenfrage im Lichte der Bibel", *Glaube und Volk* 2 (1933) 152-55.

Kittel, Gerhard, "Neutestamentliche Gedanken zur Judenfrage", *AELKZ* 66 (1933) 903-7.

Kittel, Gerhard, "Die Stellung des Jakobus zu Judentum und Heidenchristentum", *ZNW* 30 (1931) 145-57.

Kittel, Gerhard, λέγω κτλ, *TDNT* 4:77-143.

Kjaer-Hansen, Kai - Kvarme, Ole Chr. M., *Messianische Juden: Judenchristen in Israel* (ET 67), Erlangen: Verlag der Ev.-Luth. Mission 1983.

Klaiber, Walter, *Rechtfertigung und Gemeinde: Eine Untersuchung zum paulinischen Kirchenverständnis* (FRLANT 127), Göttingen: Vandenhoeck & Ruprecht 1982.

Klappert, Bertold, *Israel und die Kirche: Erwägungen zur Israellehre Karl Barths* (ThExH 207), München: Chr. Kaiser Verlag 1980.

Klappert, Bertold, *Miterben der Verheißung: Beiträge zum jüdisch-christlichen Dialog* (NBST 25), Neukirchen-Vluyn: Neukirchener Verlag 2000.

Klappert, Bertold, "Traktat für Israel (Römer 9-11)", in Martin Stöhr (ed.), *Jüdische Existenz und die Erneuerung der christlichen Theologie: Versuch der Bilanz des christlich-jüdischen Dialogs für die Systematische Theologie* (ACJD 11), München: Chr. Kaiser Verlag 1981, 58-137.

Klappert, Bertold, "Der Verlust und die Wiedergewinnung der israelitischen Kontur der Leidensgeschichte Jesu (das Kreuz, das Leiden, das Paschamahl, der Prozeß Jesu), in Hans Hermann Henrix and Martin Stöhr (ed.), *Exodus und Kreuz im ökumenischen Dialog zwischen Juden und Christen. Diskussionsbeiträge für Religionsunterricht und Erwachsenenbildung* (ABPB 8), Aachen: Einhard-Verlag 1978, 107-53.

Klappert, Bertold – Starck, Helmut, (ed.), *Umkehr und Erneuerung: Erläuterungen zum Synodalbeschluß der Rheinischen Landessynode 1980 "Zur Erneuerung des Verhältnisses von Christen und Juden"*, Neukirchen-Vluyn: Neukirchener Verlag 1980.

Klausner, Joseph, *From Jesus to Paul* ET, New York: Macmillan 1944, (^{1}1939).

Klausner, Joseph, *Jesus von Nazareth: Seine Zeit, sein Leben und seine Lehre* GT, Berlin: Jüdischer Verlag ^{2}1934, (^{1}1930) (Hebrew 1922).

Klein, Charlotte, *Anti-Judaism in Christian Theology* ET, London: SPCK 1978.

Klein, Charlotte, *Theologie und Anti-Judaismus*, München, Chr. Kaiser Verlag 1975.

Klein, Günter, "'Christlicher Antijudaismus': Bemerkungen zu einem semantischen Einschüchterungsversuch", *ZThK* 79 (1982) 411-50.

Klumbies, Paul-Gerhard, "Israels Vorzüge und das Evangelium von der Gottesgerechtigkeit in Römer 9-11", in Hans-Peter Stähli (ed.), *Wort und Dienst: Jahrbuch der Kirchlichen Hochschule Bethel*, Kirchliche Hochschule Bethel, Bielefeld NF 18 (1985), 135-157.

Knibb, M.A., "Apocalyptic and Wisdom in 4 Ezra", *JSJ* 13 (1982) 56-74.

Knibb, M.A. – Coggins, R.J., *The First and Second Books of Esdras* (CBC), Cambridge: CUP 1979.

Knight, George A.F., "Israel – the land and resurrection", in D.W. Torrance (ed.), *The Witness of the Jews to God*, Edinburgh: Handsel Press 1982, 32-41.

Knight, George W., *Commentary on the Pastoral Epistles* (NIGTC), Grand Rapids: Eerdmans/Carlisle: Paternoster 1992.

Knox, John, *Chapters in a Life of Paul* (revised by the author and edited and introduced by Douglas R.A. Hare), London: SCM ^{2}1989, (^{1}1950).

Koch, Dietrich-Alex, *Die Schrift als Zeuge des Evangeliums: Untersuchungen zur Verwendung und zum Verständnis der Schrift bei Paulus* (BHTh 69), Tübingen: J.C.B. Mohr (Paul Siebeck) 1986.

Koch, Klaus, "Einleitung", in Klaus Koch und Johann Michael Schmidt (ed.), *Apokalyptik* (WdF 365), Darmstadt: Wissenschaftliche Buchgesellschaft 1982, 1-29.

Kolde, Theodor, "Schwabacher Artikel", *RE*^{3} 18.1-2.

Köster, Helmut, τέμνω κτλ, *TDNT* 8:106-12.

Kötting, Bernhard, "Die Entwicklung im Osten bis Justinian", in Karl Heinrich Rengstorf and Siegfried von Kortzfleisch (ed.), *Kirche und Synagoge: Handbuch zur Geschichte von Christen und Juden. Darstellung mit Quellen*, 2 vols, München: DTV 1988 (repr.), ([1]1968-70), 136-175.

Kraus, Hans-Joachim, *Psalms 60-150: A Continental Commentary*, Minneapolis: Fortress Press 1993.

Kraus, Hans-Joachim, *Systematische Theologie im Kontext biblischer Geschichte und Eschatologie*, Neukirchen-Vluyn: Neukirchener Verlag 1983.

Kraus, Hans-Joachim, "Theologie als Traditionsbildung? Zu Hartmut Gese, 'Vom Sinai zum Zion'", *EvTh* 36 (1976) 498-507.

Kraus, Wolfgang, "'Eretz Jisrael'. Die territoriale Dimension in der jüdischen Tradition als Anfrage an die christliche Theologie", in Martin Karrer, Wolfgang Kraus and Otto Merk (ed.), *Kirche und Volk Gottes: Festschrift für Jürgen Roloff zum 70. Geburtstag*, Neukirchen-Vluyn: Neukirchener 2000, 19-41.

Kraus, Wolfgang, *Das Volk Gottes: Zur Grundlegung der Ekklesiologie bei Paulus* (WUNT 85), Tübingen: J.C.B. Mohr (Paul Siebeck) 1996.

Kreitzer, L. Joseph, *Jesus and God in Paul's Eschatology* (JSNTSup 19), Sheffield: JSOT Press 1987.

Kremers, Heinz, "Mission an Israel in heilsgeschichtlicher Sicht", in Heinz Kremers and Erich Lubahn (ed.), *Mission an Israel in heilsgeschichtlicher Sicht*, Neukirchen-Vluyn: Neukirchener Verlag 1985, 65-91.

Kühl, Ernst, *Der Brief des Paulus an die Römer*, Leipzig: Quelle & Meyer 1913.

Kuhn, Heinz-Wolfgang, "Die Bedeutung der Qumrantexte für das Verständnis des Galaterbriefs", in George J. Brooke (ed.), *New Qumran Texts and Studies: Proceedings of the First Meeting of the International Orgnization for Qumran Studies, Paris 1992* (STDJ 15), Leiden/New York/Köln: E.J. Brill 1994, 169-221.

Kuhn, Karl Georg, προσήλυτος, *TDNT* 6:727-44.

Kuhn, Thomas, *The Structure of Scientific Revolutions*, Chicago/London: The University of Chicago Press 1962.

Kümmel, Werner Georg, "Jesus und Paulus", in *Heilsgeschehen und Geschichte: Gesammelte Aufsätze 1933-1964* (MThS 3), Marburg: N.G. Elwert Verlag 1965, 439-56.

Kümmel, Werner Georg, "Das literarische und geschichtliche Problem des ersten Thessalonicherbriefes", in *Heilsgeschehen und Geschichte, Band I: Gesammelte Aufsätze 1933-1964* (MThS 3), Marburg: N.G. Elwert Verlag 1965, 406-16 (= *Neotestamentica et Patristica: Eine Freundesgabe Herrn Professor Dr. Oscar Cullmann zu seinem 60. Geburtstag überreicht* NovTSup 6), Leiden: E.J. Brill 1962, 213-27).

Küng, Hans, *Judaism: The Religious Situation of our Time* ET, London: SCM 1992.

Kuss, Otto, *Der Römerbrief*, 3 vols, Regensburg: Verlag Friedrich Pustet 1 1957; 2 1959; 3 1978.

Kuss, Otto, "Zu Römer 9,5", in Johannes Friedrich, Wolfgang Pöhlmann, and Peter Stuhlmacher (ed.), *Rechtfertigung: Festschrift für Ernst Käsemann zum 70. Geburtstag*, Tübingen: J.C.B. Mohr (Paul Siebeck)/Göttingen: Vandenhoeck & Ruprecht 1976, 291-303.

Kutsch, Ernst, "Gesetz und Gnade. Probleme des alttestamentlichen Bundesbegriffs", *ZAW* 69 (1967) 18-35.

Kutsch, Ernst, *Neues Testament-Neuer Bund? Eine Fehlübersetzung wird korrigiert*, Neukirchen-Vluyn: Neukirchener Verlag 1978.

Kutsch, Ernst, בְּרִית, *THAT* 1:339-52.

Lackmann, Max, *Vom Geheimnis der Schöpfung*, Stuttgart: Evangelisches Verlagswerk 1952.

de Lagarde, Paul Anton, "Über das Verhältnis des deutschen Staates zu Theologie, Kirche und Religion. Ein Versuch, Nicht-Theologen zu orientieren" (1873), in K. Fischer (ed.), *Deutsche Schriften*, München: J.K. Lehrmann 1934, 45-90.

Lake, Kirsopp, *The Earlier Epistles of St. Paul: Their Motive and Origin*, London: Rivingtons 1911.

Lake, Kirsopp – Cadbury, Henry J., in F.J. Foakes Jackson and K. Lake (ed.), *The Beginnings of Christianity, Part I: The Acts of the Apostles, Vol. IV*, London: Macmillan 1933.

Lagrange, M.-J., *Saint Paul: Épître aux Romains* (Étbib 13), Paris: J. Gabalda ^{2}1922, (^{1}1915).

Landmesser, Christof, *Wahrheit als Grundbegriff neutestamentlicher Wissenschaft* (WUNT 113), Tübingen: J.C.B. Mohr (Paul Siebeck) 1999.

Lang, Friedrich, *Die Briefe an die Korinther* (NTD 7), Göttingen: Vandenhoeck & Ruprecht 1986.

de Lange, Nicholas R.M. – Thoma, Clemens, "Antisemitismus I", *TRE* 3:113-19.

Larsson, Edvin, "Die Hellenisten und die Urgemeinde", *NTS* 33 (1987) 205-25.

Leenhardt, Franz J., *The Epistle to the Romans: A Commentary* ET, London: Lutterworth 1961.

Lenker, John Nicholas (ed.), *Sermons of Martin Luther: The Church Postils*, 8 vols, Grand Rapids: Baker Books 1995 (repr.), ^{1}1905-9.

Lenski, R.C.H., *The Interpretation of the Acts of the Apostles*, Minneapolis: Augsburg Publishing House 1961 (repr.), (^{1}1934).

Lenski, R.C.H., *The Interpretation of St. Paul's Epistle to the Romans*, Minneapolis: Augsburg Publishing House 1961 (repr.), (^{1}1936).

Levinskaya, Irina, *The Book of Acts in Its Diaspora Setting* (The Book of Acts in its First Century Setting vol. 5), Grand Rapids: Wm B. Eerdmans/Carlisle: Paternoster 1996.

Levison, John R., "Torah and Covenant in Pseudo Philo's *Liber Antiquitatum Biblicarum*", in Friedrich Avemarie and Hermann Lichtenberger (ed.), *Bund und Tora: Zur theologischen Begriffsgeschichte in alttestamentlicher, frühjüdischer und urchristlicher Tradition* (WUNT 92), Tübingen: J.C.B. Mohr (Paul Siebeck) 1996, 111-27.

Lichtenberger, Hermann, "Auferstehung in den Qumranfunden", in Friedrich Avemarie and Hermann Lichtenberger (ed.), *Auferstehung – Resurrection: The Fourth Durham-Tübingen Research Symposium, Resurrection, Transfiguration and Exaltation in Old Testament, Ancient Judaism and Early Christianity* (WUNT 135), Tübingen: J.C.B. Mohr (Paul Siebeck) 2001, 79-91.

Lietzmann, Hans, "Bemerkungen zum Prozeß Jesu II", in Kurt Aland (ed.), *Kleine Schriften II: Studien zum Neuen Testament* (TU 68), Berlin: Akademie Verlag 1958, 269-76 (= *ZNW* 31 (1932) 78-84).

Lietzmann, Hans, *An die Korinther I/II* (HzNT 9), Tübingen: J.C.B. Mohr (Paul Siebeck) [5]1969 (supplemented by Werner Georg Kümmel).

Lietzmann, Hans, "Der Prozeß Jesu", in Kurt Aland (ed.), *Kleine Schriften II: Studien zum Neuen Testament* (TU 68), Berlin: Akademie Verlag 1958, 251-63 (= *SPAW.PH* 14 (1934) 313-322).

Lietzmann, Hans, *An die Römer* (HzNT 8), Tübingen: J.C.B. Mohr (Paul Siebeck) [4]1933.

Lightfoot, John, *Commentary on the New Testament from the Talmud and Hebraica*, Peabody: Hendrickson 1995 (repr. from the OUP edition of 1859).

Lightfoot, J.B., *St. Paul's Epistle to the Galatians*, Peabody: Hendrickson 1993 (repr.), ([1]1865).

Lightfoot, J.B., *St. Paul's Epistle to the Philippians*, Peabody: Hendrickson 1993 (repr.), ([1]1868).

Lilje, Hanns, *Martin Luther in Selbstzeugnissen und Bilddokumenten*, Hamburg: Rowohlt 1965.

Lindars, Barnabas, "The Old Testament and Universalism in Paul", *BJRL* 69 (1986-87) 511-27.

Lindeskog, Gösta, *Die Jesusfrage im neuzeitlichen Judentum. Ein Beitrag zur Geschichte der Leben-Jesu-Forschung* (AMNSU 8), Uppsala: Almquist & Wiksell 1938.

Lindeskog, Gösta, "Der Prozess Jesu im jüdisch-christlichen Religionsgespräch", in Otto Betz, Martin Hengel and Peter Schmidt (ed.), *Abraham unser Vater: Juden und Christen im Gespräch über die Bibel. Festschrift für Otto Michel zum 60. Geburtstag*, Leiden: E.J. Brill 1963, 325-36.

Locke, John, *A Paraphrase and Notes on the Epistles of St Paul*, ed. by Arthur W. Wainwright (The Clarendon Edition of the Works of John Locke), 2 vols, Oxford: Clarendon Press 1987.

Lohmeyer, Ernst, *Der Brief an die Philipper* (KEK 9), Göttingen: Vandenhoeck & Ruprecht [14]1974, ([8]1930).

Lohse, Eduard, *Der Brief an die Römer* (KEK 4), Göttingen: Vandenhoeck & Ruprecht [15]2003.

Lohse, Eduard, *Colossians and Philemon* (Hermeneia) ET, Philadelphia: Fortress Press 1971.

Lohse, Eduard, "Theologie der Rechtfertigung im kritischen Disput - zu einigen neuen Perspektiven in der Interpretation der Theologie des Apostels Paulus", *GGA* 249 (1997) 66-81.

Lohse, Eduard, σάββατον κτλ, *TDNT* 7:1-35.

Lohse, Eduard, συνέδριον, *TDNT* 7:860-71.

Longenecker, Bruce W., *Eschatology and the Covenant: A Comparison of 4 Ezra and Romans 1-11* (JSNTSup 57), Sheffield: JSOT Press 1991.

Longenecker, Bruce W., *2 Esdras*, Sheffield: Sheffield Academic Press 1995.

Longenecker, Bruce W., *The Triumph of Abraham's God: The Transformation of Identity in Galatians*, Edinburgh: T. & T. Clark 1998.

Longenecker, Richard N., *Galatians* (WBC 41), Dallas, Texas: Word Books 1990.

Longenecker, Richard N., *Paul, Apostle of Liberty*, Grand Rapids: Baker Book House 1980 (repr.), ([1]1964).

de Lorenzi, Lorenzo, (ed.), *Die Israelfrage nach Röm 9-11* (MRvB.BÖA 3), Rom: Abtei von St Paul vor den Mauern 1977.

Lüdemann, Gerd, *Early Christianity according to the Traditions in Acts* ET, London: SCM 1989.

Lüdemann, Gerd, *Paul, Apostle to the Gentiles: Studies in Chronology* ET, London: SCM 1984.

Lüdemann, Gerd, *Paulus und das Judentum* (ThExH 215), München: Chr. Kaiser Verlag 1983.

Lüdemann, Gerd, *The Resurrection of Jesus*, London: SCM 1995.

Luz, Ulrich, *Das Evangelium nach Matthäus (Mt 8-17)* (EKK 1.2), Solothurn/Düsseldorf: Benziger Verlag/Neukirchen-Vluyn: Neukirchener Verlag [2]1996, ([1]1990).

Luz, Ulrich, *Das Evangelium nach Matthäus (Mt 18-25)* (EKK 1.3), Zürich/Düsseldorf: Benziger Verlag/Neukirchen-Vluyn: Neukirchener Verlag 1997.

Luz, Ulrich, *Das Geschichtsverständnis des Paulus* (BEvTh 49), München: Chr. Kaiser Verlag 1968.

Luz, Ulrich, "Das Neue Testament", in Rudolf Smend and Ulrich Luz, *Gesetz. Biblische Konfrontationen* (KT 1015), Stuttgart/Berlin/Köln/Mainz: W. Kohlhammer Verlag 1981, 58-139.

Maccoby, Hyam, *Judas Iscariot and the Myth of Jewish Evil*, New York: Free Press 1992.

Maccoby, Hyam, *The Mythmaker: Paul and the Invention of Christianity*, London: Weidenfeld & Nicholson 1986.

Maccoby, Hyam, *A Pariah People: The Anthropology of Antisemitism*, London: Constable 1988.

Macquarrie, John, *An Existentialist Theology. A Comparison of Heidegger and Bultmann*, London: SCM 1955.

Macquarrie, John, "Jesus Christus VI", *TRE* 17:16-42.

Maier, Friedrich Wilhelm, *Israel in der Heilsgeschichte nach Röm. 9-11*, in *Biblische Zeitfragen* 12 (11/12), Münster: Aschendorff 1929.

Maier, Gerhard, *Mensch und freier Wille: Nach den jüdischen Religionsparteien zwischen Ben Sira und Paulus* (WUNT 12), Tübingen: J.C.B. Mohr (Paul Siebeck) 1971.

Manson, T.W., *The Sayings of Jesus*, London: SCM 1950 (repr.), ([1]1937).

Manson, T.W., *The Teaching of Jesus: Studies in its Form and Content*, Cambridge: CUP [2]1935, ([1]1931)

Marrou, H.I., *A History of Education in Antiquity* ET, London: Sheed and Ward 1956.

Marshall, Bruce D., "Christ and the cultures: Jewish people and Christian theology" in C.E. Guton (ed.), *The Cambridge Companion to Christian Doctrine*, Cambridge: CUP 1997, 81-100.

Marshall, I. Howard, *1 and 2 Thessalonians* (NCB), Grand Rapids: Wm B. Eerdmans 1983.

Marshall, I. Howard, *The Acts of the Apostles* (TNTC), Leicester: IVP 1980.

Marshall, I. Howard, *The Gospel of Luke: A Commentary on the Greek Text* (NIGTC), Exeter: Paternoster 1978.

Martin, Raymond A., *Studies in the Life and Ministry of the Early Paul and Related Issues*, Lewiston/Queenston/Lampeter: Mellen Biblical Press 1993.

Martin, Ralph P., *2 Corinthians* (WBC 40), Dallas, Texas: Word Books 1986.

Martin, Ralph P., *Philippians* (NCB), London: Oliphants 1976.

Martin, Ralph P. - Dodd, Brian J. (ed.), *Where Christology Began: Essays on Philippians 2*, Louisville: Westminster John Knox Press 1998.

Martyn, J. Louis, *Theological Issues in the Letters of Paul* (SNTW), Edinburgh: T. & T. Clark 1997.

Marxsen, Willi, *Der erste Brief an die Thessalonicher* (ZBK), Zürich: Theologischer Verlag 1979.

Mason, Steve, *Flavius Josephus on the Pharisees: A Composition-Critical Study* (StPB 39), Leiden/New York: E.J. Brill 1991.

Matera, Frank J., "The Culmination of Paul's Argument to the Galatians: Gal. 5.1-6.17", *JSNT* 32 (1988) 79-91.

Matera, Frank J., *Galatians* (SPS 9), Collegeville: Liturgical Press 1992.

Matlock, R. Barry, "Almost Cultural Studies? Reflections on the 'New Perspective' on Paul", in J.C. Exum and S.D. Moore (ed.), *Biblical Studies/Cultural Studies: The Third Sheffield Colloquium* (JSOTSup 266), Sheffield: Sheffield Academic Press 1998, 433-59.

Mattern, Lieselotte, *Das Verständnis des Gerichtes bei Paulus* (AThANT 47), Zürich/Stuttgart: Zwingli Verlag 1966.

Maurer, Christian, ῥίζα κτλ, *TDNT* 6:985-991.

Maurer, Wilhelm, in Karl Heinrich Rengstorf and Siegfried von Kortzfleisch (ed.), *Kirche und Synagoge: Handbuch zur Geschichte von Christen und Juden. Darstellung mit Quellen*, 2 vols, München: DTV 1988 (repr.), ([1]1968-70), 1:363-452.

Mayes, A.D.H., *Deuteronomy* (NCB), London: Oliphants 1979.

McGrath, Alister E., *Reformation Thought*, Oxford: Blackwell [3]1999, ([1]1988).

McLean, Bradley H., "The Absence of an Atoning Sacrifice in Paul's Soteriology", *NTS* 38 (1992) 531-53.

MacLeod, Murdo A., "The witness of the church to the Jewish People", in D.W. Torrance (ed.), *The Witness of the Jews to God*, Edinburgh: Handsel Press 1982, 71-80.

McNeill, John T., (ed.), *Calvin: Institutes of the Christian Religion* (LCC 20-21), 2 vols, Philadelphia: Westminster Press 1960.

Mehlhorn, Paul, "Holsten", RE[3] 8:281-86.

Meier, John P., "Nations or Gentiles in Matthew 28:19", *CBQ* 39 (1977) 94-102.

Meinertz, Max, *Theologie des Neuen Testamentes (Die Heilige Schrift des Neuen Testamentes Ergänzungsband II)*, 2 vols, Bonn: Peter Hanstein Verlag 1950.

Meiser, Martin, *Paul Althaus als Neutestamentler: Eine Untersuchung der Werke, Briefe, unveröffentlichten Manuskripte und Randbemerkungen* (CThM A15), Stuttgart: Calwer Verlag 1993.

Merklein, Helmut, "Der (neue) Bund als Thema der paulinischen Theologie", in *Studien zu Jesus und Paulus II* (WUNT 105), Tübingen: J.C.B. Mohr (Paul Siebeck) 1998, 357-76 (= *ThQ* 176 (1996) 290-308)

Metzger, Bruce M., *An Introduction to the Apocrypha*, New York: OUP 1957.

Metzger, Bruce M., "The Punctuation of Rom. 9.5", in B. Lindars and S. Smalley (ed.), *Christ and Spirit in the New Testament: In Honour of Charles Francis Digby Moule*, Cambridge: CUP 1973, 95-112.

Meyer, Ben F., *The Aims of Jesus*, London: SCM 1979.

Meyer, Ben F., "A Caricature of Joachim Jeremias and His Scholarly Work", *JBL* 110 (1991) 451-62.

Meyer, Rudolf – Strathmann, Hermann, λαός, *TDNT* 4:29-57.

Michaelis, Wilhelm, *Versöhnung des Alls: Die frohe Botschaft von der Gnade Gottes*, Gümligen bei Bern: Verlag Siloah 1950.

Michalson, Carl, "Bultmann against Marcion", in Bernard W. Anderson (ed.), *The Old Testament and Christian Faith*, New York: Harper & Row 1963, 49-63.

Michel, Oskar, *Forward with Christ! Away with Paul! German Religion!*, Berlin ³1906.

Michel, Otto, *Der Brief an die Römer* (KEK 4), Göttingen: Vandenhoeck & Ruprecht ¹⁴1978, (¹⁰1955).

Michel, Otto, *Paulus und seine Bibel* (BFCTh 2.18), Darmstadt: Wissenschaftliche Buchgesellschaft ²1972, (Gütersloh: Bertelsmann ¹1929).

Mildenberger, Friedrich, *Biblische Dogmatik. Eine Biblische Theologie in dogmatischer Perspektive, Band 1. Prolegomena: Verstehen und Geltung der Bibel*, Stuttgart/Berlin/Köln: W. Kohlhammer Verlag 1991.

Mildenberger, Friedrich, "Hofmann, Johann Christian Konrad v.", *TRE* 15:477-79.

Mildenberger, Friedrich, "Systematisch-theologische Randbemerkungen zur Diskussion um eine Biblische Theologie", in Friedrich Mildenberger and Joachim Track (ed.), *Zugang zur Theologie. Fundamentaltheologische Beiträge. Wilfried Joest zum 65. Geburtstag*, Göttingen: Vandenhoeck & Ruprecht 1979, 11-32.

Millar, Fergus, "The Background to the Maccabean Revolution: Reflections on Martin Hengel's *Judaism and Hellenism*", *JJS* 29 (1978) 1-21.

Millar, Fergus, "Jews of the Graeco-Roman Diaspora", in Judith Lieu, John North and Tessa Rajak (ed.), *The Jews among Pagans and Christians in the Roman Empire*, London/New York: Routledge 1992, 97-123.

Milne, D.J.W., "Romans 7:7-12, Paul's Pre-conversion Experience", *RTR* 43 (1984) 9-17.

Mitton, C. Leslie, "Romans vii. Reconsidered - II", *ExpT* 65 (1953/54) 99-103.

Moehlman, Conrad Henry, *The Christian-Jewish Tragedy: A Study in Religious Prejudice*, Rochester, New York: Leo Hart 1933.

Moltmann, Jürgen, *The Crucified God: The Cross of Christ as the Foundation and Criticism of Christian Theology* ET, London: SCM 1974.

Moltmann, Jürgen, *Der gekreuzigte Gott: Das Kreuz Christi als Grund und Kritik christlicher Theologie*, München: Chr. Kaiser Verlag ⁵1987, (¹1972).

Moltmann, Jürgen, *Der Weg Jesu Christi: Christologie in messianischen Dimensionen*, München: Chr. Kaiser Verlag 1989.

Momigliano, A., "Review of *Judentum und Hellenismus*, by M. Hengel", *JTS* 21 (1970) 149-53.

Montefiore, Claude G., *Judaism and St. Paul: Two Essays*, New York: Arno Press 1973 (repr.), ([1]1914).

Moo, Douglas, *The Epistle to the Romans* (NICNT), Grand Rapids: Wm B. Eerdmans 1996.

Moo, Douglas, "Paul and the Law in the Last Ten Years", *SJT* 40 (1987) 287-307.

Moore, Archimandrite Lazarus, *The Parousia in the New Testament* (NovTSup 13), Leiden: E.J. Brill 1966.

Moore, Carey A., *Judith* (AB 40), Garden City, New York: Doubleday 1985.

Moore, Carey A., *Tobit* (AB 40A), New York/London/Toronto/Sydney/Auckland: Doubleday 1996.

Moore, George Foot, "Christian Writers on Judaism", *HTR* 14 (1921) 197-254.

Moore, George Foot, *Judaism in the First Centuries of the Christian Era: The Age of the Tannaim*, 3 vols, Cambridge, Mass.: Harvard University Press 1 1927; 2 1927; 3 1930.

Morris, Leon, *The Apostolic Preaching of the Cross: A Study of the Significance of some New Testament Terms*, Leicester [3]1965.

Morris, Leon, *The Epistle to the Romans*, Grand Rapids: Wm B. Eerdmans/Leicester: IVP 1988.

Morris, Leon, *The First and Second Epistles to the Thessalonians* (NICNT), Grand Rapids: Wm B. Eerdmans [2]1991, ([1]1959).

Moses, John A., "Bonhoeffer's Germany: the political context", in John W. de Gruchy, *The Cambridge Companion to Dietrich Bonhoeffer*, Cambridge: CUP 1999, 3-21.

Moule, C.F.D., "Obligation in the Ethic of Paul", in W.R. Farmer, C.F.D. Moule and R.R. Niebuhr (ed.), *Christian History and Interpretation: Studies presented to John Knox*, Cambridge: CUP 1967, 389-406.

Moule, C.F.D., "Once More, Who Were the Hellenists?", *ExpT* 70 (1958-59) 100-2.

Müller, Christian, *Gottes Gerechtigkeit und Gottes Volk: Eine Untersuchung zu Römer 9-11* (FRLANT 86), Göttingen: Vandenhoeck & Ruprecht 1964.

Müller, Gerhard, "Antisemitismus VI", TRE 3:143-55.

Müller, Jac.J., *The Epistle of Paul to the Philippians* (NICNT), Grand Rapids: Eerdmans 1991 (repr.), ([1]1955).

Munck, Johannes, *Christus und Israel: Eine Auslegung von Röm 9-11* (Acta Jutlandica, Aarsskrift for Aarhus Universitet 28.3, Teologisk Serie 7), Aarhus: Universitetsforlaget/København: Ejnar Munksgaard 1956.

Munck, Johannes, *Paul and the Salvation of Mankind* ET, London: SCM 1959.

Munro, W., "Romans 13:1-7: Apartheid's Last Biblical Refuge", *BTB* 20 (1990) 161-68.

Murphy, Frederick J., "The Eternal Covenant in Pseudo-Philo", *JSP* 3 (1988) 43-57.

Murphy-O'Connor, Jerome, *Paul: A Critical Life*, Oxford/New York: OUP 1997.

Murphy-O'Connor, Jerome, *The Theology of the Second Letter to the Corinthians*, Cambridge: CUP 1991.

Murray, John, *The Epistle to the Romans: The English Text with Introduction, Exposition and Notes* (NICNT), 2 vols, Grand Rapids: Wm B. Eerdmans 1968 (one-volume edition), (1 ¹1959; 2 ¹1965).

Mußner, Franz, *Der Galaterbrief* (HThKNT 9), Freiburg/Basel/Wien: Herder 1974.

Mußner, Franz, "'Ganz Israel wird gerettet werden' (Röm 11,26)", *Kairos* NF 18 (1976) 241-55.

Mußner, Franz, *Traktat über die Juden*, München: Kösel-Verlag 1979.

Neef, Heinz-Dieter, "Aspekte alttestamentlicher Bundestheologie", in Friedrich Avemarie and Hermann Lichtenberger (ed.), *Bund und Tora: Zur theologischen Begriffsgeschichte in alttestamentlicher, frühjüdischer und urchristlicher Tradition* (WUNT 92), Tübingen: J.C.B. Mohr (Paul Siebeck) 1996, 1-23.

Neill, Stephen C., *The Interpretation of the New Testament, 1861-1961*, Oxford: OUP ²1966, (¹1964).

Neill, Stephen C. - Wright, N. Thomas, *The Interpretation of the New Testament, 1861-1986*, Oxford/New York: OUP 1988.

Neusner, Jacob, *Ancient Judaism: Debates and Disputes* (BJS), Chico: Scholars Press 1984, pp. 127-41; 195-203.

Neusner, Jacob, *Development of a Legend: Studies on the Traditions concerning Yoḥanan ben Zakkai* (StPB 16), Leiden: E.J. Brill 1970.

Neusner, Jacob, *The Four Stages of Rabbinic Judaism*, London/New York: Routledge 1999.

Neusner, Jacob, *From Politics to Piety: The Emergence of Pharisaic Judaism*, Englewood Cliffs, N.J.: Prentice-Hall 1973 (repr.: New York: Ktav 1979).

Neusner, Jacob, "Josephus's Pharisees", in *Ex Orbe Religionum. Studia Geo Widengren*, Leiden: E.J. Brill 1972, 224-44 (= *From Politics to Piety*, Englewood Cliffs, N.J.: Prentice-Hall 1973, 45-66).

Neusner, Jacob, *Sifre to Deuteronomy: An Introduction to the Rhetorical, Logical and Topical Program* (BJS 124), Atlanta, Georgia 1987

Nickelsburg, George W.E., *Jewish Literature between the Bible and the Mishnah*, Philadelphia: Fortress Press 1981.

Nickelsburg, G.W.E., *Resurrection, Immortality, and Eternal Life in Intertestamental Judaism* (HTS 26), Cambridge, Mass.: Harvard University Press 1972.

Niebuhr, Reinhold, *Moral Man and Immoral Society*, London: SCM 1963.

Nissen, A., "Tora und Geschichte im Spätjudentum", *NovT* 9 (1967) 241-77.

Nock, Arthur Darby, *St. Paul*, London: Thornton Butterworth 1938.

Norden, Eduard, *Die antike Kunstprosa vom VI. Jahrhundert v. Chr. bis in die Zeit der Renaissance*, Stuttgart/Leipzig: B.G. Teubner 1995 (repr. of [3]1915).

Noth, Martin, *The History of Israel* ET, London: A. & C. Black [2]1960, ([1]1958).

Novak, David, *The Election of Israel: The Idea of the Chosen People*, Cambridge: CUP 1995.

Nygren, Anders, *Commentary on Romans* ET, Philadelphia: Fortress Press 1949.

Oberman, Heiko A., *The Impact of the Reformation*, Grand Rapids: Wm B. Eerdmans 1994.

Oberman, Heiko A., *The Roots of Anti-semitism in the Age of Renaissance and Reformation* ET, Philadelphia: Fortress Press 1984.

O'Brien, Peter T., *The Epistle to the Philippians: A Commentary on the Greek Text* (NIGTC), Grand Rapids: Wm B. Eerdmans 1991.

O'Donovan, Oliver, *Measure for Measure: Justice in Punishment and the Sentence of Death* (Grove Booklet on Ethics 19), Bramcote, Notts: Grove Books: 1977.

Oepke, Albrecht, *Der Brief des Paulus an die Galater* (ThHK 9), Berlin: Evangelische Verlagsanstalt 1937.

Oepke, Albrecht, "Die Briefe an die Thessalonicher", in Hermann W. Beyer, Paul Althaus, Hans Conzelmann, Gerhard Friedrich and Albrecht Oepke, *Die kleineren Briefe des Apostels Paulus* (NTD 8), Göttingen: Vandenhoeck & Ruprecht [13]1972, 157-87.

Oepke, Albrecht, "Probleme der vorchristlichen Zeit des Paulus", in Karl Heinrich Rengstorf (ed.), *Das Paulusbild in der neueren deutschen Forschung* (WdF 24), Darmstadt: Wissenschaftliche Buchgesellschaft 1982, 410-46 (= *ThStKr* 105 (1933) 387-424).

Oepke, Albrecht, διά, *TDNT* 2:65-70.

Oesterley, W.O.E., *An Introduction to the Books of the Apocrypha*, London: SPCK 1946 (repr.), ([1]1935).

Oesterreicher, John M., "Israel's Misstep and her Rise: The Dialectic of God's Saving Design in Romans 9-11", in *Studiorum Paulinorum Congressus Internationalis Catholicus 1961* (AnBib 17-18), 2 vols, Rome: E Pontificio Instituto Biblico 1963, 1:317-27.

Okeke, G.E., "I Thessalonians 2:13-16: The Fate of the Unbelieving Jews", *NTS* 27 (1980-81) 127-36.

Orchard, J.B., "Thessalonians and the Synoptic Gospels", *Bib* 19 (1938) 19-42.

Osten-Sacken, Peter von der, "Antijudaismus um Christi willen?", *BThZ* 4 (1987) 107-120 (review of Erich Gräßer, *Der Alte Bund im Neuen*) (= *Evangelium und Tora. Aufsätze zu Paulus* (ThBü 77), München 1987, 239-55).

Oswalt, John N., *The Book of Isaiah: Chapter 1-39* (NICOT), Grand Rapids: Wm B. Eerdmans 1986.

Overman, J. Andrew, "The God-Fearers: Some Neglected Features", *JSNT* 32 (1988) 17-26 (= Craig A. Evans and Stanley E. Porter (ed.), *New Testament Backgrounds: A Sheffield Reader* (BS 43), Sheffield: Sheffield Academic Press 1997, 253-62).

Packer, J.I., *Evangelism and the Sovereignty of God*, London: IVP 1961.

Packer, J.I., "The 'Wretched Man' in Romans 7", in F.L. Cross (ed.), *Studia Evangelica II* (TU 87), Berlin: Akademie-Verlag 1964, 621-27.

Pannenberg, Wolfhart, *Jesus – God and Man* ET, Philadephia: The Westminster Press 1968.

Parkes, James, *The Conflict of the Church and the Synagogue: A study in the origins of antisemitism*, London: Soncino 1934.

Parkes, James, *Whose Land? A History of the Peoples of Palestine*, Harmondsworth: Penguin [2]1970, ([1]1949).

Pate, C. Marvin, *The Reverse of the Curse: Paul Wisdom and the Law* (WUNT 2.114), Tübingen: J.C. B. Mohr (Paul Siebeck) 2000.

Pauck, Wilhelm, (ed.), *Martin Luther: Lectures on Romans* (LCC 15), Philadelphia: The Westminster Press 1961.

Pearson, Birger A., "1 Thessalonians 2:13-16: A Deutero-Pauline Interpolation", *HTR* 64 (1971) 79-94.

Pedersen, Johs., *Israel: Its Life and Culture, II-IV* ET, London: OUP/Copenhagen: Branner og Korch 1953 (repr.), ([1]1940).

Pesch, Rudolf, *Die Apostelgeschichte* (EKK 5), 2 vols, Zürich/Einsiedeln/Köln: Benziger Verlag/Neukirchen-Vluyn: Neukirchener Verlag 1986.

Peterson, Erik, *Die Kirche aus Juden und Heiden* (Bücherei der Salzburger Hochschulwochen 2), Salzburg: Verlag Anton Pustet 1933.

Pétrement, Simone, *A Separate God: The Origins and Teachings of Gnosticism* ET, San Francisco: Harper 1990.

Philipp, Franz-Heinrich, "Protestantismus nach 1848", in Karl Heinrich Rengstorf and Siegfried von Kortzfleisch (ed.), *Kirche und Synagoge: Handbuch zur Geschichte von Christen und Juden. Darstellung mit Quellen*, 2 vols, München: DTV 1988 (repr.), ([1]1968-70), 2:280-357.

Philipp, Wolfgang, "Spätbarock und frühe Aufklärung. Das Zeitalter des Philosemitismus", Karl Heinrich Rengstorf and Siegfried von Kortzfleisch (ed.), *Kirche und Synagoge: Handbuch zur Geschichte von Christen und Juden. Darstellung mit Quellen*, 2 vols, München: DTV 1988 (repr.), ([1]1968-70), 2:23-86.

Piper, John, *The Justification of God. An Exegetical and Theological Study of Romans 9:1-23*, Grand Rapids: Baker Book House 1983.

Plag, Christoph, *Israels Wege zum Heil: Eine Untersuchung zu Römer 9 bis 11* (AzTh 1.40), Stuttgart: Calwer Verlag 1969.

Plümacher, Eckhard, "Delitzsch, Franz Julius", *TRE* 8:431-33.

Plümacher, Eckhard, στοιχεῖον, *EDNT* 3:277-78.

Plummer, Alfred, *A Critical and Exegetical Commentary on the Second Epistle of St Paul to the Corinthians* (ICC), Edinburgh: T. & T. Clark 1985 (repr.), ([1]1915).

Pope, Hugh, "A Possible view of Romans X.13-21", *JTS* 4 (1903) 273-79.

Porter, J.R., "The Case of Gerhard Kittel", *Theology* 50 (1947) 401-6.

Preuß, H.D., *Theologie des Alten Testaments*, 2 vols, Stuttgart/Berlin/Köln: W. Kohlhammer Verlag 1991-92.

Quell, Gottfried – Schrenk, Gottlob, πατήρ κτλ, *TDNT* 5:945-1022.

Rabenau, Merten, *Studien zum Buch Tobit* (BZAW 220), Berlin/New York: Walter de Gruyter 1994.

von Rad, Gerhard, *Deuteronomy* (OTL) ET, London: SCM 1966.

von Rad, Gerhard, *Old Testament Theology* (OTL) ET, 2 vols, London: SCM 1975.

von Rad, Gerhard, *The Problem of the Hexateuch and other essays* ET, Edinburgh/London: Oliver & Boyd 1966.

von Rad, Gerhard, *Theologie des Alten Testaments, Band 1: Die Theologie der geschichtlichen Überlieferungen Israels*, München: Chr. Kaiser Verlag [9]1987, ([1]1957).

von Rad, Gerhard, *Theologie des Alten Testaments, Band 2: Die Theologie der prophetischen Überlieferungen Israels*, München: Chr. Kaiser Verlag [9]1987, ([1]1960).

von Rad, Gerhard – Kuhn, Karl Georg – Gutbrod, Walter, Ἰσραήλ κτλ, *TDNT* 3:356-91 (*ThWNT* 3:356-94).

Radl, Walter, θρησκεία, *EDNT* 2:154-55.

Räisänen, Heikki, "Die 'Hellenisten' der Urgemeinde", *ANRW* 2.26.2:1468-1516.

Räisänen, Heikki, "Legalism and Salvation by the Law", in Sigfred Pedersen (ed.), *Die paulinische Literatur und Theologie. The Pauline Literature and Theology* (TeolSt 7), Aarhus: Aros/Göttingen: Vandenhoeck & Ruprecht 1980, 63-83.

Räisänen, Heikki, "Did Paul Expect an Earthly Kingdom?", in Alf Christofersen, Carsten Claussen, Jörg Frey and Bruce Longenecker (ed.), *Paul, Luke and the Graeco-Roman World: Essays in Honour of Alexander J.M. Wedderburn* (JSNTSup 217), Sheffield: Sheffield Academic Press 2002, 2-20.

Räisänen, Heikki, *Paul and the Law* (WUNT 29), Tübingen: J.C.B. Mohr (Paul Siebeck) 1983.

Rajak, Tessa, *Josephus: The Historian and His Society*, London: Duckworth 1983.

Ramsay, W.M., *A Historical Commentary on St. Paul's Epistle to the Galatians*, London: Hodder and Stoughton ²1900.

Ramsey, Arthur Michael, *God, Christ and the World: A Study in Contemporary Theology*, London: SCM 1969.

Ray, Charles A., "The Identity of the 'Israel of God'", *TE* 50 (1994) 105-14.

Rees, W., "1 and 2 Corinthians", *CCHS* 1081-1111.

Refoulé, François, *"...et ainsi tout Israël sera sauvé": Romains 11,25-32* (LD 117), Paris: Les éditions du Cerf 1984.

Regner, F., *Paulus und Jesus im 19. Jahrhundert. Beiträge zur Geschichte des Themas Paulus und Jesus in der neutestamentlichen Theologie von der Aufklärung bis zur Religionsgeschichtlichen Schule*, Tübingen: Protestant Faculty dissertation 1975.

Reicke, Bo, "Judaeo-Christianity and the Jewish establishment, A.D. 33-66" in Ernst Bammel and C.F.D. Moule (ed.), *Jesus and the Politics of His Day*, Cambridge: CUP 1984, 145-52.

Reid, John K.S., "Israel – people, nation, state", in D.W. Torrance (ed.), *The Witness of the Jews to God*, Edinburgh: Handsel Press 1982, 42-57.

Reimarus, Hermann Samuel, "Von dem Zwecke Jesu und seiner Jünger", in H. Göbel (ed.), *Gotthold Ephraim Lessing Werke, Siebenter Band: Theologiekritische Schriften I und II*, Darmstadt: Wissenschaftliche Buchgesellschaft 1996 (repr.), (¹1976), 492-604.

Reinhardt, Wolfgang, "The Population Size of Jerusalem and the Numerical Growth of the Jerusalem Church", in Richard Bauckham (ed.), *The Book of Acts in Its Palestinian Setting* (The Book of Acts in its First Century Setting vol. 4), Grand Rapids: Wm B. Eerdmans/Carlisle: Paternoster 1995 237-65.

Reinmuth, Eckart, "Beobachtungen zum Verständnis des Gesetzes im Liber Antiquitatum Biblicarum (Pseudo-Philo)", *JSJ* 20 (1989) 151-70.

Reiser, Marius, *Jesus and Judgment: The Eschatological Proclamation in Its Jewish Context* ET, Minneapolis: Fortress Press 1997.

Rengstorf, Karl Heinrich, "Das Ölbaum-Gleichnis in Röm 11,16f: Versuch einer weiterführenden Deutung", in C.K. Barrett, E. Bammel, W.D. Davies (ed.), *Donum Gentilicium: New Testament Studies in honour of David Daube*, Oxford: Clarendon Press 1978, 127-164.

Rengstorf, Karl Heinrich, ἑπτά κτλ, *TDNT* 2:627-35.

Rengstorf, Karl Heinrich – von Kortzfleisch, Siegfried (ed.), *Kirche und Synagoge: Handbuch zur Geschichte von Christen und Juden. Darstellung mit Quellen*, 2 vols, München: DTV 1988 (repr.), (¹1968-70).

Rese, Martin, "Church and Israel in the Deuteropauline Letters", *SJT* 43 (1990) 19-32.

Rese, Martin, "Die Vorzüge Israels in Röm. 9,4f. und Eph. 2,12", *ThZ* 31 (1975) 211-22.

Rese, Martin, Review of David Wenham, *Paul: Follower of Jesus or Founder of Christianity?*, Grand Rapids: Wm B. Eerdmans 1995, *TLZ* 121 (1996) 672-74.

Reventlow, Henning Graf, *Problems of Biblical Theology in the Twentieth Century* ET, London: SCM 1986.

Richardson, Neil, *Paul's Language about God* (JSNTSup 99), Sheffield: Sheffield Academic Press 1994.

Richardson, Peter, *Israel in the Apostolic Church* (SNTSMS 10), Cambridge: CUP 1969.

Ridderbos, Herman N., *The Epistle to the Galatians* (NLC) ET, London: Marshall, Morgan & Scott 1976 (repr.), ([3]1961).

Ridderbos, Herman N., *Paul: An Outline of His Theology* ET, London: SPCK 1977.

Riemer, Siegfried, *Philosemitismus im deutschen evangelischen Kirchenlied des Barock* (StDel 8), Stuttgart: W. Kohlhammer Verlag 1963.

Riesner, Rainer, *Die Frühzeit des Paulus: Studien zur Chronologie, Missionsstrategie und Theologie* (WUNT 71), Tübingen: J.C.B. Mohr (Paul Siebeck) 1994.

Riesner, Rainer, *Paul's Early Period: Chronology, Mission Strategy, Theology* ET, Grand Rapids/Cambridge: Wm B. Eerdmans 1998.

Riesner, Rainer, *Jesus als Lehrer: Eine Untersuchung zum Ursprung der Evangelien-Überlieferung* (WUNT 2.7), Tübingen: J.C.B. Mohr (Paul Siebeck) [3]1988, ([1]1981).

Rigaux, Béda, *Paulus und seine Briefe: Der Stand der Forschung* (Biblische Handbibliothek 2), München: Kösel-Verlag 1964.

Robertson, Archibald - Plummer, Alfred, *A Critical and Exegetical Commentary on the First Epistle of St. Paul to the Corinthians* (ICC),`

Robinson, D.W.B., "'We are the circumcision'", *AusBR* 15 (1967) 28-35.

Robinson, J. Armitage, *St Paul's Epistle to the Ephesians*, London: Macmillan [2]1904, ([1]1903).

Roetzel, Calvin, "Διαθῆκαι in Romans 9,4", *Bib* 51 (1970) 377-90.

Roloff, Jürgen, *Die Apostelgeschichte* (NTD 5), Göttingen: Vandenhoeck & Ruprecht 1981.

Rosenberg, Alfred, *Der Mythus des 20. Jahrhunderts: Eine Wertung der seelischgeistigen Gestaltenkämpfe unserer Zeit*. München: Hoheneichen-Verlag 1944 (repr.), ([1]1930)

Rost, L., *Israel bei den Propheten* (BWANT 71), Stuttgart: W. Kohlhammer Verlag 1937.

Rowland, Christopher, *The Open Heaven: A Study in Apocalyptic in Judaism and Early Christianity*, London: SCPK 1982.

Rozenzeig, Franz, "Letter to Rudolf Ehrenberg, November 1, 1913", in Edward T. Oakes (ed.), *German Essays on Religion* (GL 54), New York: Continuum 1994, 191-93.

Rubenstein, Richard L., *After Auschwitz: Radical Theology and Contemporary Judaism*, Indianapolis: Bobbs-Merrill 1966.

Rüger, Hans-Peter, "Apokryhpen I", *TRE* 3:289-316.

Ruether, Rosemary Radford, *Faith and Fratricide: The Theological Roots of Anti-Semitism*, New York: Seabury Press 1974.

Ruether, Rosemary Radford, "The *Faith and Fratricide* Discussion: Old Problems and New Dimensions" in A.T. Davies (ed.), *Antisemitism and the Foundations of Christianity*, New York/Ramsey/Toronto: Paulist Press 1979, 230-56.

Rupp, Gordon, *The Righteousness of God: Luther Studies*, London: Hodder and Stoughton 1953.

Russell, D.S., *The Method and Message of Jewish Apocalyptic* (OTL), London: SCM 1964.

Sabatier, A., *The Apostle Paul: A Sketch of the Development of His Doctrine* ET, London: Hodder and Stoughton [4]1899.

Sacchi, Paolo, "Das Problem des 'wahren Israel' im Lichte der universalistischen Auffassungen des Alten Orients", *Jahrbuch für Biblische Theologie Band 7: Volk Gottes, Gemeinde und Gesellschaft*, Neukirchen-Vluyn: Neukirchener Verlag 1992, 77-100.

Safrai, Shmuel, "And All is According to the Majority of Deeds" (Hebrew), *Tarbiz* 53 (1983-84) 33-40.

Saldarini, Anthony J., *Pharisees, Scribes and Sadducees in Palestinian Society*, Edinburgh: T.& T. Clark 1989 (repr.), ([1]1988).

Sanday, W. - Headlam, A.C., *A Critical and Exegetical Commentary on the Epistle to the Romans* (ICC), Edinburgh: T. & T. Clark, [2]1896.

Sanders, E.P., "The Covenant as a Soteriological Category and the Nature of Salvation in Palestinian and Hellenistic Judaism", in Robert Hamerton-Kelly and Robin Scroggs (ed.), *Jews, Greeks and Christians: Religious Cultures in Late Antiquity. Essays in Honor of William David Davies* (SJLA 21), Leiden: E.J. Brill 1976, 11-44.

Sanders, E.P., "Defending the Indefensible", *JBL* 110 (1991) 463-77.

Sanders, E.P., *Jesus and Judaism*, London: SCM 1985.

Sanders, E.P., "Jesus and the Kingdom: The Restoration of Israel and the New People of God", in E.P. Sanders (ed.), *Jesus, the Gospels, and the Church. Essays in Honor of William R. Farmer*, Macon: Mercer University Press 1987.

Sanders, E.P., *Judaism: Practice and Belief 63BCE-66CE*, London: SCM/Philadelphia: TPI 1992.

Sanders, E.P., *Paul and Palestinian Judaism: A Comparison of Patterns of Religion*, London: SCM 1977.

Sanders, E.P., *Paul, the Law, and the Jewish People*, London: SCM 1985 (Philadelphia: Fortress Press 1983).

Sanders, E.P. – Davies, Margaret, *Studying the Synoptic Gospels*, London: SCM/Philadelphia: TPI 1989.

Sänger, Dieter, "Rettung der Heiden und Erwählung Israels", *KuD* 32 (1986) 99-119.

Saperstein, Marc, *Moments of Crisis in Jewish-Christian Relations*, London: SCM/Philadelphia: TPI 1989.

Sasse, Hermann, κοσμέω, κόσμος κτλ., *TDNT* 3:867-98.

Schäfer, Peter, *The History of the Jews in Antiquity: The Jews of Palestine from Alexander the Great to the Arab Conquest*, Luxembourg: Harwood Academic Publishers 1995.

Schäfer, Peter, "Der vorrabbinische Pharisäismus", in Martin Hengel and Ulrich Heckel (ed.), *Paulus und das antike Judentum: Tübingen-Durham-Symposium im Gedenken an den 50. Todestag Adolf Schlatters* (WUNT 58), Tübingen: J.C.B. Mohr (Paul Siebeck) 1991, 125-72.

Schelkle, Karl Hermann, *Paulus Lehrer der Väter: Die altkirchliche Auslegung von Römer 1-11*, Düsseldorf: Patmos Verlag ²1959, (¹1956).

Schiffman, Laurence H., *Who was a Jew? Rabbinic and Halakhic Perspectives on the Jewish Christian Schism*, Hoboken, NJ: Ktav 1985.

Schippers, R., "The Pre-Synoptic Tradition in 1 Thessalonians II.13-16", *NovT* 8 (1966) 223-34.

Schlatter, Adolf, *Der Evangelist Johannes. Wie er spricht, denkt und glaubt: Ein Kommentar zum vierten Evangelium*, Stuttgart: Calwer Verlag ⁴1975, (¹1930).

Schlatter, Adolf, *Die Geschichte der ersten Christenheit* (mit einer Einführung von Rainer Riesner), Stuttgart: Calwer Verlag ⁶1983, (¹1926).

Schlatter, Adolf, *Gottes Gerechtigkeit: Ein Kommentar zum Römerbrief*, Stuttgart: Calwer Verlag ⁵1975, (¹1935).

Schlechta, Karl, (ed.), *Friedrich Nietzsche: Werke in drei Bänden*, Darmstadt: Wissenschaftliche Buchgesellschaft 1977 (repr.), (¹1954-65).

Schlier, Heinrich, *Der Brief an die Galater* (KEK 7), Göttingen: Vandenhoeck & Ruprecht ¹⁴1971, (¹⁰1949).

Schlier, Heinrich, *Der Römerbrief* (HThKNT 6), Freiburg/Basel/Wien: Herder 1977.

Schlosser, Jacques, "Die Vollendung des Heils in der Sicht Jesu", in Hans-Josef Klauck (ed.), *Weltgericht und Weltvollendung. Zukunftsbilder im Neuen Testament* (QD 150), Freiburg/Basel/Wien: Herder 1994, 54-84.

Schmid, H.H., ירשׁ, *THAT* 1:778-81.

Schmidt, Daryl, "1 Thess 2:13-16: Linguistic Evidence for an Interpolation", *JBL* 102 (1983) 269-79.

Schmidt, Karl Ludwig, *Die Judenfrage im Lichte der Kap. 9-11 des Römerbriefes* (ThSt 13), Zollikon-Zürich: Evangelischer Verlag 1943.

Schmidt, Karl Ludwig, θρησκεία, *TDNT* 3:155-59.

Schmidt, Karl Ludwig, πταίω, *TDNT* 6:883-84.

Schmithals, Walter, *Gnosticism in Corinth: An Investigation of the Letters to the Corinthians* ET, Nashville: Abingdon 1971.

Schmithals, Walter, *Der Römerbrief als historisches Problem* (StNT 9), Gütersloh: Gütersloher Verlagshaus Gerd Mohn 1975.

Schmithals, Walter, *Die Theologie Rudolf Bultmanns. Eine Einführung*, Tübingen: J.C.B. Mohr (Paul Siebeck) 1966.

Schnackenburg, Rudolf, *Das Johannesevangelium, I Teil: Einleitung und Kommentar zu Kap. 1-4* (HThKNT 4.1), Freiburg/Basel/Wien: Herder [7]1992, ([1]1965).

Schnackenburg, Rudolf, *Das Johannesevangelium, II Teil: Kommentar zu Kap. 5-12* (HThKNT 4.2), Freiburg/Basel/Wien: Herder [4]1985, ([1]1971).

Schnackenburg, Rudolf, *Das Johannesevangelium, III Teil: Kommentar zu Kap. 13-21* (HThKNT 4.3), Freiburg/Basel/Wien: Herder [6]1992, ([1]1975).

Schnackenburg, Rudolf, "Römer 7 im Zusammenhang des Römerbriefs", in E. Earle Ellis and Erich Gräßer (ed.), *Jesus und Paulus: Festschrift für Werner Georg Kümmel zum 70. Geburtstag*, Göttingen: Vandenhoeck & Ruprecht 1975, 283-300.

Schneider, Bernardin, "The Meaning of St. Paul's Antithesis: 'The Letter and the Spirit'", *CBQ* 15 (1953) 163-207.

Schneider, Gerhard, *Die Apostelgeschichte* (HThKNT 5), 2 vols, Freiburg/Basel/ Wien: Herder 1 1980; 2 1982.

Schneider, Gerhard, παιδεύω, *EWNT* 3:3-4.

Schneider, Johannes, κλάδος, *TDNT* 3:720-22.

Schoeps, Hans-Joachim, *Paul: The Theology of the Apostle in the Light of Jewish Religious History* ET, London: Lutterworth Press 1961.

Schoeps, Hans-Joachim, *Paulus: Die Theologie des Apostels im Lichte der jüdischen Religionsgeschichte*, Tübingen: J.C.B. Mohr (Paul Siebeck) 1959.

Scholder, Klaus, *The Churches and the Third Reich, Volume 1: 1918-1934* ET, London: SCM 1987.

Scholder, Klaus, *The Churches and the Third Reich, Volume 2: The Year of Disillusionment: 1934 Barmen and Rome* ET, London: SCM 1988.

Scholder, Klaus, *A Requiem for Hitler and Other New Perspectives on the German Church Struggle* ET, London: SCM 1989.

Schrage, Wolfgang, *Der erste Brief an die Korinther: 2. Teilband 1Kor 6,12-11,16* (KEK 7.2), Solothurn/Düsseldorf: Benziger Verlag/Neukirchen-Vluyn: Neukirchener Verlag 1995.

Schrage, Wolfgang, *Der erste Brief an die Korinther: 4. Teilband 1Kor 15,1-16.24* (KEK 7.4), Zürich/Düsseldorf: Benziger Verlag/Neukirchen-Vluyn: Neukirchener Verlag 2001.

Schrage, Wolfgang, *The Ethics of the New Testament* ET, Edinburgh: T. & T. Clark 1988.

Schreckenberg, Heinz, *Die christlichen Adversos-Judaeos-Texte und ihr literarisches und historisches Umfeld (1.-11. Jh.)* (EHS.Th 172), Frankfurt am M./Bern/New York: Peter Lang 1982.

Schreckenberg, Heinz, *The Jews in Christian Art: An Illustrated History* ET, London: SCM 1996.

Schreiber, E., "Humility", *JE* 6:490-92.

Schreiner, Thomas R., *The Law and its Fulfillment: A Pauline Theology of Law*, Grand Rapids: Baker 1993.

Schreiner, Thomas R., "Paul and Perfect Obedience of the Law: An Evaluation of the View of E.P. Sanders", *WTJ* 47 (1985) 245-78.

Schrenk, Gottlob, "Der Name Israel: Der Segenswunsch nach der Kampfepistel", *Jud* 6 (1950) 170-90.

Schrenk, Gottlob, *Die Weissagung über Israel im Neuen Testament*, Zürich: Gotthelf-Verlag 1951.

Schrenk, Gottlob, "Was bedeutet 'Israel Gottes'?", *Jud* 5 (1949) 81-94.

Schrenk, Gottlob, γράφω κτλ, *TDNT* 1:742-73.

Schrenk, Gottlob, ἐκλέγομαι, *TDNT* 4:168-76.

Schunck, Klaus-Dietrich, *Benjamin. Untersuchungen zur Entstehung und Geschichte eines israelitischen Stammes* (BZAW 86), Berlin: Walter de Gruyter 1963.

Schunck, Klaus-Dietrich, "Makkabäer/Makkabäerbücher", *TRE* 21:736-45.

Schüpphaus, J., *Die Psalmen Salomos: Ein Zeugnis Jerusalemer Theologie und Frömmigkeit in der Mitte des vorchristlichen Jahrhunderts* (ALGHJ 7), Leiden: E.J. Brill 1977.

Schürer, Emil, *Geschichte des jüdischen Volkes im Zeitalter Jesu Christi*, 4 vols, Leipzig: J.C. Hinrichs'sche Buchhandlung [4]1901-11, ([1]1886-90).

Schürer, Emil, *A History of the Jewish People in the Time of Jesus Christ*, 3 vols, Peabody: Hendrickson 1994 (repr.), (Edinburgh: T. & T. Clark [1]1890).

Schürer, Emil, *The History of the Jewish People in the Age of Jesus Christ* (revised and edited by Geza and Pamela Vermes, Fergus Millar, Martin Goodman and Matthew Black), 3 vols, Edinburgh: T. & T. Clark 1973-86.

Schwartz, Daniel R., *Leben durch Jesus versus Leben durch die Torah: Zur Religionspolemik der ersten Jahrhunderte* (Franz-Delitzsch-Vorlesung 1991), Münster: Franz-Delitzsch-Gesellschaft 1993.

Schweizer, Eduard, "'Der Jude im Verborgenen . . ., dessen Lob nicht von Menschen, sondern von Gott kommt'. Zu Röm 2,28f und Mt 6,1-18", in Joachim Gnilka (ed.), *Neues Testament und Kirche: Für Rudolf Schnackenburg*, Freiburg/Basel/Wien: Herder 1974.

Schweizer, Eduard – Meyer, Rudolf, σάρξ κτλ, *TDNT* 7:98-151.

Schwemer, Anna Maria, *Studien zu den frühjüdischen Prophetenlegenden Vitae Prophetarum Band I: Die Viten der großen Propheten Jesaja, Jeremia, Ezekiel und Daniel* (TSAJ 49), Tübingen: J.C.B. Mohr (Paul Siebeck) 1995.

Schwemer, Anna Maria, *Studien zu den frühjüdischen Prophetenlegenden Vitae Prophetarum Band II: Die Viten der kleinen Propheten und der Propheten aus den Geschichtsbüchern* (TSAJ 50), Tübingen: J.C.B. Mohr (Paul Siebeck) 1996.

Scott, James M., *Adoption as Sons of God: An Exegetical Investigation into the Background of YIOΘΕΣΙA in the Pauline Corpus* (WUNT 2.48), Tübingen: J.C.B. Mohr (Paul Siebeck) 1992.

Scott, James M., "'And then all Israel will be saved' (Rom 11:26)", in J.M. Scott (ed.), *Restoration: Old Testament, Jewish, and Christian Perspectives* (JSJSup 72), Leiden/Boston/Köln: Brill 2001, 489-527.

Segal, Alan F., "Covenant in rabbinic writings", *SR* 14 (1985) 53-62.

Segal, Alan F., *Paul the Convert: The Apostolate and Apostasy of Saul the Pharisee*, New Haven/London: Yale University Press 1990.

Seifrid, Mark A., *Christ, our Righteousness: Paul's Theology of Justification* (NSBT 9), Downers Grove: IVP 2000.

Seifrid, Mark A., *Justification by Faith: The Origin and Development of a Central Pauline Theme* (NovTSup 68), Leiden: E.J. Brill 1992.

Seifrid, Mark A., "The 'New Perspective on Paul' and Its Problems", *Themelios* 25.2 (2000) 4-18.

Sellin, Gerhard, "Mythologeme und mythische Züge in der paulinischen Theologie", in H.H. Schmid, *Mythos und Rationalität*, Gütersloh: Gütersloher Verlagshaus Gerd Mohn 1988, 219 (209-23).

Siegele-Wenschkewitz, Leonore, *Neutestamentliche Wissenschaft vor der Judenfrage: Gerhard Kittels theologische Arbeit im Wandel deutscher Geschichte* (ThExH 208), München: Chr. Kaiser Verlag 1980.

Siegert, Folker, *Argumentation bei Paulus gezeigt an Röm 9-11* (WUNT 34), Tübingen: J.C.B. Mohr (Paul Siebeck) 1985.

Siegert, Folker, *Drei hellenisch-jüdische Predigten. Ps.-Philon, 'Über Jona', 'Über Jona' (Fragment) und 'Über Simson' II. Kommentar* (WUNT 61), Tübingen: J.C.B. Mohr (Paul Siebeck) 1992.

Siegfried, G., "Wisdom, Book of", *HDB*, 4:928-31.

Simon, Marcel, *Verus Israel: A Study of the relations between Christians and Jews in the Roman Empire (135-425)* (LLJC) ET, Oxford: OUP 1986.

Simpson, John W., "The Problems Posed By 1 Thessalonians 2:15-16 And A Solution", *HBT* 12 (1990) 42-72.

Sjöberg, Erik, *Gott und die Sünder im palästinischen Judentum*, Stuttgart/Berlin: W. Kohlhammer Verlag 1938.

Skehan, Patrick W. - Di Lella, Alexander A., *The Wisdom of Ben Sira* (AB 39), New York: Doubleday 1986.

Skinner, John, *A Critical and Exegetical Commentary on Genesis* (ICC), Edinburgh: T. & T. Clark ²1930, (¹1910).

Soulen, R. Kendall, "Removing Anti-Judaism" in Howard Clark Kee and Irvin J. Borowsky (ed.), *Removing the Anti-Judaism from the New Testament*, Philadelphia: American Interfaith Institute 1998, 149-56.

van Spanje, T.E., *Inconsistency in Paul? A Critique of the Work of Heikki Räisänen* (WUNT 2.110), Tübingen: J.C.B. Mohr (Paul Siebeck) 1999.

Speiser, E.A., *Genesis* (AB), Garden City, New York: Doubleday & Co. 1964.

Spicq, Ceslas, "ΑΜΕΤΑΜΕΛΗΤΟΣ dans Rom., XI,29", *RB* 67 (1960) 210-19.

Staab, Karl, *Pauluskommentare aus der griechischen Kirche*, Münster: Aschendorff 1933.

Stählin, Gustav, *Die Apostelgeschichte* (NTD 5), Göttingen: Vandenhoeck & Ruprecht ³1968, (¹1936).

Stanley, Christopher D., *Paul and the Language of Scripture: Citation technique in the Pauline Epistles and contemporary literature* (SNTSMS 74), Cambridge: CUP 1992.

Stauffer, Ethelbert, *Die Theologie des Neuen Testaments*, Stuttgart: W. Kohlhammer Verlag ⁴1948, (¹1941).

Steck, Odil Hannes, *Israel und das gewaltsame Geschick der Propheten. Untersuchungen zur Überlieferung des deuteronomistischen Geschichtsbildes im Alten Testament, Spätjudentum und Urchristentum* (WMANT 23), Neukirchen-Vluyn: Neukirchener Verlag 1967.

Stegemann, Wolfgang, "War der Apostel Paulus ein römischer Bürger?", *ZNW* 78 (1987) 200-29.

Steiger, Lothar, "Schutzrede für Israel. Römer 9-11", in Theo Sundermeier (ed.), *Fides pro mundi vita: Missionstheologie heute. Hans-Werner Gensichen zum 65. Geburtstag* (Missionswissenschaftliche Forschungen 14), Gütersloh: Gütersloher Verlaghaus Gerd Mohn 1980, 44-58.

von Stemm, Sönke, *Der betende Sünder vor Gott. Studien zu Vergebungsvorstellungen in urchristlichen und frühjüdischen Texten* (AGAJU 45), Leiden/Boston/Köln: E.J. Brill 1999.

Stendahl, Krister, "Biblical Theology, Contemporary", in *IDB* 1:418-32.

Stendahl, Krister, "Christ's Lordship and Religious Pluralism", in *Meanings: The Bible as Document and as Guide*, Philadelphia: Fortress Press 1984, 233-44.

Stendahl, Krister, "Judaism and Christianity I: Then and Now", in *Meanings: The Bible as Document and as Guide*, Philadelphia: Fortress Press 1984, 205-15.

Stendahl, Krister, "Judaism and Christianity II: A Plea for a New Relationship", in *Meanings: The Bible as Document and as Guide*, Philadelphia: Fortress Press 1984, 217-32.

Stendahl, Krister, *Paul among Jews and Gentiles and Other Essays*, London: SCM 1976.

Steudel, Annette, *Der Midrasch zur Eschatologie aus der Qumrangemeinde (4QMidrEschat$^{a.b}$)* (STDJ 13), Leiden/New York/Köln: E.J. Brill 1994.

Stock-Hesketh, Jonathan, "Law in Jewish Intertestamental Apocalyptic", Nottingham Ph.D. Thesis 1993.

Stone, David, *Fourth Ezra: A Commentary on the Book of Fourth Ezra* (Hermeneia), Minnealopis: Fortress Press 1990.

Stone, Michael E., "On Reading an Apocalypse", in John J. Collins and James H. Charlesworth (ed.), *Mysteries and Revelations: Apocalyptic Studies since the Uppsala Colloquium* (JSPSup 9), Sheffield: JSOT Press 1991, 65-78.

Stott, J.R.W., *Romans*, Leicester: IVP 1994.

Strack, Hermann L. - Stemberger, Günter, *Einleitung in Talmud und Midrasch*, München: Verlag C.H. Beck [7]1982.

Strathmann, Hermann, λατρεύω, λατρεία, *TDNT* 4:58-65.

Strecker, Georg, "Befreiung und Rechtfertigung: Zur Stellung der Rechtfertigungslehre in der Theologie des Paulus", in Johannes Friedrich, Wolfgang Pöhlmann, and Peter Stuhlmacher (ed.), *Rechtfertigung: Festschrift für Ernst Käsemann zum 70. Geburtstag*, Tübingen: J.C.B. Mohr (Paul Siebeck)/Göttingen: Vandenhoeck & Ruprecht 1976, 479-508.

Strobel, August, *Die Stunde der Wahrheit: Untersuchungen zum Strafverfahren gegen Jesus* (WUNT 21), Tübingen: J.C.B. Mohr (Paul Siebeck) 1980.

Stuhlmacher, Peter, "Achtzehn Thesen zur paulinischen Kreuzestheologie", in *Versöhnung, Gesetz und Gerechtigkeit: Aufsätze zur biblischen Theologie*, Göttingen: Vandenhoeck & Ruprecht 1981, 192-208.

Stuhlmacher, Peter, *Biblische Theologie des Neuen Testaments, Bd 1: Grundlegung. Von Jesus zu Paulus*, Göttingen: Vandenhoeck & Ruprecht 1992.

Stuhlmacher, Peter, *Der Brief an Philemon* (EKK 18), Zürich/Braunschweig: Benziger Verlag/Neukirchen-Vluyn: Neukirchener Verlag [3]1989, ([1]1975).

Stuhlmacher, Peter, *Der Brief an die Römer* (NTD 6), Göttingen: Vandenhoeck & Ruprecht 1989.

Stuhlmacher, Peter, *Gerechtigkeit Gottes bei Paulus* (FRLANT 87), Göttingen: Vandenhoeck & Ruprecht [2]1966, ([1]1965).

Stuhlmacher, Peter, "Das Gesetz als Thema biblischer Theologie", in *Versöhnung, Gesetz und Gerechtigkeit: Aufsätze zur biblischen Theologie*, Göttingen: Vandenhoeck & Ruprecht 1981, 136-65.

Stuhlmacher, Peter, "Der messianische Gottesknecht", in *Biblische Theologie und Evangelium. Gesammelte Aufsätze* (WUNT 146), Tübingen: J.C.B. Mohr (Paul Siebeck) 2002, 119-40.

Stuhlmacher, Peter, *Das paulinische Evangelium: I. Vorgeschichte* (FRLANT 95), Göttingen: Vandenhoeck & Ruprecht 1968.

Stuhlmacher, Peter, *Revisiting Paul's Doctrine of Justification: A Challenge to the New Perspective*, Downers Grove: IVP 2001.

Stuhlmacher, Peter, "Die Stellung Jesu und des Paulus zu Jerusalem", *ZThK* 86 (1989) 140-56.

Stuhlmacher, Peter, *Vom Verstehen des Neuen Testaments: Eine Hermeneutik* (GNT 6), Göttingen: Vandenhoeck & Ruprecht ^{2}1986, (^{1}1979).

Stuhlmacher, Peter, "Zur Interpretation von Römer 11$_{25-32}$", in Hans Walter Wolff (ed.), *Probleme biblischer Theologie: G. von Rad zum 70. Geburtstag*, München: Chr. Kaiser Verlag 1971, 555-70.

Stuhlmann, R., *Das eschatologische Maß im Neuen Testament* (FRLANT 132), Göttingen: Vandenhoeck & Ruprecht 1983.

Swetnam, James, "The Curious Crux at Romans 4,12", *Bib* 61 (1980) 110-15.

Tajra, Harry W., *The Trial of St. Paul: A Juridical Exegesis of the Second Half of the Acts of the Apostles* (WUNT 2.35), Tübingen: J.C.B. Mohr (Paul Siebeck) 1989.

Tannehill, Robert C., *Dying and Rising with Christ: A Study in Pauline Theology* (BZNW 32), Berlin: Alfred Töpelmann 1967.

Tcherikover, V., *Hellenistic Civilisation and the Jews* ET, Philadelphia: JPS 1959.

Theißen, Gerd, "Theologie und Exegese in den neutestamentlichen Arbeiten von Günther Bornkamm", *EvTh* 51 (1991) 308-322.

Theobald, Michael, "'Dem Juden zuerst und auch dem Heiden'. Die paulinische Auslegung der Glaubensformel Röm 1,3f.", in *Studien zum Römerbrief* (WUNT 136), Tübingen: J.C.B. Mohr (Paul Siebeck) 2001, 102-18.

Theobald, Michael, "Der 'strittige Punkt' (Rhet. a. Her. I,26) im Diskurs des Römerbriefs: Die propositio 1,16f und das Mysterium der Errettung ganz Israels", in *Studien zum Römerbrief* (WUNT 136), Tübingen: J.C.B. Mohr (Paul Siebeck) 2001, 278-323.

Theobald, Michael, *Die überströmende Gnade: Studien zu einem paulinischen Motivfeld* (FzB 22), Würzburg: Echter Verlag 1982.

Theobald, Michael, "Mit verbundenen Augen? Kirche und Synagoge nach dem Neuen Testament", in *Studien zum Römerbrief* (WUNT 136), Tübingen: J.C.B. Mohr (Paul Siebeck) 2001, 367-95.

Thiselton, Anthony C., *The First Epistle to the Corinthians* (NIGTC), Grand Rapids/ Cambridge: Wm B. Eerdmans/ Carlisle: Paternoster 2000.

Thiselton, Anthony C., "The New Hermeneutic", in I. Howard Marshall (ed.), *New Testament Intrepretation: Essays on Principles and Methods*, Exeter: Paternoster ²1979, (¹1977), 308-33.

Thiselton, Anthony C., "Truth", *NIDNTT* 3:874-902.

Thoma, Clemens, *A Christian Theology of Judaism* (with a forward by David Flusser) (SJC) ET, New York: Paulist Press 1980.

Thompson, A.L., *Responsibility for Evil in the Theodicy of IV Ezra: A Study Illustrating the Significance of Form and Structure for the Meaning of the Book* (SBLDS 29), Missoula: Scholars Press 1977.

Thompson, Michael B., *Clothed with Christ: The Example and Teaching of Jesus in Romans 12.1-15.13* (JSNTSup 59), Sheffield: Sheffield Academic Press 1991.

Thornton, Claus-Jürgen, *Der Zeuge des Zeugen: Lukas als Historiker der Paulusreisen* (WUNT 56), Tübingen: J.C.B. Mohr (Paul Siebeck) 1991.

du Toit, Andrie B., "A Tale of Two Cities: 'Tarsus or Jerusalem' Revisited", *NTS* 46 (2000) 384 (375-402).

Torrance, David W., "The witness of the Jews to God (their purpose in history)", in D.W. Torrance (ed.), *The Witness of the Jews to God*, Edinburgh: Handsel Press 1982, 1-12.

Torrance, Thomas F., "The divine vocation and destiny of Israel in world history", in David W. Torrance (ed.), *The Witness of the Jews to God*, Edinburgh: Handsel Press 1982, 85-104.

Torrance, Thomas F., "The Roman Doctrine of Grace and the Point of View of Reformed Theology", in *Theology in Reconstruction*, London: SCM 1965, 169-91.

Trevor-Roper, Hugh, (ed.), *Hitler's Table-Talk, 1941-44*, Oxford: OUP 1988 (repr.), (¹1953).

Trilling, Wolfgang, "Die beiden Briefe des Apostels Paulus an die Thessalonicher: Eine Forschungsübersicht", *ANRW* 2.25.4 (1987) 3365-3403.

Tuckett, C.M., "Deuteronomy 21,23 and Paul's Conversion", in A. Vanhoye (ed.), *L'apôtre Paul: Personnalité, style et conception du ministère* (BEThL 73), Leuven: Leuven University Press 1986, 345-50.

Twelftree, Graham H., *Jesus the Exorcist: A Contribution to the Study of the Historical Jesus* (WUNT 2.54), Tübingen: J.C.B. Mohr (Paul Siebeck) 1993.

van Unnik, W.C., "Tarsus or Jerusalem: The City of Paul's Youth", in *Sparsa Collecta: The Collected Essays of W.C. van Unnik (Part One)* (NovTSup 29), Leiden: E.J. Brill 1973, 259-320.

Urbach, E.E., *The Sages - Their Concepts and Beliefs* ET, 2 vols, Jerusalem: Magnes Press, Hebrew University 1975.

VanderKam, James C., "Anthropological Gleanings from the Book of Jubilees", in Ulrike Mittmann-Richert, Friedrich Avemarie and Gerbern S. Oegema (ed.), *Der Mensch vor Gott. Forschungen zum Menschenbild in Bibel, antikem Judentum und Koran. Festschrift für Hermann Lichtenberger zum 60. Geburtstag*, Neukirchen-Vlyun: Neukirchener Verlag 2003, 117-32.

Vermes, Geza, *The Dead Sea Scrolls: Qumran in Perspective*, London: SCM ³1994, (¹1977).

Vouga, François, "Paulus und die Juden. Interpretation aus der Zeitstimmung", *WuD* 20 (1989) 105-20.

De Vries, Simon J., *1 Kings* (WBC 12), Waco: Word Books 1985.

Wagner, J.Ross, *Heralds of the Good News: Isaiah and Paul "In Concert" in the Letter to the Romans* (NovTSup 101), Leiden/Boston/Köln: Brill 2002.

Wakely, Robin, חזק, *DOTTE* 2:63-87.

Walker, Larry – Swart, I., קשה, *DOTTE* 3:997-99.

Walker, P.W.L., *Jesus and the Holy City: New Testament Perspectives on Jerusalem*, Grand Rapids/Cambridge U.K.: Wm B. Eerdmans 1996.

Wallace, Richard – Williams, Wynne, *The Three Worlds of Paul of Tarsus*, London/New York: Routledge 1998.

Walter, Nikolaus, "Zur Interpretation von Römer 9-11", *ZThK* 81 (1984) 172-95.

Wanamaker, Charles A., *The Epistles to the Thessalonians: A Commentary on the Greek Text* (NIGTC), Grand Rapids: Wm B. Eerdmans/Exeter: Paternoster 1990.

Wanamaker, Charles A., "Philippians 2.6-11: Son of God or Adamic Christology?", *NTS* 33 (1987) 179-93.

Watson, Francis, *Paul, Judaism and the Gentiles: A Sociological Approach* (SNTSMS 56), Cambridge: CUP 1986.

Watson, Francis, "The Triune Divine Identity: Reflections on Pauline God-Language, in Disagreement with J.D.G. Dunn", *JSNT* 80 (2000) 99-124.

Watson, Philip S., (ed.), *A Commentary on St. Paul's Epistle to the Galatians by Martin Luther*, London: James Clarke 1961 (repr.), (¹1953).

Way, David V., *The Lordship of Christ: Ernst Käsemann's Interpretation of Paul's Theology* (OTM), Oxford: Clarendon Press 1991.

Weatherly, Jon A., "The Authenticity of 1 Thessalonians 2.13-16: Additional Evidence", *JSNT* 42 (1991) 79-98.

Weatherly, Jon A., *Jewish Responsibility for the Death of Jesus in Luke-Acts* (JSNTSup 106), Sheffield: Sheffield Academic Press 1994.

Weber, Ferdinand, *Jüdische Theologie auf Grund des Talmud und verwandter Schriften*, Leipzig: Dörffling & Franke 1897.

Weber, Ferdinand, *System der altsynagogalen palästinischen Theologie aus Targum, Midrasch und Talmud* (ed. by Franz Delitzsch and Georg Schnedermann), Leipzig: Dörffling & Franke 1880.

Wedderburn, A.J.M., "Paul's Collection: Chronology and History", *NTS* 48 (2002) 95-110.

Weder, Hans, "Die Externität der Mitte. Überlegungen zum hermeneutischen Problem des Kriteriums der Sachkritik am Neuen Testament", in Christof Landmesser, Hans-Joachim Eckstein and Hermann Lichtenberger (ed.), *Jesus Christus als die Mitte der Schrift* (BZNW 86), Berlin/New York: Walter de Gruyter 1997, 291-320.

Weima, Jeffrey A.D., "Gal. 6,11-18: a Hermeneutical Key to the Galatian Letter", *CTJ* 28 (1993) 90-107.

Weima, Jeffrey A.D., "The Pauline Letter Closings: Analysis and Hermeneutical Significance", *BBR* 5 (1995) 177-98.

Weinrich, Harald, *Tempus: Besprochene und erzählte Welt*, Stuttgart: W. Kohlhammer [2]1971, ([1]1964).

Weisengoff, J.P., "The Impious of Wisdom 2", *CBQ* 11 (1949) 40-65.

Weiser, Artur, *The Psalms* (OTL) ET, London: SCM 1962.

Weiß, Bernhard, *Der Brief an die Römer* (KEK 4), Göttingen: Vandenhoeck & Ruprecht [9]1899, ([6]1881).

Weiß, Johannes, *Der erste Korintherbrief* (KEK 5), Göttingen: Vandenhoeck & Ruprecht 1977 (repr.), ([9]1910).

Weiß, Johannes, *Das Urchristentum*, Göttingen: Vandenhoeck & Ruprecht 1917.

Wellhausen, Julius, *Die Pharisäer und die Sadducäer: Eine Untersuchung zur inneren jüdischen Geschichte*, Göttingen: Vandenhoeck & Ruprecht [3]1967, ([1]1874).

Wellhausen, Julius, *Prolegomena to the History of Ancient Israel* ET, Cleveland/New York: World Publishing Company 1957.

Wenham, David, *Paul: Follower of Jesus or Founder of Christianity?*, Grand Rapids: Wm B. Eerdmans 1995.

Wenham, David, "Paul and the Synoptic Apocalypse", in R.T. France and David Wenham (ed.), *Gospel Perspectives: Studies in History and Tradition in the Four Gospels, Volume II*, Sheffield: JSOT Press 1981, 345-75.

Wenham, Gordon, *Genesis 16-50* (WBC 2), Dallas, Texas: Word Books 1994.

Wenham, John W., *Christ and the Bible*, London: Tyndale Press 1972.

Wenham, John W., *Redating Matthew, Mark and Luke: A Fresh Assault on the Synoptic Problem*, London: Hodder & Stoughton 1991.

Wernle, Paul, *Paulus als Heidenmissionar*, Tübingen: J.C.B. Mohr (Paul Siebeck) [2]1909, ([1]1899).

Westerholm, Stephen, *Israel's Law and the Church's Faith: Paul and His Recent Interpreters*, Grand Rapids: Wm B. Eerdmans 1988.

Whiteley, D.E.H., *The Theology of St. Paul*, Oxford: Blackwell [2]1974, ([1]1964).

Wicke-Reuter, Ursel, *Göttliche Providenz und menschliche Verantwortung bei Ben Sira und in der Frühen Stoa* (BZAW 298), Berlin/New York: Walter de Gruyter 2000.

Wiefel, Wolfgang, "The Jewish Community in Ancient Rome and the Origins of Roman Christianity", in Karl P. Donfried (ed.), *The Romans Debate*, Peabody: Hendrickson [2]1991, ([1]1977), 85-101.

Wiesel, Elie, *Night: His Record of Childhood in the Death Camps of Auschwitz and Buchenwald*, Harmondsworth: Penguin 1969.

Wikenhauser, Alfred, *Die Apostelgeschichte* (RNT 5), Regensburg: Friedrich Pustet [4]1961, ([1]1956).

Wilckens, Ulrich, "Die Bekehrung des Paulus als religionsgeschichtliches Problem", *ZThK* 56 (1959) 273-93 (= *Rechtfertigung als Freiheit: Paulusstudien*, Neukirchen-Vluyn: Neukirchener Verlag 1974, 11-32).

Wilckens, Ulrich, *Der Brief an die Römer* (EKK 6), 3 vols, Zürich/Einsiedeln/Köln: Benziger Verlag/Neukirchen-Vluyn: Neukirchener Verlag 1 1978; 2 1980; 3 1982.

Wildberger, Hans, *Jesaja, 1. Teilband: Jesaja 1-12* (BKAT 10/1), Neukirchen-Vluyn: Neukirchener Verlag 1972.

Wiles, Gordon P., *Paul's Intercessory Prayers: The Significance of the Intercessory Prayer Passages in the Letters of St Paul* (SNTSMS 24), Cambridge: CUP 1974.

Wilkinson, J., "Ancient Jerusalem: Its Water Supply and Population", *PEQ* 106 (1974) 33-51.

Wilson, Harold, *The Chariot of Israel: Britain, America and the State of Israel*, London: George Weidenfeld & Nicholson/Michael Joseph 1981.

Windisch, Hans, *Paulus und das Judentum*, Stuttgart: W. Kohlhammer Verlag 1935.

Windisch, Hans, *Der zweite Korintherbrief* (KEK 6), Göttingen: Vandenhoeck & Ruprecht [9]1924.

Winninge, Mikael, *Sinners and the Righteous: A Comparative Study of the Psalms of Solomon and Paul's Letters* (CB.NT 26), Stockholm: Almqvist & Wiksell 1995.

Winter, Paul, *On the Trial of Jesus* (SJ 1), Berlin: de Gruyter 1961.

Winter, Paul, "The Trial of Jesus and the Competence of the Sanhedrin", *NTS* 10 (1963-64) 494-99.

Wischmeyer, Oda, "Staat und Christen nach Röm 13,1-7. Ein hermeneutischer Zugang", in Martin Karrer, Wolfgang Kraus and Otto Merk (ed.), *Kirche und Volk Gottes: Festschrift für Jürgen Roloff zum 70. Geburtstag*, Neukirchen-Vluyn: Neukirchener 2000, 149-62.

Wolff, Christian, *Der erste Brief des Paulus an die Korinther* (ThHK 7), Leipzig: Evangelische Verlagsanstalt [2]2000, ([1]1996).

Wolff, Christian, *Der zweite Brief des Paulus an die Korinther* (ThHK 8), Berlin: Evangelische Verlagsanstalt 1989.

Wolter, Michael, "Pseudonymität II", *TRE* 27:662-70.

Wood, H.G., "The Conversion of St Paul: Its Nature, Antecedents and Consequences", *NTS* 1 (1954-55) 276-82.

van der Woude, A.S., חזק, *THAT* 1:538-41.

van der Woude, A.S., קשה, *THAT* 2:689-92.

Wrede, William, "Paulus", in Karl Heinrich Rengstorf (ed.), *Das Paulusbild in der neueren deutschen Forschung* (WdF 24), Darmstadt: Wissenschaftliche Buchgesellschaft 1982, 1-97 (= Religionsgeschichtliche Volksbücher I, Halle 1904).

Wright, N.T., *The Climax of the Covenant: Christ and the Law in Pauline Theology*, Edinburgh: T. & T. Clark 1991.

Wright, N.T., *The Messiah and the People of God: A Study in Pauline Theology with Particular Reference to the Argument of the Epistle to the Romans*, Oxford D. Phil. Thesis 1980.

Wright, N.T., *The New Testament and the People of God*, London: SPCK 1992.

Wright, N.T., "The Letter to the Romans", *NIB* 10 (2002) 393-770.

Wright, N.T., *What Saint Paul Really Said*, Oxford: Lion 1997.

Wright, N.T., "ἁρπαγμός and the Meaning of Philippians 2:5-11", *JTS* 37 (1986) 321-52.

Wyschogrod, Michael, *The Body of Faith: Judaism as Corporate Election*, Minneapolis: Seabury Press 1983.

Yadin, Y., "Pesher Nahum 4QpNahum Reconsidered", in *IEJ* 21 (1971) 1-12.

Yinger, K., *Paul, Judaism, and Judgement according to Deeds* (SNTMS 105), Cambridge: CUP 1999.

Zahl, Paul Francis Matthew, *Die Rechtfertigungslehre Ernst Käsemanns* (CThM B13), Stuttgart: Calwer Verlag 1996.

Zahn, Theodor, *Der Brief des Paulus an die Römer* (KzNT 6), Leipzig: A. Deichertsche Verlagsbuchhandlung ³1925.

Zeller, Dieter, *Juden und Heiden in der Mission des Paulus: Studien zum Römerbrief* (FzB 8), Stuttgart: Verlag Katholisches Bibelwerk ²1976, (¹1973).

Ziesler, John, *Paul's Letter to the Romans* (TPINTC), London: SCM/Philadelphia: Trinity Press International 1989.

Ziesler, John, *Pauline Christianity* (OBS), Oxford/New York: OUP 1990.

Zimmerli, Walther – Jeremias, Joachim, παῖς θεοῦ, *TDNT* 5:654-717.

Index of Authors

Index of References

14. Early Christian Writings and Patristic Literature

15. Greek and Roman Authors

Index of Subjects and Names

Wissenschaftliche Untersuchungen zum Neuen Testament

Alphabetical Index of the First and Second Series

Böhm, Martina: Samarien und die Samaritai bei Lukas. 1999. *Volume II/111.*

Böttrich, Christfried: Weltweisheit – Menschheitsethik – Urkult. 1992. *Volume II/50.*

Bolyki, János: Jesu Tischgemeinschaften. 1997. *Volume II/96.*

Bosman, Philip: Conscience in Philo and Paul. 2003. *Volume II/166.*

Bovon, François: Studies in Early Christianity. 2003. *Volume 161.*

Brocke, Christoph vom: Thessaloniki – Stadt des Kassander und Gemeinde des Paulus. 2001. *Volume II/125.*

Brunson, Andrew: Psalm 118 in the Gospel of John. 2003. *Volume II/158.*

Büchli, Jörg: Der Poimandres – ein paganisiertes Evangelium. 1987. *Volume II/27.*

Bühner, Jan A.: Der Gesandte und sein Weg im 4. Evangelium. 1977. *Volume II/2.*

Burchard, Christoph: Untersuchungen zu Joseph und Aseneth. 1965. *Volume 8.*

– Studien zur Theologie, Sprache und Umwelt des Neuen Testaments. Ed. von D. Sänger. 1998. *Volume 107.*

Burnett, Richard: Karl Barth's Theological Exegesis. 2001. *Volume II/145.*

Byron, John: Slavery Metaphors in Early Judaism and Pauline Christianity. 2003. *Volume II/162.*

Byrskog, Samuel: Story as History – History as Story. 2000. *Volume 123.*

Cancik, Hubert (Ed.): Markus-Philologie. 1984. *Volume 33.*

Capes, David B.: Old Testament Yaweh Texts in Paul's Christology. 1992. *Volume II/47.*

Caragounis, Chrys C.: The Development of Greek and the New Testament. 2004. *Volume 167.*

– The Son of Man. 1986. *Volume 38.*

– see *Fridrichsen, Anton.*

Carleton Paget, James: The Epistle of Barnabas. 1994. *Volume II/64.*

Carson, D.A., O'Brien, Peter T. and *Mark Seifrid* (Ed.): Justification and Variegated Nomism.

Volume 1: The Complexities of Second Temple Judaism. 2001. *Volume II/140.*

Volume 2: The Paradoxes of Paul. 2004. *Volume II/181.*

Ciampa, Roy E.: The Presence and Function of Scripture in Galatians 1 and 2. 1998. *Volume II/102.*

Classen, Carl Joachim: Rhetorical Criticsm of the New Testament. 2000. *Volume 128.*

Colpe, Carsten: Iranier – Aramäer – Hebräer – Hellenen. 2003. *Volume 154.*

Crump, David: Jesus the Intercessor. 1992. *Volume II/49.*

Dahl, Nils Alstrup: Studies in Ephesians. 2000. *Volume 131.*

Deines, Roland: Die Gerechtigkeit der Tora im Reich des Messias. 2004. *Volume 177.*

– Jüdische Steingefäße und pharisäische Frömmigkeit. 1993. *Volume II/52.*

– Die Pharisäer. 1997. *Volume 101.*

– and *Karl-Wilhelm Niebuhr (Ed.):* Philo und das Neue Testament. 2004. *Volume 172.*

Dettwiler, Andreas and *Jean Zumstein (Ed.):* Kreuzestheologie im Neuen Testament. 2002. *Volume 151.*

Dickson, John P.: Mission-Commitment in Ancient Judaism and in the Pauline Communities. 2003. *Volume II/159.*

Dietzfelbinger, Christian: Der Abschied des Kommenden. 1997. *Volume 95.*

Dimitrov, Ivan Z., James D.G. Dunn, Ulrich Luz and *Karl-Wilhelm Niebuhr* (Ed.): Das Alte Testament als christliche Bibel in orthodoxer und westlicher Sicht. 2004. *Volume 174.*

Dobbeler, Axel von: Glaube als Teilhabe. 1987. *Volume II/22.*

Du Toit, David S.: Theios Anthropos. 1997. *Volume II/91*

Dübbers, Michael: Christologie und Existenz im Kolosserbrief. 2005. *Volume II/191.*

Dunn , James D.G. (Ed.): Jews and Christians. 1992. *Volume 66.*

– Paul and the Mosaic Law. 1996. *Volume 89.*

– see *Dimitrov, Ivan Z.*

Dunn, James D.G., Hans Klein, Ulrich Luz and *Vasile Mihoc* (Ed.): Auslegung der Bibel in orthodoxer und westlicher Perspektive. 2000. *Volume 130.*

Ebel, Eva: Die Attraktivität früher christlicher Gemeinden. 2004. *Volume II/178.*

Ebertz, Michael N.: Das Charisma des Gekreuzigten. 1987. *Volume 45.*

Eckstein, Hans-Joachim: Der Begriff Syneidesis bei Paulus. 1983. *Volume II/10.*

– Verheißung und Gesetz. 1996. *Volume 86.*

Ego, Beate: Im Himmel wie auf Erden. 1989. *Volume II/34*

Ego, Beate, Armin Lange and *Peter Pilhofer (Ed.):* Gemeinde ohne Tempel – Community without Temple. 1999. *Volume 118.*

Eisen, Ute E.: see *Paulsen, Henning.*

Ellis, E. Earle: Prophecy and Hermeneutic in Early Christianity. 1978. *Volume 18.*

– The Old Testament in Early Christianity. 1991. *Volume 54.*

Endo, Masanobu: Creation and Christology. 2002. *Volume 149.*

Ennulat, Andreas: Die 'Minor Agreements'. 1994. *Volume II/62.*

Ensor, Peter W.: Jesus and His 'Works'. 1996. *Volume II/85.*

Eskola, Timo: Messiah and the Throne. 2001. *Volume II/142.*

– Theodicy and Predestination in Pauline Soteriology. 1998. *Volume II/100.*

Fatehi, Mehrdad: The Spirit's Relation to the Risen Lord in Paul. 2000. *Volume II/128.*

Feldmeier, Reinhard: Die Krisis des Gottessohnes. 1987. *Volume II/21.*

– Die Christen als Fremde. 1992. *Volume 64.*

Feldmeier, Reinhard and *Ulrich Heckel* (Ed.): Die Heiden. 1994. *Volume 70.*

Fletcher-Louis, Crispin H.T.: Luke-Acts: Angels, Christology and Soteriology. 1997. *Volume II/94.*

Förster, Niclas: Marcus Magus. 1999. *Volume 114.*

Forbes, Christopher Brian: Prophecy and Inspired Speech in Early Christianity and its Hellenistic Environment. 1995. *Volume II/75.*

Fornberg, Tord: see *Fridrichsen, Anton.*

Fossum, Jarl E.: The Name of God and the Angel of the Lord. 1985. *Volume 36.*

Foster, Paul: Community, Law and Mission in Matthew's Gospel. *Volume II/177.*

Fotopoulos, John: Food Offered to Idols in Roman Corinth. 2003. *Volume II/151.*

Frenschkowski, Marco: Offenbarung und Epiphanie. Volume 1 1995. *Volume II/79 –* Volume 2 1997. *Volume II/80.*

Frey, Jörg: Eugen Drewermann und die biblische Exegese. 1995. *Volume II/71.*

– Die johanneische Eschatologie. Volume I. 1997. *Volume 96. –* Volume II. 1998. *Volume 110.*

– Volume III. 2000. *Volume 117.*

Frey, Jörg and *Udo Schnelle (Ed.):* Kontexte des Johannesevangeliums. 2004. *Volume 175.*

– and *Jens Schröter* (Ed.): Deutungen des Todes Jesu im Neuen Testament. 2005. *Volume 181.*

Freyne, Sean: Galilee and Gospel. 2000. *Volume 125.*

Fridrichsen, Anton: Exegetical Writings. Edited by C.C. Caragounis and T. Fornberg. 1994. *Volume 76.*

Garlington, Don B.: 'The Obedience of Faith'. 1991. *Volume II/38.*

– Faith, Obedience, and Perseverance. 1994. *Volume 79.*

Garnet, Paul: Salvation and Atonement in the Qumran Scrolls. 1977. *Volume II/3.*

Gemünden, Petra von (Ed.): see *Weissenrieder, Annette.*

Gese, Michael: Das Vermächtnis des Apostels. 1997. *Volume II/99.*

Gheorghita, Radu: The Role of the Septuagint in Hebrews. 2003. *Volume II/160.*

Gräbe, Petrus J.: The Power of God in Paul's Letters. 2000. *Volume II/123.*

Gräßer, Erich: Der Alte Bund im Neuen. 1985. *Volume 35.*

– Forschungen zur Apostelgeschichte. 2001. *Volume 137.*

Green, Joel B.: The Death of Jesus. 1988. *Volume II/33.*

Gregory, Andrew: The Reception of Luke and Acts in the Period before Irenaeus. 2003. *Volume II/169.*

Gundry, Robert H.: The Old is Better. 2005. *Volume 178.*

Gundry Volf, Judith M.: Paul and Perseverance. 1990. *Volume II/37.*

Hafemann, Scott J.: Suffering and the Spirit. 1986. *Volume II/19.*

– Paul, Moses, and the History of Israel. 1995. *Volume 81.*

Hahn, Johannes (Ed.): Zerstörungen des Jerusalemer Tempels. 2002. *Volume 147.*

Hannah, Darrel D.: Michael and Christ. 1999. *Volume II/109.*

Hamid-Khani, Saeed: Relevation and Concealment of Christ. 2000. *Volume II/120.*

Harrison; James R.: Paul's Language of Grace in Its Graeco-Roman Context. 2003. *Volume II/172.*

Hartman, Lars: Text-Centered New Testament Studies. Ed. von D. Hellholm. 1997. *Volume 102.*

Hartog, Paul: Polycarp and the New Testament. 2001. *Volume II/134.*

Heckel, Theo K.: Der Innere Mensch. 1993. *Volume II/53.*

– Vom Evangelium des Markus zum viergestaltigen Evangelium. 1999. *Volume 120.*

Heckel, Ulrich: Kraft in Schwachheit. 1993. *Volume II/56.*

– Der Segen im Neuen Testament. 2002. *Volume 150.*

– see *Feldmeier, Reinhard.*

– see *Hengel, Martin.*

Heiligenthal, Roman: Werke als Zeichen. 1983. *Volume II/9.*

Hellholm, D.: see *Hartman, Lars.*

Hemer, Colin J.: The Book of Acts in the Setting of Hellenistic History. 1989. *Volume 49.*

Hengel, Martin: Judentum und Hellenismus. 1969, ³1988. *Volume 10.*
– Die johanneische Frage. 1993. *Volume 67.*
– Judaica et Hellenistica.
 Kleine Schriften I. 1996. *Volume 90.*
– Judaica, Hellenistica et Christiana.
 Kleine Schriften II. 1999. *Volume 109.*
– Paulus und Jakobus.
 Kleine Schriften III. 2002. *Volume 141.*
Hengel, Martin and *Ulrich Heckel* (Ed.): Paulus und das antike Judentum. 1991. *Volume 58.*
Hengel, Martin and *Hermut Löhr* (Ed.): Schriftauslegung im antiken Judentum und im Urchristentum. 1994. *Volume 73.*
Hengel, Martin and *Anna Maria Schwemer:* Paulus zwischen Damaskus und Antiochien. 1998. *Volume 108.*
– Der messianische Anspruch Jesu und die Anfänge der Christologie. 2001. *Volume 138.*
Hengel, Martin and *Anna Maria Schwemer* (Ed.): Königsherrschaft Gottes und himmlischer Kult. 1991. *Volume 55.*
– Die Septuaginta. 1994. *Volume 72.*
Hengel, Martin; Siegfried Mittmann and *Anna Maria Schwemer* (Ed.): La Cité de Dieu / Die Stadt Gottes. 2000. *Volume 129.*
Herrenbrück, Fritz: Jesus und die Zöllner. 1990. *Volume II/41.*
Herzer, Jens: Paulus oder Petrus? 1998. *Volume 103.*
Hoegen-Rohls, Christina: Der nachösterliche Johannes. 1996. *Volume II/84.*
Hofius, Otfried: Katapausis. 1970. *Volume 11.*
– Der Vorhang vor dem Thron Gottes. 1972. *Volume 14.*
– Der Christushymnus Philipper 2,6-11. 1976, ²1991. *Volume 17.*
– Paulusstudien. 1989, ²1994. *Volume 51.*
– Neutestamentliche Studien. 2000. *Volume 132.*
– Paulusstudien II. 2002. *Volume 143.*
Hofius, Otfried and *Hans-Christian Kammler:* Johannesstudien. 1996. *Volume 88.*
Holtz, Traugott: Geschichte und Theologie des Urchristentums. 1991. *Volume 57.*
Hommel, Hildebrecht: Sebasmata. Volume 1 1983. *Volume 31* – Volume 2 1984. *Volume 32.*
Hvalvik, Reidar: The Struggle for Scripture and Covenant. 1996. *Volume II/82.*
Johns, Loren L.: The Lamb Christology of the Apocalypse of John. 2003. *Volume II/167.*
Joubert, Stephan: Paul as Benefactor. 2000. *Volume II/124.*
Jungbauer, Harry: „Ehre Vater und Mutter". 2002. *Volume II/146.*
Kähler, Christoph: Jesu Gleichnisse als Poesie und Therapie. 1995. *Volume 78.*

Kamlah, Ehrhard: Die Form der katalogischen Paränese im Neuen Testament. 1964. *Volume 7.*
Kammler, Hans-Christian: Christologie und Eschatologie. 2000. *Volume 126.*
– Kreuz und Weisheit. 2003. *Volume 159.*
– see *Hofius, Otfried.*
Kelhoffer, James A.: The Diet of John the Baptist. 2005. *Volume 176.*
– Miracle and Mission. 1999. *Volume II/112.*
Kieffer, René and *Jan Bergman (Ed.):* La Main de Dieu / Die Hand Gottes. 1997. *Volume 94.*
Kim, Seyoon: The Origin of Paul's Gospel. 1981, ²1984. *Volume II/4.*
– Paul and the New Perspective. 2002. *Volume 140.*
– "The 'Son of Man'" as the Son of God. 1983. *Volume 30.*
Klauck, Hans-Josef: Religion und Gesellschaft im frühen Christentum. 2003. *Volume 152.*
Klein, Hans: see *Dunn, James D.G..*
Kleinknecht, Karl Th.: Der leidende Gerechtfertigte. 1984, ²1988. *Volume II/13.*
Klinghardt, Matthias: Gesetz und Volk Gottes. 1988. *Volume II/32.*
Koch, Michael: Drachenkampf und Sonnenfrau. 2004. *Volume II/184.*
Koch, Stefan: Rechtliche Regelung von Konflikten im frühen Christentum. 2004. *Volume II/174.*
Köhler, Wolf-Dietrich: Rezeption des Matthäusevangeliums in der Zeit vor Irenäus. 1987. *Volume II/24.*
Köhn, Andreas: Der Neutestamentler Ernst Lohmeyer. 2004. *Volume II/180.*
Kooten, George H. van: Cosmic Christology in Paul and the Pauline School. 2003. *Volume II/171.*
Korn, Manfred: Die Geschichte Jesu in veränderter Zeit. 1993. *Volume II/51.*
Koskenniemi, Erkki: Apollonios von Tyana in der neutestamentlichen Exegese. 1994. *Volume II/61.*
Kraus, Thomas J.: Sprache, Stil und historischer Ort des zweiten Petrusbriefes. 2001. *Volume II/136.*
Kraus, Wolfgang: Das Volk Gottes. 1996. *Volume 85.*
– and *Karl-Wilhelm Niebuhr* (Ed.): Frühjudentum und Neues Testament im Horizont Biblischer Theologie. 2003. *Volume 162.*
– see *Walter, Nikolaus.*
Kreplin, Matthias: Das Selbstverständnis Jesu. 2001. *Volume II/141.*
Kuhn, Karl G.: Achtzehngebet und Vaterunser und der Reim. 1950. *Volume 1.*
Kvalbein, Hans: see *Ådna, Jostein.*

Nissen, Andreas: Gott und der Nächste im antiken Judentum. 1974. *Volume 15.*

Noack, Christian: Gottesbewußtsein. 2000. *Volume II/116.*

Noormann, Rolf: Irenäus als Paulusinterpret. 1994. *Volume II/66.*

Novakovic, Lidija: Messiah, the Healer of the Sick. 2003. *Volume II/170.*

Obermann, Andreas: Die christologische Erfüllung der Schrift im Johannesevangelium. 1996. *Volume II/83.*

Öhler, Markus: Barnabas. 2003. *Volume 156.*

Okure, Teresa: The Johannine Approach to Mission. 1988. *Volume II/31.*

Onuki, Takashi: Heil und Erlösung. 2004. *Volume 165.*

Oropeza, B. J.: Paul and Apostasy. 2000. *Volume II/115.*

Ostmeyer, Karl-Heinrich: Taufe und Typos. 2000. *Volume II/118.*

Paulsen, Henning: Studien zur Literatur und Geschichte des frühen Christentums. Ed. von Ute E. Eisen. 1997. *Volume 99.*

Pao, David W.: Acts and the Isaianic New Exodus. 2000. *Volume II/130.*

Park, Eung Chun: The Mission Discourse in Matthew's Interpretation. 1995. *Volume II/81.*

Park, Joseph S.: Conceptions of Afterlife in Jewish Insriptions. 2000. *Volume II/121.*

Pate, C. Marvin: The Reverse of the Curse. 2000. *Volume II/114.*

Peres, Imre: Griechische Grabinschriften und neutestamentliche Eschatologie. 2003. *Volume 157.*

Philip, Finny: The Originis of Pauline Pneumatology. *Volume II/194.*

Philonenko, Marc (Ed.): Le Trône de Dieu. 1993. *Volume 69.*

Pilhofer, Peter: Presbyteron Kreitton. 1990. *Volume II/39.*

– Philippi. Volume 1 1995. *Volume 87.* – Volume 2 2000. *Volume 119.*

– Die frühen Christen und ihre Welt. 2002. *Volume 145.*

– see *Ego, Beate.*

Plümacher, Eckhard: Geschichte und Geschichten. Aufsätze zur Apostelgeschichte und zu den Johannesakten. Herausgegeben von Jens Schröter und Ralph Brucker. 2004. *Volume 170.*

Pöhlmann, Wolfgang: Der Verlorene Sohn und das Haus. 1993. *Volume 68.*

Pokorný, Petr and *Josef B. Souček:* Bibelauslegung als Theologie. 1997. *Volume 100.*

Pokorný, Petr and *Jan Roskovec* (Ed.): Philosophical Hermeneutics and Biblical Exegesis. 2002. *Volume 153.*

Porter, Stanley E.: The Paul of Acts. 1999. *Volume 115.*

Prieur, Alexander: Die Verkündigung der Gottesherrschaft. 1996. *Volume II/89.*

Probst, Hermann: Paulus und der Brief. 1991. *Volume II/45.*

Räisänen, Heikki: Paul and the Law. 1983, ²1987. *Volume 29.*

Rehkopf, Friedrich: Die lukanische Sonderquelle. 1959. *Volume 5.*

Rein, Matthias: Die Heilung des Blindgeborenen (Joh 9). 1995. *Volume II/73.*

Reinmuth, Eckart: Pseudo-Philo und Lukas. 1994. *Volume 74.*

Reiser, Marius: Syntax und Stil des Markusevangeliums. 1984. *Volume II/11.*

Rhodes, James N.: The Epistle of Barnabas and the Deuteronomic Tradition. 2004. *Volume II/188.*

Richards, E. Randolph: The Secretary in the Letters of Paul. 1991. *Volume II/42.*

Riesner, Rainer: Jesus als Lehrer. 1981, ³1988. *Volume II/7.*

– Die Frühzeit des Apostels Paulus. 1994. *Volume 71.*

Rissi, Mathias: Die Theologie des Hebräerbriefs. 1987. *Volume 41.*

Roskovec, Jan: see *Pokorný, Petr.*

Röhser, Günter: Metaphorik und Personifikation der Sünde. 1987. *Volume II/25.*

Rose, Christian: Die Wolke der Zeugen. 1994. *Volume II/60.*

Rothschild, Clare K.: Luke Acts and the Rhetoric of History. 2004. *Volume II/175.*

Rüegger, Hans-Ulrich: Verstehen, was Markus erzählt. 2002. *Volume II/155.*

Rüger, Hans Peter: Die Weisheitsschrift aus der Kairoer Geniza. 1991. *Volume 53.*

Sänger, Dieter: Antikes Judentum und die Mysterien. 1980. *Volume II/5.*

– Die Verkündigung des Gekreuzigten und Israel. 1994. *Volume 75.*

– see *Burchard, Christoph*

Salier, Willis Hedley: The Rhetorical Impact of the Sēmeia in the Gospel of John. 2004. *Volume II/186.*

Salzmann, Jorg Christian: Lehren und Ermahnen. 1994. *Volume II/59.*

Sandnes, Karl Olav: Paul – One of the Prophets? 1991. *Volume II/43.*

Sato, Migaku: Q und Prophetie. 1988. *Volume II/29.*

Schäfer, Ruth: Paulus bis zum Apostelkonzil. 2004. *Volume II/179.*

Schaper, Joachim: Eschatology in the Greek Psalter. 1995. *Volume II/76.*

Schimanowski, Gottfried: Die himmlische Liturgie in der Apokalypse des Johannes. 2002. *Volume II/154.*

– Weisheit und Messias. 1985. *Volume II/17.*

Schlichting, Günter: Ein jüdisches Leben Jesu. 1982. *Volume 24.*

Schnabel, Eckhard J.: Law and Wisdom from Ben Sira to Paul. 1985. *Volume II/16.*

Schnelle, Udo: see *Frey, Jörg.*

Schröter, Jens: see *Frey, Jörg.*

Schutter, William L.: Hermeneutic and Composition in I Peter. 1989. *Volume II/30.*

Schwartz, Daniel R.: Studies in the Jewish Background of Christianity. 1992. *Volume 60.*

Schwemer, Anna Maria: see *Hengel, Martin*

Scott, James M.: Adoption as Sons of God. 1992. *Volume II/48.*

– Paul and the Nations. 1995. *Volume 84.*

Shum, Shiu-Lun: Paul's Use of Isaiah in Romans. 2002. *Volume II/156.*

Siegert, Folker: Drei hellenistisch-jüdische Predigten. Teil I 1980. *Volume 20* – Teil II 1992. *Volume 61.*

– Nag-Hammadi-Register. 1982. *Volume 26.*

– Argumentation bei Paulus. 1985. *Volume 34.*

– Philon von Alexandrien. 1988. *Volume 46.*

Simon, Marcel: Le christianisme antique et son contexte religieux I/II. 1981. *Volume 23.*

Snodgrass, Klyne: The Parable of the Wicked Tenants. 1983. *Volume 27.*

Söding, Thomas: Das Wort vom Kreuz. 1997. *Volume 93.*

– see *Thüsing, Wilhelm.*

Sommer, Urs: Die Passionsgeschichte des Markusevangeliums. 1993. *Volume II/58.*

Souček, Josef B.: see *Pokorný, Petr.*

Spangenberg, Volker: Herrlichkeit des Neuen Bundes. 1993. *Volume II/55.*

Spanje, T.E. van: Inconsistency in Paul? 1999. *Volume II/110.*

Speyer, Wolfgang: Frühes Christentum im antiken Strahlungsfeld. Volume I: 1989. *Volume 50.*

– Volume II: 1999. *Volume 116.*

Stadelmann, Helge: Ben Sira als Schriftgelehrter. 1980. *Volume II/6.*

Stenschke, Christoph W.: Luke's Portrait of Gentiles Prior to Their Coming to Faith. *Volume II/108.*

Sterck-Degueldre, Jean-Pierre: Eine Frau namens Lydia. 2004. *Volume II/176.*

Stettler, Christian: Der Kolosserhymnus. 2000. *Volume II/131.*

Stettler, Hanna: Die Christologie der Pastoralbriefe. 1998. *Volume II/105.*

Stökl Ben Ezra, Daniel: The Impact of Yom Kippur on Early Christianity. 2003. *Volume 163.*

Strobel, August: Die Stunde der Wahrheit. 1980. *Volume 21.*

Stroumsa, Guy G.: Barbarian Philosophy. 1999. *Volume 112.*

Stuckenbruck, Loren T.: Angel Veneration and Christology. 1995. *Volume II/70.*

Stuhlmacher, Peter (Ed.): Das Evangelium und die Evangelien. 1983. *Volume 28.*

– Biblische Theologie und Evangelium. 2002. *Volume 146.*

Sung, Chong-Hyon: Vergebung der Sünden. 1993. *Volume II/57.*

Tajra, Harry W.: The Trial of St. Paul. 1989. *Volume II/35.*

– The Martyrdom of St.Paul. 1994. *Volume II/67.*

Theißen, Gerd: Studien zur Soziologie des Urchristentums. 1979, ³1989. *Volume 19.*

Theobald, Michael: Studien zum Römerbrief. 2001. *Volume 136.*

Theobald, Michael: see *Mußner, Franz.*

Thornton, Claus-Jürgen: Der Zeuge des Zeugen. 1991. *Volume 56.*

Thüsing, Wilhelm: Studien zur neutestamentlichen Theologie. Ed. von Thomas Söding. 1995. *Volume 82.*

Thurén, Lauri: Derhethorizing Paul. 2000. *Volume 124.*

Tolmie, D. Francois: Persuading the Galatians. 2005. *Volume II/190.*

Tomson, Peter J. and Doris Lambers-Petry (Ed.): The Image of the Judaeo-Christians in Ancient Jewish and Christian Literature. 2003. *Volume 158.*

Trebilco, Paul: The Early Christians in Ephesus from Paul to Ignatius. 2004. *Volume 166.*

Treloar, Geoffrey R.: Lightfoot the Historian. 1998. *Volume II/103.*

Tsuji, Manabu: Glaube zwischen Vollkommenheit und Verweltlichung. 1997. *Volume II/93*

Twelftree, Graham H.: Jesus the Exorcist. 1993. *Volume II/54.*

Urban, Christina: Das Menschenbild nach dem Johannesevangelium. 2001. *Volume II/137.*

Visotzky, Burton L.: Fathers of the World. 1995. *Volume 80.*

Vollenweider, Samuel: Horizonte neutestamentlicher Christologie. 2002. *Volume 144.*